Competency 5: Engage in Policy Practice

A. Identify social policy at the local, state, and federal level that impacts well-being, ~~service delivery~~, and access to social services	6, 7
B. Assess how social welfare and economic policies impact the delivery of and access to social services	2, 3, 7
C. Apply critical thinking to analyze, formulate, and advocate policies that advance human rights and social, economic, and environmental justice	3, 4, 7

Competency 6: Engage with Individuals, Families, Groups, Organizations, and Communities	1, 9, 10, 12
A. Apply knowledge of human behavior and the social environment, person-in-environment, and other multidisciplinary theoretical frameworks to engage with clients and constituencies	1, 10, 12
B. Use empathy, reflection, and interpersonal skills to effectively engage diverse clients and constituencies	9, 12

Competency 7: Assess Individuals, Families, Groups, Organizations, and Communities	5, 6, 9, 13
A. Collect and organize data, and apply critical thinking to interpret information from clients and constituencies	5, 6, 9
B. Apply knowledge of human behavior and the social environment, person-in-environment, and other multidisciplinary theoretical frameworks in the analysis of assessment data from clients and constituencies	5, 6, 9, 13
C. Develop mutually agreed-on intervention goals and objectives based on the critical assessment of strengths, needs, and challenges within clients and constituencies	5, 6, 9
D. Select appropriate intervention strategies based on the assessment, research knowledge, and values and preferences of clients and constituencies	5, 6, 9, 13

Competency 8: Intervene with Individuals, Families, Groups, Organizations, and Communities	6, 8, 9
A. Critically choose and implement interventions to achieve practice goals and enhance capacities of clients and constituencies	6, 8, 9
B. Apply knowledge of human behavior and the social environment, person-in-environment, and other multidisciplinary theoretical frameworks in interventions with clients and constituencies	6, 8, 9
C. Use inter-professional collaboration as appropriate to achieve beneficial practice outcomes	6, 8, 9
D. Negotiate, mediate, and advocate with and on behalf of diverse clients and constituencies	6, 8, 9
E. Facilitate effective transitions and endings that advance mutually agreed-on goals	6, 8, 9

Competency 9: Evaluate Practice with Individuals, Families, Groups, Organizations, and Communities	7, 8, 12
A. Select and use appropriate methods for evaluation of outcomes	7, 8, 12
B. Apply knowledge of human behavior and the social environment, person-in-environment, and other multidisciplinary theoretical frameworks in the evaluation of outcomes	7, 8, 12
C. Critically analyze, monitor, and evaluate intervention and program processes and outcomes	7, 8, 12
D. Apply evaluation findings to improve practice effectiveness at the micro, mezzo, and macro levels	7, 8, 12

Sara Miller McCune founded SAGE Publishing in 1965 to support the dissemination of usable knowledge and educate a global community. SAGE publishes more than 1000 journals and over 800 new books each year, spanning a wide range of subject areas. Our growing selection of library products includes archives, data, case studies and video. SAGE remains majority owned by our founder and after her lifetime will become owned by a charitable trust that secures the company's continued independence.

Los Angeles | London | New Delhi | Singapore | Washington DC | Melbourne

Human Behavior Theory for Social Work Practice

Terry L. Koenig

University of Kansas

Rick Spano

University of Kansas

John B. Thompson

St. Ambrose University

Los Angeles | London | New Delhi
Singapore | Washington DC | Melbourne

FOR INFORMATION:

SAGE Publications, Inc.
2455 Teller Road
Thousand Oaks, California 91320
E-mail: order@sagepub.com

SAGE Publications Ltd.
1 Oliver's Yard
55 City Road
London EC1Y 1SP
United Kingdom

SAGE Publications India Pvt. Ltd.
B 1/I 1 Mohan Cooperative Industrial Area
Mathura Road, New Delhi 110 044
India

SAGE Publications Asia-Pacific Pte. Ltd.
18 Cross Street #10-10/11/12
China Square Central
Singapore 048423

Acquisitions Editor: Joshua Perigo
Editorial Assistant: Noelle Cumberbatch
Production Editor: Kelle Clarke
Copy Editor: Terri Lee Paulsen
Typesetter: C&M Digitals (P) Ltd.
Proofreader: Eleni Maria Georgiou
Indexer: Beth Nauman-Montana
Cover Designer: Scott Van Atta
Marketing Manager: Katherine Hepburn

Library of Congress Cataloging-in-Publication Data

Names: Koenig, Terry, author. | Spano, Rick, author.

Title: Human behavior theory for social work practice / Terry Koenig, University of Kansas, Rick Spano, University of Kansas, John Thompson, St. Ambrose University.

Description: Thousand Oaks : SAGE Publications, [2019] | Includes index.

Identifiers: LCCN 2018048767 | ISBN 9781506304915 (pbk. : alk. paper)

Subjects: LCSH: Social service. | Human behavior.

Classification: LCC HV40 .K594 2019 | DDC 150.2/436132—dc23
LC record available at https://lccn.loc.gov/2018048767

This book is printed on acid-free paper.

19 20 21 22 23 10 9 8 7 6 5 4 3 2 1

DETAILED CONTENTS

PREFACE

John, Rick, and I have discussed several reasons for wanting to write this book. As authors, we bring a unique and rare balance of social work practice and teaching experience as well as a love of theory and philosophy to our writing. When we began to discuss a new approach to a human behavior theory textbook for social work students, which equally addressed theory and social work practice, we were already keenly aware that there were virtually no human behavior theory texts that took on this reciprocal application of theory to practice. We observed our students at all levels of the curriculum (BSW, MSW, and PhD) having difficulties making sense of theories and struggling to apply these theories and their attendant ideas and concepts to practice. Theory was often seen as cumbersome and not very relevant to social work practice. As educators, we had discovered how theory could come alive for students—once it was linked directly to social work case examples. We thought students might change their minds or at least be open to the richness and benefits of using theory if we examined a variety of case examples from social work practice through the multiple lenses of theories (e.g., critical, moral, and cognitive development; systems, empowerment, and psychodynamic). Theories could be used to understand behavior at individual, family, group, community, and even societal levels; and theories could also suggest and even point the way for social work interventions, as well as research, advocacy, and policy-based efforts.

In our teaching, we discovered it is much harder for most of our students to move from a broad theory that "takes in the kitchen sink" to its application in practice. In contrast, students are often astute in their inductive skills, moving from specific cases to more abstract ideas; they are able to discuss a case from social work practice and "back in" (with some reflection and discussion) to broader ideas and theories. And, so we were determined in this book to start with, integrate, and end with a wide range of cases from our own practice, teaching, and in some cases, our research experiences. Of course, the specifics of these cases have been disguised to protect clients' privacy, but they reflect our diverse practice experience with combat veterans, older adults, and those with head injuries, in mental health, foster care, and in private practice with survivors of sexual abuse.

Over the years, we have also interacted with numerous social work faculty members who felt that human behavior theory textbooks did not draw on original scholars and their writings and instead these primary writings were being glossed over, watered down, and treated with very little depth. It was for this reason that we agreed to not only provide a succinct theory overview within each chapter but also to feature one or two scholars in an in-depth section that typically follows the overview of every theory. This kind of writing—a thorough overview that incorporates original as well as current source material and an in-depth feature on a theorist for every chapter—was challenging, but it was very rewarding for us. We hope that our readers will enjoy these in-depth scholar features and will be less intimidated to "go to the source" and read their original writings.

Educators also told us that they wanted more theories that address macro-level practice. We have responded with robust treatment of macro theories including critical theories, systems theories, and theories of the natural environment and social work.

We have also been frustrated with the limited critique of theories and conceptual ideas for social work scholarship. Although some scholars, such as Stan Witkin, have explored critique questions that reflect the ideals and values of the social work profession, in most instances theory critique is absent from social work scholarship. This forced us to try to define key elements that reflect social work values and ethics, are rooted in our history and current understandings of social work, and that can be used for critique of any theory or idea. Our objective was not to encourage students to memorize key ideas in theories, but through a process of engaging in ongoing critique, we were hoping students might "learn how to learn." Theories and models come and go as trends in social work and our society. For those of you old enough to remember, think of neurolinguistic programming, and for those of you new to the profession, think of mindfulness, trauma-informed care models, and eye movement desensitization techniques. It does matter what theories are currently being employed and what will be reimbursed for by insurance companies in our often resource-starved agencies, but it is also important to know how consistent these theories, models, and techniques are with social work values (e.g., whether or not the theoretical premises ignore the dignity and worth of each person or encourage the social worker's ongoing competence and growth through critical self-reflection). For these reasons, we included introductory chapters that encourage students to critique theory and to understand a theory's historical context. Further, each of our theory chapters includes a separate section on theory critique.

Finally, we were also intentional about including theory overviews, in-depth features, and case examples that reflect growing human diversity within our society based on, but not limited to, race/ethnicity, gender, class, age, sexual orientation and gender expression, (dis)ability, and religion. Our goal was to let our clients and scholars speak for themselves. As authors who know White privilege, we have been witnesses to the marginalization and oppression experienced by so many and, in turn, hope to help our students and colleagues alike in waking up, in moving, as Paulo Freire remarks, from a naïve consciousness to a critical consciousness as a way to make our world a better and more equitable place to live in.

ABOUT THE AUTHORS

Terry L. Koenig, PhD, LSCSW, professor, School of Social Welfare, University of Kansas, teaches human behavior theory, ethics, social work philosophy, and qualitative research methods. Sparked by relationships with her Kazakh daughter-in-law and grandchildren, she pursued a Fulbright scholarship to Kazakhstan in 2011 where she taught social policy with social work students on the Siberian steppe. Dr. Koenig's scholarship examines ethical decision-making and cross-cultural aspects of social work practice. In addition, she has developed and supported a cross-cultural social work course between the School of Social Welfare and social work faculty at the Universitá del Sacro Cuore in Milan, Italy.

Rick Spano, PhD, LSCSW, Professor Emeritus, School of Social Welfare, University of Kansas, has taught social work policy, practice, ethics, and social work history and philosophy for nearly five decades. He developed and supported bilingual and comparative studies social work courses between the School of Social Welfare and Escuela de Trabajo Social, University of Costa Rica. In addition, Dr. Spano's practice experience includes extensive work in foster care, and he maintains a private practice where he uses a family systems approach to treat sexual abuse of children and adults. He remains active in developing and presenting materials on social work ethics.

John B. Thompson, PhD, MSW, MA, MATS, is associate professor at the School of Social Work, St. Ambrose University. Dr. Thompson's interests, scholarship, and teaching are interdisciplinary, bringing together wisdom from Christian theology, philosophy, and the social sciences. His courses focus on understanding human behavior and addressing multiple social issues such as mental illness, the opioid crisis, environmental degradation and mass homicide. Publications include work on the intersection of theology and psychiatry, pragmatism and social work, and a book on Christian theology and social justice (in process).

ACKNOWLEDGMENTS

Terry:

I would like to acknowledge the scholars whose shoulders I stand upon and who have provided me with great support, including Ann Weick, Dennis Saleebey, Edith Freeman, Rick Spano, and John Thompson. These writers and thinkers encouraged me to integrate my Lutheran theological background with my growing interests in theory as it applies to real-world experience and social work practice. I would also like to acknowledge my husband, Randy, whose rural roots in Nebraska continue to ground me in the present, and my family, including Nicole, Josh, Kuanysh, Adelric, and Aurelyon. Their love has fueled my energy and focus in writing this book.

Rick:

I wish to acknowledge families that have deeply contributed to my participation in this book project. First, my professional family at the KU School of Social Welfare. which has been my academic home for the past 43 years. The formal and informal support provided by Ann Weick, Dennis Saleebey, Charlie Rapp, Don Chambers, Dennis Dailey, Terry Koenig, and Alice Lieberman was central to helping me to translate ideas from the strengths perspective into practice. Second, my personal family including my wife, Penny, who lived with this additional creature (this book) living in our house for three years. And, to my children, Jake and Kate, who also allowed me space to wander down unfamiliar paths that took my time and attention away from them and their children; thank you. Without their support none of this could have happened.

John:

I would like to thank my coauthors, Terry and Rick, for their dedication and integrity; my colleagues at St. Ambrose University for their friendship and dialogue about many topics relevant to this book; and my wife, Kendra, for her ongoing inspiration and support.

The authors would like to thank the following reviewers:

Patricia Carl-Stannard, Sacred Heart University

Noelle L. Fields, The University of Texas at Arlington

Chris Garland, Northeastern State University

Patricia Kolar, University of Pittsburgh

Daniel Liechty, Illinois State University

Rose McCleary, CSU Bakersfield

Scott Meyer, Plymouth State University

Claudia Moreno, Dominican College

Ericka Robinson-Freeman, The University of Texas at Arlington, School of Social Work

James L. Scherrer, Dominican University, Graduate School of Social Work

Sherita Williams-Tompkins, Jackson State University

INTRODUCTION TO THEORY AND ITS APPLICATION TO SOCIAL WORK PRACTICE

PHOTO 1.1
Opening the door to theory: Moorish palace door, Granada, Spain

CASE EXAMPLE
YOUR NEW CLIENT AT THE COMMUNITY MENTAL HEALTH CENTER

Imagine you are working in a community mental health center in your area. A new client has been referred to you for counseling. Her name is Martha, and as she walks into your office you notice she smells a bit like patchouli and is wearing a "hippie" type dress and has matted hair. She appears to be in good spirits today, but you detect a certain sadness and anxiety as you observe her mannerisms, speech, and affect.

As you get to know this person you understand that she is Caucasian, 60 years old, recently divorced (after 40 years of marriage), has five adult children, and also recently left her lifelong, conservative religious affiliation. She reports feeling increasingly discontent with her life over the past several years, especially after her youngest child left for college two years ago, leaving her and her now ex-husband "empty nesters." Since the divorce last year, Martha has been mostly "couch surfing," hanging out with a much-younger crowd, smoking marijuana (something she had never tried before), and joined a drum circle that meets in the local town square. She reports feeling confused about her life and concerned for her future because she has no income, health benefits, or job prospects. She says that she has mostly enjoyed her new young friends, but she also believes their relationship is time-limited because they know she is "old." She reports feeling "lost" because she has been rejected by her religious community that she belonged to for decades, yet she doesn't "fit in" all that well with the young "partying" crowd either. Her stated goal for seeking counseling is to "figure out my life" and to "feel better," as she says she is "always tense, yet bummed—especially because my kids just don't seem to understand, I hardly see them anymore."

As we begin to think about theory and its use in social work practice, consider the following case example and the many questions it raises—questions that all relate to a variety of theoretical perspectives.

Much more could be said about this client, of course, but this should suffice to begin our discussion. At this point, anyone reading even this much about another person will have many interpretations of the situation, likely with many more thoughts about what Martha "ought" to do. But what is the role of the professional social worker when serving in the role of a counselor? Our NASW *Code of Ethics* (2015) prescribes, among other things, that we focus on the relationship with the client and recognize the client's self-determination. This is a start to professional work as it moves beyond simple advice giving and imposing our own beliefs, ideologies, and agendas on other people. This is a good place to pause for just a moment—think about Martha and her situation again and note your own initial emotional reactions and thoughts about what is going on with her, and why. Do you think these thoughts and emotions have anything to do with Martha and her reality (something you presently know very little about), or do they simply reflect your own life history, personality, religious and political views, and so on? Note that I've offered a dichotomy: either your views accurately reflect Martha's life, or they merely reflect your own biases. Strict dichotomies, of course, tend to be false, and, since you and Martha are both human beings from the same planet, chances are that there will be some degree of overlap between your thoughts and her situation. With patience and good listening skills, a therapeutic relationship can develop that will hopefully benefit the client, while disabusing you of your projections and simple inaccuracies about Martha, her life, and what she should do.

But if we're not in the simple advice-giving game as professionals, does this leave us with nothing more to offer clients than the usual counseling clichés such as "how does that make you feel?" or "what do *you* think it means?" To what does a professional appeal in order to help her or his client? Or, in other words, how should we try to understand what might be going on with this person? Social workers, like psychologists and other helping professionals, always rely on the emerging (and always changing) body of empirical research related to their particular field of practice (e.g., empirically supported treatments for depression and anxiety). We also inevitably rely on a variety of perspectives or theories to help us make sense of the research information, to help us navigate the complexities of our relationships with clients, and to offer clients perspectives and information that will hopefully help them navigate their own diverse life circumstances. Most importantly, of course, we rely on the perspectives of clients and their own theories about what is happening in their life to guide the co-creative dialogue that hopefully typifies client–practitioner exchanges. This is the art of social work practice.

Consider Martha's case further (granting, again, that we know little about her). What thought paths did you start down? Perhaps you thought sociologically and imagined that Martha had been stuck in a prescribed, traditional familial role as wife and mother and was finally breaking free from oppression following the "empty nest" situation that changed her immediate social environment. Some feminist theorists have actually proposed that this is a developmental process that women may go through at this or other times in their lives (Belenky, Clinchy, Goldberger, & Tarule, 1986; Gilligan, 1982). Maybe you thought Martha had been caught in an abusive relationship with her husband for all these years and finally had had enough and left once the kids had grown. On the other hand, maybe you thought more psychologically—Martha might have a diagnosable mental health disorder such as bipolar disorder. She may be in a near-psychotic state, on the "way down" from a manic episode in which she left home to pursue a fantasy dream of becoming a 1960s-style traveling musician who "cuts loose" from societal norms and experiments with mind-expanding drugs and "free love." In this case her loved ones might be desperately seeking to find her and help her restore their view of a balanced and stable life, not hers. Or perhaps you are more existentially minded. Maybe Martha recently learned that she has cancer, and though she has no regrets about her choice to marry, have children, and lead a more conventional lifestyle, she is having a spiritual crisis because her religious community believes that if she just has more faith that she will be healed. Perhaps you have assumed that Martha is a victim in this situation, or that she has the moral high ground. Maybe Martha cheated on her husband for a number of years and he divorced her when he finally found out. Maybe her religious community, and children, while seeking reconciliation, have held her accountable for her behavior. Martha, in this case, may have rejected them because she still thinks she deserves to have a husband and a lover on the side. Or perhaps Martha was an abusive mother who alienated her children over the years and finally divorced her husband, sued him, and won a large settlement of money, and blew it all doing drugs and gambling and now has nothing to show for it.

In any case the point should be clear: there are many possibilities in Martha's case (and all others) and they all relate to different meta-theories, perspectives, theories, or practice models. At the broadest, most abstract level, we can consider meta-theories such as social constructionism, broad critical theory, or positivism that help us to very broadly understand Martha's situation or just about anything else. These meta-theories may be developed and used by diverse disciplines such as psychology, sociology, culture or gender studies, biology or political science. In addition, we may consider meta-theories or perspectives from the humanities such as philosophy, history, or theology. Each broad "angle" offers a somewhat different view of the same situation. It is very much like describing a mountain (or other geographical location)—do you focus on the trees, the wildlife, the atmosphere, the soil, the recreational possibilities, the potential timber harvest, the people who have lived there over time, or the way it feels to finally reach the summit (among many other possibilities)? Each "view" roughly corresponds to a different discipline or perspective (and likely overlaps with others): trees to botany; wildlife to zoology; timber harvest to economics; summit reaching to literature; and so on. Scientists in many fields have for many decades suggested that the best way to understand or describe the environment is to consider the situation holistically as each part and "view" is mutually interdependent with the others. This is the ecological perspective, which social work has also adopted and utilized for many years (Germain & Gitterman, 1980). Whether trying to understand the health and status of a mountain or a human situation like Martha's, we consider many points of view—or "angles"—in order to make sense of things.

The different points of view may include, as just stated, different broad meta-theories or disciplinary perspectives within psychology or biology. They may also involve more specific theories from within such disciplines. For example, a psychological perspective may include or support psychodynamic (e.g., Freudian), humanistic, cognitive–behavioral or community psychology theories (among others). Narrowing further, each of these have subcategories, multiple theorists, and in our case, practice models and strategies, which reflect different views. The same holds for all fields of study such as sociology or history.

Although authors have defined meta-theories, perspectives, theories, and practice models in different ways, for our purposes, a **meta-theory** is defined as a theory concerned with the investigation, analysis, or description of theory itself. For example, social constructionism, among other things, discusses knowledge, how we know what we know, and espouses multiple truths not a singular truth as a way to understand Martha's situation. Examples of meta-theories include pragmatism, positivism, broad critical theory, and social constructionism. A **perspective** is a worldview or way of perceiving the world such as the strengths perspective, ecological perspective, feminist perspective, or person-in-environment perspective. A **theory** (e.g., psychodynamic, symbolic interactionism, empowerment, moral development, and systems) is defined as a set of statements aimed at explaining or proving why something happens. A **practice model** such as cognitive–behavioral, narrative, and task-centered describes how social workers can apply and implement theories in their practice. Practice strategies flow from practice models and can include a range of skills such as active listening, advanced accurate empathy, community organizing, and the use of eco-maps and genograms. Further, meta-theories, perspectives, theories, and practice models interact with and can inform each other (see Diagram 1.1). For example, a meta-theory such as broad critical theory can be understood as supporting a feminist perspective. A feminist perspective can support empowerment theory and a narrative model. Meta-theory is the broadest and most abstract term, while a model with its accompanying practice strategies is the most concrete term reflecting what is closest to what a social worker might do in practice. It should be noted that many of us may use a practice model without understanding its conceptual roots. We don't know what meta-theory, perspective, or theory supports the model. As we grow and develop as practitioners, we may explore or "back into" a meta-theory, perspective, or theory that supports a particular practice model and this can deepen our understanding and use of the model with clients.

It is natural for each of us to have our own personal and cultural history, biases, and viewpoints that shape who we are and how we interpret various events and situations we encounter, including those of our clients. In addition, because we each have our own (somewhat) unique histories and ideologies, we will each have a more naturally occurring affinity toward some meta-theories, perspectives, theories, and models, and an aversion to others. One of the great benefits of having a deep and broad theoretical understanding is that it helps us to develop self-awareness by recognizing where our own viewpoints fit with the multitude of theoretical ideas that are out there. When we do this we are better equipped for intentional and ethical practice with clients, individually and/or collectively. Theoretical understanding also permits us to better assist clients by enabling us to offer them theoretical concepts—as appropriate (usually informally)—as a means of facilitating interpretation,

DIAGRAM 1.1   ■   Conceptual Relationship Among Meta-Theory, Perspective, Theory, and Model

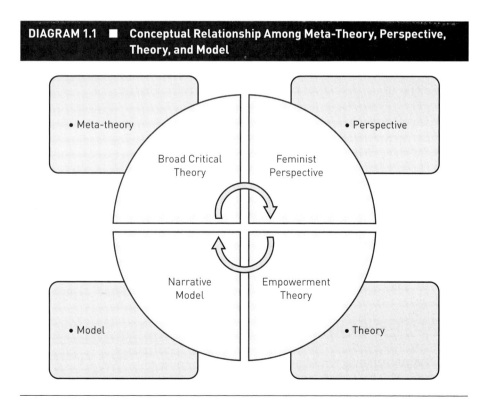

education, and action. In Martha's case, for instance, if she was experiencing a sense of existential confusion and social alienation because of a choice to explore life beyond the strict confines of prescribed gender roles, it may be liberating and empowering to learn that many other women have experienced the same thing and that those espousing a feminist developmental perspective have argued that this is a legitimate process, thus validating her experience. As stated, there are many other possibilities, and a professional social worker will have many different ideas from which to draw. We are assuming of course that the worker always begins with the client's story and goals, and does not merely superimpose a perspective or theory in an oppressive manner upon the client (e.g., Rossiter, 2011).

HOW THIS BOOK IS ORGANIZED

A broad and deep understanding of theory is essential for professional social work practice and is something cultivated throughout one's career. We are tempted here to say that this book represents a beginning to this lifelong study, but it is not. You have taken many courses in your life already and have likely read (or, perhaps, are currently reading, depending on where you are in your academic career) many books on topics ranging from history to world religions to statistics. As social workers we draw upon all relevant knowledge, client expertise, and practice wisdom in order to accomplish our goals. This book is a formal continuation of your education, focusing on theory for professional practice. Our aim is to provide you with an overview of a broad spectrum of theories, ranging from the ecological (e.g., deep ecology) to the psychological (e.g., psychodynamic thinkers such as Otto Rank) to the sociopolitical (e.g., theories of culture and White privilege). We also aim to offer significant depth to each topical area by focusing in on one or two particular theorists and exploring their ideas in some detail. Therefore, each chapter (following the first section of the book) will be structured as follows:

1. General overview of the theory that identifies basic vocabulary, historical developments, and primary thinkers

2. In-depth focus on one or two theorists, identifying key concepts, arguments, and orientation

3. Critique of the theory and specific theorist(s) including commentary, comparison, and opinion

4. Application of the theory to diverse social work practice settings, case situations, and levels of practice. This section also includes classroom exercises and/or questions for student reflection and discussion

CHAPTER SUMMARIES

We have organized this book into two main sections. Chapters 1 through 3 are introductory chapters that help set the stage for the deeper look at multiple theories discussed in Chapters 4 through 13. We have summarized each chapter as follows:

Chapter 2: Critique of Theory for Use in Social Work Practice. This chapter presents a conceptual framework (or set of five questions) for critiquing any theory. This conceptual framework is based on assumptions that have their roots in the history and philosophy of knowledge and values as understood in the profession of social work. Each question in this conceptual framework attempts to get you to look at theories through different lenses just as you would facets of a gemstone. These critique questions are discussed in every theory chapter (Chapters 4–13) and include: What does this theory say about human behavior? How does this theory address growth and change (e.g., for the individual and community)? How holistic is this theory? How consistent is this theory with social work values and ethics? What sources of knowledge does this theory support (e.g., client's voice, social worker's practice wisdom, and qualitative and quantitative research studies)?

Chapter 3: Contextualizing Human Behavior Theory. This chapter explores the impact of historical context on our understanding of human behavior. The authors discuss how larger social conditions such as trends, ideologies, and events have a direct impact on not only our understanding of human behavior, but also the theories we choose to use in social work practice. We present an historical framework designed to ask important questions about these choices including: What are the assumptions about human behavior in the social environment that shape our responses to social conditions (policy) and interpersonal behavior (direct practice)? Why is this particular theory or perspective emerging at this moment in time? Is this theory or perspective a new understanding of human behavior? What is it that makes this understanding of human behavior important to our current context?

Chapter 4: Critical Theories. This chapter discusses the importance of critical theory as an overarching, central theory (or meta-theory) for social work practice. Our overview examines critical theory from its inception to more current streams (e.g., critical race theory, feminist criticism, and critical queer theory). We also feature an in-depth analysis of the writings of Paolo Freire, a Brazilian educator and critical theorist whose broad international influence has also been particularly felt in American progressive education. Freire advocated for a radically different educational approach to empowering marginalized or oppressed populations. We pose questions of critical theory for its use in social work practice and examine potential applications of critical theory to a range of social work education and practice situations.

Chapter 5: Psychodynamic Theory. Psychodynamic theory is discussed from its beginnings in Freud's work (which examines intrapsychic and unconscious processes that contribute to human development) to current efforts (e.g., acknowledging people's creativity and strengths; and the crucial role of the mother–infant bond on adult development). This chapter also traces the influence of psychodynamic theory on the social work profession as it developed the diagnostic school that espoused a medical or deficit-based approach to practice. Otto Rank, as a proponent of the contrasting functional school, which emphasized individual creativity and will, is featured as our in-depth theorist. Finally, this chapter provides a critique of psychodynamic theory that takes into account its current evolutions; case examples are provided that illustrate psychodynamic theory's persistent influence on social work practice.

Chapter 6: Systems Theories. In this chapter, we explore two major system theories: structural functionalism and general systems theories (GST). GST, which views all matter as holistic systems whose elements interact with each other, combined with ecology, the study of living organisms within their environment, led to the development of social work's ecosystems theory and the Life Model. The importance of this theory and model to social work cannot be overestimated; consequently, key writers of ecosystems theory and the Life Model are featured in the in-depth section of this chapter. We draw on newer writings to address systems theories shortcomings (e.g., lack of attention to the impact of oppression on human growth) and we discuss this theory's application to social work practice (e.g., use of eco-maps and genograms).

Chapter 7: Environmental and Ecological Theory in Social Work. This chapter provides an overview of ecological theories and environmental ethics and makes a case for this foundation as a way to strengthen social work's attention to the natural world. We examine not only the impact of the natural world on humans (shallow ecology) but also the intrinsic worth of the natural world (deep ecology). Arne Naess, a Norwegian philosopher, is featured as the progenitor of deep ecology. A critique of ecological theories incites us to expand our definitions of core social work values such as the dignity and worth of each person and social justice to include both human and non-human life. Several case examples are provided that reflect ameliorative, but also proactive social work practices as well as potential new roles for social work.

Chapter 8: Life Span Theories, Family Life Course Perspectives, and Historical Trauma. This chapter examines the prominent role of life span theories in social work education while acknowledging its limitations (e.g., in accounting for influences of diversity, such as gender, race, ethnicity, and sexual orientation). We explore newer ideas about human development such as emerging adulthood as a distinct stage, nigrescence theory (which depicts Black identity development), and multiracial identity theories. Maria Yellow Horse Brave Heart and Venida Chenault, both Native American social work scholars, are featured for their work on historical trauma as it impacts human growth and development. Finally, we present a separate section on family development. Case examples are provided throughout this chapter to illustrate the application of individual and family life cycle development to social work practice.

Chapter 9: Symbolic Interactionism. This chapter provides an overview of symbolic interactionism (SI). Key ideas and assertions undergirding this human behavior theory include human behavior is an interpretation of what we do and how we perceive what others do; our minds are vehicles designed to tell us how others see things; as others act, we put ourselves into their perspective in order to understand the meaning their acts have for them; by taking the role of others, we engage in discovery and development of our own perspectives; and because SI is an interpretive theory it does not claim objectivity. We examine the contributions of three prominent sociologists—Mead, Cooley, and Goffman—and discuss the usefulness of SI at multiple levels (micro to macro) for social work practice.

Chapter 10: Behavior Theory, the Cognitive Turn, and the Influence of Mindfulness. This chapter focuses on behavior theory, its turn toward cognitive development, and its more recent turn toward mindfulness. Three generations of behavior therapies are also described: the first generation, which emphasized the mutual influence of environment on behavior and cognitive processes; the second generation, which introduced the pivotal role played by cognition in shaping human behavior; and the third generation, which moved away from the fundamental belief that individuals sought pleasure and/or avoided pain. The goal of third generation therapies is for clients to actively accept (through such strategies as mindfulness) psychological discomfort or pain as inevitable instead of viewing them as obstacles to achieving their goals. Our in-depth section on mindfulness features the writings of Thich Nhat Hanh and John Kabat-Zinn. The chapter concludes by applying concepts taken from behavior theory and its therapies to a series of case examples.

Chapter 11: Theories of Culture and White Privilege. This chapter examines social work's expanded view of culture as encompassing many different forms of diversity including, but not limited to, race and ethnicity, sexual orientation, gender and gender expression, age, (dis)ability, and class. Our in-depth section features Kimberlé Crenshaw's groundbreaking work on intersectionality, and we assert that social workers need to develop their own critical consciousness through praxis, a process of action and self-awareness, self-reflection, and dialogue with others. The chapter provides examples that identify both the processes and potential outcomes that result when we begin doing our own work as it relates to diversity in social work practice. We also examine the complex interactions between our own personal narratives and our professional lives as they relate to practice at all levels.

Chapter 12: Empowerment Theory and the Strengths Perspective. This chapter closely examines the roots of empowerment theory in social work dating back to the 1890s. It looks at the evolution of the strengths perspective through the eyes of some of its major contributors and its very close connection to empowerment theory. More specifically, we focus on a cadre of academics and practitioners over the last three decades who together developed a conceptual framework for a strengths-based approach to practice. Ann Weick and Dennis Saleebey are featured in our in-depth section as two key progenitors of the strengths perspective. Through case examples, we examine the application of the strengths-based model for case management in numerous fields of practice including mental health, child welfare, health, and aging.

Chapter 13: Cognitive and Moral Development. In this chapter we discuss cognitive and moral development featuring Piaget, Kohlberg, and Carol Gilligan. Special attention is paid to the growth in cognitive reasoning and the concomitant progression of moral development. We examine the differences among the varying perspectives with special attention to Gilligan's challenges of Kohlberg's reliance on social justice with her emphasis on the importance of a care orientation. We identify ongoing challenges, yet to be addressed, from current theorists including questions about roles played by culture, race, and religion as they relate to cognitive and moral development. Finally, we examine the concept of moral dialogue, developed by Spano and Koenig (2003), which attempts to connect cognitive and moral development to a framework of questions used to guide a process whereby social workers can focus on cognitive and moral aspects of practice situations in order to manage their own interactions with clients in ways that are congruent with our *Code of Ethics*.

WHAT IS THEORY?

Perhaps the broadest definition of theory is that it simply refers to the vast array of ideas we use to make sense of ourselves and the world around us. We theorize every time we try to understand something, whether simple or complex. Our clients also develop personal theories about why they are struggling or have overcome a particular problem. For example, if we're out rowing on a lake and we seem to be sinking, we might theorize that either we have a hole in the boat, letting water in, or maybe air is leaking and deflating the boat. We could theorize further that maybe we are not actually sinking, but our perception is mistaken because a wind came up and the waves are larger now, which causes them to rise higher on the sides of the boat. This is an example of simple, practical theorizing related to an immediate need. Of course, more formal and complex theories are required when we try to understand bigger questions in cosmology or human behavior, the latter being the focus of this book. Theories and models of the more simple, practical, or immediate need tend to be related to, and interdependent with more complex, overarching, and broad-reaching perspectives. In the boating example, many big ideas are in play as well, including the physics of water and waves, gravity and flotation, psychological ideas about how humans react in stressful situations, and existential ideas about the meaning of human life and death, the (possibly) sinking raft literally and metaphorically representing the precarious nature of human existence. This is to name just a few of the many practical, scientific, and philosophical ideas that are relevant. Can you think of a few more? Perhaps trauma theory (for the possible after effects), best practice ideas about small vessel rescue at sea, or even more practical ideas about when to begin bailing vs. attempting a raft repair on the water vs. paddling like hell toward shore! Consider as well how deep and interconnected ideas can be. For instance, if the boaters come from a highly individualistic culture and (implicitly) greatly value self-sufficiency, they might, on this theory, decide not to call for help. Alternatively, they might decide not to call for help out of a sense of embarrassment because this has happened before—the idea of saving face being prioritized over personal safety. The point is to recognize the importance of our ideas, the ongoing need for "big" and "small" ideas to work together, and the necessity of our understanding of these various ideas in order to navigate our world. There is, of course, no substitute for good, critical thinking.

THEORY AND SCIENCE

Students come to social work from many different fields such as biology, theology, and English, though most tend to come from the social sciences such as psychology and sociology. All fields of study are relevant to social work and of course all students are welcome to bring their knowledge and wisdom to bear for social work ends. It seems that the humanities tend to prepare students with a fairly broad understanding of meta-theories or perspectives, whereas the sciences (including social sciences) tend to focus more on theory (if they focus on theory at all) as it pertains to empirical research. This only makes sense, but in any case it is worth exploring the relationship of theory to science, especially since so many students come with this background, and hence have fairly empirically focused ideas about the nature of theory.

Scientific theory typically includes overarching ideas and themes that are developed inductively based on the results of many empirical research studies (e.g., Godfrey-Smith, 2003). Consider a simple example about birds: if, say an evolutionary biologist is studying the color of a particular bird, she or he might scientifically observe a sample of birds in a broad geographical location and note that all of the birds in the sample are black. A second sample of the same species of bird in a different geographical location may be observed as being white. This would lead the biologist to theorize about why the colors are different. Using evolutionary theory as a broad background, the biologist might suggest that the birds in one region are white because this area is further north, or perhaps at a higher elevation, either of which could lead to snowfall, which would potentially increase the probability of survival for white birds who could therefore camouflage themselves to avoid predators. Contrariwise, the black birds may have better camouflage in non-snowy regions.

Note the different levels of theory working in this example. The most abstract, most explanatory, or broad theory, evolution, must already be understood by the biologist in order to participate in thinking within the biological discourse in the first place. Then empirical research is undertaken that yields data about bird color and geography. The biologist must have both a broad theoretical knowledge, information about birds (e.g., anatomy and social behavior), scientific study skills, and then the ability to use critical thinking skills to synthesize all of the information and offer some interpretation—this too is an idea, a theory about why some birds of the same species differ in color according to geographical region. If we take the analogy one step further, thinking of social work, we might imagine that the biologist is not just interested in understanding birds, as social workers are interested in more than merely understanding human behavior (or birds, for that matter), but also wants to do something positive to protect the bird species. Let's say the bird being studied is on the endangered species list. Now the biologist, like the social worker, needs not just good theoretical knowledge, information about his subjects, scientific skills, and an interpretation, but also the various practical skills necessary for doing something, whether medical, perhaps aiding an individual injured bird, or political, perhaps helping to pass legislation protecting bird habitat in order to prevent extinction.

Note as well that practical skills are often necessary for doing the science (for biologists as well as social workers). Practical strategies or skills can involve anything from building a bird blind to having basic outdoor skills to political keenness in networking. As with previous examples, the confluence of scientific information, practical skills, professional experience, and the ongoing dynamic relationships with clients (i.e., their perspectives) to make something happen denotes the *art* of social work practice. The art of social work practice involves an acknowledgment of the practice wisdom and experience of the practitioner, which may incorporate, but moves beyond empirical evidence (Gitterman & Knight, 2013). The practitioner may develop hunches or insights as to what is going on with a client. For example, a social worker may sense that there is a reason why the client is not fully motivated to participate in rehabilitation (even if the client has never said anything) after having a below-the-knee amputation of his leg. She may pursue questions to ascertain what the client is thinking and feeling that may contribute to his lack of motivation, though there is no clear evidence to support her intuitive hunch. This represents her tapping into the *art* of social work and may also reflect the fact that she has worked with other unmotivated clients and knows it is important to pursue what is going on with this particular client.

DOES THEORY REALLY MATTER? THEORY MYTH BUSTERS

Social work is a complex field of study and social action that involves theory at multiple levels (see next section), but it always remains practical in many ways as well. Addressing human (and non-human) needs in society as a professional social worker requires both mind, spirit, and body: full engagement of both the intellect and practical skill sets. When the focus for social action becomes overly intellectual, or overly practical, this can cause problems. In the former case, we can lose our connection with the real lives of those whom we aim to serve. In the latter we can become subject to all kinds of ideological agendas, marketing schemes, and even professional trends, the worst of which can lead us to unwittingly work against our clients' best interests. (See the in-depth section on Paulo Freire in our chapter on Critical Theories.) In any case, some will question the need for, and value of, theory for social work practice, so we address a few common misunderstandings here.

Myth #1 – *Theory is too difficult and complicated for social workers to understand*. This is perhaps the worst misunderstanding. Social workers, as people who bring together theory, knowledge, values, sanction, purpose, and practical skills from multiple disciplines in order to affect positive social change, actually have the somewhat ominous task of understanding the broadest range of theories. Since we operate at both the interpersonal and sociopolitical levels we must learn many more theories than most in order to do our work. It is true that some theories are challenging to understand (at least initially) and that some are complex. This is a challenge we accept in order to do our work as professional social workers. It is also true in the many years of experience of the present authors that social work students are highly adept at understanding, critiquing, and applying theory in a beneficial way.

Myth #2 – *Theory is just ivory tower nonsense with no practical import*. It is true that not every theory or idea is relevant to social work practice. This holds true for every sort of practice, and just about anything else for that matter. That said, there is a surprising multitude of theories that *are* relevant and useful for social work practice. Theory is actually inescapable—even if we wanted to avoid theory, or tried to reason that theory is not necessary, we would at best be (ironically) theorizing about how theory is not necessary. At worst, we would render ourselves ignorant about key ideas, past and present, that are essential for competent, professional-level practice (not to mention that we would leave ourselves vulnerable to charges of incompetence by licensing boards or other helping professions, all of which also recognize the essential nature of theory for practice).

Consider what is called a **shared decision-making model** (SDM) in the mental health field (Goscha, 2009). This is a relatively simple, practice-level model (see next section for more on this) that basically states that there are two "experts" involved in making decisions about the use of psychiatric medications: the psychiatrist *and* the patient (or *client*—the use of terms, or labels, is also important, which comes from "labeling theory"). SDM, now a few decades in the making, contrasts with conventional psychiatric practice that did not take much interest in clients' goals, interests, and values when prescribing drugs. Research is currently being conducted to consider empirical questions about SDM, such as whether clients adhere to their medications more when SDM practices are used, or whether clients show more improvements in their symptoms when SDM practices are used instead of the older, "one expert" practice. This SDM model is consistent with social work ethics such as client self-determination (NASW, 2015) and may serve to significantly improve the lives of many people suffering with mental illnesses. In this case it should be clear how important this realm of thought—models, theories, perspectives, and values—is to social work practice because the ideas we use (or assume, if we are not very self-aware or theoretically trained) have a dramatic impact on what we *do* with clients in practice settings.

One may argue that this SDM model involves just practical-level thinking and is therefore not really linked to one of our "academic" theories such as empowerment or psychodynamic theory. Consider then a much more complex theory (or body of theories) we tend to speak of in short hand as "social justice." Bringing about more social justice in the world is also called for in the NASW *Code of Ethics* (2015). But what does the term *mean*? Does it mean that everyone in society should have the exact same amount of money, or assets, or property, or opportunities, or rights, or capabilities, or land? Who is responsible for social justice? Does it mean that the government should take care of all social services, or should the private sector still be involved, and at what level? Does social justice imply socialist economic policies? Does social justice include ecological justice? If so, how? And how exactly does social (and ecological) justice shape practice for social work?

Many more questions could be asked here. Social justice is rather complex and requires additional understanding about political and economic theories, among others. The point is that if social workers are called to bring about more social justice, then the ideas—the theories—about what social justice *is* and how it shapes social work practice could not be more relevant to our profession. It is worth noting at this point that not every social worker needs to know all the same theories; nor do they all need to know them at the same depth of understanding. All professionals need at least a basic, working knowledge of a wide range of theories (such as those covered in this book), but each person will also specialize to some degree in her or his particular field of practice. So, for example, a social service administrator will likely need to know more about management theory than a counselor working independently in private practice, and a lobbyist will need more knowledge about political theory than a community gardener. No social worker can afford a narrow theoretical focus, however: a mental health treatment facility administrator, for instance, must maintain a high level of working knowledge of direct practice models and theories, in addition to management theories, in order to engage in ethical and effective decision-making processes regarding the agency's clients and mental health employees.

Myth #3 – *The use of theory in social work practice should be avoided because it leads to oppression.* This myth raises some warranted caution about the use of theory, but it is ultimately false as well. As mentioned earlier in this chapter, it is impossible to avoid theory, at least in the broadest sense, because to do so would imply that it is actually possible to approach any person, group of people, or situation with no set of theoretical ideas informing one's interaction with that person, persons, or situation—as if humans could (or would want to) become some sort of theoretical blank slate when doing social work practice. This is as absurd as it is counterintuitive—it is precisely our theoretical ideas, combined with our own history, values, and culture (including scientific knowledge), that make us who we are, and to suggest otherwise simply doesn't make sense. That said, it is also true that not every theory is applicable or relevant to every situation. And in some cases it *would* be oppressive or otherwise harmful to apply a particular theory to a particular person or situation. For example, if a case manager in a substance abuse treatment center pre-determined to use Freudian theory at the expense of all other ideas, this could be potentially detrimental to the client and inconsistent with professional ethics. In this situation the client may be a person of faith who wants to work through the 12 steps and considers God his or her "higher power." The case manager, applying strict Freudian principles, may then attempt to treat the patient using free association in order to help her or him with rescue fantasies of a projected ideal father figure. Here the case manager would be ignoring the client's beliefs and wishes (an ethical violation in this case—though there are exceptions to following clients' wishes), and also ignoring the potential benefits of not only an AA program, but also the many other ideas (theories) and scientific developments since Freud about the most effective treatments for substance abuse disorders.

More generally, we can say that the seemingly arbitrary application of one theory to a client or situation without considering the client's wishes (and values, goals, beliefs, etc.), the context, the multitude of other theories and scientific information (among other things like race, class, gender, age, etc.) *does* equate to an unethical and oppressive use of theory (Rossiter, 2011). It also denies the collaborative, artistic nature of social work practice. This need not be the case: with a solid foundation in theoretical knowledge, combined with a high degree of maturity and self-awareness, the dyadic (or group) interactions between social workers and clients can be ethical, healing, and helpful. This sort of positive scenario is the goal and is the type of situation where a social worker can then bring theoretical ideas to bear in a useful way, whether in making decisions about what to say or do, by explicitly offering interpretive ideas, or simply education to the client (remember the story at the beginning of the chapter).

THE INTERACTIVE ABSTRACT/CONCRETE CONTINUUM

There are so many different theories out there that it can be difficult to know how to think about them, or categorize them. Even in this chapter so far we've discussed quite a variety of ideas, from ethics, to meta-theories such as social constructionism, to human behavior theories and perspectives, practice models, and strategies. So far all we know is that there are a lot of theories and that they differ from one another in a variety of ways. What we would like to do here is offer a rough sketch of how we think about theories for social work. Keep in mind that this is over-simplified and, at least in our opinion, there isn't any way to offer a comprehensive taxonomy or fully satisfactory categorization of theories. That said, we find it useful to think about meta-theories, perspectives, theories, and practice models and strategies by placing them on a broad spectrum or continuum from the more abstract, complex, and explanatory, on one side, to more concrete, simple, and practical on the other. So, for instance, the "biggest," broadest ideas out there that tend to act as umbrella or meta-theories over many others (e.g., perspectives, theories, models, or strategies) and fall on the more abstract, explanatory side of the continuum. These would include epistemological perspectives or meta-theories such as social constructionism, broad critical theory, pragmatism, or **positivism** (see the upper-left quadrant in Figure 1.1). In the lower-left quadrant are perspectives such as the strengths, ecological, feminist, and person-in-environment perspectives. In the lower-right quadrant of the spectrum are theories such as cognitive behavioral theory, empowerment theory, and systems theory; and in the fourth or upper-right-hand quadrant are the more concrete models and practice strategies such as shared decision-making (SDM), mindfulness, the Life Model, and the use of eco-maps and genograms.

Models and practice strategies differ from our broader meta-theories and perspectives in that they do not attempt to explain the nature of reality (**ontology**), the ways we come to know truth (**epistemology**) or even explain what ethics are and how we apply them. Instead, meta-theories examine philosophical questions or the "big" questions that continue to be addressed by theorists in every field (including social work) and the answers to them have rippling effects on many other ideas and practices. For example, if a social worker tends to be positivistic in her or his epistemology—or way of knowing things—this means she or he believes that, in large measure, there is an objective truth that can be discovered through systematic inquiry. The social worker may highly value quantitative scientific methodologies that delineate outcomes and would therefore likely utilize only social work practice methods (e.g., evidence-informed mindfulness strategies). In the mental health field this practitioner would likely find value therefore only in cognitive-behavioral theory or similarly quantifiable practice methods. Note how the "big" ideas have a profound impact on actual practice with clients. The way we conceptualize our world—our orientation to the big theoretical questions about truth, reality, ethics, and politics—ultimately shapes how we view ourselves, other people, social situations, and also our research and practice methods. Similarly, if a practitioner is more affectionate toward **social constructionism** as a meta-theory that acknowledges the importance of subjectivity, multiple ways of knowing, and that knowledge is time and context-bound, she or he would be more likely to value a different array of therapeutic methods that are conceptualized and researched to take into account a wide range of situations faced by unique client groups. Said practitioner (again thinking of the mental health field) would be more likely to use empowerment or narrative theories, which are more amenable to social constructionism.

Understanding how these meta-theories, perspectives, theories, models, or practice strategies link together provides us with a continuum for determining their rough intellectual location. This is a loose term we use to refer to where a perspective or theory fits according to the aforementioned scheme, and also to consider its assumptions and arguments for its validity. This is a dialectical process between the individual social worker's experiences and her or his theoretical orientation (Palmer, 1969). In other words, the individual, with his or her own personal history, values, culture, and personality, is in a constant interaction with the ideas/theories she or he inherited automatically from personal history and culture, as well as those encountered (and continuing to encounter) more formally from reading and studying, or even from analyzing, synthesizing, and inventing new ideas based on her or his current life and professional practice. The goal, again, is understanding the diversity of ideas, and self-awareness—if practitioners are

FIGURE 1.1 ■ **The Interactive Abstract/Concrete Continuum: Meta-Theories, Perspectives, Theories, and Practice Models**

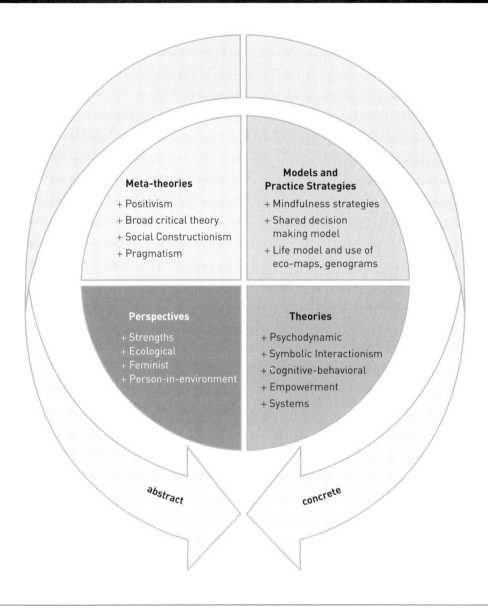

aware of the theories at play in a conversation with others then this empowers them to make more informed, intentional choices about how to proceed with clients in any social work practice situation. A high level of theoretical self-awareness is necessary in order to fulfill professional ethical obligations such as avoiding the tendency to push one's own beliefs, values, and opinions onto clients. If a practitioner is unaware of his or her own biases in this regard, then as a matter of course she or he will more easily make assumptions about what clients think, how they feel, or what they should do (Levy, 1976; Spano & Koenig, 2007/2008).

For example, consider a situation where a White child welfare services worker is assisting a Native American client with various services such as housing, employment, and child care. Let's say that the social worker in this case is unable to form a positive, working relationship with the client and that overall her work is proving ineffective despite feeling that she was rather polite and really tried to be helpful. Now as always, many things could be influencing the client–practitioner relationship and the outcome of the situation overall. One of the many potential problems could be theoretical—the practitioner, despite her good intentions, may be ignorant about Native American history, spiritual beliefs, and thought, and may be making assumptions about the nature of the relationship with the client that are leading to a breakdown in the relationship. The practitioner may assume, for instance, that as an "empowerment" social worker, she has all the power (e.g., referral sources, helpful tips, a good listening ear), while the client remains in the role of a recipient to her benevolence. This sort of theoretical assumption (to be sure, a flawed understanding of empowerment theory; for example, see Pease, 2002) overlooks the possibility that this sort of power structure in the relationship may be oppressive and trigger a justifiably negative response from the client (whether Native American or not). If the practitioner had a deeper, more accurate understanding of empowerment theory (i.e., that recognizes power in the client and community as well), and also a broader understanding of, say, historical trauma theory (which recognizes the generational transmission of trauma among Native Americans, etc.), then perhaps an ethical, effective, and healthy relationship could be formed with this client that might lead to positive outcomes. This level of theoretical awareness would, as stated above, include the practitioner understanding theory with some depth and breadth, including intellectual location, and an understanding, or self-awareness, of how this interacts with her own history, culture, and personal views.

META-THEORIES AS OVERARCHING THEORIES: THEIR CONTRIBUTIONS TO PRACTICE

Thus far in the chapter we have argued for the central role played by theories, at all levels, as important sources of influence on our behavior as practitioners. The reality is that there is no one "theory of everything" that underlies all professional practice. We have identified lenses that can be useful in analyzing theories from multiple sources including economics, political science, sociology, psychology, biology, and so on. We now shift our attention to two meta-theories, pragmatism and critical theory, for their relevance and application to social work practice.

Pragmatism as an Overarching
Theory for Social Work Practice

Pragmatism as an American philosophical approach or meta-theory has much to offer social work practitioners. In fact, the development of social work in the United States goes hand in hand with the development of pragmatism (Thompson, 2012). So what is pragmatism? Pragmatism is a distinctly American philosophy developed by Jane Addams and John Dewey (among others) in Chicago, Illinois, in the early 1900s (Thayer, 1982; Thompson, 2012). Both Addams and Dewey were great thinkers and practitioners, and their achievements in the development of social work and education are well known (Dewey, 1977; Fischer, 2009; Fishman & McCarthy, 2007; Franklin, 1986; Hamington, 2009; Thayer, 1982).

In short, pragmatism is a philosophical school or general orientation to thinking about ontology, ethics, epistemology, and political theory (among other things) that starts with the assumption that human beings are biological organisms (following Darwin) linked to the earth and multiple non-human species in various interdependent relationships (Dewey, J., in Hickman & Alexander, 1998). As such, we humans, unlike much previous thought about the "big" questions of life (e.g., how we know things, or what is really real), should not think of ourselves as having disembodied minds that are necessarily capable of somehow grasping eternal, universal, capital-T truths. Instead, with proper humility we can acknowledge our limitations and fallibility (as history has proven time and again, especially with ethical failures of various sorts) and set out to create the best society we can, given the tools (including theories) we have available (and inventing new ones!). This means that pragmatists don't start with the assumption that they have the one, true political perspective, or social theory, or knowledge-generating method (e.g., a particular approach to science), but instead start with an ethics-based quest for democracy, equality, justice, and freedom for all people. In other words, pragmatism is ultimately about setting the conditions of society such that all people have the maximum opportunity to be healthy and thrive. Pragmatists use multiple theories, practice models, and strategies to achieve these goals. The two following examples should help to illustrate how pragmatism fits with social work.

First, the origins of the current "person in environment" (PIE) concept—central to the NASW *Code of Ethics* (2015), and the Council on Social Work Education accreditation standards for academic programs (2015)—can be traced back to John Dewey's "organism in environment" perspective, a central tenet of pragmatism (Hickman & Alexander, 1998; Thompson, 2012). This concept, one main facet of pragmatism, states that humans are biological animals, like the rest of the animal kingdom, and are not disembodied minds seeking abstract truths. As such we are placed within the world (not above it), originating, like other species, via evolutionary processes. But this is only half of the equation—we also originate in specific geographical, biological, and cultural *environments* that, from the outset, shape all aspects of our lives. This is not to say that we are somehow predetermined to be what we are. Pragmatists actually focus instead on our human capacity to reason, to learn, and to make choices that not only interact with our environments by responding, but also by acting upon the environment to modify it in various ways. As organisms in our various environments—whether physical, social, political, and so on—we are influenced by the environment, yet we also shape that environment. The concern is about how and to what extent the environment shapes us, and how and to what extent we shape the environment. This is a constant and dynamic interaction that is always in process. When it comes to social work of course we're concerned with values like justice and well-being. So we are particularly interested in how we can actualize these values. The organism-in-environment aspect suggests that change should occur at multiple levels. In other words, when looking to bring about, say, justice, we should consider both the organismic (or individual) level, as well as that of the environment(s). This is what social work is all about.

For instance, social workers interested in justice for prisoners would need to consider individual concerns such as the reasons for, and length of stay in, solitary confinement, and who gets punished that way according to race, class, gender, and so on. This would be considered work at the organism level and also reflects our values such as the dignity and worth of every human being. A pragmatist understands that change needs to take place at the environmental level too, given the perspective just discussed. So this social worker would be seeking change as well at the policy level, perhaps with the prison or with state and/or federal legislation. To sum up, the organism-in-environment perspective of pragmatism is the historical origin of current social work thinking (i.e., called the person-in-environment thinking) that continues to offer theoretical insight into how we go about achieving our ends.

Second, pragmatism considers ideas (theories and practice models) to be primarily useful as tools, or instruments, for humans (and non-humans) to use for multiple purposes including describing the world around us, understanding ourselves individually and collectively, and for solving all sorts of problems by way of applying our ideas, or by inventing new ideas and/or physical tools of various sorts (Dewey, in Hickman & Alexander, 1998; Thompson, 2012). Consider the vast amount of thought (and variety of theories) involved in human inventions, from the wheel to the space shuttle, from the idea of democracy and individual rights to the *Diagnostic and Statistical Manual of Mental Health Disorders* (DSM-5). These represent many ideas, many created devices, many uses. Consider again the previous example about the social worker concerned with justice in the corrections system. The worker would need to decide which ideas to use as tools to address the particular aims she or he had in mind. As a pragmatist, the worker would not presume to have just one tool—say a particular criminal justice theory, or perhaps a political theory—that she or he would use in all cases and for every reason. The worker would have many different theory tools in his or her "kit" that would offer the flexibility to make an informed decision about which one(s) to use.

This orientation applies to the simpler, less explanatory theories and practice models as well as to some of the broader perspectives. For example, social workers would not necessarily assume that the best political approach is always their personal favorite political party line. They may decide that policy changes that would increase justice for prisoners would be best served using ideas from a different theory. Diversity of ideas is highly valued, and the complexities of the issues that social workers address usually demand flexibility. Keep in mind that the tool/kit analogy, while useful, also quickly breaks down when we consider that the ideas (tools) and the source of the ideas (kit) do not reside with the practitioner alone; not only do clients bring their own tools and kit, but new ideas and sources are hopefully generated by way of the creative, collaborative relationship between practitioner and client in context of multiple environments.

Pragmatism also includes humility with regard to the ideas themselves; this is called **fallibilism** (Hickman & Alexander, 1998; Thompson, 2012). This means that the ideas are not considered finished or perfect as they stand but are always in process and able to be revised and improved. This allows social workers great opportunities for analyzing and synthesizing extant ideas, as well as the possibility of inventing new ideas. This is all part of the great critical thinking process that is necessary for effective social work practice, whether at the individual or societal level. In our opinion, this is also psychologically healthy as it seems to reduce anxiety when we don't assume we have the one, right answer to everything from the outset, but instead approach problems with an array of ideas at our disposal. These "instruments" can then be utilized in order to achieve the ethical ends such as freedom and justice that define social work.

Overall, pragmatism provides a nice overarching perspective or meta-theoretical orientation because of its non-presumptuous flexibility, and also because it has (arguably) already been the broad theory informing and shaping social work since Jane Addams and John Dewey developed it over 100 years ago. Pragmatism permits social work practitioners to select the ideas they believe will best serve their clients (alongside the clients' own ideas). It also permits researchers to utilize not only quantitative and qualitative scientific methods but also wisdom and expertise from both practitioners and clients. In sum, by putting ethics first (e.g., justice and equality) pragmatism keeps these goals at the forefront, making all knowledge-making and practice-related concerns serve these ends.

Critical Theory as an Overarching Theory for Social Work Practice

Critical theory, beginning with Marx through authors like Paulo Freire, provided a conceptual foundation for early empowerment writings rooted in social work's core mission to serve those who are poor, dejected, oppressed, and who live on the margins of our society. In fact, social work writers have long been referring to the works of Marx, Freire (a key contributor to critical and empowerment-based theories and featured in our text), and others to describe how to assist clients in developing a critical consciousness or awareness of their oppression, and the means to take their power back. These early writers describe assisting clients to engage in a process of reflection (on their oppressive situation), dialogue with others in similar circumstances, and take action to bring about changes in their situation.

It is no accident that this book has been created to provide a framework for helping social work students to think about and critique any theory or set of ideas. Our critique framework (which is presented in Chapter 2) asks us to take into account the nature of each theory, whether or not the theory attends to holistic thinking and supports growth as well as social work values (e.g., the dignity and worth of each person), and if the theory acknowledges multiple types of knowledge (i.e., empirical studies, professional expertise), but also the working knowledge and wisdom that clients bring to their own experiences. In essence, broad critical theory insists that we engage in this kind of thinking or critique of any theory or ideas, making certain that we consistently connect up what are often intimate, personal experiences with larger, unjust social structures and behaviors. For example, take the woman who was sexually abused by a priest when she was child, who now "wakes up" through news media and conversations with her friends to the unjust religious structures that refuse to acknowledge the cancer in their institution—relegating the abuse to a handful of individual priests that they mislabel as psychologically deviant. In this example, having access to research studies is helpful because we know that heterosexual men are more likely than gay men to sexually abuse a child. And, knowing this, we can analyze the institutional behavior of the Catholic Church as an attempt to deflect blame and avoid being held accountable for their abusive behavior and for the ensuing cover-up by church leadership. For this individual woman, her experience is not simply a "personal problem," but it is all bound up in the harm and willful blindness of leaders at the helm of a powerful and corrupt religious institution.

Critical theory requires much from those of us who live in a democratic society. It insists that large social structures, such as a diocese or government, can only be held accountable (having their corruption curtailed or stamped out) in a democracy when citizens—from all walks of life based on class, race, ethnicity, sexual orientation and gender expression, (dis)ability, age, religion, and other forms of diversity—have an equal place at the decision-making table (e.g., in the voter's booth, at city council meetings, in state government, as members of the church institution or the foster care agency. Critical theorists hold to a creed that mirrors social work values having long been concerned about power within democratic societies and across a broad set of relationships and oppressive situations (See race, queer, and feminist criticism in Chapter 4). They put forth the idea that the transformation of society is only possible when people move from a culture of silence (where they passively accept what happens to them) to genuine participation in democracy through an analysis of the assumptions and actual practices of their society as played out within a historical and political context. Without any challenges to "progress" in which efficiency and outcomes or results are placed above individual well-being and freedom, our society faces negative social and moral consequences. Critical theorists emphasize the important role of social work and other social disciplines (in contrast to the humanities or natural sciences) to challenging all forms of oppression and to continuing to engage in a critique of our current social reality. In our age of shrinking resources for a range of needs and services (e.g., quality public education, mental health, disability, aging, and child welfare services), social workers who espouse a critical theoretical perspective are called on to provide a critique of our society's abandonment of the welfare and needs of the majority of our citizens, including the "least among us." And, social workers can point to our core professional principles (e.g., social, economic, and ecological justice, and the dignity and worth of each person) that reflect the best of our American society and the human spirit. As Hubert H. Humphrey (1977, p. 37287) once remarked:

The moral test of government [and hence, a society] is how it treats those who are in the dawn of life, the children; those who are in the twilight of life, the aged; and those in the shadows of life, the sick, the needy and the handicapped.

Key Terms (in order of appearance)

Meta-theory 4	Shared decision-making	Epistemology 15
Perspective 4	model 12	Social constructionism 15
Theory 4	Positivism 15	Pragmatism 18
Practice model 4	Ontology 15	Fallibilism 20

References

Belenky, M. F., Clinchy, B. M., Goldberger, N. R., & Tarule, J. M. (1986). *Women's ways of knowing: The development of self, voice, and mind.* New York, NY: Basic Books.

Council on Social Work Education (CSWE). (2015). *Educational policy and accreditation standards.* Alexandria, VA: Author.

Dewey, J. (1977). *The philosophy of John Dewey: A critical exposition of his method, metaphysics and theory of knowledge.* The Hague, Netherlands: Martinus Nijhoff Publishers.

Fischer, M. (2009). *Jane Addams and the practice of democracy.* Chicago: University of Illinois Press.

Fishman, S., & McCarthy, L. (2007). *John Dewey and the philosophy of hope.* Chicago: University of Illinois Press.

Franklin, D. (1986). Mary Richmond and Jane Addams: From moral certainty to rational inquiry in social work practice. *Social Service Review, 60,* 504–525.

Germain, C. B., & Gitterman, A. (1980). *The Life Model of social work practice* (1st ed.). New York, NY: Columbia University Press.

Gilligan, C. (1982). *In a different voice.* Cambridge, MA: Harvard University Press.

Gitterman, A., & Knight, C. (2013). Evidence-guided practice: Integrating the science and art of social work practice. *Families in Society, 94,* 70–78.

Godfrey-Smith, P. (2003). *Theory and reality: An introduction to the philosophy of science.* Chicago, IL: University of Chicago Press.

Goscha, R. J. (2009). *Finding common ground: Exploring the experiences of client involvement in medication decisions using a shared decision making model* (Doctoral dissertation). Retrieved from ProQuest Dissertation Publishing. (3386638)

Hamington, M. (2009). *The social philosophy of Jane Addams.* Chicago: University of Illinois Press.

Hickman, L. A., & Alexander, T. M. (Eds.). (1998). *The essential Dewey: Pragmatism, education, democracy* (Vol. 1). Bloomington: Indiana University Press.

Humphrey, H. H. (1977). Remarks at the dedication of the Hubert H. Humphrey Building, *Congressional Record,* November 4, 1977, *123,* p. 37287.

Levy, C. S. (1976). *Social work ethics.* New York, NY: Human Sciences Press.

National Association of Social Workers (NASW). (2015). *Code of ethics.* Retrieved from http://www.socialworkers.org/pubs/code/default.asp

Palmer, R. E. (1969). *Hermeneutics.* Evanston, IL: Northwestern University Press.

Pease, B. (2002). Rethinking empowerment: A postmodern reappraisal for emancipator practice. *British Journal of Social Work, 32,* 35–147.

Rossiter, A. (2011). Unsettled social work: The challenge of Levinas' ethics. *British Journal of Social Work, 32,* 35–147.

Spano, R., & Koenig, T. L. (2003). Moral dialogue: A worker-client interactional model. *Social Thought, 22,* 91–104.

Spano, R., & Koenig, T. (2007/2008). What is sacred when personal and professional values collide? *Journal of Social Work Values and Ethics, 4.* Retrieved from http://www.socialworker.com/jswve

Thayer, H. S. (1982). *Pragmatism: The classic writings.* Indianapolis, IN: Hackett Press.

Thompson, J. (2012). *Rethinking the clinical vs. social reform debate: A dialectical approach to defining social work in the 21st century.* (Doctoral dissertation). Retrieved from ProQuest Dissertation Publishing (3522069)

CRITIQUE OF THEORY FOR USE IN SOCIAL WORK PRACTICE

PHOTO 2.1
Taking into account multiple viewpoints: Walled city, Dubrovnik, Croatia.

This chapter introduces you to a process for analyzing and critiquing theory. This process involves two key steps. First, you will summarize the theory, define its key concepts, and create a working thesis with examples or evidence of the main point or claim of the theory. For example, systems theories, in general, support the key idea of holism or that everything is connected to everything else. For example, when working with a teenager who wants to stop abusing alcohol, from a systems' viewpoint, we will want to assess the client's internal world, the client's social (and natural) environment, and how the two interact with each other. The client may need to develop new friends at school in his or her environment in order to maintain sobriety. A key thesis of systems theories is that when we ignore the interactions between the environment and the client's internal world such as the impact of friendships that may help the client sustain sobriety, then we will not be as effective in helping the client reach life goals. Our thesis about systems theories may also change over time as we "dive in," analyze, and critique the theory in more depth.

Second, you will use a framework (or a set of questions) for critiquing theory. In this chapter, we will present a set of questions that are consistent with our historical context chapter (see Chapter 3) and reflect major themes in social work's development. We will not only introduce theory critique questions as a way of exploring a theory's overall usefulness and limitations, but we will give you ways to think about a theory's usefulness and limitations in relationship to social work practice. For example, a theory such as behaviorism or social learning theory has ample knowledge or evidence to support its effectiveness in addressing behavior change with diverse populations (Akers & Jensen, 2003; Miller, 2011). However, this theory can support the use of coercive and even abusive practice strategies to bring about client behavior change (e.g., yelling at a client who is disabled to get her or him to fold towels in a residential facility) that are not consistent with social work values such as the dignity and worth of clients or in seeking social justice for marginalized groups of people. Consequently, even if a theory has "evidence" to support its effectiveness, the application of a theory may be ethically questionable and therefore social workers must exercise caution and perhaps even refrain from using it in practice.

Social work has drawn upon and uses multiple sources of knowledge (such as diverse human behavior theories, practice wisdom, or client expertise) as a way to work with people in solving a variety of problems they face within their social and natural environments. However, social work scholars have not often discussed distinct elements of theory critique (Robbins, Chatterjee, & Canda, 2011; Witkin & Gottschalk, 1988). Some of this may be due to practitioners' lack of awareness of social work's rich history and intellectual rigor, which can indeed be used to help critique theories and their conceptual ideas. Current social work educational curriculum devotes minimal attention to social work history that addresses our profession's key purposes, our values, and the development of our knowledge or intellectual ideas (e.g., our belief and emphasis on clients' growth and change in contrast to pathology and illness; Koenig & Spano, 2007; Saleebey, 2005; Simon, 1994). Some of this may also be due to our discomfort with philosophy and our lack of experience in analyzing ideas and in developing a stance or argument to support our positions. Social work educators have strongly supported a liberal arts education in which social work students can develop these critical thinking skills through their coursework in philosophy, world history, human biology, religious studies, languages, and other subjects. It is our belief that the capacity to engage in theory critique is an essential skill that social workers can learn how to do.

What follows is an examination of our questions for theory critique. Each question is described in more depth, more detailed follow-up questions are suggested, and examples are given for how critique questions can be applied to a range of theories.

- What does this theory say about human behavior?

- How does this theory address growth and change (e.g., for the individual and community)?

- How holistic is this theory?

- How consistent is this theory with social work values and ethics?

- What sources of knowledge does this theory support (e.g., client's voice, social worker's practice wisdom, or qualitative and quantitative research studies that reflect the profession's worldview)?

WHAT DOES THIS THEORY SAY ABOUT HUMAN BEHAVIOR?

In order to examine the possibilities for using a theory in social work practice, it becomes important for practitioners to be able to summarize the theory and its key ideas and articulate a thesis that explains (with examples and evidence) the main point or claim of the theory. In order to engage in this process, we will want to become familiar with some philosophical terms (e.g., ontology and epistemology) so that we can use these terms in our theory analyses. Our capacity to analyze theories can help us to understand if a particular theory is a "good fit" or applicable to our particular practice as a social worker. These theoretical assumptions are discussed by many different social work scholars and philosophers (see Burrell & Morgan, 2003) and can be categorized along two broad dimensions: the **subjective–objective dimension** and the **stability–radical change dimension** (see Figure 2.1). The subjective–objective dimension involves the debate over whether or not theorists can treat the social world just like the natural world as being real and external to the individual (objective) or whether the world ought to be viewed as having a more personal and subjective quality to it, one in which individuals create their own meanings. The stability–radical change dimension involves an emphasis by some theorists on stability, integration, the nature of social order, and equilibrium (Comte, 1853; Durkheim, 1938; Homans & Curtis, 1934) in contrast to those theorists who are concerned with conflict, coercion, and change as a way of understanding human affairs (Marx, 1867/1976; Marx & Engels, 1932).

FIGURE 2.1 ■ **Two Assumptive Dimensions of Human Behavior Theories**

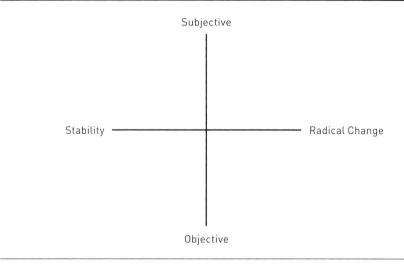

The Subjective–Objective Dimension

For our purposes, the subjective–objective dimension will encompass two central philosophical concepts: ontology and epistemology. What follows is a description of each key concept with questions that you might ask when you are considering the use or application of a theory to social work practice.

Ontology

Ontology is concerned with the very essence of reality; scholars have long debated what we mean by reality (Keat & Urry, 1975; Kolakowski, 1972). Does our social reality exist outside of our awareness of it? If a tree falls in a forest and no one is around to hear it, does it make a sound?

Some assume that the social world or "reality" is external to an individual and that it consists of concrete, tangible, and objective structures. For them, the social world is just as real as the natural world. And, so, we are born into an external world that has a reality of its own; it is not something that we create. It is prior to the existence or consciousness of any human being. No one needs to be in the forest to hear the tree make a sound as it falls; indeed trees fall independently of human sensation and awareness all the time.

However, others view reality as made up of names and concepts that create our social world. Human beings create their own meaning and sense of purpose in the world and this meaning-making or our understandings of how the world operates can and do change all the time. In order to illustrate how humans' perceptions of reality are constantly changing and defined by the person who is observing the reality, the following well-known story is told by a respected Buddhist monk who one day passed by two other monks engaged in lively exchange:

Two monks were watching a flag flapping in the wind. One said to the other, "The flag is moving." The other replied, "The wind is moving." Huineng (the respected Buddhist monk) overheard this. He said, "Not the flag, not the wind, mind is moving." (Aitken, 1995).

Like the Buddhist monks, the meanings that we make of our social (and physical world) can change dramatically and are based on how our mind perceives that reality at that moment in time. Certainly in this way, reality is constantly in the process of change, and how we understand or make meaning of our social world changes based on our perceptions. An ancient philosopher, Heraclitus, once remarked that we cannot step into the same river twice (T. M. Robinson, 1987). Our subjective perceptions define our reality. In its extreme form, nothing exists outside of human awareness or consciousness of it. If a tree falls in the forest and no one hears it fall, then, it has no meaning for humans and in effect, it did not happen. As we examine theories in this textbook, here are some ontological questions we might ask:

- Does this theory view reality as tangible, concrete, and external to the individual, or is reality based on the meanings that human beings give to it?

- Does this theory honor the ways in which our clients perceive their reality?

- When reality is viewed differently by the client, the social work professional, or others (e.g., physician, judge, family member), how do we manage differences between ourselves, our clients, and others?

Epistemology

Epistemology is concerned with how we know what we know and privileges certain kinds of knowledge. It also involves distinguishing justified belief from mere opinion (Giddens, 1974). Key epistemological approaches (or meta-theories) that will be addressed in our text (and that undergird many human behavior theories) include positivism, social constructionism, and pragmatism. *Positivism*, which developed out of the Enlightenment and the Age of Reason, began in England in the 17th century (Crotty, 1998). Positivism emphasized unambiguous knowledge of the world grounded in direct experience through careful scientific observation, not speculation (Comte, 1853). Positivism has ascribed great status to scientific findings, which are viewed with absolute objectivity. However, more recent scholars (Heisenberg, 1930; Murdoch, 1987) have shifted this position and refer to postpositivism, which strives for probabilities (not certainties) and still touts a level of objectivity (but not absolute objectivity).

Social constructionism (Berger & Luckmann, 1966) is rooted in broader notions of postmodernism and deeply challenges positivist claims to objectivity. Social constructionists view all knowledge and meanings as constructed in our interactions between human beings and their world. Our social reality is a function of shared meanings; societies and cultures develop these shared meanings in interactions with others and through language. Social constructionism ascribes great status to multiple, ignored, and at times competing understandings of human beings' narratives in order to uncover the meanings that these participants ascribe to their contextual experiences.

Pragmatism assumes that humans are biological organisms linked to the earth and multiple non-human species in various interdependent relationships (Addams, 1902/2002; Dewey, 1916). Pragmatists believe that we move forward to create the best society we can by humbly acknowledging our fallibility. Pragmatists start with an ethics-based quest for democracy, equality, justice, and freedom for all people and are interested in developing societal conditions to support these ideals. Pragmatists ascribe status to the systematic analyses of societal conditions that can best support democracy for all people.

As social workers, we may strive but struggle to obtain some kind of certainty, objective knowledge, scientific explanations of human behavior, or even ways to predict human behavior. The following case example is provided to explore the difficulties social workers face in drawing upon theories to reach a level of certainty in practice. An older male client shared with the social worker that he was being financially exploited by a family member. In practicing from a critical theoretical perspective, the social worker worked with the older adult to encourage him to participate in a support group with other elders who had experienced financial exploitation. Critical theories indicate that it is often through dialogue with similar others that this older adult can develop a critical consciousness or awareness of his experience of exploitation as part of a larger social problem that many elders experience. This broader knowledge and awareness can in turn impact the older adult to take action to address the financial exploitation (e.g., advocating with policy makers to develop harsher penalties for financial exploitation). However, there is no way for the social worker to predict whether or not the older adult will participate in a support group. And, minimal evidence suggests exactly what the social worker should do to help raise the older adult's critical consciousness of the exploitation. Even though practitioners may be able to make effective use of theories, therapeutic models, or skills, we caution readers in that any theory or "evidence" is a guide at best, and often oversimplified. Practice is filled with messy and important situations in which there are no technical solutions. Practitioners' personal beliefs and assumptions can also unduly impose their reality on clients. In general, human behavior theories and perspectives are at best inadequate, partial, often contradictory, or even wrong.

We encourage readers to search for an epistemology of practice that includes artistic and intuitive processes (as well as scientific research) to bring to our situations of instability, uncertainty, value conflicts, and uniqueness. Human behavior is often unpredictable: people surprise us and are resilient in ways we think not possible. As social workers, our practice with human beings is not like conducting a chemical experiment, where the results are predictable and most often turn out the same way. Social work authors, such as Jane Addams and others, have discussed how social workers' growth involves learning to develop a trial-and-error method of working with clients that includes managing our discomfort, our not-knowing and uncertainty, and which as discussed in Chapter 1, involves a pragmatic approach in which we take into account our clients' unique characteristics and environmental context in order to adjust our thinking and actions (Addams, 1902/2002; Chappell Deckert & Koenig, 2017).

Our growth as professionals often occurs as we reflect upon our practice and are able to adjust what we are doing to best serve our clients. Schön (1983) describes this as reflecting-in-action and indicates that professionals become skilled in learning to "think on their feet." They can think, reflect, and change their responses toward a client in the very moments that they are working with that client. This takes practice to be able to do and involves working in the swampy lowlands and with messy problems that do not have easy solutions. Many social workers, seeing the limits of using scientific evidence to solve these messy practice problems, are not interested in searching for laws or underlying regularities in the social world. Instead, social work professionals often view their understanding of the world as relativistic and contextual. Social workers operate in a relativistic world of "grays," where not much is quickly or easily solvable.

Further, social workers believe that it is only possible to understand human behavior from the point of view of the individuals who are directly involved in the behavior. This has been referred to as contextual knowing, and there are many ways of knowing that include the use of our practice wisdom, our capacity to reflect-in-action, our awareness of clients' stories, and the patterns we might see in those stories that help us with current and future clients. Also, this contextual knowing occurs for clients themselves through dialogue in which they discover new meanings to their narratives (Mehrotra, 2010; Netting & O'Connor, 2005; Weick, 2000; Woodcock, 2012). For example, a social work practitioner worked with a veteran who had experienced childhood sexual abuse by his now-deceased father. After several sessions with the social worker, the veteran was still unable to tap into his emotions and experiences of the abuse and expressed that he felt stuck in his work with the social worker. Unexpectedly, the veteran was called to return home to attend the funeral of a family friend. This spontaneous trip brought back many memories of the sexual abuse that the veteran was able to share in subsequent sessions with the social worker. Returning home provided a social context for the veteran that helped him remember details about the sexual abuse and begin to come to terms with how helpless he was as an 8-year-old boy. The social worker encouraged the veteran to tell his stories of abuse and also suggested that the veteran might make another visit home to not only remember the abuse but also how he had coped with the abuse (e.g., the client had built a make-shift tent near a creek so that he could periodically escape from the abuse). Through this storytelling, the veteran was able to more fully remember the abuse and also honor his capacities for resilience. This example of contextual knowing reflects a social constructionist epistemology, honors the client's knowledge or expertise about his own situation, as well as the practitioner's intuition and capacity to use spontaneous client experiences.

As we examine theories in our textbook, here are some questions that we might ask about the epistemological assumptions of each theory:

- What kind of knowledge does this theory support? (e.g., intuition, research-based evidence, practice wisdom, or a particular epistemological approach such as social constructionism)

- Does this theory seek to explain or predict human behavior?

- Does this theory value knowledge that is subjective, based on personal experience, or even spiritual?

- Does this theory view clients as having expert knowledge about their own experiences?

The Stability–Radical Change Dimension

The stability–radical change dimension involves examining the degree to which a theory emphasizes stability, unity, and cohesiveness in human affairs. This is in contrast with theories that provide explanations for radical or transformative change at an individual, family, group, community, and/or societal level (Burrell & Morgan, 2003). As social workers, we will want to examine if a theory ignores the centrality of growth or change and instead views stability, unity, and cohesiveness as more important than pursuing this change and growth. For example, a social worker who uses family systems theory (which often values helping couples to work through conflict and stay together) may experience major difficulties in using this theory if the couple is engaged in intimate partner violence because systems theory does not provide guidance about which direction the social worker should take (i.e., stability or radical change). For example, in instances of violence, ethical considerations are essential (e.g., a woman's safety) in determining the direction the social worker may need to take in working with the couple. These ethical concerns are not addressed by systems theory.

Social work is very interested in how individuals, families, and communities grow, change, and strive toward health and well-being, and so it also becomes pivotal for us to analyze the assumptions that a theory makes about whether or not change, health, and growth are even possible. Because these ideas will be much more fully addressed in the next section, we will not present questions about growth and change here.

As we examine theories in our textbook, here are some questions that we might ask about stability as part of the stability–radical change dimension:

- Is this theory concerned with stability, unity, or cohesiveness within individuals, families, communities, or societies? How do you know?

- What importance does this theory place on stability, unity, or cohesiveness in contrast to growth and change for individuals, families, communities, or societies?

HOW DOES THIS THEORY ADDRESS GROWTH AND CHANGE?

Social work has used many theories and perspectives for understanding human behavior. Two important historical streams that have impacted our view of how growth and change happens in practice have been expressed through the diagnostic and functional schools. The **diagnostic school** emphasized an approach to practice that involved the expertise of the social work professional in assessing, diagnosing, and treating clients (Hamilton, 1940; Hollis, 1935; Towle, 1945). This school of thought has been prominent in social work's history and still impacts the profession today (e.g., psychodynamic theory, ego psychology; Fleischer & Lee, 2013). However, the **functional school** has provided a meaningful historical alternative rooted in the belief that everyone, no matter how difficult their life circumstances, has a place within them that propels them toward growth and change (See our chapter on psychodynamic theory for a discussion of Otto Rank.)

(Hofstein, 1964; Rank, 1945; V. P. Robinson, 1930; Taft, 1937, 1962). This view of growth and development has been supported by empowerment theory and the strengths perspective (Saleebey, 2005; Simon, 1994) as well as robust empirical findings on a trans-theoretical model of practice, which points to the centrality of the practitioner's hope and belief in the client's capacity to grow and change (Duncan, Miller, Wampold, & Hubble, 2010; Koenig & Spano, 2007).

Along with social work's emphasis on individual and/or family growth and change, social work has long been concerned with how to help communities participate in social change. This has especially been evident in its community practices that involve helping communities organize, develop, plan, and engage in progressive social change for a wide range of challenges that emerge at global and local levels. These challenges include human rights for women and girls, the needs of diverse ethnic and cultural groups, injustices due to class and economic need, and the emerging needs of the natural environment. For example, social workers have been involved in helping South American women organize to combat extreme violence and its impacts on their families (Chappell Deckert, 2013); in supporting grassroots food movements (e.g., local farmers in the development of well-functioning farmer's markets; Cobb, 2011); in organizing community-based youth HIV prevention programs (Chowdhury et al., 2013); and in combatting the erosion of voter rights in the United States (Congressional Social Work Caucus, 2013).

As we examine theories, we will want to ask questions about a theory's assumptions regarding growth and change:

- Does this theory support the belief that individuals and communities can grow and change no matter how difficult the circumstances?

- How does this theory say that growth, development, and/or change occur?

- What is the social worker's role in helping client systems to grow and change?

HOW HOLISTIC IS THIS THEORY?

Holistic thinking involves an awareness that reality needs to be understood in terms of whole patterns; a pattern loses its meaning and imbalance occurs if it is broken down or reduced into parts (Koenig & Spano, 1998; Spano, Koenig, Hudson, & Leiste, 2010). Holistic thinking is highly valued by social work practitioners as evidenced by our emphasis on understanding people within their environments (Gordon, 1969) (See our discussion of pragmatism in Chapter 1.); our expansive perspective of micro-mezzo-macro and now global social work practice (Grise-Owens, Miller, & Owens, 2014); in regard to our view of human nature and reasoning in human activities; and in social work's holistic awareness of growth as including both difficulties and strengths. Social workers place importance on a person-in-environment perspective, which acknowledges the holistic and dynamic interaction between people and their social/natural environments (Bartlett, 1958; Germain, 1973; Gitterman & Germain, 2008; O'Brien & Young, 2006). Our mission has always involved a dual purpose of supporting human capacities and at the same time engaging in social and political efforts to bring about greater societal responsiveness to individual needs. This is reflected in our conception of micro-mezzo-macro practice, which involves working across all levels: with individuals and families, in small groups, at community and social policy levels, in regard to the natural world (Besthorn, Koenig, Spano, & Warren, 2016; Hudson, 2014), and within a global context. This also means that our assessment and treatment practices are holistic, taking into account bio-psycho-social-spiritual elements of our client systems (Bergeron, 2013; Canda & Furman, 2010).

Human nature addresses the question of what it means to be human and encompasses key ideas, such as the impact of free will and the environment on human behavior and humans' use of reason in problem solving. Social workers have long grappled with and embraced holistic views of the role of the environment on human nature and the contrasting role of a person's free will to act autonomously without environmental constraints (Bartlett, 1970; Gordon, 1969). Although some thinkers have described human nature as having fixed, innate qualities that a person is born with, social workers and others have increasingly called this view into question, noting the related and even simultaneous influence of environment and experience on human nature. Scholars and practitioners alike point to the artificial dichotomy between nature and nurture and instead refer to the constant, holistic influences of both nature and nurture on phenomena such as major depression and fetal development (Esposito, Grigorenko, & Sternberg, 2011; Griffiths, 2009). This holistic awareness of the multiple sources or causes of behavior impacts social work at many levels; for example, social work practitioners engage in holistic assessment and treatment with clients and conduct research that acknowledges the complex contexts of clients' lives.

Reason is viewed as a defining feature of human nature and involves the capacity for humans to consciously make sense of their world by establishing and verifying information; changing and adapting beliefs, practices, and institutions based on new and existing information; and by drawing on multiple and integrated sources of knowledge to engage in creative activities and address problems (Freeman, 2008). Reason is closely associated with human activities such as art, science, language, and philosophy and helps us in developing our capacities to make holistic connections and to integrate these multiple sources of knowledge.

A holistic mindset helps us to expand our view of human behavior, which emphasizes health and positive growth along with an awareness of illness and pathology. Through our empowerment, critical feminist, and strengths perspectives, the profession of social work recognizes the potential of people for growth and the capacity to maintain integrity in body, mind, and spirit in spite of crises and difficulties (Collins, 1986; Lee, 2001; Saleebey, 2005). We put forth the idea that holistic thinking includes the view that human qualities can be both a strength and a weakness; that healing is often found right next to the wound (not outside of the person who is wounded); and that growth includes both difficulties and also strengths or triumphs in human functioning.

As we examine theories in our textbook, here are some questions about holistic thinking that we might ask:

- How does this theory view the role of the social and/or physical environment on determining human behavior?

- What does this theory say about the role of biology or genetics on human behavior?

- What does this theory say about the transactions (interactions) between people and their environments?

- Does this theory support the idea that human beings, in spite of difficulties, can reason, act upon, and creatively change their environments?

- How does this theory view the importance of a broad range of bio-psycho-social-spiritual characteristics in shaping the client or community's worldview?

HOW CONSISTENT IS THIS THEORY WITH SOCIAL WORK VALUES AND ETHICS?

Many social work writers have insisted that social work is primarily a value-driven profession and as such view any perspective, theory, practice model, or strategy as needing to be scrutinized for its consistency with our profession's unique core values (Bartlett, 1970; Gordon, 1965). In this section, we will define and discuss these core values as delineated in the Preamble of our *Code of Ethics* (NASW, 2008). These values include: (1) service, (2) social justice, (3) dignity and worth of the person, (4) importance of human relationships, (5) integrity, and (6) competence. Two more social work values will be discussed within the context of these six core values. Client self-determination will be examined in relationship to the value of social justice. Cultural competence will also be discussed as it adds depth to our understanding of the dignity and worth of the person.

People are often drawn to social work because of the profession's distinct emphasis on serving others. Social work scholars have referred to the profession as having a mission to serve others: to help individuals in need and also address broader social problems (Bartlett, 1970; Gordon, 1965). Social work practitioners value their *service* to others above self-interest. For example, many social workers volunteer some portion of their skills and expertise without any expectation of financial compensation (e.g., working for Habitat for Humanity to help build houses, volunteering to provide counseling one evening per week).

Social workers also highly value *social justice* in which they strive to ensure that all members of a society have the same human rights, protections, social benefits, and opportunities. Social workers acknowledge historical and current inequalities, which contribute to vulnerability that many experience within our society. Consequently, social workers engage in practice and policy-based advocacy to confront discrimination, oppression, and institutional inequities across many levels within our society. For example, social workers are engaged in efforts to address issues of unemployment, access to health care, education and housing, child and adult violence (e.g., child abuse, intimate partner violence), poverty, and other forms of social injustice. Social workers strive to support clients' self-determination and freedom as they access services, other information, and resources and as they meaningfully participate in their own decisions and broader life goals. Self-determination and social justice go hand-in-hand. Social justice supports the idea that individuals and society have both rights and responsibilities that they owe each other and further recognizes both individual self-determination and the common social good. Social workers also promote the responsiveness of communities and other social institutions to meet individual needs. Recent authors have also insisted that we expand our view of social justice to include ecological justice (Besthorn et al., 2016). Increasingly, social work educators and practitioners alike are encouraging us to include the natural environment in our clinical and social justice work (e.g., supporting clients in meditating in the beauty of the natural environment; initiating sustainability efforts for clean air and water).

Social workers also value the *dignity and worth of each person*. They treat each client with care and respect, mindful of individual differences (e.g., race, ethnicity, sex, sexual orientation, gender identity or expression, age, marital status, political belief, religion, immigration status, or mental or physical disability). In order to be vigilant about their own prejudices and biases, social workers engage in ongoing education, supervision, and other activities to increase their self-awareness, knowledge, cultural sensitivity, humility, and competence in working with diverse groups of clients. For example, social work educators and practitioners can visit cultural centers (e.g., Native American) in their region and learn from indigenous people about their oppression and resiliency.

Social workers recognize the *importance of human relationships* and understand that relationships are vital for client change and growth. Social workers engage people as partners in the helping process and seek to strengthen clients' relationships with others as a means of enhancing the well-being of individuals, families, social groups, organization, and communities. For example, if we are working with a client who has experienced life events that we are unfamiliar with (e.g., military combat; racial, gender, or age discrimination; intimate partner violence), we can let the client know that we are unaware and even ignorant of the client's experiences. We can encourage clients to tell about their experience and support their expertise and knowledge of these experiences.

Social workers value *integrity*, which can be defined as behaving in a trustworthy manner, while also monitoring their own practice so that it remains consistent with the profession's mission, values, ethical principles, and ethical standards. Social workers' integrity extends to their ethical practice within the organizations with which they are affiliated. For example, if you are a rural social worker, it can be very difficult to maintain boundaries because you are likely to see your clients in the community grocery store or at the movie theater. One way to manage these likely boundary crossings is to have conversations with the client early in your professional relationship. You can let the client know that you will never initiate conversation with the client in a public place. If the client wants to talk with you, then, the client can choose to do so.

Social workers practice within their areas of *competence* and strive to develop and enhance their professional expertise. Social workers are charged with increasing their professional knowledge and skills and are further encouraged to pursue supervision and ongoing training to ensure competence. Social workers should aspire to contribute to the knowledge base of the profession. For example, many social work practitioners pursue training and intensive supervision in specific clinical areas such as motivational interviewing or trauma-informed care. In these ways, social workers can become more knowledgeable about an area of practice.

As we examine theories in our textbook, here are some questions about social work's core values that we might ask:

Service

(1) How can this theory support the client's unique needs and interests?

(2) What emphasis does the theory place on your involvement in addressing broader social or community-based needs?

(3) According to this theory, what is the role of the social worker in advocating for clients to have access to needed resources?

Social Justice

(4) How does this theory address clients' experiences of oppression and discrimination?

(5) What, if any, aspects of service delivery in our agency supports or hinders social justice for this client system?

Self-Determination

(6) How does this theory support (or not support) clients' self-determination and participation in their own growth and change?

Dignity and Worth of Each Person; and Cultural Competence

(7) How does this theory take into account culture, race, age, sexual orientation, gender expression, and other forms of diversity?

Importance of Relationships

(8) Based on this theory, what is your role in supporting or nurturing clients' key relationships with family members, friends, and other support networks?

Integrity

(9) Does your use of this theory require that you persuade, coerce, or deceive clients?

Competence

(10) What kinds of skills and expertise do you need in order to use this theory in social work practice?

(11) What does this theory say about how you monitor and adjust your work to ensure you are meeting agreed-upon client goals?

(12) What education, training, and ongoing supervision will you need?

WHAT ARE THE SOURCES OF KNOWLEDGE THAT SUPPORT THIS THEORY?

In this section, we will examine "evidence" that supports theories presented in this textbook. The evidence we will focus on includes not only empirical research studies but also the client's expertise and your growing practice wisdom and use of critical thinking as a social work professional (See Figure 2.2).

Using Empirical Research

Social work scholars have advocated for an evidence-based approach to practice. They call on practitioners to be ethically competent by identifying and evaluating evidence for intervention strategies that can be used to meet the specific needs of clients (Cournoyer, 2004). Although this is perhaps a laudable goal, there continues to be great concern among social work scholars and practitioners about the use of this kind of "evidence" in social work practice; a growing number of scholars describe limitations of this narrow approach to evidence (Gitterman & Knight, 2013; Witkin & Harrison, 2001). In contrast and for our purposes, the term **evidence-guided practice** will be used to encourage you to explore the theories that will be presented in this text (e.g., theories about human growth and development, psychological and societal processes) and the range of evidence for these theories that comes from multiple sources such as

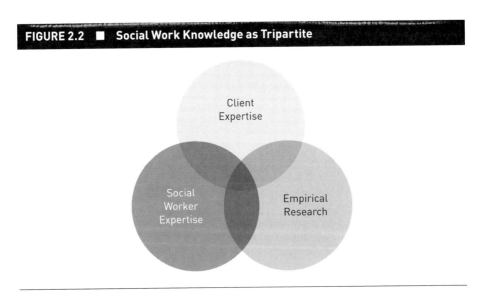

FIGURE 2.2 ■ Social Work Knowledge as Tripartite

the narratives of clients, the critical thinking and creativity of practitioners, and empirically based research studies.

Evidence-guided practice (EGP) is an approach in which interventions are suggested, not prescribed by research. EGP acknowledges the especially broad nature of the social work profession, and the multiple types of knowledge and skills that social workers need in working with clients and communities (e.g., critical thinking, legislative advocacy skills, and respecting and drawing upon clients' expertise about their life experiences). The purpose of social work is much broader than individual client work, and social workers are charged with improving clients' social and psychological functioning, enhancing transactions between people and their environments, and influencing communities, organizations, and political processes (Gitterman & Germain, 2008). Consequently, it is difficult for the social work practitioner to only draw upon narrow intervention research that is unable to acknowledge the broader social context in which social workers practice (e.g., poverty-stricken neighborhoods; communities with high rates of violence, crime, and oppressive or limited police presence; substandard housing; and a lack of social services). These complex social problems do not lend themselves to narrow evidence-based, clinical interventions.

Practitioner Expertise

Instead, EGP acknowledges the use of research studies but places the practitioner and client in the driver's seat in determining if these studies have any relevance for their work together given the broader social context in which the client lives and the responsibilities of the social worker (Betts-Adams, LeCroy, & Matto, 2009; Nevo & Slonim-Nevo, 2011). Authors argue that this is more ethically consistent with social work values of respecting the dignity and worth of our diverse clientele and their self-determination in making decisions that fit best with their life experiences. EGP, unlike evidence-based practice, also values the importance of theory (e.g., theories on multiracial identity development, gender expression, and women's moral development) and views theories in combination with empirical research as providing meaningful information for practice (Gitterman & Knight, 2013; Walker, Koroloff, Briggs, & Friesen, 2007). However, theories and research are not enough to guide practice. Social workers must use their critical thinking, creativity, hunches, self-reflection, and other skills to monitor their practice as well as actively listen to and engage clients in a collaborative process that acknowledges their real-world experiences and expertise. Evidence indicates that practitioners who adhere strictly to interventions are much less able to be authentically present or listen to their clients (Henry, Strupp, Butler, Schacht, & Binder, 1993).

Client Expertise

Taking into account the client's voice and expertise and letting the client take the lead or direct the work has also been a longstanding approach within social work practice. Increasingly, others are acknowledging the importance of client feedback and in letting clients teach us what we need to know about working with them (Duncan, 2012; Koenig & Spano, 2007; Saleebey, 2005; Lambert & Shimokawa, 2011; Shimokawa, Lambert, & Smart, 2010; Slone, Reese, Mathews-Duvall, & Kodet, 2015). Robust studies indicate that client feedback can be obtained across all types of theoretical orientations or diagnoses of individual clients and can be tailored to the individual worker/client relationship (Duncan, 2012). We know much less about how to involve groups and communities in obtaining their feedback on our work.

One Final Note: Common Factors Research

Although common factors researchers limit definitions of practice to psychotherapeutic approaches such as cognitive-behavioral, psychodynamic, or person-centered therapies, what they have found is relevant for our work with individual clients. The general success rate in treated persons using these therapies (which have their roots in many of the theories we discuss in this book) is 67% compared with that of 33% for untreated persons over the same period of time (Lambert, 2013). And, the benefits of these therapies can be found in diverse settings (e.g., public mental health clinics, managed care settings, university counseling settings). However, what is truly fascinating is that none of these proclaimed therapies or models are superior to any other systematically applied psychotherapy approach (Duncan, Miller, Wampold, & Hubble, 2010; Stiles, Barkham, Mellor-Clark, & Connell, 2008). And, although we know that treatment works, Duncan (2014) describes elements that are troubling. First, clients who seek mental health or substance abuse services drop out or quit therapy at significant rates averaging at least 47%. Second, not everyone benefits from treatment; many clients go home without obtaining help. Third, practitioners vary significantly in their clinical effectiveness and they struggle to identify clients who are not doing well. It is important to learn about models, theories, and techniques, but becoming enamored with or believing that salvation can be brought about with any approach is not a good idea. These treatment models account for so little of the clients' growth and change, whereas the client and practitioner—and their relationship—account for so much more.

Five common factors, as highlighted by Duncan (2014), comprise a **transtheoretical perspective**, are interdependent and interactive, and include client, practitioner, the client/practitioner relationship, model/technique, and client feedback. (Because of the overlap and interacting nature of these factors, the percentages for each factor do not add up to 100%.)

First, the client's contribution, which is unique and idiosyncratic (e.g., a supportive partner, spiritual beliefs, a difficult divorce) is the largest contributor, or 40%, of the change that occurs in the therapeutic process. Clients are indeed what drive any change, and our capacity to draw upon their unique characteristics and to help engage them in the work is the most important determinant of client change. Second, the practitioner's effects (e.g., successful therapists attended more to identifying client resources and channeling them toward achieving client goals; successful therapists also have specified skills such as with couple's therapy) (Gassman & Grawe, 2006; Owen, Duncan, Reese, Anker, & Sparks, 2014) account for approximately 36% to 57% of client change. Third, those practitioners who are able to develop strong, positive relationships with clients (and from the client's point of view) represent 36% to 50% of client change. The relationship, or alliance, is one of the best predictors of client outcomes. The alliance refers to the worker–client relationship that focuses on achieving the client's goals. Fourth, the model or technique (and theory) are the beliefs and strategies unique to any given approach. Only 7% of client change is due to the model or technique. However, it is really broader, general effects of treatment including: (a) client's expectancy for improvement; (b) the worker's hope and belief in the client's natural growth, development and change; along with (c) the worker's allegiance to the approach being used that matter much more than any specific model or technique. At least 28% of client change is attributed to these general effects. Fifth, the practitioner's process of obtaining formal, ongoing client feedback and using this feedback to tailor services also impacts client growth and change (Reese, Duncan, Bohanske, Owen, & Minami, 2014). (Although no percentage is attributed to client feedback because this is a newer area of study, indications are that client feedback has an impact on the work.) This client feedback interacts with and integrates all the other common factors.

As we examine theories in this textbook, here are some questions about evidence that we might ask:

- What evidence guides or supports this theory?

- What importance does this theory place on the social worker's expertise?

- What importance does theory place on the client's expertise (e.g., life experiences)?

- Given that a meaningful relationship (or alliance) between the client and worker greatly impacts client growth and change, what importance does this theory place on the development of that professional relationship?

- What does the theory say about how the professional relationship is used to obtain goals for the work? (For example, who defines the goals in the professional relationship? Is it appropriate for practitioners to coerce clients to achieve socially acceptable goals?)

CHAPTER SUMMARY

In this chapter, we have used a conceptual framework (or set of questions that represent key themes) for critiquing theory. This conceptual framework is based on assumptions that have their roots in the history and philosophy of knowledge and values as understood in the profession of social work. Each question in this conceptual framework attempts to get you to look at theories through different lenses just as you would facets of a gemstone. For example:

- If you are exploring the epistemological assumptions behind a theory, you will be examining what kinds of knowledge (e.g., clients' life experience, empirically guided studies, or the practitioner's practice wisdom) are valued by the theory.

- If you want to examine the question of ontology (or what is real), you will want to know how the theory acknowledges the client's views and intimate knowledge of his or her real-world life experiences and challenges.

- If you are exploring a theory to see how holistic it is, this will draw your attention to whether or not the theory can be applied only to individuals, or if it is applicable to community or advocacy-based work.

- If you are examining the theory's emphasis on growth and change, you will want to know how your theory views the possibilities and capabilities of change for the client. Is the theory hopeful or guarded about the prospects for growth in the clients and communities that you work in?

- If you want to know how consistent a theory's major ideas are with social work values and ethics, you will want to explore how the theory addresses oppression and discrimination or how it supports and enhances social justice for diverse groups of people that we are called to work with as social workers.

- Finally, if you are interested in exploring the evidence for a given theory, you will want to examine, among other things, how the theory views the importance of the client's contribution to the work (e.g., a supportive partner, a recent death in the family), the practitioner's capacity to identify client resources that support client goals, and the relationship (or alliance) between the worker and client.

We also provided specific, more detailed questions (that have been included as bullet points) throughout this chapter that flow from the five key questions in our conceptual framework. As we move forward in the text, our goal is to present each theory, taking an in-depth look at a central theorist with relevance for social work practice, and then engage in a critique of the theory using these key questions. Because each theory has different emphases of attention (e.g., some theori focus primarily on internal, psychic processes of individuals while others examine the role of socialization and societal oppression on human behavior), our questions may be responded to in a variety of ways and some may be addressed in much greater detail than others. Theory critique involves not only examining the shortcomings of a theory but also its strengths in being useful for social work practitioners and scholars alike. Your growing practice wisdom will play a major role in determining whether or not a theory is useful to you in your practice.

Key Terms (in order of appearance)

Subjective–objective dimension 25	Diagnostic school 30	Transtheoretical perspective 38
Stability–radical change dimension 25	Functional school 30	
	Reason 32	
	Evidence-guided practice 36	

References

Addams, J. (1902/2002). *Democracy and social ethics*. Urbana: University of Illinois Press.

Aitken, R. (Trans.). (1995). *The gateless barrier: The Wu-men kuan (Mumonkan)*. New York, NY: North Point Press/Farrar, Straus, and Giroux.

Akers, R. L., & Jensen, G. F. (2003). "Taking social learning global": Micro-macro transitions in criminological theory. In R. L. Akers and G. F. Jensen (Eds.), *Social learning theory and the explanation of crime* (pp. 9–38), New Brunswick, NJ: Transaction Publishers.

Bartlett, H. M. (1958). Working definition of social work practice. *Social Work, 3*(2), 5–8.

Bartlett, H. M. (1970). *The common base of social work practice*. New York, NY: National Association of Social Workers.

Berger, P. L., & Luckmann, T. (1966). *The social construction of reality: A treatise in the sociology of knowledge*. Garden City, NY: Doubleday.

Bergeron, M. Y. (2013). The interface of institutional, socio-political, and relational trauma in clinical encounters: The case of Adelita and Mrs. Diaz. *Smith College Studies in Social Work, 83*, 213–232.

Besthorn, F. H., Koenig, T. L., Spano, R., & Warren, S. L. (2016). A critical analysis of social and environmental justice: Reorienting social work to an ethic of ecological justice. In R. Hugman & J. Carter (Eds.), *Rethinking values and ethics in social work* (pp. 146–163). London, England: Palgrave-Macmillan.

Betts-Adams, K., LeCroy, W. C., & Matto, H. C. (2009). Limitations of evidence-based practice for social work education: Unpacking the complexity. *Journal of Social Work Education, 45*(2), 165–186.

Burrell, G., & Morgan, G. (2003). *Sociological paradigms and organizational analysis*. Burlington, VT: Ashgate.

Canda, E. R., & Furman, L. D. (2010). *Spiritual diversity in social work practice*. New York, NY: Oxford University Press.

Chappell Deckert, J. (2013). From persecution to hope: Mennonite mothering in the context of violence. In K. Fast & R. Epp Buller (Eds.), *Mothering Mennonite* (pp. 293–307). Toronto, Canada: Demeter Press.

Chappell Deckert, J. & Koenig, T. L. (2017). Social work perplexity: Dissonance, uncertainty and growth in Kazakhstan. *Qualitative Social Work*, https://doi.org/10.1177/1473325017710086

Chowdhury, J., Alicea, S., Jackson, J. M., Elwyn, L., Rivera-Rodriguez, A., Miranda, A., . . . McKay, M. M. (2013). Collaboration with urban parents to deliver a community-based youth HIV prevention program. *Families in Society, 94*(3), 150–156.

Cobb, T. (2011). *Reclaiming our food: How the grassroots food movement is changing the way we eat*. North Adams, MA: Storey Press.

Collins, B. (1986). Defining feminist social work. *Social Work, 31*, 214–219.

Comte, A. (1853). *The positivist philosophy*, Vol. 1. (H. Martineau, Trans.). London, England: Chapman.

Congressional Social Work Caucus. (2013, March). *Membership in 113th Congress*. Retrieved July 24, 2015, from http://socialworkcaucus-lee.house.gov/membership

Cournoyer, B. (2004). *The evidence-based social work skills book*. Boston, MA: Pearson Education.

Crotty, M. (1998). *The foundations of social research: Meaning and perspective in the research process*. London, England: Sage.

Dewey, J. (1916). *Democracy and education*. New York, NY: Simon & Schuster.

Duncan, B. L. (2012). The partners for change outcome management system (PCOMS): The heart and soul of change project. *Canadian Psychology, 53*(2), 93–104.

Duncan, B. L. (2014). *On becoming a better therapist: Evidence-based practice one client at a time* (2nd ed.). Washington, DC: American Psychological Association.

Duncan, B. L., Miller, S. D., Wampold, B. E., & Hubble, M. A. (2010). *The heart and soul of change: Delivering what works in therapy* (2nd ed.). Washington, DC: American Psychological Association.

Durkheim, E. (1938). *The rules of sociological method.* Glencoe, IL: Free Press.

Esposito, E. A., Grigorenko, E. L., & Sternberg, R. J. (2011). The nature-nurture issue (an illustration using behaviour-genetic research on cognitive development). In A. Slater & G. Bremner (Eds.), *An introduction to developmental psychology* (pp. 79–114). West Sussex, UK: BPS Blackwell & John Wiley & Sons.

Fleischer, L., & Lee, E. (2013). Ego psychological contributions to understanding psychopharmacology and clinical practice in social work education. *Smith College Studies in Social Work, 83,* 446–465.

Freeman, E. M. (2008). Methods of practice interventions. *Encyclopedia of Social Work.* Washington, DC: National Association of Social Workers and Oxford University Press.

Gassman, D., & Grawe, K. (2006). General change mechanisms: The relation between problem activation and resource activation in successful and unsuccessful therapeutic interactions. *Clinical Psychology and Psychotherapy, 13,* 1–11.

Germain, C. B. (1973). An ecological perspective in casework practice. *Social Casework, 54,* 323–330.

Giddens, A. (1974). *Positivism and sociology.* London, England: Heinemann Educational Publishers.

Gitterman, A., & Germain, C. B. (2008). *The life model of social work practice: Advances in knowledge and practice* (3rd ed.). New York, NY: Columbia University Press.

Gitterman, A., & Knight, C. (2013). Evidence-guided practice: Integrating the science and art of social work. *Families in Society, 94*(2), 70–78.

Gordon, W. E. (1965). Toward a social work frame of reference. *Journal of Social Work Education, 1,* 19–26.

Gordon, W. E. (1969). Basic construct for an integrative and generative conception of social work. In G. Hearn (Ed.). *The general systems approach: Contribution toward an holistic conception of social work* (pp. 5–12). New York, NY: National Council on Social Work Education.

Griffiths, P. (2009). The distinction between innate and acquired characteristics. In E. N. Zalta (Ed.), *The Stanford Encyclopedia of Philosophy.* Retrieved July 25, 2015, from http://plato.stanford.edu/archives/fall2009/entries/innate-acquired/

Grise-Owens, E., Miller, J. J., & Owens, L. W. (2014). Responding to global shifts: Meta-practice as a relevant social work practice paradigm. *Journal of Teaching in Social Work, 34,* 46–59.

Hamilton, G. (1940). *Theory and practice in social case work.* New York, NY: Columbia University Press.

Heisenberg, W. (1930). *The physical principles of the quantum theory* (C. Eckart & F. C. Hoyt, Trans.). Chicago, IL: University of Chicago Press.

Henry, W. P., Strupp, H., Butler, S. F., Schacht, T. E., & Binder, J. L. (1993). Effects of training in time-limited dynamic psychotherapy: Changes in therapist behavior. *Consulting and Clinical Psychology, 61,* 434–440.

Hofstein, S. (1964). The nature of process: Its implications for social work. *Journal of Social Work Process, 14,* 13–53.

Hollis, F. (1935). Some contributions of therapy to generalized case work practice. *The Family, 15,* 328–334.

Homans, G. C., & Curtis, C. P. (1934). *An introduction to Pareto, his sociology.* New York, NY: Alfred Knopf.

Hudson, J. W. (2014). *The natural environment in social work education* (Doctoral dissertation). Retrieved from ProQuest, UMI Dissertations Publishing. (3641717)

Keat, R., & Urry, J. (1975). *Social theory as science.* New York, NY: Routledge & Kegan Paul.

Koenig, T. L., & Spano, R. N. (1998). Taoism and the strengths perspective. *Social Thought, 18*(2), 47–65.

Koenig, T., & Spano, R. (2007). The cultivation of social workers' hope in personal and professional practice. *Journal of Religion and Spirituality in Social Work Practice: Social Thought, 26*(3), 45–61.

Kolakowski, L. (1972). *Positivist science.* Harmondsworth, England: Penguin.

Lambert, M. J. (2013). Outcome in psychotherapy: The past and important advances. *Psychotherapy, 50,* 42–51.

Lambert, M. J., & Shimokawa, K. (2011). Collecting client feedback. *Psychology, 48*(1), 72–79.

Lee, J. A. B. (2001). *The empowerment approach to social work services: Building the beloved community* (2nd ed.). New York, NY: Columbia University Press.

National Association of Social Workers (NASW). (2008). *The code of ethics*. Washington, DC: NASW Press.

Marx, K. (1867/1976). *Capital: A critique of political economy*, Vol. 1 (B. Fowkes, Trans.). Harmondsworth, England: Penguin Books.

Marx, K., & Engels, F. (1932). *The German ideology*. London, England: Lawrence and Wishart.

Mehrotra, G. (2010). Toward a continuum of intersectionality theorizing for feminist social work scholarship. *Affilia: Journal of Women and Social Work, 25,* 417–430.

Miller, P. H. (2011). *Theories of developmental psychology*. New York, NY: Worth.

Murdoch, D. (1987). *Niels Bohr's philosophy of physics*. Cambridge, England: Cambridge University Press.

Netting, F. E., & O'Connor, M. K. (2005). Lady boards of managers: Subjugate legacies of governance and administration. *Affilia: Journal of Women and Social Work, 20,* 448–464.

Nevo, I., & Slonim-Nevo, V. (2011). The myth of evidence-based practice: Towards evidence-informed practice. *British Journal of Social Work, 41,* 1176–1197.

O'Brien, P., & Young, D. S. (2006). Challenges of formerly incarcerated women: A holistic approach to assessment, *Families in Society, 87,* 359–366.

Owen, J., Duncan, B., Reese, J., Anker, M., & Sparks, J. (2014). Accounting for therapist variability in couple therapy outcomes: What really matters? *Journal of Sex and Marital Therapy, 40,* 488–502.

Rank, O. (1945). *Will therapy*. New York, NY: Knopf.

Reese, R. J., Duncan, B., Bohanske, R., Owen, J., & Minami, T. (2014). Benchmarking outcomes in a public behavioral health setting: Feedback as a quality improvement strategy. *Journal of Consulting and Clinical Psychology, 83,* 731–742.

Robbins, S. P., Chatterjee, P., & Canda, E. R. (2011). *Contemporary human behavior theory: A critical perspective for social work*. Boston, MA: Allyn & Bacon.

Robinson, T. M. (1987). *Fragments* (Heraclitus, Trans.). Toronto: University of Toronto Press. (Original work published approximately 600 BCE)

Robinson, V. P. (1930). *A changing psychology in social work*. Chapel Hill, NC: University of North Carolina Press.

Saleebey, D. (2005). *The strengths perspective* (4th ed.). Boston, MA: Allyn & Bacon.

Schön, D. A. (1983). *The reflective practitioner: How professionals think in action*. New York, NY: Basic Books.

Shimokawa, K., Lambert, M. J., & Smart, D. W. (2010). Enhancing treatment outcome of patients at risk of treatment failure: Meta-analytic and mega-analytic review of a psychotherapy quality assurance program. *Journal of Consulting and Clinical Psychology, 78*(3), 298–311.

Simon, B. L. (1994). *The empowerment tradition in social work: A history*. New York, NY: Columbia University Press.

Slone, N. C., Reese, R. J., Mathews-Duvall, S., & Kodet, J. (2015). Evaluating the efficacy of client feedback in group psychotherapy. *Group Dynamics, Theory, Research, and Practice, 19*(2), 122–136.

Spano, R., Koenig, T. L., Hudson, J. W., & Leiste, M. R. (2010). East meets west: A non-linear model for understanding human growth and development. *Smith College Studies in Social Work, 80,* 198–214.

Stiles, W. B., Barkham, M., Mellor-Clark, J., & Connell, J. (2008). Effectiveness of cognitive-behavioural, person-centred, and psychodynamic therapies in UK primary-care routine practice: Replication in a larger sample, *Psychological Medicine, 38,* 677–688.

Taft, J. (1937). The relation of function to process in social case work. *Journal of Social Work Process, 1,* 1–18.

Taft, J. (1962). Time as the medium of the helping process. In V. P. Robinson (Ed.), *Jessie Taft: Therapist and social work educator* (pp. 305–324). Philadelphia, PA: University of Philadelphia Press.

Towle, C. (1945). *Common human needs*. Ann Arbor: University of Michigan.

Walker, J., Koroloff, N., Briggs, H., & Friesen, B. (2007). Implementing and sustaining evidence-based practice in social work. *Journal of Social Work Education, 43,* 361–375.

Weick, A. (1987). Reconceptualizing the philosophical perspective of social work. *Social Service Review, 61*, 218–230.

Weick, A. (2000). Hidden voices. *Social Work, 45*, 395–402.

Witkin, S. L., & Gottschalk, S. (1988). Alternative criteria for theory evaluation. *Social Service Review, 62*, 211–224.

Witkin, S. L., & Harrison, W. D. (2001). Whose evidence and for what purpose? *Social Work, 46*, 293–296.

Woodcock, R. (2012). Knowing where you stand: Neoliberal and other foundations for social work. *Journal of Comparative Social Welfare, 28*, 1–15.

CONTEXTUALIZING HUMAN BEHAVIOR THEORY

PHOTO 3.1
Ancient ruins as historical context: Forum Romanum, Rome, Italy.

RATIONALE FOR THE CHAPTER

Why is historical context important to our understanding of human behavior in the social environment? What can be said about how we understand ourselves and our environments is that these understandings are shaped by the larger belief systems that transcend the profession's thinking. While some writers see professions as shaping society's perceptions (Young & Muller, 2014), others argue that professions are shaped by their social contexts (Etzioni, 1969; Flexner, 1915; Greenwood, 1957). Our belief is that our understanding of human beings and their environments reflects the ongoing interactions of the professions with larger social systems (e.g., economic, political, cultural, educational, and historical) that exist at any moment in time.

It is only by breaking down the scope of our examination of human behavior to include interactions of people in their environments that we can begin to understand how "context stripping"—isolating our focus on individuals while excluding their environments—limits our ability to engage in social work practice. Practice requires us to examine the complex interactions between client systems and their respective contexts. Unfortunately, too many theories that guide our understanding of the human condition are based on person *or* environment. We often divide our HBSE (human behavior and the social environment) theory content into "micro" or "macro" level courses. In the micro courses, we focus on individuals, small groups, and families. In the macro courses, we emphasize content related to communities and organizations (Forte & Root, 2011). This structure often results in our attention being focused on one side of the person/environment perspective, which limits the usefulness of the content since what social workers are focused on is finding the optimal matches for maximizing the potential for both personal growth and enhancement of the environment. In addition, we expand the definition of environment beyond the human element of environment (social interactions among humans), to include the physical environment (the built environment such as housing), and the natural environment (non-human elements such as plants, animals, boulders, and the air we breathe) (Besthorn, Koenig, Spano, & Warren, 2016; Gordon, 1962).

For example, beginning in the 1970s, social norms shifted away from an emphasis on community responsibility to provide rehabilitation for incarcerated individuals toward punishment of individuals who were deemed to be personally accountable for their behaviors (Phelps, 2011). This was part of a larger shift suggesting community responsibilities were to be reduced, leaving individuals who needed either rehabilitation or other social services to fend for themselves. This trend has continued in nearly all areas of social services. In some fields of practice, like corrections, it resulted in increased prison populations across the country. In other areas, like public assistance, states sought to reduce the number of people receiving Temporary Assistance for Needy Families (TANF), thereby reducing costs with no attempt to determine the negative impacts on those in need of the resources provided by the policy (Matthews, 2013) (See Table 3.1).

Today, we continue to emphasize personal responsibility over community accountability in many areas of our social services. The popular phrase that captures this neoliberal ideology is that we need to make "government smaller" and emphasize "individual freedom," meanwhile more and more individuals find themselves homeless, hungry, and hopeless, while a small fraction of the population garners more and more resources (Harvey, 2005) (see Critical Theories chapter, Figure 4.2). What is inescapable is that social work exists in political contexts and is shaped by those contexts irrespective of their conservative or liberal trends.

TABLE 3.1 ■ TANF's Decline as a Safety Net for Families

TANF's Role as a Safety Net Has Declined Sharply Over Time

Number of families receiving AFDC/TANF benefits for every 100 families with children in poverty

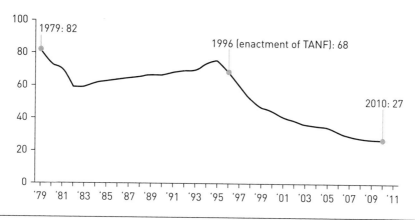

Source: CBPP analysis of poverty data from the Current Population Survey and AFDC/TANF caseload data from Health and Human Services and (since 2006) caseload data collected by CBPP from state agencies.

In summary, the unique challenge that social workers face is that the profession's purpose requires that we focus on people in their environments. As noted above, in human behavior theory, most of the literature focuses on *either* human behavior "or" the environment. This is why we are providing you with conceptual lenses in Chapter 2 that allow you to critique how individual theories relating to HBSE can be helpful or limiting based on their capacity to inform you about the interactions of individuals in their environments within the larger purpose of social work, which focuses on matching individuals and environments to optimize potential growth for both.

ASSUMPTIONS REGARDING OUR DISCUSSION OF HBSE THEORIES AND THEIR CONNECTION TO PRACTICE

The following material identifies a set of assumptions about HBSE theory that we believe is essential to framing the use of human behavior theory for social work practice. Our intention is to articulate the impacts of systems beyond social welfare (e.g., political, economic, cultural) that shape the translations of human behavior theory into practice. These assumptions speak to the need for social workers to employ a complex under-standing of human behavior theories that connect the interactions of small systems (e.g., individuals, small groups, families) to larger systems (neighborhoods, communities, and organizations) at all levels of practice, which occur in a specific **historical context** that shapes those interactions.

The following case example reflects the need to understand individual interactions within the broader social context in which they occur.

CASE EXAMPLE
BEING AFRICAN AMERICAN IN A DOMINANT WHITE SCHOOL

One of the authors was asked to see a 12-year-old African American student who was involved in a series of altercations on the playground at his grade school. Before seeing the student, the worker met with both parents to discuss their concerns. The focus of the school staff was on efforts to improve the student's social and inter-personal skills as a way to reduce the fighting. The mother accepted the school's assessment of the situation. The father had very direct concerns about a White male social worker "messing" in his son's life. What ensued was a lengthy (four hour) conversation that focused on the worker's racial attitudes, beliefs, behaviors, and experiences. The conversation was very personal on both sides of the discussion. It involved focusing on both the father's experience with White people, and the social worker's own experiences as a White social worker working in Black communities. In the end, the worker and the father developed an alliance that sanctioned the creation of a working plan to address the situation. After meeting with the son for a brief period of time he shared with the worker that he was being taunted on the playground and in the halls by White students who referred to him using racial slurs. He was the only African American student in his class, and he experienced himself as an "outsider," estranged from his peers and isolated within the school community.

After the initial contacts with the family, the worker shifted focus to seeking access to the school's administrators and to the staff to rede-fine the "problem" from solely an individual issue to broader concerns about the community norms in the school, which related to the school's stated policies of emphasizing inclusion and respect for diversity as a part of their culture. The result of the staff/administrative meetings included a more open discussion about how they could implement steps to more carefully monitor their own and White students' behaviors and as a way to ensure support for the organizational culture that they sought to create. They set organizational goals including respectful reflection on their own behav-iors, and examination of curriculum issues related to race and in opening up dialogue about racism. Their emphasis was on how they could achieve their stated goals and foster respect and human dignity, for all students in that school.

In this instance, the worker was challenged to address the realities of the racism that exists in America (historical context) by entering into discussion related to how race was influencing this specific family and the worker's ability to help. The social worker must simultaneously address the interpersonal interactions, commonly defined as problems, and their definition by the more powerful members of the community. To examine relationships between the individual and his or her environment, the following assumptions are active in shaping the social worker's responses in this situation.

First, the larger social conditions (trends, ideologies, and events) have direct impacts on our understanding of human behavior in the social environment. The interactions of these larger systems directly impinge on the development of milieus which shape our practice. In this instance, large-scale trends related to race, violence, and education played a role in creating and sustaining the circumstances facing this 12-year-old client, his peers, and his school. Clearly, our young children take in information on a regular basis about how racial issues are playing out in the larger society. They are not immune to the messages that they get suggesting how they should perceive each other. In this instance, some of his peers had messages that the use of racial slurs was somehow acceptable. Whether that came from watching television, interacting with their peers, or off the Internet, it created an environment in which interpersonal aggression was viewed as acceptable among some of his fellow students. Clearly, concerns related to race were central to the relationship between the worker and the client's parents. Thus, race permeated all of the relationships of key people involved, including the family, teachers, the principal, the students, and the worker. To ignore that fact would have significantly thwarted any opportunity for improving this child and his environment. By directly engaging and supporting the participants at the micro level, individual family and staff, the larger issues could be acknowledged by the participants in such a way as to allow a change in perceptions held by all the participants (Lynn & Parker, 2006). This understanding of human behavior in the social environment was crucial to the development of strategies that allowed all of the participants to find new ways to address the underlying issues that were impacting the situation. This perspective created a situation that fostered growth for both the person and the environment.

Second, human beings and communities are mutually interdependent. Humans cannot live without communities, and communities will disintegrate when they fail to meet the needs of their individual members. As Aristotle observed, human beings are social animals and therefore they must understand the reality that without communities, humans cannot prosper. And, communities will wither without the participation of individuals who make up the community. In this situation, the connection between the individuals and the community required the practitioner to integrate human behavior theory (e.g., Erikson's (1950) life stage model regarding individual development and family systems theory) with organizational theory and critical race theory as perspectives for understanding the complex interactions among the family, school staff, the student and his peers, and himself. No one human behavior theory exists that can address all aspects of this common but complex practice situation, which requires connections to be made between individual needs and community needs. Acknowledging this client's need for community and the need for the community to include him in order to reach their goals became the focus of the work.

Third, there are many ways to understand the interactions of individuals and their environments. The use of human behavior theory is a product of a specific historical context in which these theories occur. They represent the beliefs we hold at a particular moment in time. If this case example had occurred in the 1920s, after Freud had completed a lecture tour across the United States and his ideas had begun permeating the culture, social workers would have likely used psychodynamic theory to define the situation. This would have led to an emphasis on working with the student on his intrapsychic dynamics, or struggles with authority. The work would have focused on helping him to resolve these intrapsychic problems as a way to address his behaviors. Given what the theory suggests about the dynamics of the situation, the focus would have been on the student and possibly on any family problems that could be found. Today, with the emergence of critical race theory, social workers have a perspective that orients them toward the larger social conditions. In this situation, racism is a factor that connects larger system issues with the immediate situation on the playground. Current reactions to police violence expressed in the phrase, "Black lives matter" demonstrates this point. In other words, feminist authors when speaking about gender, have asserted that the *personal is political* (Mills, 1959; Morgan, 1970). By expanding our understanding of the situation to include the interactions of both the community and the individual we are able to more comprehensively develop practice strategies that allow us to be more effective in our work at both levels of intervention.

Fourth, historical context is a framework that consists of important questions about events and situations surrounding our work that define our understanding of human behavior in the events we face each day as practitioners. In this instance, while our entry point is the individual in the school, we must look at the broader forces that are shaping both the school's and the children's behaviors. Some trends affecting the current historical context include the constant focus on racial tensions in many communities across the nation, the turmoil in schools due to policies that redefine the role of the school to encompass many more activities (e.g., providing students with food on the weekends) and defund education, and related economic policies that currently have impacts on many families. To ignore the reality that our local institutions are directly affected by these national trends means that social workers could focus solely on working at an individual level isolated from the larger forces shaping those behaviors. We would be left with no alternative but to use human behavior theories that reduce their focus to idiosyncratic and individual series of events and thereby participate in context stripping.

Fifth, historical context is also a way to ask important questions about our role in the choice of human behavior theory used in specific practice situations. From its inception, social work has had a dual purpose: social control and social change. Social control consists of activities that attempt to induce conformity to existing community standards, and social change focuses on reforming or replacing institutional structures in our society. Trying to find an appropriate balance between these two, often conflicting aspects of our practice creates significant tension for most workers. Since most social workers, like the one described in this example, are asked to deal with "problems" in the agencies in which we are employed, we are often pressured to emphasize the social control components of our practice. Most of the agencies in which we work have as a part of their stated function elements of social control. We often feel pressured by law, agency policy, administrative practices, and often peers to get clients to conform to larger social norms.

In our example, the "problems" were defined as individual in nature and the solution was to reduce the existing behaviors without examining the deeper causes leading to those behaviors. Had the worker stayed at the level of accepting the staff's definition of the problem as having to do with authority and poor peer socialization skills, it would have allowed the institution to ignore what were the underlying problems for both the student and the school. The need to incorporate both the individual and the environment in our perspective without prejudging where the problem is located is what differentiates social work from other helping professions. Our job to match persons and environments in order to support the maximization of their respective growth is the fundamental purpose of social work. It cannot be achieved if one separates the interactions between the two components.

DEFINING HISTORICAL CONTEXT

This portion of the chapter connects the preceding assumptions about human behavior with the contribution that history makes to our understanding of the study of human behavior in the social environment. More specifically, it will focus on the historical context as a critical factor in shaping specific thinking and benefits as they impact our practice. It acknowledges the reality that history is most often taught in small segments that are disconnected from the primary subject matter of a course. For example, most social work students are introduced to some historical materials but it consists of recitation of dates, brief mention of individuals in the profession's history, and certain key benchmarks like the passage of the Social Security Act (Spano, 1986). However, in most courses this information is disconnected from any direct application to the main content of the course.

Our focus here is connecting the events occurring in the larger society with their impact on human behavior in the social environment. Historical context is the dirt in which ideas about human behavior in the social environment are grown. It consists of understanding how economic, religious, political, and social welfare systems interact and how these interactions shape our understanding and application of material to human behavior (Spano, 1986). For example, the current emphasis on using models to drive our practice, flourishes in an historical context that emphasizes efficiency in all arenas of practice. The neoliberal context in which we practice presumes that unless outcomes can be measured, they have no value. Therefore, if we are not using evidence-based practices (EBPs) (and certain types of EBPs are valued over others) we are likely not to obtain resources by funders in order to do our work. In other words, the criteria used to define "success" are often driven by the larger economic, political, educational, and social welfare systems that exclude the voices of clients and often marginalize the voices of professionals who are charged with the delivery of services. For example, in the past few years, many state governments enacted measures to "reform" TANF and defined success as reducing the number of people who receive benefits and, in turn, reducing costs to states. There has been no mention of improving the conditions in which recipients live (Matthews, 2013).

CASE EXAMPLE
UNDERSTANDING A TEENAGER'S ANGRY OUTBURSTS

This case situation involves a faith-based group home for children. The director was describing to board members the behavior of one of the residents. The resident was a 13-year-old male who had been in 11 different foster placements. He had been in this home for approximately four months when he began to experience significant behavioral issues. He had numerous incidents of uncontrollable rage both at home and at the school. The police had been called on two occasions to assist in controlling his outbursts.

(Continued)

(Continued)

One of the board members had learned about the incidents from his wife who was a teacher in the student's school building. The board member raised questions about the situation at the next board meeting. His concerns were both about the child and the staff. The director described the specific incidences that the staff had been handling and their responses to what happened, with no mention of diagnoses. What followed was an intense discussion among the board members reflecting their concerns and their understanding of this situation. All of the members expressed concern about the child, and about three-fourths of the members expressed interest in the guidelines that were being used for the management of the situation and expressed the belief that these behaviors were driven by intense psychological pressures experienced by this child. The director had information that the child was diagnosed with reactive attachment disorder (RAD) but had not shared that during the discussion. The other one-fourth of the board members were focused on his behavior as a manifestation of "evil" and wanted to have the staff bring him and the other children to church services every week as a means to help rid him of these behaviors. These different interpretations of human behavior lead to very different responses based on divergent meanings given to the same behavior.

The following four questions illustrate how historical context can be helpful in the study of human behavior in the social environment.

First, what are the assumptions about human behavior in the social environment that shape responses to social conditions (policy) and interpersonal behavior (direct practice)? The following example demonstrates how people see the same thing and arrive at very different conclusions.

Second, why is this particular theory or perspective emerging at this specific time? For instance, what were the forces that were in play in the late 1800s and the early 1900s that shaped the development of psychodynamic theory? Understanding how sexuality was defined during the Victorian Era is extremely informative when you read how these larger ideas were translated into Freud's writings. For example, you may very well ask questions about the "sexist" elements of psychodynamic theory but any critique should include an understanding of the Victorian perceptions of gender and specifically about how women were viewed in that context. When you understand the context within which the theory was developed, you are in a much stronger position to both understand the theory and to analyze its usefulness, or lack of usefulness, in our present context. Without an understanding of the evolution of the theoretical ideas, you are forced to accept or reject them based solely on your own personal perspectives, which are also embedded in a specific or current historical context. By connecting the current context to the historical context you have a tool that allows you to not only understand but analyze the usefulness of specific elements of the theory. In this instance, Freud's notion about gender may not be transferable to your practice. However, concepts like transference and countertransference may be quite useful in your current practice.

Third, ask the question, is this a new understanding of human behavior? The proliferation of human behavior theory from the late-1800s until the present is quite extensive. Often, what happens is that there are multiple iterations of ideas that are given new names or there is a high degree of overlap among many theories as they are translated into practice models. For example, the utilization of psychodynamic theory in social work began in the 1920s. Social work's understanding of its translation into practice was much closer to Freud's interpretation of his theory. As time moved forward, the psychosocial approach and ego psychology supplanted the original understandings of psychodynamic theory and modified them in such a way that they became more appropriate to practice in social work. Thus, years on a couch, four times a week, projecting one's thoughts and feelings, was inappropriate to the tasks expected to be performed by social workers. Our clientele, our agency context, and limited resources all required that social work modify this particular understanding of the human condition in such a way that it was possible to use within the social work profession.

Fourth, what is it that makes this understanding of human behavior important in our current context? An outstanding example of how human behavior theory gets used to explain connections between human beings and the larger systems plays out in the area of poverty. There are essentially two divergent perspectives that have competed for nearly 600 years. The first rests on the notion that poverty is created by problems associated with social structures in the larger society (Hunter, 1912; Orshansky, 1969; Wolfer, 2014). The second rests on the notion that poverty is a personal matter that represents some kind of character flaw in the individual (Lei, 2013; Shaw, 1890). This will be taken up in greater detail later in the chapter. What is important here is to acknowledge that depending on the perspective you apply, you come out with very different strategies to impact clients based on your definition of this condition. In reality, as social workers, we need to be able to examine multiple perspectives that may in fact suggest how to focus on both the individual and the environment in order to develop practice strategies useful to mitigate the impact of poverty on the individual while simultaneously focusing on system changes that also need to be in place in order to address this complex situation.

In summary, our historical context framework focuses on the four questions in Table 3.2. These questions, taken together, provide social workers with useful information that moves beyond focusing solely on the development of skills to deliver professional services, toward examining the impacts of larger social, structural, and cultural forces that shape what we are doing in our relationships with clients. The use of this historical context framework connects human beings to their environments and with larger social trends to more directly critique and to operationalize the feminist adage that the *personal is political*. Using this framework creates opportunities for social workers to explore ways to unite people and their environments in order to simultaneously achieve a balance between our roles as agents of social control and advocates for social change.

TABLE 3.2 ■ Historical Context Framework Questions

1. What are the assumptions about human behavior in the social environment that shape our responses to social conditions (policy) and interpersonal behavior (direct practice)?

2. Why is this particular theory or perspective emerging at this moment in time?

3. Is this theory or perspective a new understanding of human behavior?

4. What is it that makes this understanding of human behavior important to our current context?

APPLICATION OF HISTORICAL CONTEXT FRAMEWORK

This section examines and applies the historical context to two different periods of time in order to demonstrate how it may be useful to you as a social work practitioner when you read human behavior theory as well as its translation into practice. The Elizabethan Period and later half of the 1800s up until WWI serve as exemplars for using historical context as a means to integrate both old and new material into your knowledge base and as a way to avoid what we earlier identified as "context stripping" when applying human behavior theory. This section begins with a brief overview that illustrates how responses to social and personal concerns were present from the outset of the creation of human communities, not just during the past 600 years.

Overview

Long before people developed what we now call human behavior theory, societies drew upon numerous belief systems that explained why people behaved in certain ways. Many of these ideas were drawn from emerging religious traditions that suggested how we should live and respond to each other. There were two strong themes in these early moral traditions: charity and social justice. An early example of this type of thinking can be found in the Egyptian *Book of the Dead*, published in 3500 BC. In this book, "acts of mercy" were required by individuals to protect others from harm (Popple & Leighninger, 2005). Similarly in the Jewish *Torah*, the Christian *Bible* and Muslim *Quran*, we see strong assertions about how people ought to behave toward each other in their community. Because of their emphasis on morality, or behaving ethically, their perceptions were deeply rooted in their respective moral foundations. And, these moral foundations had direct connections to how each tradition understood human behavior. In addition to theology, parallel belief systems were developed by individuals drawing on the thinking of philosophers, including Aristotle, Socrates, Plato, and Cicero, as well as many other classical and medieval thinkers.

The importance of these traditions is they were applied in ways that established community norms that determined what "charity" and "social justice" meant for the people in their respective communities. For example, people who needed assistance were sorted into categories called "worthy" and "unworthy." People who were physically or mentally challenged, orphaned, or unable to take care of themselves based on circumstances beyond their control were deemed to be "**worthy poor**." The explanations for why these people needed help were most often rooted in a belief that these afflictions had been visited upon them by God or were circumstances beyond their control. People who chose not to work or engaged in stealing, abuse, assault, lying, and cheating received the label "**unworthy poor**." They were seen as individuals whose conditions were created by their own choices, and therefore, worthy of punishment. These early perceptions divided people into categories of good and evil, which reflected the community's understanding of human behavior and its sources. Hence, early responses to social welfare were often the purview of the churches. Religious leaders took a central role in dispensing resources for those who deserved charity and punishing or admonishing those they felt were undeserving of help.

The preceding information provides an exceptionally brief overview of some of the sources for the early development of responses to individual and community struggles, later to emerge as components of a social welfare system in more advanced societies. Its purpose is simply to introduce the reality that the problems we have in our societies are long-standing, complex, and a product of interactions among all of the systems that make up communities including economic, political, religious, and cultural as well as social welfare. The following two descriptions provide exemplars of certain themes that remained central to our understanding of human behavior from our earliest communities to the present time. First, the most important themes center on the role the interactions of these systems play in shaping our understanding of human behavior theory. Although there have been many different arrangements of the systems, we will pay special attention to the influence of religious traditions especially those that emphasized individual responsibility, while recognizing that there were many other religious traditions that also influenced social welfare at various points in time. The rationale for this choice rests on the direct influence these traditions had as they related to assigning individual responsibility as a primary cause for many social problems. This was especially true in the Elizabethan Era, during which time the poor laws were codified. It is less the case when we look at the Progressive era (1895 to 1917), during which time there was much more active involvement by churches that represented views guided by beliefs that balanced charity with the need to aspire to social justice. Second, we will also see how social science ideas took on greater importance as a rival explanation for social conditions during the Progressive era.

The importance and persistence of the tensions between these two paradigms continues to this day. For example, you need only look at the current arguments about the nature of homosexuality to see a continuing clash between these two perspectives. On one side of the argument, some conservative Christians have drawn theological explanations to frame homosexuality as abominable, sinful, and a matter of personal choice. On the other side, some individuals rely on social science explanations based on genetics, biology, and the need for more information to understand this aspect of human behavior. The point to be made here is that this is not a blanket condemnation of all theological views nor an endorsement of the social sciences; however, the very real and continuing tensions between those who hold very different beliefs continue to have an impact on our current debates and shape our understanding of human behavior.

Elizabethan Poor Laws

The following discussion attempts to use the emergence of the **Elizabethan Poor Laws** as an example of how human behavior theory defines a problem, gives meaning to people's behavior in relationship to a problem, and defines appropriate responses to those behaviors based on the community's understanding of human behavior. Most of you have some information about this topic, the poor laws, based on courses you took in social policy and in your introductory social welfare classes. What follows is a summary of the themes that existed during that period of time and how those themes interacted to create the historical context that produced these documents.

The development of the responses that later came to be known as the Elizabethan Poor Laws came on the cusp of significant social, cultural, and intellectual developments that impacted our understanding of human beings. What you are exposed to in your policy classes regarding the definition of the Elizabethan Poor Laws actually represents a two-and-a-half-century compilation of rules, regulations, and laws that came in response to the larger social changes impacting society. The beginnings of public relief occurred in the first half of the 16th century, with the passage of the Statute of 1536, which contained most of the elements of the English responses to the poor. Elements of the statute included whipping individuals for not finding work, returning those individuals to the town of their birth, and indenturing children, between the ages of 5 and 14, who were found begging. In addition, provisions were made to collect charitable contributions by church wardens and created systems of accountability for charitable expenditures (de Schweinitz, 1961).

So what was happening during this period that would account for these kinds of responses? The answers to this question are complex but important to understand. One of the major themes has to do with the changing social structures that came as English society moved through a process that allowed for the transition from feudal society to the early beginnings of the capitalist economy. Both the transition from feudal structures to capitalist structures and the development of new responses to these changes required significant alterations of both social institutions and the people who lived in these communities. In essence, the existing economic, political, religious, and emerging social welfare systems were faced with new sets of problems that could not be solved using traditional means. For example, in the feudal system there was a very clearly structured relationship between nobles and the peasant population. Nobles were able to run their estates, which included tasks like food production, protection of their lands, and the productions of goods for consumption on a daily basis like clothing and shelter. Workers received a small portion of what they produced and were provided protection by the lord of the manor from incursions by outsiders. By the mid-1300s, wages were beginning to replace the feudal system. With the creation of wages, peasants began to leave the feudal estates for urban areas in an effort to sell their labor for wages rather than continuing subsistence living. The result was greater freedom and mobility for workers. These social changes led to a decade, in the 1590s, of widespread food scarcity, higher prices, thievery, and social disorder. In essence, these changes helped destabilize the fundamental structures that had previously bound the community together.

In part, the English response to these changes was to more formally codify prior laws and regulations into a document that reflected their understanding of the current challenges, including their perspectives about why people were behaving in new and troubling ways and what could be done to change their behavior. The following are the basic elements of what we refer to as English Poor Laws of 1601 (Berg-Weger, 2013; de Schweinitz, 1961):

1. Parents were responsible for their children and grandchildren

2. Children were responsible for their parents and grandparents

3. Vagrants who refuse to work were committed to a house of correction, whipped, branded, stoned, or put to death

4. There was an assumption of state responsibility for the maintenance of life, as a legal right

5. There were three categories of "worthy" dependents: needy children (apprenticeships); able-bodied (provided with work); and the impotent, who could receive indoor relief (poorhouse) or outdoor relief (in their own homes or the homes of others in the community)

6. Help was to be provided by the local community where the individual was born

7. Money was collected either voluntarily or through taxes when necessary

8. Amounts to be received by the poor were governed by the concept of "less eligibility," which meant that the amount of assistance provided would be lower than the lowest paid worker in the community

In addition, the poor were divided into two broad categories, the "worthy" and the "unworthy" poor. People who physically, mentally challenged, orphaned, or unable to take care of themselves based on circumstances beyond their control were deemed to be "worthy" poor. People who had no physical defects but were without employment or engaged in stealing, abuse, assault, lying, and cheating received a label of "unworthy" poor. The unworthy poor had no moral claim on the community for assistance and in fact were to be punished because their maladies were created by their own choices for which they should take full responsibility. On the other hand, the worthy poor, who were the poor through no fault of their own should be extended reasonable help.

Coupled with the political and economic changes outlined above, there were additional dimensions that were reflected by this language of designating people as worthy or unworthy poor. These ideas were based in some Christian traditions that highly emphasized moral explanations for the behavior of the poor. They moved from the assumption that human beings were essentially lazy and that character flaws caused them to be poor. It is important to acknowledge that not all religious institutions shared these views; however, this particular perspective had significant influence on the development of the Elizabethan Poor Laws in ways that other theological perspectives did not. Sermons from the churches that influenced the Elizabethan Poor Laws gave warnings to parishioners about being careful not to encourage any level of dependence on charity. Their concern focused on pauperism, not poverty. George Herbert's *The Country Parson* (see Hutchinson, 1941, p. 274) illustrates this view,

> the great and nationall [sic] sin of this Land [the Parson . . . should] . . . esteem to be idleness. . . . For men [who] have nothing to do . . . fall into drink, to steal, to whore, to scoffe, to revile to all sorts of gamings . . . idleness is twofold, one of having no calling, the other is walking carelessly in our calling.

Their concern focused on pauperism, or the moral character of the poor, and not the fact that poverty existed.

Summary. Our role as social workers and many of our sectarian agencies remains rooted in moral traditions that impact our practice. We are often sanctioned to work with clients based on conflicting belief systems rooted in both religion (values) and science (knowledge) that shape how we understand human behavior, and how we develop our responses based on those understandings. The Elizabethan Era initiated the collaboration between religion and the emerging political structures that continue to provide services for people in our communities. The persistence of these belief systems often clash when social workers are faced with difficult questions about what they "should do" based on opposing interpretations of client behaviors. For example, if a social worker works with a woman who is struggling with the decision about whether to continue or terminate a pregnancy, the social worker will face ethical dilemmas that are not answered fully in the NASW *Code of Ethics* (2017). Our knowledge base clearly indicates that for each client, such decisions create challenges at the psychological, interpersonal, social, and spiritual levels. Ensuring that social workers have adequate knowledge to address these complex interactions is central to competent practice. In addition, managing clients' moral perspectives and our own, often complicates the decision-making process. Knowing the differences between these two very differing sources for understanding human behavior is central to competent practice.

Human Behavior Theory From the Mid-1800s to 1920

As we noted in the previous section of the chapter, the emergence of the Elizabethan Poor Laws represented a codification of 250 years of beliefs about human behavior, administrative rulings, and the social change that impacted English society. We will now look at the mid-1800s to the outset of World War I in the United States. The reason we chose this time period is that it demonstrates both the continuities and the significant changes occurring as a result of emerging human behavior theories. It also represents a period of time when the social sanction for providing help to individuals in need transitioned from religiously based local institutions and local community political structures (e.g., local sheriffs and church "wardens") to more complex institutions specialized in providing resources and services to specific groups (e.g., children's institutions, correctional facilities, and large hospitals for the mentally ill) (Rothman, 1971). It also represented a period of time in which the actual services in many of these areas moved from unpaid volunteers to the emergence of paid professionals to provide services for these same populations (Pumphrey & Pumphrey, 1964; Spano & Koenig, in press; Trattner, 1974).

From the time that the first European immigrants arrived in North America, they developed responses to the same types of problems that they had faced in Europe. Their responses were shaped by their views about human behavior, which ran very parallel to what we identified in the preceding section. First, they were strongly influenced by the religious traditions that existed in their countries of origin. For the most part, that meant largely Christian perspectives held by the immigrants continued to hold sway with regard to their understanding of human behavior. Furthermore, they were influenced by the new context in which they had settled that provided access to large tracts of land and became part of America's response to handling social problems (Turner, 1935). A second influence was the fact that they lived in small, isolated communities that had subsistence economies, where there were often no excess resources to respond to problem behaviors. Finally, they retained beliefs suggesting wealthy members of the community were morally superior to those individuals who had little or no resources (Weber, 1930). These conditions supported existing beliefs that when people behaved badly, it was their responsibility to correct their action and the community meted out punishment based on the assertions underlying that belief system. Because they had meager resources, they depended on families to take care of any problem behaviors of their members or they utilized inexpensive responses such as "stocks" to allow the community to punish wrong-doers. These patterns remained fairly stable from colonial times to the mid-19th century.

By the **Jacksonian era**, 1830s to 1850s, significant social change began occurring. These changes affected peoples' understanding about new social problems that were challenging the very foundations of American society. Native-born European Americans were faced with trying to understand the increase in the numbers of new immigrants coming to their shores. They came from different cultures, spoke different languages, and represented different religious traditions (Rothman, 1971). As a result, there was concern about the need to control the diversity that was represented by the influx of these newcomers. In his book, *The Discovery of the Asylum*, Rothman traces the emerging views about how human behavior theory played out in the development of new social institutions including those developed for children (orphanages), individuals with mental illness (asylums), and people convicted of crimes (prisons). Each of these responses shared the belief that human behavior could be shaped and corrected if people were subjected to a strict regimen that would teach them the proper way to behave. The above-named institutions shared in common very specific and highly structured environments that were used to shape individual responses along more socially acceptable lines (Rothman, 1971). The idea behind the creation of these institutions was that they would serve as experimental communities that would allow the larger society to replicate their practices by translating them into the larger society. One of the goals was to ensure a sense of order, and with that order came a certain amount of control over the behaviors of the immigrants as well as others who were refusing to behave in ways that the dominant groups believed to be appropriate.

As these efforts began to take hold, a transition occurred that began expanding the type of people who were delivering the services. New organizations emerged, like the Association for Improving the Conditions of the Poor (AICP). The AICP developed a better-trained group of volunteer women who visited the poor. Their perspective on human behavior rested on the belief that their responsibility was to be role models for poor families. They saw themselves as teachers who had a moral responsibility to show the poor how they should lead their lives. They carried with them a heavy dose of moral authority based on their particular religious belief systems. Hence, they were very concerned about addressing issues related to alcohol and drug abuse as well as sexual behaviors, and more specifically on "pauperism" (i.e., "unworthy" poor who had the capacity to work but did not seek employment) (Axinn & Levin, 1975). Their approach combined saving the poor by providing "moral character development" as well as educating them on proper social behaviors. The former was based on long-standing religious belief systems about the causes of human behavior and the latter suggested that part of their work was to model correct behavior, which introduced the view that human beings can be taught new behaviors. However, no matter which method was being used, the workers' belief system was based on moral frameworks held by the service providers rather than those of their clients.

The most important transition was the development of systematic collection of information about the conditions in which the poor lived. This marked the beginning of the shift toward connecting individual behaviors with the social environments in which people lived. This led to an expansion of information that would later become the basis for the inclusion of a rival paradigm for understanding human behavior theory.

Human Behavior Theory in the Late 1800s

During the latter half of the 1800s, as the population grew, cities and farming communities underwent significant changes. These changes were driven by immigration, urbanization, and industrialization (Hofstadter, 1955). These three trends changed nearly every aspect of American communities and required new responses that redefined our understanding of human behavior theory. The challenges demanded more complex understanding of the emerging social forces that were shaping not only people's behavior, but also their opportunities to function in acceptable ways in the larger society. These changes demanded a further expansion of our understanding of human behavior to include the impacts of political, economic, cultural, social welfare, and educational systems on people's behavior. The responses still contained large elements of religion, but now they included emerging awareness that human behavior had to be understood in the context in which it was occurring. Connections were made between larger social events and individual behaviors that were observed by those providing services to others in need (Popple & Leighninger, 2005; Pumphrey & Pumphrey, 1964; Richmond, 1906). For example, social problems were connected to cyclical economic depressions, the Civil War, massive waves of immigration, and significant increases in migration that fed urbanization. In addition, the arrival of industrialization was viewed by those early social welfare workers as a contributing factor that went beyond the realm of personal responsibility.

The more narrow moralistic views of the AICP gave way to the emergence of the Charity Organization Societies (COS), which further developed this transition. Like their predecessors, the COS organizations were concerned about ending pauperism and in providing minimal charity for those who could not work due to some incapacity such as age, physical illness, or blindness (Leiby, 1978). What the COS workers did was to collect information about their clients and their environments in order to apply what they called "scientific charity." While this approach remained quite different from our understanding of human behavior, it began to include ideas for understanding human behavior that were coming from the emerging disciplines of political science, economics, psychology, sociology, and education (Lewis, 1954; Lubove, 1965).

In the beginning, the COS organizations never challenged the basic assumptions about the causes of poverty. Instead, they used scientific charity to achieve two goals: to make more efficient use of the money given to private agencies and to keep the poor from becoming dependent on charity, which could hinder their path to self-sufficiency. Meanwhile, some of the new COS workers, including Mary Richmond, who was the secretary of the COS in Baltimore, Maryland, and a leader in the development of casework, were beginning to explore newer human behavior theories such as those identified in the preceding paragraph along with an emerging "medical model." The medical model emphasized collection of information about not only the individuals but also the environments in which they were operating as a way to explain their behavior (Richmond, 1917, 1930).

Meanwhile, as the charity organization societies began their transition from an individually oriented theological perspective toward the use of social sciences to understand and explain people's behavior, another group of social reformers emerged in connection with a broader social movement called the **Social Gospel movement**. This group was led by Protestant progressives who were focused on the same social problems: industrialization, urbanization, and immigration. The Social Gospel adherents were different from their COS counterparts when it came to their theological perspectives. The theology that informed the early work in the COS movement was focused on individual salvation whereas the Social Gospel adherents focused on social salvation, based on community action aimed at changing social structure. (Davis, 1967). Their influence coincided with the development of the Settlement House Movement in social work. While most of the settlement house workers were not directly involved in the Social Gospel movement, they often cooperated in attempting to bring about reforms related to improving urban housing, shorter working hours, better working conditions for women, and unemployment insurance (Addams, 1897).

During the **Progressive era**, unlike the Elizabethan era, we can see the active participation of more liberal theologians' reform perspectives directly impacting our understanding of human behavior and offering alternative understandings of the problems facing human beings and connecting their behavior to the context in which it occurred. This perspective remains an important influence, though often cyclical, in the development of social welfare and social work. For example, the civil rights movement in the 1960s was driven by participation among a number of groups including labor unions, church leaders like Martin Luther King, and community activists.

Consistent with social reform and more liberal theological perspectives, the emergence of social and natural sciences created what Thomas Kuhn (1962) referred to as a "**scientific revolution**," which started after the Civil War. The tension between moralistic and social reform elements continues in present debates about human behavior theory and its interaction with social issues. This new paradigm pushed social workers to move beyond prior historical explanations to explore their understanding of human behavior. For example, up until this time social workers believed that people were poor because of extravagance, improvidence, indolence, and intemperance (Shaw, 1890). Each of these concepts focused on pauperism, which emphasized attention on the individual person and what service providers believed were moral character flaws that created their maladies. By the turn of the century, Richmond and her COS contemporaries began collecting information about clients that challenged existing views of what caused problems for the poor (Richmond, 1917). They found that patterns of structural barriers such as unemployment; inadequate food, clothing, and shelter; periodic economic depressions; and physical illnesses or death were contributing factors in most cases. These were significant shifts in perspectives that changed the language used to describe the poor. It resulted in early social workers moving from a concern about pauperism to concern about poverty. This language shift signals the influence of a social science paradigm that recognized social problems like poverty as having structural components far beyond the control of any individual or family. This perspective was articulated in Robert Hunter's landmark book, *Poverty* (Hunter, 1912).

The foundation for this paradigm shift had been laid over the preceding 100 years by such well-known thinkers as Adam Smith, Karl Marx, Charles Darwin, William Sumner, and Albion Small, who were all social scientists writing about the nature of conflict in societies. Others, including William James, Charles Cooley, George Herbert Mead, and W. I. Thomas, provided new theories of human behavior out of the school of thought called symbolic interactionism. In social action theory, Max Weber, Thorstein Veblen, John R. Commons, and Robert MacIver spoke about the relationship between larger social structures and their impact on individual human beings (Martindale, 1960). From the emerging field of psychology, the following luminaries stand out: Sigmund Freud,

Alfred Adler, Carl Jung, Adolph Meyer, and Otto Rank. While this represents only a partial list of contributors to this new knowledge base, these individuals, nearly all of whom are White males, had a strong impact on the broader cultural milieu in which our understanding of human beings developed. All of these authors were attempting to utilize scientific principles to examine and understand human behavior from different perspectives. A more comprehensive examination of the historical context during the Progressive era can be found in Robert Bremner's (1972) outstanding book, *From the Depths: The Discovery of Poverty in the United States.*

Among the many consequences this new social science paradigm created was the movement toward professionalization in nearly all aspects of society. Some professions, like medicine, had established formal educational curriculums that were already moving toward standardization by the early 1900s. This trend also impacted nursing, business, government, education, and social services. What transcended these individual disciplines was an emphasis on the use of social and natural science ideas as a way to impact society (Hofstadter, 1955).

In social work, agencies had always provided the training for their volunteers to deliver the services needed by their clients. By the 1890s, there was a call for social work to develop formal training as a part of the preparation for practice and that training should occur in university settings. By 1898, the New York School of Philanthropy was formed, and by 1910 it became the New York School of Social Work. As early as 1875, social workers had come together for the First National Conference of Charities and Corrections. This conference was held annually and provided opportunities for social workers from many different fields of practice to share knowledge and develop skills over a broad range of fields of practice (child welfare, delinquents and correction, health, public institutions, families, mental hygiene, and industrial and economic problems). By 1917, social work developed an organizational structure designed to further the members' interests. The Bureau of Occupations became the Social Workers Exchange, and by 1921 it became the American Association of Social Workers (AASW) (Bruno, 1948).

In summary, the intellectual and social history of this period can be characterized as one in which there were significant changes that have a direct relationship to the development of social welfare services and social work as a profession. It is filled with profound changes in society and the way we think about our understandings of society. However, like all periods in human history, it has both positive and negative consequences. Like preceding periods in history, ideas are always connected to values. During this period, the adoption of a more "scientific" approach to understanding human behavior emphasized the role of objectivity in understanding human behavior. This created different consequences for the application of the ideas. In many instances the new social sciences were used in ways that actually created harms for the people who receive services. For example, Charles Darwin's ideas about evolution were translated into explanations about the organization of societies. These translations emphasized the application of the principles of "survival of the fittest" to society. The consequence of this translation had a significant negative impact on vulnerable people. Following Darwin's thinking, Herbert Spencer argued against every form of state assistance, including public education, sanitary supervision, regulation of housing, state protections for medical malpractice, tariffs, and government postal service (Martindale, 1960). Another example involves housing reform efforts that emphasized inclusion of fresh air and light in the construction of housing, creating what were known as "dumb-bell tenements," that contributed to significant fire hazards and deaths for many of their inhabitants (Bremner, 1972). What both the Elizabethan era and progressiveness have in common is that they applied ideas and values toward specific social aims. In the former, the emphasis was on how people "should" behave; in the latter, the emphasis was on ideas that explained the "why" in people's behavior without recognizing the role of values in the application of those ideas. This tension between values and ideas continues to exist in social work practice today.

HISTORICAL CONTEXT QUESTIONS APPLIED TO THE LATE 1800s TO 1920

1. *What are the assumptions about human behavior in the social environment that shape our responses to social conditions (policy) and interpersonal behaviors (direct practice)?*

The Elizabethan period resulted in profound changes in our understanding of human behavior theory. It began with largely morality-based assumptions drawn from various theologies about the nature of human behavior. Peoples' behaviors were classified as good or evil, worthy or unworthy, immoral or moral, and sinful or virtuous. While many different sacred scriptures provided differing interpretations of human behavior, most people shared the notion that human beings were fundamentally flawed and without the external help provided by God they were doomed to failure (Axinn & Levin, 1975; de Schweinitz, 1961; Popple & Leighninger, 2005). They emphasized the role of charity for individuals who could not work, for example, orphaned or displaced children, widows, people with physical disabilities, and people with mental illness. However, their central focus was on ensuring that people who had the capacity to work became employed. Pauperism, not poverty, was the focus of their attention, and they believed pauperism was caused by moral flaws that led to laziness and personal choices that created the person's circumstances.

During the 1800s, the emerging social science paradigm offered a rival set of assumptions about the nature of human behavior. With the advent of sociology, economics, psychology, political science, and education, the focus shifted to the development of new knowledge bases that could be tested, understood, and applied by developing expertise in these various disciplines. Most social science beliefs also put human behavior in the context of its social environment (Booth, 1902–1903; Taylor, 1908–1909). This required a broader and more complex understanding of the connections between individual human behavior and social environments. This new paradigm sought to understand how environments contributed to or shaped choices that people made in their lives. Until this time, there was no explicit connection between human behavior and the environment. For example, assumptions about the reasons why some people were rich and some people were poor began to be challenged. At the beginning of 1800s, morality-based assumptions rested on the belief that the wealthy were being rewarded by God for their hard work in virtue. Poor people were seen as having character flaws that resulted in their lack of resources (Weber, 1930). By the end of the 1800s, sociologists, political scientists, and economists were arguing that existing political structures, economic arrangements (capitalism), and unequal distribution of opportunities explained the ever-widening gap between rich and poor.

It must be emphasized that ideologies reflecting both morality-based and social science-based paradigms coexisted. However, the tension between morality-based understandings and social science persisted and competed for prominence from the 1800s to our current discussions. One only needs to look at the public debate about structuring resource allocation for the poor to hear these two very distinct points of view being expressed. One side argues for work requirements in order to receive benefits; the other side argues that structural barriers, like low wages, hinder any hope of progress for the poor. According to social science proponents and those involved in the Social Gospel and settlement house movements, until those inequities are remediated, we have a responsibility to provide for the poor.

2.   *Why is this particular theory or perspective emerging at this moment in time?*

During the Elizabethan era, the churches were a source of both relief to the poor and needy as well as in providing the personnel to deliver those services. For the most part, the more conservative churches took the lead in shaping our understanding of human behavior and the services required to meet people's needs. However, at the same time, there were individuals who began to explore what would later become the natural and social sciences. These two perspectives began to clash as they presented their views on human behavior.

First, religiously based explanations for human behavior were closely in line with the political and economic structures that allowed them to exert significant influence on what we now call the social welfare system. They played key roles in shaping discussions about how people "should" behave as well as the reasons for their behavior. As the Elizabethan era progressed, the social science paradigm shifted to positivism as a primary way to understand human behavior.

Second, by the 1800s, the emergence of the social sciences had gathered significant momentum with regard to its impact on our understanding of both human beings and their environments. With the emergence of multiple perspectives (e.g., economic, political, sociological, cultural, and social welfare), there was an emphasis on moving beyond the application of strongly held religious values as a way to understand human behavior. The emerging positivist approach argued to replace a reliance on scripture with an emphasis on the collection of "objective data." That data would allow for more efficient and effective ways of dealing with the poor. In reality, both perspectives have values and ideas embedded in them. Neither recognized the full impact of this interaction on shaping their work.

3.   *Is this theory or perspective a new understanding of human behavior?*

As we noted in this chapter, many of the morality-based explanations for human behavior are as old as humankind. They speak to what people, in their respective communities, believed to be the right or the wrong ways to behave. They also give an explanation for those beliefs that emphasizes the importance of values in some theistic or nontheistic tradition. First, during the Elizabethan era, communities became intertwined with political and economic systems. They became powerful influences shaping broader norms, and therefore, also shaped the behavior of individuals in those communities. The Crusades and the Inquisition illustrate the close ties between religious and political systems. Second, by the 1800s, different theological perspectives also influenced the social welfare system. The proponents of these perspectives emphasized the need to reform society as a way to realize biblical injunctions on social justice. While this was not a new belief system, it began to influence aspects of the definition of social problems, the explanation for human behavior, and prescribed courses of action to alleviate human misery.

Third, social scientists put forth different ideas about the nature of human behavior that provided significant viable alternatives to the older morality-based traditions. Their strong belief in science as a way to understand and solve human problems created significant conflict with the older religious traditions. Many early scientists found themselves at odds with the powerful religious institutions in their communities and on occasion incurred their wrath (e.g., Galileo, Copernicus). To this day, these two traditions put forward very different arguments about current social issues. For example, discussion about creationism versus evolution often engendered great passion and irreconcilable differences of opinion (AAAS, 2006; Gallop, 2011).

4. *What is it that makes this understanding of human behavior important in our current historical context?*

As we have alluded to in answering the other questions in this section, these two different paradigms have remained important to our understanding of human behavior over the last four centuries. In the policy arena, we constantly hear the tension between these two perspectives expressed on a broad range of topics. For example, in corrections, we talk about the relative merits of the effectiveness of punishment versus the effectiveness of rehabilitation (Phelps, 2011). In public assistance, we argue that without stringent work requirements, recipients will not work unless they are forced to do so. Others argue that without dealing with issues such as the loss of day care and medical benefits, low income wage rates, and problems with public transportation, these structural barriers will ensure individuals cannot succeed (Cheng, 2009). In child welfare, we hear those who argue that only "good" families, who are heterosexual, married, and active in their churches, should be licensed as foster families. Others argue that the research suggests that children who grow up in gay and lesbian families function at as high or higher levels than those raised in heterosexual families (APA, 2012).

The tensions between these two paradigms directly track to our work as social workers and create ethical dilemmas for many of our social workers whose personal belief systems may not fit with the profession's *Code of Ethics* or they may work in agencies whose policies run counter to what research suggests may be best for their clients. There is every likelihood that the answers to the above questions will continue for the foreseeable future to create tensions between the paradigms and among social workers who are charged with delivering services based on both values and theories of human behavior.

CHAPTER SUMMARY

The purpose of this chapter is to provide you with ways to think creatively about what you are learning in your human behavior courses. There are several important issues embedded in the preceding portions of this chapter.

1. No one human behavior theory is sufficient to explain the complexity of people's behavior when taken in the context of their environments. As a result you will need to learn how to examine both current and emerging theories as you expand your knowledge in the area of HBSE.

2. Our understanding of human behavior reflects both belief systems about "why" people behave in certain patterns and how people "ought" to behave. This reality creates troubling intellectual and ethical challenges for social workers in all practice contexts, whether micro or macro, fields of practice, and agency contexts.

3. All theories of HBSE reflect the historical context in which they are developed as well as the current context in which they are being translated, and sometimes transformed, in current practice.

4. There are competing and conflicting broader social trends that shaped and continue to shape the translation of HBSE theories into policy, research, and practice. Broadly stated, human behavior theories are drawn from a broad range of disciplines, each of which captures different elements of the complexity of human behavior.

5. As professional social workers, we are charged with understanding human behavior theories that inform us about the interaction between people and their environments as it relates to helping *both* people and environments develop to their full potential while minimizing the harm that can come by ignoring one or the other.

These issues interact in ways that create significant and ongoing challenges for social work practitioners. They not only require the mastery of intellectual skills, like critical thinking, reflection, and self-awareness, but they also require the development of skills related to identifying value conflicts, framing ethical dilemmas, and vigilance to ensure that the application of our intellectual skills remains within the framework of the NASW *Code of Ethics* (2017). Understanding the historical context within which we practice helps identify pressures that you will experience in your practice.

Classroom Exercise: Analyzing Current Events

The following exercise is designed to help you put into practice the elements in this chapter. Find an article in the newspaper or magazine that describes individual, family, small group, community, or societal behavior.

Read Through the Article and Discuss the Following Questions

1. How is the person, family, small group, community, or societal behavior described?

2. What are the assumptions being made about the behavior?

3. How are the behaviors of the actors characterized—good or bad; ill; deviant; in need of medical, psychological, and/or social interventions? Or are they characterized as healthy and adaptive?

4. Does the description and/or analysis of the behaviors fit with other explanations that you have heard, or is it novel to you?

5. Does the author appear to believe that change or growth is possible? How can you tell?

6. Do the people have free will? Where is the behavior determined by internal or external forces outside their control?

Directions for Completing the Assignment

1. Break up into small groups. Discuss the questions and provide a spokesperson to report back to the other groups in class.

2. Share with the class your answers to the above questions and identify those areas where you are unsure about what might account for the writer's description and analysis of the situation.

3. In what ways do you agree or disagree with the author's description and analysis of the situation?

4. What are the implications for social work practice in this situation?

Key Terms (in order of appearance)

Historical context   48

Worthy poor   54

Unworthy poor   54

Elizabethan poor laws   55

Jacksonian era   59

Social Gospel movement   60

Progressive era   61

Scientific revolution   61

References

Addams, J. (1897). Social settlements. *National Conference of Charities and Corrections, Proceedings*, 338–346.

American Association for the Advancement of Science (AAAS). (2006). *Statement on the teaching of evolution*. St. Louis, MO: Author.

American Psychological Association (APA). (2012). *APA on children raised by gay and lesbian parents*. Retrieved from http://www.apa.org/news/press/response/gay-parents.aspx

Axinn, J., & Levin, H. (1975). *Social welfare: A history of American response to need*. New York, NY: Harper & Row.

Berg-Weger, M. (2013). *Social work and social welfare: An invitation*. New York, NY: Routledge.

Besthorn, F. H., Koenig, T. L., Spano, R., & Warren, S. L. (2016). A critical analysis of social and environmental justice: Reorienting social work to an ethic of ecological justice. In R. Hugman & J. Carter (Eds.), *Rethinking values and ethics in social work*. London, England: Palgrave-Macmillan.

Booth, C. (1902–1903). *The life and labour of the people of London*. London, England: Macmillan.

Bremner, R. H. (1972). *From the depths: The discovery of poverty in the United States*. New York: New York University Press.

Bruno, F. J. (1948). *Trends in social work*. New York, NY: Columbia University Press.

Cheng, T. C. (2009). Racial inequality in receiving transitional support services and being sanctioned among TANF recipients. *Journal of Social Service Research, 35*, 115–123.

Davis, A. F. (1967). *Spearheads for reform: The social settlements and the progressive movement 1890–1914*. New York, NY: Oxford University Press.

de Schweinitz, K. (1961). *England's road to social security*. New York, NY: Perpetua.

Erikson, E. H. (1950). *Childhood and society*. New York, NY: W. W. Norton.

Etzioni, A. (Ed.). (1969). *The semi-professions and their organization: Teachers, nurses, social workers*. New York, NY: Free Press.

Flexner, A. (1915). Is social work a profession? *National Conference of Social Work, Conference Proceedings, 42*, 576–590.

Forte, J. A., & Root, V. (2011). To ITV or not to ITV: A comparison of hybrid and web- enhanced approaches to teaching a macro-course in human behavior in the social environment, *Journal of Human Behavior in the Social Environment, 21*, 82–96.

Gallop, R. G. (2011). *Evolution: the greatest deception in modern history* (2nd ed.). Ponte Vedra Beach, FL: Red Butte Press.

Gordon, W. E. (1962). A critique of the working definition. *Social Work, 7*, 3–13.

Greenwood, E. (1957). Attributes of a profession. *Social Work, 2*, 45–55.

Harvey, D. (2005). *A brief history of neoliberalism*. New York, NY: Oxford University Press.

Hofstadter, R. (1955). *The age of reform*. New York, NY: Vintage Books.

Hunter, R. (1912). *Poverty*. New York, NY: Macmillan & Co.

Hutchinson, F. E. (Ed.). (1941). *The works of George Herbert*. New York, NY: Clarendon Press.

Kuhn, T. S. (1962). *The structure of scientific revolutions*. Chicago, IL: University of Chicago Press.

Lei, K. (2013). Employment, day labor, and shadow work among homeless assistance clients in the United States, *Journal of Poverty, 17*, 253–272.

Leiby, J. (1978). *A history of social welfare and social work in the United States*. New York, NY: Columbia University Press.

Lewis, V. S. (1954). *The development of the Charity Organization Movement in the United States 1875–1900: Its principles and methods*. Cleveland, OH: Privately published.

Lubove, R. (1965). *The professional altruist: The emergence of social work as a career*. Cambridge, MA: Harvard University Press.

Lynn, M., & Parker, L. (2006). Critical race studies in education: Examining a decade of racism on U.S. schools. *The Urban Review, 38*, 257–290.

Martindale, D. (1960). *The nature and types of sociological theory*. Boston, MA: Riverside Press.

Matthews, D. (2013, June 18). Welfare reform took people off the rolls. It might have also shortened their lives. *Washington Post*. Retrieved from http://www.washingtonpost.com/blogs/wonkblog/wp/2013/06/18/welfare-reform-took-people-off-the-rolls-it-might-have-also-shortened-their-lives/

Mills, C. W. (1959). *The sociological imagination*. New York, NY: Oxford University Press.

Morgan, R. (1970). *Sisterhood is powerful: An anthology of writings from the Women's Liberation Movement*. New York, NY: Random House.

National Association of Social Workers (NASW). (2017). *The code of ethics*. Washington, DC: Author.

Orshansky, M. (1969). How poverty is measured, *Monthly Labor Review, 92*, 37.

Phelps, M. S. (2011). Rehabilitation in the punitive era: The gap between rhetoric and reality in U. S. prison programs. *Law and Society Review, 45*, 33–68.

Popple, P. R., & Leighninger, L. (2005). *Social work, social welfare, and American society*. Boston, MA: Pearson.

Pumphrey, R. E., & Pumphrey, M. W. (1964). *The heritage of American social work: Readings in its philosophical and institutional development* (2nd ed.). New York, NY: Columbia University Press.

Richmond, M. E. (1906). The retail method of reform. *International Journal of Ethics, 16*, 171–179.

Richmond, M. E. (1917). *Social diagnosis*. New York, NY: Russell Sage Foundation.

Richmond, M. E. (1930). *The long view*. New York, NY: Russell Sage Foundation.

Rothman, D. J. (1971). *The discovery of the asylum: Social order and disorder in the new republic*. Boston, MA/Toronto: Little, Brown & Company.

Shaw, J. L. (1890). Economic and moral effects of outdoor relief. *National Conference of Charities and Corrections, Proceedings, 81*–91.

Spano, R. (1986). Creating the context for analysis of social policies: Understanding historical context. In D. E. Chambers, *Social policy and social programs: A method for the practical public policy analyst* (pp. 38–51). New York, NY: Macmillan.

Spano, R., & Koenig, T. L. (in press). Social work values and ethics. In S. Kapp, *Introduction to social work*. Thousand Oaks, CA: Sage.

Taylor, G. (1908–1909). The standard for city's survey. *The Charities and the Commons, 21*, 508.

Trattner, W. I. (1974). *From poor law to welfare state: History of social welfare in America*. New York, NY: Free Press.

Turner, F. J. (1935). *The frontier in American history*. New York, NY: Henry Holt & Company.

Weber, M. (1930). *The protestant ethic and the spirit of capitalism*. New York, NY: Routledge.

Wolfer, T. A. (2014). Community-led total sanitation: A "new frontier" for international social work practice. *Social Development Issues, 36*, 67–77.

Young, M., & Muller, J. (2014). *Knowledge, expertise and the professions*. New York, NY: Routledge.

CRITICAL THEORIES

PHOTO 4.1
State's power to quash freedom: Parthenon of censored books created for Documenta Art Festival, Kassel, Germany, 2017

©Terry Koenig

ETHICS SPOTLIGHT
A TWO-TIERED FOSTER CARE SYSTEM

In a Midwestern state, the legislature is debating changes to the foster care system. You have been asked to speak to members of your community about this proposal. The legislation being debated creates a two-tiered system where current foster parents' payments remain the same, while a whole new group of foster parents receives substantially higher levels of payment. The criteria for receiving higher payments include both husband and wife are a team and one of them cannot work outside the home, the husband and wife have to be married and faithful for the past seven years, they cannot smoke or drink in the home, they must attend church services or other community group meetings on a regular basis, and they must either home school or send the foster children to private schools.

Discussion Questions

(1) What are the values that underlie the definition of the "problems" that this proposed law is trying to address?

(2) How do these values support existing social structures and disadvantage or advantage certain groups in the larger society?

(3) When these kinds of distinctions are made between foster care parents, who are the winners and losers?

(4) What evidence supports that good parenting is based on the characteristics that have been chosen (e.g., heterosexual married couple, don't smoke and drink, and must attend church)?

As you continue to read our chapter on critical theory, think about how you might analyze and respond to this case example.

CRITICAL THEORIES AND THEIR ROOTS IN MARXISM

Critical theories can be broadly understood as having their roots in Karl Marx's ideas (Marx & Engels, 1948; Marx, Engels, & Tucker, 1978). Marx viewed getting and keeping economic power as the motive behind all social and political activity (e.g., education, philosophy, religion, government, science, the arts, technology, and the media). Human events must be understood within their economic context, which he referred to as "material circumstances," and within the social, political, and ideological atmosphere generated by these economic conditions (i.e., "the historical situation"). We cannot understand human affairs by searching for timeless abstract principles; instead, our understanding comes through an examination of their specific economic, social, and political causes as they play out in the real world. Further, we must pay attention to the distribution and dynamics of economic power, which in Marx's view is the most significant way in which people are divided and excluded from participation in society. The following cartoon in Figure 4.1 illustrates the view that those who are rich become so literally off the backs of the poor (Felice, 2014).

FIGURE 4.1 ■ **Getting rich off the backs of the poor**

In our current context, Marx would draw battle lines between the 1 percent of the American population whose after-tax income tripled between 1979 and 2007 (see Figure 4.2); and the middle and poorest fifths of our country, many of whom live in substandard conditions, do not have enough food to eat, perform manual labor, and whose efforts fill the pockets of the rich (Sherman & Stone, 2010).

FIGURE 4.2 ■ **Income Gains at the Top Dwarf Those of Low- and Middle-Income Households**

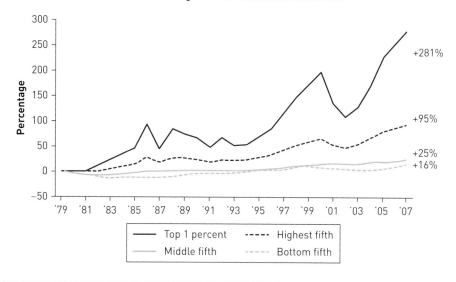

Percent Change in After-Tax Income Since 1979

Source: CBPP calculations from Congressional Budget Office data.

BROAD AND NARROW DEFINITIONS OF CRITICAL THEORY

In the narrow sense, critical theory refers to several generations of German philosophers and social theorists whose roots are in the Western European Marxist tradition and who founded the Institute for Social Research (also known as the Frankfurt School). The Frankfurt School began in 1929–1930 with Max Horkheimer and Theodor Adorno and stretches to Herbert Marcuse and Jürgen Habermas. Over the next 40 years, these intellectuals developed theoretical strategies for a thorough critique of Western culture (known as critical theory) (Horkheimer, 1987; Horkheimer & Adorno, 1972). They experienced persecution (e.g., were forbidden to lecture in their academic settings) and were driven out of Germany in 1933 by the National Socialist party (the Nazis). Consequently, Horkheimer and his colleagues moved the Institute to New York until 1949, when they returned to Frankfurt, Germany (Althusser, 2004).

The first phase for critical theorists (in the narrow sense) involved focusing on human beings as self-creating producers of their own history who could engage in real consensus and thereby transform social life to make it more democratic (Horkheimer, 1982). In the second phase, critical theorists examined antidemocratic trends such as increased tighter connections between states and the market in advanced capitalist societies and the emergence of the fascist state. Horkheimer came to view these antidemocratic trends as eroding freedom and solidarity. In response, Habermas encouraged societies to develop a "public sphere" or public space where citizens are on equal footing with each other, share information, engage in criticism about the state and economy, and insist on mutual accountability (Habermas, 1989).

Critical theories, in their broad meaning, encourage us to analyze power, but within an expansive range of relationships and across multiple dimensions of the domination of humans in modern society (e.g., race, feminist, queer, and post-colonial). Due to the contextual nature of social criticism that occurs in a particular time and with a specific audience that has its own demands and needs for liberation, critical theorists came to the place of rejecting a scientific or objective basis for criticism grounded in a grand theory. The critical social scientist moved away from seeking a unified theory toward employing many theories in diverse historical, political, economic, and social situations.

KEY THEMES IN CRITICAL THEORY AND ITS DEVELOPMENT

In general, critical theorists have addressed several key themes. These are described immediately below and include a critique of Enlightenment ideas, the challenging of uncritical acceptance of progress, questioning and acting on all forms of oppression, initiating a public process of self-reflection, and supporting equality and participation in the public sphere.

Critique of the Enlightenment

The Enlightenment put forth the belief that all societies can and should be changed by the power of reason according to universally valid criteria. True humanity is embodied in universal human nature, not in customs, diverse beliefs, or practices. Cultural progress and increased productivity occur through the advance of science and technology. Critical theorists viewed this Enlightenment effort as having been perverted into egoism, possessiveness, and the domination of Western individualism. Critical theorists came to regard advanced capitalist societies as a "totality," in which the tight integration of states and markets threatened to eliminate individual freedom. In the Enlightenment (and Kantian) view, knowledge is portrayed in universal terms, individuals and institutions are simply a given, and the goal of science is to state the facts about them objectively. Critical theorists viewed the Enlightenment's emphasis on individual freedom as artificial; mass culture posed the greatest obstacle to radical transformation of society in that people are discouraged from genuine participation in democracy. Instead, they are encouraged to passively accept what happens and not engage in analysis of their historical and political context. Critical theorists challenged this view arguing that individuals and institutions can only be understood by examining the assumptions and actual practices of a particular society.

Challenging Uncritical Acceptance of Progress

In our contemporary society, individual autonomy or freedom is sacrificed for efficiency and pursuing actions that will achieve the best results in any situation. This is defined as "instrumental reason." The question of how to do something is placed above any critical reflection on why we should or should not do something. Critical theorists were most concerned with the negative social and moral consequences that result from uncritical acceptance of scientific and technological progress.

Questioning and Acting on All Forms of Oppression

Critical theorists emphasize a future in which individuals use reason not as a means to achieve a universal, objective goal but to identify specific, subjective ways to respond to the world by defining and leading the good life. In particular, Habermas (1971) referred to the important role of the social sciences (in contrast to the humanities or natural sciences) in critically questioning all forms of oppression. It is the social sciences that are in the best position to challenge oppression. Horkheimer (1982) indicated that a critical theory is adequate only if it explains what is wrong with current social reality, identifies people who can change this reality, provides standards or norms for criticism, and puts forth achievable practical goals for social transformation.

Initiating a Public Process of Self-Reflection

For Habermas, the goal of critical theory is not to control or influence the decisions others make; instead, the goal is to initiate a public process of self-reflection

(Habermas, 1971). The critic seeks to promote a process that makes reflection most possible, even reflection on the democratic process itself. Habermas and other critical theorists rightly call technocratic any social inquiry that only develops optimal problem solving strategies based on third-person knowledge of impersonal consequences for all courses of action. Evidence-based practitioners who do not readily take into account the social and political context in which they practice or researchers who conduct studies as detached observers represent examples of this technocratic model (Lorenz, 2008). In contrast, the social work practitioner or researcher who is a reflective participant acknowledges that any problem-solving strategy needs to involve the clients, agencies, communities, and/or institutions as actors in the decision-making process; this decision-making process must take into account the broader social, political, and economic context.

An example of this shared decision-making process has been societies' difficulties in developing effective medical practices and treatment for AIDS (Bohman, 1999). The continued spread of the AIDS epidemic and lack of effective treatment brought about a crisis in expert authority. Lay participants, in cooperation with researchers and patients, were integral in reshaping the medical community's treatment practices for addressing AIDS. Just as in this example, critical theorists indicate that there have to be opportunities for the public to engage in reflective inquiry about scientific practices and other forms of expertise. In this way, citizens are able to test and hold accountable the research and medical communities. Critical theorists would support this type of problem solving in that it acknowledges the need to include multiple perspectives of people who represent varying degrees of authority or power (e.g., patients, physicians, lay participants).

Supporting Equality and Engagement in the Public Sphere

Habermas discussed the importance of public interactions that occur within the intimate family, in coffee houses, and in political debates and viewed that at the core of these interactions, members should not control or influence others' decisions, but instead interact with each other as equals (Habermas, 1989). He understood social differences and pluralization as positive features of modern society (Habermas, 1975). Habermas also criticized the state, indicating that the state is "crisis ridden" and unable to solve structural problems of unemployment, economic growth, and environmental destruction. These crises open up public space for citizens to contest and consider their involvement in new social movements. He envisioned a public sphere for modern societies in which information about the state and economy is shared, but also one in which criticism is encouraged and citizens can make demands for mutual accountability across multiple domains, countries, cultural groups, or other boundaries. Instead of an assumed set of practices, a cosmopolitan public sphere is created when at least two culturally rooted spheres begin to overlap (Habermas, 1989). Some critical theorists have viewed the European Union, with the inclusion of multiple states and cultures, as an incomplete or imperfect example of this cosmopolitan public sphere (Habermas, 2001; Ruggie, 2000).

CRITICAL THEORY IN THE 20th CENTURY: FEMINIST CRITICISM AND CRITICAL RACE THEORY

As new forms of critical theory emerge related to racism, sexism, colonialism, and disability, scholars and activists alike have worked to transform democratic ideal and practices for the purpose of emancipation (Bell, 2004; Cook-Lynn, 2012; Rich, 1979; Tyson, 2015). It makes sense that there might be many different critical theories that reflect different historical contexts. Marx referred to this as the "struggles and wishes of the age" (Marx & Ruge, 1844). What follows is a description of two of these streams of critical theory: feminist criticism and critical race theory.

Feminist Criticism

Feminist criticism examines ways in which literature and other elements in society undermine the economic, political, social, and psychological emancipation of women (Delphy, 1984; Tyson, 2015; Woolf, 1929). Feminists refer to a patriarchal ideology that keeps men and women in traditional gender roles, marginalizes and objectifies women, and supports male dominance. Feminists also engage in activism to promote women's equality (e.g., public demonstrations, involvement in voter registration, provision of shelters for survivors of rape and other abuse). They continue to lead the struggle for better family policies such as high-quality affordable day care and better nutrition and health care for mothers and children. The newer term, "feminisms," is used to support multiple viewpoints, to move beyond binary opposites (e.g., male or female) and offer ways of thinking that challenge the notion of a single best point of view (Cixous, 1997). Feminist theorists believe we should be cautious of drawing upon Marx's insights because although Marx viewed economic forces as determining the lives of both sexes, he did not take into account the many types of oppression that women face despite or beyond their economic class.

French feminists, who influenced Anglo-American feminists, emphasized (1) materialist feminism (social and economic oppression of women); and (2) psychoanalytic feminism (patriarchy's impact on women's psychological experiences). Simone de Beauvoir (1949) did not use the term "material feminist," but her groundbreaking book, *Second Sex*, represents the theoretical basis for material feminists. Delphy (1984), influenced by de Beauvoir, coined the term materialist feminist and understood marriage to trap and stunt a woman's intellectual growth and economic freedom. Women have difficulty recognizing their own subjugation and taking action to change it. They have been written out of history and have no record of their shared culture, traditions, or oppression; and although the numbers of women living independently or as single parents is growing, women have typically been dispersed among men and attached through unpaid work (e.g., housework) and social standing (as a kind of slavery or serfdom) (see Guillaumin, 1996).

French feminist psychoanalytic theory examines patriarchy's impact on women's psychological identity, growth, and creativity. Because most psychological subjugation occurs at the level of language, language must be investigated. Cixous (1997) argues that language reveals what she calls patriarchal binary thought, seeing the world in polar opposites, one of which is considered superior to the other. For Cixous (1997), Irigaray (1986), Kristeva (1996) and others, women are the source of life, and are themselves the source of power and energy. They encourage the development of a new language that eliminates binary thinking which, in turn, oppresses and silences women.

Multicultural feminism has become especially important as White, middle-class, heterosexist feminists, who have held leadership in the women's movement in the United States, are finally recognizing the way in which their policies and practices may indeed ignore the experiences of women of color, lesbians, poor, and the undereducated in the United States and throughout the world. African American feminists have been especially helpful in revealing the political and theoretical limitations of White mainstream feminists' neglect of cultural experiences different from their own. Many African American women advocate for ethnic cultural feminism, which is concerned more with the particular female cultural values of their own ethnic group rather than with women in general (see Bethel, 1982; Walker, 1984). These interpretations demonstrate the importance of understanding the intersectionality of gender issues within a cultural context.

In summary, feminist criticism is concerned with the emancipation of women; newer iterations (e.g., feminisms) encourage us to move beyond binary opposites and to challenge a single, best point of view. French feminists who focus on the economic and psychological oppression of women have influenced Anglo American feminists. Newer forms of feminism have also included the experiences of diverse women of color, lesbians, those who are poor, and others.

Critical Race Theory

Critical race theory (CRT) sprang up in the mid-1970s as a number of activists and scholars in the United States became interested in studying and transforming the relationships among race, racism, and power. These activists and scholars attended to W. E. B. DuBois's prediction that the "problem of the twentieth century is the problem of the color-line—the relation of the darker to lighter races of men [sic] in Asia and Africa, in America and the islands of the sea" (1903/2003, p. 15). The movement considers many of the same issues that conventional civil rights and ethnic studies address but places them in a broader historical, economic, political, and social context. Critical race theorists drew upon critical legal studies, radical feminism, and other scholarly elements (e.g., European critical theorists) to fight this new, more subtle form of racism that was gaining ground. Derrick Bell, professor of law at NYU; Alan Freeman, who taught at SUNY-Buffalo law school; and others began to put forth pointed critiques that questioned the gains made in American society during the civil rights era. For them, the advances of the civil rights era had stalled and were retreating. For example, these authors viewed more favorable legal decisions (e.g., *Brown v. Board of Education*) as deteriorating over time, cut back by narrow lower court interpretations, and as actually supporting elite White interests (Bell, 2004; 1980a, 1980b).

Although there are many subgroups of CRT (e.g., Latino-critical, queer-critical, and Indian critical), most CRT scholars support the following key premises:

(1) Racism, defined as unequal power relations that grow from the sociopolitical domination of one race by another and that results in systematic discriminatory practices (e.g., segregation), is a common or ordinary experience for people of color in the United States. Racism represents the way our society does "business as usual." Because it is ordinary and claims of objectivity and meritocracy are camouflaged as self-interest, power, or privilege for Whites, racism is difficult to cure or address.

Color-blind conceptions of equality, which state that one should treat all persons equally without regard to their race, only remedy the most blatant forms of discrimination (e.g., mortgage redlining that limits, for example, where a person of color can live or buy property). In contrast, affirmative action strives for increased minority membership and involvement in certain environments such as the workplace or school in an attempt to diversify these settings.

(2) The majority group tolerates advances in racial justice only when it suits their interests to do so. This can be referred to as interest convergence or material determinism and is a thesis put forth by Derrick Bell in his critique of the *Brown v. Board of Education* decision, which supposedly helped Blacks in their quest for educational equality. Bell proposed that this legal decision, considered a triumph in civil rights litigation, may have resulted from the self-interest of Whites and not a desire to eliminate racism (Bell, 1980a, 1980b).

(3) Race is socially constructed. Race is not an inherent or fixed category with moral or intellectual characteristics that represent racial superiority, inferiority, or purity. Instead, races are categories that society invents, manipulates, and recreates. Further, everyone's identity is a product of intersectionality in which individuals and classes often have shared or overlapping interests and traits.

(4) The experiences of racial minorities have given them what might be called a legitimate and unique voice of color. Consequently, they are competent in explaining the meaning and consequences of racial oppression.

In summary, CRT places race, as it intersects with other human characteristics and elements in society (e.g., ethnicity, class, gender, sexual orientation), at the center of critical analysis and scholarship, and political, legal, and social action. CRT has an activist agenda that moves beyond scholarly critique toward the elimination of racial oppression, and like other forms of critical theory is interested in the transformation and liberation of society.

Critical Theory in Social Work

Critical theory has been slow to gain acceptance among American social workers due, in part, to its critique of unjust institutions and other social structures in which social workers are gainfully employed (e.g., child welfare, schools, health care settings). American social work's turn toward clinical and psychotherapeutic practice has also contributed to its lack of participation over the last several decades in broader social reform. That being said, within the last 15 years, social workers have increasingly drawn upon critical theoretical writings to tease out confusion about the meanings and uses of critical theory (Brookfield, 2009; Keenan, 2004; Kondrat, 2002; Salas, Sen, & Segal, 2010) and to encourage social work to not only help individuals and families understand oppression but to take action to change unjust societal practices and institutions (Fook & Askeland, 2006; Fook & Gardner, 2007; Salas et al., 2010). Social work authors refer to critical theorists from the broader tradition (e.g., Habermas and Horkheimer), and more current social work applications of critical theory draw upon Freire, Fook, and Gardner, and Giroux (Brookfield, 2009; Hegar, 2012; Scanlon & Saleebey, 2005).

Brookfield (2009) challenges our profession by noting that it is unfortunately possible to practice without acting to change existing social injustices. He indicates that social workers may view an unjust society as normal or may ignore power dynamics and wider structures that impact our clients and social work practice. He posits that social workers who operate from a critical theory perspective need to be able to identify unjust practices and institutions and then challenge and change them. And so, while empowerment theories and proponents of the strengths perspective in social work (Koenig & Spano, 2007; Saleebey, 2005; Simon, 1994; Solomon, 1976) demonstrate the potential to transform individuals and society, critics point out that often their focus has been on personal and interpersonal empowerment. For an example, see Lee's (2001) empowerment model, which emphasizes a process of self-efficacy or self-confidence, the development of a **critical consciousness** that emerges in dialogue with others, and out of this, the power to take effective change to reach personal goals. This model is commendable in that it appropriately links individual empowerment to collective empowerment, and it has been applied to social work practice with marginalized populations (e.g., women experiencing domestic violence, those dealing with poverty). However, these empowerment practices are viewed by some critical theorists as having shortcomings because they lack emphases on sociopolitical empowerment.

Overview Summary

This overview has attempted to provide both broad and narrow understandings of critical theory, from its inception in the Frankfurt School to more current streams of critical theory such as feminist criticism and critical race theory. What follows is an in-depth examination of Paulo Freire's writings. Freire was a Brazilian educator, critical theorist, and practitioner who advocated for a radically different educational approach to empowering marginalized or oppressed populations. His influence has been particularly felt in American progressive education and across the globe in Central and South America, Europe, Africa, and India. American social work scholars have nominally addressed the impact of Freire's writings on social work thinking and practice even though some have called for social work to more fully embrace Freire's writings for their consistency with our mission of pursuing broader social structural change.

IN-DEPTH: PAULO FREIRE (1921–1997)

Paulo Freire was born in Recife, Brazil, to middle-class parents, but by the time he was in elementary school, economic depression resulting from the United States' Great Depression had thrust his family into an impoverished situation (Collins, 1977). At this early age he experienced what it was like to go hungry and to lack the basic material necessities of life. Even at this young age he decided to dedicate himself to ending hunger so that other children would not have to experience the same deprivations he and his family went through. Despite his struggles with impoverishment, Freire was able to enter the university, where he studied psychology, law, and philosophy, earning a doctoral degree in 1959. Throughout his career he held many education and social service–related positions that involved direct contact with many of Brazil's poorest families (many of whom were illiterate). Career highlights include his professorship in the history and philosophy of education department at the University of Recife, his brief imprisonment and exile to Chile in 1964 (his ideas were thought subversive by a military coup), and his time as a consultant to Harvard University's School of Education (Freire, 1970). Freire's ideas stemmed from his Catholic faith tradition and were used by the Catholic Church for mission work (e.g., literacy programs). He also served as a consultant to the World Council of Churches. It is an understatement to assert that Freire's social justice–centered thought and life works have been influential not only in Brazil but worldwide. Moreover, his thought has influenced not only the field of education but has reached well beyond that into most academic disciplines and professions, including social work.

The Oppression of Human Consciousness: The Brazilian Situation

The Portuguese began colonization of Brazil in 1500. The motivation was fairly straight forward: exploit the people and land for profit. And this is what took place. For the next several hundred years the natural resources of Brazil were taken—from timber to gold—and the peoples were enslaved and/or oppressed. Freire, based on his own experiences and knowledge nearly 500 years later, described his own Brazilian society and culture as slavocratic, anti-democratic, and dominated by an oppressive outside force (Freire, 1976). This was the cultural history of his society, which had little experience with democracy and self-governance. The goal of this section is to introduce Freire's ideas by explaining some of his basic concepts as they relate to these conditions of oppression. This will involve discussion of human nature and vocation, the cultural facets of oppression, and the odd relationship that exists between oppressors and the oppressed.

Freire's View of Human Beings as Subjects Not Objects

In order to understand Freire's thoughts on oppression, it is first necessary to understand how he thinks about human beings. Human beings, says Freire, should be considered *subjects* and not *objects*. As mere objects, people are relegated to a state of disengaged passivity. Freire states,

> [w]e began with the conviction that the role of man [sic] was not only to be in the world, but to engage in relations with the world—that through acts of creation and re-creation, man makes cultural reality and thereby adds to the natural world, which he did not make. (Freire, 1976, p. 43)

As an object of an oppressive regime, people may have a basic understanding of the activities of "biological necessity" for survival (e.g., hunting for food), but they do not have either the awareness or the power to intentionally and creatively shape the socio-cultural, economic, or political forces that dominate them. When people are objectified they are not able to fulfill their vocation as human beings, which is to develop their consciousness and in so doing become more fully human. What Freire means by this is that when conditions are oppressive, people are prevented from developing an increasingly larger awareness of the causal forces that are ever present in human societies, which in turn shape those societies. He states that oppressed people are stuck in a **naïve consciousness**. In Brazil (like so many parts of the world today), this was characterized not only by illiteracy but by a collective ignorance of the aforementioned forces and dynamics of human society. Naïve consciousness is "characterized by an over-simplification of problems; by a nostalgia for the past; by underestimation of the common man [sic]; by a strong tendency to gregariousness; by a lack of interest in investigation, accompanied by an accentuated taste for fanciful explanations" (Freire, 1976, p. 18).

Threats to Liberation: Internalized Oppression and a Culture of Silence

The oppressive class is always at the ready with various sloganized explanations to impose upon the powerless. Freire states that there is usually a "magical" sort of quality to peoples' understanding of how things work. In other words, people's illiteracy includes a form of credulity that makes them easy prey to those who exploit them. While they do have culture (something Freire emphasizes as an empowering feature of every human group), there is no critical dialogue between the people and their governing bodies, nor between the people and each other, whether in the form of gathering relevant information, discussion and debate, and definitely not in decided sociopolitical action. This naïve state of being leaves people without the power to change the fact that they do not have civil and political rights such as the right to vote, with which they might otherwise raise their voices to an authoritarian regime.

Freire considered his people in Brazil to have been in transition—in a slow process of awakening from their cultural alienation to an awareness of the macro issues that so impacted their lives and well-being (1976). This is a dangerous process fraught with perils both internal and external. These are additional factors that tend to keep oppressed cultures from fighting for their own best interests. Internally, there is what Freire calls the **culture of silence**. This is concomitant with naïve consciousness and stems from people's internalization of the oppressor's world view, specifically as it pertains to messages about the identity of the oppressed class and the reasons for them being in an impoverished and otherwise disadvantaged state. Koenig et al. (2017) state,

> According to Freire, the dominant group's narrative that characterizes those in poverty as ignorant and lethargic derives from the larger economic, political, and social structures designed to oppress certain groups in society . . . the dominant narrative rests on the belief that poverty is a personal problem, not a structural problem. (p. 13)

In other words, individuals are blamed for their lot in life when in fact they had no valid opportunity to do otherwise—yet they remain silent because they have internalized the mythologies of the oppressors. These mythologies include the following:

> the myth that the oppressive order is a "free society"; the myth that all men [sic] are free to work where they wish, that if they don't like their boss they can leave him and look for another job; the myth that this order respects human rights and is therefore worthy of esteem; the myth that anyone who is industrious can become an entrepreneur—worse yet, the myth that the street vendor is as much an entrepreneur as the owner of a large factory; the myth of the universal right of education. . . . the myth of the equality of all. (Freire, 1970, p. 135)

Forceful propaganda and slogans supplant any real dialogue between classes in order to maintain the status quo. Thus, the culture of silence is really an internal and an external threat. When people continue to believe that they are inferior, helpless, and responsible for their own abject state, they do not engage in a process of liberation.

Fear of Freedom as a Threat to the People's Liberation

Another factor that threatens the liberation from oppression is the *fear of freedom*. This begins with the idea of adaptation.

> [T]he adaptive person is person as *object*, adaptation representing at most a weak form of self-defense. If man [sic] is incapable of changing reality, he adjusts himself instead. Adaptation is behavior characteristic of the animal sphere; exhibited by man, it is symptomatic of his dehumanization. (Freire, 1976, p. 4)

Believing they have no capacity for changing oppressive conditions, people tend to develop a fatalistic attitude, often fearing the very possibility of their own liberation. They tend to believe their condition is static, that they have no choice, that it is "just the way it is," possibly attributing it to the desires of various deities or other magical or supernatural forces.

> The oppressed, having internalized the image of the oppressor and adopted his [sic] guidelines, are fearful of freedom. Freedom would require them to eject this image and replace it with autonomy and responsibility. Freedom is acquired by conquest, not by gift. It must be pursued constantly and responsibly. Freedom is not an ideal located outside of man; nor is it an idea which becomes myth. It is rather the indispensable condition for the quest of human completion. (Freire, 1970, p. 31)

This quote highlights the centrality and significance of freedom in Freire's thought. It also points to the importance of responsibility (more on this later) and action. But fear, individual and collective, is arresting, an anesthetic to the societal transformation required for liberation. Seeking freedom requires great collective energy and taking big risks, things virtually impossible for those resigned to, and dehumanized by, the oppressors' mythology. Freire states that not only are the oppressed dehumanized by the situation of oppression, but the oppressors too are dehumanized because they dehumanize others. However, authentic change must come from the oppressed themselves—they must lead the way to a new situation.

External Threats to Liberation: Divide and Rule, and Assistentialism

There are external threats to changing oppressive situations as well. First, a common dimension of subordination of the large majority by a small, powerful minority is to *divide and rule*. "The minority cannot permit itself the luxury of tolerating the unification of the people, which would undoubtedly signify a serious threat to their own hegemony" (Freire, 1970, p. 137). Instead, the oppressors must quell any purportedly subversive action, by force if necessary. The oppressed are not allowed to find unity, to organize themselves so as to threaten the status quo. One of the best strategies, according to Freire, is to isolate individual groups within the majority and either create or deepen rifts between them. There are many effective strategies used to do this such as "localizing" communities by stressing just the needs of a particular community, possibly suggesting that neighboring communities are competitors or scapegoats for the first community's problems. In any case, keeping communities alienated from each other helps to prevent anyone from seeing the big picture. Another strategy is for the oppressive class to deny class distinctions and offer "peace" and harmony between them, which in reality only serves as another, likely sloganized piece of propaganda—another myth to be internalized.

A second external barrier to liberation is **assistentialism**. This involves the use of many well-meaning professionals as an instrument to keep people in their respective socioeconomic positions (Freire, 1976). Freire stated,

> Assistentialism is an especially pernicious method of trying to vitiate popular participation in the historical process. In the first place, it contradicts man's [sic] natural vocation as subject in that it treats the recipient as a passive object, incapable of participating in the process of his own recuperation; in the second place, it contradicts the process of "fundamental democratization." The greatest danger of assistentialism is the violence of its anti-dialogue, which by imposing silence and passivity denies men conditions likely to develop or to "open" their consciousness (Freire, 1976, p. 15).

Assistentialism is thus inconsistent with people moving beyond being mere objects, it is inconsistent with actual democratic processes, and it elides any process of real dialogue, both within the oppressed majority, or between the oppressed and their oppressors. Particular strategies vary, but two are worth mentioning here. First, when the oppressive class notes any subversive movement among the masses—anything to indicate that they are renouncing their submerged state and have unified to demand change—they band together in self-defense. "[T]hey create social assistance institutions and armies of social workers; and—in the name of supposedly threatened freedom—they repel the people" (p. 14). This "army" of social workers is charged with the task of helping people "adjust" to the conditions of their environment. Second, this is best accomplished by also employing "crisis theoreticians" to invent and spread propaganda about the looming chaos supposedly caused by non-conforming "subversives." In this new facsimile of reality, the people are "unwell" and require "medicine"—whereas in fact their "ailment" is the wish to speak up and participate (p. 14). In this strange situation, what is considered "healthy" is silence, passivity, and inaction.

Those supposed professionals who step in to help only serve the ends of the elite class by pacifying the oppressed, keeping them in a state of **massification**. Massified people are still objects, not a true people who have been able to take responsibility for their own liberation. The professionals take ideas and superimpose them upon the massified class in a paternalistic fashion—they are *for* the people (perhaps in spirit) but not *with* the people. Helping professionals insult people's natural vocation as *subjects* who participate in their own destinies, who join in democratic *dialogue*, and who jointly take the *risks* necessary to develop their own consciousness and well-being.

The Liberation of Human Consciousness: Freire's Utopian Ideals

Freire's ideas about liberation basically run counter to all the ways people are oppressed. Liberation is an ongoing process that can never stop because the threat of oppression always exists, and because the vocation of humans is to continue developing and cultivating their lives as subjects. There are a number of dichotomies to expect: instead of objects, subjects; instead of oppression, freedom; instead of fear, hope; instead of complacency, risk taking; instead of silence, reflective dialogue and action; instead of naïve consciousness, critical consciousness; instead of the status quo, transformation. In this section we will explain Freire's main ideas about the liberation process, including attention to his theory of education.

The movement from *objects* to *subjects* denotes a profound transformation in people. "During the phase of a closed [oppressed] society, the people are *submerged* in reality. As that society breaks open, they *emerge*. No longer *mere spectators*, they uncross their arms, renounce expectancy, and demand intervention. No longer satisfied to watch, they want to participate" (Freire, 1976, p. 13). The ability to effectively participate in sociopolitical processes is predicated upon a people developing what Freire calls *critical consciousness*. This is arguably the heart and soul of his social justice message. Simply put, critical consciousness signifies an expanded human awareness—one that recognizes social, economic, and political factors as causal forces that shape human behavior. Critical consciousness is characterized by depth in the interpretation of problems; by the substitution of causal principles for magical explanations; by the testing of one's "findings" and by openness to revision; by the attempt to avoid distortion when perceiving problems and to avoid preconceived notions when analyzing them; by refusing to transfer responsibility; by rejecting passive positions; by soundness of argumentation; "by the practice of dialogue rather than polemics" (Freire, 1976, p. 18).

What Freire has in mind with critical consciousness is a politically active form of critical thinking that avoids common pitfalls such as "group think," hasty generalizations, and irrational fanaticism. He advocates a more humble stance that recognizes the fallibility in all forms of inquiry, with an openness to revision—all of this is part of his understanding of how authentic, democratic dialogue takes place.

Critical Consciousness and the Transformation of Society

One of Freire's educational methods—called "culture circles"—when teaching literacy was to gather people in small groups and show them slides of various cultural artifacts, such as an image of people working (Freire, 1976). While teaching reading and writing skills, he did so in a "problem posing" fashion that invited discussion about who works, why they work, how much they work, who profits from their work, when they work, who else works, what kind of work they do, and so on. The goal was to engage them in discussion and debate about the structural realities that surround various issues such as work. With this method, Freire hoped to encourage independent, critical thinking about the topic without imposing his own ideologies. In other words, he was *for* the people as a literacy instructor, yet *with* the people as a collaborator and not an agent of cultural enforcement from the elite class. The goal is to get people in dialogue with each other, to expand their knowledge and awareness about the important issues that impact their lives, which creates the possibility for choices to be made. Freire's critical consciousness concept is achieved by a process he calls *conscientization*. Conscientization is a broad term indicating the ongoing humanization of people as subjects. Freire remarks,

> For us, men and women, being in the world means being with it and with others—acting, speaking, thinking, reflecting, meditating, seeking, creating intelligence, communicating that intelligence, dreaming and always referring to a tomorrow, comparing, evaluating, deciding, falling into transgression of principles, embodying them, breaking away, opting, believing, or disbelieving. (Freire, 2004, p. 112)

What Freire is talking about is becoming a presence in the world, specifically, becoming a better human presence in the world by moving from basic awareness and choice to taking responsibility for an expanded ethical consciousness as well—at the macro levels of economy and politics. Becoming a person in the world means embodying one's hopes and freedoms, as well as all of the great responsibilities for ethical decision making and the resultant actions that go with them—both individually and collectively. Freire does not suggest that we are unlimited, for we are "conditioned" beings—meaning that we all have a biological, cultural, sociological, economic, geographical, and political history that has shaped the present—but with understanding of said conditioning, paired with ethics, hope, and action, real changes can take place in an ever-unfolding process.

Conscientization and the Liberatory Model of Education

Conscientization is also an educational process that includes techniques such as the culture circles previously discussed. More generally, Freire has had a tremendous impact on the world of education (among others) with his *banking model* vs. *liberatory model*. The **banking model of education** is what is typically used by an oppressive class in order to maintain the current order. In this way of thinking, the teacher talks about reality as a predictable, static entity that is completely cut off from the day-to-day realities of the students (Freire, 1970). The teacher's task is to "fill" the students with prefabricated information: facts, dates, names, and so on, all devoid of any meaning they might have for any particular individual or group. This content is then memorized and rehearsed by the student in a mechanical fashion. "Education thus becomes an act of depositing, in which the students are the depositories and the teacher is the depositor" (p. 58). As such, the teacher–student is dichotomized and there is always one all-knowing expert (the teacher), and one ignorant, empty vessel (the student) (Collins, 1977). There is no room for creativity, debate, or invention. A common example of this type of education comes in the form of technical education for the massified herd. Technical training, including preparation for various skilled labor, and even professional training of sorts, can be introduced in a form devoid of any sense of critical consciousness. The intended result, of course, is maintaining passivity by preventing a macro level awareness. The banking approach, as nugatory pseudo-education, "masks the effort to turn men [sic] into automatons—the very negation of their ontological vocation to be more fully human" (Freire, 1970, p. 61).

In contrast, the **liberatory model of education** has as its center the reconciliation of the teacher–student contradiction: teachers are simultaneously teachers and students (Freire, 1970). Students and teachers work collaboratively such that teachers' "efforts coincide with those of the students to engage in critical thinking and the quest for mutual humanization. His [sic] efforts must be imbued with a profound trust in men and their creative power" (p. 62). Education becomes a profoundly hopeful endeavor forming solidarity between teachers and students, as well as between student groups. "Founding itself upon love, humility, and faith, dialogue becomes a horizontal relationship of which mutual trust between the dialoguers is the logical consequence" (p. 80). The resulting education is a mutual effort as part of the conscientization process: education that goes somewhere. "There are questions all of us must ask insistently that make us see the impossibility of *studying for study's sake*. It is impossible to study without any commitment" (Freire, 2004, p. 60). Instead, liberatory education is problem-posing, which aims at demythologizing the oppressor's insidious messages. Liberatory education is thus prophetic as it also looks to the future as people begin to develop their own capacity for praxis. Freire defines praxis as the ability to reflect (i.e., using critical consciousness) and to act (i.e., to take intentional, collaborative action). This is part of authentic dialogue—thinking about acting, and acting based on critical thinking. Both mind and body are engaged in this ongoing dialectical. People's critical "activity consists of action and reflection: it is praxis; it is transformation of the world. And as praxis, it requires theory to illuminate it. Men's [sic] activity is theory and practice; it is reflection and action" (Freire, 1970, p. 119). The following case example set within an American social work classroom illustrates many of Freire's ideas about liberatory education.

CLASSROOM EXAMPLE
THE APPLICATION OF FREIREAN CONCEPTS TO AN AMERICAN SOCIAL WORK CLASSROOM

In the American experience, the instructor presented material related to ethical decision-making in social work practice. The students were asked what they would do if they were working with a woman who was struggling with relationship issues, and they learned in the second session that the woman was referring to her relationship with a same-sex partner. What ensued was an intense discussion among members of the class who had very strong feelings about homosexuality. One group argued that social workers have a responsibility to work with people without discriminating based on sexual orientation. Other students took the position that they would end the relationship based on the fact that they had strong religious beliefs that defined homosexuality as immoral and that they should not be forced in some way to violate their personal moral beliefs. In this instance, the two most adamant students were African American women with strong Orthodox Christian beliefs, and they chose to leave the classroom rather to engage in any further discussion.

A Freirean analysis of this situation suggests key ideas from critical theory may be helpful in moving through this difficult classroom interaction. The first concept that sheds some light on the situation is the concept of naïve consciousness. One group of students held fast to the NASW Code of Ethics (2015) to answer the question. The other group grounded their responses in their personal worldviews. Both groups found it difficult to move beyond the external rules to seek a solution that would be appropriate for a professional social worker. The interpretations of questions related to the meaning of the two very different positions were difficult for the students to grasp. At one point the two students who most strongly voiced the opinion that they had a right to their own moral beliefs as it related to their practice, got up and left the room. The instructor chose to take a break and use the time to reach out to these two students.

During the break, the instructor found the two students (who had gone to the administrative offices of the school to lodge a complaint about being discriminated against based on their Orthodox Christian views). After some conversation they agreed to come back into the classroom to reengage in the discussion. What became abundantly clear is that they could identify themselves as oppressed people but only as it related to their religious views and not their race or gender. In this instance they were both oppressors and oppressed. The instructor moved the discussion to focus attention on the social contexts that were shaping the students' individual responses. The connection was made between the events occurring in the classroom and the larger social contexts in which the students were operating beyond social work education. At that point, students were able to talk more directly about how they experienced oppression, sometimes in the form of censoring ideas, as well as how both groups needed to learn the same skills to develop a better sense of how these larger issues could be addressed in a classroom to create an awareness of assistentialistic, oppressive behavior. The emphasis for the instructor was to focus on awareness, reflection, critical thinking, and action by tying their discussions to the larger issues of homophobia, racism, and sexism. This process attempted to create a classroom that reflected the liberatory model of education where critical thinking, on all sides of the issues, can be explored and tied to the larger social context in which the discussion is occurring. This required both students and the teacher to engage in critical thinking as a means to reduce the **culture of silence**, which often is exhibited in these situations.

In contrast, the banking model suggests that the teacher would state simply that the Code of Ethics (NASW, 2015) is the only source for dealing with these complex issues; the teacher would insist that the students follow that Code without exploring the deeper meaning of the values or the struggles necessary to decide how to balance personal views with professional responsibilities. When the teacher becomes the only expert in a classroom, this engenders a culture of silence where students do not learn critical thinking skills necessary to develop and manage these conflicts in order to better serve their clients.

In sum, Freire's ideas, which sit at the heart of both narrow and broad understandings of critical theory, are centered upon a prophetic hope (2004) that through a collaborative conscientization process, oppressed communities can develop critical consciousness sufficient to empower them toward collective social, economic, and political action that will transform their society such that freedom and well-being may prevail for all.

THEORY CRITIQUE

In this section, elements of theory critique will be discussed and applied to our understanding of critical theories and their relevance for social work practice. Our analysis of critical theories involves examining not only the limitations but also the benefits of incorporating a critical theoretical perspective into social work practice. Critical theories, along with Paulo Freire's ideas, have the potential to strengthen and enrich the difficult work that social workers undertake as they partner with oppressed populations and take on their role as prophets to advocate for those on the margins of society with our government and private sector leaders. As we observe the shrinking of the middle class and the growing gap between the wealthy and everyone else across our planet, the relevance of these theories and the social action they insist upon becomes an imperative, or shall we say "critical" approach, for social work practitioners.

What Does This Theory Say About Human Behavior?

Marx viewed humans as focused on getting and keeping economic power; the human drive for economic power influences, although does not completely determine, all social and political behavior. Critical theorists are engaged in a critique of democratic and "totalizing" societies which, in their view, continue to concentrate power in the hands of a small, wealthy elite. Consequently, they encourage those who have experienced oppression and discrimination (and are in the technical majority but have been excluded from societal participation, for example, through voter suppression) to engage in critical analyses or consciousness about their place in society and how economic power is distributed. The oppressed and marginalized can then participate in action and ongoing reflection to make changes in society that support broad, equitable social participation for all citizens. Marx in particular viewed discrimination based on class as the most important way in which people are excluded from social life and that when the elite or powerful try to divide people based on gender, race and ethnicity, age, ability, sexual expression, or other characteristics, this masks the need for all people to work together to address class and economic power as the most important and distinguishing feature of society.

Although critical theorists view humans as creators and producers of their own history and able to engage in radical transformation of social life, they came to view government's increasing connections with business and "free markets" as eroding individual and collective freedom or "free will" and solidarity. Some critical theorists (e.g., Habermas, 1984, 1989/1961) have attempted to elevate the role of individual citizens (and clients) as having equal footing no matter their place, status, and power in society;

this equality can occur through societies' development of public spheres or spaces where citizens can share information, engage in criticism about their government and economy, and insist on mutual accountability. As we have seen in United States Congressional politics, it is very difficult for government to hold itself accountable and instead, the effective running of government requires that citizens play a much greater role as equal partners in pursuing mutual accountability no matter how much economic power or money a politician, interest group, banking institution, wealthy elite, or lobbyist pumps into the political system.

How Does This Theory Address Growth and Change?

This theory emphasizes that growth and change occur when people of similar circumstances (e.g., those who are poor or have been abused) engage in dialogue with each other about their experiences of oppression. This dialogue involves raising questions and challenging immediate, lived experience. Critical theorists refer to a process of growth and change that occurs as people "wake up" to their oppression and begin to take effective action to not only change their individual lives but to insist on changes in larger social structures to impact broader society. Freire describes how people move from naïve consciousness, accepting the larger, dominant narrative that defines and limits who they are and fosters a culture of silence to an awakening or critical consciousness that enables them to become aware of unjust structures. This awareness or self-reflection involves translation into action, which is indeed what Freire and others refer to as praxis.

How Holistic Is This Theory?

Critical theorists, including Freire, argue for broad social structural change that must come from the people (i.e., from those who are oppressed) and not from those in power. Humans are not truly free, independent agents and so in effect critical theorists would never argue for social workers to engage only in individual treatment or family work without concomitantly participating in broader social change. Freire, in particular, was skeptical of the role of social workers because they are often used by the state to engage in social control (e.g., social workers help provide government-supported food stamps and other resources that only minimally allow the poor, disabled, and others to survive). In providing minimal levels of support, social workers in effect help to silence the masses from protesting or organizing themselves to resist those in power. Critical theorists challenge social work professionals to work with those who are marginalized so that they too have a place at the table as societal decisions are made (e.g., policy making) and not settle as workers whose only function is as agents of social control.

How Consistent Is This Theory
With Social Work Values and Ethics?

Critical theories are very consistent with social work values and ethics. These theories support the *dignity and worth of every human being* and encourage social work practitioners to join with and *serve* those in our society who face oppression and possess less economic and political power. Social workers who practice from a critical theoretical perspective strive to develop meaningful dialogue and *relationships* with those who experience oppression as a means of helping them to "wake up" or move from naïve to critical consciousness regarding their powerless conditions. As noted by Habermas (1989), this process would also result in having the poor and marginalized take their place next to those with considerable power as equal participants in public dialogue about the difficulties, possibilities, and ways of constructing a more democratic society. Social work is rooted in a definition of *social justice* that insists on equal and meaningful participation for everyone. In order for social workers to *competently* engage in this kind of advocacy and join with those who experience oppression, they would need to become politically, socially, and economically aware about current societal conditions and unjust political and economic structures. Critical theorists call social workers to act with *integrity* by continually nurturing their professional self-awareness and engaging in a process of attending to and educating themselves about emerging broader societal developments.

What Are the Sources of Knowledge That Support This Theory?

Critical theories were created in a particular historical and cultural context that involved the oppression of many people (e.g., intellectuals, Jewish people, and those with mental and physical disabilities) during Nazi Germany; this context shaped critical theory's central emphasis on theory as being incomplete without participant actions that seek the emancipation of those who have experienced oppression or persecution. Because critical theorists' great project is to bring about social change for the poor and others, some scholars have challenged the effectiveness of its core ideas (e.g., how to help the oppressed develop a critical consciousness) in actually bringing about this needed social change. Scholars in social work and other disciplines have argued that it is very difficult, if not impossible, to evaluate the process of emancipation and social change in a community using rigorous empirical methods (randomized studies). However, critical theorists do use qualitative and community-based participatory action (CBPR) research, which is very compatible with its emphasis on working *with*, not for, those who have experienced oppression. These methods involve research participants at various levels in helping to design, carry out, and take ownership, even authorship, for publishing findings from research studies.

APPLICATION OF CRITICAL THEORIES TO SOCIAL WORK

Here are some guiding questions to keep in mind as you read this section:

1. Social work has two contradictory purposes that include *social control* (e.g., supporting the use of medication as a chemical restraint with nursing home residents) and *social change* (e.g., active involvement in voter registration where certain groups are being disadvantaged). How do we connect these contradictory purposes in practice?

2.   Critical theory is most often pitched at an analysis of broad social situations: racism, homophobia, sexism, ageism, and so on. Since 90% or more of social workers are employed at the direct practice level, how can this theory be useful?

3.   Beyond the reality that social workers are engaged in direct service practice, most social workers struggle to find sanction (e.g., permission from the agency to engage in critique of agency policy) to engage in social action activities. How do we identify people and other resources to support social change efforts?

4.   Most social work curriculums devote relatively little time to studying critical theories as tools to be used by practitioners. Does social work education currently emphasize a "banking concept" of education or a "liberatory concept" of education? Support your response with examples.

What the first three sections of the chapter do is to provide you with an understanding of the development of critical theory within its historical context and to examine the work of Paulo Freire as an example of how critical theory has been understood. Finally, we have provided a critique of this theory in order for you to have a balanced view from both adherents and critics of the theory. Our goal here is to provide possible applications of these ideas to the day-to-day practice of social workers.

The central problem for most social workers is to take abstract, complex theories like critical theory to a concrete level where they can be translated into actions for our clients. We believe critical theory has usefulness at all levels of practice. At the most abstract level, these ideas include ways to connect social contexts to individual behaviors. For example, critical feminist theory provides ways of viewing the impact of current perceptions of gender on broad issues like pay differentials between men and women who are doing the same job (macro level). To use the ideas expressed earlier in the chapter, this is an example of women being treated as "objects" not subjects in their own lives. At another level, critical theory suggests how the development of consciousness in women (e.g., through meeting in small groups) is essential to raise their awareness in defining their experience from "private troubles" to "public issues" (at the mezzo level) or, as Freire describes, this process involves moving from naïve consciousness to critical consciousness and praxis (action and reflection) on their own behalf. When a social worker sits with a woman who has been sexually abused by a male, she may ask, "Why did this happen to me?" A social worker can respond with psychological or family systems explanations or can place important parts of her experience within the larger social narratives that are based on ideologies that objectify women, create power imbalances that disadvantage women, and suggest that males should be in dominant positions and women should be subservient to them.

This example suggests how to use critical theory as a means to move beyond our traditional approaches that define social work based on what we do (e.g., individual therapy or community organization) to a broader perspective that informs social work practice at all levels. It allows us to incorporate persons within environments rather than persons as separate from their environments. Critical theory requires us to look upon both these elements in our perspective, and it begins to suggest how to analyze contexts and their impacts on an individual's growth, empowerment, and social justice. It shifts the focus from an individual's problems and pathologies to the social, economic, and political structures that shape individual behaviors. Figure 4.3 provides a more detailed view of how these complex interactions have challenged social work professionals in their day-to-day work. While Figure 4.3 lays out traditional elements of the various levels of practice—macro, mezzo, and micro—and identifies roles played by social workers at each of these levels, it also identifies the impact of social or environmental conditions on social work roles.

ENVIRONMENTAL CONDITIONS

What Figure 4.3 adds is the importance of critical theory as a way to shape the activities at all levels of practice. What unifies social work practice is a theoretical perspective (such as critical theory) that allows social workers to connect persons/environments no matter where their specific point of entry. Therefore, if we are working with poor people we can be policy analysts focusing on large populations of individuals who live in poverty, the poor. But as social workers we must understand the impact that poverty has on a single person who is homeless and needs our assistance. In fact, critical theory suggests that it is necessary for us to engage in both systemic change through use of the development of critical consciousness as well as addressing our clients as the "subjects," not "objects," of our efforts.

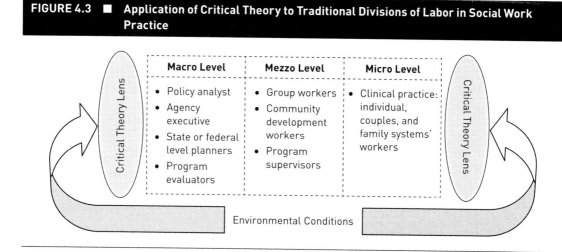

FIGURE 4.3 ■ Application of Critical Theory to Traditional Divisions of Labor in Social Work Practice

In addition, Figure 4.3 provides a way to examine levels at which social workers practice. As noted above, some see themselves as community organizers, social planners, and group workers; others see themselves as family therapists and individual therapists. The reliance on descriptions of what we do reflects our ties to specific organizations and professional education as they relate to employment priorities. In other words, social work is reduced to a set of skills that we are expected to perform in the agencies in which we are employed. The problem with this approach is that it focuses the majority of our attention on what is different among social workers rather than what we have in common. Instead of emphasizing skills, we presume that theoretical perspectives are more central to unifying our approach to social work. What theory in general, and in this instance, critical theory specifically, does is to focus our attention at multiple levels of a situation in order to take complex person-in-environment elements into account no matter what our specific level of function. It requires clinicians to ask questions not just about where to place a child of color in our child welfare system, but to acknowledge and to act (praxis) on the issues that create the overrepresentation of children of color in our system. Again, as in this case example, the worker and client need to move beyond combating negative messages, including personal failure, lack of effort in school systems, interpersonal violence, and psychological trauma. Instead, critical theory suggests understanding the circumstances in a broader perspective so that both the client and the worker develop a critical consciousness that allows them to name and to seek to act against the dominant narratives that create many of the situations in which clients experience major barriers.

In summary, what critical theory does is provide a bridge focusing simultaneously on individuals and their environments. It allows professionals and clients to concurrently integrate appropriate activities that empower individuals to reach their potential while at the same time addressing circumstances that create environmental barriers to their progress.

Application of Critical Theory to Social Work Education

Paulo Freire's work (1970, 1976), which is outlined earlier in the chapter, uses several key concepts that can be useful in analyzing social work contexts including social work education. Freire critiques the role of professionals, asserting they often participate in the ongoing process of oppression, and he puts forth several concepts for re-examining aspects of our educational preparation:

(1) Assistentialism, which involves the use of well-meaning professionals as instruments to keep people in their respective socioeconomic positions.

(2) Massification, which defines people as "objects" who are unable to take responsibility for their own liberation. In contrast, as "subjects" people can participate in democratic dialogue seeking to jointly take risks to develop their own consciousness and well-being.

(3) Naïve consciousness, in which people are unaware of the conditions in which they live and how those conditions oppress them.

(4) Critical consciousness, which is a politically active form of critical thinking that avoids such pitfalls as group think, hasty generalizations, and irrational fanaticism. People can engage in a process to move from naïve consciousness to critical consciousness.

(5) The banking model of education, which involves the teacher filling the students with prefabricated information (e.g., facts, dates, and names), all devoid of any meaning they might have to a particular group. Education thus becomes an act of depositing in which the students are the depositories and the teacher is the depositor.

(6) A liberatory model of education (which is in contrast to a banking model) involves the leveling of the relationships between teachers and students, in which they work collaboratively to engage in creative thinking directed toward mutual humanization.

(7) A culture of silence, which develops because individuals are blamed for their lot in life with no recognition that they have little valid opportunity to act differently. They remain silent because they have internalized the mythologies of the oppressors.

The following is a second example parallel to the previously presented case on the American social work classroom. While these two case examples appear to be quite disparate on the surface, they share common processes that illustrate challenges to creating critical thinking in classrooms. The first example, found in the in-depth section on Paulo Freire, is set in an American classroom focused on teaching social work practice; the second example described below reflects one of the author's social policy teaching experiences in a Central Asian social work classroom.

CLASSROOM EXAMPLE
THE APPLICATION OF FREIREAN CONCEPTS TO SOCIAL WORK EDUCATION IN A CENTRAL ASIAN CONTEXT

In the Central Asian classroom, the challenge faced by the educator was to establish a process whereby students might begin to raise their own questions about social policy and ethics without imposing external perspectives on the situation and/or possible responses that were embedded in a different cultural context (e.g., American or European). This was especially difficult given the students' perspectives that teachers had all the answers based on their prior experience with a "banking concept" of education. In addition to their perspective on education, they divided themselves into two separate language groups, Russian and Kazakh. The Russian speaking

(Continued)

(Continued)

students represented the dominant group in the country and the Kazakh speaking students were subservient to them. This was carried over into the classroom where translations were made from English to Russian and only on occasion translated into Kazakh. The interactions between the Russian and Kazakh students clearly indicated that the Russian speaking students saw their needs as more important than those of the Kazakh students. In addition both groups did not see any value in listening to or interacting with each other. They wanted the teacher to lecture based on their perception that the teacher had the only worthwhile information to share with the group (banking concept). They reflected a view of massification in which they were objects, not subjects able to engage in democratic dialogue; students resisted any attempts to work in small groups because they did not see their colleagues as having anything useful to contribute to class discussions (Koenig et al., 2017).

At one point, while discussing social policy related to domestic violence, the instructor asked the students to think about how discrimination played out in their country. This posed a significant challenge for both the interpreter and the class. They did not understand the concept of discrimination nor did they think that there were any groups in the country who might be experiencing discrimination. In this instance, students were unaware of domestic violence shelters that were being established by the government. Both groups expressed views about the appropriateness of creating shelters. What they shared in common with their concerns was that they were deeply rooted in existing cultural norms that emphasized domestic violence as a family issue not a governmental concern. What the instructor did was to begin to help students engage in a process of critical consciousness where they connected family structure to the larger social norms that in many instances support the subservience of women to men. The instructor shared web-based materials on the Kazakh domestic violence shelters, which included photos of ethnic Kazakh women who had been physically beaten but were now getting help in the shelter. As was the case in the preceding American classroom example, the teacher's role was to raise questions that allowed students to search through their existing thinking to determine potential alternatives that fit within their own life experience and professional responsibilities.

CLASSROOM EXERCISES: THE APPLICATION OF CRITICAL THEORY TO SOCIAL WORK PRACTICE EXAMPLES

The following case examples provide an opportunity to apply the ideas presented in this chapter drawn from critical theory. The authors have provided discussion questions that can be used in the classroom to examine these cases.

Case Example: Jennifer's Dilemma

Jennifer is a 28-year-old woman who has had a successful academic career. She is currently enrolled in a graduate nursing program. She is single and recently began dating a man who is highly invested in creating a relationship between the two of them. She comes to see you because she is having panic attacks that interfere with her work and schooling. Jennifer shares a story that includes an unstable and disconnected set of family relationships, death of two family members, and a history of drug use and sexual assault that occurred throughout her high school years. She lacks any hope that she can "fix" herself because she is "broken" and will never be able to engage in a healthy relationship with anyone. How can you use critical theory to analyze and respond to Jennifer's situation?

Case Example: Funding Challenges in Community Mental Health

You are the director of a mental health center in a rural state where the economy has still not fully recovered from the events surrounding the 2008 recession. Your state Mental Health Association members have lost nearly $30 million in state aid. They no longer can provide services to middle-class families who cannot afford standard agency fees ($132 per hour). The agencies are unable to expand their client base because the state legislature is one of many who have refused to support Medicaid expansion. How can you use critical theory to analyze and respond to the situation with the other directors of the Mental Health Association?

DISCUSSION QUESTIONS

1. How does critical theory shape your understandings of these case situations and potential responses relevant to social work practice?

2. How holistic is critical theory in taking into account how you respond to the situation no matter what your specific job function?

3. Can you use critical theory, in these situations, to examine the personal and social aspects of oppression and connect your analysis to social work values? Please describe.

4. Can you generate ideas about how you could move beyond your specific functions in the agency to address additional areas of concern? Please describe.

5. What if any "evidence" can you generate to suggest that your use of critical theory could have positive outcomes for client systems?

CHAPTER SUMMARY

This chapter includes four major sections. First, we examined the development of critical theory based on the works of Karl Marx and a group of authors who collectively were a part of the Frankfurt School. What these writers shared in common was a perspective about the interactions between individuals and the larger society. While Marx focused primarily on the role played by economic structures in the oppression of certain groups within society, the Frankfurt School emphasized a view that human beings were self-creating producers of their own history and that this was accomplished when social life was more democratic. All of these writers engaged in a critique of capitalism as a threat to individual freedom. Their solution to these dangers rested on creating public dialogue that allowed people to engage in the free flow of ideas that led to more open and equal participation of all citizens.

Second, we looked at the writings of Paulo Freire. His view of critical theory was born out of Brazil's 500-year history of exploitation. This specific application of critical theory shares the fundamental belief expressed by his predecessors, namely the work that needs to be done involves reducing oppression experienced by poor people through a process he called conscientization. This is achieved by creating a process in which poor people come together to develop their awareness that oppression occurs in their daily lives. According to Freire, the oppression of poor people creates a culture of silence where there is no dialogue that explores the causes for their living conditions. The process he advocates is one that moves people from naïve consciousness to critical consciousness. He describes how people move from naïve consciousness, accepting the larger dominant narrative that defines and limits who they are, and fosters a culture of silence, to awakening or critical consciousness, which enables them to become aware and act on unjust social structures. This awareness or self-reflection involves translation into action that addresses injustice, which is indeed what Freire and others refer to as praxis. We also examined some of the more current iterations of critical theory used by social workers to analyze more specific levels of oppression (e.g., critical race theory, feminist criticism, critical queer theory, and postcolonial criticism).

Third, we provided a series of questions that can be used to examine how critical theory relates to our work as social workers. Some of these dimensions include how critical theory can be used to examine the causes of human behavior, causes of human behavior, if critical theory is holistic enough to be used across multiple levels of intervention, supports growth and change, and is consistent with social work values and ethics.

Fourth, we examined potential applications of critical theory to a range of social work education and practice situations. These examples and analyses of case situations suggest how critical theory can be useful for addressing several important questions faced by social work practitioners whether they are working with individuals, groups, or communities. What critical theory provides for social workers is a way to integrate their work by simultaneously focusing on the immediate situation (e.g., addressing a culture of silence; transitioning from naïve to critical consciousness and developing a liberatory stance toward professional education) while incorporating a larger systems perspective. Since critical theory is a product of examining the lives of marginalized groups of people, it allows social workers to explore the immediate needs of people as well as the systematic changes that must be addressed to reduce the impact of oppression that pervades their daily lives.

Key Terms (in order of appearance)

Critical theories 72

Critical consciousness 80

Naïve consciousness 82

Culture of silence 82

Assistentialism 84

Massification 85

Banking model of
education 86

Liberatory model of
education 87

References

Althusser, L. (2004). Critical theory. In S. H. Daniel (Ed.), *Contemporary continental thought* (pp. 25–158). New York, NY: Pearson.

Bell, D. A., Jr. (1980a). Brown v. Board of Education and the interest-convergence dilemma. *Harvard Law Review, 93,* 518–533.

Bell, D. A., Jr. (1980b). *Shades of brown: New perspectives on school desegregation.* New York, NY: Teachers College Press.

Bell, D. A., Jr. (2004). *Silent covenants: Brown v. Board of Education and the unfulfilled hopes for racial reform.* Oxford: Oxford University Press.

Bethel, L. (1982). This infinity of conscious pain: Zora Neale Hurston and the black female literary tradition. In G. T. Hull, P. B. Scott, & B. Smith (Eds.), *All the women are White, all the Blacks are men, but some of us are brave* (pp. 176–188). Old Westbury, NY: Feminist Press.

Bohman, J. (1999). Critical theory. In E. N. Zalta (Ed.), *The Stanford encyclopedia of philosophy.* Retrieved April 8, 2015, from http://plato.stanford.edu/archives/spr2015/entries/critical-theory/

Brookfield, S. (2009). The concept of critical reflection: Promises and contradictions. *European Journal of Social Work, 12*(3), 293–404.

Cixous, H. (1997). Sorties: Out and out: Attacks/ways out/forays. In C. Belsey & J. Moore (Eds.), *The feminist reader* (pp. 91–103). Malden, MA: Blackwell.

Collins, D. (1977). *Paulo Freire: His life, works and thought.* New York, NY: Paulist Press.

Cook-Lynn, E. A. (2012). *A separate country: Postcoloniality and American Indian nations.* Lubbock, TX: Texas Tech University Press.

de Beauvoir, S. (1949). *The second sex (Le deuxième sexe).* Paris, France: Éditions Gallimard.

Delphy, C. (1984). *Close to home: A materialist analysis of women's oppression* (D. Leonard, Trans.). London, England: Hutchinson.

DuBois, W. E. B. (1903/1973). *The souls of black people: Essays and sketches.* New York, NY: Kraus.

Felice, E. (2014, July 14). *About the historic gap between rich and poor Italians.* Retrieved April 8, 2015, from https://nephist.wordpress.com/2014/07/14/about-the-historic-gap-between-rich-and-poor-italians/

Fook, J., & Askeland, G. (2006). The critical in critical reflection. In S. White, J. Fook, & F. Gardner (Eds.), *Critical reflection in health and social care* (pp. 40–54). Buckingham, UK: Open University Press.

Fook, J., & Gardner, F. (2007). *Practising critical reflection: A resource handbook.* Maidenhead, UK: Open University Press.

Freire, P. (1970). *Pedagogy of the oppressed.* New York, NY: Herder and Herder.

Freire, P. (1976). *Education: the practice of freedom.* London, England: Writers and Publishing Cooperative.

Freire, P. (2004). *Pedagogy of indignation*. Boulder, CO: Paradigm Publishers.

Guillaumin, C. (1996). The practice of power and belief in nature. In D. Leonard & L. Adkins (Eds.) *Sex in question: French materialist feminism* (pp. 72–108). London, England: Taylor & Francis.

Habermas, J. (1971). *Knowledge and human interests*. Boston, MA: Beacon Press.

Habermas, J. (1975). *Legitimation crisis*. Boston, MA: Beacon Press.

Habermas, J. (1984). *Theory of communicative action*. Boston, MA: Beacon Press.

Habermas, J. (1989/1961). *Structural transformation of the public sphere*. Cambridge, MA: MIT Press.

Habermas, J. (2001). *The postnational constellation*. Cambridge, MA: MIT Press.

Hegar, R. L. (2012). Paulo Freire: Neglected mentor for social work. *Journal of Progressive Human Services*, *23*, 159–177.

Horkheimer, M. (1982). *Critical theory*. New York, NY: Continuum.

Horkheimer, M. (1987). *Eclipse of reason*. Boston, MA: Beacon Press.

Horkheimer, M., & Adorno, T. W. (1972). *Dialectic of enlightenment*. New York, NY: Seabury.

Irigaray, L. (1986). *The Irigaray reader*. Oxford: Blackwell.

Keenan, E. K. (2004). From sociocultural categories to socially located relations: Using critical theory in social work practice. *Families in Society*, *85*, 539–548.

Koenig, T., & Spano, R. (2007). The cultivation of social workers' hope in personal and professional practice. *Journal of Religion and Spirituality in Social Work Practice: Social Thought*, *26*(3), 45–61.

Koenig, T. L., Spano, R., Kaufman, D. V., Leiste, M. R., Tynyshbayeva, A. A., Madyarbekov, G., & Makhadiyeva Karataevna, A. (2017). A Freirean analysis of Kazakhstani social work education. *International Social Work*, *60*(1), 156–169.

Kondrat, M. E. (2002). Actor-centered social work: Re-visioning "person-in-environment" through a critical theory lens. *Social Work*, *47*, 435–448.

Kristeva, J. (1996). *The Kristeva reader*. Oxford, UK: Blackwell.

Lee, J. A. B. (2001). *The empowerment approach to social work services: Building the beloved community* (2nd ed.). New York, NY: Columbia University Press.

Lorenz, W. (2008). Paradigms and politics: Understanding methods paradigms in an historical context: The case of social pedagogy. *British Journal of Social Work*, *38*(4), 625–644.

Marx, K., & Engels, F. (1948). *The communist manifesto*. New York, NY: International Publishers.

Marx, K., Engels, F., & Tucker, R. C. (1978). *The Marx-Engels reader* (2nd ed.). New York, NY: W. W. Norton.

Marx, K., & Ruge, A. (1844, February). *Letter from Marx to Arnold Ruge*. Paris, France: Deutsch-Franzosische Jahrbucher.

National Association of Social Workers (NASW). (2015). *Code of ethics*. Washington, DC: NASW.

Rich, A. (1979). *On lies, secrets and silence: Selected prose*. New York, NY: W. W. Norton.

Ruggie, G. (2000). *Constructing the World Polity*. London, England: Routledge.

Salas, L. M., Sen, S., & Segal, E. A. (2010). Critical theory: Pathway from dichotomous to integrated social work practice. *Families in Society*, *91*(1), 91–96.

Saleebey, D. (2005). *The strengths perspective* (4th ed.). Boston, MA: Allyn & Bacon.

Scanlon, E., & Saleebey, D. (2005). Is a critical pedagogy for the profession of social work possible? *Journal of Teaching in Social Work*, *25*(3–4) 1–18.

Sherman, A., & Stone, C. (2010, June 25). *Income gaps between very rich and everyone else more than tripled in last three decades, new data show*. Washington, DC: Center on Budget and Policy Priorities.

Simon, B. L. (1994). *The empowerment tradition in social work: A history*. New York, NY: Columbia University Press.

Solomon, B. B. (1976). *Black empowerment: Social work in oppressed communities*. New York, NY: Columbia University Press.

Tyson, L. (2015). *Critical theory today: A user-friendly guide* (3rd ed.). London & NY: Routledge.

Walker, A. (1984). *In search of our mother's gardens*. San Diego, CA: Harcourt Brace Jovanovich.

Woolf, V. (1929). *A room of one's own*. New York, NY: Harcourt Brace.

5

PSYCHODYNAMIC THEORY

PHOTO 5.1
Unconscious processes: Going underground to understand behavior, Labryinthic grotto, Sintra, Portugal

CASE EXAMPLE
MITCH'S REPRESSED MEMORIES

As an intensive care unit (ICU) social worker within a veterans' hospital in the Midwest, I met with Mitch while he was lying flat on his back in a hospital bed. He had attempted suicide; Mitch and I began the sensitive process of getting to know each other and of him helping me to understand what had brought him to the place of considering suicide. After Mitch was discharged from the hospital, we began to meet regularly for outpatient sessions.

As our relationship continued to unfold, Mitch described himself as a combat veteran who had served as an advisor in Vietnam. What ensued was a discussion about his 30-year history of substance abuse, several inpatient admissions to substance abuse treatment facilities and subsequent failed attempts at getting sober, and now his first experience with a three-month period of sobriety. Mitch indicated that he had never talked about his combat experiences and that he felt it was now important for him to do so.

What became so clear for both of us was that Mitch began to stutter as he attempted to speak about his combat experiences. He further described being teased by substance abuse treatment professionals, including social workers, about his stuttering. They viewed his stuttering as fake and as a way for Mitch to gain attention from others. However, as we stepped further into his stories of combat, Mitch described his responsibilities for the men that served under him and how, in one decisive battle, all of them

had died and he had used their bodies as a barricade to save himself. The horror of this scene was palpable to Mitch; because he could only discuss a small portion of it during several sessions, I didn't realize it was only one of many battles that Mitch had participated in. Mitch also experienced flashbacks and nightmares, which although difficult to manage, helped him remember details of his combat experiences that he had long forgotten. As Mitch worked through these experiences of combat, his stuttering decreased until it was nearly gone.

Mitch's substance abuse and stuttering seemed linked to the trauma he had experienced in combat. Mitch had also tried desperately to bury or forget these awful memories, but they re-emerged in his sober state and in increasing flashbacks and nightmares. Mitch's behavior can be viewed as an attempt to "repress" or push down difficult memories. Psychodynamic theories examine unconscious or buried elements of our psyche, pointing to the fact that even if we try to protect our ego by pushing these unacceptable impulses and experiences out of our conscious memory, they will continue to have a powerful impact on our current functioning. Like a festering thorn long buried under the skin, Mitch's repressed experiences exert great influence over his current behavior. Once Mitch acknowledges and works through these experiences, he can increase his coping skills and capacities for health and growth.

BRIEF INTRODUCTION
TO FREUDIAN IDEAS

Psychodynamic theory, as a general category of theories, addresses the psychological, intrapsychic elements of human functioning that are continually changing, contribute to motivation, and influence behavior (Berzoff, Flanagan, & Hertz, 1996; Dean, 2002). Although sometimes used interchangeably with psychoanalytic theory, psychodynamic theory is the more expansive term, encompassing a broad range of theories and perspectives. Largely based on the work of Sigmund Freud, psychodynamic theory developed at the beginning of the 20th century in Vienna against the backdrop of the Enlightenment philosophies of Europe and ultimately the social developments of democracy. Freud's ideas were radical in that he challenged the repression of sexuality common in the Victorian society of his day (Danto, 2013). Freud proposed a method of treatment, psychoanalysis, in which the professional as expert could help the "patient" closely examine unconscious processes that contribute to failures in social and emotional functioning. By developing insight into these unconscious processes, Freud believed we can obtain optimum human functioning and freedom, and develop into mature and thoughtful human beings (Brandell, 2004).

Freud's 1909 historic U.S. lectures at Clark University represented a call for American society to acknowledge and address the mental health needs of all people. In these lectures, Freud repudiated the Victorian era's attempts to disdain psychopathology, to repress sexuality all together, and to ignore the effects of trauma (e.g., sexual abuse) on children (S. Freud, 1910). Freud's lectures addressed the distress that interfered with people's everyday functioning, traumatic familial and institutional abuse in which society had typically blamed the child for the abuse, repressed wishes (e.g., sex with a parent), infantile sexuality in which he viewed all infants as bisexual at birth, and finally, he took up the issue of people who truly needed mental health treatment but would not seek it due to societal stigma.

KEY CONCEPTUAL ELEMENTS OF FREUD

What follows is a discussion of key concepts that are central to Freud's intrapsychic orientation. These concepts still undoubtedly influence social work practice today.

Id, Ego, and Superego

Freud's psychoanalytic orientation includes many interacting perspectives (e.g., structural, genetic, dynamic, economic). According to Freud's structural perspective, the human psyche is composed of interdependent elements: the **id**, **ego**, and **superego**. The id, or unconscious, houses key drives (e.g., sex and aggression) that seek gratification. The ego, whose functions include the use of judgment, reason, frustration tolerance, problem solving, and relationship skills, erects protective defenses against anxiety. The ego mediates the demands of the id and the superego's role as a conscience or seat of morality.

Ego Defense Mechanisms

An important function of the ego is to defend itself against anxiety generated by intolerable or unacceptable impulses or threats from conscious awareness. Examples of **ego defense mechanisms** include repression, which involves keeping unwanted thoughts and feelings out of awareness or unconscious, and projection, which involves unconsciously attributing one's unacceptable thoughts and feelings onto others. Ego defenses, broadly understood to help individuals navigate or adapt to their environment, have been further developed by theorists associated with ego psychology and will be discussed later in this chapter (e.g., A. Freud, 1936; Laughlin, 1979).

Childhood Experiences and
Their Impact on Adult Development

Freud put forth the idea that childhood experiences and relationships contribute to and shape adult development and functioning. Individuals' current perceptions and behavior are actually an effort to make sense of a painful past.

Resistance

Resistance involves the individual's means of coping with anxiety by refusing to engage in self-reflection or self-analysis that could lead to change and growth. Freud viewed self-reflection as necessary for client growth. However, a client's resistance can be viewed as normal and reflects how difficult it is for any of us, including our clients, to make life changes.

Transference and Countertransference

In treatment, clients often ascribe or transfer character traits and attitudes of significant others in their past to the social worker. If the social worker does not understand how she or he is perceived by the client, then it is very difficult to be helpful in the therapeutic process. Practitioners using a psychodynamic approach view **transference** as necessary in order to help clients explore their distorted views of ambivalence, love, or hatred toward others.

Countertransference is the same phenomenon as transference except that it refers to the professional attributing character traits and feelings of significant others to the client. Countertransference is a very common phenomenon, and Freud believed that this contributed to "blind spots" in the practitioner's own work with clients. He suggested that practitioners participate in their own analysis to enhance self-reflective capacities and address those "blind spots" (S. Freud, 1910, 1937). For example, if a social worker is uncomfortable with her or his own sexuality, this may interfere with and make it difficult to help a client explore his or her own sexuality.

PSYCHODYNAMIC THEORIES' EARLY INFLUENCES ON SOCIAL WORK PRACTICE

The earliest historical influence of psychodynamic theory on the social work profession occurred in the late 1920s. Social workers began to work in hospitals and newly developed child guidance clinics where they interacted with psychiatrists and became increasingly exposed to psychodynamic ideas; some even sought out psychoanalysis as part of their own personal and professional growth (Taft, 1958). As increased numbers of social workers joined the Red Cross, they began to work with WWI soldiers who were experiencing "shell shock" or the psychological trauma of combat. These changing work environments reflected major shifts in societal openness toward addressing mental health needs.

Virginia Robinson became one of the first social work scholars to describe the pivotal impact of Freud's ideas on social work theory and practice (Robinson, 1930). Other social work writers including Gordon Hamilton, Florence Hollis, and Charlotte Towle, who espoused a **diagnostic theory of case work**, pointed to the use of Freudian ideas to help social workers individualize their treatment with clients and families (Hollis, 1970; Smalley, 1970; Strean, 1993). Mary Richmond's emphasis on "study, diagnose and treatment" (1917) represented the use of a "medical model" approach to practice, grounded in ideas about the professional's role in first studying, assessing, and then treating a client who is having difficulties in adapting to the real world.

Psychodynamic theory provided a model for the impact of childhood experiences and conflicts on adult relationships and that often played out as a kind of parallel process within the worker/client relationship (Woods & Hollis, 2000). In an attempt to assist clients to have positive experiences with an authority figure, social workers interacted with clients in such a way as to help them have a "corrective emotional experience" (Strean, 1993). This meant, for example, that the social worker might provide limits and structure or provide a warm, inviting relationship with clients who had not experienced these healthy relational elements in childhood. However, as some have cautioned, in making psychodynamic theory their own, many social workers placed this theory, with its focus on curing mental illness, above social work's more established purpose of pursuing greater opportunities for those who are economically and socially disadvantaged, and strengthening individuals, families, and communities in accessing needed resources.

The **functional theory of case work**, developed by Virginia Robinson and Jessie Taft at the Pennsylvania School of Social Work in the 1930s, was influenced by the philosophy and teachings of George Herbert Mead, John Dewey, and later Otto Rank, one of Freud's earliest and most beloved disciples. The functional school differed from the diagnostic school in that it operated not from a psychology of illness, but from a psychology of growth and with an emphasis on creativity and the impact of social and cultural influences on human development. The functionalists also put the client and his or her goals, rather than the worker's expertise and ability to diagnose and treat, at the center of the social work relationship. Social workers in the functional school rejected the classical psychoanalytic ideas that the diagnostic school embraced, characterizing them as mechanistic, deterministic views of humans, who had gotten caught up in the dark forces of the unconscious and harsh restrictive influences of parental dictates in the early years of development (Smalley, 1970).

Otto Rank broke from Freud and countered his emphasis on the uncontrollable wishes and desires of the unconscious. Instead, as we shall see later in this chapter, Rank emphasized human growth, the development of the self, and the will as a controlling and organizing force. Rank's work also emphasized ideas such as the significance of time as a factor in the helping process (an idea that Taft and others used as the basis for the functional model). Robinson noted that the Rankian concept of the psychoanalytic situation was a dynamic one in which the patient works out his or her own will, conscious desires, and unconscious and unaccepted strivings against the attitude of the analyst (Robinson, 1930).

EXTENSIONS OF PSYCHODYNAMIC THEORY

Psychodynamic theory has been extended to include four core models: **ego psychology**, drive theory, object relations, and self-psychology (see Table 5.1).

While these theories have all shaped social work practice today, for our purposes, we will examine ego psychology and more current developments influenced by infant research and attachment, social constructionism and feminist and other diversity perspectives.

EGO PSYCHOLOGY

It was not until Sigmund Freud's *The Ego and the Id* (1923) that the importance of the environment in ego development was emphasized which, in turn, opened the way for the

TABLE 5.1 ■ Extensions of Psychodynamic Theory	
Four Core Models	**Description**
Ego psychology	The most widespread model in the United States is ego psychology, which was taken up by social workers in the 1940s and centers on the executive ego as a mediating hub for a system of functional, protective defenses (Goldstein, 2011). Ego psychology uses practice interventions that are designed to enhance human coping, motivation, self-esteem, and resilience and works in tandem with the strengths perspective (Saleebey, 2005).
Drive Theory	Those clinicians who adhere to drive theory explore dreams, transference, and countertransference in professional relationships, and examine client difficulties caused by deeply repressed conflicts due to childhood trauma and that may emerge in adulthood. Drive theorists promote client responsibility through self-awareness and reflection (Pine, 1990).
Object Relations	The object relations model suggests that the way people relate to others and to the environment in adult life is shaped by caregiving experiences during infancy. Practitioners using an object relations perspective help clients assess whether their current perceptions of reality and behavior are actually an effort to make sense of painful childhood experiences (Klein, 1948; Sullivan, 1953; Winnicott, 1965).
Self-Psychology	Those practitioners, including social workers, who use self-psychology (Goldstein, 2001) view the self as the core of human personality, which requires ongoing affirming and empathic relationships with others. They work with clients to address difficulties faced by inadequate early nurturing (Kohut, 1971, 1977).

development of ego psychology. Ego psychology gained recognition in the United States in the late 1930s and 1940s and deeply influenced social work practice (e.g., development of the strengths perspective) (Saleebey, 2005). Ego psychology included such prominent thinkers as Anna Freud, Heinz Hartmann, Rene Spitz, Margaret Mahler, Erik Erikson, and Edith Jacobson. As noted by Goldstein (2011), ego psychology emphasizes human potential, people's strengths, and resilience; drew attention to adaptive, conflict-free, autonomous ego functions (Hartmann, 1939); supported an individual's problem-solving capacities, defenses, coping mechanisms (A. Freud, 1936) and the human drive for competence and mastery (R. W. White, 1959); described individual's growth and development within a life cycle perspective (Erikson, 1950, 1959); emphasized the impact of interpersonal relationships (including the mother–infant bond), society, and culture in shaping human behavior (Jacobson, 1964; Mahler, Pine & Bergmann, 1975; Spitz, 1965); and examined the application of ego psychology to practice (Blanck & Blanck, 1974/1994).

For example, Anna Freud made a significant contribution to ego psychology in her clarification of defense theory and the principle mechanisms of defense. She and other scholars identified ego defense mechanisms, which are often now referred to as both mal-adaptive, but also adaptive. Many of these defenses are delineated in Table 5.2.

TABLE 5.2 ■ Defense Mechanisms	
Defense Mechanism	**Description**
Repression	Pushing unwanted thoughts and feelings out of conscious awareness
Reaction Formation	Taking an opposite view in an attempt to hide true feelings or desires, which may be socially or morally unacceptable
Projection	Known as "blame shifting"; attributing to others' unacceptable thoughts and feelings that the person himself or herself has but that are not conscious
Isolation	Creating a gap between unpleasant or threatening thoughts or feelings from other thoughts or feelings; attempting to avoid unpleasant thoughts/feelings by objectifying and detaching oneself from them
Undoing	Negating or acting out in reverse an unacceptable or guilt-provoking act, thought, or feeling
Regression	Reverting to an earlier stage of development in order to avoid anxieties of the present
Introjection	Taking on the behaviors, attributes, and ideas of another person in order to deal with difficult feelings or situations; commonly associated with the internalization of external authority such as parents
Sublimation	Channeling an expression of anxiety into socially acceptable ways

(Continued)

TABLE 5.2 ■ (Continued)

Defense Mechanism	Description
Intellectualization	A form of isolation in which one wards off anxiety-producing emotions by thinking about them, rather than experiencing them directly
Rationalization	Using faulty, yet convincing reasoning to justify certain ideas, feelings, or actions
Displacement	Shifting feelings or conflicts about a person/situation to more acceptable, safer outlets
Somatization	Converting intolerable impulses or conflicts into physical symptoms
Compensation	Overachieving in one area in an attempt to make up for other deficits or deficiencies
Altruism	Obtaining satisfaction through service or self-sacrifice to others as a means of dealing with unacceptable feelings and conflicts
Splitting	When an individual is unable to integrate difficult feelings, the tendency is to view people or events as either all bad or good; involves compartmentalizing opposite affect states and failing to integrate positive and negative qualities of self or others
Denial	Refusing to accept reality because it is too anxiety producing or threatening

Ego psychologists view defense mechanisms as operating unconsciously; the person is not aware of using a particular defense. A defense can be maladaptive in that it can severely limit a person's ability to perceive reality or to cope effectively. However, a defense may also be adaptive and actually serve as a healthy coping mechanism. When a person uses a defense or coping mechanism in a flexible rather than rigid fashion and the person is able to function well, the defenses are said to be adaptive.

MORE CURRENT DEVELOPMENTS

Although some current social work scholars and practitioners have been dismissive of the relevance of psychodynamic theories for social work practice (Danto, 2013; Dean, 2002), recent developments in psychodynamic theory demonstrate increased consistency with social work values and practices. These developments have come from many sources including (1) newer infant research and attachment theory; and (2) social constructionism, feminist perspectives, and in relationship to other forms of diversity (e.g., gay and lesbian growth and development).

Infant Research and Attachment Theory

Early classical psychodynamic theorists placed minimal to no importance on the relationship between parents and the infant in shaping the infant's ego development. Infants were seen as initially autistic, overrun with drives, dependent on caregivers for emotional regulation, but unable to interact with their caregivers. In contrast, more current infant research has examined the conditions for the infant's normal, healthy development, and has shown that babies actively participate in interactions with their caregiver from birth as a kind of mutual attunement, and that this need is over and above any need for physical care or protection. Within this interactive caregiver–infant relationship, the baby learns to regulate emotions and share in the caregiver's subjective and social world (Jacobson, 1964; Mahler, Pine, & Bergmann, 1975; Spitz, 1965). The infant's development is not about the resolution of competing needs as described in earlier classical psychodynamic theory, but instead it occurs in a "conflict free" setting (Hartmann, 1939) where needs (e.g., for attachment and independence) are integrated (Lachmann, 2001).

Attachment theory, as an outgrowth of psychodynamic theory, examines the caregiver's emotional availability and response to the child's needs as a way of providing a "safe haven" for the child. Once a secure attachment relationship has developed, the caregiver can function as a "secure base" from which the child can increasingly explore new environments (Ainsworth, 1969; Bowlby, 1969, 1988). This early caregiver–infant relationship serves as a foundation and template for all the child's subsequent relationships. If the caregiver is not responsive or emotionally unavailable, the child is likely to develop a less than ideal pattern of attachment (e.g., insecure, avoidant), contributing to later behavioral, cognitive, and mental health difficulties in adulthood. Attachment theory has found substantial support from neurobiological research to the point that scholars conceptualize individual development as holistic, arising out of the interactions and integration of the brain, mind, body, and spirit of both infant and caregiver and "held within a culture and environment that supports or threatens it" (Schore & Schore, 2008, p. 10). Social work professionals have viewed attachment theory as very applicable to practice across a variety of situations (e.g., child abuse and neglect; later-life resiliency; risk-taking behaviors, and romantic relationships) (Black-Hughes & Stacy, 2013; Lawler, Schaver, & Goodman, 2011; Saini, 2012; Shemmings, Shemmings, & Cook, 2012; Young, 2013).

Other Challenges to Psychodynamic Theory

Social constructionism, as defined in Chapter 2, has its roots in a postmodern perspective that contests positivist notions of objectivity (Berger & Luckman, 1967; Gergen, 1985). Specifically, social constructionists have challenged psychodynamic theory regarding its traditional notions of the practitioner as being able to stand outside of the therapeutic process as an objective observer who is able to make expert judgments about the client's reality that are not accessible to the client (Hoffman, 1983; Slavin, 2001). Social constructionism decentered the expert role of the practitioner in favor of knowledge that is co-constructed by all of the participants (i.e., both the practitioner and client give meaning to the therapeutic encounter). This has enabled the practitioner to participate more fully and openly in the clinical relationship and further encourage clients' views and expertise on their own lived experience as it shapes the therapeutic encounter. Contemporary theorists have broadly referred to this as a two-person encounter that emphasizes genuineness, openness, mutuality, and dialogue in the therapeutic process (Brandell, 2004; Goldstein, 2011; Goldstein, Miehls, & Ringel, 2009).

Psychodynamic theory has been soundly critiqued for its depiction of women as inferior to men, for its oppressive views of gender roles (e.g., for Freud, women were incomplete psychologically and biologically, and envied men) (Buhle, 1998; Firestone, 1970; Friedan, 1974), and as noted earlier, for its dismissal of the pervasive impact of sexual abuse on women's growth and development. At one point, Freud acknowledged that he just did not understand women and viewed them as mysterious and complex. In contrast, newer perspectives have augmented ego psychology and provide a more comprehensive understanding of women's development as well as that of gay, lesbian, and culturally diverse populations. Scholars have challenged classical psychodynamic views of women as inferior and have studied women's femininity and healthy psychosexual development (Chodorow, 1978, 1989; Horney, 1967). Further, others at the Stone Center for Developmental Studies, which include prominent writers such as Jean Baker Miller (1976), Judith Jordan, Alexandra Kaplan, Irene Stiver, Janet Surrey, and Jessica Benjamin, have delineated women's development as evolving more from connections and relationships rather than from separateness or differentiation of self from others (see Erikson, 1950). Women grow optimally in meaningful relationships with others and out of a sense of responsibility and commitment to those relationships. Ego psychology has also shifted and expanded to address healthy views of gay and lesbian development.

Summary of Overview

This overview of psychodynamic theory addresses Freud's traditional psychodynamic perspective, which examines intrapsychic and unconscious processes that contribute to human functioning as well as current developments (e.g., infant research and attachment theory; and influences of social constructionism, feminist, and other diversity perspectives). The authors discuss key concepts central to Freud's orientation (e.g., ego defense mechanisms; the impact of childhood experiences on adulthood; transference and countertransference) that still impact social work practice today. The earliest influences of psychodynamic theory on the social work profession occurred in the late 1920s as the first social work scholars representing the diagnostic school drew upon Freudian ideas and espoused a medical model to individualized treatment with clients. In contrast, the functional school influenced by Virginia Robinson, Jesse Taft, Otto Rank, and others operated from a psychology of growth and emphasized a person's creativity and will as an organizing force, as opposed to unconscious processes. Four core models (i.e., ego psychology, drive theory, object relations, and self-psychology) that flow from psychodynamic theory are described and a more in-depth examination is provided of ego psychology and its substantial impact on social work (e.g., the development of the strengths perspective; and growth and development within a life cycle perspective).

IN-DEPTH: OTTO RANK

Otto Rank (1884–1939) is a significant, yet usually overlooked figure in the development of psychodynamic theory (Costa, 2014; Lieberman, 1985). He has also had a significant influence on the development of theory for a broad range of social work practices, especially those related to case management and psychotherapy. As we will see, his existential, relationship-focused ideas can be observed today in multiple approaches to social work.

Unlike many of his medically educated contemporaries such as Freud, Otto Rank's professional training was in clinical psychology, and he was well versed in philosophy and literature/arts (Costa, 2014; Lieberman, 1985). Rank, nearly 30 years younger than Freud, was practically adopted by him and considered a son and co-creator of certain aspects of Freud's psychoanalytic theory (Rank actually coauthored a portion of Freud's (1955) *The Interpretation of Dreams*). Young Rank quickly integrated as a central figure in the Psychoanalytic Society, becoming its secretary at age 21. He served in this capacity for approximately 18 years (1906–1924). By this time, Rank had developed (and widely published) his own ideas about psychoanalysis that de-emphasized the Oedipal complex, introduced the idea of birth trauma (he published a book called *The Trauma of Birth*, 1929), and refocused the psychotherapeutic relationship on collaborative, here-and-now interactions between the therapist and client. Rank's psychoanalysis was primarily concerned with liberating the creative will of the individual, which ran counter to many of Freud's ideas.

By 1926, when Rank was nearly 42, he paid Freud a farewell visit, as the two men's ideas, and their relationship, had become incompatible. Rank was subsequently disassociated from the Psychoanalytic Society, was ostracized, and considered pathological by most of his former friends and colleagues. Even Rank's former students and trainees were required to be re-analyzed according to orthodox Freudian form in order to continue their affiliation and sanctioned practice with the society. Rank moved from Vienna to Paris and eventually settled in the United States, finding a teaching position in the School of Social Work at the University of Pennsylvania (Taft, 1958). Rank's relationship with Freud, his associations (and disassociation) with the Psychoanalytic Society, and subsequent relationships with Jesse Taft (professor of social work at the University of Pennsylvania) are a fascinating history in their own right—and significant to the development of Rank's ideas and social work theory. A detailed examination of this history is well beyond the scope of our present text; we'll focus instead on Rank's own psychoanalytic ideas in what follows. It is noteworthy, however, that Rank, rejected and professionally oppressed by his former psychoanalytic community, was apparently only able to find an academic home with the Social Work faculty at the University of Pennsylvania. The subsequent merging of his ideas with those of other social work scholars into what became known as the "functional school" of social work has had a profound influence to this day, as we shall see.

Will Psychology

In contrast to the tripartite geography of the mind in Freud's theory—the id, ego, and superego—Rank's psychology focuses instead on the human *will* (Rank, 1996). This is a radically different approach to understanding human psychology and its application to therapeutic ends. On the one hand, Freud's psychology is medical and, as Rank puts it, "pedagogical" (Rank, 1936, p. 22). What Rank means by "pedagogical" is that Freud (like many other contemporaries such as Alfred Adler) offers a psychology that presumes to impose predetermined morals on people, namely clients in therapy. Freud's psychology assumes the human will is "bad" because it represents genetically inherited aggressive/sexual instincts that must be somehow overcome or sublimated. As such, the will is also considered "resistant" to the treatments of the psychoanalyst—the will is something negative in any case, something which must be broken.

Rank finds this thinking flawed and wanting of a more pure psychological (as opposed to moralistic) approach. Rank states, "why must we always deny the will . . . the essential problem of psychology is our abolition of the fact of will" (1936, p. 10). Instead, Rank valued the will as a life-giving and transformative force. It is neither "good" nor "bad," but it is a distinctly human capacity that can be awakened and self-directed. The will, as centerpiece to Ranks's psychology, is also a major locus of human difficulties. Rank understood human beings to be plagued by conflicts of the will, which potentially lead to guilt and inhibitions that create problems for people in various ways in their lives, from family relationships to work life to social life. But he also held out hope because he also believed in the capacity for creative regeneration of self and relationships. He generally labeled his approach a "constructive therapy," the focus of which is "not the overcoming of resistance, but the transformation of the negative will expression . . . into positive and eventually creative expression" (p. 19).

By moving from Freud's biocultural determinism, to his own creative free-will focus, Rank opened new possibilities in the understanding of human development. Instead of assuming that the human individual merely *reflects* her or his external biological and cultural milieu, he asserts that the individual also has the power to "alter the external" (Rank, 1936, p. 3). The individual, as a creative force, has the power of self-determination, which can be used intentionally to shape her or his psychosocial world. In other words, there are both external forces (i.e., biocultural) and more importantly, internal forces (i.e., will) that act as determining factors in human behavior (as well as in the construction of identity, meaning, purpose, and values).

How does Rank define the will? What Rank has in mind is a conscious, volitional, and creative force in every human being. What each person does with his or her will is highly variable of course, but he believes there is potential in everyone to use this important capacity for positive growth and change (Menaker, 1982). In order to really engage life intentionally and use one's creative will, one must, in a sense, become psychologically "reborn." Rank doesn't have anything religious in mind with the idea of psychological rebirth; he means that all people (hopefully) become aware at some point of their own internal ability to decide who they are and what they will do with their life. He does not deny the influences of culture and genetics, but he also asserts that people have the capacity to make their own choices about who they become and what they do. This runs counter to the prevailing positivistic ideas at the time (and still today), which attempt to explain human behavior in a deterministic, mechanistic, and reductionistic manner. Positivist (as well as some social constructionist) perspectives tend to understand human behavior merely as a function of the past—of external causes such as behavioral shaping, genetic predispositions, and cultural mores. "[F]or Rank there resides a causality *within* the individual so that every act is not reducible to the deterministic influence of past experience as a cause" (Menaker, 1982, p. 41). In fact, Rank believes that the will as an internal causal force is the most essential and defining characteristic of humanity.

According to Costa (2014), Rank's **will psychology** is about becoming fully human, or developing "more life." His understanding of Rank places a tension between the creative, authentic individual (hopefully undergoing a psychological rebirth) and the reified biocultural factors, or milieu that each individual grows up in as a necessary matter of course. For Rank, the unconscious (again breaking with Freud) is a complex shared symbolic experience between individuals in each culture that consists of that culture's mythology, art, religion, philosophy, and so on. These are generated by people's collective will, values, creations, and search for the eternal. Rank's definition of spirituality is composed of these aspects of human life, aspects which mark human existence from non-human animals. He considers them supernatural in the sense that things like values do not exist as physical objects, though he maintained an atheistic perspective. Psychological awakening consists in developing an awareness of one's milieu in this sense and then making intentional choices about how one's will defines oneself according to one's own decisions about values, meaning, purpose, and creative endeavors. The subjectivity, or individual life, of the individual quickly becomes the focus in Rank's thinking as each person becomes "more human" by embracing more authentic life-giving endeavors.

Rank recognized a number of life-thwarting activities and ideologies such as drug addiction, hate, exploitation, oppression, hyper-conformity, violence, and Nazism—anything that crushes the will, creativity, values, and the search for the eternal (Costa, 2014). In contrast, "more life" involves recognizing and valuing the diversity of mythologies, arts, religions, and world philosophies, all as artifacts of human will and creative intelligence. Anything less—such as devaluing one culture's art over another—is considered the denial of people's humanity. Yet each culture is composed of individuals, and the value of the individual is prime. Becoming more human means transcending will-crushing forces, and self-creating according to one's own will and values—this adds a third dimension beyond the Freudian idea that the composed is trapped between the id impulses and superego parental/societal values. Rank's hope is that people transcend not just Freud's dichotomous thinking but potentially break free from their inherited culture's mores altogether (as well as from base instincts) and live life on their own terms. In Rank's thinking, one's personality and lifestyle themselves are the canvas upon which the (life) artist—the highest form of being human—"paints."

The Guilt Problem

While the will is the centerpiece for Rank's theory, and the means by which people may develop "more life," the oppressed, or neurotic will, can also become an internal source of problems. In a sort of ironic twist, Rank states that willing often generates a state of guilt in people (Rank, 1936). This isn't the sort of guilt that one experiences as a result of behaving in an unethical manner such as getting caught stealing and feeling bad about it. With the idea of guilt he intends more of an existential condition, a state of being that humans, as a matter of course, find themselves in, often not consciously. It is a bit of a "catch-22" and works like this: people have two options in life—first, they may follow the pack or herd (starting with what their parents want) and conform to some external standard preestablished by family, culture, or other social condition. The second option is to follow one's own will and intentions, to be authentically oneself, and make choices in accord with one's internal desires and motivations—to self-create. Everyone is constantly navigating the tensions inherent in this condition and nobody is purely self-created, nor purely conformist (though many more tend toward the latter than the former). Guilt arises in both cases. If one conforms to one's internal will and desires, then guilt comes about as a result of the awareness that one must be in defiance of, or at least acting inconsistently with one's parents, first of all (a necessary aspect of growing up), and then one's peer groups and (at least some) social mores and institutions. There is some deep-seated awareness that one is acting at the "expense of the other" as one separates from others. Rank considers this a normal tension that comes with maturation as one negotiates between the wish to separate and the wish to merge.

Guilt also accompanies *not* separating—if we choose to ignore our inner will and conform (or merge into the collective) then there is guilt over not being true to oneself, not being authentic (Rank, 1936). Another way to say this is that we are all different from each other in many respects, yet there are always overlaps as well—say in our appearance, political views, relationship styles, or even our personal preferences about music and food. When we recognize these differences there is a tendency to either find something wrong with ourselves (because we are different than the other[s]), or to find something wrong with those who differ from us. In the first case, we deem ourselves "bad" because we don't fit in; in the latter case, the other is considered "bad" because they are different. In either case we can become flooded with the kind of existential guilt Rank describes, as well as the concomitant negative emotions. This state of affairs can then negatively impact our relationships with family, friends, entire communities, and especially with ourselves.

Therapy nearly always includes the **guilt problem** as a central feature, the goal being to find a way to will, but without guilt (or at least not as much). Willing without guilt requires at least a basic understanding and acceptance of this human condition, and the ability to make choices—to will—by taking ownership of those choices, accepting responsibility and consequences for one's actions, and moving forward, becoming "more human" (Costa, 2014). Above all, this requires *self*-acceptance.

The Trauma of Birth

The guilt problem begins with what Rank calls the "trauma of birth" (Menaker, 1982; Rank, 1936). Rank initially considered **birth trauma** more literally, understanding it as the traumatic *physical* event of being born. Over time, however, Rank came to understand birth trauma as a more symbolic and existential event. Being born does literally separate each person from her or his mother physically, yet it also begins the long process of becoming a separate individual, *psychologically* different from the mother (and father and/or other caregivers). In this sense, the trauma of birth refers to the birth of individuality: "The resulting anxiety serves either to produce a fixation on the wish to return to the mother, in which case the individual becomes neurotic, or to propel him [sic] into future-directed, creative productivity" (Menaker, 1982, p. 69). The fixation on returning to the mother, or, stated more existentially, the desire to merge or conform, derives from a neurotic need for security and the avoidance of responsibility for one's life—basically, a fear of living. The alternative, which denotes proper human development, is the embrace of life, with

> driving growth toward separateness, uniqueness, and individuation of the ego. To be born means to be responsible for one's own separate existence and survival; and in this separateness man [sic] comes to experience his [sic] finiteness; he [sic] comes to know death, to fear the loss of his [sic] hard won individuality. (p. 64)

In other words, the trauma of birth (psychologically/existentially speaking) symbolizes what it means to become more human—to mature into an adult person who takes on the challenges of life. The idea of birth trauma, alongside the guilt problem, tends also to become a focus for therapy with Rank as dynamics similar to those just mentioned between mother and child play out between therapist and client (Rank, 1996).

Will Therapy

Will therapy, or constructive therapy, as Rank also calls it, is the application of his will psychology toward therapeutic ends. Rank's therapy is similar to Freud's in that people with some sort of life difficulty meet one-on-one with a trained therapist for approximately one hour, one or more times per week, to engage in a "talking cure." That said, Rank takes the therapeutic mechanisms, methods, and goals of psychotherapy in radically new and different directions. The contrasts, like with his will psychology, begin with his whole approach to understanding the human condition: unlike Freud, Rank does not offer a disease/pathology-based theory or therapy (Menaker, 1982; Rank, 1936). With regard to people who are experiencing life difficulties severe enough to warrant psychoanalytic intervention he states, "that even if they show quite marked disturbances of functioning in their so-called 'symptoms,' they are not sick in the medical sense. Their sufferings are emotional. The causes are rooted in the human development and human adjustment" (Rank, 1936, p. 1). As such, there is no universally prescribed cure for some set of symptoms collected under a generic disease label. Rank recognizes the reality of suffering that people experience, but he asserts that it is rooted in their existential condition (e.g., guilt).

Change Mechanisms and Therapeutic Methods

Rank's ideas about therapy do not include a list of techniques or methods. "I have attempted to write in place of a technique of psychotherapy, a 'philosophy of helping'" (Rank, 1936, p. 2). Instead of techniques, Rankian therapy focuses on the relationship between the client and therapist, the content of which centers upon existential themes that are particular to each individual client. "In each separate case it is necessary to create, as it were, a theory and technique made for the occasion without trying to carry over this individual solution to the next case" (p. 3). Instead of applying a universalized and predetermined psychological construct (i.e., Freud's theory) to each individual, Rank states that each client is unique—the therapist should "learn the speech of the other, and not force upon him [sic] the current idiom" (p. 4). Instead, the therapeutic relationship and experience are the change agents. Rank called his therapy "constructive" because the intent is to generate something new with each client, based on that client's particular life experiences. Change occurs as a growth process, not as an interpretation, or fitting of each client's life story with a theoretical construct in the therapist's mind. Rank hoped to keep his will psychology free from moralism, yet his psychotherapy (arguably, like all approaches) did contain values. "It values the individual in his [sic] uniqueness and his [sic] capacity for understanding and feeling, growth, and creativity" (Menaker, 1982, p. 102). "Therefore, therapy is less a process of acquiring understanding than of experiencing one's own functioning in the context of a new relationship" (p. 103).

The big question for Rank then, is what is it about the relationship between therapist and client that is so therapeutic? If the therapist is neither applying psychotherapeutic techniques, nor offering some grand interpretation, then what about the relationship dynamics actually help the client grow and change? It is important to understand that a Rankian therapist is not an analyst—someone who sits, detached and likely behind the client, who lies "on the couch." Instead, the therapist is a listener, a collaborator, and essentially, just another human being. In order to be therapeutic, the therapist must affirm the client's will and assist the client in accepting her or his own individuality.

There are two functional aspects to this (Menaker, 1982; Rank, 1936). First, the simple act of being accepted has basic therapeutic value—having someone else listen to the honest details of one's thoughts, emotions, and history. If there is anything "cathartic" about Rank's therapy it is the ability to honestly and freely express emotions in the safe and caring environment of the therapeutic relationship. In other words, clients can be authentic—they can "be themselves" without fear of moralistic judgment or manipulative interpretations. Second, as clients identify with the therapist, they develop self-acceptance. This occurs as a result of internalizing the therapist's acceptance as an aspect of the identification that takes place in a proper therapeutic encounter. The identification process is a form of merging, or becoming a "we," at least for a time. There is a danger of irony here because the therapeutic agent aimed at fostering individuality requires a degree of union between therapist and client. Rank was all too aware of this and attempted to remedy the situation by setting strict time limits for the duration of therapy (which are different for each client). Time limits serve as a constant reminder to both therapist and client that their union is temporary, not just temporally, but that in the end they remain individuals. Time limits serve a secondary existential function as they force the client (and therapist) to face the inevitability of separation and ends (i.e., their own death). The psychotherapeutic relationship, like conscious, subjective human life itself, exists only between apparent nothingness both before it begins and after it ends. The Latin phrase *carpe diem* (seize the day!) may well characterize Rank's approach in sum.

If there is anything that approximates a method to Rank's therapy it is the therapist's ability to maintain an active awareness of the relationship dynamics with the client as they play out in the present moment (Menaker, 1982). Helping clients by affirming their will and individuality is something the therapist does by inviting clients to explore the aforementioned existential concerns and emotions, recognizing the importance of their social context. Being therapeutic requires a high degree of self-awareness on the part of practitioners, which permits them to maintain an awareness of their own life concerns and emotions as they observe the ways in which the client relates to them. For instance, a therapist may notice that the client tends to over-relate with her or him by agreeing with everything she or he says, possibly to the detriment of the client's own opinions and feelings (or it could be vice versa). This relational feature would be something the therapist would bring up (as appropriate) to discuss with the client, inviting her or him to explore ideas, express related emotions, and consider his or her authentic beliefs, values, and intentions. Through this healing relationship, clients may develop the most important characteristic of psychological health, which is self-acceptance. Self-acceptance denotes the acceptance of one's own will and uniqueness, which should diminish the sense of guilt and enhance clients' abilities to take ownership of who they are, who they have been, and who they will become in the future. Rankian therapy is not about dwelling on the past (e.g., anal fixations) but about taking responsibility for oneself and making intentional decisions and decisive actions for the future.

At this point, critical thinking may raise a question about ethics—does Rank approve of and endorse every kind of "willed" behavior that clients may have done in the past, or are currently engaged in? Such behavior may include violence, dishonesty, cruelty, addictions, or lawlessness. Rank does not view therapy as an attempt to force people into conformity with any ethical or other type of regulatory thought or behavior system. He believed people's thoughts, emotions, and behavior, even when harmful to self or others, tend to be creative mechanisms, adaptive to the given life circumstances of the individual (i.e., their history, social context). Rank was therefore not interested in whether people are "good" or "bad," but he sought to really understand each person's struggle with the existential conditions we all face. Life necessarily involves a certain amount of pain and discomfort. "The suffering associated with it [willing], as well as the responsibility for mastering it, must be borne by each individual" (Menaker, 1982, p. 105). Rank would likely assert here as well that when people are caught up in addictions, hyper-conformity, or other destructive behavior, they are most likely not acting from a place of freedom, with a self-aware, creative, and intentional will.

Goals of Therapy

The goals of Rankian therapy, like with his will psychology, are existential, and there-fore relative to the individual. That said, Rank did have some general ends in mind. According to Menaker, the goal of Rankian therapy is "to liberate the individual's inher-ent capacities. It should help the individual to accept the nature of his [sic] own being and of his [sic] emotional life; in this sense it is affirmative" (Menaker, 1982, p. 102). People often get "stuck" in various ways such as the ambivalence that results from guilt and fear. This could manifest itself in many ways, such as sabotaging one's own romantic relation-ships when they become "'serious," out of a fear of not having found the "best" mate, or perhaps due to doubts in one's ability to maintain a healthy, long-term relationship. People become developmentally stunted as well when they blame others for their own mishaps in an attempt to avoid responsibility and deny their own will and intentions. This may tie into a broader existential concern, the "fear of living"—meaning, if people can evade responsibility for their own will and actions, then in a sense they can avoid this often anxiety-provoking aspect of human life, and not really "living" may facilitate the denial of the inevitability of death. Moreover, not really "living" also lets one off the hook when things go badly in life (e.g., occupational failures), in which case other people or external conditions can always be scapegoated and blamed.

Rank did not judge people for "getting stuck" in life—in fact, he thought of these problems as creative attempts to cope, often with rather unfortunate life circumstances (e.g., neglectful and/or cruel parenting). Thus, the goal of Rankian therapy is to engage life and live without guilt or excuse; to take responsibility for one's decisions, mistakes, successes—to mature into an adult who recognizes her or his uniqueness, creativity, abilities, and limitations; and lives into her or his "will to be" and will to "more life" (Costa, 2014). Successful therapy means the liberation of the individual will toward self-determined creative expression (Rank, 1936).

THEORY CRITIQUE

In this section, psychodynamic theory, Rankian therapy, and more current theoretical developments (e.g., ego psychology) will be critiqued for their relevance to social work practice. One of the difficulties in engaging in a critique of psychodynamic theory is that some of the criticisms of this theory are based in its classical or older Freudian ideas, which although novel in challenging American society to address sexuality and the mental health needs of citizens, had many flaws (e.g., sexist, silent about diversity in all its forms, and unwilling to acknowledge the impact of the mother–infant bond on a child's ego development; which indeed Otto Rank emphasized in contrast to Freud). Newer developments of psychodynamic theory, as described in the overview of this chapter, have begun to address these shortcomings. What follows is an examination of both classical psychodynamic theory, Rankian therapy, and newer developments (e.g., ego psychology, attachment theory).

What Does This Theory Say About Human Behavior?

Classical psychodynamic theory includes many assumptions about human behavior and places importance on

- the existence of the unconscious and its impact on ego development;
- the use of a medical model or deficit-based approach to working with clients;
- childhood experiences as contributing to adult growth and development; and
- defense mechanisms, which can be maladaptive or lead to healthy ego development.

More current developments (e.g., functional school and Rankian ideas, ego psychology, attachment theory, and feminist perspectives) contradict or expand on classical psychodynamic theory and emphasize

- people's creativity, their will, potential and strengths, not just their pathology or deficits, as central to human growth and development;
- the crucial role of the mother–infant bond in contributing to adult growth and development;
- the professional's role and involvement (e.g., two-person therapy) in the clinical relationship; and
- diversity in all its forms as pivotal for understanding human development.

Classical psychodynamic theory has been soundly critiqued in social work for its focus on clients' weaknesses, deficits, and problems as opposed to healthy development (Greene, 2002; Saleebey, 2005). Although this was likely true in its beginnings, newer theoretical developments have placed importance on the professional's humanity and reciprocity within a client-based relationship that highlights the client's healthy or normative development. Ego defense mechanisms, once viewed as largely maladaptive, have been recast in ego psychology to potentially function as healthy coping strategies. What makes any critique of psychodynamic theory complicated is that mental health treatment is regulated in the United States through health insurance companies, which require psychiatric diagnoses for payment of services. An emphasis on the use of these diagnoses makes it difficult for the social work practitioner (working in an agency dependent on health insurance payments) to consistently support healthy development let alone preventative practices, which are likely not covered by insurance but can assist a diverse range of clients in strengthening the development of their creative will and their coping, problem solving, and other adaptive skills. Further, health insurance companies and trends in social work education have supported the use of short-term treatment, which some have said is a Band-Aid approach for addressing complex client needs that require longer-term treatment (e.g., in addressing childhood physical and sexual abuse; in working with combat veterans). Finally, most private insurance companies categorize work with couples and families with diagnoses that are not reimbursed.

Psychodynamic theory presumes the existence of an unconscious and of universal stages that house intrapsychic conflicts in childhood that, if not resolved, may persist into adulthood. It also points to the tendency for people to repeat early childhood conflicts in adult relationships and that may be played out in a parallel process within the client–worker relationship (e.g., through transference and countertransference). By examining these psychological and often unconscious processes, humans are viewed by these theorists as able to reach their potential. With the advent of ego psychology, less emphasis was placed on these unconscious processes and more on the autonomous and even "conflict-free" zones in which a child could grow and develop aided by the infant–mother bond and within a context that acknowledged diversity (e.g., ethnicity, race, gender, sexual orientation and sexual expression, disability, and age).

ETHICS SPOTLIGHT
MARILYN AND HER FAMILY ARE IN CRISIS

Marilyn is a 43-year-old woman who comes to talk with you about her struggles around parenting of three children, Angela (age 13), Harvey (age 15), and Samuel (age 16). Each of them are acting out in their respective schools. She begins by describing being overwhelmed by the constant flow of information from her children's schools, clearly indicating that they are unable to control their behavior and their grades have dropped significantly in the past 18 months. These behaviors coincide with her husband abandoning the family after losing his job at a local factory. Marilyn has had no contact with him since he disappeared. She is undoubtedly overwhelmed by the intensity of the events that are unfolding within her family, as well as the external pressures as they relate to her inability to pay rent and provide food and clothing for her children.

Toward the end of the session, Marilyn says that she wants you to know that since her husband left, she has been having memories of being sexually abused by her uncle when she was

(Continued)

(Continued)

approximately 8 years old. She expresses concerns about whether this has actually happened or if it is a product of her current state of mind. In either case, she cannot sleep and fears she will have a "breakdown" if she is unable to get clear about what happened.

The agency requires that you give a diagnosis at the end of the first session in order to bill for services.

Discussion Questions

(1) Do you believe you have enough information to make a diagnosis, and should that diagnosis focus on the family or Marilyn's issues? (Note: Most insurance companies do not pay for family-focused work—only individual diagnoses are linked to resources.)

(2) How do you balance decisions about where to focus your work when there is clear evidence (i.e., the acting out of the children) against the less verifiable emergence of Marilyn's repressed memories of sexual abuse?

(3) How do you define what is in the best interests of this family?

How Does This Theory Address Growth and Change?

Classical psychodynamic theorists viewed human beings as caught up in the unseen forces of the unconscious and also restricted by parental authority in early childhood development. Childhood experiences greatly contributed to adult development, and classical theorists adhere to a more deterministic view of this growth and development. For the classical theorist, this meant that a child was constrained by parents and other societal forces and was less free to grow and develop independently or creatively. In effect, childhood experiences and conflicts predicted or causally determined adult development.

This idea of determinism has been contrasted with notions of free will, which are so central to Rankian ideas and later developments in ego psychology. Free will encompasses the belief that we do have a choice in how we behave and we can act free from the causal influences of past events. Determinism and free will are often viewed as opposing ideas; they have long been debated but are much more than philosophical concepts. Determinism has real-world consequences for people who have lived, for example, through traumatic experiences, such as childhood sexual abuse. In our recent past, helping professionals believed that if a woman had experienced sexual abuse as a child, she was "damaged goods" and more likely to sexually abuse her own children than a woman who had not experienced childhood sexual abuse. In other words, a woman who had experienced sexual abuse was unlikely to recover, heal, grow, and work through this past abuse; consequently, this would contribute to her being more likely to abuse her own children. It was only when scholars discovered that in the general population women were very likely to be sexually assaulted or abused by age 18 (i.e., nearly 1 out of 3 women), that these myths were thoroughly challenged (Briere & Elliott, 2003).

This idea of determinism supports a deficit or medical model approach, which can be very harmful to clients: practitioners are guarded at best and less hopeful about their clients' capacities for growth and change. As discussed in Chapter 2, the practitioner's hope in a client's capacities greatly contributes to client growth. Newer developments in Rankian therapy, ego psychology, and beyond broke from this Freudian determinism and emphasized not only the professional's expertise but the client's resiliencies, creative will, strengths, and capacities. No matter what their circumstances or experiences, human beings are able to overcome great adversity and strive for healthy adaptation.

How Holistic Is This Theory?

Many social workers have repudiated psychodynamic approaches as being narrowly and individually focused. Certainly, early in the development of psychodynamic theory, Freud viewed the environment (e.g., the mother–infant bond) as nearly irrelevant to human growth and development. Although newer developments have addressed the impact of interpersonal and familial relationships on an individual's growth and development (see Bowlby, 1969; Winnicott, 1965), these approaches have still been accused of not being sufficiently appreciative of the larger environment's impact on shaping the client's world. Psychodynamic theories have also been indicted for shifting social work's professional responsibilities away from addressing political change, community-based advocacy, social policy, and other social justice efforts that can better address the problems clients face while living within increasingly complex, global environments (Specht & Courtney, 1994).

Psychodynamic theories are charged with being reductionist in that they encourage practitioners and researchers alike to give very little attention to broader societal injustices or problems in favor of examining and changing individual client behaviors. For others, a human being's behavior cannot be understood apart from the social, economic, spiritual, and environmental contexts in which it occurs (see "Systems Theories," Chapter 6). By reducing down the focus of attention to the individual, psychodynamic theorists engage in a kind of "context stripping." In effect, by being reductionist, psychodynamic theorists may be asking smaller, more specific questions about human behavior, thereby ignoring the larger picture. Although some elements of psychodynamic theory have attempted to support not just individuals but also larger community and social systems in becoming more "self-reflective," tolerant, and democratic in their views (Danto, 2013; Freud, 1937), it is hard to ignore psychodynamic theorists' emphasis on *individual* growth and development.

How Consistent Is This Theory With Social Work Values and Ethics?

Psychodynamic theory, especially its classical form, has faced challenges regarding its consistency with social work values and ethics. Classical psychodynamic theory has ignored, been silent, or put forth negative views of women and other diverse populations (e.g., those who are ethnically/racially diverse; people who are gay, lesbian, bisexual or transgender). Freud placed heterosexual male growth and development as the subject (or at the center) of his theory, and other diverse groups were viewed as deficient or incomplete (e.g., women had penis envy and were morally inferior to men; homosexuality was a form of psychopathology). Because of these biases, classical psychodynamic theory has often been viewed as inconsistent with social work's core values of respecting the worth and dignity of all people and striving for social justice (e.g., failing to address violence against women). For example, although Freud became aware of the profound impact of women's experiences of childhood sexual abuse and rape through his work as a psychoanalyst, the Viennese medical establishment pressured him to recant his views about the real problem of sexual violence perpetrated against women (Masson, 1984).

More current feminist writers have challenged these early gender biases and have developed their own contributions to the study of female psychosexual development (e.g., environmental influences on women's development; femininity and mothering as part of a socialization process and not genetic in origin) (Chodorow, 1978, 1989; Horney, 1967; Miller, 1976). Ego psychology has now integrated newer knowledge about diversity and the strengths and coping capacities of these groups as well as the special challenges they may face as part of their growth and development (Drescher, 1998; Goldstein & Horowitz, 2003; Gutierrez, 1990; Berzoff, Flanagan, & Hertz, 1996). Further, more contemporary theorists view the professional relationship, involving the participation of both client and worker, as pivotal to client growth (Goldstein, Miehls, & Ringel, 2009). These current developments support social justice, self-determination, the freedom of human sexuality, the importance of human relationships, and the dignity and worth of all people including marginalized populations.

What Are the Sources of Knowledge That Support This Theory?

Psychodynamic theorists have studied the actual internal processes of their treatment modalities as well as their outcomes (Tuckett, 2001). Researchers have been able to establish evidence for the effectiveness of adult psychoanalytic psychotherapy as well as its relevance to child psychiatry (Fonagy, 2003). Further, more current brain research (e.g., attachment theory and the infant–caregiver bond as well as the pervasive influences of unconscious processes on emotions and intellect) increasingly supports psychodynamic theories (Gabbard, 2000). Research methods based in psychodynamic approaches have typically involved real-world case studies and qualitative approaches in contrast to quantitative studies that require more highly controlled conditions (e.g., randomized control trials). Because of this, psychodynamically oriented researchers have been viewed by some as not meeting the "gold standard" for highly rigorous quantitative research (Brandell, 2004). It must be noted that by employing qualitative and case study methods, these research studies take into account not only the professional's expertise but also clients' narratives regarding their own struggles and growth. Research that supports psychodynamic theory draws upon multiple sources of knowledge (e.g., empirical studies; practitioner and client expertise) and places great importance on empirically studying the development of a meaningful relationship between the practitioner and the client.

APPLICATION OF PSYCHODYNAMIC THEORY

Introduction

What you have read in the early sections of this chapter attempts to emphasize psychodynamic theory as a set of ideas consisting of a dynamic and evolving framework for understanding human behavior. This may be the theory that has had the most persistent impact on the helping professions, including social work, and it continues to influence public perceptions of human behavior. Its critiques often focused on its original conception by Freud, which reflected his particular historical context, and therefore, reflect his attitudes and those of his contemporaries toward gender, race, and so on that were prevalent at the turn of the 20th century. However, as we have suggested, psychodynamic theory continues to evolve from its original form to include ego psychology, drive theory, will therapy, object relations, self-psychology, and attachment theory. Unfortunately, there has been a tendency to discount the useful elements of this theory that continue to provide meaningful ideas that have relevance to current practice. We see the theory as a resource that remains a useful way for understanding important aspects of our current clinical work. Classical psychodynamic theory includes the following assumptions about human behavior:

- The existence of the unconscious and its impact on ego development

- The use of a medical model or deficit-based approach to working with clients

- Childhood experiences as contributing to the adult growth and development

- Defense mechanisms that can be maladaptive or lead to healthy ego development

When we combine more current developments (e.g., functional school, ego psychology, attachment theory, and feminist perspectives) we get a more full understanding of human behavior, which allows us to expand the usefulness of these ideas. The following represent both some contradictions and expansion on classical psychodynamic theory:

- People's creativity, potential, and strengths, not just their pathology or deficits, are central to human growth and development.

- The role of the mother–infant bond is crucial in contributing to adult growth and development.

- Importance is placed on the professionals' role and involvement in two-person therapy or with multiple people, e.g., couples, families and groups in clinical relationships.

- Diversity in all its forms is pivotal for understanding human development.

THE APPLICATION OF PSYCHODYNAMIC THEORY TO CASE EXAMPLES

The following case example provides an opportunity to look at some of the conceptual elements of this theory that were presented in the first few pages of this chapter.

In the first session, we can see the impact of childhood experiences on the current interactions between the worker and the client. For example, the client begins to work with a "safe problem" that allows her to check out the worker to determine how she can navigate or adapt to this new environment that includes an older White male worker. Her behavior reflects the connection between her childhood experiences in the current conversation with the therapist who has similar characteristics to her father (White, older, and male). Her strategies reflect what psychodynamic theory characterizes as ego defense mechanisms. Unfortunately, given the theory's roots in a medical model, it suggests these behaviors have only negative consequences and must somehow be "overcome." For social workers to be able to use psychodynamic theory to support a client's growth, it is more useful to see these behaviors as "coping strategies." This is not simply a superficial change in language, but it reflects a shift in perspective that helps us to ask different questions—not how is this behavior a problem, but how is this behavior useful to helping this client navigate this new situation and what benefits come from this behavior that support the client's functioning.

CASE EXAMPLE
EGO DEFENSE MECHANISMS OR COPING STRATEGIES?

A 65-year-old White male social worker in a mental health center received a referral involving a White female in her mid-30s. In the first session, her presenting concerns had to do with the deteriorating relationship between herself and her husband. During the whole first session, she focused on "communication" problems they were experiencing. She asked numerous questions about how the therapist thought that couples "ought" to communicate. Then, before the session ended, she asked more directly about how she should respond to her husband's insistence that she remain at home with their three sons rather than pursue a degree in psychology. The remainder of the session was spent focusing on how she felt devalued and that "men" were incapable of respectful communication with women. The session ended shortly after this comment and a brief discussion about how her experiences might play out with the worker, who pointed out that she might be concerned about his ability to really hear what she was trying to tell him. And, that he wanted her to feel free to tell him when she felt that he was not hearing what she was telling him. She paused, then she agreed to come back for one more session.

The second session began with the client saying that she really didn't want to focus on her marriage. She wanted to talk about some things that had to deal with what happened between her and her father. What unfolded was a history of sexual abuse that persisted from the age of 6 through age 17, at which time she escaped her family by marrying her current husband. Her father used a number of strategies over time to control her behavior, from physically and emotionally abusive behaviors, to bribes, to promises that he would leave her younger sister alone if she acquiesced to his demands.

The translation suggested above allows the social worker to more easily transition from the original psychodynamic ideas put forward by Freud to Rank's notion of "will." Freud's original emphasis was on struggles associated with internal drives, housed in the id, which would be moderated by rules externally imposed onto those drives, housed in the superego. It was only later, as noted earlier in the chapter, that Freud began to emphasize the autonomous role of the ego and its capacity for generating growth (1929). Rank, on the other hand, saw the will as a primary force in integrating ongoing healthy growth and development for individuals. The use of this perspective allows the possibility of translating our focus from dealing with behaviors as pathological to understanding behaviors as expressions of people's attempts to grow and develop. This emphasis began with Rank's perspective and can be found in current psychodynamic writings (Danto, 2013; Dean, 2002; Goldstein & Horowitz, 2003).

A second example illustrates the power of the concepts of transference and counter-transference in current practice:

CASE EXAMPLE
TWO-WAY CLIENT AND WORKER RELATIONSHIP

A social worker has been seeing a client for an extended period of time in helping her to deal with her family's abusive and neglectful behaviors. The relationship between the worker and client was well established, and the work was proceeding in a productive fashion. The client asked the worker to see a colleague who was in need of help with some substantial problems that were getting in the way of her professional performance. The following exchange occurred over several sessions in which there was a great deal of time spent on exploring the potential impacts of this decision on their existing relationship, which the worker believed to be his primary ethical obligation. The end result was to move forward to see both individuals in a manner where the primary client's privacy was protected and a clear agreement was made to exclude any discussion of the new client's relationship with the worker.

The primary client became quite angry after the worker began to see her colleague. She stated that the worker was abandoning her for her colleague. She accused the worker of not caring because he had "replaced" her with this new client whom he liked much better than he liked her. She asserted that she knew she would lose out to this other person and would be "kicked to the curb." Unlike prior difficult times in the work, she was unable to enter into any active participation in examining her responses to what was happening. When the worker confronted her behavior more directly, pointing out how it was different from prior situations, she blurted out, "you are going to leave me for the other person just like my father left me to create a new family when he divorced my mom." This projection of her feelings of abandonment onto the worker represents the

(Continued)

(Continued)

client's transference onto the worker of her feelings that originated in the relationship between her and her father.

Meanwhile, on the worker's side of the relationship, there was a great deal of concern related to the reality that he had talked about protecting the primary relationship with his existing client prior to making any decision about seeing the client's colleague. The worker held strong beliefs about upholding ethical standards for himself as related to his work with clients. His attempts to try to have a significant conversation with his client about the potential hazards of his becoming involved with her colleague seemed to indicate that she understood and would be able to handle the existence of the two relationships. However, he had failed to see the depths of the problems associated with this decision. His own frustration with himself for not having seen the clinical implications that might flow from his decision led him to try to convince his client that her fears about him abandoning her were unwarranted. Those frustrations began to interact with the client's fears of abandonment, and the process became counterproductive in that his reaction to his own guilt and frustration simply reinforced her beliefs. In the end, it was necessary to seek consultation from a colleague in order to get clarity on how his behavior was adding to the problem rather than reducing the negative impacts on the relationship.

In short, the client's transference of her pain related to her father's abandonment onto the worker and his response to the transference, which translated into his own unspoken fears that he might make a mistake that would harm a client, interacted in such a way that a useful and productive clinical relationship was significantly harmed. Only through the use of outside consultation would the worker sort out and begin to take charge of the issues that were inhibiting the client's growth and development. This example illustrates not only how transference and countertransference can impact clinical relationships, but it also reinforces the idea, presented by newer psychodynamic theorists, that the relationship is not a one-way but a two-way interaction involving both the social worker and the client.

CONNECTIONS TO USEFULNESS IN PRACTICE

First, one of the most profound and important aspects of psychodynamic theory is the influence it has exerted on the connections between early life experiences and later life behaviors. What started out with a more medically oriented emphasis on causality between early life experiences and later life behaviors has evolved into a more nuanced view of the relationships that exist between early life experiences and later life development. For example, even other models not directly connected to psychodynamic theory like narrative therapy emphasize understanding clients' life stories as central to current behaviors (White & Epston, 1990). However, this approach assumes the malleability and creativity that individuals possess to reinterpret their early understandings of events in such a way that they can identify resources and capacities that can be brought to bear in their current circumstances. Behavior modification is another example of an approach that requires the collection of data to establish "baseline" information focused on patterns of behavior that exist prior to the actual encounter with a social worker (Thomlinson & Thomlinson, 2011). Finally, the continuing presence of social history information in most agency records suggests that no matter how "present focused" we become there is still a strong thread of reliance on the collection of information to establish historic patterns of behavior and their connection to the current context.

Second, we have emphasized the evolution of psychodynamic theory over the course of the last century. One of its more important changes relates to the use of social constructionism as a way of beginning to understand the importance and the dynamics involved in seeing the helping relationship as a two-party process (Dean, 2002). Early iterations of psychodynamic theory did recognize concepts including transference, countertransference, and projection, all of which require a focus on the interactions between the professional and the client. In order to examine ourselves as a part of the process, there is an inherent requirement that professionals develop certain skills that are central to all levels of practice. In order to utilize psychodynamic theory, workers are required to develop a sense of self-awareness, the capacity for reflection, the ability to think critically, and to develop analytical skills that help them more fully understand the processes that are taking place in their practice.

Third, we specifically focused on the work of Otto Rank for the application of the broader notion of psychodynamic theory. This choice was based on the belief that Rank's reinterpretation of Freud's original work, with its emphasis on the concept of "will," "constructive therapy," and his emphasis on placing human growth and development in the context of larger social and cultural systems, is more compatible with social work's values and purpose. It also lays the conceptual foundation that ties to current efforts related to the development of the strengths perspective. Rank's theory emphasized the uniqueness of each individual's capacity for understanding and feeling, growth, and creativity. Therefore, his perspective ties very closely with the value base of social work, as well as situating people in relation to their environments, which is the focus of all levels of social work practice.

Finally, as you enter professional roles within the context of our current agencies you will see the footprints of psychodynamic theory on a daily basis. Many of you will practice in agencies that require social histories, diagnoses, and the development of treatment plans (often instigated and developed by professionals with little input from clients). You will also encounter the residual impacts of the medical model in its various forms as it continues to challenge social workers to adhere to social work's *Code of Ethics*, and purposes, which include both social control and social change.

CHAPTER SUMMARY

As we pointed out in this chapter, psychodynamic theory had a pervasive and complicated relationship with social work. It began its impact in the early 20th century with the arrival of Sigmund Freud, who did a series of lectures in the United States. Freud's impact was significant in all aspects of American society. It was particularly influential in the emerging mental health fields. Given that social work was active in a broad range of agencies, including child guidance clinics, mental health centers, work with veterans, school social work, and medical social work, psychodynamic theory's influence permeated many professional helping settings. However, psychodynamic theory broke into two separate schools of thought within the social work profession. The first, and the largest group, were those social work professionals who became known as the "diagnostic school," which relied on interpretations of Freud's perceptions about the human condition and the translation of those ideas into a broad range of practice strategies to be used to bring about growth and change. The second, and smaller group, in social work focused on the ideas provided by Otto Rank, who had been in Freud's inner circle but broke with his mentor when he developed different interpretations of what was central to human growth and development. Rank was unable to secure a position until he came to the United States where he met Jesse Taft and Virginia Robinson, both social work professors, who helped him attain a position at the University of Pennsylvania. Through their efforts to translate his work into English and publish their own interpretations of his ideas, a second group of social workers emerged called the "functional school" (see Table 5.3).

TABLE 5.3 ■ Comparing Functional and Diagnostic Themes		
Characteristics of Approach	**The Diagnostic Approach**	**The Functional Approach**
Purpose of Intervention	Help individuals realize their own capacities for change and growth	Within the function of an agency or social program, help individuals reach their creative potential
Theory	Freudian psychoanalytic and personality theory, Richmond, anthropology (cultural roots and customs)	Otto Rank and "will," concept of separation, psychoanalytic techniques, Mead and Dewey (e.g., social and cultural aspects of human development)
Philosophy	Concept of norms in psychic functioning, therapist as expert in working with clients, human events consist of person and situation (i.e., subjective and objective reality)	Emotional development is self-determined, deep concern for the social problems with which agencies are set up to deal with
Knowledge	Motivations and needs, verbal and nonverbal communication, self-awareness, personality structure, conscious utilization of techniques	Knowledge of self, conflicting forces within individuals, workers' attitudes toward clients, relationship process, agency function (e.g., rules and procedures)

Characteristics of Approach	The Diagnostic Approach	The Functional Approach
Values	Self-help, social productivity, acceptance of differences, respect for others	Social responsibility, self-determination
Workers' Attributes	Provider of gratification, protection, and guidance; other-centered, objective, warm, assumes responsibility for direction of treatment	Attitude of understanding and acceptance, and promise of help
Terminology	Treatment	Helping process, constructive new environment
Definition	Mutual process of shared responsibilities	The constructive new environment in which the client is given an opportunity to strive for better solutions
Key Elements	Worker assumes responsibility for direction and goals of treatment, authority (suggestions, advice, restraint), and psychosocial help	Sense of security, positive transference, time (structural importance of), authority (re: time, attention, relief, constructive plan), internal process, structured out of agency functions
View of Clients	Responsible participants, stimulated by worker to participate in the study of their particular situation, fashioned by interrelationship between clients' basic needs and their physical and social environment	At the center of the social work relationship (responsible for choices, goals, outcomes, direction of change)

As the above table suggests, there are significant differences in how the two schools of thought understood the professional relationship and the nature of the work. As the chapter points out, from Freud's perspective, the nature of the professional's work with clients was to create positive individual experiences with an authority figure that would provide a "corrective emotional experience" (Strean, 1993), which emphasized limits and structure as well as an inviting, nurturing environment in which to correct for unhealthy interactions clients experienced in their childhood. Its assumptions were built on a medical model focusing on internal conflicts among the id, ego, and superego. It focused on the reduction of pathology as its primary goal, but it remained silent about the capacity of both social and cultural factors on human development. The functional school emphasized the concept of "will" as a conscious, volitional, and creative force for growth and change that supported a person's capacity for creative regeneration of self in relationships. The emphasis was on an individual's capacity to be a creative force through the power of self-determination, which could not only shape one's internal world but also the environments in which the person lived. Finally, the functional school emphasized the importance of both the time-limited nature of the professional relationship and the context in which the relationship occurred (i.e., the agency setting) as important elements that shaped the work.

As we noted earlier, psychodynamic theory has had multiple iterations that remain relevant in current models of practice (e.g., ego psychology, drive theory, object relations, self-psychology, and the functional school's interpretation of Rank's work), which appear in the strengths perspective (Saleebey, 2005). In many instances, the critiques that have been leveled at psychodynamic theory focus on its original form in which its reliance on a medical model emphasized reductionist thinking, isolation of clients from their environments, lack of attention to diversity, a focus on the professional relationship as a one-way exchange with all of the attention on the client, and negative connotations embedded in the original writing as it relates to gender. Many of these criticisms have been addressed in ways that allow social workers to adapt the theory to fit practice in the 21st century (Danto, 2013; Dean, 2002; Goldstein, 2011).

Classroom Exercise

CASE EXAMPLE
EARNING A LIVING AS A STRIPPER

You are the social worker in a local mental health agency. You are working with a 28-year-old White female client who is in a relationship with a man (not married). They have two children ages 5 and 3, and she is supporting her family through her job as a stripper in a local bar. She comes asking for assistance with ongoing panic attacks that started when the owner of the club refused to enforce the "no touch" rules. She has supported her family for approximately nine years in this occupation.

The client shared with you that she was raised in a Pentecostal tradition, and as a result, her parents do not know that she's not married to her partner nor that she is earning a living as a stripper ($6,000 dollars per month). Her husband is not employed and on occasion has put his hands on her during arguments between the two of them. She has just learned that she is pregnant with her third child and will need to stop her employment in her sixth month of the pregnancy. She does not see her parents as a resource since they are unaware of the details of her current family situation.

Directions

Please answer the following questions based on viewing yourself as the worker in this situation. After you have answered the following questions, come together in groups of four or five students to share your answers. Use the time to examine how your responses are similar and different than those of your colleagues. The emphasis is on your reflection and your analysis based on the interactions between you and the client as seen through the theoretical lens of psychodynamic theory.

Discussion Questions

1. According to what you have read about transference and countertransference, there is a process that goes on between workers and clients. What thoughts and feelings could you imagine this client might place on you (e.g., your gender, race, your age, your religious background) as she thinks it may affect the meaning and understanding you have of her situation? What might be the

thoughts and feelings engendered in you based on the client's characteristics (e.g., her gender, her parents, her occupation, her deception of her family, her determination to support her family)?

2. What ego defense mechanisms, or coping strategies, are present that are helping the client to navigate or adapt to her environment? Which ones would you try to strengthen, and which ones would you attempt to have her replace with some other behaviors? What is your rationale for your analysis?

3. How do her childhood experiences (e.g., being raised in a religiously conservative family and at times a verbally abusive family, the fact that she's currently not married but living with a man without telling her family) impact her current levels of functioning?

4. What role does resistance play in creating barriers to change? How could resistance be useful in helping this client to keep some level of stability in her situation? What resistance would you support, and what areas of resistance would you try to confront in order to create change? Provide a rationale for your answers to both questions.

Last Step

Now come together as a class and share your group's responses to this case situation and examine how psychodynamic theory connects to the importance of the reality that the helping process is shaped not only by the client's understanding but how you as a person interact with the client by bringing your own beliefs, knowledge, values, skills, and your attributes into the work.

Key Terms (in order of appearance)

References

Ainsworth, M. D. S. (1969). Object relations, dependency and attachment: A theoretical review of the infant–mother relationship. *Child Development*, *40*, 969–1025.

Berger, P. L., & Luckman, T. (1967). *The social construction of reality*. New York, NY: Doubleday Anchor.

Berzoff, J., Flanagan, L. M., & Hertz, P. (1996). *Inside out and outside in*. Northvale, NJ: Jason Aronson, Inc.

Black-Hughes, C., & Stacy, P. D. (2013). Early childhood attachment and its impact on later life resilience: A comparison of resilient and non-resilient female siblings. *Journal of Evidence-based Social Work*, *10*, 410–420.

Blanck, G., & Blanck, R. (1974/1994). *Ego psychology: Theory and practice.* New York, NY: Columbia University Press.

Bowlby, J. (1969). *Attachment and loss.* Vol. 1: Attachment. New York, NY: Basic Books.

Bowlby, J. (1988). *A secure base* (2nd ed.). New York, NY: Basic Books.

Brandell, J. R. (2004). *Psychodynamic social work.* New York, NY: Columbia University Press.

Briere, J., & Elliott, D. M. (2003). Prevalence and psychological sequelae of self-reported childhood physical and sexual abuse in a general population sample of men and women. *Child Abuse & Neglect, 27,* 1205–1222.

Buhle, M. (1998). *Feminism and its discontents: A century of struggle with psychoanalysis.* Cambridge, MA: Harvard University Press.

Chodorow, N. (1978). *The reproduction of mothering: Psychoanalysis and the sociology of gender.* Berkeley: University of California Press.

Chodorow, N. (1989). *Feminism and psychoanalytic theory.* New Haven, CT: Yale University Press.

Costa, J. (2014). *To be more person: A reading of Otto Rank.* Rio de Janeiro, Brazil: Julio Roberto Costa Publisher.

Danto, E. A. (2013). Psychoanalysis. *Encyclopedia of social work.* Washington, DC: National Association of Social Work and Oxford University Press.

Dean, R. G. (2002). Teaching contemporary psychodynamic theory for contemporary social work practice. *Smith College Studies in Social Work, 73,* 11–27.

Drescher, J. (1998). *Psychoanalytic therapy and the gay man.* Hillsdale, NJ: Analytic Press.

Erikson, E. (1950). *Childhood and society.* New York, NY: Norton.

Erikson, E. (1959). *Identity and the life cycle.* Vol. 1: Selected papers, psychological issues. New York, NY: International Universities Press.

Firestone, S. (1970). *The dialectic of sex: The case for feminist revolution.* New York, NY: Morrow.

Fonagy, P. (2003, June). Psychoanalysis today. *World Psychiatry, 2*(2), 73–80.

Freud, A. (1936). *The ego and mechanisms of defense.* New York, NY: International Universities Press.

Freud, S. (1910). The origin and development of psychoanalysis (H. W. Chase, Trans.). *American Journal of Psychology, 21,* 181–218.

Freud, S. (1929). The ego and the id. *The standard edition of the complete psychological works of Sigmund Freud, 19,* 12–66 (J. Strachey, Trans.). London, England: Hogarth.

Freud, S. (1937). Analysis terminable and interminable. *The standard edition of the complete psychological works of Sigmund Freud, 23,* 209–253 (J. Strachey, Trans.). London, England: Hogarth.

Freud, S. (1955). *Interpretation of dreams* (J. Strachey, Trans.). New York, NY: Basic Books.

Friedan, B. (1974). *The feminine mystique.* New York, NY: Dell.

Gabbard, G. O. (2000). A neurobiologically informed perspective on psychotherapy. *British Journal of Psychiatry, 177,* 117–122.

Gergen, K. J. (1985). The social constructionist movement in modern psychology. *American Psychologist, 40,* 317–329.

Goldstein, E. G. (2001). *Object relations theory and self psychology.* New York, NY: Free Press.

Goldstein, E. G. (2011). Ego psychology and social work treatment. In F. J. Turner (Ed.), *Social work treatment* (pp. 144–156). New York, NY: Oxford University Press.

Goldstein, E. G., & Horowitz, L. G. (2003). *Lesbian identity and contemporary psychotherapy: A framework for practice.* Hillsdale, NJ: Analytic Press.

Goldstein, E. G., Miehls, D., & Ringel, S. (2009). *Advanced clinical social work practice: Relational principles and techniques.* New York, NY: Columbia University Press.

Greene, R. R. (2002). *Resiliency: An integrated approach to practice, policy, and research.* Washington, DC: NASW Press.

Gutierrez, L. M. (1990). Working with women of color: An empowerment perspective. *Social Work, 35,* 149–154.

Hartmann, H. (1939). *Ego psychology and the problem of adaptation.* New York, NY: International Universities Press.

Hoffman, I. Z. (1983). The patient as interpreter of the analyst's experience. *Contemporary Psychoanalysis, 19,* 389–422.

Hollis, F. (1970). The psychosocial approach to the practice of social casework. In R. Roberts and R. Nee (Eds.), *Theories of social casework* (pp. 33–75). Chicago, IL: University of Chicago Press.

Horney, K. (1967). *Feminine psychology.* New York, NY: W. W. Norton.

Jacobson, E. (1964). *The self and the object world.* New York, NY: International Universities Press.

Klein, M. (1948). *Contributions to psychoanalysis: 1921–1945.* London, England: Hogarth Press.

Kohut, H. (1971). *The analysis of self.* New York, NY: International Universities Press.

Kohut, H. (1977). *The restoration of the self.* New York, NY: International Universities Press.

Lachmann, F. M. (2001). Some contributions of empirical infant research to adult psychoanalysis. *Psychoanalytic Dialogues, 11,* 167–185.

Laughlin, H. P. (1979). *The ego and its defenses* (2nd ed.). New York, NY: Jason Aronson.

Lawler, M. J., Shaver, P. R., & Goodman, G. S. (2011). Toward relationship-based child welfare services. *Child and Youth Services Review, 33,* 473–480.

Lieberman, J. (1985). *Acts of will: The life and work of Otto Rank.* New York, NY: Macmillan.

Mahler, M., Pine, F., & Bergman, A. (1975). *The psychological birth of the human infant.* New York, NY: Basic Books.

Masson, J. M. (1984). *The assault on truth: Freud's suppression of the seduction theory.* New York, NY: Farrar, Straus, and Giroux.

Menaker, E. (1982). *Otto Rank: A rediscovered legacy.* New York, NY: Columbia University Press.

Miller, J. B. (1976). *Toward a new psychology of women.* Boston, MA: Beacon Press.

Pine, F. (1990). *Drive, Ego, Object, And Self: A Synthesis For Clinical Work.* New York, NY: Basic Books.

Rank, O. (1929). *The trauma of birth.* New York, NY: Dover.

Rank, O. (1936). *Will therapy.* New York, NY: A. A. Knopf.

Rank, O. (1996). *A psychology of difference: The American lectures* (R. Kramer, Ed.). Princeton, NJ: Princeton University Press.

Richmond, M. (1917). *Social diagnosis.* New York, NY: Russell Sage Foundation.

Robinson, V. (1930). *A changing psychology in social casework.* Chapel Hill: University of North Carolina Press.

Saini, M. (2012). Reconceptualizing high-conflict divorce as a maladaptive adult attachment response. *Families in Society, 93*(3), 173–180.

Saleebey, D. (2005). *The strengths perspective in social work practice.* New York, NY: Longman.

Schore, J. R., & Schore, A. N. (2008). Modern attachment theory: The central role of affect regulation in development and treatment. *Clinical Social Work, 36,* 9–20.

Shemmings, D., Shemmings, Y., & Cook, A. (2012). Gaining the trust of "highly resistant" families: Insights from attachment theory and research. *Child & Family Social Work, 17,* 130–137.

Slavin, M. O. (2001). Constructivism with a human face. *Psychoanalytic Dialogues, 11,* 405–430.

Smalley, R. (1970). The functional approach to casework practice. In R. Roberts & R. Nee (Eds.), *Theories of social casework* (pp. 77–128). Chicago, IL: University of Chicago Press.

Specht, H., & Courtney, M. E. (1994). *Unfaithful angels: How social work abandoned its mission.* New York, NY: Free Press.

Spitz, R. A. (1965). *The first year of life: A psychoanalytic study of normal and deviant development of object relations.* New York, NY: International Universities Press.

Strean, H. (1993). Clinical social work: An evaluative review. *Journal of Analytic Social Work, 1,* 5–23.

Sullivan, H. S. (1953). *The interpersonal theory of psychiatry.* New York, NY: William Alanson White Psychiatric Foundation.

Taft, J. (1958). *Otto Rank.* New York, NY: Julian Press.

Thomlinson, R. J., & Thomlinson, B. (2011). Cognitive behavior theory and social work treatment. In F. J. Turner (Ed.), *Social work treatment* (pp. 77–102). New York, NY: Oxford University Press.

Tuckett, D. (2001). Evidence based psychoanalysis: An imperative and an opportunity. *International Forum on Psychoanalysis, 10,* 211–215.

White, M., & Epston, D. (1990). *Narrative means to therapeutic ends.* New York, NY: W. W. Norton.

White, R. W. (1959). Motivation reconsidered: The concept of competence. *Psychological Review*, *66*(5), 297–333.

Winnicott, D. W. (1965). *Maturational processes and the facilitating environment*. New York, NY: International Universities Press.

Woods, M., & Hollis, F. (2000). *Casework: A psychosocial therapy*. New York, NY: McGraw Hill.

Young, S. M. (2013). Attachment style and risk taking: A theoretical approach to understanding young men who have sex with men. *Journal of Human Behavior in the Social Environment*, *23*(8), 869–678.

SYSTEMS THEORIES

PHOTO 6.1
Everything is connected: Moorish tile, Granada, Spain

CASE EXAMPLE
SMALL-TOWN SOCIAL WORK PRACTICE

A social worker has recently moved from an urban environment to a very small town in upstate New York. Her rural community has very few practitioners that provide mental health services to individuals and families, and so she makes the decision to set up a private practice in this rural environment. As she assesses the town and surrounding areas to determine where she might best set up her practice, she discovers an office building located on a major street that runs through the center of town. Her initial thoughts are that this location is ideal because the office could be made into a very inviting space for potential clients and it publicizes and draws attention to the importance of mental health services in this "tucked away" rural community where mental health services have been scarce. However, because she is in such a rural environment, the social worker knows that in order to grow her private practice, she must take extra precautions to try to protect client privacy and she must find ways to positively introduce her new community to the importance of mental health services.

In examining this case from a systems perspective, the following questions might be explored:

(1) What systems (or elements of this practice situation) would be important for the social worker to examine in trying to adequately address the issues of client privacy and confidentiality?

(2) For example, what would the social worker want to take into consideration when examining her physical environment?

(3) How might she assess her social environment (e.g., neighbors, other community members or leaders, potential and actual clients) to determine how best to ensure client privacy?

(4) How do the values and beliefs of members of the larger community (e.g., mental health professionals at local agency) impact the delivery of services in the community?

In the above case example, the social worker's practice situation can be analyzed using a systems theoretical approach. In effect, how will the social worker assess and act on a plan to address client privacy? How will she address concerns the small town has about these mental health services? How will she create a fit among herself, her office and the services she provides, potential clients, and her physical environment? The profession of social work has historically embraced and continues to draw upon social systems theories unlike any other set of theories. Systems theories, and specifically general systems theory (GST), are concerned with the adaptive "fit" of individuals with their environments (e.g., family and friends, neighborhoods, agencies, housing, and natural surroundings) and the means by which they grow and obtain a dynamic equilibrium or balance.

The following diagram (Figure 6.1) helps us to examine important elements or parts of the system that interact to create a whole picture or case. Social workers who use a systems approach often draw diagrams or eco-maps like this one as a way to think holistically about the case situation and to be sure not to ignore elements that are connected and will likely interact with each other. In an eco-map, relationships are depicted as nurturing (solid straight line), conflictual (dashed line), or absent (no line) (Hartman, 1978; Iverson, Gergen, & Fairbanks, 2005).

FIGURE 6.1 ■ Eco-Map of Case Example

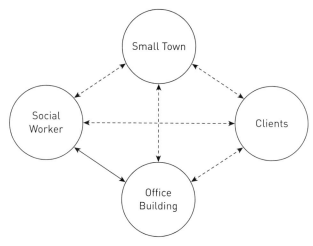

In this case example, the social worker has developed a positive agreement with the landlord for renting the office building (solid line between the social worker and office building), but there are potential conflicts (dashed lines) with the small town and prospective clients in terms of how they will view her efforts to establish an office and publicize mental health services. The small town may also struggle to accept clients' needs for mental health services. Further, prospective clients may be hesitant to access mental health services due to potential stigma from the community.

INTRODUCTION TO SYSTEMS THEORIES

Systems theories have had a dominant and lasting influence on social work practice through the development of the ecosystems or the ecological perspective and the Life Model (Germain & Gitterman, 1980). Two major types of systems theories will be discussed in this theory overview: structural functionalism and general systems theory. These two broad types of systems theories have been chosen for their very different approaches to stability, equilibrium, and change and for their impact on social work practice (See Chapter 1 for a discussion of the role of stability and change on theory).

Structural Functionalism

Key ideas in **structural functionalism** can be traced back to the ancient Greeks who attempted to apply concepts and methods of the natural sciences to the realm of human affairs (e.g., political science). Structural functionalism uses a biological analogy to describe social systems in the tradition of Comte, Spencer, and Durkheim.

Auguste Comte believed that knowledge and society were in the process of an evolutionary transition that involved giving up the vain search for absolute truths and instead supported reasoning and observation to study the laws of any phenomena. Comte believed that this study (or positive method), which had already triumphed in math, astronomy, and physics, would eventually prevail in politics and in a positive science of society (e.g., sociology). Indeed, structural functionalism has had a deep and some would say, unfortunate, lasting impact on the field of sociology due to its reliance on a systems' self-regulation, cohesiveness, and unity without accounting for a system's change and growth (Burrell & Morgan, 2003).

In keeping with this notion of studying the laws of a phenomena, Herbert Spencer is viewed as having developed structural functionalism. This theory views society as a self-regulating system that can be understood by studying its various elements and the way these elements are related. Spencer applied Darwin's human evolution to the development of societies, referred to as social Darwinism. He coined the term "survival of the fittest" and regarded societies as naturally evolving, super organisms, who strive for unity and interdependence as a way to survive (1864). Durkheim added to Spencer's ideas and believed that regulation, stability, and order were the predominant forces in social affairs and saw traditional societies as being held together on the basis of mechanical solidarity deriving from similarity of parts (1893; 1895). For example, societies were based on a system of shared values, customs, norms, and beliefs. He recognized that in the process of a transition from traditional to industrial societies, solidarity could break down—creating a state of anomie or normlessness (e.g., class conflict, unregulated competition, and degrading, meaningless work). However, he saw this all as an abnormal state of affairs and a pathological deviation from the natural course of development, which involved stability and order. In addition, Pareto (1935) put forth the idea that society could largely be explained in terms of equilibrium. Society was a system of interrelated parts, which although in a state of flux, were also in a state of unchanging equilibrium, in that movements away from equilibrium were balanced by changes tending to restore it.

In social anthropology, Malinowski and Radcliffe-Brown also contributed to the development of structural functionalism. For example, Malinowski (1945) thought primitive social systems and cultures could be understood in terms of the functions that they perform and he made parallels between biological organisms and human societies. And, Radcliffe-Brown (1952) analyzed society and social life noting that societies represent a network of relationships among its various social structures that have a certain continuity. In order for societies to exist, they need to perform certain functions (e.g., marital ceremonies, funeral rituals), which contribute to the life and maintenance of a community. He saw social institutions as contributing to the integration, stability, and maintenance of the social system as a whole.

As a key author in the development of structural functionalism, Talcott Parsons analyzed social systems as a whole and the conditions necessary for the system's survival, functioning, and equilibrium (Parsons, 1937, 1951). Unlike critical theorists (e.g., Marx) who focused on the occurrence of radical change, Parsons examined why societies are stable and able to function. In his AGIL model, which involves four conditions (i.e., adaptation, goal attainment, integration, and latency), Parsons outlined functions or minimum conditions that a system must perform if it is to survive (Parsons, 1959; Rocher, 1974):

- Adaptation—the capacity of the system to interact with the environment and acquire sufficient resources

- Goal attainment—the way a system defines and prioritizes its goals for the future and makes decisions accordingly

- Integration—the system's actions to establish control, inhibit deviance to its shared values and norms, and coordinate the relationships of various parts of the system

- Latency or pattern maintenance—the way a system addresses and integrates challenges and changes in order to maintain and transmit its cultural values

Parsons's ideas have been criticized for their inability to adequately account for a system's growth and change; Merton (1968) was one of the first scholars to address some of the theory's limitations. Merton indicated that not all social systems function to contribute to unity, and not all social activities are functional for an entire societal or cultural system. He studied the social and cultural sources of deviant behavior and examined the ways in which social structures exert pressure upon people in society to engage in nonconformist rather than conformist conduct. For example, when society provides little or no resources to help a young adult pay for higher education, these adults may use drugs or engage in criminal behavior because they feel that an education is beyond their reach.

Although social and cultural structures define certain goals as legitimate and determine the acceptable ways or means for reaching these goals, Merton (1968) described discrepancies between these cultural goals in society and the means to achieve those goals. For example, Merton refers to American society as a stable society that expects its people to conform to specific goals and to pursue acceptable or societally legitimate means for reaching these goals. Genuine failure only consists of lessening or withdrawing one's ambition. Merton puts forth five types of adaptive responses that human beings might engage in due to the mismatching of goals and the means for reaching those goals. These responses can lead to conformity or deviance.

- Conformity—internalize social goals and have access to socially approved means to reach them

- Innovation—internalize goals for success, but don't have access to the means to achieve these goals (e.g., the development and growth of corrupt business practices)

- Ritualism—have access to the means to achieve goals but have lost sight of the goals (e.g., this may occur when people are not able to or do not want to participate in a highly competitive, achievement-oriented society)

- Retreatism—people who adapt by neither accepting the goals or means to achieve these goals (e.g., high school dropouts, artists, those addicted to abusive substances, hermits)

- Rebellion—envision new goals through nonconformist behavior (e.g., the revolutionary who wants to set up a new society, new goals and means for achieving these goals)

Merton did not see these deviant adaptations as forms of psychopathology but as role responses that were a result of a breakdown between expectations for success and the means to achieve it. The following case example examines concepts from structural functionalism and Merton's adaptive responses as applied to a large institution, the Veterans' Administration (VA).

CASE EXAMPLE
POSTTRAUMATIC STRESS DISORDER (PTSD) IN THE VA HOSPITAL

You are a medical social worker in a VA hospital in a large Midwestern city. You have worked with many veterans who are suffering from posttraumatic stress due to their combat experiences in Afghanistan and Iraq. Nearly all of the combat veterans you have worked with express a strong commitment and loyalty to the military and are proud of their military service. However, many are afraid to formally ask for help for their posttraumatic symptoms, which involve difficulties in maintaining relationships, substance abuse as a means of helping them cope with the violence they experienced or contributed to in combat, and nightmares and flashbacks. These combat veterans say that even though the military has encouraged them to pursue professional help to treat symptoms of their posttraumatic stress, many military leaders are very vocal, indicating that those combat veterans who ask for this help are emotionally unstable and give the military a "bad name."

(1) As a large bureaucratic system, how has the military reacted to those veterans with posttraumatic stress?

(2) How does the military define its goals as they conflict with the needs of the combat veterans?

(3) How does the military control and inhibit deviance to its shared values and norms when working with combat veterans who have posttraumatic stress?

(4) How does the military system address and integrate combat veterans with posttraumatic stress in order to maintain and transmit its culture and norms?

In this case example, adherents of structural functionalism would likely view these combat veterans with posttraumatic stress as representing a threat to military order and stability. Because these structural functionalist theorists adhere to an organismic analogy in which the system always adapts or returns to a level of stability and cohesion, they demonstrate conservatism and a return to unity or regulation; these theories struggle to address high degrees of change within a system or society. The structural functionalists have had the most difficulty in examining how new types of social structures are created or come into existence. For example, how might an institution such as the VA need to change in order to take into account the needs of combat veterans? Finally, it is important to note that even at the beginning of the 21st century, structural functionalist ideas, which have been slow to acknowledge new and diverse social structures, are profoundly critiqued in discourse about societal, institutional, and familial behavior (Mann, Grimes, Kemp, & Jenkins, 1997). For example, structural functionalism has not adequately addressed lesbian, gay, bisexual, and transgender people; diverse forms of women's growth and development and feminist perspectives; racially and ethnically diverse families; or the prevalence of family violence.

Person-in-Environment Perspective and General Systems Theory

A **person-in-environment (PIE) perspective** is a guiding principle in social work and associated with the earliest definitions of the scope and purpose of social work (see the Milford Conference report in American Association of Social Workers, 1929). The definition of PIE is that there is reciprocity between individuals and environments: individuals can impact various elements of the environment, and the environment can exert conducive or inhibiting influences on the individual. Two of the progenitors of social work, Jane Addams and Mary Richmond, while engaged in public debate about what social work practice should look like (social environmental change versus individual treatment), understood the importance of a combined person-in-environment perspective that involved work with both individuals *and* larger systems (Thompson, 2012; Thompson, Spano, & Koenig, in press). This PIE perspective gave social workers a framework for engaging in assessment and practice interventions aimed at the individual, the environment, or both. Key governing elements of the social work profession identify attention to the individual-in-environment as a crucial and defining element of social work practice (Council on Social Work Education [CSWE], 2015; National Association of Social Workers [NASW], 2005).

The PIE perspective has been conceptually linked to general systems theory (GST) and the ecosystems perspective in social work. As the social work profession developed, scholars began to look for ways to better conceptualize the person-in-environment perspective. By the 1970s, this concern had become a major quest in the disciplinary discourse. Over the next several decades, two major, interrelated frameworks were advanced specifically for the purpose of giving theoretical substance to the PIE perspective: (a) ecological or ecosystems perspective and the Life Model; and (b) general systems theory (GST).

Ecosystems theory in social work (see Germain, 1973; Germain & Gitterman, 1996; Meyer, 1983) draws on GST and the science of ecology, which is the study of living organisms within their environments (Dubos, 1972). GST is largely based on the work of theoretical biologist Ludwig von Bertalanffy (1950, 1967) and was viewed as a means of cutting through differences among diverse disciplines, and assumed increasing importance in various areas (e.g., sociology, anthropology, organizational theory, and psychology). General systems theory became ascendant in social work in the 1960s and 1970s and remained the prevailing paradigm in social work until the introduction of ecological systems theory (ecosystems theory) and the Life Model in the late 1970s and 1980s (see Figure 6.2). Hearn (1969) is usually credited with introducing GST into the social work literature along with others including Pincus and Minahan (1973), Meyer (1976), and Goldstein (1973).

FIGURE 6.2 ■ Development of the Ecosystems Perspective

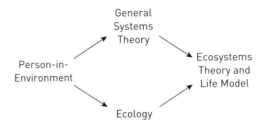

General systems theory (GST) is based on the assumption that all living and nonliving matter can be regarded as systems that are holistic and whose elements interact with each other. All systems have properties that are capable of being studied (e.g., individuals, small groups, families, organizations, neighborhoods and communities), and social work is typically involved with all of these systems. For example, social workers often must address difficulties due to a client's behavior. From a GST perspective, behavior is considered to be a consequence of the total situation in which a person (e.g., internal biological, psychological, social, and spiritual systems), group or other social system (e.g., community) finds itself. The person in the family or group, the group within the larger community or neighborhood, and the community within a region or society are all illustrations of the interaction among and within various systems that interact with each other and help shape individual behavior. Systems in GST have certain distinguishing properties (see Table 6.1).

TABLE 6.1 ■ Key Properties of Systems Theories

Properties	Description
Boundaries	Systems have boundaries, which is how they can be defined; and they have patterned relationships. For example, the social worker's judgment, coupled with clients' views, are involved in developing conceptual boundaries of the case and in creating an eco-map. Who should be included or left out in the eco-map? The diagram that is finally drawn will shape the client's and worker's understanding of the case.
Open systems, negative entropy, and entropy	All organic, living systems are open in that their boundaries are permeable and they can exchange energy or interact with their environments. Open systems import more energy than they expend (negative entropy). This exchange enables the system to grow and develop. Closed systems are self-contained, will not thrive, and instead decline or entropy because they do not exchange energy with their environments.
Homeostasis	Systems tend to preserve their structures and characteristics, even when the relatedness of their elements shifts (e.g., in couples therapy, partners may choose to stay together, but they may want to change their roles and behaviors). Because of the need to preserve their structure, systems engage in a balance between a steady state and ongoing growth and change, referred to as dynamic homeostasis. A functioning system seeks to maintain its equilibrium through negotiations with the environment.

Properties	Description
Reciprocity and equifinality	Elements of the system are potentially reciprocal, in that they act upon each other. Change in one part of the system generates change in all its parts, and thus any intervention always has a reciprocal effect on all the elements of the case (i.e., this is equifinality).
Multifinality	As an open system, your growth and development as a student can be viewed as independent from your earlier experiences. If you have grown up in poverty or experienced intimate partner violence, these prior experiences do not have to determine what happens to you in the future and this provides an optimistic view of systematically oriented social work practice. A single event can be introduced into your life that will have multiple effects on you as a system (this is multifinality) and can change the way you view these difficulties.

The ecological perspective combined with the principles of GST have contributed to social work's development of the ecosystems perspective and the use of the ecomap, which represents a "case system." General systems theory helps us to understand the importance of case boundaries, which determine what elements are part of a case system; that individuals, families, and communities are open systems that can grow and change; case elements are related and interactive; that we as social workers can work to impact client systems in many different ways (equifinality); and that one event can have a "ripple effect," impacting all of the adjacent elements of the case (multifinality). Once you view a case systematically, in which people, events, the natural environment, and organizations are all connected and interact with each other, it is difficult to return to a more linear view of a case in which each element is examined in isolation from other elements of the case. When you use an ecosystems perspective in your practice, you are involved in a process of visualizing the case through the development of an ecomap, which can then contribute, in collaboration with clients, to the creation of many different strategies or options (Meyer, 1983).

Proponents of ecosystems theory have begun to address shortcomings of its early development (Gitterman, 2011). First, this theory now addresses discrimination and oppression by emphasizing the need for social workers to gain competence in community and legislative efforts (as well as direct practice) in order to holistically and systemically work with clients. Second, clients' coping styles, which were used to address "problems in living," are now understood as strengths-based coping mechanisms for managing normal life stressors. Third, in an attempt to take into account client system's diverse backgrounds, current ecosystems writings have moved away from fixed, linear, and universal life cycle stages to a life course approach that acknowledges the variety of ways in which individuals, families, organizations, and communities change and develop (e.g., single-parent and blended families; ethnic and sexual minority diversity within communities). Finally, authors of the ecosystems theory and Life Model have broadened and deepened the ecological metaphor to include the natural environment (e.g., see writings on deep ecology and ecofeminism) (Besthorn & Canda, 2002; Besthorn & McMillen, 2002; Gitterman & Germain, 2008; Mack-Canty, 2004).

Summary of Overview

This overview has examined two major systems theories: structural functionalism and general systems theories. Although structural functionalism continues to embrace more conservative ideas that emphasize a system's cohesion and unity, scholars such as Merton have challenged the singular focus of all systems as engaged in reaching a value consensus among its members. Merton described discrepancies people experience between societal goals and the means to achieve those goals which, in turn, contribute to deviant or nonconformist behavior. General systems theory (GST) developed out of social work's early practice emphasis on understanding people within their environments (PIE). General systems theory, which views all matter as holistic systems whose elements interact with each other, combined with ecology, the study of living organisms within their environments, led to the development of ecosystems theory and the Life Model. As the ecosystems theory has evolved, it has attempted to better address oppression, the natural as well as social environment, coping mechanisms that reflect healthy adaptation, and diversity over the life course. Ecosystems theory continues to function as a prevailing theoretical and practice-based perspective in social work.

IN-DEPTH EXPLORATION OF SYSTEMS THEORIES AS APPLIED TO SOCIAL WORK PRACTICE

As we noted earlier in this chapter, social work had a long history that emphasized the importance of the inclusion of both human beings and their environments as the focus of our attention. This perspective is one of the more important distinctions between social work practice and other disciplines that fall into the broad category of helping professions (e.g., psychology, psychiatry, and counseling). For most of the 20th century, social workers struggled to implement their dual purpose, focused on both individual remediation and social change. One of the major problems they faced was that the knowledge base from which they were drawing, social science theory, tended to focus on either individuals *or* the environments. There was no set of ideas that spoke to how to examine the transactional space between individuals and their environments. As a result, there were continual tensions about how to realize the need for both—individual remediation and social change—to be integrated into all practice situations.

Unfortunately, the opportunities to achieve this task were difficult given that most social workers were employed in agencies designed to address problems through individual remediation rather than larger-scale social change. In 1929, Porter Lee's presidential address to the National Conference of Social Work, *Cause and Function*, urged participants to acknowledge the need for *both* cause and function to be viewed as part of social work. As we just observed, the fundamental problem faced by the profession was that the social sciences structured their knowledge bases to focus on understanding individuals or environments. Thus, psychology provided a range of templates for understanding human beings' behavior but remained relatively silent about how human behavior was impacted by a person's environmental contexts. Sociology, political science, anthropology, and economics spoke to how large-scale social and cultural structures acted but this knowledge seldom addressed how the systems impacted individuals living in these social contexts.

By the late 1950s and early 1960s, new sources of knowledge began developing as we have noted earlier in the chapter. Within social work, a new group of scholars, including Harriet Bartlett, Bill Gordon, Howard Goldstein, Allen Pincus, and Ann Minahan, began efforts to apply the work of Gordon Hearn and his colleagues, who were translating general systems theory into social work. In his edited book, Hearn (1969) and his coauthors explored systems theory's value as a tool that might allow social work to move in the direction of integrating our understanding of human beings *in* their environments (PIE). Figure 6.2 tracks the development of system concepts from general systems theory and ecological theory to ecosystems theory, which became known as the Life Model as it was translated into practice.

SOCIAL WORK FRAME OF REFERENCE BASED ON SYSTEMS THEORY

Figure 6.3 represents a social work frame of reference that attempts to synthesize the work of Bartlett (1970) and Gordon (1962, 1965) as it contributed to helping practitioners focus on the interactions between persons and their environments. In addition, this diagram rests on the belief that systems theory can be utilized as a means to integrate a more complex point of view for understanding human behavior.

FIGURE 6.3 ■ Social Work Frame of Reference

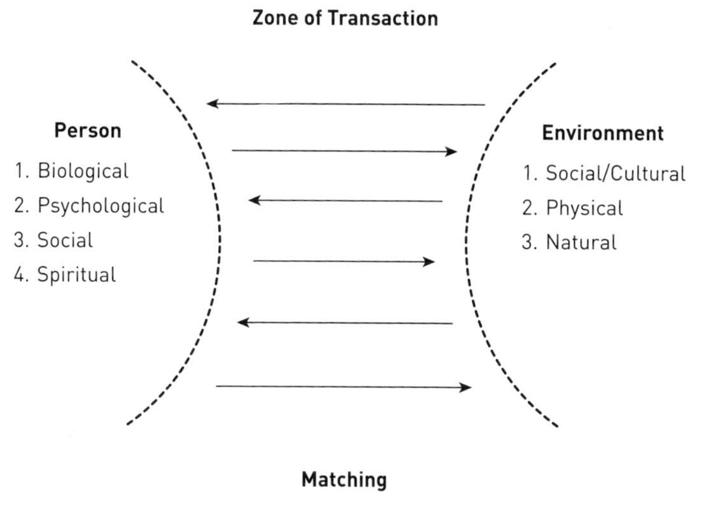

In essence, Figure 6.3 includes four interacting components: person, environment, zone of transaction, and matching. First, the person is understood to be made up of subsystems that include biological, psychological, social, and spiritual components. These subsystems interact within the person in various ways that impact their responses to events in their environments. For example, a father in a family of four has a heart attack, which originates in his biological system, and could have long-term physical consequences. If the family depends on resources earned by the man's physical labor, the family may be at risk of losing economic resources needed to sustain its current balance. The heart attack also impacts his psychological system, which also responds to the event. Some individuals react with extreme fear, others may interpret this as a wake-up call to change habits that may have contributed to the condition. In the social realm, there are likely to be ramifications such as changing habits that may lead to new and different activities and acquaintances based on an exercise regimen. In addition, it may change how family members view him or, if other family members saw him as exceptionally strong, they now have to integrate the notion of their husband or father as vulnerable. Finally, from the spiritual component, a heart attack often causes people to reflect on what is important in their lives as they come to accept their own mortality and the mortality of others. Systems theory provides tools for examining the interactions of these various subsystems within the person, allowing us to begin to more fully understand their responses and the responses of those surrounding them.

Second, the environment—like the person—consists of various subsystems that interact to shape people's experience. The concept of environment includes the social, physical, and natural components. In social work, there is a great deal of attention paid to people's social environments, which are made up of those persons with whom clients interact. Assuring that people have others in their lives who contribute positively to individual growth and development is certainly important. However, it is not a sole source of either resources or barriers to those goals. In this example, if the man is lodged in a family system and has a partner and children, they have a direct impact on him and his reactions to the heart attack. If this same individual lives in a single-room occupancy hotel with no friends or family, his experience would be quite different. The social environment provides both resources, and sometimes barriers, that are central to understand in order for us to help elements of the systems to develop new homeostatic balances. Another aspect of environments are the physical components made up of constructed elements of our environment, including houses, sidewalks, cars, elevators, bridges, highways, and furniture. For example, if this family lives on the fifth floor of a building in which there are no elevators, that physical environment is likely to require very different responses in order to effectively adapt to the new conditions in which the family finds itself. Finally, there is the natural environment, which consists of water, trees, flowers, climate, mountains, and land. Again in this instance, if the family lives in a rural area on the farm, which functions as their sole source of income, it requires a great deal of physical exertion in order to make a living. The consequences and adaptations necessary would be quite different than they would if they lived in a more populated area where obtaining goods and services required less physical effort.

The third element of the figure is the zone of transaction, which is the space between the person and the environment. Systems theory directs the worker's attention to what is going on between systems in order to determine how those systems are interacting with each other in ways that promote positive interactions or destabilize their interactions. For example, in the family situation we have been talking about, a social worker might focus on the interactions between the economic system and the needs of the family system. If the employer recognizes that the employee, the father in this case, needs some time to be able to recoup his physical health, then there is likely to be less stress on the family, which may help them re-stabilize by focusing on the husband's health and their reaction to the changes. If the employer needs the father to be at work because the business has certain tasks that must be performed in a timely fashion, the family may very well be destabilized because of the conflicting demands placed on one of its members and the consequences created for others in the family.

The final element in Figure 6.3 focuses on the goals for the interactions in any specific situation. In essence, the worker is seeking to make a "good match" between the needs of both systems. A "bad match" is one in which the decisions made have a negative impact on either side of the equation. In other words, the social worker is looking in the zone of transaction to attempt to employ strategies that create positive outcomes for both the person and the environment. This attention to the interacting systems allows the worker to perceive what is happening as a product of the adjustments occurring in the interactions among the various systems. As we pointed out above, if the employer demanded the father immediately return to work in order to remain employed and have access to medical coverage, systems theory would suggest the destabilization of the family and the likelihood of significant problems emerging (anxiety, anger, and fear) that would interrupt the family's capacity to sustain themselves. Should those interactions continue over a period of time, we would expect the family to reestablish its homeostatic balance at a lower level. Thus, the needs of the family would be sacrificed in order for the employment system to function more smoothly.

Ecosystems theory provides practitioners with a perspective that allows workers to be able to identify, organize, and analyze information in ways that are more congruent with social work's purposes, which include both taking remedial actions in order to re-stabilize systems, as well as examining ways in which systems need to change in order to better function for the people who constitute those systems. However, while it directs our attention at systems, it does not necessarily provide specific direction about how to intervene in those systems in order to bring about change. In most instances, systems theory needs to be paired with more specific models that give workers tools with which to work to bring about change. In this example, systems theory would allow us to understand who is inside the boundaries of the family, how they interact with each other, and how those interactions lead to a homeostatic balance. It does not tell us what specific actions are necessary to assist the family in reorganizing itself based on the new challenges required as a result of the father's heart attack. For that level of specificity, we have to pair systems theory with models of practice that allow us to translate our understanding of the situation into a course of action that can be used to actually help the family. Examples would include the use of narrative therapy, structural family therapy, strategic family therapy, and conjoint family therapy because they provide specific strategies such as examining family members' roles in this changing situation.

Transition From General Systems Theory to the Life Model

General systems theory, as noted earlier in the chapter, evolved over a long period of time through the writings of numerous authors in the field of sociology. Both Talcott Parsons and Robert Merton were actively developing their respective positions on the nature of general systems theory. By the late 1960s, social workers began to view systems theory as a perspective that might be used to create a more unified perspective on practice. In 1969, the Council on Social Work Education hosted a workshop chaired by Gordon Hearn. This workshop led to the publication of a series of presentations in the form of a book, *The General Systems Approach: Contributions toward an Holistic Conception of Social Work*. This collection of essays addressed the application of systems theory to social work practice, field education, and direct work with clients (Hearn, 1969). Shortly thereafter, Pincus and Minahan (1973) published their text, *Social Work Practice: Model and Method*, which became a broadly used resource for organizing the teaching of social work practice. Its impact shifted the focus of practice classes from methods to levels of practice. Instead of courses focused on casework, group work, and community organization, this text emphasized refocusing on the use of systems theory as a perspective to be utilized at all levels of practice. It substituted language that remains prevalent in social work practice today. For example, with systems as a unifying perspective, it applied those ideas to differing levels of practice including micro, mezzo, and macro; change agent system; client system; target system; action system; homeostatic balance; and entropy. As a result, people were seen as being made up of internal systems that then interacted with other systems in their environment. Systems theory became a means of understanding families and small groups as well as organizations and communities that interacted with individuals to shape their respective reactions.

This transition created some significant challenges for educators teaching in practice classes. The challenges included the mastery of an array of new terms, helping students to shift their focus from individual persons *or* their environments to mastering what was called a "simultaneous dual focus" (looking in the zone of transaction between systems as a focal point), and helping students move from using systems theory as their orienting frame of reference to developing specific behaviors that flowed from their new understanding of systems theory. The struggle to move from an orienting framework to specific behaviors persisted over the first few years, particularly in developing answers to questions that students posed including, "What do we do once we understand a system's dynamics?" The search for answers to this question led social workers to examine emerging systems–oriented theories that would address potential strategies to give more guidance to practitioners. The next step in the evolution of systems theory was the inclusion of ecological theory as a means to translate systems theory into social work practice.

Combining Ecological and Systems Theories

During the 1970s, social workers continued to try to refine translations of systems theory into the practice of social work. In 1980, Carel Germain and Alex Gitterman published their book, *The Life Model of Social Work Practice*. This book was the culmination of their efforts to develop curriculum using ecological theory as a metaphor for practice. According to the authors, "this book represents the beginning attempt to work out the dimensions of an integrated method of practice with individuals, families, groups, organizations, and selected aspects of neighborhoods and communities" (Germain & Gitterman, 1980, p. x). The **Life Model of social work practice** drew from larger trends that made up the intellectual context in which it was developed. At the broadest level, it acknowledged the pitfalls in traditional Western scientific thinking that tended to be reductionist and included elements of Eastern thinking that tended to connect people with their environments. They also acknowledged the work of Bartlett and Gordon, who described social work's purpose as the importance of matching individuals in environments in order to produce maximum growth and development in both people and their environments. Finally, they asserted that the Life Model integrates social work's dual purpose of social change and individualized treatment with the ecological perspective and the conceptual framework for social work practice (Germain & Gitterman, 1980).

True to the ecological metaphor used to define practice, the model has continued to evolve and adapt in the face of significant changes in the environments in which social work has practiced. In the last 27 years, since the original publication of the book, two subsequent editions have been published. Each of the subsequent editions attempted to address significant social change that created new challenges and new social problems. Gitterman (2011) identified four specific trends that required adaptation of the Life Model. First, between 1980 and the present, social workers found themselves dealing with the devastating impact of homelessness, drug addiction, AIDS, child abuse, and community violence. This occurred in the context in which the "safety net" had been dismantled. Second, because of the complexity of social problems, social workers needed to be able to intervene at multiple levels, not just the individual level, to respond to these complex problems. Third, there was an emphasis on attempting to avoid blaming oppressed people for their problems, which was a dominant theme in the larger social discourse. Fourth, social workers needed specific assistance to help them deal more effectively with diverse populations who were being more and more marginalized in American society. Finally, in the most recent edition, material was added to emphasize assessment, practice monitoring, and practice evaluation, which have taken center stage in current literature related to social work practice.

CURRENT CONCEPTUALIZATION OF THE LIFE MODEL

Assumptions of the Life Model

The following materials attempt to summarize the fundamental ecological assumptions upon which the Life Model of social work practice rests. First, human beings act within physical, social, and cultural environments. Physical environments include the natural world; structures built by people; the space that supports and contains, or arranges these structures; and the rhythms of environmental and human biology. Second, the model has a holistic view of people and their biological, cognitive, emotional, and social processes as well as the physical and social environments that can be fully understood only in the context of the relation between and among them. Third, human growth and development is an evolutionary process in which adaptations are made between individuals and their environments (Gitterman & Germain, 2008).

Purposes of the Life Model

According to Germain (1973), the use of ecosystems theory, with its focus on transactional and interface phenomena, achieves three purposes. First, the Life Model of practice helps guide us in our efforts to engage "progressive forces and adaptive potentialities of the person, mobilizing the environmental processes as helping media, and altering elements of the environment." Second, "it fosters passionate concern, human aspirations and for the development of milieus to promote them" (p. 326). Third, it provides a way to conceptualize problems, formulate objectives, and widens the arena of help and expands the role of the caseworker. Germain's description of these three purposes continues to express important elements of the Life Model for practice. However, in Gitterman and Germain's (2008) synthesis of the advances in this model of practice, he defines the Life Model's purpose at the direct practice level as to improve the level of fit between people's (individual, family, group, community) perceived needs, capacities, and aspirations and their environmental supports and resources.

In addition to the general statement of purpose outlined above, Gitterman and Germain (2008) operationalize at the direct practice level how this can be done through a process of mutual assessment in which "the worker and the service recipient(s) determine practice focus choosing to:

1. Improve a person's (collectivity's) ability to manage stressor(s) through more effective personal and situational appraisals and behavioral skills

2. Influence the social and physical environments to be more responsive to a person's (collectivity's) needs

3. Improve the quality of the person: environment exchanges" (p. 285).

What he adds in his critique of social conditions is the need to include additional professional functions that address the ever-growing social inequities in society. Specifically, he defines professional functions to include mobilization of community resources to improve community life, efforts to influence organizations to develop responsive policies and services, and efforts to exert political influence at the local, state, and federal levels to address legislation and regulations (Gitterman & Germain, 2008).

Focus of the Life Model

From its inception, the Life Model has consistently drawn on systems theory as a means to focus our attention on the interactions within and between systems and individual persons. In the newer literature there are some important changes that attempt to recognize the new challenges that face both individuals and their environments. For example, given the fact that the "safety net" for many people has been dismantled, it becomes essential for social workers to include careful assessment of both the barriers as well as the potential resources that exist in the environment. This suggests the development of skills that can support efforts to ameliorate environmental issues, not just interpersonal issues, by developing community, organizational, and legislative skills necessary to effect change in any given situation.

A second shift in focus identified by Gitterman and Germain (2008) emphasized the move from "problems in living" to "life course," which is a conception of human development that replaces "life cycle" models. The concept of life course moves away from a more linear conception of human growth and development toward one that suggests many different possibilities for growth and development that are more hospitable to the diverse expressions of individuals, families, and communities. For example, Erikson's (1950) epigenetic model for human growth and development suggests linear stages through which all human beings pass as they grow and develop. However, it is silent on issues of race, gender, and sexual orientation. The life course approach to understanding human behavior essentially includes the uniqueness of each system and requires us to suspend judgment about whether or not this particular system is behaving "normally." It places diversity directly at the heart of growth and development and demands that we be open to understanding how the person and environments interact in ways that do not apologize or blame either system. Our job is to focus on how to establish a more positive fit between the needs of people and their environments so that neither is harmed in their interactions and our focus is on the strengths that can be brought to bear to create a more harmonious fit among the systems.

THEORY CRITIQUE

This critique involves an analysis of broader systems theories and when appropriate will provide commentary on both structural functionalism and general systems theory (GST) for their varying applications to social work practice. What may become immediately clear to you as a student is that systems theories are very abstract and only provide you with a way of understanding, describing, and perhaps assessing a client system (e.g., through the use of an eco-map or genogram). Although systems theories can be more specifically applied to social work practice through the use of the ecosystems perspective or Life Model, they certainly do not lend themselves to being able to predict what kind of practice strategy will work best with a particular client at a specific moment in time.

What Does This Theory Say About Human Behavior?

Structural functionalism and GST emphasize the integration, stability, adaptation, and unity of systems. Unlike critical theories (see Chapter 4), systems theories are not typically concerned with conflict and coercion as a way of understanding or changing individual or societal behavior. Further, structural functionalism and GST view ontology (or the nature of reality) as concrete, objective, and external to the individual. For structural functionalists, society is understood to be a tangible structure with its members cohesively coming together around a shared set of values. If we and our clients accept these societal values, then we are able to function and adapt within this societal system. Merton challenged this systemic, integrated view of society indicating that there are often members in our society who may not agree with or share the same values as the majority of society and are then considered deviant and nonconformist. This is in great contrast to GST and the ecosystems perspective, which both acknowledge the changing realities and the potential growth and possibilities of human beings intimately linked to their social and natural environments. The following Ethics Spotlight highlights potential differences in the ways that structural functionalism, GST, and an ecosystems approach understand human behavior.

ETHICS SPOTLIGHT
GAY AND LESBIAN COUPLES AS FOSTER PARENTS

As a social worker in a public child welfare agency in a very politically conservative region, how would you address your agency's traditional views of marriage and their unwillingness to certify gay and lesbian couples as foster parents? If you are operating within a structural functionalist mindset, you might view gay and lesbian couples as deviant, nonconformist, and harmful to the stability or cohesiveness of society. Therefore, these couples would not be "fit" to be foster parents. If you are practicing within a GST framework and are cognizant of social work values that support the dignity and worth of all human beings, then you might view this same couple as representing a new, emerging family structure that has the potential to provide a child in need of care with ample opportunities for love and growth.

Discussion Questions

(1) Engage in self-reflection about your personal views of gay and lesbian people and their capacity to function as foster parents. Share these personal perspectives, values, and beliefs with at least one student colleague in your class.

(2) How might your personal values impact your work at this agency?

(3) What might the application of general system theory or the Life Model suggest about how to appropriately confront your state agency's traditional view of marriage?

(4) How could you go about supporting nonconformist or nontraditional views of the "perfect" foster parents?

(5) If you were working in a private or religiously based foster care agency, how might this change your behavior as a social worker?

How Does This Theory Address Growth and Change?

When we examine structural functionalism, we realize that this theory is largely silent about individual and societal change and growth. Structural functionalists view society as having its own consciousness, which creates values that contribute to stability and cohesiveness and imposes them on the individuals within that society. This view of society coalescing around a shared set of values excludes people who think and act innovatively, creatively, and/or with a different set of values and beliefs. However, GST supports a system's growth and change. As with the concept of multifinality, one small change in a system can positively interact with and affect all of its elements (e.g., the birth of a baby into a young couple's life; the restored health of the water system in a community such as Flint, Michigan). The ecosystems theory notes that person/environment exchanges are dynamic and influence and shape each other over time. People need to receive resources from their environment for their survival and growth; the environment needs for us to care and support its health and flourishing. Newer additions to the ecosystems perspective have also attempted to better account for a system's growth and change (e.g., clients' coping strategies may inhibit their well-being, but they may also function as a positive resource and means for clients' growth and development) (Gitterman & Germain, 2008).

How Holistic Is This Theory?

As social work scholars and practitioners struggled to find an overarching way to link their diverse practice contexts and variety of client populations together, GST and ecosystems theories represented one of the best and most holistic theoretical perspectives to draw upon. This theory helped the practitioner to define a case based on its boundaries (e.g., individual, family, and community) and to incorporate many different types of interventions (e.g., community and legislative as well as direct practice efforts), which could lead to change and growth within a case. In particular, proponents of the ecosystem framework and the Life Model of practice have insisted on considering the whole human context in any practice situation; newer developments of this framework (Congress, 2005; Gitterman & Germain, 2008) have paid closer attention to the growing diversity among people within a variety of contexts (e.g., the role of culture and race, gender, sexual orientation, and gender expression).

Some scholars have also attempted to redefine the person-in-environment concept to indicate that there is no separation at all between people and their environments. Human beings are the environment. These developments have been seen most dramatically in current writings on deep ecology and the social worker's role in including natural environmental concerns in professional education and practice (e.g., environmental degradation, toxic waste) (Besthorn & Canda, 2002; Hudson, 2014) and in neuroscience developments, which concretely support the interdependence of persons and their environments (Green & McDermott, 2010).

How Consistent Is This Theory With Social Work Values and Ethics?

Because systems theories help us to build a bridge among micro, mezzo, macro, and global practice, they are consistent with our values of service, social justice, and the importance of human relationships. If we only focus on an individual client or families' circumstances, we will ignore the broader societal context that impacts the family. Systems theories encourage us to look for links between individual troubles and larger public issues. In particular, GST brings a hopefulness to our work with individuals, families, and even larger communities in that it supports the idea that change can occur at various points in a system and serve as a catalyst for subsequent changes in other areas. In this way, we honor the relationships and connections clients make within the larger social and natural environment. For example, one urban high school student's experience of racism can encourage an entire group of students to protest for fair and equal treatment by school educators and administrators. In using a GST and ecosystems theoretical approach, social workers can help students to see the connections among racist policies in urban schools starved for educational resources, racist language, and an individual student's experience of racism.

It is also important to note that structural functionalism, GST, and the ecosystems theory have been soundly criticized for not directly addressing clients' experiences of oppression and discrimination. Even newer writings on the Life Model (Gitterman & Germain, 2008) and structural functionalism (as one of sociology's central theories) have not readily integrated the experiences of marginalized groups into their theoretical framework. These theories continue to ignore or have difficulties integrating newer developments on race, gender, class, ability, religion, sexual orientation and gender expression, diverse family forms (e.g., single-parent and blended families), and the experiences of intimate partner violence or other forms of sexual assault. Systems theories have been more useful for describing and assessing a client's situation, including assessing the existence of discrimination or oppression on the client. However, these theories have been largely silent about the role of power in relationships that can contribute to injustice, nor do they offer much guidance for what you might do as a social worker to address or intervene in these oppressive situations.

What Sources of Knowledge Does This Theory Support?

Epistemologically, structural functionalism seeks to explain how systems best function and emphasizes knowledge that is hard, real, and tangible. For example, if we observe a family, institution, or community from a structural functionalism perspective, we are concerned with how this system develops social order, integration, and consensus among all of its members. Structural functionalism does not readily take into account knowledge based on personal experience such as the family or community members' experiences or the professional's knowledge and expertise. In contrast, practitioners who draw upon GST, ecosystems, and the Life Model view this same family or community as an inherently open system with mutually interacting elements and with ample possibilities for change and growth. Social workers who use an ecosystems approach value family or community members' direct experiences and work collaboratively with them to explore their fit or adaptation with the larger social and natural environment. For example, the social worker who uses an eco-map as a practice strategy is encouraged to work "shoulder-to-shoulder" with the client (e.g., family member) to develop the eco-map. In using this approach, the social worker places value on the client's knowledge or expertise, and knows the eco-map is not an "end product" or a fixed, static assessment, but it instead grows and changes with the client and can even help the client to revision her future (Hartman, 1978; Iverson et al., 2005).

Because systems concepts are abstract and take into account the connected and interacting nature of many elements within a case system that change over time, it is difficult to operationalize these concepts (e.g., boundaries, open systems, equifinality) and thereby conduct quantitative studies. However, qualitative inquiry that addresses time- and context-bound knowledge seems much more fitting to capture a client's current situation and ongoing growth and development. That being said, it is very difficult to study the impact of the natural and social environment on a client system—and systems theorists have had major difficulties handling the unexpected, creative ways in which growth and change occur.

APPLICATION OF THE LIFE MODEL TO SOCIAL WORK PRACTICE: ECO-MAPS, GENOGRAMS, AND BEYOND

This section of the chapter focuses on the use of eco-maps and genograms as practical tools for the applications of the Life Model to an actual practice example. The following example demonstrates how complex practice situations can be mapped, and questions can be asked that can inform our practice as social workers.

CASE EXAMPLE
CARL'S JOURNEY THROUGH FOSTER CARE

Carl was a 13-year-old adolescent who had been taken from his home as a result of his mother's inability to control his behavior. He had been placed with two other foster families before coming to a group home in a small Midwestern city. His behavior included both physical and verbal aggression toward peers and adults. He was failing in school and had been referred to the juvenile court after he attempted to break into his grade school. He was an extremely intelligent young man who cared deeply about his mother and his younger brother (Kent) and older sister (Cheryl). Carl's mother, Susan, a Caucasian woman, worked at a local transportation company where she was a dispatcher. Susan had significant bouts with depression and at one point had attempted to take her own life. Her last attempt involved the use of a rifle, which severed her spinal cord and she was now a paraplegic. In addition, she lost her housing and was sleeping on the floor at her workplace.

Carl's father, who is Native American, was incarcerated in a state prison after having been convicted of second-degree murder. He had approximately seven more years to serve on his sentence. At the time Carl came to the group home, he had no prior contact with his father over

the past five years. According to court records, both the father and the son had expressed a strong interest in being able to visit each other. The case plan clearly stated that Carl was to be reunited with his biological family as soon as it was feasible.

During the next two years of Carl's placement at the group home, he showed remarkable progress. He went from failing grades in every subject to As in all of his classes. His anger was no longer expressed in physical or verbal aggression. His teachers and the staff at the group home were advocating that he be given a chance to return to the care of his mother. However, Carl's mother needed handicap-accessible Section 8 Housing and had been on a waiting list for almost 14 months, with no immediate likelihood that she would have a home available. She continued to be homeless and was sleeping in the back room office at her work site.

Carl came to the group home director to have a conversation about his future. He had been told by the judge, his mental health worker, as well as his foster care providers that he would be able to return home when he met the treatment plan goals. He insisted that he had done his part and it was time for him to be able to be

(Continued)

(Continued)

with his mom as he had been promised. Toward the end of the discussion he became angry and stated, "Why should I work so hard when nothing is going to happen?" After his conversation, the group home director requested a meeting that included all of the relevant actors in his treatment plan (school social worker, court worker, mental health therapists for both Carl and his mother, classroom teacher, protective service worker, Housing Authority staff, and foster care team). All of the members of the team agreed that he had met the requirements outlined in the treatment program. With the exception of the group home director and classroom teacher, all of the other actors stood firm in their belief that his mother was not able to care for him and returning him to her care would lead to a failed placement. The group home director and the classroom teacher both argued that if he wasn't given a chance to be with his mother, there was every likelihood that he would give up and return to the very behaviors that had gotten him in trouble. After lengthy discussion, the group home director made arrangements to have an additional slot opened up at his facility, which would be used only for instances when one of his residents was unable to stay with her or his family after reunification efforts. This meant that Carl could come back to the facility and the staff would work with him on managing his reactions should the placement fail. During the prior 14 months, the Housing Authority had failed to find his mother suitable housing, which led to several contentious team meetings. Finally, the Housing Authority was able to get his mother an apartment and arrangements were made for Carl to return to his mother's home.

As the majority of the team predicted, his mother was unable to care for him and his acting out became more frequent. Arrangements were made to bring Carl back to his group home placement. However, at the moment that he was to be returned to the group home, his father was released from prison on parole. Since Carl was registered with the tribe, the tribe asserted its right to place Carl with his father based on the Indian Child Welfare Act (ICWA) provisions, arguing that this policy took precedence over any plan that the team had developed. This made the team's plan impossible to execute. Carl was moved into his father's apartment in a neighboring city where both of them faced very difficult challenges that eventually led to Carl being returned to the foster care system. However, he was not allowed to return to his original placement because the protective service worker had disagreed with the plan and now asserted her authority to send him to a new placement in another group home. Approximately six months later he experienced abuse in the new group home, and his overall functioning deteriorated significantly until he committed a crime for which he was sentenced to a juvenile detention facility until the age of 21.

Eco-Maps

One of the important tools used to help us understand a client's situation is through the use of **eco-maps**. This tool provides us with a visual image of the individuals', families', groups', communities', networks', and organizations' capacities to deal with stressors that require change (Gitterman & Germain, 2008). Its purpose is to help both the worker and the client quickly organize what are often complex numbers of systems as well as to characterize their interactions. Figure 6.4 attempts to synthesize the preceding case illustration.

FIGURE 6.4   ■   Carl's Eco-Map

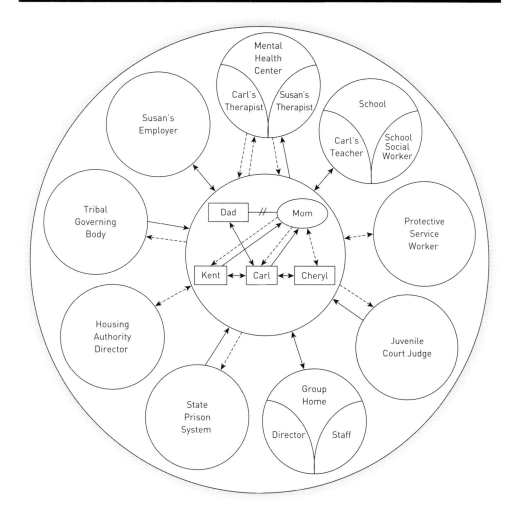

Carl's eco-map represents a picture of his narrative at this particular moment in his life. His situation is both complex and common. In nearly all our practice encounters there are multiple systems impacting, and impacted by, these complex forces. There are nine interacting systems that are all active in this one individual's life. While we might want to assume that they all work together, the reality is each system has its own dynamic energy that may or may not support the activities of the surrounding systems.

In Carl's situation, the school teacher and the group home staff shared the same vision about what might be in this child's best interest. However, the Housing Authority and Susan's therapist were concerned about what was in his mother's best interest. The protective service worker and the juvenile court judge emphasized their respective systems' concern with reducing potential risks for this child. Later the tribal government asserted the need for Carl to be placed with his father in order to protect his cultural heritage. Each of these systems has its own boundaries, structures, functions, energy, dynamics, and roles, which often clash when they come in contact with each other in a specific situation. It is often the case that the surrounding systems' agendas override the voices in the family. In this instance, the eco-map was used to help Carl understand what these various systems were doing in relationship to what he wanted. Unfortunately, what systems theory is unable to do is to provide the ability to predict the outcome of the interactions. For Carl, no matter how clearly his situation had been documented, organized, and analyzed, none of the professionals were able to predict the outcomes of their interventions. As systems theory suggests, attempting to impose cause-and-effect thinking in these situations ignores the reality that events are multi-causal and the prediction of outcomes is uncertain. In Carl's case, each of the interacting systems brought its respective views to the situation. Their perspectives clashed and the resulting outcomes proved unacceptable to any of the individual systems and harmful to Carl and his family.

The eco-map provides a means to translate systems theory from a general understanding of how systems interact to a more concrete level that allows us to personalize each person in their situations (PIE). It allows us to gather, organize, and analyze how these specific systems are interacting in ways to create both barriers and resources that can be used to improve the situation. In addition, how we collect this information becomes extremely important. In order to effectively develop an eco-map, it is necessary for the professional to follow the client through the description of his or her understanding of the situation. This approach fosters an atmosphere of mutuality between the professional and the client by supporting the client's attempts to define her or his own situation. It also helps both the professional and the client come to understand the complexity of most situations. When clients are able to use their own words to characterize their situation, they often reach a much deeper understanding of what is happening and what they need to do to improve the situation. The process of identifying problem areas, resources needed to make change, and potential strengths, as well as developing an action plan to bring about change, are all inherent in the process of developing a contract between the worker and the client (Hartman, 1978).

Genograms

Genograms, like eco-maps, are tools that have been developed as part of an array of strategies connected to the Life Model (Hartman, 1978, 1979; Hartman & Laird, 1983). Their functions include identifying generations within a family, major family events, intergenerational communications, family aspirations, alignments, and role assignments (Gitterman & Germain, 2008). Their purpose is to provide both the worker and the client with a graphic representation of the potential resources and barriers that can be brought to bear in a current situation. In addition to producing information, the diagram can be used to develop mutuality in the relationship between the worker and the client and as a tool to track changes as the work unfolds.

Figure 6.5 provides a genogram of Carl's family. It provides basic information about how Carl defined his family and allowed for the exploration of relationships that existed within that family. For example, Carl identified his father as an important figure in his life, though neither of his siblings shared his perspective. While developing the genogram, he expressed a strong desire to visit his father, whom he had not seen since his imprisonment. Arrangements were made for them to have semiregular contact through visits, as well as through artwork his father shared with him. There was no indication in any of the foster care case materials that he had any interest in his father nor had there been any efforts to foster any connection with his Native American heritage. In addition, arrangements were made for him to participate in activities at a Native American educational institution that did outreach into the community.

FIGURE 6.5 ■ Carl's Genogram

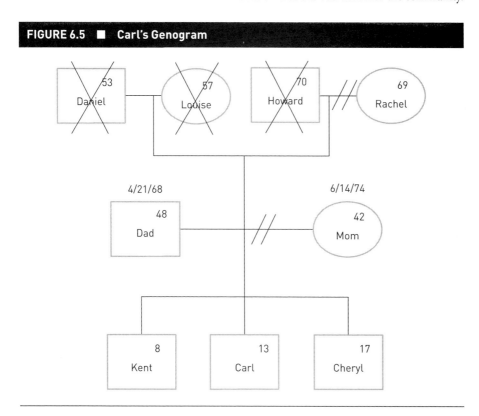

In addition to eco-maps and genograms, there have been numerous other tools associated with the Life Model. Each of them is designed to provide more specific lenses through which to view client systems. The following are examples of these mapping tools: culturagrams (Congress, 1994, 2005), spiritual genograms (Hodge, 2005), and gendergrams (White and Tyson-Rawson, 1995). The common thread that runs throughout each of these tools is that they employ systems theory to focus our attention on the interactions among people in their environments (PIE); they serve as frameworks to collect, organize, and prescribe general directions for action whether you are practicing at the individual, family, group, organizational, or community levels.

CHAPTER SUMMARY

This chapter attempts to trace the evolution of general systems theory (GST) from a broad explanatory theory used to examine and describe the interactions of various components of society, to its adaptation in the social sciences especially ecology, and for use in social work. Its importance to social work cannot be overestimated. For nearly 100 years, social workers tried to use social science ideas that tended to focus on either understanding human beings (biology and psychology) or some aspect of human's environments (sociology, economics, political science). However, from its inception, social work maintained the importance of understanding both individuals and their environments. What the profession lacked was a set of ideas that brought together the interactions of both persons and environments in ways that helped organize, analyze, and act on information focusing on the interactions of both components: the person-in-environment (PIE) perspective. While most other professions, including psychiatry and psychology, narrowed their focus of attention to one side of the interaction, social workers persisted in their belief that only by looking at both individuals in environments could we fashion useful responses to the complex factors creating social problems in peoples' individual responses within an increasingly complex industrial society.

We have examined the emergence of structural functionalism from the perspectives of both Talcott Parsons and Robert Merton as beginning efforts to introduce the use of systems theory to explain social interactions. This new framework provided a more complex way of understanding social interactions at the individual, group, organizational, and community levels. The major challenge for social work was to develop additional ideas that could be used with systems theory for it to be adapted to the purposes of social work. Therefore, both Parson's and Merton's contributions are included to not only view systems' characteristics in sustaining themselves (Parsons) but also as a means of understanding how systems could change (Merton). For social workers, it is essential to be able to adapt theories in ways that make them fit into the social work profession's value base, which includes the importance of both stability and change.

The ecological metaphor gave rise to the Life Model for social work practice. This model focuses practitioners on the interactions between individuals in their environments. In addition, it suggests that all systems have certain characteristics in common, which means that there are certain basic processes that transcend the importance of method (casework, group work, and community organization).

From the 1960s up until to the present, social work has been dominated by the extension of ideas utilizing systems theory, especially ecosystems theory as a central framework for practice. From its early beginnings, it has provided professional social workers with ways to gather, organize, and analyze information in their day-to-day practice. More recently, this approach has been refined with the addition of more specific models of practice that relate to different levels of systems, like family therapy models, that were mentioned earlier in the chapter. In essence, systems theory helps us to understand the interacting systems within human beings (biopsychosocial spiritual), interpersonal interactions between human beings (interpersonal communication systems), small group interactions, as well as processes that contribute to community and organizational structures. Social workers are also attempting to expand their use of systems into the physical and natural environments as yet another application of these theories. In conclusion, as you move into your professional life you will find ongoing current examples of how ecological systems theory can be useful in building knowledge in various fields of practice.

One Final Example: Systems Theories as Applied to Alcohol and Drug Addiction

The following example, knowledge building in the area of drug and alcohol addiction, illustrates how research and practice can be interwoven and understood using ideas from systems theories. First, in the mid-20th century, drug and alcohol treatment focused on the intrapersonal systems within the individual. The creation of Alcoholics Anonymous as well as Narcotics Anonymous developed treatment responses that emphasized the importance of spirituality, a higher power, as essential to regaining sobriety (Alcoholics Anonymous World Services [AAWS], 1939; Narcotics Anonymous World Services [NAWS], 1983). Second, alcohol treatment focused on the importance of social support groups as essential to maintaining sobriety. Third, professionals from psychiatry, psychology, social work, and drug and alcohol counseling used varying models emphasizing the psychological aspects of the work. In addition, they expanded the focus to include family systems as an essential part of the treatment response. Fourth, most recently, new avenues of brain research, based on neuroscience, focused on developing brain studies that examine the role that the person's brain plays in the addiction process (Johnson, 2014). This latter development will require examining the interactions of all four intrapersonal systems in order to more fully understand the addiction process. Changes in the knowledge about one system will interact with what we know about the other systems. Therefore, this information will need to be added to what we currently know about the social systems that immediately surround the individual, AA groups, families, and outpatient treatment to understand how those interactions support or fail to support recovery. Lastly, we will need to examine larger social structures that create policy that either provides resources, or deny them to those who suffer from addiction. Comprehensive treatment for drug and alcohol problems will require integrating systems that stretch from brain research to national social policy in order to create and coordinate treatment responses that acknowledge the multicausal and mutually interacting nature of this significant social problem.

Classroom Exercises

The following exercises are provided to help you explore the use of the eco-map and genogram with another student colleague. Pay close attention to what each of you learns through your joint discussion about the structure of your family and the processes that impact that system.

Exercise 1: Creating an Eco-Map

The following exercise has two parts. The first part is to identify a family problem that is (or was) of some importance to you. Based on what was happening in that situation, you are asked to prepare an eco-map that describes who was involved and the nature of their relationships in this specific situation. The second part is to bring that eco-map to class and pair up with another student colleague. Each of you shares your eco-map and description with your partner and what you have learned from mapping out this situation.

Exercise 2: Creating a Genogram

Create a genogram that represents your family over three generations. Bring it to class and share it with a student colleague. Be sure to answer the following questions:

(1) How did you determine who to put in your family?

(2) Where did you obtain the information about the relationships among your family members?

(3) Can you identify important aspects of your current behavior that connects you with the people in the genogram? Please describe.

Key Terms (in order of appearance)

Structural functionalism   137

Person-in-environment (PIE) perspective   141

Ecosystems theory   141

General systems theory (GST)   142

Life Model of social work practice   149

Eco-maps   156

Genograms   158

References

Alcoholics Anonymous World Services (AAWS). (1939). *Alcoholic anonymous*. New York, NY: Author.

American Association of Social Workers. (1929). *Social case work, generic and specific: A report of the Milford Conference*. New York, NY: Author.

Bartlett, H. M. (1970). *The common base of social work practice*. New York, NY: National Association of Social Workers.

Bertalanffy, L. V. (1950). The theory of open systems in physics and biology. *Science, 3*, 23–29.

Bertalanffy, L. V. (1967). General systems theory. In N. Demerath & R. A. Peterson (Eds.), *Systems change and conflict* (pp. 119–129). New York, NY: Free Press.

Besthorn, F. H., & Canda, E. R. (2002). Revisioning environment: Deep ecology for education and teaching in social work. *Journal of Teaching in Social Work, 22*, 79–101.

Besthorn, F. H., Koenig, T. L., Spano, R., & Warren, S. L. (2016). A critical analysis of social and environmental justice: Reorienting social work to an ethic of ecological justice. In R. Hugman & J. Carter (Eds.), *Rethinking values and ethics in social work* (pp. 145–163). London, England: Palgrave-Macmillan.

Besthorn, F. H., & McMillen, D. P. (2002). The oppression of women and nature: Ecofeminism as a framework for an expanded ecological social work. *Families in Society, 83*, 221–232.

Burrell, G., & Morgan, G. (2003). *Sociological paradigms and organizational analysis*. Burlington, VT: Ashgate.

Congress, E. P. (1994). Use of culturagrams to assess and empower culturally diverse families. *Families in Society, 75*, 531–540.

Congress, E. P. (2005). Cultural and ethical issues in working with culturally diverse patients and their families. *Social Work in Health Care, 39*, 249–262.

Council on Social Work Education (CSWE). (2015). *Educational policy and accreditation standards*. Alexandria, VA: Author.

Dubos, R. J. (1972). *A god within*. New York, NY: Charles Scribner's Sons.

Durkheim, E. (1893). *The division of labor in society* (G. Simpson, Trans.). Glencoe, IL: Free Press.

Durkheim, E. (1895). *The rules of sociological method* (S. A. Solovay & J. H. Mueller, Trans.). Chicago, IL: Chicago University Press.

Erikson, E. H. (1950). *Childhood and society*. New York, NY: W. W. Norton.

Germain, C. B. (1973). An ecological perspective in casework practice. *Social Casework, 54*(6), 323–330.

Germain, C. B., & Gitterman, A. (1980). *The Life Model of social work practice* (1st ed.). New York, NY: Columbia University Press.

Germain, C. B., & Gitterman, A. (1996). *The Life Model of social work practice* (2nd ed.). New York, NY: Columbia University Press.

Gitterman, A. (2011). Advances in the Life Model of social work practice. In F. J. Turner (Ed.), *Social work treatment: Interlocking theoretical approaches* (5th ed.; pp. 279–292). New York, NY: Oxford University Press.

Gitterman, A., & Germain, C. B. (2008). *The Life Model of social work practice: Advancements in theory and practice* (3rd ed.). New York, NY: Columbia University Press.

Goldstein, H. (1973). *Social work practice: A unitary approach*. Columbia, SC: University of South Carolina Press.

Gordon, W. E. (1962). A critique of the working definition. *Social Work, 7*(4), 3–13.

Gordon, W. E. (1965). Toward a social work frame of reference. *Journal of Education for Social Work, 1*(2), 19–26.

Green, D., & McDermott, F. (2010). Social work from inside and between complex systems: Perspectives on person-in-environment for today's social work. *British Journal of Social Work, 40*, 2414–2430.

Hartman, A. (1978). Diagrammatic assessment of family relationships. *Social Casework, 59*(8), 465–476.

Hartman, A. (1979). *Finding families: An ecological approach to family assessment in adoption*. Beverly Hills, CA: Sage.

Hartman, A., & Laird, J. (1983). *Family centered social work practice*. New York, NY: Free Press.

Hearn, G. (1969). *The general systems approach: Contributions toward an holistic conception of social work*. New York, NY: Council on Social Work Education.

Hodge, D. R. (2005). Developing a spiritual assessment toolbox: A discussion of strengths and limitations of five different assessment methods. *Health and Social Work, 10*(4), 314–323.

Hudson, J. (2014). *The natural environment in social work education*. (Doctoral dissertation, University of Kansas). Dissertation Abstracts International, 6341717.

Iverson, R. R., Gergen, K., & Fairbanks, R. P. (2005). Assessment and social construction: Conflict or co-creation? *British Journal of Social Work, 35*, 689–705.

Johnson, H. C. (2014). *Behavioral neuroscience for the human services*. New York, NY: Oxford University Press.

Lee, P. (1929). Social work: Cause and function. *Proceedings*. National Conference of Social Work (pp. 3–20). New York, NY: Columbia University Press.

Mack-Canty, C. (2004). Third-wave feminism and the need to reweave the nature/culture duality. *National Women's Studies Association (NWSA) Journal, 16*(3), 153–179.

Malinowski, B. (1945). *The dynamics of culture change*. New Haven, CT: Yale University Press.

Mann, S. A., Grimes, M. D., Kemp, A. A., & Jenkins, P. J. (1997). Paradigm shifts in family sociology? Evidence from three decades of family textbooks. *Journal of Family Issues, 18*, 315–349.

Merton, R. K. (1968). *Social theory and social structure*. Glencoe, IL: Free Press.

Meyer, C. H. (1976). *Social work practice* (2nd ed.). New York, NY: Free Press.

Meyer, C. H. (1983). *Clinical social work in the eco-systems perspective*. New York, NY: Columbia University Press.

Narcotics Anonymous World Services (NAWS). (1983). *Narcotics anonymous*. Chatsworth, CA: Author.

National Association of Social Workers (NASW). (2005). *NASW standards for clinical social work in social work practice*. Washington, DC: Author.

Pareto, V. (1935). *The mind and society* (Vols. 1–4). (A. Bongiorno & A. Livingston, Trans.). New York, NY: Harcourt Brace.

Parsons, T. (1937). *The structure of social action*. New York, NY: Free Press.

Parsons, T. (1951). *The social system*. New York, NY: Free Press.

Parsons, T. (1959). *Economy and society*. London, England: Routledge and Kegan Paul.

Pincus, A., & Minahan, A. (1973). *Social work practice: Model and method*. Itasca, IL: Peacock Publisher.

Radcliffe-Brown, A. (1952). *Structure and function in primitive society*. Glencoe, IL: Free Press.

Rocher, G. (1974). *Talcott Parsons and American sociology* (B. Mennell & S. Mennell, Trans.). London, England: Nelson.

Spencer, H. (1864). *Principles of biology* (vol. *1*). London and Edinburgh: Williams & Norgate.

Thompson, J. B. (2012). *Rethinking the clinical vs. social reform debate: A dialectical approach to defining social work in the 21st century*. (Doctoral dissertation, University of Kansas). Dissertation Abstracts International, 3522069.

Thompson, J. B., Spano, R., & Koenig, T. L. (in press). Back to Addams and Richmond: Was social work really a divided house in the beginning? *Journal of Sociology and Social Welfare*.

White, M. B., & Tyson-Rawson, K. J. (1995). Assessing the dynamics of gender in couples and families: The gendergram. *Family Relations, 44*(3), 253–260.

ENVIRONMENTAL AND ECOLOGICAL THEORY IN SOCIAL WORK

©Terry Koenig

PHOTO 7.1
Interaction between humans and nature: Gyeongbokgung
Palace, Seoul, South Korea

CONNECTING SOCIAL WORK WITH THE NATURAL ENVIRONMENT

The following case example helps us explore the complex relationships between people and their natural environments.

CASE EXAMPLE
LAKE POOPÓ

A recent *New York Times* (NYT) article (Ives, 2016) tells the story of a Bolivian people called the Uru, and the imminent demise of not just their livelihood, but of their culture and way of life, as the lake their people have been fishing for generations has all but dried up over the last several years. The cause? Climate change—the Uru are among the first of many whose lives will be significantly altered due to the effects of climate change such as rising sea levels, desertification (i.e., where fertile land becomes desert usually due to deforestation or inappropriate agriculture), and an overall increase in the number and severity of extreme weather conditions such as droughts and hurricanes (Earl, 2009; National Academy of Sciences, 2015; Wilson, 2017). Many other groups and nations are also threatened such as the Kiribati nation, whose islands span the size of Alaska in the South Pacific, yet do not rise more than six feet above sea level (Ives, 2016). The Uru, one of the remaining indigenous peoples of Bolivia, have for centuries cultivated a lifestyle surrounding Lake Poopó [accent last "o"], their primary source of food and culture (Casey, 2016). Until the recent changes leading to the dying of the fish, the Uru were a proud, self-reliant people who lived simply from their surroundings, having passed down for generations the wisdom of fishing and making a life on the banks of the lake. Many of their rituals and celebrations related directly to the fishing season and finding a sustainable catch. The lake provided not just fish but a sufficient ecosystem to sustain life as they knew it. Flamingos, for instance, once prevalent at the lake (now gone), were hunted and used for a variety of things such as an analgesic made from fatty tissues.

Several factors are responsible for the climate change that dried up Lake Poopó. First, the average temperature increased significantly—over 1.6 degrees Fahrenheit just between 1995 and 2005 (Casey, 2016). Second, the popularity of quinoa in wealthier, Northern countries such as the United States led to water being drawn from the few rivers supplying water to the lake. Third, sediment from upstream mining operations ran downstream, clouding the water and making the lake more shallow and susceptible to drought. The resulting ecosystemic effects are perilous as the fish drowned and baked in the silt-clouded, overheated shallows; the birds (flamingos) who fed on the fish died off or left; and the Uru are the latest lake residents to abandon their homeland or face dire circumstances.

So what does the drying up of Lake Poopó have to do with social work? In a word: everything. There may not be a regional county social services center nearby for American social workers to find a convenient job with a modest salary, but that is not where we begin our thinking in this field (granted, we all do need jobs and sufficient salaries somehow). The situation that the Uru people are facing today is a prime example of just the kinds of people and situations that social workers care about and have a duty to intervene in at multiple levels. Our *Code of Ethics* states our concerns for social, economic, and environmental justice and our duty to provide assistance to individuals and groups who are in need (Council on Social Work Education [CSWE], 2015; National Association of Social Workers [NASW], 2017). This mandate includes those nearby but does not have geographical, national, racial/ethnic, or even species-related boundaries. Our concern is for those who are vulnerable, exploited, harmed, and/or threatened anywhere on the earth. The Uru and the Lake Poopó ecosystem are therefore of concern.

Social work professionals could address a variety of issues, from clinical to political. Perhaps most obvious, when people are displaced, in this case as "climate change refugees" (Ives, 2016), social workers have often taken a prominent role in assisting them with resettlement. This includes developing expertise in the culture(s) of those displaced, the culture(s) of the new location, gaining knowledge of the relevant transportation and legal procedures, and finding the best, most practical ways to help people navigate their new surroundings, such as finding a place to live and coping with changes (among many other things). Additional traditional social work roles could be in counseling/mental health therapy for grief and loss, mental health and substance abuse issues, and normal psychosocial adjustments. Particularly vulnerable people would be of special concern, such as children, those who are disabled, and the elderly. These and more concerns would be relevant to social work, but in the micro/mezzo, and ameliorative sense what must also be addressed are prevention and macro perspectives. In other words, social work is always concerned with the sociopolitical conditions that lead to the issues and problems. In this case, one may immediately begin to question the policy decisions that led to water being diverted from Lake Poopó for agricultural use, who benefited from the diversion, and who had the power to make those decisions (and who didn't). Similar questions should be raised about the decisions to permit sediment from mining operations to enter the lake. This is just the beginning, though; the point is always to find solutions, to challenge the status quo when it means people are suffering—in this case from a complete loss of culture, land, and livelihood—by taking various social and political actions (e.g., community organizing) to affect positive change. This, in a nutshell, is the traditional social work perspective that includes both micro and macro levels of concern, research, and action. What we'd like to do is push this boundary even further to include not just the human sociopolitical arena but also concern, research, and action for non-human species, land, habitats, and even entire ecosystems.

In the case of the Uru and the demise of the Lake Poopó ecosystem, instead of just thinking of the well-being of the human individuals, families, and cultures, we expand our thinking to include vulnerable non-human species (e.g., flamingos, fish), the land and the lake itself, as well as the complex interrelationships that are affected among all of the above—when one aspect of the ecosystem is degraded, there are significant detrimental impacts to other aspects of the system. This broadened view expands the social work purview to include care/concern and a duty to investigate and take action on an even larger scale. It includes interventions from micro to macro, yet adds many potential roles for professional social workers. This chapter will concern itself with exploring the ecological theories (especially ecological ethics) that we can use to deepen our vision of a just, healthy, and thriving world. It means we must face challenging but promising questions, such as:

- Why exactly should a social worker care about fish and flamingos?

- Do environmental concerns such as pollution disproportionately affect people who are poor, oppressed, and marginalized?

- What have social workers done historically with regard to the natural environment?

- How do environmental and ecological ethics line up with our NASW *Code of Ethics*?
- What would a social worker do to help not just the humans but also the non-humans and the entire Lake Poopó ecosystem?
- Who (or what) are social work clients? (Do we need to think in terms of *clients*?)
- Are social workers also "environmental activists"?
- What new jobs and roles could social workers take on as advocates for the environment?
- How, where, and when should social workers take action on behalf of non-human species or ecosystems?
- What knowledge and methods should social workers use to address environmental concerns?
- What are the relationships between humans and non-human species and natural environments?

There are a number of ways currently used to label the thinking about the natural environment we are concerned with in this chapter. Terms such as "environmental movement" or "ecological crisis" or "inconvenient truth" may come to mind, and no discussion of the natural environment can escape the multitude of political ideologies and perspectives that often raise tension and anxiety at the mere mention of this topic. What seems an agreeable starting point is the recognition that the natural environment is important to us all since we all breathe the air, drink the water, and otherwise require sustainable habitat for mere survival! Our aim with this chapter is not to survey all of the relevant ideologies, nor to provide a comprehensive history of environmental concerns. Instead, we hope to offer a cogent discussion of key concepts and themes related to environmental thought (focusing on ethics) and explore the relationships and roles that social work has had, and potentially can have, with regard to environmental concerns.

We are using the term **ecological social work** in order to emphasize social work's interest in ecology (the study of macro biophysical and social systems, their relationships and interdependencies) as opposed to older "person in environment" thinking (Gitterman & Germain, 2008) that only includes human individuals and groups in their respective sociopolitical environments. The term "ecology" immediately denotes a concern with an entire biotic community that includes humans, but it also concerns itself with non-human species, from black bears to grasshoppers to bluegreen algae. In addition, an ecological focus transcends narrowly defined human interests to concerns with habitats, geophysical systems, and their interrelationships with their biological inhabitants. The terms "environment" and "ecology" are often used interchangeably, and given social work's history of the use of both terms to mean just humans in their sociopolitical environments, it can get confusing (reference ecological social work). To be sure, we do not intend to diminish the importance of human sociopolitical relations; we hope instead to expand our thinking beyond the merely human, or **anthropocentric** world view. Social work has since its inception concerned itself with the needs and issues of individuals and groups who have been oppressed, exploited, and threatened—with this in mind our attention now turns toward the inclusion and application of our ethics-based profession to ecosystemic thinking.

IS ENVIRONMENTAL THOUGHT NEW?

In a word, no—the environmental movement that arguably began with the publication of Rachel Carson's book *Silent Spring* in 1962 represents a modern public discourse and multi-faceted activism in response to pollution, contamination, and other forms of environmental degradation caused by modern industrial, military, and farming practices (among others). But ideas, or theories, about the natural environment date back to antiquity as all societies and cultures have asked questions about the essence and value of human beings, non-human animals, and the environment around us. Modern technological societies are also not the first to think about what we should do with our garbage or whether we should cut down all of the trees or not (Diamond, 2005). But we are the first society with the power to alter the natural environment (and in effect, ourselves and other Earth inhabitants) in such drastic and potentially devastating ways. We have seen the costs of our modern, technological society, from the Chernobyl nuclear disaster in the former Soviet Union to the recent British Petroleum oil spill in the Gulf of Mexico. And there are many interrelated ecosystemic threats including climate change, deforestation, species extinction, air and water pollution, coral reef disappearance, landfills, urban sprawl, and the list goes on (Earl, 2009; Landsberg & Warring, 2014; McKibben, 2011; National Academy of Sciences, 2015; Wilson, 2017).

Fortunately, there are many ideas, or theories, we can use to develop our understanding of the ecosystems beyond (but including) the human world. These ideas (see next section) also have historical roots, grounding them in wisdom from ancient to more recent times. For instance, many current thinkers often make linkages to religious and/or spiritual figures such as St. Francis (1182?–1226) in the Christian tradition (de Steiguer, 2006; Delio, 2003). Francis recognized the value of all living creatures, including not just non-human mammals but also birds, plants, trees, and so on. In his sermon to the birds, he stated that religious devotion should include concern for the welfare of non-human creatures. In his famous canticle to the sun, he even refers to the sun and moon as "brother" and "sister." There are other thinkers, especially starting with the industrial revolution—some hopeful, offering new and/or applied ethical ideas, others speculating about future environmental disasters. Thomas Malthus (1776–1834), for instance, an English economist and clergy person, famously argued that the ever-increasing human population would not be able to produce enough food for itself, which would lead to ruinous famine, disease, and war. This argument has its proponents still today, offering updated versions of the "Malthusian" dystopia or place in which everything is in ruins and has deteriorated. However, not all writers of the industrializing era have such a bleak outlook. Henry David Thoreau (1817–1862), author of the well-known book *Walden, or Life in the Woods* (1854), penned a romantic treatise based on his two-year stint in a small cabin on Walden Pond (Thoreau, 1995). While there he swam in the pond, walked in the woods, grew a garden, and enjoyed a sort of idyllic life in the natural environment—a contrast to the urbanization and industrialization going on around him. With *Walden*, Thoreau offered a unique perspective in American literature and philosophy that is still influential today. He believed that all creatures were valuable, and not just for human-centered needs. He extolled the beauty and value of wild lands and the need for humans to spend time in the mountains, valleys, rivers, and other natural areas. While we are not able to offer a comprehensive survey of environmental thought here, the following will address key themes in the development of environmental ethics (mostly 20th century), then offer a more in-depth examination of deep ecology and the application of these ideas to social work practice.

ENVIRONMENTAL ETHICS

The history of **environmental ethics**, especially as it has developed over the past century or so, is a history of thinking that begins with a purely anthropocentric ethic, then to one that transcends concern just for ourselves (humans) to include non-human animals (zoocentrism), all life forms (biocentrism), and eventually entire ecosystems (ecocentrism). One convenient way to think about this development is to consider it in three rough stages as a movement from "light green" or "shallow" environmentalism, to a "mid-green" ethic, and finally to a "deep green" ecological ethic (Curry, 2011).

Light Green Ethics

According to Curry (2011), **light green ethics** limits direct value only to human beings. Non-human animals, and all other biological species, habitats, and ecosystems have value only as they pertain to the use and service of humans. This is called *instrumental value*: anything non-human has value only as it is instrumental for our use somehow. For example, in the Lake Poopó case, the fish would have value *only* because they serve human needs as a food source (or otherwise). Beyond this limited ethical purview, the fish would be considered expendable as they possess no value of their own, and are therefore not considered in ethical deliberation. Our values—including *what* we value—tend to shape law and policy, which leads to very divergent outcomes depending on our values. At Lake Poopó, if the people all move away to find work elsewhere, an instrumental value-based, light green ethic may suggest policy that leads to further degradation of the lake ecosystem because there would no longer be immediate and direct human concerns. Note as well that the "light" in light green also refers to the general lack of depth of ecological analysis; the idea that humans are not affected by the degradation of the Lake Poopó ecosystem just because the people who lived in the immediate vicinity of the lake have moved on, shows a rather sophomoric understanding of the complex interrelationships that comprise the natural world and the place of humans within it (more on this later).

We have just defined *instrumental value*; the contrasting term is called *intrinsic value*. Intrinsic value means that non-human species or individual members of a species or ecosystems have value *without* regard for their usefulness to human beings. The non-human entity or entities may in fact have instrumental value to humans; but if so, their value transcends their relation to humans, and is therefore not dependent upon it. This raises an important question about the origin of the intrinsic or inherent value that a creature or species may have, which often leads to deep roots in religious, spiritual, and/or philosophical traditions. There are many different arguments and perspectives (mostly beyond our discussion here). Holmes Rolston, for instance, a well-known environmental philosopher, has argued that the intrinsic value of non-human animals is evident in the fact that they tend to *value* their own survival, well-being, and offspring (among other things) (Rolston, 1988). Thus, the animal that *values*, is *valuable, intrinsically*, and therefore it is our duty as humans to consider it as such in our ethical deliberations. This would include the fish at Lake Poopó as well as many, if not all, other creatures. The idea that something is intrinsically valuable will be considered again in upcoming sections.

Perhaps not surprisingly, environmental ethics, light green or otherwise, are highly politicized. Those adhering to a light green ethic tend to be considered politically right-wing (Curry, 2011). The tendency is toward thinking that centers upon human action, for human benefit. The assumption is that humans are the most advanced life form to have evolved thus far, and as such we have a duty to take control of the natural environment and to the extent possible, manage and control the next steps of evolution. Natural environments are considered "natural resources," a term that implies their instrumental value—literally, nature as a resource for human use and consumption. As such, humans and human political processes should "speak" for nature; we should use our vast technological resources to shape and exploit the natural world in an ongoing cycle of growth and prosperity (for humans). According to these perspectives, terms such as "sustainability" tend to serve the interests of neoliberal capitalism as "natural resources" are commodified and simply become another part of the human global economy.

Mid-Green Ethics

With **mid-green ethics** we move from an anthropocentric perspective to a biocentric one (Curry, 2011). The ethical purview is extended to include non-human animals, with special attention to individuals as opposed to entire species. Biocentric views basically extend the concern for human rights and welfare to non-human animals. There is also still no inherent value ascribed to habitats, nonliving things, or ecosystems. A prime example of this type of thinking and action is the animal liberation movement that began with Peter Singer's book *Animal Liberation* (1975). This movement has been primarily concerned with the extreme suffering endured by animals in factory farms, laboratories, and so on. Since non-human animals can experience pain the same way humans do, recognition of this fact creates a primary obligation or duty to prevent avoidable suffering such as occurs when cows are processed and slaughtered for human consumption. Moreover, if animals such as cows, pigs, or chickens are considered to have rights, or some inherent value, then killing them for food itself raises ethical concerns, especially since in the United States alone more than 10 billion animals are slaughtered for food each year, not including the 100 million that die in laboratories or the 50 million killed for fur (Curry, 2011). Since we tend to value human life, despite the ability to reason or to have certain sorts of experiences (e.g., in young children or people with dementia), the failure to extend the same consideration to non-humans amounts to what Singer would call *speciesism*, a human prejudice or chauvinism that always places the interests of one's own species above other animals. Of course, the idea of speciesism is also subject to the criticism that it is a prejudice for *sentient* life and does not value biological life otherwise. The focus on sentience and suffering also leads to a potential overfocus on individual animals, as opposed to considering the broader value of a species of animal (or plant or fungus, etc.) within an ecosystem. In sum, what we get with a biocentric perspective is a change in attitude or orientation to the human–nature (or human to non-human) relationship such that humans are recognized as a part of the biotic community, with a duty to consider other species, especially sentient ones, in our ethical deliberations. There is also recognition of the interdependence of humans with at least some other animal species. Finally, biocentric perspectives also tend to recognize that non-human animals may have the capacity for their own pursuits, according to the type of animal they are (e.g., dolphins, while they may not pursue careers in business, do have relationships, raise young).

Deep Green Ethics

Deep green ethics are basically inclusive macro environmental ethics. What we mean is that deep green ethics are ecocentric: they are holistic in their consideration of entire ecosystems, including the complex interrelationships among species, geography, climate, and so on. They are inclusive because they do not ignore the sentience, self-determination, or suffering of *individuals* within species but consider the needs of the individual in light of the health of the entire species in its particular habitat. Deep green thinking also means that there is at least the potential for humans to "lose" when conflicts arise between human needs (and wants) and the needs of other species or ecosystem health (Curry, 2011). With deep green ethics the goal is the "deepest" level of ecological analysis. This is necessarily non-anthropocentric as it ascribes intrinsic value to non-humans (similar to biocentrism) but transcends the mid-green perspectives by also ascribing intrinsic value to entire species, habitats (including non-biological elements), and ecosystems themselves, from micro to macro (including the idea that the entire earth is itself an ecosystem). Thinking again of Lake Poopó, deep green thinking would begin with the value of the entire lake ecosystem (in its broader context with nearby mountain ranges and plains, etc.). Analysis would be required to understand (to the extent possible—this can be very difficult!) the food chains including the insects, fish, humans, birds, and others, along with the sources of water, any pollutants (e.g., farm runoff, sediment), climate concerns, the history of the system, and more. A close analysis can be costly and time consuming, and it always involves competing interests between humans and non-humans—and often between non-human species as well.

There are a number of deep green ethical theories that explore the above-mentioned principles in much more detail, each offering its own particular perspective. One well-known idea is Aldo Leopold's (1887–1948) Land Ethic. With his book *A Sand County Almanac* (among others), he offered a reflective piece that describes a new ethics (e.g., specifying what is right/wrong, good/bad) centering upon the land itself (Curry, 2011; Leopold, 1949). His oft-cited central tenet is that "a thing is right when it tends to preserve the integrity, stability and beauty of the biotic community. It is wrong when it tends otherwise" (Leopold, p. xx). By "biotic community," he intends more than just biocentrism as he extends ethical thinking to include soils, plants, and waters—all considered "land." Leopold's ideas set limits on what humans should, and more importantly, should *not* do, with regard to the land. This ethic offers a needed contribution to human thinking, but it also raises many difficult questions. For example, if doing the right thing means preserving the integrity, stability, and beauty of the land *as a whole*, then won't certain individuals, or even individual species, need to be sacrificed for the greater good? And who should decide what exactly amounts to the "integrity," and especially the "beauty" of the whole biotic community? Does this mean that humans cannot cut trees for wood, or mine for metals, or build houses? Despite the difficulty of these and many more questions raised by the land ethic, perhaps the significance and contribution of this ethic is that the questions are raised at all, and that careful consideration of the overall health of mountain ranges, riparian systems, and prairies is valued and deliberated.

Another group of theories that also raise important questions and have served to reorient thinking about the environment are those broadly labeled **ecofeminist**. Generally speaking, feminist ideas challenge the status quo of patriarchal or masculinist thinking, which can lead to domination and exploitation of not just women and other human populations but also the natural environment (Curry, 2011). Ecofeminist analyses also tend to range from the concerns of individuals to the sociopolitical institutions and structures that lead to thought and action that propagates continued oppressions of various groups of people, non-human animals/species, and the land. Ecofeminists attempt to upend pathological masculinist thinking by calling attention to the value systems inherent to it, such as the idea that all life exists according to dualistic hierarchies where there is a master and slave, or a higher and lower. According to this type of hyper-masculine thinking, males have priority and power over females; reason rules over emotion; the abstract intellectual is valued over the body; humanity (the apex of which is male) rules over and against nature, which is instinctual and carnal. Like the land ethic (and so many others), ecofeminism has brought important considerations and social action to bear upon multiple environmental issues. Ecofeminist ideas also raise more questions, such as the concern that attempting to replace masculinist thinking with feminist only reifies the very essentialisms (i.e., that female and male are separate, opposing, and stereotyped) and dualisms that are of concern in the first place. Sex and gender discussions are highly complex, but the contribution of ecofeminists cannot be overstated, and like the other theories discussed here, thinking and debates (internally and externally) continue to develop. We now turn our attention to one of the most prominent and enduring deep green theories, deep ecology. We selected this theory for our in-depth section not only because the theory offers much for ecological consideration but also because of its utility for social work practice.

IN-DEPTH: ARNE NAESS AND DEEP ECOLOGY

Deep ecology was invented by a Norwegian philosopher named Arne Naess in the early 1970s and has been widely influential to this day, especially in the United States (Curry, 2011). However, though it was started by a philosopher, the deep ecology movement has long since taken on a life of its own with proponents from diverse nations, religions, political orientations, and so on. One of its great strengths is that it does not presume to dictate an adherent's metaphysics, or their view of the nature of reality, specific politics, or detailed methods of action. Deep ecology is more a platform for ecological thinking and action than it is a comprehensive ecological theory of its own. That said, it does have eight ecological principles (plus two optional) that offer a rough trajectory that can be used by people from multiple walks of life. But before diving into the details of the eight principles, it is worth asking what is it that is so "deep" about deep ecology. Naess responds that the "deep" in deep ecology refers to two primary aspects: questioning and change. First, deep ecology means deep questioning in the public sphere. This means that deep questioning is not just for academics and other professional ecologists, but it is a conversation that should take place in bar rooms, elementary schools, and around family tables as well (to name a few). His hope is that the questions asked will transcend (or "go deeper" than) the usual political spin and media hype. "[W]hat characterizes the deep movement (in relation to the shallow) is not so much the *answers* that are given to "deep questions" but rather *that* "deep questions" are raised and taken seriously (Naess, 1995, p. 210).

Deep dialogue continues to ask hard questions about why things are the way they are, who is responsible for them, what values are at play, and what actions can be taken to affect change. This last point is the second essential aspect of "deepness": "the necessity of a substantial change in economic, social, and ideological structures" (p. 211). For example, politicians may feign concern for the environment, offering that they find intrinsic value in trees, mountains, and bald eagles, but then support policies that are inconsistent with those values and supposedly create jobs while lining the pockets of corporate executives. Deep questions don't assume that all companies and politicians are malevolent, but they also don't fail to ask deeper economic questions, such as "why do we assume that continued economic growth and extremely high levels of consumption are so important?" Deep questions involve asking what kind of society fulfils our most basic human needs like loving relationships with family and friends, time to develop and enjoy those relationships, and access to nature. If those are things we value, then what kind of economy and work life, what kind of religion, what kind of education is congruent? What kinds of lifestyles are beneficial to all forms of life on the planet, not just a small percentage of ultra-wealthy humans? (Bodian, 1995, p. 27).

Eight Principles of Deep Ecology

Naess, in 1986, working with his friend George Sessions, generated eight principles that "are meant to express important points which the great majority of supporters accept, implicitly or explicitly, at a high level of generality" (Naess, 1995, p. 67). Deep ecology is thus both descriptive of what became of the movement (and hence not just "top down" from Naess), as well as prescriptive of what supporters of it should accept. Table 7.1 illustrates the basic platform of deep ecology.

TABLE 7.1 ■ Eight Principles of Deep Ecology Platform

1. The well-being and flourishing of human and non-human life on Earth have value in themselves (synonyms: intrinsic value, inherent worth). These values are independent of the usefulness of the non-human world for human purposes.

2. Richness and diversity of life forms contribute to the realization of these values and are also values in themselves.

3. Humans have no right to reduce this richness and diversity except to satisfy vital needs.

4. The flourishing of human life and cultures is compatible with a substantially smaller human population. The flourishing of non-human life *requires* a smaller human population.

5. Present human interference with the non-human world is excessive, and the situation is rapidly worsening.

6. Policies must therefore be changed. These policies affect basic economic, technological, and ideological structures. The resulting state of affairs will be deeply different from the present.

7. The ideological change will be mainly that of appreciating life quality (dwelling in situations of inherent value) rather than adhering to an increasingly higher standard of living. There will be a profound awareness of the difference between bigness and greatness.

8. Those who subscribe to the foregoing points have an obligation directly or indirectly to try to implement the necessary changes.

A Few Comments

The first point pretty much sums up the non-anthropocentric nature of deep ecology and comprises the foundation for what follows. It is worth noting that the term "life" (that which has inherent value) is not limited to biocentrism but, according to Naess, is intended to be more comprehensive and includes rivers, landscapes, and ecosystems (Naess, 1995, p. 68). In the second principle, the term "complexity" should not be confused with "complicated." Working 10 hours per day, commuting in rush hour traffic, all while trying to raise children, get adequate exercise, sleep, and eat healthy (not to mention spending valuable time in natural environments)—that is *complicated*. Complexity, on the other hand, refers to the "multifaceted quality" of life that has naturally evolved over time and denotes the richness of life (Naess, 1995, p. 69). The third principle refers to "vital need" as the only justification for human actions that reduce richness and diversity of life, yet the term is rather vague. Naess states that this is intentional in order for the differences in societal structure, climate, and other related factors to be taken into consideration when making ethical deliberations. Principle four can raise concerns about the rate of human population reduction and the possibility of exploitation of vulnerable groups. What Naess has in mind is a gradual reduction (possibly over hundreds of years), with proper, ethical planning, realizing there will be continued species extinctions no matter what we do. Principles five and six refer to human "interference" with the non-human world. The caution here is only that Naess does not intend for humans to somehow magically vanish from the global scene—we always have, and will continue, to manage and modify the natural world. The concern is the extent, which must be reduced. Principles seven and eight refer to life quality and the obligation to act. These too are left intentionally vague and open. The goal is for action leading to more flourishing, but there is room for a variety of foci, priorities, opinions, and many different types of actions that can lead to positive change.

Ecosophy and the "Apron" Diagram

Ecosophy is Naess's preferred term to describe wisdom about ecology: the word is literally composed of roots that mean this: "eco" as in ecology, and "Sophia," which is the feminine word for wisdom. Ecosophy represents another "layer" to deep ecology—the eight principles are one part of a larger system of thinking, or wisdom, of which there are four levels.

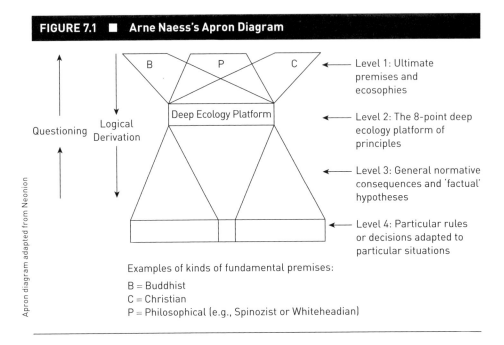

FIGURE 7.1 ■ Arne Naess's Apron Diagram

Level 1: Ultimate premises and ecosophies

Level 2: The 8-point deep ecology platform of principles

Level 3: General normative consequences and 'factual' hypotheses

Level 4: Particular rules or decisions adapted to particular situations

Examples of kinds of fundamental premises:

B = Buddhist
C = Christian
P = Philosophical (e.g., Spinozist or Whiteheadian)

Apron diagram adapted from Neonion

We can think of ecosophy as a response to the question of justification for the eight principles. In other words, one might ask for a rationale for the eight principles, something for them to be founded upon. The four levels of ecosophy offer room for diverse justifications, as well as for more particular empirical research and decisions to be made about policy. *Level 1* of ecosophy (see Figure 7.1) includes the ultimate premises, or foundations for the eight principles. Naess does not state what those foundations must be, but he insists that there may be multiple foundations, depending on the individual or group. For example, one may logically generate the eight principles based on a Christian understanding of the inherent value of God's creation, which includes non-human animals as well as the land (e.g., see Bouma-Prediger, 2010). This more recent understanding (among others) upends theologies of violence and domination as it offers a reinterpretation of often-referenced environment-related biblical passages that have been misunderstood and misused. In Genesis 1:28, for instance, God tells the newly created human (Adam) to "be fruitful and multiply, and fill the earth and subdue it; and have dominion over the fish of the sea and over the birds of the air and over every living thing that moves upon the earth (NRSV, 2001). The key term here is "dominion" and its meaning. Does dominion mean domination, exploitation, destruction? Bouma-Prediger offers fairly decisive argumentation to show that the use of the term dominion does not mean these things. When interpreted in light of other biblical references to dominion (e.g., the ideal kingly dominion in Psalm 72), a very different view emerges. "The psalm unequivocally states that such a ruler executes justice for the oppressed, delivers the needy, helps the poor, and embodies righteousness in all he [sic] does" (Bouma-Prediger, 2010). Thus, the proper interpretation of dominion leads to a definition of shalom—the flourishing of all creation. Humans are to follow a Christ-like ethic of dominion as service and protection for the earth and its inhabitants. Naess's point, however, is not to champion one religious or philosophical system over others (assuming one can logically derive the eight principles), but to suggest that there are many paths that lead to them.

Level 2 of ecosophy is composed of the eight principles themselves, the deep ecology platform (just outlined), which leads to *level 3*, which Naess opaquely labels "general normative consequences" and "factual hypotheses" (Naess, 1995, p. 77). It seems that what he has in mind is a movement from the more abstract eight principles to more concrete ideas that utilize information from the empirical sciences such as sociology or ecology. For instance, a principle such as valuing life quality over economic growth (#7) requires further information in order to apply it to any real-world situation. In order to form policies that reflect the principle, one would need to know quite a bit about the details of the economy they're dealing with, the historical and current sociopolitical situation (e.g., see the example at the end of this chapter on Kettleman City, CA), environmental/ecological information (and more), in order to evaluate multiple options, face difficult dilemmas, and ultimately make hard choices. This brings us to *level 4*, the final level, which specifies "particular rules or decisions adapted to particular situations" (Naess, 1995, p. 77). This level indicates the actual policy (or other) decisions that are made, along with general rules that can guide current and future practice. Rerouting heavy truck traffic around a school zone in order to avoid air pollution and the concomitant health hazards to children would be one example.

We mentioned earlier that there are two "optional" principles in Naess's deep ecology. Briefly, these include self-realization and maximizing diversity (Naess, in Sessions, 1995). The first of these, self-realization, is not meant to denote the self as an ego-focused, navel-gazing entity who tries to self-actualize or maximize their individual success, wealth, or power. Quite the opposite. With this principle Naess offers a developmental concept that aims at maturity in the sense that over time we begin to identify "self" more broadly, not just including our own individual self-interest, but expanding to include all forms of life in a universal symbiosis. As such we would incorporate the idea of other human individuals and groups, as well as non-human species, into our self-concept. This way ethics and values align to produce motivation that is beneficial to all life—a sort of internalizing of the principles of deep ecology into one's very identity. The second idea grows out of the first: if we incorporate others (including non-human species) into our identity, then the diversity of life will become a value. But it is more than an abstract value since we will have incorporated others into our self-concept. In other words, it is a move beyond just philosophizing and reasoning to an existential, psychological level of becoming a different sort of people who will as a matter of course change our lifestyles to fit our new and developing identities. As people with the wisdom of ecology, we would develop lifestyles that are "simple in means but rich in ends" (Naess, 1995, p. 80).

CRITIQUE OF ENVIRONMENTAL AND ECOLOGICAL THEORY

What Does This Theory Say About Human Behavior?

Left to our own devices, human beings in industrialized nations have viewed the natural environment as an endless resource for their benefit. Except in rare circumstances (e.g., among indigenous tribes, ecofeminists), people have taken from, but not given back, to nature or treated the natural world as an actor with equal moral standing to humanity. Social work's history is no exception in that the natural environment has rarely been acknowledged except for its impact on human well-being. Shallow ecology has dominated social work's responses to the natural environment.

However, this dominant perspective may be changing as humans begin to understand that their fate is indistinguishably linked to the health and well-being of the natural world. Deep ecologists draw upon views of reality as tangible (e.g., climate change is a "fact" agreed upon by 97% of the scientific community [Karl, Melillo, & Peterson, 2009]) but also acknowledge that our reality is constantly changing as we become increasingly aware that real environmental devastation does interact with human life. Writers have called for us to develop or "socially construct" a new creation story that understands we are not at the center or pinnacle of creation but are part of a vast web of life (Coates, 2003; Naess, 1973) in which all elements of the web (e.g., animals, plants, soil) have an equal claim to life and if negatively impacted, can have unpredictable effects on the entire web (e.g., the destruction of earthworms can vitally hinder human beings' capacities to grow crops and thereby flourish).

How Does This Theory Address Growth and Change?

This theory holds out hope that human beings will wake up and make changes in their behavior before it is too late. Authors such as Naess (2008) indicate that the changes we make now will make the world a better, more livable place for our children's children. For example, human overpopulation is understood by deep ecologists to be a major factor in contributing to environmental degradation (Butler, 2015). And, overpopulation is something we can positively address if we choose to do so. We also need a major shift in our view of growth as striving for economic gains through increased production, consumption, and wealth, and instead we need to explore how to create a better, richer quality of life. In this sense, small and local is more beautiful and healthier for the natural world and for humans (Jackson, 1994). In particular, social workers who embrace deep ecology will likely have to embrace not only individual but community-based practices as a means of creating the kind of growth and change needed to restore our natural world. As noted in the overview, social workers already function as, and can develop future roles for, mediation and negotiation, community organizing, and policy development as a means of more adequately addressing the moral and equal claims of humanity and the natural world.

How Holistic Is This Theory?

Social work has always understood itself to have a wider lens than other helping professions in that it focuses on the person-in-environment, always taking into account the larger social context in which individuals, families, and communities cope with and are resilient. However, as noted in the overview, social work has been slow to include not only the physical environment, such as housing, but also the natural world such as streams, landscapes, and air or water quality as they directly impact human well-being. Deep ecologists, ecofeminists, and green social workers encourage us to examine our wholeness, integration, and harmony with the totality of creation (i.e., living and nonliving entities) and to view our humanity as part of the natural cycles of life, death, and interdependence. This means that we would want to engage in social work practice by moving beyond a bio-psycho-social-spiritual approach, which often focuses on persons to the exclusion of a more inclusive definition of environments, and this would include the natural world in our assessment, treatment, and proactive practices with clients.

How Consistent Is This Theory With Social Work Values and Ethics?

At a broad level, deep ecology is very consistent with social work values and ethics. However, our understanding and definitions of core social work values need to be expanded to more fully incorporate the natural world as an important actress in social work practice. From a deep ecological perspective, the dignity and worth of each person, the importance of relationships, social justice, and self-determination all need to be reframed in order to take into account the natural environment. For example, the dignity and worth of each person can be expanded to include not only human but non-human life (e.g., rivers, natural terrains, ecosystems) in all its forms of richness and diversity.

Social justice by its very definition excludes the natural world. The profession of social work can also reshape social justice, which many believe to be at the center of our value-base, and instead refer to an ecologically sensitive justice (deep green) that views the natural world on equal footing with humanity. Some scholars in social work have already called for this reframing of social justice into ecological justice (Besthorn, 2013; Besthorn, Koenig, Spano, & Warren, 2016). Further, ecological, green, ecofeminist approaches require us to examine the connections between social problems and the unequal distribution of the planet's resources, which unduly affect quality of life for poor and marginalized populations. An ecologically just response would insist that social workers respond by challenging and addressing poverty, understanding full well poverty's connections to ecological problems (Rogge, 2000).

When we examine the value of the "importance of relationships," social workers can ask themselves how human beings relate to the non-human world. Many would say that human beings are already part of the natural world and that it is "unnatural" to exclude ourselves from an intimate, perhaps even spiritual, relationship with the planet. These ideas run counter to our Western epistemologies that celebrate the split between nature and humanity, and it is here again where we look to indigenous, ecofeminist, Eastern views such as Taoism and other beliefs to help us understand that we are already one with all of creation (Koenig & Spano, 1998).

Self-determination, although also a central social work value, must be examined in relationship to human and non-human rights and responsibilities. Deep ecologists point out that although humanity has a right to satisfy (or self-determine) vital needs, it has no right to excessively interfere and irreparably harm the non-human world (e.g., through the destruction or overdevelopment of natural environments for human's recreational use). Further, human beings have a responsibility to change economic and political structures to protect and support the flourishing of the natural world.

Competence and integrity would require that social workers develop skills and expertise in understanding the natural world and humanity's place in it. And, this directly implies that social work educators need to develop and put forth an expanded ecological orientation to better equip social workers who will indeed address the effects of climate change and environmental damage on humans. This expanded orientation would counter the narrower conceptualization of the social environment, which continues to dominate human behavior coursework in social work education.

Jones (2013) proposed an expanded ecological approach in social work education that focuses on the understanding that students have of the natural world, its processes and systems (e.g., the cycling of matter through the web of life and the sustaining of life through the energy of the sun), and the place humans occupy within the planet. Jones called for students and faculty alike to develop this ecological literacy (Orr, 1992), which is vital for transforming social work education. Jones also suggested that this transformed social work education would include encouraging students to explore indigenous ways of knowing, other forms of spirituality, and their roles in shaping the human and natural world relationship (Zapf, 2005, 2008). Teaching students about humans' place within the larger universe would require different pedagogical approaches and greater use of self-reflective and contemplative practices. Students would need to develop an even more robust critical approach for understanding the natural world (e.g., how the environmental crisis began, the analysis of scientific data and impact of government policies on the environment).

What Sources of Knowledge Does This Theory Support?

Deep ecologists call us to develop ecological literacy, to be involved in a quest of learning new and ever-changing knowledge about our planet, to relearn ideas about the natural world (e.g., its cycles and processes that we have long forgotten), and to teach this ecological literacy at all levels of our education (e.g., elementary and secondary schools, in our liberal arts, and social work programs). Our knowledge of the symbiotic relationship between humans and the planet can be developed through examination of ample scientific studies demonstrating the negative effects of human activity on our natural world (e.g., climate change and environmental degradation) (Butler, 2015) and from the personal experiences and knowledge clients and professionals have obtained as they work to integrate the natural world into their lives and practices.

As deep ecological writers point out, in order to develop this increased understanding or knowledge, we will be required to move beyond our Western dualistic views that support the epistemological split between humans and the natural world and instead develop a deeper, spiritual perspective that sees all of the earth and humans as interconnected (e.g., indigenous and shamanic traditions, which view humans and animals as involved in a necessary and relational exchange). For example, in Kazakh indigenous traditions that reflect Central Asian beliefs about links between humans and nature, a creation story is told about the Baiterek or sacred Tree of Life (see Photo 7.2). Each year, in the crown of the tree, a sacred bird lays an egg and the sun and dragon living at the foot of the tree swallow the egg. This symbolizes the holistic connections between opposites such as day and night, good and evil, and summer and winter.

Many indigenous spiritual helpers also believe that humans, sustained by the natural world in eating animals, fish, and birds, are then responsible for giving

©Terry Koenig

PHOTO 7.2
Baiterek or sacred Tree of Life reflecting indigenous traditions: Astana, Kazakhstan

CASE EXAMPLE
EXPERIENTIAL LEARNING AND INTEGRATING THE NATURAL WORLD: A CASE EXAMPLE ON THE SIBERIAN STEPPE

A social work educator developed a meaningful relationship with her Kazakh language interpreter, his wife, and baby while teaching social policy for a semester on the Siberian steppe in Kazakhstan. Through interactions with the interpreter about his spiritual beliefs reflecting shamanistic traditions that emphasized humans' deep connections with nature, this author returned home, changed her behavior, and now regularly cycles several miles through wheat fields, communing with red-tailed hawk and wild turkey that frequent her bike path. Developing a relationship with her interpreter, who represented a different culture with diverse beliefs and values, reawakened her connections to and knowledge of the natural world. She now grows vegetables and herbs from seed in her garden.

In small groups, discuss the following questions:

(1) Describe an experience in which you developed a deeper connection to nature.

   a. How did this come about?

   b. What did you learn?

   c. And, how did it change you?

(2) How could you deepen your experiences and behavior so as to have a more intimate relationship with nature?

(3) How might your experiential learning and self-reflection on the natural world change the way you practice social work?

back to or compensating the natural world (Hamayon, 1999). This means, for example, that businesses need to move beyond being "socially responsible" to being responsible for giving back to the natural world when their production and other activities exploit natural resources. The following case example is provided to encourage you to explore the "give and take" between humans and the natural world and your role as a social worker in mediating or participating in a kind of exchange between human well-being and the natural world.

Critique Summary

Deep ecologists view reality as tangible and concrete, but they also acknowledge that reality is constantly changing as humans interact with the natural world. Social work scholars encourage us to write a new creation story that understands we are not at the center or pinnacle of creation but are one part of the vast web of life in which all elements of the web have an equal claim to life (animals, plants, and soil). Deep ecologists hold out hope that human beings will "wake up" and make changes in their behavior before it is too late. These changes or growth may not be fully realized for several generations, but they are necessary to begin now (e.g., addressing overpopulation). We are also encouraged to examine our wholeness, integration, and harmony with the entirety of our natural world, thereby expanding our traditional social work notions of the social environment. Deep ecology is very consistent with social work values, but it incites us to expand and reframe our definitions of core social work values such as the dignity and worth of each person, social justice, and self-determination to include not only human but non-human life in all its richness and diversity. Finally, deep ecologists call us to develop ecological literacy, to be involved in learning new knowledge about our planet, and to relearn ideas about the natural world (e.g., its cycles and processes that we have long forgotten), and to teach this literacy at all levels of education.

The following example identifies a current situation faced by citizens in northern Minnesota. It provides an opportunity to explore the complex and conflicting values embedded in current situations, i.e., the values of immediate economic gain in relationship to long-term environmental degradation and potential harms to human beings in the area. It raises important questions about how social workers can position themselves in ways to influence the debates about relative costs and benefits to the environment and individuals who will face significant challenges no matter which direction the debate takes.

CASE EXAMPLE
COPPER AND NICKEL MINING IN THE SUPERIOR NATIONAL FOREST

International mining companies from Canada, Chile, and Switzerland have put forth proposals to extract copper and nickel from Superior National Forest near Duluth, Minnesota. Mining production promises to pump vast financial resources into Minnesota's public education and other economic efforts, but will most certainly pollute Lake Superior; the Boundary Waters Canoe Area Wilderness; the Red River, which flows into Canada; and other bodies of water for hundreds of years beyond the life of the mining plants. Over 50,000 Minnesotans have expressed objections to this mining production. According to some environmentalists, there are moral quandaries that this proposed mining extraction creates because there is uncertainty about how long the polluted water from the mining site will need to be treated once the mines close. What is clear is that there is growing opposition to people in the state of Minnesota having to shoulder all the long-term

environmental and financial risks while external mining corporations financially benefit from the profits (Marcotty, 2017).

Assume that you are a school social worker working in Minnesota Public Schools and are concerned about the lack of resources to support public education. Explore the following questions:

(1) How would you mediate or balance out the educational benefits for children (promised by the copper and nickel mining companies) with the public health of Minnesotans and others due to long-lasting water pollution?

(2) Is it morally acceptable to meet immediate educational needs of children while ignoring the long-term impact of the effects of water pollution? Explain your answer using ideas and concepts from the overview of this chapter.

SOCIAL WORK'S HISTORICAL RELATIONSHIP WITH THE NATURAL ENVIRONMENT

In Chapter 2, we introduced a framework for analyzing human behavior that challenged readers to answer for themselves, how holistic is this theory? We argued for the necessity of a holistic approach because social work requires us to understand both persons and the environments in which their behavior occurs (Gordon, 1965; Koenig & Spano, 1998; Spano, Koenig, Hudson, & Leiste, 2010). While social work has always understood the importance of environments, we have often focused on the social (people) and physical (constructed) but often ignored the natural environment (earth, sky, water, forests). What follows is an examination of social work's relationship to the natural environment from the 1830s to our present day. In each time period, the characteristics of a person-in-environment perspective in social work are described, including assumptions that drive the person-in-environment perspective, the relationship between humanity and environments, and the role of the social worker related to persons and their environments. A table that synthesizes these ideas is provided at the beginning of each time period and a more detailed analysis follows each table (see Table 7.2 through Table 7.9).

1830–1870

During the mid to latter half of the 19th century, some early social service providers, who were the forerunners of social work, used the natural environment as a metaphor to provide the rationale for placing homeless children from urban areas to rural communities. These providers were individuals that were influenced by the larger Transcendentalist Movement, which centered on the healing, restorative, and regenerative powers of Nature as well as defining the belief that divinity pervades all nature and humanity, and its members held progressive views on feminism and communal living. Among the leading figures of this movement were Ralph Waldo Emerson, Henry David Thoreau, and Walt Whitman (Emerson, 2010; Parrington, 1957).

During this period, what we have come to know as orphan trains came on the scene. This movement was a reaction to complex social changes occurring as we transitioned from an agrarian to a more industrialized economy. One aspect of this large-scale social transition, industrialization required redistribution of labor between rural and urban areas of the country. There were many orphaned and dependent children, as a result of industrialization and its attendant changes, in the large cities on the East Coast. In addition to the overcrowding in the cities, there were numerous epidemics that left many children homeless (Holt, 1992). One of the most well-known social service providers concerned with the plight of children was Charles Loring Brace, a philanthropist and reformer who was born in 1826 in Connecticut and later was seen as the father of the foster care movement. He recognized many of the "evils" in the cities and developed the idea that children would grow up to be productive adults if they were "transplanted" into

TABLE 7.2 ■ The Moralistic Period, From 1830 to 1870		
Person-in-Environment Assumptions	**Relationship Between Humanity & Environments**	**Role of Social Worker Related to Persons & Their Environments**
Humans are deeply flawed (sinful); natural environment given to humans by God for their use	Humans created by God in his [sic] image and humans are to rule over all elements of the natural world	Focus on individual with little attention to environments

the rich soil and fresh air found on the farms in middle America. As a result, thousands of children were removed from their living conditions in the large cities to be placed with Midwestern families where they could be integrated into these families as well as provide a source of labor to assist in the family farming operations. The results of the use of this agrarian metaphor were mixed at best. Many of the children did in fact have positive interactions with their families; others were unable to adjust to these very different surroundings and got into trouble in their new communities (Holt, 1992; Popple & Leighninger, 1990).

1870–1890

Social workers practicing in various fields, including the Association for Improving the Conditions of the Poor (AICP), combined their moral perspectives with the very early emergence of a shifting paradigm that emphasized not only moral understandings of human behavior but the use of reason as a way to understand human behavior. They began to collect and record information about their clients that seemed important in developing their understanding of why the poor were poor. They continued their emphasis on "moral character development" as a method for changing people's behavior. However, they began to look at the surrounding conditions in which the poor lived as a way to understand their clients. Their approach specifically began focusing on the constructed environments in which people lived as a way to understand problems related to reducing need among the poor. They began to see connections between poor housing, lack of garbage collection, accidental deaths of workers on the job, and health-related concerns as they related to the creation of poverty. This began the process of shifting from their moralistic views about the poor (pauperism) toward redefining these notions as "poverty," which became the focus of the Charity Organization Societies (COS). This period can be seen as the beginning of the tensions that have existed between two competing paradigms: those who define the poor as a product of personal irresponsibility, and those who emphasize the role that environments played in the creation of poverty. They represent a transition from solely focusing on individuals to including the potential

TABLE 7.3 ■ The Pre-Professional Era, From 1870 to 1890		
Person-in-Environment Assumptions	**Relationship Between Humanity & Environments**	**Role of Social Worker Related to Persons & Their Environments**
Association for Improving the Conditions of the Poor (AICP) focuses solely on moral character development of poor and other marginalized groups. Its only concern is the role played by the social environment with minor attention to the physical environment (i.e., poor housing).	Paradigm shift from moralistic tradition toward use of social science to collect data on the impact of social and physical elements of human problems.	Continue to be "role model" for poor; focus remains on saving poor from their moral defects. Orphan trains are a response to evils in city and its unhealthy lifestyle; agrarian living is a healthier way to grow and develop.

impact that environments (both constructed and social) played in the challenges faced by the poor (Spano & Koenig, in press). They also romanticized the role of the natural environment as a potential source of healing for those who lived in the urban centers.

1890–1920

By the 1890s, the combination of industrialization, urbanization, and immigration gave rise to the Progressive era. These reformers were driven by the fundamental beliefs that emerging social sciences, embedded in Jeffersonian values, which idealized agrarian life, could be used to solve the complex problems society faced (Hofstadter, 1955). In essence, the Progressives subscribed to the notion that cities were inherently evil and dangerous, especially for children. They too believed rural settings, the yeoman farmer ideal, would allow people to grow up in healthier circumstances; therefore, they would be more productive citizens (Hofstadter, 1955; Leiby, 1978; Spano & Koenig, in press; Wiebe, 1967). However, Progressives focused their attention primarily on the emerging problems facing those who were living in urban areas.

The one major exception focused on the tension between two influential personalities in the Progressive era, whose competing and conflicting views of the natural environment played an important role in providing the context for social work's emerging appreciation for environments in their work related to the delivery of services. At the national level, John Muir and Gifford Pinchot presented competing and conflicting views of the natural environment. For Muir, the ideas of the Transcendentalists about the natural world having its own spirit and independent value were paramount, while Pinchot viewed nature as a reservoir of resources to be used on behalf of human beings (Besthorn, 1997). At the national level, Pinchot's perspective won out and social work followed the direction of the larger discussion about the natural environment. This resulted in social workers including the environments in their ongoing work with clients but focused more on the social and physical aspects of the environment rather than the natural environment.

TABLE 7.4 ■ The Emergence of Social Work, From 1890 to 1920		
Person-in-Environment Assumptions	**Relationship Between Humanity & Environments**	**Role of Social Worker Related to Persons & Their Environments**
Charity Organization Societies (COS) start with moralistic, individual approach and transition to social science to study and solve individual/social problems. COS emphasizes social and physical world with some attention given to preserving natural environment for human benefit.	Emergence of an ideological view of the natural environment (Jeffersonian idealism) and emergence of "shallow ecology" approach with some recognition of the need to preserve nature as a healthy influence on humans.	Applies scientific principles to urban problems as way to better conditions for humans. Major focus on understanding social movements through psychology, sociology, and economics. Applies science to physical environment (e.g., Pittsburgh Survey, child labor studies, and housing reform). In addition, open spaces in cities, camping programs, and creation of national parks are examples acknowledging importance of nature to people (shallow ecology).

An excellent example of social workers moving beyond simply focusing on individual charity to include the environment was the Pittsburgh Survey. This survey examined the impact of steel production on the workers in the city of Pittsburgh and focused on collecting information about the impact of environmental hazards created by steel mills. It was a six-volume work that examined women in the trades, the connection between wages and health conditions, child poverty, racial hiring practices, the emotional and physical tolls taken on workers' mental as well as physical health, housing's impact on families, and the impact of industrial accidents on workers and their families (Kellogg, 1909–1914). This extensive work was spearheaded by Paul Kellogg, who later became the editor of *Survey* and *Survey Graphic*, which were journals to which social workers, journalists, artists, and other social reformers contributed to support social action.

This is the first foray by early social workers into a serious examination, using social science principles, of the interactions of people and their environments. Their focus was on what we call "shallow ecology," which means their concern was primarily about the negative impact the environment was having on people and focused on the social and physical environments. They emphasized changes needed to be made to improve the human side of the equation rather than practicing from a "deep ecology" perspective and seeing the environment as having its own intrinsic value.

In addition to the Pittsburgh Survey, social workers in the settlement house movement turned their attention to issues related to creating green spaces in cities, developing camping programs for inner-city children, as well as advocating for improving sewer systems, garbage collection, improved tenement housing, and industrial regulation. All of these activities were based on the recognition that many of these realities of urban life created deleterious effects on the well-being of people who lived in the poor neighborhoods they served (Addams, 1910; Bremner, 1966).

1920–1930

During the decade of the 1920s, Americans refocused their attention from the international scene that had created World War I toward a more isolationist perspective emphasizing the application of capitalist ideology as a means to achieve prosperity. For example, Americans rejected President Wilson's call for a League of Nations that would have encouraged Americans to broaden their focus to include world events. President Calvin Coolidge summed up the role of government in his often-quoted statement, that "the business of government is business."

Social workers turned their focus to the newly emerging theories of human behavior, which emphasized understanding the individual person. Narrowing their focus to the individual was fed by their obsession with being viewed as a profession, by demonstrating the knowledge base and specific skills necessary to achieve that status. These efforts were fueled by Abraham Flexner's 1915 address in which he asserted that social work was not a profession because it did not possess distinct and educationally transmittable techniques (Bruno, 1948). Thus, social work began a search for a series of techniques that could somehow be based in the social sciences. The search for science and techniques led them to the work of Sigmund Freud, whose influence was spreading throughout America during this period of time (See Chapter 5). They looked to use

TABLE 7.5 ■ Social Work Approaches, From 1920 to 1930		
Person-in-Environment Assumptions	**Relationship Between Humanity & Environments**	**Role of Social Worker Related to Persons & Their Environments**
Emphasis shifts from efforts to create reforms to improve physical and social environments to focusing on individuals with emphases on intra- and interpersonal dynamics as social work seeks professional status.

Some efforts continue in the areas of structural change (e.g., social insurance). However, the environment is treated as a resource pool for human use. Pollution and exploitation environment for profit continues. | Social work struggles to operationalize focus on both person/environments. Most social workers attempt to develop sophistication in techniques that focus on individual adaptation to social environment.

Some continue to work toward structural changes by promoting social insurance through collection of data like their Progressive forbearers. The natural environment is seldom addressed in any professional literature. The impact of the physical environment is recognized for its detrimental effects on children, minors, and other industrial workers. | Majority of social workers focus on internal landscape of humans and their maladies. A few social workers emphasize need for social insurance in response to industrialization and impacts of social environment on workers, women, and children harmed by working in factories.

Social workers advocate for better housing in urban environments. |

his psychodynamic theory as a basis for work in mental health, schools, children services, and family services. A competing perspective was presented by Mary Richmond. She placed her understanding of human behavior in its environmental context. Her definition of the environment was the social environment and, to some extent, the physical environment in which clients lived. The psychodynamic and person-and-environment perspectives dominated the conversation among about 90% of the social work profession. Meanwhile, there were some social workers who continued to advocate for social insurance and other broader social programs (Chambers, 1963). However, they remained a small segment of the profession.

Further, the profession emphasized developing professional status. In the 1920s, social work focused on its organizational structures (American Association of Social Workers, AASW) and numerous university-based social work education programs banded together to create the American Association of Schools of Social Work. Finally, social work began its development of a range of journals to establish itself as having a unique knowledge base. Among those journals were *Survey, Survey Graphic, Social Service Review,* and *The Family* (Spano & Koenig, in press). With the exception of camping programs developed in the YMCA and YWCA programs and some settlement houses, social work, like the larger society, paid little attention to the role of the natural environment in its professional literature.

1930–1945

The events shaping this decade actually occurred in October 1929 with the infamous stock market crash, which created national and international depression. Until those cataclysmic events unfolded, social work had remained essentially a small enterprise housed primarily in the private sector. Most formally educated social workers were located in small agencies typically funded by various religious groups—for example, Catholic Social Services and Lutheran Social Services—or they were in small, locally funded children's guidance clinics and ethnically based helping organizations. Their focus was almost exclusively on helping individuals and families adjust to their respective environments and most operated with very limited funding. Shortly after the Crash in 1929, these social workers recognized that the problems they were facing went far beyond the individuals with whom they were working, and far beyond their ability to respond to the magnitude of the need created by the social and economic forces unfolding before their eyes. By 1930, they began to call for help from public sources, the federal government, to offset the overwhelming conditions that far outstripped their meager resources to help those in need.

TABLE 7.6 ■ The Social, Physical, and Natural Environments, From 1930 to 1945

Person-in-Environment Assumptions	Relationship Between Humanity & Environments	Role of Social Worker Related to Persons & Their Environments
Professionally trained social workers focus on social environment, but new recruits to positions in the New Deal directly address both physical environments as related to working conditions in manufacturing, social insurance, and the natural environment (e.g., Civilian Conservation Corps [CCC]; Tennessee Valley Authority [TVA]; Agricultural Adjustment Act [AAA]).	As noted above, during the Depression, large numbers of untrained social workers enter the profession to work in social services. Many head or develop programs like the CCC, TVA, AAA, and others. Some take active stances against the New Deal because it has not fundamentally changed our relationship to economic and political structures.	Trained (MSW) social workers focus on schools, mental health, and family services in private sector. When Depression begins, there is a strong growth in public social services and need to distribute resources to new segments of the population.
These programs believe natural environment should be exploited for human benefit. However, CCC engages in some reclamation efforts.	They link racism, poverty, toxic policies for land use, and control of production of goods and services. They call for more equal distribution of goods to all groups, based on their "shallow" ecology perspective.	New emphasis on social insurance to help feed and clothe population and reclaim land to produce food, replant forests, and create power through use of natural resources. "Science" is applied to farming and production of electricity—all directed toward human consumption with some emphasis on preserving natural resources, but with a focus on nature in service to humans.

Historian, Arthur Schlesinger describes the situation faced by Roosevelt as he took the oath of office in 1932. He stated,

> The national income was less than half of what it had been four short years before. Nearly 13 million Americans—about a quarter of the labor force—were desperately seeking jobs. The machinery for sheltering and feeding the unemployed was breaking down everywhere under the great burden. And a few hours before, in the early morning before the inauguration, every bank in America had locked its doors. It was now just a matter of staving off hunger. It was a matter of seeing whether representative democracy could conquer economic collapse. It was a matter of staving off violence, and even (at least some thought) revolution. (1959, p. 3)

The overwhelming social and economic conditions required a shift in attention from helping individuals to focusing social workers' attention to the larger environmental issues that created the individual responses they were seeing. Soon they found themselves awash in a sea of newly created federal and local responses designed to deal with the complex social and economic factors shaping the new reality in America.

Roosevelt's New Deal provided a context in which new agencies and new personnel were recruited into what was to become the public social service arena. This fast-paced transition had direct impacts on social work. First, it created an influx of new recruits who did not have formal social work training, and therefore, were less indoctrinated into social work's culture that emphasized professionalism. Second, many of these new social work recruits had very recently been clients before obtaining positions in the social service agencies. They often came from other disciplines and neither knew, nor were particularly interested in, the workings of their clients' minds. They did understand many of the hardships faced by the people with whom they were working and were much less likely to frame their understanding in psychological terms. Some of these social workers offered a more radical critique of the structural, economic, and political problems by the nation. One group of social workers called the Rank and File Movement aligned itself with members of the Communist Party to argue for more systemic changes than the reforms put forward by the new dealers (Spano, 1982). Finally, as a result of the Great Depression, social work came in contact with unprecedented attempts to incorporate the natural environment as a part of a comprehensive response to the cataclysmic effects of the crisis.

What the New Deal provided was a series of adjustments in the existing economic, political, and social structures designed to ward off more serious structural challenges to the arrangement of our social institutions (e.g., the threat of revolution). In terms of the natural environment, the New Deal created a number of initiatives that funded agencies directly affecting the natural environment (Badger, 1989; Degler, 1970; Goldston, 1968; Leuchtenburg, 1963). The following list provides a brief overview of their work.

- The Bureau of Agricultural Economics became a central planning agency whose goal was to enable every American farmer to grow crops that were best fitted to their soil, their available machinery, and market conditions.

- The Agricultural Adjustment Act (AAA) was developed to attempt to control the overproduction of many crops, which drove the prices down, thus causing farmers to lose money even though they had adequate crops.

- The Commodity Credit Corporation offered price support loans on stored crops.

- The Soil Erosion Service ran projects to demonstrate the benefits of terracing and contour plowing, planting cover, utilizing wind-resistant crops, and turning land over to pasture.

- In the south, the Tennessee Valley Authority (TVA) was created to revitalize one of the most deprived areas, creating a role to both create and distribute public power, engage in conservation, and control flooding.

- The Civilian Conservation Corps (CCC) served as a means of providing work for unemployed urban youths, whose jobs included reforesting denuded slopes, cutting woodland breaks to prevent forest fires, demonstrating soil conservation to farmers, and working on irrigation.

- Finally, the Works Project Administration (WPA) and its various components set about the rebuilding of roads, bridges, parks, public buildings, and other projects that left an enduring footprint on the natural environment.

There were common threads that ran through these programs as it related to social work's perceptions of the natural environment. First, social work assumed that nature was to be seen as a resource to be utilized for human betterment. Second, there was a fundamental belief that the continued and more effective use of the resources in the natural environment did not have to take into account its long-term impacts on those natural environments. Third, there was no willingness to entertain the idea that there was a connection between immediate consumption of the resources in the natural environment and long-term negative effects for human beings as well as the environment. As we have seen in the earlier periods, "shallow ecology" dominated social work's interactions with the natural environment.

1940–1945

While the first decade of this period of time was focused on responding to the Great Depression, after 1938, the social conditions rapidly changed as war loomed on the horizon based on events in Europe and Asia. For example, the unemployment rate in 1938 remained at 9.9% but by 1944 it had dropped to 1.2% (Ehrenreich, 1985). The growing external threats led the government, business, and labor to engage in efforts to reduce their divisions in order to be able to meet production for the upcoming war.

Social workers who had graduate education continued their ongoing feud related to the relative merits of the functional and diagnostic schools. The newly recruited public social service workforce was deeply engaged in the development and delivery of programs and services in this greatly expanded public social service sector. Neither group added new ideas that moved social work beyond a focus on the social and economic environment. After December 7, 1941, when the Japanese attacked Pearl Harbor, the entire country was focused on the development and use of our natural resources as a major weapon to be used against the Axis powers (e.g., Germany, Italy, and Japan). In large part, the natural resources available in the United States proved to be critical to winning the war when paired with its military and industrial complexes, and there was little discussion of questioning the use of these natural resources to achieve our political ends.

The vast majority of social workers stood behind the goals for World War II. Many social workers offered their services to the Red Cross and involved themselves in mental health services at the Veterans Administration and in mental health centers. The focus of these services was on assisting soldiers to transition back in to the larger society to resume their prior lives. The postwar focus of their work combined attention to individual needs as well as reconstructing people's social environments.

1945–1960

In 1945, any illusion of cohesion among the Allies (e.g., United States, France, Great Britain, and the Soviet Union) quickly crumbled. The end of World War II gave way to a new war, the Cold War. One of the consequences for the United States was that, just as we experienced a Red Scare after World War I, a similar wave of fear spread across the nation. The United States focused its fear on anti-Soviet foreign policy and the growing paranoia about the dangers of domestic communism. One of the consequences of fear was to shut down any further attempts at the reforms initiated during the New Deal (Ehrenreich, 1985). For approximately four years, from 1950 to 1954, Senator Joe McCarthy from Wisconsin initiated an endless sea of subpoenas designed to purge the government of anyone who had even a vague connection to the Communist Party (Leuchtenburg, 1963).

TABLE 7.7 ■ Emphasis on Person Not Environments, From 1945 to 1960		
Person-in-Environment Assumptions	**Relationship Between Humanity & Environments**	**Role of Social Worker Related to Persons & Their Environments**
Social work continues to develop "person" focused practice drawn from multiple psychologies with little incorporation of roles played by physical and natural environments. Even with emergence of group and family therapy, focus is on social environment, which ignores all other aspects of environment or relegates their importance to the meaning given them by the individual. Twin forces of professionalization and broader political, economic, and cultural factors support disconnect between persons-in-environments.	Imbalance between focus on person rather than environments accelerates during this period. Multiple new theories develop that all share an emphasis on the prominence of individual need, wants, and meaning as it related to environments. "Problems" are products of people's perspectives and emphasis is on helping them adapt to existing environmental constraints or supporting their use of the natural environment for self-interests.	Social work transitions to pervasive emphasis on individuals and small groups. It sustains focus on social environment. The physical environment receives some attention as it relates to the emergence of suburbs and their impact on families. There continues to be emphasis on camping programs through settlement houses, Boy and Girl Scouts, and the YWCA and YMCA as well as some church-sponsored programs with no attention toward reciprocity between the natural environment and humans.

Social work continued its ongoing discussions about the merits of both the functional and diagnostic schools until the early 1950s. A large contingent of new social workers, in what was now identifiable as the public social service sector, were immersed in the further development and refinement of many of the new social insurance programs that were born from the New Deal. Their optimism about continuing to develop reforms was short-lived due to the emerging conservative atmosphere in the larger society. During the 1950s, social work theorists continued to develop and refine models of practice, including the Psychosocial Approach (Florence Hollis), the Functional Approach (Ruth Smalley), Behavior Modification in Casework (Edwin Thomas), Crisis Intervention (Lydia Rapaport), and the Problem-Solving Model in Social Casework (Helen Harris Perlman). Many of these models of practice reached fruition by the early 1960s (Roberts and Nee, 1970). For the most part, there was little new in these theories that required social workers to include anything more than the social and physical environments. However, as Besthorn points out, Perlman at least acknowledged the impact of climate and other natural forces in shaping the human psyche (Besthorn, 1997).

There is minimal literature for this time period that suggests social workers were expanding their understanding of the role environment played beyond human interaction, and broad scale social changes would set the stage for many of the problems that surfaced in the late 1960s. For example, the Veterans Administration and the Federal Housing Authority garnered funds that allowed them to underwrite the costs of mortgages for middle-class families. This legislation focused on freestanding homes, which created an explosion in the development of suburbs but failed to subsidize multiple-unit apartment houses or renovation of existing houses. This meant the core of the cities would be less able to compete with the suburbs for attractive housing. In addition, this legislation allowed for racial discrimination against non-White buyers. Even though the Supreme Court, in 1949, ruled that this was unconstitutional, the practice continued (Ehrenreich, 1985). In 1956, the federal government launched a massive campaign to promote the use of cars and trucks by passing the Interstate Highway Act. The building of roads and subsidizing housing and fuel resulted in the creation of significant commuter travel for workers to get from their home to their workplace. These changes had profound effects then and continue to create significant environmental problems that have only escalated with the passage of time.

Unfortunately, this period of time may reflect the nadir of social work's ability to move beyond the concept of social environment to include the natural environment. However, there were some papers published at least acknowledging the importance of a broader perspective for social work. Each year the Social Welfare Forum published papers by a handful of participants who acknowledged the need for broader conceptualization of social work. For example, Ralph Bunche (1954), American Ambassador to the United Nations, presented a paper that focused on social welfare as a world concept, in which he talked about America's promise as an international ideal for the Western world. Philip Hauser (1956), then president of the American Sociological Association, presented a lecture, "Demography and Human Ecology in Relation to Social Work," which analyzed broad-scale social forces affecting various elements of society. However, he did not include the natural environment in his calculations. In conclusion, while there were significant social policy changes that were affecting the natural environment as well as the physical environment, social work remained relatively silent and continued down the path of refining its place among the professions. Those who attempted to provide a broader environmental perspective were relegated to the side tent, while those in the main tent focused more narrowly on persons.

1960–1980

Up until this era, the profession of social work had developed a variety of distinct methods such as casework, group work, community organization, and policy development. However, beginning in the 1960s and 1970s, social work scholars began to look for a theory or paradigm that would allow them to bring together these diverse strands of social work practice. General systems theory (GST), with its assumptions that all elements within a system interact with each other and are capable of being studied (e.g., individuals, small groups, families, organizations, neighborhoods, and societies), was introduced as a means of unifying these diverse methods (Hearn, 1969; Pincus & Minahan, 1973; Meyer, 1976; Goldstein, 1973). GST defines a system as including living and nonliving matter that are holistic and interact with each other (Bertalanffy, 1950, 1967). This theory made room for social work to begin to consider the natural environment. However, agencies only employed social workers to focus on work with individuals, families, and groups and so there was little expectation that the natural environment would be taken into account in social work practice. Because of this agency context, social work primarily ignored the nonliving elements of a system (e.g., lakes, prairie, air, or mountains), nor did it examine the impacts of nonliving matter on human beings. This truncated version of GST remained the prevailing paradigm

TABLE 7.8 ■ Increased Holistic Approach to Social Work Practice, From 1960 to 1980

Person-in-Environment Assumptions	Relationship Between Humanity & Environments	Role of Social Worker Related to Persons & Their Environments
In an attempt to unify diverse strands of practice (e.g., casework, group work, community- and policy-based work), social work embraces a systems perspective. The profession develops the life model and ecosystems approach, which take into account the transactions and adaptations of people with their "social" environments.	Increasing focus on transactions between clients and social environments leads to more holistic practice. With the emergence of the Vietnam War, the feminist movement, and other large-scale protests by citizens, societal and governmental structures are viewed as contributing to people's personal "problems."	Social workers engage in assessment and intervention designed to determine individual adaptation within social environments, although there are some radical social workers who advocate for broader structure changes in governmental and societal systems. The built environment, such as affordable and adequate housing needs of the poor, garners some attention by social workers, however, natural environment is virtually not considered in this ecosystems approach.

in social work until the introduction of the ecosystems theory and the Life Model in the late 1970s.

The ecosystems approach and Life Model were attempts to assist social workers in applying abstract GST ideas to social work practice. For example, the ecosystems approach and Life Model aided social workers in defining the boundaries of their case systems, in visualizing their cases through the development of an eco-map that they could jointly create with their clients, and in helping their clients largely adapt to their intractable social environments (See Chapter 6). These newer developments helped the field to develop an increasingly holistic stance that moved away from universal, linear, life cycle stages; political and social happenings (e.g., Vietnam War and feminist movement) contributed to social work's greater attention to unjust societal structures as they impacted individual work (e.g., radical social workers who advocated for governmental and broader societal change); and others fought for affordable and adequate housing for the poor. However, both approaches typically failed to incorporate the natural environment as part of the system of focus for social work practitioners and also largely ignored environmental inequities (e.g., ethnically and racially diverse people living disproportionately in toxic natural environments that contributed to "personal" problems). The early roots of both the ecosystems approach and Life Model emphasized the clients' social environment and it is not until the turn of the 21st century that these approaches deepened or broadened their scope to include the natural environment (see Besthorn & Canda, 2002; Gitterman, 2011).

1980 to the Present

In the 1980s and 1990s, some social work scholars exhorted our profession to expand its conceptual understanding of the context of practice to include the natural environment (Germain, 1981; Weick, 1981). As a part of systems thinking, these environmental social workers argued for the natural environment to be viewed as a system that social workers needed to consider in their practice because of its potentially harmful or beneficial effects on the well-being of humans. In particular, these scholars, who reflected a shallow ecological perspective, called for social work to address the disproportionate effects of environmental degradation on the poor and other marginalized groups at local, national, and international levels. During this time period, social work writings on the natural environment proliferated; scholars began to write on a myriad of topics to urge the profession to address the implications of integrating the natural world into practice and policy-based efforts as well as in conceptualizing how our professional education needed to be augmented and transformed. For example, new CSWE educational standards (2015) now address social work's role in addressing environmental justice in addition to social and economic justice. These pioneers have challenged our profession to expand its long-standing commitment to social justice to include ecological justice, which views the natural world as not simply one system but in full partnership with humanity. They have also encouraged us to move toward a deep ecological stance that values the flourishing of both human and non-human life and understands non-human life as intrinsically valuable beyond its benefits or use for humans.

TABLE 7.9 ■ Inclusion of the Natural World, From 1980 to the Present		
Person-in-Environment Assumptions	**Relationship Between Humanity & Environments**	**Role of Social Worker Related to Persons & Their Environments**
First concerns raised about absence of natural environment in social work's theoretical approaches. Scholars call on social work to extend ecosystems approach to address larger societal oppression of marginalized groups and to address environmental crises. Conceptual, practice, and policy-based appeals made to extend social justice to include environmental, and although still debated, ecological justice.	Ecosystems approach remains largely unchallenged, however many critique its lack of acknowledgment of societal, political, and economic structures that interact with and contribute to oppressive harms, not only to humans, but to the natural world (shallow ecology). In more recent writings, the natural world is viewed by some as having equal moral standing with humanity (deep ecology).	Some social workers begin to raise alarms about growing impact of environmental decline on human well-being and advocate for profession to engage in practices, policy development, advocacy, and educational efforts to address natural environment at local and international levels. Burgeoning literature on social work and natural environment develops. Social work governing bodies approve policy statement, making natural environment part of professional purview and incorporating environmental justice in accrediting standards.

SOCIAL WORK AND THE NATURAL ENVIRONMENT: CURRENT DEVELOPMENTS

In the present era, environmental crises and their impacts on diverse, global populations have challenged social work by their complexity, frequency, and damage to the natural environment and the well-being of many people. Social workers are already providing direct services to help clients, particularly those from marginalized and poor communities, who have been disproportionately harmed by environmental damage and degradation (e.g., floods, drought, earthquakes, and radioactive contamination) (Gray, Coates, & Hetherington, 2013). Yet, social workers have been less involved or not heard by decision makers who formulate policies that are set up to nurture, protect, and sustain the natural world and its central role and relationship to humanity. Few in social work have raised the consciousness of a community, geographic region, or larger society regarding the physical environments of their clients (e.g., repairing senior housing; cleaning up low-income properties with lead contamination), yet they work in these neighborhoods and know full well the effects of environmental problems on human beings (Dominelli, 2012a). It is for these and other reasons that we have included this chapter on deep ecology.

©Terry Koenig

PHOTO 7.3

Humanity as it interacts with the natural world: Boboli Garden sculpture, Florence, Italy

Environmental Social Work, Shallow Ecology, and Nature-as-System

In the 1980s and 1990s, some social work scholars began to insist that the social work profession expand its traditional focus on the "social" environment to include the natural environment (Berger & Kelly, 1993; Germain, 1981; Hoff & McNutt, 1994; Penton, 1993; Soine, 1987; Weick, 1981). These scholars primarily operated from a systems theoretical perspective (see Chapter 6) and made inextricable links among the health of the natural environment, the well-being and survival of human beings, and the disproportionate effects of environmental degradation experienced by poor and marginalized groups of people with whom we work.

They advocated for **environmental social work**, rooted in a systems perspective, which viewed nature as its own system. This was a monumental step forward in insisting that the profession include the natural world in its understanding of social work practice. However, this environmental approach represented a "shallow ecology" (light green ethics) in that it was "concerned with ecological problems because of their impact on human beings" (Besthorn, 2012, p. 250); the environment was still viewed as an object, with endless resources that humans could act upon and use.

Deep Ecology and Ecological Justice

Although there is some confusion in the social work literature regarding the concept of deep ecology (see Dominelli, 2012a), for our purposes, the term deep ecology, or deep green ethics, is defined as a belief in the flourishing of both human *and* non-human life. Social work scholars, educators, and practitioners alike who espouse a deep ecological perspective understand non-human life, in all its richness and diversity, as independent and intrinsically valuable beyond its usefulness for humans (Besthorn, 2013; Hudson, 2014). These social workers embolden us to view our current interference with the non-human world as excessive, and that social work's call to social justice needs to embrace a more

---

FIGURE 7.2 ■ **Relationship of the Natural Environment to Humanity and Marginalized Populations**

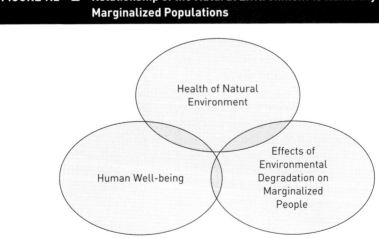

expansive ecological justice that treats the natural world as a major actress, with equal moral standing to humanity, in competing claims for well-being.

Ecological justice not only critiques capitalist goals of pursuing economic growth at the expense of the natural world, but views modern environmental justice movements as ignoring the earth on which any capital is constructed and only nipping at the edges (e.g., saving a reservoir or an endangered species) of the exploitive nature of capitalism and corporate interests (Besthorn, Koenig, Spano, & Warren, 2016; Harvey, 2014; Ife, 2008; Parr, 2013). Photo 7.4 illustrates this idea of an equal, albeit competing, partnership between humanity and the natural world with Milan, Italy's beautiful sky embracing the magnificent Duomo.

Ecological justice encourages social workers to be involved in enriching and sustaining human and non-human quality of life (e.g., decreasing the human population; supporting protections for biodiversity and wilderness areas) and, in turn, not adhering to an increasingly higher standard of living and economic growth for humans (Naess, 1984, 2008). This can be defined as sustainable development and includes qualitative improvement without growth or quantitative increase. For example, human population growth and consumption must be kept in balance with the planet's capacity to manage the loss of and, in turn, regenerate renewable resources such as forests (Daly, 1996).

©Terry Koenig

PHOTO 7.4
The natural world and humanity in equal albeit competing moral standing: Earth's sky and Milan's ancient Duomo, Milan, Italy

The Natural World as a Living Organism: Nature-as-Subject

A deep ecological view also challenges the notion of nature as just one of many systems within the context of humanity and human well-being; instead, it emphasizes nature as an alive, yet fragile, threatened, finite resource that is its own subject and needs to be protected, not simply exploited. Nature-as-subject taps into connections between the natural world and spirituality much more directly, and there are social work practitioners and scholars who understand the whole earth as a living, self-regulating organism (e.g., see writings on green social work, ecofeminism, and indigenous views of nature) (Besthorn & McMillen, 2002; Dominelli, 2012a; Gray, Coates, & Yellow Bird, 2012; King, 1989; Rogge, 2001).

An example from our own indigenous history, which challenges Western views of nature as an object, can be found in Chief Seattle's 1854 reply to the Great White Chief in Washington who made a monetary offer for a large area of Indian land in return for an Indian "reservation" (Smith, 1887). Chief Seattle described the earth, in deep ecological terms, as alive and intimately related to human beings. He stated,

Ever[y] part of this soil is sacred in the estimation of my people. Every hillside, every valley, every plain and grove, has been hallowed by some sad or happy event in days long vanished. Even the rocks, which seem to be dumb and dead as they swelter in the sun along the silent shore, thrill with memories of stirring events connected with the lives of my people, and the very dust upon which you now stand responds more lovingly to their footsteps than yours, because it is rich with the blood of our ancestors, and our bare feet are conscious of the sympathetic touch. (Smith, 1887)

Green Social Work and an Analysis of Power

Scholars have also critiqued environmental approaches to social work stating that they tend to ignore political, economic, and societal power as it impacts natural environments and the individuals and communities that live in these environments. These green, ecofeminist, and eco-critical social workers encourage us to partake in a critical perspective that analyzes the connections between social problems and the unequal distribution of the planet's resources, which unduly affect quality of life for poor and marginalized populations. They insist that we take action to respond to our ecological crises by challenging and addressing poverty (as it is often connected to ecological problems), socioeconomic disparities, corporate practices and responsibilities, limited natural resources, consumption patterns, diverse global contexts, and global interdependencies (Dominelli, 2012a; Rambaree, 2013; Rogge & Combs-Orme, 2003; Ross, 2013).

In order to support the well-being of the planet, social workers are beginning to practice in a holistic manner, securing not only the well-being of people but also animals and plants within the context of human rights and active citizenship. What follows is a discussion of the ecologically oriented roles that social workers currently engage in that reflect both ameliorative and proactive practices. New and future roles for social workers are also examined for their incorporation of deep ecological justice principles into practice.

Social Work Roles: Ameliorative and Proactive

Social work has been increasingly called upon to ameliorate the effects of environmental crises through activities such as addressing hunger and food insecurity, assisting low-income families to manage energy costs, supporting refugees displaced from their homeland due to environmental crises, and managing the health consequences of climate change (Alston, 2007). These activities can be referred to as reactive or tertiary social work practice and typically represent shallow ecology or environmental social work concerns. This is in contrast to more proactive, or positive, social work practices (e.g., working with individuals and families to adapt to new environmental realities, advocating for and making a contribution to wider social and political discussions and decisions, as well as, contributing to the development of sustainable communities) (Dominelli, 2012a). These proactive practices can represent both shallow and deep ecological activities in that the natural world becomes a key participant in any decision-making process. The following Ethics Spotlight examines how the established role of a social worker in a mental health agency might be expanded to address clients' concerns and interactions with the natural world.

ETHICS SPOTLIGHT
MENTAL HEALTH AND COMMUNITY GARDENS

You are a community mental health center social worker working within an urban, poor, African American community. A growing number of clients have expressed their concerns about having to obtain transportation to travel to nearby neighborhoods to obtain groceries because their own community has virtually no grocery stores with fresh produce. You are aware of the positive relationship between physical health and mental health and want to do something to help these clients.

(1) How do you see your role as a social worker in addressing this situation?

   For example, should you get involved in helping to organize your clients and others to develop community gardens? Why or why not?

(2) How might you make a case for the connection between mental health and food deserts with your supervisor and with funders for dedicating time to work on this issue?

(3) Ground your decision in values from the NASW *Code of Ethics* Preamble (i.e., social justice, service, dignity and worth of each person, importance of human relationships, competence, and integrity). Which values apply to this case situation and why?

(4) Is this an example of shallow or deep ecology? Explain your answer.

Current and Future Social Work Roles

In this section, we will examine current and future ecological social work roles (see Table 7.10) that represent ameliorative and also increasingly proactive practices.

TABLE 7.10 ■ Eco-Oriented Social Work Roles and Examples

Eco-Oriented Social Work (SW) Roles	Current (C) or Future (F) Examples
Activist, advocate, and community organizer to hold corporations accountable	Help communities organize to hold firms accountable for consequences of their decisions; use case studies to show how SW can operate at a local level to demand accountability (C & F)
Health care SW practitioner	Work with individuals/families to address effects of industrialization and pollution (e.g., increased rates of cancer, congenital defects) (C)
Developer of micro-renewable energy technologies	Develop demonstration projects tackling issues like fuel poverty and unemployment through creation of electricity for domestic use (C)
Mediator of conflict	Mediate conflicts among newcomers who have migrated in response to deteriorating conditions, established dwellers, and with the nation-state in addressing these conditions (C)

(Continued)

TABLE 7.10 ■ (Continued)	
Eco-Oriented Social Work (SW) Roles	**Current (C) or Future (F) Examples**
Community mobilizer	Help communities become full partners in disaster and preventative plans (C & F); help develop healthy food sources through creation of community gardens (C)
Organizational developer	Engage in action at local, national, international levels and use self-created organizations to advocate equal distribution of resources to protect Earth (F)
Researcher	Demonstrate suffering of poor and marginalized globally, their lack of access to resources, and promote alternative modes of production and consumption (F)
Policy developer and reformer	Help society reorient itself and not focus on technical fixes (e.g., create ecological tax reforms, respond to environmental health challenges, restructure global economy) (F); reform policies related to drought management (C)
Animal rehabilitator	Rehabilitate distressed, injured animals due to ill health of oceans or other natural environments (C)
Clinical practitioner	Help clients heal through therapeutic interactions with nature (e.g., youth offenders) (C)
Educator	Cultivate ecological literacy in SW education and in our communities (C)
Direct service practitioner	In your work with individuals, groups, and families, include assessments that incorporate the interactions between clients and their natural environments (F)

Currently, social workers in health care settings are working with individuals and families to help them address the effects of industrialization and pollution (e.g., due to increased rates of cancer and congenital defects) (Rogge, 2000; Rogge & Combs-Orme, 2003). Social workers have a long-standing history of helping communities deal with the impact of natural disasters, have been nominally active in social policy (e.g., as policy reformers for drought management and in holding corporations accountable for their decisions), and less active in the creation of preventative measures designed to head off disasters (Dominelli, 2012b; Ross, 2013). Social workers have also been involved in mediating conflicts due to environmental degradation (e.g., among newcomers who have migrated in response to these conditions, established dwellers, and the nation-state) (Dominelli, 2012a; Ramon, 2008). Social workers also engage in therapeutic work to help people heal through interactions with nature and in helping animals heal from the impacts of industrialization and pollution on our water, land, and air (Heinsch, 2012; Norton, 2010; Taylor, 2013). Finally, social work educators and practitioners are involved in cultivating ecological literacy in social work education and in promoting this literacy in their communities (Hayward, Miller, & Shaw, 2013; Hudson, 2014; Jones, 2006; Zapf, 2008).

Nearly all of the previously described practices involve social work's ameliorative responses to ecological destruction and other harms. However, social workers are also increasingly engaged in proactive practices including the development of micro-renewable energy technologies to tackle fuel poverty and unemployment, in assisting communities to develop healthy food sources such as through community gardens (Dominelli, 2011, 2012a; Shepard, 2013), and in cultivating ecological literacy in our communities and in social work education (e.g., through deeper awareness of the cycles and processes of nature) (Hudson, 2014; Jones, 2013). Finally, scholars point to future roles that social workers could pursue—for example, using case studies to show how social workers can operate at the local level to demand corporations' accountability; engaging in action at local, national, and international levels to demand equal distribution of resources to protect the planet; researching the suffering of globally poor and marginalized who lack access to resources and promoting alternative modes of production and consumption; and as a policy developer helping society reorient itself through ecological tax reforms and in restructuring the global economy (Dominelli, 2012a, 2013; Pandey, 2010; Pyles, 2007; Stehlik, 2013; Zapf, 2009).

SUMMARY OF SOCIAL WORK AND THE NATURAL ENVIRONMENT

This overview discusses ecological ethics and the elements of deep ecology as a theoretical perspective for its application to social work practice. The authors provide a historical and current examination of professional social work's understanding of and involvement in the natural world at both a shallow level for how the environment impacts humans and at a deeper ecological level in which nature is intrinsically valued and has equal, albeit competing moral standing with humanity. Several case examples are provided that reflect ameliorative but also proactive social work practices as well as potential new roles for social work.

IN-DEPTH CASE EXAMPLE

JUAN AND KETTLEMAN CITY

(Contributed by Dr. Kris Clarke, Professor, University of Helsinki, Faculty of Social Sciences)

Alma, a new social worker in Kings County, California, received a referral to work with the family of Juan, a 12-year-old child living in Kettleman City, who had been chronically truant from school. The child had many unexcused absences and the School Attendance Review Board (SARB) wanted to know if Juan's family had any needs for human services. Alma's task was therefore to assess their situation and connect them with any necessary services that could help support Juan's attendance at school.

Initially, Alma examined the SARB form letter to the parents. It emphasized that poor attendance, even due to chronic health problems and other unavoidable circumstances, had a big impact on school success. She then considered that her first steps would be a psycho-social assessment of Juan with a home visit and perhaps referrals to various community agencies. She therefore set up a time to meet Juan's family and traveled to Kettleman City for the first time.

Kettleman City is so small that it is not a city, not a town, not even a village, but an unincorporated "census-designated place" that lies in the Central Valley of California at the halfway point between San Francisco and Los Angeles.

(Continued)

(Continued)

Approximately 1,500 people live in this place that is hot and dusty in the summer and shrouded in damp Tule or ground fog characteristic of the San Joaquin valley in the winter. You might even miss Kettleman City when driving through California, except that it is often used as a pit stop for travelers looking for a quick hamburger or cup of coffee.

Most of the people who live in Kettleman City are farm laborers. They work in the fields on the west side of the San Joaquin Valley, one of the most fertile agricultural regions in the world. Yet, these farm workers are also among the poorest in the state, with a median yearly income of $22,500. Residents have little access to many of the amenities that most of us take for granted such as shops, grocery stores, gyms, pharmacies, and movie theaters. There are no sidewalks or street lights for people to feel safe walking at night. Roaming and feral dogs are frequently encountered in Kettleman City, which makes parents afraid to let their children out to play. Most social and health care services are a long drive away, and many residents have no cars. The local elementary school is 98% Latino and less than half of students are on grade level in English and math, with especially low scores in history. There is a relatively large proportion of undocumented immigrants residing in the area. In recent years, there has been a marked increase in birth defects in children born in Kettleman City.

Kettleman City faces many environmental challenges. It is located next to a major interstate highway, where hundreds of passing trucks add to the poor air quality. There are five gas stations in the town of 1,500 to serve the busy highway traffic. Gas fumes from these pumps have been identified by the Environmental Protection Agency (EPA) as a possible source of local birth defects. Oil was first discovered in Kettleman City in 1928, and its fields were once some of the most productive in the United States. Drilling continues today, though the resulting collateral contamination of toluene, a colorless liquid known to cause neurological harms, has been identified as having a possible link to birth defects. Residents use drinking water from wells that have elevated

levels of arsenic and benzene, which are known carcinogens. Kettleman City is the site of a massive 1,600-acre hazardous waste dump, one of the largest in the western part of the United States, which trucks in a massive amount of toxic material from Southern California every day. The dump takes asbestos, PBCs, and other dangerous materials and was recently fined by the EPA for improperly disposing of some of the waste. Farm workers labor in fields laced with pesticides that seep into the groundwater. Bad air, unsafe water, and toxic land creates a profoundly unhealthy environment, particularly for the most vulnerable in Kettleman City (California Department of Public Health [CDPH], 2010). Despite the fact that nearly a dozen babies have been born with birth defects in the small town in recent years, it has been difficult to point to single or clear causes because of the small population and many sources of toxic pollution (Leslie, 2010).

Social work is guided by a person-in-environment approach, which requires social workers to take into account the many layers of a person's context in understanding the issue that bring them to the encounter with human services. As we discuss in this chapter, increasingly, social work has come to recognize the need to incorporate a deep green ethics in response to grasping the complexity of human life in conditions of climate change in the 21st century. As Alma quickly realized when mapping out Juan's situation, the role of the natural environment was as important as the social environment.

Alma met with Juan and his family to better understand why he was missing so much school. Juan was one of six children, all of whom struggled with asthma. Both parents worked in the fields but their employment had become more precarious as the region struggled with a drought and limited water supplies for growing. The family lived in dilapidated camp housing within two miles of the school, but they had no car for transportation to travel further, which is especially difficult in an area lacking mass transportation and extreme heat. Finally, Juan's parents were undocumented and were always worried about potentially being picked up by the immigration authorities without warning. Being undocumented has meant that Juan's parents have often tried to avoid contact with various systems out of fear their status would be disclosed. The social worker tried to unpack each of the issues to better understand how they led to excessive school absences.

As the social worker began to ask more about why Juan had not been in school, the struggles he and his siblings have with asthma seemed to be a significant issue. Asthma is triggered for many reasons. The extreme heat of the summer, wood fire, and the car exhaust of winter worsens asthma. It is estimated that 400 trucks pass within four miles of Kettleman City daily, with 100 of them bearing hazardous waste for the dump. This toxic miasma made every day a struggle for the children to breathe and affected how often Juan was able to go to school. He often could not breathe so his mother had him stay home where he could rest with his head elevated. Sometimes Juan was expected to stay home to care for ill younger siblings because his parents could not take a day off of work without substantial financial loss.

Alma's agency provided in-service training that presented research that emphasized when asthma is not properly managed, children are often forced to rely on emergency room interventions, which is very costly to society. Poor management of asthma leads to missed days of children's school, missed days of parents' work, and limitations on children's activities, which impairs children's emotional, intellectual, and physical development. Improperly managed asthma can even lead to premature death. In areas like Kettleman City, childhood rates of asthma are much higher than in other parts of the state while access to care is much worse (CDPH, 2010).

The social worker thought that focusing on getting better medical treatment for Juan could be the key to the solving the chronic absences from school. However, she soon found that Juan's asthma was deeply entwined with many other issues. The undocumented status of Juan's parents, together with their precarious economic existence as farm laborers, had a strong impact on the family's ability to put food on the table and gain access to services. The grinding poverty of farm labor meant that the family was often food insecure and unable to meet many other basic needs, such as paying for gas to go to appointments. Alma learned that farm workers often face abusive practices by growers that include wage theft, job insecurity, and unhealthy working conditions that include a lack of rest breaks and pesticide exposure. The constant fear of deportation meant that Juan's parents were reluctant to participate in school events, seek justice for working conditions, or reach out for human services. The family was often anxious and uncertain about the future.

Finally, Alma considered the physical environment in which Juan lived. There had been a rash of babies born with birth defects in Kettleman City, though investigations could point to no definitive cause. The vast toxic dump took hazardous waste with arsenic, petroleum products, and all kinds of chemical compounds. The diesel fumes from hundreds of trucks that rumbled through the town hung low. With so many sources of pollution, public health officials could not point to a single cause of the ill-being of residents. Alma wondered, how did Kettleman City become entwined in such a toxic stew of pollution, pesticides, and poverty?

To answer this question, she had to consider the historic legacy of region. The San Joaquin Valley, which comprises about 10,000 square miles and lies in Central California and stretches 250 miles from the Sacramento–San Joaquin River Delta to the Tehachapi Mountains north of Los Angeles, was originally inhabited by the Miwok and Yokut tribes, who were hunters and gatherers. Indigenous people caught salmon in the northern part of the Valley and after the Gold Rush of 1848, White Europeans began to encroach on tribal lands, bringing railroads and yeoman cattle farming, which dramatically changed the landscape and economy of the San Joaquin Valley. The Valley was originally an austere open landscape with high grasses and wetlands with most people living in the hills.

(Continued)

(Continued)

As Europeans began to arrive in the mid-1800s, they fundamentally altered the ecology and landscape of the Valley. Early cattle farming gave way to the emergence of agriculture. In a hot and arid region such as the Valley, agriculture required water and early farmers freely diverted the water from rivers into canals. By 1910, nearly all surface water had been diverted, which led to the search for groundwater sources to irrigate the rapidly growing agribusiness industry. By the mid-20th century, a complex system of dams and reservoirs was constructed to support the rapidly growing agricultural industry and expanding population.

A diversity of people including African Americans from the south, Chinese and Japanese laborers, Armenians fleeing the genocide, and Latinos came to work in the emerging agricultural industry. Large ranches and farms tended to be owned by European Americans, so a patchwork of farm towns grew in the Valley often divided by ethnicity. City centers were dominated by European Americans. As sewerage lines, water pipes, and sanitation were developed, these types of infrastructures often bypassed "Mexican towns" or "Black towns" because they were not designated as incorporated areas with their own municipal councils and resources. As years have gone by, a growing gap thus emerged between incorporated areas with infrastructure and unincorporated places with very poor infrastructure. Kettleman City is one such place. Alma thus realized that Juan's situation was deeply related to the historic legacy of racism and oppression in California.

Settler population incursion in the San Joaquin Valley since the 19th century fundamentally altered the biodiversity of the environment. Since the start of the Gold Rush in 1849, water has been diverted in California as miners built flumes and waterways in search of gold. As the agricultural industry grew, vast tracts of land were plowed under, which displaced wildlife and decimated much of the pristine natural environment. Tulare Lake, the largest lake west of the Mississippi, once dominated the

San Joaquin Valley and lay just some miles due east of Kettleman City. The Tachi tribe had lived on the banks of Tulare Lake for centuries in high densities along with abundant fish and fowl. Four major rivers (the Kings, Kaweah, Tule, and Kern) fed into Tulare Lake, which was 4.5 times larger than Lake Tahoe and even bigger than the Great Salt Lake. The unending thirst of agriculture for irrigation meant that dams, embankments, and canals diverted much of the flow of the rivers, and early farmers drained marshlands surrounding Tulare Lake. These actions resulted in rendering Tulare Lake dry by the 20th century. Lost was not only the profuse complexity of biodiversity of plant and animal life, but the sustainable practices of Indigenous peoples who lived in harmony with their environment were destroyed as settlers competed for water rights and farmland. The belief in placing personal profit above the rights of nature and community interests thus became solidified in the region.

As Alma began to see the links among the many different issues that led to Juan's school absences, she made some notes to try to map out Juan's situation (see Figure 7.3): Frustrated with the systemic nature of social and environmental oppression in Kettleman City, Alma wondered what she could do as a social worker beyond direct services, which seemed inadequate for Juan's situation and largely inaccessible to the family. She heard about an environmental justice group in the San Joaquin Valley, so she attended a meeting and learned that there were many community groups working on a variety of issues throughout the Valley, from water and air quality to zoning and land use. At the meeting, Alma saw that many of the skills that she had learned in her graduate social work courses, such as community organizing and policy development, could be utilized to help develop the capacity of the group to have an impact on the local natural environment.

Someone in the group suggested that Alma come with one of the organizers to visit an elementary school in Fresno, a city 60 miles north of

FIGURE 7.3   ■   An Environmental Map of Juan and Kettleman City

National Park Service

PHOTO 7.5
San Joaquin Valley air pollution

Kettleman City. Fresno schools fly a flag each day that follows the color coding of the EPA air quality index. On a red day, for example, outside activities are restricted. At the behest of the elementary school nurse who treated nearly 25% of the school students with asthma, an after-school meeting of parents, school officials, and environmental justice activists had assembled to advocate for a healthier school. They met two days a month after school to map out the intertwined social and environmental challenges that pupils at the school faced. The school group identified issues such as the trucking plant next door to the school, the use of leaf blowers by janitorial staff during school hours, as well as the substandard housing of impoverished families, which was often infused with mold, dust mites, and secondhand smoke that were triggers for students' asthma. They prioritized issues and defined next steps to tackle school, city, and state policies that allowed practices that harmed the natural environment and produced a toxic situation for students.

Alma returned to Kings County and realized that she had to go beyond her work with the county and engage with local environmental justice groups to make real change that would benefit clients like Juan.

Discussion Questions

1. Describe the environmental issues in Kettleman City.

2. How do these environmental issues interact with the people of Kettleman City and in particular the health of Juan?

3. What are the likely impacts of historical trauma on both human and natural environments (e.g., biodiversity and water) for Kettleman City's current situation?

4. Reflect on the plan and actions that Alma decided to take in relationship to this case. Based on concepts used in this chapter

(Continued)

(Continued)

(e.g., light green and deep green ethics, sustainability), discuss Alma's current actions and explore other potential actions she could take as a social worker.

5. Think more broadly. How do natural environments intertwine with ethical and direct social work practice issues in your locality?

6. What are some of the steps that social workers could take to draw attention to environmental conditions that impact poor and marginalized people in your geographic region (light green ethics or shallow ecology)?

7. What actions could you as a social worker take to place attention on the health of the natural world in your locality (e.g., deep ecology)? And, how might you make a case with your agency for doing this?

8. What can we do to prepare social workers for the social impacts of degradation of the natural environments in which we work?

CHAPTER SUMMARY

This chapter has provided an overview to help you explore the fundamental theoretical foundations currently available in understanding the natural environment. It has provided a rationale for the involvement of social work and issues related to preserving and protecting the natural environment. It has tracked the evolution of social work's relationship to the natural environment in various historical contexts. This chapter has also critiqued the concept of deep ecology as it relates to our understanding of human behavior. And, finally, it provides a series of case examples to help you understand the challenges facing social workers as we move forward in a world where the natural environment is under great stress.

There are certain central themes that can be found in each of the elements of this chapter. First, from its inception, social workers have sought to connect their understanding of human behavior to various aspects of the environments in which those behaviors take place. This person-in-environment provides social workers a more complex and nuanced understanding of human behavior. Second, social work has drawn on the ideas in the larger historical context to inform its understanding of the relationship between people and their environments. For example, the AICP was created at a moment in time when individual moralistic theologies were dominant. Therefore, social work utilized those ideas and values to explain the behavior particularly of the poor. Later, the charity organization societies drew from both the emerging social sciences and the emergence of theologies that valued social change to alter prior understandings of human behavior. Third, as we tracked this history, social work relied on what we have characterized as a "shallow ecological approach," which emphasized the utilization of the natural environment for human well-being. Not until the 1980s was there an infusion of what has now been called "deep ecology," which acknowledges the importance and the rights of the natural environment to be protected on its own merits. Fourth, the chapter suggests we are entering into a new era where we must rethink our impact on nature and how our current practices are doing what may be irreparable harm to the environment. The consequences of this stance toward the environment requires we focus on issues of global warming, air pollution, the availability of potable water, and the disposal of toxic waste as examples of issues that fall disproportionately on the poor and other marginalized groups of people, thus raising fundamental issues related to our responsibility to promote social, environmental, and ecological justice on behalf of our clients.

Classroom Exercises

1. Arrange yourselves in small groups of 4 or 5 students. Take a case situation, current or past, from your practice or practicum, that you believe has some elements of the natural or constructed environment that are relevant to the situation. For example, you may have worked with some clients whose living conditions were compromised by a lack of food, water, and clean air or contained chemical toxins. Review what you did in that situation in the light of the potential for "light green" or "dark green" strategies you now see as important for your practice as a social worker.

2. For one week, look at sources where you get your news [newspapers, television coverage, online news sources (e.g., news aggregators that synthesize syndicated articles such as *Huffington Post* or *Reddit*)]. Choose any article that focuses on environmental issues that impact a "marginalized group" as defined in the NASW *Code of Ethics*. Discuss how you might use your social work skills to assess, develop helping strategies, and evaluate the results in this situation with a focus on the realization of social and ecological justice.

Key Terms (in order of appearance)

Ecological social work   168
Anthropocentric   168
Environmental ethics   170
Light green ethics   170

Mid-green ethics   171
Deep green ethics   172
Ecofeminist   173
Deep ecology   173

Environmental
    social work   196

References

Addams, J. (1910). *Twenty years at Hull-House*. New York, NY: Macmillan Press.

Alston, M. (2007). Globalisation, rural restructuring and health service delivery in Australia: Policy failure and the role of social work? *Health & Social Care in the Community, 15*, 195–202.

Badger, A. J. (1989). *The New Deal: Depression years 1933–1940*. New York, NY: Noonday Press.

Berger, R., & Kelly, J. (1993). Social work in the ecological crisis. *Social Work, 38*, 521–526.

Bertalanffy, L.V. (1950). The theory of open systems in physics and biology. *Science, 3*, 23–29.

Bertalanffy, L. V. (1967). General systems theory. In N. Demerath & R. A. Peterson (Eds.), *Systems change and conflict* (pp. 119–129). New York, NY: Free Press.

Besthorn, F. H. (1997). *Reconceptualizing social work's person-in-environment perspective: Explorations in radical environmental thought* (Unpublished doctoral dissertation). University of Kansas, Lawrence, KS.

Besthorn, F. H. (2012). Deep Ecology's contributions to social work: A ten year retrospective. *International Journal of Social Welfare, 21*, 248–259.

Besthorn, F. H. (2013). Radical equalitarian ecological justice: A social work call to action In M. Gray, J. Coates, & T. Hetherington (Eds.), *Environmental social work* (pp. 31–45). London: Routledge.

Besthorn, F. H., & Canda, E. R. (2002). Revisioning environment: Deep ecology for education and teaching in social work. *Journal of Teaching in Social Work, 22*, 79–101.

Besthorn, F. H., Koenig, T. L., Spano, R., & Warren, S. L. (2016). A critical analysis of social and environmental justice: Reorienting social work to an ethic of ecological justice (pp. 146–163). In R. Hugman & J. Carter (Eds.), *Rethinking values and ethics in social work*. London, England: Palgrave-Macmillan.

Besthorn, F. H., & McMillen, D. P. (2002). The oppression of women and nature: Ecofeminism as a framework for an expanded ecological social work. *Families in Society, 83*, 221–232.

Bodian, S. (1995). Simple in means, rich in ends: An interview with Arne Naess. In G. Sessions (Ed.), *Deep Ecology for the 21st century: Readings on the philosophy and practice of the new environmentalism* (pp. 26–36). Boston, MA: Shambhala.

Bouma-Prediger, S. (2010). *For beauty of the Earth*. Grand Rapids, MI: Baker.

Bremner, R. H. (1966). *From the depths: The discovery of poverty in the United States*. New York, NY: New York University Press.

Bruno, F. J. (1948). *Trends in social work as reflected in the Proceedings of the National Conference of Social Work 1874–1946*. New York, NY: Columbia University Press.

Bunche, J. (1954). *Social welfare – A world concept*. Proceedings of the National Conference of Social Work. New York, NY: Columbia University Press.

Butler, T. (Ed.). (2015). *Overdevelopment, overpopulation, overshoot*. San Francisco, CA: Foundation for Deep Ecology.

California Department of Public Health (CDPH). (2010, November). Investigation of birth defects and community exposures in Kettleman City, CA. Retrieved from: https://www.cdph .ca.gov/Programs/CCDPHP/DEODC/EHIB/ EES/CDPH%20Document%20Library/FINAL_ KettlemanDraftReportFactsheet_English_ADA .pdf#search=Kettleman%20City%20Repor

Carson, R. (1962). *Silent spring*. Boston, MA: Houghton Mifflin.

Casey, N. (2016, July 7). Climate change changes a lake, and an identity. *New York Times*.

Chambers, C. A. (1963). *Seedtime of reform: American social service and social action 1918–1933*. Minneapolis: University of Minnesota Press.

Coates, J. (2003). *Ecology and social work: Toward a new paradigm*. Halifax, Nova Scotia: Fernwood Publishing.

Council on Social Work Education (CSWE). (2015). *Educational policy and accreditation standards*. Alexandria, VA: Author.

Curry, P. (2011). *Ecological ethics: An introduction* (2nd ed.). Cambridge, UK: Polity Press.

Daly, H. E. (1996). *Beyond growth*. Boston, MA: Beacon Press.

de Steiguer, J. E. (2006). *The origins of modern environmental thought*. Tempe: University of Arizona Press.

Degler, C. N. (1970). *New Deal*. Chicago, IL: Quandrangle Books.

Delio, I. (2003). *A Franciscan view of creation: Learning to live in a sacramental world*. St. Bonaventure, NY: The Franciscan Institute.

Diamond, J. (2005). *Collapse: How societies choose to fail or succeed*. New York, NY: Penguin Group.

Dominelli, L. (2011). Climate change: Social workers' roles and contributions to policy debates and interventions. *International Journal of Social Welfare, 20*, 430–438.

Dominelli, L. (2012a). *Green social work: From environmental crises to environmental justice.* Cambridge, MA: Polity Press.

Dominelli, L. (2012b). Social work in times of disaster: Practicing across borders. In M. Kearnes, F. Klauser, & S. Lane (Eds.), *Critical risk research: Practices, politics and ethics* (pp. 197–218). Oxford: Wiley-Blackwell Publishers.

Dominelli, L. (2013). Social work education for disaster relief work. In M. Gray, J. Coates, & T. Hetherington (Eds.), *Environmental social work* (pp. 280–297). New York, NY: Routledge.

Earl, S. (2009). The world is blue: How our fate and the ocean's are one. *National Geographic Society.* Washington, DC.

Ehrenreich, J. H. (1985). *Altruistic imagination: A history of social work and social policy in the United States.* Ithaca, NY: Cornell University Press.

Emerson, R. W. (2010). *Nature.* New York, NY: American Renaissance Books.

Germain, C. (1981). The physical environment and social work. In A. N. Maluccio (Ed.), *Promoting competence in clients: A new/old approach to social work practice* (pp. 103–124). New York, NY: Free Press.

Gitterman, A. (2011). Advances in the Life Model of social work practice. In F. J. Turner (Ed.), *Social work treatment: Interlocking theoretical approaches* (5th ed.). (pp. 279-292). New York, NY: Oxford University Press.

Gitterman, A., & Germain, C. B. (2008). *The Life Model of social work practice: Advancements in theory and practice* (3rd ed.). NY: Columbia University Press.

Goldstein, H. (1973). *Social work practice: A unitary approach.* Columbia: University of South Carolina Press.

Goldston, R. (1968). *The Great Depression: The United States in the Thirties.* Greenwich, CN: Fawcet.

Gordon, W. E. (1965). Toward a social work frame of reference. *Journal of Education for Social Work, 1,* pp. 19–26.

Gray, M., Coates, J., & Hetherington, T. (Eds.). (2013). *Environmental social work.* New York, NY: Routledge.

Gray, M., Coates, J., & Yellow Bird, M. (Eds.). (2012). *Indigenous social work from around the world: Towards culturally relevant education and practice.* Burlington, VT: Ashgate.

Hamayon, R. N. (1999). Shamanism in Siberia: From partnership in supernature to counter-power in society. In N. Thomas & C. Humphrey (Eds.), *Shamanism, history and the state* (pp. 76–89). Ann Arbor: The University of Michigan Press.

Harvey, D. (2014). *Seventeen contradictions and the end of capitalism.* New York, NY: Oxford University Press.

Hauser, P. M. (1956). *Demography and human ecology in relation to social work.* Proceedings of the National Conference of Social Work. New York, NY: Columbia University Press.

Hayward, R. A., Miller, S. E., & Shaw, T. V. (2013). Social work education on the environment in contemporary curricula in the USA. In M. Gray, J. Coates, & T. Hetherington (Eds.), *Environmental social work* (pp. 246–259). New York, NY: Routledge.

Hearn, G. (1969). *The general systems approach: Contributions toward an holistic conception of social work.* New York, NY: Council on Social Work Education.

Heinsch, M. (2012). Getting down to earth: Finding a place for nature in social work practice. *International Journal of Social Welfare, 21,* 309–318.

Hoff, M., & McNutt, J. G. (Eds.). (1994). *The global environmental crisis: Implications for social welfare and social work.* Brookfield, VT: Ashgate Publishing.

Hofstadter, R. (1955). *The age of reform.* New York, NY: Vintage Books.

Holt, M. I. (1992). *The orphan trains: Placing out in America.* Lincoln: University of Nebraska Press.

Hudson, J. (2014). *The natural environment in social work education* (Unpublished doctoral dissertation). Lawrence: University of Kansas.

Ife, J. (2008). *Human rights and social work: Towards rights-based practice.* Cambridge, MA: Cambridge University Press.

Ives, M. (2016, July 2). A remote Pacific nation, threatened by rising seas. New York Times.

Jackson, W. (1994). *Becoming native to this place*. Berkeley, CA: Counterpoint.

Jones, P. (2006). Considering the environment in social work education: Transformations for eco-social justice. *Australian Journal of Adult Learning, 46*, 364–382.

Jones, P. (2013). Transforming the curriculum: Social work education and ecological consciousness. In M. Gray, J. Coates, & T. Hetherington (Eds.), *Environmental social work* (pp. 213–230). London and New York, NY: Routledge.

Karl, T. R., Melillo, J. M., & Peterson, T. C. (Eds.). (2009). *Global climate change impacts in the United States*. Cambridge, MA: Cambridge University Press.

Kellogg, P. U. (Ed.). (1909–1914). *The Pittsburgh Survey* (Vols. *1–6*). New York, NY: Russell Sage Foundation.

King, Y. (1989). The ecology of feminism and the feminism of ecology. In J. Plant (Ed.), *Healing the wounds: The promise of ecofeminism* (pp. 18–28). Philadelphia, PA: New Society Publishers.

Koenig, T. L., & Spano, R. N. (1998). Taoism and the strengths perspective. *Social Thought, 18*, 47–65.

Landsberg, J., & Warring, R. (2014). *Forests in our changing world: New principles for conservation and management*. Washington, DC: Island Press.

Leuchtenburg, W. W. (1963). *Franklin D. Roosevelt and the New Deal, 1932-1940*. New York, NY: Harper and Row.

Leiby, J. (1978). *The history of American social welfare and social work in the United States*. New York, NY: Columbia University Press.

Leopold, A. (1949). *A Sand County almanac*. New York, NY: Oxford University Press.

Leslie, J. (2010, July/August). What's killing the babies of Kettleman City? *Mother Jones*. Retrieved from https://www.motherjones.com/environment/2010/09/kettleman-city-toxic-birth-defect-cluster/

Marcotty, J. (2017, December 20). State predicts PolyMet would need $1B from copper-nickel mines. *Star Tribune*.

McKibben, B. (2011). *Eaarth: Making a life on a tough new planet*. New York, NY: Times Books.

Meyer, C. H. (1976). *Social work practice* (2nd ed.). New York, NY: Free Press.

Naess, A. (1973). The shallow and the deep, long-range ecology movement: A summary. *Inquiry, 16*(2), 95–100.

Naess, A. (1984). A defence of the deep ecology movement. *Environmental Ethics, 6*, 265–270.

Naess, A. (1995). Deepness of questions and the Deep Ecology movement. In G. Sessions (Ed.), *Deep Ecology for the 21st century: Readings on the philosophy and practice of the new environmentalism* (pp. 204–212). Boston, MA: Shambhala.

Naess, A. (2008). The basics of the deep ecology movement. In A. Drengson & B. Devall (Eds.), *The ecology of wisdom* (pp. 105–119). Emeryville, CA: Counterpoint Press.

National Academy of Sciences. (2015). *Climate intervention: Carbon dioxide removal and reliable sequestration*. Washington, DC: National Academies Press.

National Association of Social Workers (NASW). (2017). *Code of ethics*. Washington, DC: Author.

Norton, C. L. (2010). Exploring the process of wilderness therapy: Key therapeutic components in the treatment of adolescent depression and psychosocial development. *Journal of Therapeutic School and Programs, 4*(1), 24–46.

NRSV. (2001). *Bible*. Cleveland, OH: World Publishing.

Orr, D. (1992). *Ecological literacy: Education and the transition to a postmodern world*. Albany: State University of New York Press.

Pandey, A. (2010). Greening Garhwal through stakeholder engagement: The role of ecofeminism, community, and the state in sustainable development. *Sustainable Development, 18*(1), 12–19.

Parr, A. (2013). *The wrath of capital: Neoliberalism and climate change politics*. New York, NY: Columbia University Press.

Parrington, V. L. (1957). A romantic revolution in America, 1800-1860 (Vol. *2*). In V. L. Parrington (Ed.), *Main currents in American thought* (pp. 386–414). Norman, OK: University of Oklahoma Press.

Penton, K. (1993). Ideology, social work, and the Gaian connection. *Australian Social Work, 46*(4), 41–48.

Pincus, A., & Minahan, A. (1973). *Social work practice: Model and method*. Itasca, IL: Peacock Publisher.

Popple, P. R., & Leighninger, L. H. (1990). *Social work, social welfare and American society*. Boston, MA: Allyn & Bacon.

Pyles, L. (2007). Community organizing for post-disaster social development: Locating social work. *International Social Work, 50*, 321–333.

Rambaree, K. (2013). Social work and sustainable development: Local voices from Mauritius. *Australian Social Work, 66*, 261–276.

Ramon, S. (Ed.). (2008). *Social work in the context of political conflict*. Birmingham, UK: Venture Press.

Roberts, R. W., & Nee, R. H. (1970). *Theories of social casework*. Chicago, IL: University of Chicago Press.

Rogge, M. (2000). Children, poverty and environmental degradation: Protecting current and future generations. *Social Development Issues, 22*(2/3), 46–53.

Rogge, M. (2001). Social development and the ecological tradition. *Social Development Issues, 23*(1), 32–41.

Rogge, M., & Combs-Orme, T. (2003). Protecting our future: Children, environmental policy, and social work. *Social Work, 48*, 439–450.

Rolston, H. (1988). *Environmental ethics: Duties and values in the natural world*. Philadelphia, PA: Temple University Press.

Ross, D. (2013). Social work and the struggle for corporate social responsibility. In M. Gray, J. Coates, & T. Hetherington (Eds.), *Environmental social work* (pp. 193–209). New York, NY: Routledge.

Schlesinger, A., Jr. (1959). *The age of Roosevelt: Coming of the New Deal*. Boston, MA: Houghton Mifflin.

Sessions, G. (1995). *Deep Ecology for the 21st century: Readings on the philosophy and practice of the new environmentalism*. Boston, MA: Shambhala.

Shepard, B. (2013). Community gardens, creative community organizing, and environmental activism. In M. Gray, J. Coates, & T. Hetherington (Eds.), *Environmental social work* (pp. 121–134). New York, NY: Routledge.

Singer, P. (1975). *Animal liberation: The definitive classic of the animal movement*. New York, NY: HarperCollins.

Smith, H. (1887, October 29). *Chief Seattle's treaty oration*. Seattle, WA: Seattle Sunday Star.

Soine, L. (1987). Expanding the environment in social work: The case for including environmental hazards content. *Journal of Social Work Education, 23*(2), 40–46.

Spano, R. (1982). *The Rank and File Movement in social work*. Washington, DC: University Press of America.

Spano, R., & Koenig, T. L. (in press). Social work ethics. In S. Kapp (Ed.), *Introduction to social work*. Thousand Oaks, CA: Sage.

Spano, R., & Koenig, T., Hudson, J. W., & Leiste, M. R. (2010). East meets west: A non-linear model for understanding human growth and development. *Smith College Studies in Social Work, 80*, 198–214.

Stehlik, D. (2013). Social work practice with drought affected families: An Australian case study. In M. Gray, J. Coates, & T. Hetherington (Eds.), *Environmental social work* (pp. 135–155). New York, NY: Routledge.

Taylor, S. A. (2013). Social science research in ocean environments: A social worker's experience. In M. Gray, J. Coates, & T. Hetherington (Eds.), *Environmental social work* (pp. 88–101). New York, NY: Routledge.

Thoreau, H. D. (1854). *Walden*. New York, NY: Simon & Brown.

Thoreau, H. D. (1995). *Walden*, (2nd ed.; C. W. Bigsby, Trans.). Appleton, WI: Tuttle.

Weick, A. (1981). Reframing the person-in-environment perspective. *Social Work, 26*, 140–143.

Wiebe, R. H. (1967). *The search for order 1877–1920*. New York, NY: Hill and Wang.

Wilson, E. O. (2017). *Half earth: Our planet's fight for life*. New York, NY: Liveright.

Zapf, M. (2005). The spiritual dimension of person and environment: Perspectives from social work and traditional knowledge. *International Social Work, 48*, 633–642.

Zapf, M. (2008). Transforming social work's understanding of person and environment: Spirituality and the 'common ground.' *Journal of Religion & Spirituality in Social Work*, *27*, 171–181.

Zapf, M. (2009). *Social work and the environment. Understanding people and place*. Toronto, ON: Canadian Scholars Press.

8

LIFE SPAN THEORIES, FAMILY LIFE COURSE PERSPECTIVES, AND HISTORICAL TRAUMA

©Terry Koenig

PHOTO 8.1
The life cycle from birth to death: Well of life, Zagreb, Croatia

CASE EXAMPLE
MICHAELA'S EXPLORATION

You are a social worker who works in a veterans' outpatient mental health clinic. One of your clients, Johanna, is a mother of multiracial descent (i.e., White, Native American, and African American). Johanna is worried about her daughter, Michaela, age 16, and has asked that you meet with her. In your first session with Michaela, who identifies herself as African American, it becomes clear to you that she is articulate and very bright. She admits to using drugs, struggling to develop friendships in school, and being lost and unmotivated. Over the next few sessions and as you develop a more meaningful relationship with Michaela, she indicates that her father, who is African American, left when she was 6 years old and Michaela has not seen him since this

time. You wonder if Michaela might benefit from exploring the relationship with her father and if possible, even reconnecting with him. What might help Michaela to feel less lost, more grounded, and able to develop a deeper sense of self?

(1) What stage of life span theory (e.g., Erikson's eight stages) might be applicable to this case situation?

(2) How does life span theory influence what you might do in your work with Michaela and her mom?

(3) What might be the shortcomings of using life span theory to address gender, race, ethnicity, and oppression?

In this case example, Michaela can be characterized as representing Erikson's pivotal fifth stage, which reflects the crisis or conflict of *Identity vs. Role Confusion*. Michaela appears to be struggling to develop her own individual identity. If she can obtain knowledge about herself through interactions with others and perhaps even her father, she may be able to more easily forge a strong sense of self. Life span theories, however, are largely silent about the influences of gender, race and ethnicity, historical oppression, and other characteristics such as sexual orientation and gender expression on identity development. Numerous scholars have developed avenues from Erikson to better account for diversity in individual growth and development (Cross, 1971, 1991; Helms, 1995; Root, 1996).

OVERVIEW OF LIFE SPAN THEORIES

Life span theories are a centerpiece in social work education and featured prominently in human behavior and the social environment (HBSE) courses and on social work licensing examinations. Frequently and despite their limitations in addressing diverse pathways to growth and development, **life span theories** are understood to represent "normal" human growth and development and are thereby viewed as readily applicable to social work practice (Apgar, 2016; Ashford & Lecroy, 2013; Carter, Preto, & McGoldrick, 2015; Hutchison, 2015; Robbins, Chatterjee, & Canda, 2011;

Rogers, 2016; Zastrow & Kirst-Ashman, 2016). For the purposes of this overview, a life span approach to human development as described by Erikson will be delineated, and then, other scholarly writings (i.e., life course perspectives, emerging adulthood as a distinct developmental stage, and racial identity theories) will be showcased for their diversion, expansion, or critique of Erikson's work.

A life span approach to human growth and development originated in the 1950s with the work of Erik H. Erikson (1950, 1963) in his development of the eight stages of man [sic]. Although influenced by Freud, Erikson emphasized the role of the ego in shaping human development (in contrast to the influences of the id, the unconscious, and other psychodynamic processes as described by Freud in Chapter 5). Erikson was also one of the first scholars to put forth the idea of physical and psychological developmental stages as occurring throughout adulthood and in adaptation to the larger social environment.

According to Erikson, each developmental stage is defined by a crisis or conflict in which the ego assists the individual in attaining a balance between two opposing basic attitudes or personality traits such as *Industry vs. Inferiority*. These two basic attitudes are defined by Erikson as (1) ego "syntonic," representing behaviors, values, and feelings in harmony with the needs and goals of the ego, and (2) ego "dystonic," referring to behaviors, values, and feelings seen as distressing or unacceptable to the needs and goals of the ego. At each stage of development, healthy resolution of the crisis or turning point involves a balance toward the syntonic or integrative quality

PHOTO 8.2
These horseshoe arches are like cascading life stages: Mosque in Cordoba, Spain

©Terry Koenig

while maintaining some of the dystonic tendency (see Photo 8.2). The resolution of each crisis further leads to the development of ego qualities described as virtues or strengths (e.g., hope, competence, freely pledged loyalties, love, or devotion to others).

Erikson understood personality development to be epigenetic, that is, arising from a genetic blueprint in which all stages are dependent on one another; unfold in a linear, prescribed order; and exist in some form before their critical time or ascendency (Erikson, 1950, 1963; Smelser & Erikson, 1980). Originally, Erikson delineated eight stages of growth and development (see Table 8.1). What follows is a brief description of each stage.

TABLE 8.1 ■ Erikson's Original Eight Stages of Human Development			
Stage	**Age**	**Conflict or Crisis**	**Syntonic Ego Quality**
1	Birth to 1 year	Basic Trust vs. Mistrust	Hope that wishes can be fulfilled
2	2 to 3 years	Autonomy vs. Shame and Doubt	Willpower or capacity to freely make decisions
3	3 to 5 years	Initiative vs. Guilt	Purpose or capacity to reach goals
4	6 to 12 years	Industry vs. Inferiority	Competence
5	12 to 18 years or so	Identity vs. Role Confusion	Fidelity or freely pledged loyalties
6	Early to late 20s	Intimacy vs. Isolation	Love or devotion to others
7	Late 20s to 50	Generativity vs. Stagnation	Care for others
8	After 50	Integrity vs. Despair	Wisdom

Stage 1, Basic Trust vs. Mistrust (Birth to 1 Year)

Through swallowing and sucking, the child "takes in" nourishment and is dependent on the mother for food and care. As the child grows and becomes more active, the child is able to bite or "hold onto" objects. If the mother meets the child's needs with consistency, basic trust will develop that includes the child's self-trust or inner certainty of being able to cope with urges. Successful resolution of this stage leads to a lasting ego quality of hope that wishes can be fulfilled. Unsuccessful resolution leads to a sense of mistrust in oneself and others.

Stage 2, Autonomy vs. Shame and Doubt (Age 2–3 Years)

The child learns to hold on and let go through retention and elimination of feces and urine. If successfully resolved, the child experiences "self-control without loss of self esteem" (Erikson, 1950, p. 70) and develops the ego quality of willpower or the capacity to freely make decisions. If not resolved, the child experiences long-lasting feelings of shame and doubt.

Stage 3, Initiative vs. Guilt (Age 3–5 Years)

Children master language and locomotion skills and are ready to take initiative in their learning and behavior. During this time, the Oedipal wishes for the opposite-sex parent must be repressed to avoid guilt. Parents can encourage the child to participate in acceptable activities (to divert the sex drive). At this point, the superego or conscience is developed that places moral boundaries on initiative. Successful resolution of this stage leads to the ego quality of purpose or the capacity to pursue goals. Unsuccessful resolution leads to feelings of shame.

Stage 4, Industry vs. Inferiority (Age 6–12 Years)

The child enters school and learns to win recognition from others by creating things. If successful, the child develops a sense of industry and the ego quality of competence. If not successful, the child experiences a sense of inferiority and inadequacy.

Stage 5, Identity vs. Role Confusion (Age 12–18 or So)

This stage is characterized by rapid physical growth. Adolescence begins and childhood ends. At this stage, adolescents engage in efforts to integrate views of self with how others view them and strive to obtain self-knowledge through relationships with others. If this stage is successfully resolved, a strong individual identity is forged, the adolescent engages in new and meaningful societal roles, and he or she gains a lasting ego quality of fidelity or freely pledged loyalties. Unsuccessful resolution of this stage results in role confusion or identity diffusion in which the individual is left with strong doubts about self-identity.

Stage 6, Intimacy vs. Isolation (Early to Late 20s)

In this stage, a young adult emerges from the search and development of ego identity eager and ready for interpersonal relationships encompassing psychological and sexual intimacy. Failure to achieve intimacy leads to a deep sense of isolation, the avoidance of intimate contacts, and self-absorption. Successful resolution leads to the lasting ego quality of love or devotion to others.

Stage 7, Generativity vs. Stagnation (Late 20s to 50)

Erikson viewed this stage as key because it leads to mature "genitality," procreation, and the individual's concern for establishing and guiding the next generation. When people fail to be creative, invest in the next generation, and move beyond self-interest, a sense of stagnation and personal impoverishment takes place. Successful resolution of this stage leads to a lasting ego quality of care for others.

Stage 8, Integrity vs. Despair (After 50)

Each individual, to become a mature adult, must to a sufficient degree develop all the previously mentioned ego qualities to reach the final stage of ego integrity. Ego integrity is defined as an acceptance of past choices and one's particular life cycle. Unsuccessful resolution of this stage leads to despair and a fear of death. If successfully resolved, the individual develops the ego quality of wisdom.

Although Erikson's first five stages are closely tied to Freud, Erikson shifted emphasis from the instincts of the id, and the primary role of childhood in shaping adult functioning and personality, to the reality orientation of the conflict-free ego. With focus on the ego rather than the id and unconscious processes, Erikson emphasized the ability of the individual to achieve mastery in each stage. In his later writings, Erikson modified his life span theory to include religious development (e.g., the impact of deeply held religious views on an individual's development). (See Erikson's 1962 and 1969 biographical analyses of Luther and Gandhi, respectively.) Erickson's wife, Joan M. Erikson, extended the original life span theory to include a ninth stage (Erikson & Erikson, 1997).

This ninth stage of lifespan development incorporates all previous stages and acknowledges that elders face greater challenges than in earlier stages at developing an integrative personality. The concept of gerotranscendence, understood as a greater delineation of the ego quality of wisdom, is used to augment Erikson's final stage of *Ego Integrity versus*

Despair. Gerotranscendence is viewed in a nonreligious sense as a natural part of the aging process whereby some people may transcend any developmental crises (Erikson & Erikson, 1997; Tornstam, 1989, 2005).

ADVANCES BEYOND ERIKSON

Life Course Perspectives

In the 1960s, scholars began to examine historical or broader societal events such as immigration from Europe to the United States and wartime experiences (e.g., combat in WWII) for their impact on individuals' growth and development (Neugarten, 1996; Stouffer, Suchman, DeVinney, Star, & Williams, 1949; Thomas & Znaniecki, 1918–1920). These scholars developed advances in methods for studying people over the course of their lives (e.g., people born at the same time [birth cohort] or in relationship to events and transitions such as health and illness) (Butz & Torrey, 2006).

Life course writings, distinct from life span theory in their emphasis on variations over the life course and in relationship to cohorts and historical context (Elder & Giele, 2009), reflect a new paradigm linking social change, social structures, and individual behavior (Elder, 1998; Giele, 1995). **Life course perspectives** address four core elements that move beyond distinct stages of development and instead cut across the full span of a person's life. The four elements are: historical and geographical location, social embeddedness, agency and personal control, and timing (Elder & Giele, 2009). Historical and geographic context refers to the idea that people born in a specific year are members of a birth cohort with a particular historical experience and range of life opportunities that depend on geographic location (e.g., the historical and regional background of early feminist leaders set them apart from others born in a different region and time period). Social embeddedness examines how lives change as intergenerational relationships and social roles change (e.g., from the birth of children, to their departure, and their own childbearing, which is referred to as a family life cycle) (Hill & Foote, 1970) or how a new heterosexual marriage often leads to turnover in the husband's friends (Wellman, Wong, Tindall, & Nazer, 1997). Agency and personal control refers to the process by which people plan and make choices to control their lives. This element of individual choice and planning is balanced by the reality that people live within a particular historical and geographic social context that can constrain their decision making. Timing refers to when events or transitions occur (e.g., whether early or late relative to other people or normative expectations); and the impact of historical events on the life course that may continue over several generations (Hareven, 2000). As noted by these four themes, life course theories are distinguished from life span theories in their emphases on human development as understood within a broader historical, social, and cultural context.

Emerging Adulthood as a Distinct Developmental Stage

Emerging adulthood is understood as a new conception or stage of human development for the period from late teens through the early 20s, with a focus on ages 18–25 (Arnett, 2000, 2004, 2007). Although Erikson (1968) described a kind of prolonged adolescence in which people were given a *psychosocial moratorium* to freely experiment without stepping into normative adult roles, he did not view this phenomena as a separate developmental stage. However, scholars are now increasingly viewing emerging adulthood as a stage of development involving individuals' exploration regarding work, love, and worldviews; as distinct from adolescence and young adulthood; and as likely existing for majority populations who are middle class and above and who live in industrialized cultures. These characteristics contribute to and provide young adults the opportunity to pursue a prolonged period of independent role exploration.

Emerging adulthood is punctuated by individuals' relative freedom from taking on prescribed roles, by diversity in residential status (e.g., living at home with parents for periods of time, living with a romantic partner, or living in a college dorm), as well as varied pathways for post-secondary education (e.g., going to school, taking off from school to pursue employment, and engaging in graduate work). When interviewed, American people in this age period view themselves in some ways as adults and in other ways not as adults (Arnett, 2001). This newly identified period has, in part, emerged due to sweeping demographic shifts over the past 50 years, including later marriages (if at all), later age of first childbirth, and steep increases in the proportion of young people in myriad countries obtaining an education. Consequently, it is no longer normative for young adulthood to be a time of entering and settling into long-term adult roles and instead this stage of emerging adulthood is typically a period of instability and exploration. The following Ethics Spotlight explores challenges for social workers in addressing the stage of emerging adulthood.

ETHICS SPOTLIGHT
AUTONOMY AND DIVERSITY IN EMERGING ADULTHOOD

You are a social worker employed in a family clinic at Lutheran Social Services. A young couple in their early 20s comes to see you due to increased problems in their interactions with each other. The husband is White, the wife is Latina, and they have just had a baby. Both husband and wife are employed and are also students in an undergraduate program in architecture. In order to help cover their college expenses, the couple has lived with the wife's parents for the past two years. You wonder if their communication problems may be due to the fact that they live with the wife's parents and are not independently taking care of themselves. Discuss the following questions.

(1) What are your personal beliefs about what it means to be an independent adult?

(2) Would you consider the husband and wife to fully be adults? Why or why not?

(3) How might your personal beliefs about "being independent" negatively (or positively) influence your work with this couple?

(4) For you as a worker, how might cultural issues become important in understanding this couple's movement toward independence?

Diversity in Human Growth and Development

Early life span and life course theorists viewed their understandings of human development as universally applicable to all groups of people regardless of their diversity (e.g., race, ethnicity, gender, and sexual orientation and expression). However, this universal appeal has undergone increasing scrutiny and critique because life span and life course theories (as well as perspectives of emerging adulthood) have been based largely on the experiences of White, American, heterosexual, middle-class men and are less applicable to other groups of people (Syed & Mitchell, 2013). Even with life course theorists' emphasis on the impact of historical time periods in which people grow and develop and the accumulation of advantage or disadvantage over the life course (Seabrook & Avison, 2012), these writers have typically ignored the broader impacts of discrimination and oppression experienced by marginalized groups of people. In this section, we have chosen to examine pivotal theories of growth and development that address racial diversity. Specifically, we will discuss nigrescence, a ground-breaking theory depicting African American identity development (Cross, 1971, 1991), and newer multiracial identity development theories (Root, 1996).

Nigrescence Theory

First developed during the civil rights movement in the United States, **nigrescence theory**, which refers to a French term for turning or becoming Black, depicts a process of moving from Black self-hatred to an affirmation of a Black identity (Cross, 1971). As Cross (1991) deepened his understanding of Black or African American racial identity development, he revised his original theory to emphasize the pivotal role of social interactions that inform an individual's identity as a member of a social reference group, and incorporated "race salience" or the significance of race in a person's approach to life (Vandiver, 2001). Cross's revised theory depicts four identity stages and reflects a process of self-acceptance: Pre-Encounter, Encounter, Immersion-Emersion, and Internalization.

The first stage, Pre-Encounter, describes the importance of race to the development of a Black person's identity. In this stage, people may assimilate to and adopt pro-American, mainstream societal values or they may have an anti-Black identity that includes miseducation and self-hatred. Miseducation involves believing the larger society's negative stereotypes about being Black (e.g., not intelligent, lazy, violent). Self-hatred can contribute to poor self-esteem, impaired identity development, and difficulties in mental health functioning.

In the second stage, Encounter, Black people experience events that can be transformative and lead them to question their Pre-Encounter beliefs about race in American society. These events contribute to a re-examination of their belief systems and racial identity and propels them into Immersion-Emersion (stage three).

The third stage, Immersion-Emersion, is characterized as an emotionally volatile transition from an old racial identity into a new one. At the beginning of the third stage, people immerse themselves in Black culture, which manifests itself in many ways (e.g., exclusive involvement with Black friends and activities). Individuals also develop either a strong pro-Black identity or a strong anti-White identity. As stage three progresses, they become emotionally more settled and move into the Internalization stage.

In the fourth stage of Internalization, the person develops an intellectual and emotional acceptance of being Black. Cross (1991) indicated that in this stage an individual would develop one of three identities: Black Nationalist, Biculturalist, or Multiculturalist. The Black Nationalist views being Black as the only salient identity that is actualized through activism to bring about larger societal change. The Biculturalist integrates two identities, typically a sense of being Black with a sense of being American. The Multiculturalist integrates three or more cultural frames of references (e.g., gender, class, sexual orientation, or a racial reference group other than Black). When a person moves through these stages, nigrescence theorists have viewed this as a move from psychological illness to psychological health and well-being.

Multiracial Identity Development and Border Crossings

Newer multiracial identity development theories (Choi-Misailidis, 2010; Root, 1996) challenge monoracial racial identity development as described by Cross (1971, 1991), Helms (1995), and others; and biracial identity development theories, which examine the development of persons who have to reconcile two racial heritages (Hall, 2000; Kerwin & Ponterotto, 1995; Poston, 1990). Multiracial identity development theorists, who point to the growth of multiracial families in the United States (Sue & Sue, 2003) and note our government's reticence and ambivalence about even acknowledging persons of multiracial identity (e.g., it has only been in the last 30 years that the United States has collected census data on multiracial populations), suggest that racial identity development is even more complex and fluid than it is for persons who claim a monoracial or biracial identity. For example, monoracial individuals typically do not have to choose their racial identity, and both biracial and monoracial theories generally assume one's racial identity develops within linear stages and is fixed and stable over time. In contrast, theorists describe persons engaged in multiracial identity development as having multiple realities that they explore in the development of their identity, and that are likely to change across their development (Choi-Misailidis, 2010; Hitlin, Brown, & Elder, 2006; Root, 1996). One prominent multiracial identity development theory is depicted by Root (1996), who emphasized the fluidity and self-definition of identity development for multiracial individuals.

Root (1996) indicates that multiracial individuals address, experience, and negotiate their identity by one of four possible border crossings, and although these crossing may be found among many diverse racial groups, they appear most prominent among people with multiracial identities.

- The first border identity involves the person having "both feet in both groups," with the individual able to interact with, embrace, and respect multiple racial groups simultaneously (Root, 1996, p. xxi).

- The second border crossing occurs when individuals match their identity based on the demands of their particular racial and ethnic social context. In this border context, the individual does not switch loyalties but practices situational ethnicity and race based on various contexts.

- The third border identity involves individuals decisively sitting on the border of their racial groups and using this border as their reference point.

- As part of the fourth border crossing, the individual creates a home in one racial group for an extended period of time and then may change identification with one group to explore other racial groups. The choice to identify with a particular group may be based on which context provides emotional, social, and political support.

Finally, multiracial individuals may also change their identity several times and move in and out of these four border crossings in the process of developing their multiracial identity.

Summary of Overview

This overview examines life span theory (Erikson, 1950) as foundational to social work education while also acknowledging its limitations in addressing diverse pathways (e.g., gender, race, ethnicity, and sexual orientation) and the influences of historical oppression on human growth and development. More recent theoretical advances are explored, including life course theories and emerging adulthood as its own distinct developmental stage. Life course perspectives are distinct from life span theory in their emphasis on variations over the life course and in relationship to cohorts and historical context that impact identity development. Further, scholars have examined emerging adulthood as a more newly defined stage of human development (from late teens through mid-20s) in which people have a prolonged period of independent role exploration regarding work, love, and their worldviews. Both life course perspectives and emerging adulthood as a distinct stage are advances to our understanding of human growth and development, but their universal appeal has undergone increasing scrutiny and critique because they have been based largely on the experiences of White, American, heterosexual, middle-class men and are viewed as less applicable to other groups of people.

This chapter moves forward with a deeper examination of pivotal theories of human growth and development that address racial diversity. Specifically, we discuss nigrescence theory, a ground-breaking theory depicting African American or Black identity development and the process of moving from Black self-hatred to an affirmation of a Black identity (Cross, 1971, 1991). We also explore newer multiracial identity theories, acknowledging the growth of multiracial families in the United States. These multiracial identity theories challenge monoracial identity development (e.g., nigrescence theory) and biracial identity theories in their depiction of multiracial identity development as increasingly complex and fluid. We conclude by spotlighting Root's (1996) multiracial identity development theory, which examines the border crossings multiracial individuals experience and negotiate as part of their development.

IN-DEPTH: MARIA YELLOW HORSE BRAVE HEART AND VENIDA S. CHENAULT

Introduction: Weaving of Personal and Professional Experiences

Two key social work scholars, Maria Yellow Horse Brave Heart and Venida S. Chenault, who are significant but often ignored figures in the development of social work's understanding of racism and oppression, will be examined in this section. These two scholars are featured in this chapter because they explore the role of historical trauma and unresolved historical grief in individual and community-based identity development among First Nations or indigenous peoples (Brave Heart, 1998; Chenault, 2004, 2011). Our in-depth exploration of Chenault and Brave Heart will incorporate elements from a range of their scholarly writings.

First, Chenault will be examined for her attention to structural injustices that contribute to what has been termed an *American Holocaust* perpetrated toward indigenous people (Legters, 1988). Second, Brave Heart will be examined for her development of the concepts of historical trauma, unresolved historical grief, and psycho-educational interventions designed to address cumulative trauma and psychic wounds experienced by indigenous people (Brave Heart & DeBruyn, 1998; Weaver & Brave Heart, 1999). Third, we return to Chenault to discuss the long-term impacts of this cataclysmic violence on indigenous people's health and mental health with a specific emphasis on empowerment processes for indigenous women who have experienced violence and abuse.

Chenault, who is Prairie Band Potawatomi and Kickapoo, provides a broad, social structural understanding of imperialist ideals and colonization of indigenous people by European Americans. European Americans have viewed themselves as superior, with the right to dominate or colonize other groups, such as First Nations people. This colonization contributed to indigenous peoples' oppression and experiences of historical trauma, unresolved historical grief, and ensuing public health problems such as high suicide and homicide rates, high rates of intimate partner violence (IPV), and substance abuse. Chenault, who completed her BSW, MSW, and PhD in social work from the University of Kansas and is currently president of Haskell Indian Nations University in Lawrence, Kansas, closely examines the prevalence of IPV in First Nations' communities. Chenault also systematically explores an empowerment process (i.e., the development of self-esteem, sense of belonging, social support, and social action), which can occur for indigenous women who have faced IPV.

Brave Heart, who has over a decade of clinical social work experience in working with Lakota communities

©Terry Koenig

PHOTO 8.3
Native American painting: Haskell Indian Nations University, Lawrence, Kansas

in urban and reservation settings, became increasingly aware of the complexities of traditional Lakota cultural and spiritual beliefs and their impact on helping First Nations people to heal from ongoing violence perpetrated by European Americans. Lakota beliefs stress ongoing relationships with one's ancestors and with the spirit world those ancestors inhabit. Brave Heart was led to believe that these spiritual views can contribute to Native communities' open wounds regarding their **American Holocaust** and inability to recover from such calamitous atrocities committed against their ancestors. Brave Heart, who is Lakota, first developed the concept of **historical trauma** as involving indigenous people's experiences of oppression and suffering, which led to "collective and compounding emotional and psychic wounding (Niederland, 1989)—both over the lifespan and across generations" (Brave Heart, 1998, p. 288). Brave Heart-Jordan (1995) describes that during her post-graduate clinical social work training she experienced a kind of awakening in which she "concurrently became aware of personal grief about the genocide of indigenous people and began making a conscious association between the American Indian historical trauma and the [Jewish] Holocaust" (p. 8).

Brave Heart was also initially inspired by psychoanalytic beliefs (See Psychodynamic Theory, Chapter 5) that childhood experiences impact and can determine adult development, including the presence of mental health difficulties. She describes being drawn to the field of social work because, unlike many helping professions, social work placed great importance on discrimination, racism, and oppression as they impact human growth and development. This inspiration fueled Brave Heart's examination of multigenerational trauma as a contributing factor in the development of long-standing mental health problems for indigenous people.

Structural Injustices and the American Holocaust

Chenault notes that best practices for healing of First Nations people involve helping them to acknowledge and grieve over traumatic experiences associated with colonialism and the massive structural violence committed by their European American oppressors. The violence committed against First Nations people has been referred to as an American Holocaust in that the victims of this genocide are estimated to be from 3.5 to 13 million of the original indigenous peoples (Stannard, 1992; Thornton, 1987). Scholars report a range of estimates, from two-thirds to nearly 99% of all indigenous people in North America were destroyed between 1500 and 1900 (Stiffarm & Lane, 1992; Weaver & Brave Heart, 1999). For our purposes, several concepts drawn from multiple disciplines, such as social work, indigenous studies, law, and political science, are defined by Chenault (2011, pp. 19–22) to help us better understand this structural violence and genocide (GlenMaye, 1998; Mullaly, 1997; Said, 1993; Yellow Bird & Chenault, 1999).

- **Imperialism** refers to practices, attitudes, and perspectives supporting the rights or sense of entitlement of one culture (e.g., European Americans) to dominate or rule over another culture (e.g., First Nations people). Imperialism serves as a foundation for colonialism.

- **Colonialism** can be understood as a "sustained series of events enacted by an invading power on another culture, which facilitates and perpetuates the development of a worldview" (Chenault, 2011, p. 20) or an ideology that supports oppression and unjust social structures. This worldview supports the superiority of the invading power over groups viewed as inferior or different.

- **Oppression** is viewed as "a condition of powerlessness that cuts across every system within a culture" (Chenault, 2011, p. 20) and, in turn, requires holistic, structural responses and practice-based strategies at multiple levels (e.g., individual, family, and community-based change efforts; and social and political action) in order to adequately combat and eradicate.

- **Colonization** is the ongoing process and maintenance of oppressing a group, culture, or nation and involves multiple layers of domination and exploitation to make sure that oppressive conditions (e.g., violence, abuse, dehumanization) stay in place. People who experience ongoing deleterious effects of these oppressive conditions (e.g., shame, self-blame, and feelings of craziness) can end up internalizing negative images of themselves and their capacities, beliefs, and worldviews.

- **Indigenous decolonization** describes the conscious actions and planned strategies that indigenous people engage in to reconnect with and reclaim their knowledge, philosophies, and practices. Allies of indigenous people can also engage in practices to support needed tribal-based solutions and change efforts (e.g., teaching language skills to help revitalize a tribal language).

- Structural frameworks are used to help understand the dynamics that contribute to existing social problems for indigenous peoples, such as abuse and violence against indigenous women. These frameworks contrast with more narrowly focused, deficit, and victim-based models and instead call for multidimensional analysis and action that refrain from short-term "fixes" and instead support long-term change.

Although the narratives of First Nations people are punctuated with the effects of imperialism and colonialism, these narratives also include seeds of hope and stories of the use of structurally based, decolonizing strategies that combat the process of colonization. It is here that we turn to the work of Brave Heart, who not only defines historical trauma and unresolved grief as experienced by indigenous people, but she has carried out psychoeducational interventions tailored to the unique needs of indigenous people that have contributed to their growth and healing.

Historical Trauma, Historical Unresolved Grief, and Healing Strategies

As noted earlier, Brave Heart was the first scholar to define the concept of historical trauma and examine its relevance for First Nations people. She notes that those who have experienced massive historical and generational group trauma (e.g., Native American and Jewish Holocaust descendants) may also develop a *historical trauma response* (HTR), which can include many symptoms such as anxiety, flashbacks of traumatic events, depression, and substance abuse as a means of coping with the trauma (Brave Heart, 2013; Krystal, 1984; van der Kolk, 1987); and they may experience *historical unresolved grief* or unsettled bereavement in which they are unable or prohibited from working through devastating losses due to genocide and societal denial of the violence (Doka, 1989; Fogelman, 1988).

Generations of Loss Resulting in Unresolved Grief

For indigenous peoples, such as the Lakota, historical unresolved grief involves the profound, unsettled bereavement that results from generations of devastating losses. Brave Heart (1998) describes these numerous losses, including

- loss of traditional spiritual leadership through the assassination of Tatanka Iyotake (Sitting Bull), who was very involved in the resistance to the "White man's" genocide policies;

- the Wounded Knee Massacre, in which hundreds of Lakota were slaughtered and buried in mass graves;

- the deliberate extermination of the buffalo by the U.S. government, which contributed to the starvation of the Lakota people;

- the forced removal of Lakota and other indigenous children to boarding schools where they were severely abused, separated from their families, and died fleeing the boarding schools in an attempt to return home to their tribal communities (for example, see the indigenous children's cemetery and documentation of boarding school practices at the Cultural Center, Haskell Indian Nations University, Lawrence, Kansas);

- the practice of deficient health standards and overcrowding at boarding schools, which contributed to a tuberculosis epidemic (i.e., between 1936 and 1941, more than one-third of the Lakota population over the age of 1 year died due to the effects of tuberculosis) (Brave Heart, 1998; Hoxie, 1989);

- the loss of land in which the best land was turned over to European Americans, thereby displacing hundreds of Lakota ranchers and farmers; and

- the loss of traditional modes of self-governance that operated through consensus—instead, European Americans forced their "hierarchical models of government [which resulted] in factionalism and conflict" (Brave Heart-Jordan, 1995, p. 28) among Lakota people.

The American government and its people further denied the magnitude of Native American genocide and prohibited Native Americans from practicing indigenous ceremonies, e.g., the Ghost Dance, purification ceremonies, and the wiping of the tears ceremony which would have helped them to resist oppression and heal from these losses (Doka, 1989). What follows is a description of one indigenous ceremony, the Ghost Dance, for its significance to the Lakota people as they struggled to address unresolved grief and cope with these cumulative, traumatic losses.

The Ghost Dance and Unresolved Grief

Brave Heart-Jordan describes the Ghost Dance as a "spiritual movement initiated in 1889 by Wovoka, a Paiute prophet, who predicted the coming of the Messiah and visions of deceased ancestors if Indians would perform this dance. This movement spread among several Plains Indian tribes" (1995, p. 14) including the Lakota, who were facing starvation due to the U.S. government's deliberate extermination of the buffalo. In 1890 and despite the U.S. government prohibition against traditional ceremonies, the Lakota developed and observed their own version of the Ghost Dance, or *Wanagi Wacipi*, on several reservations. Brave Heart states that the Lakota version of the Ghost Dance focused on "a) the reunification with deceased relatives, b) the return of the buffalo and the traditional way of life, and c) the disappearance of the white man" (1995, pp. 14–15). She further remarks that,

> The devastating impact of the loss of the buffalo and the Lakota response suggest the existence of historical unresolved grief as early as 1890, evident in the tenets of the *Wanagi Wacipi*—the fantasy of the return of the buffalo and the reunion with deceased relatives. . . . It is clear that the *Wanagi Wacipi* came to the Lakota at a time of desperate conditions and may be viewed as both an attempt to cope with the traumatic reality and a process of unresolved grief. (Brave Heart-Jordan, 1995, p. 16)

The Ghost Dance reflects the traditional concepts of death for the Lakota in that they continue to maintain relationships with the deceased. As Brave Heart notes,

> In traditional Lakota culture, the spirits of the deceased are alive; the Lakota remain very involved with the spiritual world and seek contact with the spirits through the ceremonies such as the *Hanbleca* or vision quest, the *Wiwanyag Wacipi* or Sun Dance, and the *Yuwipi* or healing ceremony. (Brave Heart-Jordan, 1995, p. 16)

With the U.S. government's prohibition of these and other ceremonies, as well as the indigenous structure of extended relationships (*tiospaye*), which expands far beyond European American understandings of a family system, the Lakota and other First Nations people were unable to engage in healthy adaptation to cataclysmic, massive losses and instead experienced prolonged, unresolved grief. It is at this juncture that we introduce Brave Heart's scholarly efforts to develop an intervention to address this unresolved trauma and grief.

Brave Heart's Psychoeducational Intervention to Address First Nations's Grief and Loss

Brave Heart combines her clinical social work experience with scholarly efforts to create "an originally designed, culturally syntonic, four-day psychoeducational intervention designed to initiate a grief and trauma resolution for 45 Lakota human service providers" (1998, p. 292) at the sacred Black Hills near Harney Peak, which is considered the center of the Lakota universe. This healing intervention involved four components: (1) Stimulating remembrance of Lakota trauma through a presentation and videotape about the Wounded Knee Massacre and boarding school trauma followed quickly by small group activities designed to develop group cohesiveness, bonding, and symptom normalization (e.g., each participant diagrammed a lifeline of traumatic experiences which they shared with partners and in small groups); (2) review of the elements of unresolved trauma and grief; (3) co-facilitation by a Lakota man and woman (with similar trauma experiences to the participants) of small group exercises and discussion; and (4) the carrying out of the *oinikage/inipi* or Lakota purification and traditional wiping of the tears ceremonies. These spiritual ceremonies help Lakota people to renew, recreate, and strengthen their self-identity through the incorporation of traditional Lakota cultural beliefs, opportunities for collective mourning, emotional release, and with the expectation of healing from grief and loss (p. 293). Key findings from this intervention study show that participants overwhelmingly reported heightened awareness of historical trauma and its impact, would lead to cathartic relief, and facilitated a grief resolution process leading to reduction in grief-related emotions and "a more positive group identity coupled with a commitment to continuing this healing work" (p. 299). Further, these findings hold promise in being generalizable to other tribes.

Indigenous Women, Violence and Abuse, and Empowerment-Based Strategies

Chenault (2004, 2009) has conducted what appears to be the only doctoral research study and subsequent follow-up study using quantitative methods to examine American

Indian college women's experiences with violence and abuse (i.e., emotional or verbal abuse, physical victimization, sexual victimization, being threatened, or stalked) and to examine their empowerment processes (i.e., self-esteem, social support/sense of belonging, and social action). Chenault defines empowerment "as a set of characteristics present at various levels—personal, interpersonal, community or political—that can be altered or reduced as a result of experiences such as violence and abuse" (2004, p. 105). Chenault justifies her use of quantitative methods to document the incidence and prevalence of her participants' experiences with violence and abuse although simultaneously acknowledges the limitations of these methods in capturing First Nations women's narratives of violence and empowerment. As a way to manage these shortcomings, Chenault augments her work with participatory methods (e.g., engaging in dialogue and feedback with female Native college participants about her study's design and findings).

The results for both studies, which use a national tribally diverse sample, demonstrate similar disturbing prevalence and incidence rates of violence and abuse for indigenous women. Specifically, in the 2004 study, the overwhelming majority of participants (85.7%) reported having experienced at least one form of violence or abuse. However, in examining personal, interpersonal, community, or political levels of empowerment, Chenault's findings suggest that while the development of self-esteem (at the personal level) can be impacted by violence and abuse, it may be reinforced or strengthened by additional protective factors that exist in the community in which one is raised (i.e., in a reservation setting). At the interpersonal level, Chenault's findings suggest no differences exist between women who have experienced violence and abuse and those who have not. However, her findings "suggest that reservations, tribal lands, pueblos, and villages foster . . . social support networks and the sense of belonging" (p. 124).

Chenault also explores the social action (community or political) dimension of empowerment in her study. She examines participants' engagement in behaviors such as cultural or healing practices and/or ceremonies (e.g., talking circles or sweat lodges) that contribute to change at the family, community, society, or global levels. Chenault points out that intervention research on violence against women has largely ignored this social action dimension of empowerment that plays a crucial role in helping women achieve positive group identity. Her findings suggest that participants "who have experienced emotional abuse or been threatened are more likely to engage in social action, as well as the use of cultural practices for preventing harm to oneself, protecting oneself or correcting injustices to oneself" (p. 126).

Finally, Chenault (2011) illustrates an indigenous mother's experiences with helping her teenage daughter to grow and develop in the face of ongoing oppressive structures and systems:

> As my daughter learns to negotiate high school, the cliques and strongholds
> of privilege, I am reminded of the difficulty of being and raising [a] strong
> Indigenous [woman]. We face oppression on many levels and in virtually every
> structure and system, including relationships in which we are less valued as
> companions and wives. The added trauma of misogynist violence in our home,
> family, communities and the larger society we interact with daily can produce a
> tremendous burden. (p. 133)

Summary. This section has explored the contributions of two key indigenous social work scholars, Chenault and Brave Heart. These authors provide us with an in-depth look at the role of cumulative historical trauma and grief as it impacts individual, family, and community identity for First Nations peoples. Chenault systematically examines violence and abuse against indigenous women as well as their empowerment processes; Brave Heart evaluates the effectiveness of a psychoeducational intervention designed to help First Nations people heal from cataclysmic, massive trauma.

CRITIQUE OF LIFE SPAN THEORIES AND BEYOND

What Does This Theory Say About Human Behavior?

As we have previously discussed (see Chapter 2), theories can be analyzed based on their undergirding assumptions, such as where they fit on the subjective–objective dimension or the stability–radical change dimension. The subjective–objective dimension asks us to examine whether a theory views the world as real and external to the individual (objective) or more personal and subjective. Life span and life course theorists as well as proponents of emerging adulthood are definitely more inclined to view the world as tangible and concrete; people do not simply create their own meanings and life paths. However, proponents of racial identity theory, especially those who support multiracial perspectives, which are fluid and dependent on individuals' experiences within their social context at a particular point in time, reflect a much more subjective standpoint and take into account individuals' experiences of growth as well as discrimination and oppression. Historical trauma, as depicted by Brave Heart and Chenault in this chapter, also illustrates a more subjective perspective that examines not only an individual's experience but the long-lasting effects of oppression, trauma, and growth that affect multiple generations of Native American people.

The stability–radical change dimension asks us to examine the emphases that a theory places on stability, integration, social order, or equilibrium in contrast to conflict, coercion, or change as a way of understanding human behavior. Life span theories, in particular, acknowledge a crisis or conflict at distinct stages in human development, but the positive goal of these crises or conflicts is to *integrate* syntonic or more positive ego qualities in order to reach a "higher" level of growth. Nigrescence theory, in contrast, actively discusses eye-opening, transformative events for African American individuals, which create a level of conflict leading the person to potentially develop a strong, self-accepting African American identity. The four border crossings that Root (1996) describes in her understanding of multiracial identity development support the complex, incomplete, and fluid relationships that a multiracial individual navigates in social interactions. These incomplete, fluid relationships, such as when individuals decide to stand on the border of any racial group as a way to explore their identity, reflects an awareness and comfort with *change* as part of multiracial identity development. The following Table 8.2 was created to show the placement of this chapter's key theories/concepts on our two assumptive dimensions.

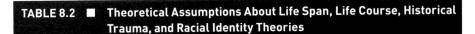

TABLE 8.2 ■ Theoretical Assumptions About Life Span, Life Course, Historical Trauma, and Racial Identity Theories

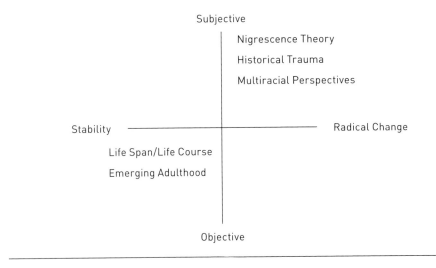

How Does This Theory Address Growth and Change?

Life span theorists view human growth and development as having predictable, linear stages. Each person is understood as already having a "genetic blueprint" that determines (and perhaps even predicts) how she or he will develop over the life span. Proponents of emerging adulthood, as its own distinct developmental stage, also continue to draw attention to stage development linked to a specific age (i.e., 18–25). In contrast, life course theorists are much less concerned with stages of individual development and instead describe broader societal themes, such as historical events or processes that impact cohorts of people (e.g., war-time combat or immigration) and shape their growth and development over the life course. In large measure, these life course theories do not address the historically pervasive impact of oppression, discrimination, and genocide, which continue to impact the identity development of racially diverse groups of people such as Native Americans or African Americans. Historical trauma theorists reflect the belief and need for whole communities to experience generational and community-based change and growth. Scholars who put forth this perspective view individual identity development as intimately and inseparably linked to community and generational identity development. An individual's growth and change is viewed as incomplete without concomitant family, tribe, and communal growth and change.

Racial identity development theorists (e.g., those who put forth nigrescence theory) do describe a linear process that involves an African American person moving toward greater self-acceptance and healthy identity development. However, theories such as nigrescence do not link ages to the stages of identity development for the African American person. Nigrescence theory implies that an individual may "wake up" to oppression and discrimination at any time over the course of her or his chronological lifetime. Somewhere in the growth process, a person may be exposed to and reflect on eye-opening events or processes that serve as a catalyst for a growing awareness of oppression. How and why growth and development happens can vary greatly across individuals. What is implied in nigrescence theory is that greater health and self-acceptance is likely to occur by waking up to this oppression.

Scholars have been slow to explore the experiences of identity development for multiracial individuals; this is in part due to our federal government and broader American society's lack of acknowledgment of the growth and distinct experiences of multiracial individuals. However, newer multiracial identity development perspectives are being developed, and these theorists view change and potential growth as the centerpiece of multiracial identity development (Root, 1996). For these scholars, identity is understood to be complex and fluid. Individuals who identify as multiracial may change their identity more than once as they move in and out of border crossings, which allow them to explore identification in one racial group, simultaneous identification in more than one racial group, or as they may stand outside of any racial groups to explore what it means to live "on the border" in their development of a multiracial identity.

How Holistic Is This Theory?

Nearly all of the theories, perspectives, and concepts that we have discussed in this chapter emphasize individual development over societal and community development. Historical trauma is an exception in that it holistically links individual identity development to generational and community growth and development. For example, these theorists stress the importance of Native American communities and our larger American society in acknowledging historical oppression; this acknowledgment serves as a means of assisting individuals, families, and tribes in developing healthy self and community-based identities. Further, life span theory and life course perspectives typically do not support social work's emphases on a holistic understanding of individuals as bio-psycho-social-spiritual beings. For example, these theories do not readily address intellectual and spiritual development as their focus is linked to Freudian thought and to intrapsychic identity development. Life span theorists such as Erikson represent some of the first to acknowledge an individual's identity as being influenced by her or his social environment. Yet, these early theorists depicted the social environment in more narrow terms (e.g., acknowledging how the social world exists within an individual's psychological makeup).

In this section, we can also examine the artificial "nature versus nurture" debate described in Chapter 2 regarding the causes of human behavior as being biologically based (nature) versus the primacy given to the social environment in shaping behavior (nurture). Life span theory, in particular, views human growth and development as emerging from a genetic blueprint. This blueprint implies an emphasis on a fixed, innate state of development (with all the stages already within a person at birth, reaching ascendency at a particular time). This is in contrast to life course and racial identity development theories as well as historical trauma, all which take into account the impact of a broad range of historical and social environmental "causes" of identity development. However, it must be noted that life course theories continue to ignore broader societal phenomena such as discrimination and oppression as they impact individual and community growth and development.

How Consistent Is This Theory With Social Work Values and Ethics?

In this section, we will examine our theories for their consistency with key social work values including social justice, the dignity and worth of each person, and professional competence—specifically, cultural competence. Social workers value social justice, seeking to ensure that all members of our society have the same human rights, protections, and opportunities. In this chapter, our racial identity theories and our examination of historical trauma challenge us to broaden our personal and professional views of the long-lasting impact of oppression and injustice, and at the same time to acknowledge the potential growth over the life course for these individuals and communities. Racial identity development theorists are interested in helping to illuminate the unique, complex, and fluid human development journey for those from diverse racial backgrounds. In contrast, and due to their focus on the growth and development of White, European, heterosexual men, life span and life course theories (including writings about the newer stage of emerging adulthood) are limited in their capacity to be applied to groups of marginalized or vulnerable populations. Even life course theorists, who point to their sophistication in studying longitudinal data, continue to ignore the pervasive influences of oppression or discrimination for whole communities. Consequently, as social workers who support the pivotal value of social justice, we should be cautious in using these narrow conceptions of human growth and development. Other than historical trauma, our theories are also limited in their emphasis on taking action to expand or change existing social policies to better address the needs and capabilities of diverse racial groups.

With the exception of life span theory and the newer conception of emerging adulthood, the theories and perspectives put forth in this chapter overwhelmingly support the dignity and worth of each person and are mindful of diversity (e.g., race, ethnicity, gender, (dis)ability, sexual orientation, immigration status, and religion). Some of the theories discussed in our chapter characterize human development in progressive stages (e.g., life span theory and nigrescence theory) and others point to the fluidity and contextual nature of human development (e.g., life course perspectives and multiracial identity development theory). Both stage-based and more fluid theories of human development may be useful for social workers to pay attention to in their work with clients. For example, the stage of *Generativity vs. Stagnation* may be helpful for social workers to address in their work with adults who are living with a chronic illness as they struggle to give something back to future generations or take on a project that has personal significance. However, these same adults may also benefit from the social workers' knowledge and awareness of human development as fluid, indicating that not all adults may go through this prescribed stage, may address it much later than indicated by the ages assigned to the stage, or may not go through this stage at all due to their identification in multiple racial groups, which leads them to explore a variety of opportunities. All this is to say that the social worker must take care to filter any theory of human growth and development through a value-based lens that supports the dignity and worth of all people.

Becoming competent and in particular, culturally competent, has also been described as a central value for the social work profession. For example, social work scholars, such as Venida Chenault and Maria Yellow Horse Brave Heart, have increasingly described post-colonial practices with indigenous and other populations who have experienced systematic oppression (e.g., Native American, African American people and Mexican American people). These scholars discuss the importance of cultural humility and sensitivity for White social workers as they meet with and learn from their clients who represent these diverse racial groups. Some have indicated that White social workers can thoughtfully engage in social work practice with racially diverse groups. However, in order to be vigilant about their own prejudices and biases, these White social workers will need to develop the stance of a learner, of "not knowing," and will want to pursue ongoing self-awareness and participation in activities that provide opportunities to learn from indigenous people about their oppression and resiliency.

What Sources of Knowledge Does This Theory Support?

For over 60 years, Erikson's theory of life span development has inspired numerous conceptually oriented and research-based writings. In general, Erikson's successive life span stages, although now understood to be experienced in a more flexible or fluid way (Kroger, 2002), have been supported by countless empirically based studies (Sokol, 2009). One of the difficulties in examining this empirical literature is the lack of agreement on how identity development is defined; Erikson's writings were no exception and have been criticized for their ambiguity (e.g., using a variety of identity-related terms, including identity formation, identity development, identity consolidation, and identity resolution), making it difficult to determine a consistent understanding of identity across a broad range of scholarly writings.

Life span and life course theorists as well as proponents of emerging adulthood, as its own distinct developmental stage, have been soundly critiqued for their views of human growth and development as being *universally* applicable to all groups of people. These critics have indicated that life span theory and life course perspectives are most readily applicable to White, European, middle-class, heterosexual men and fail to account for the experiences of diverse groups of people (e.g., based on gender, race, ethnicity, or sexual orientation). Critics also note the paucity of studies that examine emerging adulthood as a distinct stage among diverse racial and ethnic groups (Miller & Joe, 2008). In general, life span and life course theories describe developmental stages, but they fail to take into account the unique voices and perspectives of diverse groups of people and, for example, do not address the role or expertise of practitioners in assisting clients to work through these developmental crises or turning points at each stage of development, or to examine the historical timing of their birth and its impact on identity development.

In response, scholars have put forward a myriad of developmental perspectives (e.g., nigrescence theory and multiracial identity development as discussed in our overview). These perspectives, with varying degrees of empirical support, have been advanced to better account for human growth and development among diverse groups of people (e.g., based on gender) (Jordan, 2001; Frey, 2013), race or ethnicity (Root, 1996; Worrell, Cross, & Vandiver, 2001), sexual orientation (Cass, 1979), and involving the intersection of two or more identities such as for lesbian and gay Native Americans (Adams & Phillips, 2009). Further, these perspectives acknowledge the client's unique voice and experiences of identity development.

Historical trauma as experienced by Native American people is a relatively new phenomenon, having been first conceptualized by Maria Yellow Horse Brave Heart. Brave

Heart worked as a clinical social worker with Native American people, and this served as the impetus for her doctoral work and ongoing scholarship (Brave Heart, 1998, 2000; Brave Heart-Jordan, 1995). Although historical trauma powerfully illustrates the experiences and responses of people who have dealt with oppression and its emotional wounding over the lifespan and across multiple generations, this concept has also been critiqued due to confusion about the variety and complexity of its meanings. For example, authors describe historical trauma as a response, a syndrome, and a process through which trauma is transmitted across generations (Crawford, 2014). Preliminary qualitative and quantitative studies have provided increasing depth as to the experiences and narratives of people who have experienced historical trauma. In effect, it is the expertise of individuals and community members who are intimately acquainted with oppression and its impacts over multiple generations that has shaped not only an understanding of historical trauma but also shed light on strategies that might be effective in contributing to healing and growth (Brave Heart, 2003). Social work practitioners who work with Native American people are likely to develop professional "expertise" through their careful attention to relationships with clients and communities who have experienced historical trauma. Of all the theories, perspectives, and ideas that we have discussed in this chapter, historical trauma most elevates the expertise of clients and their relationships with practitioners.

INTRODUCTION TO SOCIAL WORK'S UNDERSTANDING OF LIFE SPAN THEORY

As we noted in the Overview section of the chapter, Erikson's perceptions of life span theory (LST) gained significant traction among psychiatrists, psychologists, and especially social workers. This was particularly true for social workers who were working in the fields of health, mental health, and child welfare. LST was nearly always the centerpiece, and sometimes the exclusive focus, for human behavior classes in schools of social work. To this day it continues to be one of the more central theories taught in both BSW and MSW programs in the United States. By the 1960s, social workers were looking for human behavior theories that moved beyond the constraints of the more person-focused psychodynamic theories (Perlman, 1965; Scherz, 1970; Smalley, 1967). What most social workers struggled to do was to expand existing approaches that almost exclusively attended to the person side of the person/environment focus while remaining silent about the transactions between individuals and their environments (i.e., P/e vs. P/E). Erikson's work and social work's response was at the front end of a two-decade period during which social workers incorporated both LST and, in the late 1960s, together with systems theory, these frameworks allowed a more comprehensive understanding of the interactions of individuals and environments in affecting human behavior.

Assumptions Underlying Life Span Theory

The following is a summary of the key underpinnings of life span theory as it relates to its translation into social work practice.

- Erikson' discusses his theory as though he is describing "normal" human development. What he fails to recognize is that his understanding of human development is based on White, Western, male, heterosexual development. It does not account for the important role diversity plays in shaping both human beings and their environments.

- LST is a product of the psychodynamic tradition. However, Erikson's work begins shifting the emphasis from intra-psychic dynamics, among the id, ego, and superego, to placing the ego at the center of the developmental process. This opens the door for a deeper emphasis on interactions between persons and their environments. This made the theory much more congruent with social work's focus on person-in-environment.

- Another assumption in Erikson's work is the connection between physical and psychological development in the context of the environment. LST, sometimes called an "age-stage" theory, conceives human growth and development as an interaction of temporal and psychological processes unfolding simultaneously.

- Erikson sorted behaviors into two categories: first, ego "syntonic," those behaviors, values, and feelings in harmony with the needs of the ego and, second, ego "dystonic," those behaviors, and values that are distressing or unacceptable to the needs and goals of the ego.

- Erikson understood personality development to be epigenetic—arising from a genetic blueprint in which all the stages are dependent on one another; unfolding in a linear, prescribed order; and existing in some form before their critical time for ascendancy.

- Resolution of the crisis in each stage, when successfully traversed, was seen as virtuous or a strength. When the crisis "failed" to be resolved, the person's growth was truncated and therefore problematic.

- Each of his original eight stages identified crises that needed to be addressed in order for individuals to progress in their development. In most instances, these crises were framed in somewhat mutually exclusive categories, for example, trust vs. mistrust.

Taken together, these assumptions created a model for understanding human behavior that was much more useful for social work. First, it shifted our attention from focusing solely on the intrapsychic processes among the id, ego, and superego to include the importance of the social, physical, and natural environments that shaped human behavior. Second, these assumptions provide markers, e.g., trust, identity development, generativity through which individuals, and also families, e.g., couple intimacy, regrouping and binding could be understood; they both describe developmental processes that create "normal" tensions rather than expressions of pathology. Third, it provided a context in which social workers could begin to take a more balanced view for understanding human behavior as a product of both persons and their environments. Fourth, it fit well with the emerging emphasis in social work on social systems theory, which began in the late 1960s.

Early Lifespan Theory Applied to Understanding Family Development

This section of the chapter provides an opportunity to illustrate how LST can be applied to our work, not only with individuals but also families. We chose its application to families because Erikson's work is most often applied solely to individual development, but it has parallels in the family development literature. One area of social work practice where LST and systems theory came together was in the field of family therapy. In 1977, Sonya Rhodes suggested a perspective that offered a way to understand the interface between individual growth and the family environment. Her perspective was deeply rooted in psychodynamic theory but also provided a set of tasks that needed to be addressed in order for a family to successfully negotiate the various stages through which it must move to meet its needs as well as the needs of its individual members. Table 8.3 presents one way to utilize LST as it applies to family development.

TABLE 8.3 ■ Stages of Family Developmental Life Cycle (Rhodes)	
1.	**Intimacy vs. Idealization or Disillusionment**
A.	*Overall task*—to create a relationship between the two adults that allows for appropriate degrees of intimacy.
Subtasks	
1.	Come to grips with the total person you married (good and bad).
2.	Create an acceptable degree of intimacy to build the relationship.
3.	Make the transition from being "in love" to loving the partner.
4.	Negotiate conflicts and find mutually satisfying ways to support each other.
2.	**Replenishment vs. Inward Turning—Childbirth to Entry Into School**
A.	*Overall task*—to develop nurturing patterns among all family members so that emotional, physical, and spiritual sustenance is available to adults as well as their children.
Subtasks	
1.	Engage in succoring and be available and responsive to the needs of the child.
2.	Manage triadic relationships.
3.	Find and capitalize on opportunities to replenish adults' emotional energy.
4.	Adapt to new financial demands on the family.
3.	**Individuation vs. Pseudo-Mutual Organization**
A.	*Overall task*—the family must shift its focus of energy from family concerns to individual interests.

Subtasks	
1.	Create a level of independence that allows the child to create its identity outside the family (structurally and emotionally).
2.	Shift energies of adults to recreating their identities outside the realm of childrearing.
3.	Bring back new information and experiences to the family for them to pursue.
4.	Redefine the nature of the relationship between the adults.
4.	**Companionship vs. Isolation**
A.	*Overall task*—to create opportunities for the children to leave the family and make the transition to the broader community and for the adults to find companionship with partners and those outside the family.
Subtasks	
1.	Deal within the family with the overt sexuality of children and parents.
2.	Revitalize and/or renew the marital relationship that has been submerged during childrearing years (couple activities).
3.	Learn how to negotiate with teenage children.
4.	Redefine the parent/child roles.
5.	**Regrouping vs. Binding and Expulsion**
A.	*Overall task*—to allow the departure of the children as a natural outgrowth of their growth and maturity. The marital relationship and peer relations are key to success in this stage.
Subtasks	
1.	Reconstitute the family's structure and relationships.
2.	Balance the need for independence without loss of intimacy.
3.	Develop the capacity to tolerate experimentation that violates family norms.
4.	Redefine power and control, authority, and trust that allows ongoing contact and supports psychological as well as physical separation.
6.	**Rediscovery vs. Despair**
A.	*Overall task*—to reestablish marital balance that includes rediscovery of one's partner and reconnecting with children on a multigenerational dimension.
Subtasks	
1.	Renegotiate the adult relationship devoid of parental roles.
2.	In general, the adults shift their attention toward each other and begin to accept the losses related to children leaving.

(Continued)

TABLE 8.3 ■ (Continued)	
3.	Reroute maturing and conflict resolution strategies.
4.	Re-approach members on an adult-to-adult basis.
7.	**Mutual Aid vs. Uselessness**
A.	*Overall task*—to create a system by which transgenerational support and mutual aid are available to members.
Subtasks	
1.	Respect intergenerational differences as a source of support rather than something to be avoided.
2.	Engage in mutually beneficial relationships that draw on the strengths each generation possesses.
3.	Create a willingness to support family members who have problems.
4.	Deal with the losses that are inevitable in this stage (emotional, psychological, financial, etc.).

Interpretation of the work of Rhodes (1977)

Table 8.3 provides social workers with the conceptualization of what they are likely to face when working with families. It must be acknowledged up front, as we noted in the preceding section, that these early efforts have many of the same limitations found in Erikson's framework for understanding individual development. Suffice it to say that Table 8.3 does not provide specific information on the many diverse interactions and processes as they relate to family development. In order to fully translate the LST material, social workers need to develop an understanding of issues related to ethnicity, race, sexual orientation, gender, and variations in family structure (e.g., single-parent families, and blended families). However, these stages of the **family life cycle** do provide a broad, useful framework for approaching common themes that are given unique expression in our work with families. For example, "creating a relationship between two adults that allows for appropriate degrees of intimacy" is a task that many families face (see Table 8.3, Stage 1, Subtask 2). However, there are instances when a child is conceived at the outset of a relationship, before there is any real intimacy between the two adults. This situation often places significant stress on the couple's relationship due to the lack of opportunity to develop intimacy, which impacts the trajectory of the family's development and responses to the child. Or, there are instances when couples conceive a child and shortly after the conception they go in separate directions. At some point, the child will ask questions about who the absent parent is and why that parent left. However, in both of these examples, if the parents have not developed some level of intimacy, this will have significant impacts on the child.

Another way in which Rhodes's family developmental framework can be helpful is that it lays out a variety of tasks facing the family without requiring a single focus for understanding the family's challenges. For example, there are numerous theories that speak to the development of intimacy in coupling relationships, including role theory, psychodynamic theory, object relations theory, symbolic interaction theory, critical race theory, and feminist theories. All of these theories could be used to frame various aspects of the internal and external dynamics that are part of a couple's struggles in developing an intimate relationship. The worker and the family needs opportunities to jointly explore what sets of ideas seem the most reasonable in their specific context.

Finally, this family developmental framework allows us to move from a focus on pathology toward a focus on the challenges being faced by the families with whom we work. It allows workers to examine the connections between behaviors that were successful in earlier developmental stages and how those behaviors may create barriers for families as they face new challenges that create crises. For example, some families are able to provide nurture for their very young children. They do this by refocusing their attention from broader interactions that are useful in their attempts to develop their relationship as a couple to redefining boundaries that refocus their energies within the family in order to add a nurturing environment for the child. However, when a child gets old enough to enter school, that same family has to develop new skills. Still later, in Stage 2, it is necessary for the family to help the child develop the capacity to integrate ideas and values that go beyond those beliefs held within their family.

The following case example provides you with an opportunity to utilize elements of the framework in Table 8.3. This particular case focuses primarily on the first four stages of family development.

CASE EXAMPLE
ELLEN AND SAM

Ellen and her husband, Sam, came to see a school social worker at their son's middle school. They had been summoned to the school because their son William has recently begun acting out in school and refusing to turn in his homework in a timely fashion. Prior to this time, the school social worker described William as a model student with a solid "B" average. He now refuses to hand in his homework and is in danger of failing five of his six classes, and all of his teachers are concerned about him withdrawing from his interactions with peers. During the past three months, Ellen and Sam report that at home he is also vacillating between being uncommunicative and engaging in angry outbursts in his interactions with them. After some discussion, they share with the worker that they checked his computer, and they found evidence that he had been on several gay porn sites. Both parents are extremely upset and they are taking steps to "straighten" him out. They assure the school that they have been proactive in restricting his use of the computer and that they believe this is just a "phase." They are going to take him to their parish priest who will instruct him on the moral dangers of his behavior. Place yourself in the role as social worker and utilize the first four stages in Table 8.3 to begin to identify how you might assess the challenges facing this family, and develop a plan to work with them. The following are a few questions to help you get started:

1. How has this family created a nurturing environment for this child? (Try to focus on what they have done that was useful prior to the current challenges.)

2. Does this family understand their own sexuality as well as their child's sexuality?

3. How open is this family to new information that emerges from outside its boundaries?

4. What skills and abilities do these parents have to assist in the transitions necessary to negotiate the current challenges?

Contemporary Life Course Theory (LCT)
Applied to Family Development

As we previously noted, early life span theory had the advantage of beginning to reach out to connect individuals to their environments; subsequent life course theorists placed a stronger emphasis on the environments' role in shaping families' development. These writers began to fill in the gaps that had gone unaddressed in the earlier conceptions of life span theory. Historical context, geography, social embeddedness, agency and personal control, and timing all contributed to a closer look at the environmental side of the person/environment focus for social work (Hareven, 2000). Life course theorists began to question important assumptions upon which the earlier conceptions of family development had been based. For example, they challenged what was assumed to be "normal" family development, the impact of divorce on family development, the role diversity plays in families, how sexual orientation impacts family life, the role of spirituality in family development, and the role that poverty plays in family functioning. These are among the many elements that created a more nuanced set of lenses to examine our work with families (Biblarz & Savci, 2010; Boyd-Franklin, 2003; Walsh, 2012).

McGoldrick and Shibusawa (2012) provide a definition for families that opens up our understanding to include the various social conditions and structures that are shaping our 21st-century understanding of families. According to McGoldrick and Shibusawa, families comprise those who have a shared history and shared future. They encompass the entire emotional system of at least three, four, or even five generations, held together by blood, legal, and/or historical ties. Relationships with parents, siblings, and other family members go through transitions as they move along the life cycle. Boundaries shift, psychological distance among members changes, and roles within and between subsystems are redefined. It is extremely difficult, however, to think of the family as a whole because of the complexity involved. As "a system moving through time" the family has basically different properties from all other systems (McGoldrick & Shibusawa, 2012). This systems language allows us to look at families in ways that encourage understandings of the many aspects that make families in the 21st century much more complex. However, there is significant crossover between current understandings by scholars of life course theory (LCT), such as McGoldrick, and those put forward by family life cycle (FLC) scholars, such as Rhodes. First, early FLC writers built their understandings of families with a much heavier emphasis on the individual's development within families rather than fully articulating a more transactional view of the interactions between individuals, their families, and environments. However, both groups acknowledged the importance of connecting an individual's growth and development to her or his family's growth and development.

Second, both early and current writers shared the view of families as developmental entities that progressed through stages impacting the lives of their individual members. Both groups conceived of family systems as developmental and temporal. The challenges included predictable stressors, for example, transitions that required adapting parent–child interactions based on the age and temperament of the child, as well as unpredictable disruptions in the life cycle process, including serious illness of a family member, untimely death of a member, and job losses. Third, systems theory provided a way to create a balanced view that looked at the interactions among the members of the family. Emphasis was placed on the system's structure and processes, rather than a more narrow focus on the individuals who existed in the family system's structure.

The major differences between the early writers and current scholars is that current scholars put forward much more complex understandings of the context in which families exist and how these varied social changes impact family development. The original group of writers based their inquiry on what they referred to as "normal" families, whom we now call "traditional" families that included two parents who are White and heterosexual, with the father working outside the home and the mother inside the home tending to 2.5 children. Contemporary writers are challenging this narrowly constructed view of families, including what it means to be a "normal" family. They point out that the understanding of "normal" is a social construction and that many of the early writers, as well as some current writers (e.g., Bowen and Haley), continue to draw from White, middle-class groups reflecting Euro-American norms (McGoldrick & Shibusawa, 2012). And, these writers' membership in the dominant groups in our society often contributes to seeing families, whose experiences are different from their own, as pathological. Finally, newer writings are producing knowledge that focuses on issues related to diversity, oppression, discrimination, and a broad range of "isms," each emphasizing the empowerment of families to meet their unique challenges rather than characterizing unique adaptation as pathological (Chodorow, 1974; Dilworth-Anderson, Burton, & Johnson, 1993, LaSala, 2007).

Context for Family Life Course Thinking

In the prior section we began by identifying the assumptions that helped shape early life span authors' thinking. As we move into the discussion of the current writing on life course theory, we will look at the contextual issues that cut across the application of life course theory to family systems. According to McGoldrick and Shibusawa (2012),

- It is necessary to find a balance between applying a **family life course perspective** in a more linear or rigid manner, where families are pathologized in contrast to viewing families as "systems moving through time," acknowledging the importance of diverse paths for family development.

- Families pass from one stage to the next and that requires them to develop new skills that were not present in prior stages. For example, skills necessary to nurture family members are present in all stages. However, the skills necessary to nurture an infant are quite different than the skills needed to nurture an adolescent.

- In all stages, families are negotiating expansion, contraction, and realignment of their relationships to support the development of their members. For example, anyone who has seen parents standing at a school bus stop or in front of their neighborhood elementary school can attest to the challenges required to support their child's transition into the larger community. This requires them to expand the boundaries of the family system so that the child can move away from the safety of their home.

- Family development is not wedded to age or dependent on one type of family. All families develop based on their own contexts, structures, and processes. For example, when a child enters school, the two-parent families face issues related to refocusing the couple's attention on their own relationship and their shared development to adjust to the new circumstances. A single parent may be dealing with a sense of grief and loss and possible isolation as the child enters school. In both instances, the tasks require new or significantly modified skills to master the challenges the family faces.

- Current family life course writers do not use a single sequential pathway for understanding family development. Life course perspectives require that we reach out to emerging scholarship that emphasizes how gender, diversity, economic impacts, cultural elements, and broader social economic and political trends provide a more nuanced view of the challenges facing families.

We encourage you to keep these contextual elements in mind as you move through the following material that illustrates how both frameworks can be useful in your practice. Table 8.4 provides an interpretation of the work of McGoldrick and Shibusawa (2012), with some additional elements that come from other family theory scholars. The table takes their work and breaks it not only into stages but also the tasks faced by families as they traverse the challenges of developing through time.

TABLE 8.4 ■ Stages of Family Life Course (McGoldrick)	
1.	*Coupling: The Journey of Families*
A.	*Overall task*—to define the couple relationship within the context of both partners including their families of origin.
Subtasks	
1.	Come to grips with importance of both family of origin systems as they influence a couple's current life.
2.	Move beyond the stereotypes, fallacies, and myths they bring to the marriage.
3.	Create partnerships educationally and in emotional connectedness.
4.	Reintegrate family status by establishing healthy boundaries (separate but connected family of origins).
2.	**Families With Young Children**
A.	*Overall task*—to transition from a two-person system to a three-person system within their environmental context (physical, psychological, social, and spiritual).
Subtasks	
1.	Adults must move up a generation to become caretakers to the younger generation.
2.	They must make a shift to take responsibility and deal with challenges posed by parenting a young child.
3.	Learn to handle the child care responsibilities and chores that conflict with obtaining sufficient resources; recreate nurturing activities inside the family.
3.	**Families With Adolescents**
A.	*Overall task*—to develop new definitions of the roles and responsibilities of both children and parents based on changing cognitive, emotional, physical, and social needs.
Subtasks	
1.	Allow for the integration of close adolescent–parent relationships with the need for development of greater independence in these relationships.

2.	Integrate new information coming from outside the family; gender roles, technology, values, and aspirations may challenge existing family norms.
3.	Learn the process of negotiations to traverse the balance in dependence/independence/interdependence.
4.	**Families at Midlife: Launching Children and Moving On**
A.	*Overall task*—to manage the challenges that face families as their children move between independent living and the need to return to their families as they attempt to establish themselves outside the family.
Subtasks	
1.	Children must complete education, lead independent lives, and find partners or decide not to partner.
2.	Parents need to reorient their attention and attachments toward each other and toward new pursuits.
3.	Manage the disruptions that occur as adult children leave the family and return on multiple occasions.
5.	**Between Families: Young Adulthood**
A.	*Overall task*—to manage the transition from having a young adult live inside the family to establishing a trajectory that is shaped by the young adult's reality.
Subtasks	
1.	For the young adult, to separate from their family of origin without cutting off.
2.	For the family, to manage the realities of the current emotional context, which creates significant pressure that challenges the young adult in achieving independent status.
3.	For the young adult, formulate life goals and plans to move toward those goals.
6.	**The Family in Later Life**
A.	*Overall task*—the remaining family members need to develop strategies that allow for them to sustain relationships within the family as well as sustain connections with their informal (e.g., friends) and formal resources in the broader social context.
Subtasks	
1.	Members need to develop adjustments to retirement, which requires individuals to assume their new status and its meaning to themselves and others in the family.
2.	Develop skills necessary to manage new challenges, including the death of family members and friends, the addition of new roles, and grandparenting.
3.	Develop the ability to manage new challenges as they relate to financial security, declining health, and the complex tasks associated with gerotranscendence, which involves the ability to better integrate personality to transcend any developmental challenges.

Interpretation of the work of McGolderick and Shubusawa (2012)

Rhodes's and McGoldrick's Frameworks for Understanding Family Social Work Practice

This section provides an opportunity to look at glimpses of a single family and the challenges they face over the course of time. Our purpose is to provide you with opportunities to practice using the frameworks you have just examined. It will also ask you to take material provided in the preceding sections of the chapter on development of racial identity, oppression, and strengths-based work.

In the following case example, you are a social worker working in a family social service agency and you receive a call from the Jackson family requesting assistance.

A number of years pass and you receive a message that Winona and Carl have called the agency asking to come see you because they are having some problems. They arrive in your office and share the following information.

CASE EXAMPLE

THE JACKSON FAMILY – PART ONE

Winona and Carl met each other at the age of 20 and married one year later. Winona is a member of the Pottawatomie Prairie Band Tribe, reflecting her mother's heritage. Carl is a product of the family in which his mother is African American and his father is White. Carl secured employment at an automobile manufacturing plant in a medium-size Midwestern city. He completed his GED and worked on the assembly line. Winona finished high school and went on to become a Certified Nursing Assistant (CNA). They rented a small house in a working-class neighborhood and began having children. They had two children in the first three years of their marriage. Aaron is their 3-year-old son and they have a 1-year-old daughter named Charlotte. Aaron had some problems with his lungs and received a diagnosis of chronic asthma. Charlotte appears to be healthy. The family has always struggled to meet their financial needs, but they have been able to keep a roof over their heads and feed their children. However, Carl's parents have expressed concern about the fact that Winona is taking the children to spiritual ceremonies with members of her tribe.

Her in-laws are concerned about the moral development of the children and are pressing Carl to intervene to stop Winona for the sake of the children's "souls." Carl and Winona are both concerned about the tensions being created between themselves by their respective family members.

Discussion Questions

(1) How can the major themes in Stages 1 and 2 of both frameworks be used to guide your understanding of what you are seeing?

(2) How can you formulate and share your assessment of the situation with the parents?

(3) What are some of the tasks that need to be addressed to reduce their tensions?

(4) How do your own beliefs and characteristics related to gender and race impact your understanding of this situation?

(5) As you use these frameworks, how do they affect your thoughts and feelings about the nature of your work with this family?

CASE EXAMPLE
THE JACKSON FAMILY – PART TWO

The couple has remained together and continue to experience financial tensions. Winona was able to go back to school and is now a Licensed Practical Nurse (LPN). She is working at a local health clinic making $14.50 an hour. Carl continues to work at the auto plant but has had two lengthy layoffs due to the downsizing of the workforce and because of the necessity to retool the assembly line. He has lost about four months' wages over the last two years.

They continued to live in the same area, but they had to move to an apartment because they couldn't afford the rent increases in their old house. They are living in a multifamily unit with two townhouses. They report having more blow-ups during the past two years. These are triggered by family tensions, and they are feeling that they are "losing ground." They also are very concerned about Aaron, who is now a senior in high school, while Charlotte is in her sophomore year. The White neighborhood and the high school is populated largely by lower-middle-income children who are from similar economic circumstances. According to Winona and Carl, Aaron is struggling in school. They say it started in middle school when he began to get in fights with classmates who had used racial slurs toward him and he struck back. He withdrew from playing sports because his grades made him ineligible. They have found evidence he is smoking marijuana and is getting more and more withdrawn. Carl's parents have recently expressed a desire to have Aaron come and live with them until he "finds out who he is." Neither Carl nor Winona are open to Carl's parents' suggestions, but it does put pressure on them because they see these comments as a condemnation of their

parenting. Winona and Carl also express concerns that Aaron will be drawn into the racial unrest that is prominent in their community. Charlotte continues to attend school regularly and maintains a "C" average but has begun to talk about bullying she is experiencing at school. Right now the parents' concerns are focused on their children's challenges and the tensions that these create for their own relationship.

Discussion Questions

How can you use the two-family systems development frameworks (Rhodes and McGoldrick) along with material on nigrescence and historical trauma to answer the following questions as they relate to the Jackson case?

(1) How do the themes in the tasks outlined in both frameworks assist you in identifying what is happening? How does that understanding translate into your work with this family?

(2) What are the potential stressors operating for the children?

(3) What new skills do the parents need to learn in order to support their children's ongoing development?

(4) How do your own experiences, beliefs, and characteristics shape the meaning you give to what you're seeing?

(5) How do the ideas in the chapter about identity (nigrescence and historical trauma) relate to this situation?

A substantial amount of time has passed and Winona and Carl are again seeking assistance. As a new social worker, you receive the information outlined in the preceding two encounters with this family.

CASE EXAMPLE
THE JACKSON FAMILY – PART THREE

Winona and Carl's presenting concern is that they are currently experiencing an increase in the tensions between them, and they cannot understand why they continue to experience struggles now that they are in their "golden years." Both children have established themselves outside the home. Aaron has a job in a small fabrication plant that provides a meager but steady income. He is married with three children and there have been times when tensions in his own family have required that he move back home with his parents for a few weeks at a time. Carl and Winona report that the problems Aaron has are just "normal issues" that all couples face. However, they report conflicts between Aaron and his wife and that in the last year there has been one instance in which he hit his wife. Charlotte has not married and is the owner of a small shop that focuses on selling southwestern Native American art. She makes enough money to sustain herself. She has recently been diagnosed with stage 3, treatable breast cancer, but she has no health insurance.

Carl and Winona identify some of their struggles; neither of their children will listen to the suggestions they make about their situations, and both have concerns about the children's circumstances (Aaron's unstable marriage and Charlotte's health). Carl is also concerned about a lack of retirement income due to the 2008 recession. He also expresses concern that Aaron is caught in a dead-end job and won't be able to take care of his family, and Winona will want to help them financially. Winona's immediate concern is that she wants to provide money for Charlotte's care and that takes precedence over their own needs. She is pressing to sell the house and move into a small apartment. Carl is opposed to this because he has "worked all of his life" to provide a home for himself and Winona.

Discussion Questions

The following are some questions you can ask that will help you tie the life course frameworks to the assessment and development of a plan of action and that can help evaluate your progress.

(1)   How could you engage in a discussion with this couple regarding ways to deal with the changing nature of their relationship?

(2)   How can you explore ways they have handled conflict in the past as it relates to the current tensions?

(3)   How can they enter into a discussion regarding managing tensions that center on redefining their parental roles with their adult children?

(4)   What skills should they employ to talk with each other about the newly emerging challenges regarding their different definitions of priorities in their retirement?

Discussion of the Frameworks

Now that you have had the experience of using these two frameworks, we will share some observations about how they are similar and different; we will also examine their strengths as well as some of their limitations. First, both frameworks have significant levels of overlap. For example, for McGoldrick and Shibusawa (2012) and Rhodes (1977) both discuss the tasks of parenting children in Stage 2. However, McGoldrick's language is clearly broader and allows the social worker to focus on both the internal systems in a family and the context in which the family exists. Rhodes's language focuses attention more specifically on the internal dynamics of the family and the individuals within the family with much less emphasis on the context within which these tasks are being completed.

Second, both authors look at families as "systems moving through time," even though only McGoldrick uses this specific phrase. What both perspectives do is to put forward the idea that families are developmental, with identifiable stages, and this development occurs over time. They do have differences in the specific stages that reflect their own historical context. McGoldrick identifies Stage 5, *Between Families: Young Adulthood*, which focuses on the realities of current families whose children have extended periods between the time they originally leave home and are fully emancipated. This elongated process is a product of the current social context that did not exist at the time that Rhodes created her framework. This additional stage is important because current literature suggests that young adults in the 21st century are taking longer to finish their education, find jobs, establish committed relationships, and are delaying decisions about whether or not to have children (Arnett, 2000).

One of the limitations in both models is that they have fairly linear presentations of the stage-based process. For example, in both models, Stage 3 focuses on identity development. However, we would say that identity represents a central theme in *all stages* of family development. For example, Carl and Winona had to redefine their identities as husband and wife to include new roles having to do with being parents. In their last encounter with the agency, their work involved identity issues in connection to the tensions emerging from redefining their identities from workers to retirees. Their children began developing their identities at birth (i.e., locating themselves in relationship to gender [male and female] when they were two years old). In subsequent stages, portions of their work deal with integrating new identities such as being a student, becoming an employee, grappling with what it means to be an adult, being a partner, and being a parent. This is not intended to be a comprehensive list but simply to demonstrate how themes are located in, and actually flow throughout, all of the stages rather than being isolated in one stage.

Third, both frameworks, in and of themselves, do not address the myriad of permutations and combinations that shape families' trajectories, structure, and processes. Thus, no one framework speaks to what happens in all families. However, frameworks do provide a beginning format that can be used to suggest what you will need to look for in order to work with your specific families. One example would be the managing of "triadic relationships" in families' lives. If a child is born into a family where the parents live separately and the child lives with one parent and only visits the other parent, the tasks related to developing intimacy between the couple are focused on their parental roles, not their spousal relationship. In addition, unique challenges may emerge if that child decides as an adolescent that she or he wants to live with the parent who has not been the custodial parent. In this instance, the family structure requires different skills that need to be mastered.

Fourth, metaphorically, both frameworks provide a skeletal snapshot of the nature of families, and that picture is based on one type of family, a "traditional" family. Current trends suggest that these families are becoming fewer and fewer, while families with differing structures and dynamics are on the rise. The example of Carl and Winona illustrates identity issues for their family members that are significantly different from other families due to their racial complexity as compared with more homogeneous families located in a dominant racial group. In order to be able to address these issues, we have to rely on a more nuanced view of the frameworks in this chapter. The inclusion of nigrescence theory represents a framework to assist the social worker in helping the Jackson family address complex dynamics that confront their family and the challenges presented by the context in which their work is occurring. The concept of historical trauma also plays out in Winona's responses to her children and in the larger community attitudes she must confront.

Finally, if we include current knowledge that looks more closely at the relationship between social context and family development we can help ourselves understand and confront the pressures impacting families' ability to do their work. For example, what do we need to know about sexual orientation in order to help Sam and Ellen deal with William's exploration of his sexual orientation? If William is in fact gay, how can we help them struggle with the spiritual dimensions of their understanding of his behavior? What are the challenges they face as they seek to deal with their own fears about what might happen should this information come to light with their extended family? How can we help them explore their own sense of grief and loss as they absorb this new information? How can they deal with the fears they have that William will become a target for violence based on the larger community's homophobia? In the work with Winona and Carl, how might their own diverse backgrounds impact their ability to develop an intimate relationship? If the community in which they live views their relationship as unacceptable, what additional pressures will they face in developing a healthy relationship? What are the special challenges that they may face as they try to support their children and their identity development? How will their ability to accrue limited resources during their working life impact their relationships between themselves and their children during retirement?

Reflections

In this section of the chapter we have attempted to provide a set of maps or frameworks that can be helpful in two ways. First, these frameworks allow us to see families as growing and developing systems that are in constant change based on the environments in which they exist. Second, while there are common themes in their developmental processes, each family is unique and must be understood based on its own characteristics and contexts. Third, using developmental frameworks is one way in which social workers can focus their attention on helping families address the challenges they are facing by normalizing those challenges rather than pathologizing families. Finally, helping families to understand themselves in developmental terms allows us to share with them how current issues may come up in the future and provides some guidance about how those challenges can be managed.

CHAPTER SUMMARY

In this chapter we began our journey looking at the work of Eric Erikson, who proposed an epigenetic developmental process that provided a blueprint for tracking a linear, prescribed order of development that unfolds at specific times. His focus was on the individual, but his work was later expanded on by social workers to include family life. In both individual and family development, early life span theory was based on assumptions rooted in a largely male heterosexual and European worldview. While these frameworks provided a way to view individual and family development, they both shared rather narrow, "Eurocentric" biases. Current applications broaden these lenses to view families by including the impact of diverse pathways (e.g., gender, race, ethnicity, sexual orientation) and diverse structures (e.g., single-parent, couples, extended family and multigenerational families). Newer writings from the social sciences provides a more complex understanding of racial identity development (e.g., nigrescence and multiracial identity development theories). Further, historical trauma is being used to deepen our understanding of the ways in which identities are developed as a response to the larger social conditions and challenges faced by current families.

While life span, life course, racial identity development, and historical trauma theories are not a panacea for our work with individuals and families, they help connect the dual aspects of person/environment. This allows us to focus on the transactions occurring between people and contexts that account for both development and barriers central for social workers to understand in working with client systems. Finally, our discussion helps set the stage for the use of these materials as a means to assist families in responding to challenges, by capitalizing on their strengths rather than pathologizing their adaptations.

Key Terms (in order of appearance)

Life span theories   214

Life course perspectives   218

Nigrescence theory   220

American Holocaust   223

Historical trauma   223

Imperialism   224

Colonialism   224

Oppression   224

Colonization   224

Indigenous decolonization   225

Family life cycle   236

Family life course
   perspective   241

References

Adams, H. L., & Phillips, L. (2009). Ethnic related variations from the Cass Model of Homosexual Identity Formation: The experiences of two-spirit, lesbian and gay Native Americans. *Journal of Homosexuality, 56,* 959–976.

Apgar, D. (2016). *Social work ASWB advanced generalist exam guide: A comprehensive study guide for success.* New York, NY: Springer Publishing.

Arnett, J. J. (2000). Emerging adulthood: A theory of development from the late teens through the twenties. *American Psychologist*, *55*, 469–480.

Arnett, J. J. (2001). Conceptions of the transition to adulthood: Perspectives from adolescence through midlife. *Journal of Adult Development*, *8*(2), 133–143.

Arnett, J. J. (2004). *Emerging adulthood: The winding road from late teens through the twenties.* New York, NY: Oxford University Press.

Arnett, J. J. (2007). Emerging adulthood: What is it, and what is it good for? *Child Development Perspectives*, *1*, 68–73.

Ashford, J. B., & LeCroy, C. W. (2013). *Human behavior in the social environment: A multidimensional perspective* (5th ed.). Boston, MA: Brooks/Cole.

Biblarz, T., & Savci, E. (2010). Lesbian, gay, bi-sexual, and transgender families. *Journal of Marriage and Family*, *72*, 480–497.

Boyd-Franklin, N. (2003). *Black families in family therapy: Understanding the African American experience* (2nd ed.). New York, NY: Guilford Press.

Brave Heart, M. Y. H. (1998). The return to the sacred path. Healing the historical trauma and historical unresolved grief response among the Lakota through a psychoeducational group intervention, *Smith College Studies in Social Work*, *68*(3), 287–305.

Brave Heart, M. Y. H. (2000). Wakiksuyapi: Carrying the historical trauma of the Lakota. *Tulane Studies in Social Welfare*, *21-22*, 245–266.

Brave Heart, M. Y. H. (2003). Historical trauma response among Natives and its relationship with substance abuse: A Lakota illustration. *Journal of Psychiatric Drugs*, *35*, 7–13.

Brave Heart, M. Y. H. (2013). *Historical trauma and parenting.* Retrieved on May 2, 2017 at: https://www.ihs.gov/telebehavioral/includes/themes/newihstheme/display_objects/documents/slides/historicaltrauma/htparenting0113.pdf

Brave Heart, M. Y. H., & DeBruyn, L. M. (1998). The American Indian holocaust: Healing historical unresolved grief. *American Indian and Alaska Native Mental Health Research*, *8*(2), 56–78.

Brave Heart-Jordan, M. Y. H. (1995). *The return to the Sacred Path: Healing from historical trauma and historical unresolved grief among the Lakota.* Doctoral dissertation, Smith College School of Social Work, Northampton, MA.

Butz, W. P., & Torrey, B. B. (2006). Some frontiers in social science. *Science*, *312*(5782), 1898–1900.

Carter, B., Preto, N. A. G., & McGoldrick, M. (2015). *The expanding family life cycle: Individual, family and social perspectives* (5th ed.). Boston, MA: Pearson.

Cass, V. C. (1979). Homosexual identity formation: A theoretical model. *Journal of Homosexuality*, *4*(3), 219–235.

Chenault, V. S. (2004). *Violence and abuse against indigenous women.* Unpublished doctoral dissertation. University of Kansas, School of Social Welfare, Lawrence, KS.

Chenault, V. S. (2011). *Weaving strength, weaving power: Violence and abuse against indigenous women.* Durham, NC: Carolina Academic Press.

Chodorow, N. (1974). Family structure and feminine personality. In M. Z. Rosaldo & L. Lamphere (Eds.), *Women, culture and society* (pp. 43–66). Stanford, CA: Stanford University Press.

Choi-Misailidis, S. (2010). Multiracial-heritage awareness and personal affiliation (M-HAPA): Understanding identity in people of mixed-race descent. In J. Ponterotto, J. Casas, L. Suzuki, & C. Alexander (Eds.), *Handbook of multicultural counseling* (pp. 301–311). Thousand Oaks, CA: Sage.

Crawford, A. (2014). "The trauma experienced by generations past having an effect in their descendents": Narrative and historical trauma among Inuit in Nunavut, Canada. *Transcultural Psychiatry*, *5*(3), 339–369.

Cross, W. E., Jr. (1971). The Negro-to-Black conversion experience. *Black World*, *20*, 13–27.

Cross, W. E., Jr. (1991). *Shades of black: Diversity in African-American identity.* Philadelphia, PA: Temple University Press.

Dilworth-Anderson, P., Burton, L., & Johnson, L. B. (1993). Reframing theories for understanding race, ethnicity and families. In P. G. Boss, W. J. Doherty, R. Larossa, W. R. Schum, & S. K. Steinmetz (Eds.), *Sourcebook of family theories and methods: A contextual approach* (pp. 627–646). New York, NY: Plenum.

Doka, K. J. (1989). *Disenfranchised grief: Recognizing hidden sorrow*. Lexington, MA: D. C. Heath and Company.

Elder, G. H. Jr. (1998). The life course as developmental theory. *Child Development, 69*(1), 1–12.

Elder, G. H., Jr., & Giele, J. Z. (2009). *The craft of life course research*. New York, NY: Guilford Press.

Erikson, E. H. (1950). *Childhood and society*. New York, NY: Norton.

Erikson, E. H. (1962). *Young man Luther: A study in psychoanalysis and history*. New York, NY: Norton.

Erikson, E. H. (1963). *Childhood and society* (2nd rev. ed., enlarged). New York, NY: Norton.

Erikson, E. H. (1968). *Identity, youth and crisis*. New York, NY: W. W. Norton.

Erikson, E. H. (1969). *Gandhi's truth*. New York, NY: Norton.

Erikson, E. H., & Erikson, J. M. (1997). *Life cycle completed (Extended version)*. New York, NY: Norton.

Fogelman, E. (1988). Therapeutic alternatives of survivors. In R. L. Braham (Ed.), *The psychological perspectives of the Holocaust and of its aftermath* (pp. 79–108). New York, NY: Columbia University Press.

Frey, L. L. (2013). Relational-cultural therapy: Theory, research and application to counselling competencies. *Professional Psychology: Research and Practice, 44*(3), 177–185.

Giele, J. Z. (1995). *Two paths to women's equality: Temperance, suffrage, and the origins of modern feminism*. New York, NY: Twayne.

GlenMaye, L. (1998). Empowerment of women. In L. M. Gutierrez, R. J. Parsons, & E. O. Cox (Eds.), *Empowerment in social work practice: A sourcebook* (pp. 29–51). Pacific Grove, CA: Brooks/Cole Publishing Co.

Hall, R. E. (2000). The racial canons of American sociology: Identity across the lifespan as biracial alternative. *American Psychologist, 31*, 86–93.

Hareven, T. K. (2000). *Families, history and social change: Life-course and cross-cultural perspectives*. Oxford, UK: Westview Press.

Helms, J. (1995). An update on Helms' White and people of color racial identity models. In J. Ponterotto, J. Casas, L. Suzuki, & C. Alexander (Eds.), *Handbook of multicultural counseling* (pp. 181–198). Thousand Oaks, CA: Sage.

Hill, R., & Foote, N. N. (1970). *Family development in three generations: A longitudinal study of changing family patterns of planning and achievement*. Cambridge, MA: Schenkman.

Hitlin, S., Brown, J. S., & Elder, G. H. (2006). Racial self-categorization in adolescence: Multiracial development and social pathways. *Child Development, 77*, 1298–1308.

Hoxie, F. E. (1989). *A final promise: The campaign to assimilate the Indians, 1880–1920*. Cambridge, MA: University Press.

Hutchison, E. D. (2015). *Dimensions of human behavior: Person and environment* (5th ed.). Thousand Oaks, CA: Sage.

Jordan, J. V. (2001). A relational-cultural model: Healing through mutual empathy. *Bulletin of the Menninger Clinic, 65*, 1, 92–103.

Kerwin, C., & Ponterotto, J. G. (1995). Biracial identity development: Theory and research. In J. Ponterotto, J. Casas, L. Suzuki, & C. Alexander (Eds.), *Handbook of multicultural counseling* (pp. 199–217). Thousand Oaks, CA: Sage.

Kroger, J. (2002). Identity processes and contents through the years of late adulthood. *An International Journal of Theory and Research, 10*, 317–337.

Krystal, H. (1984). Integration & self-healing in post-traumatic states. In S. A. Luel & P. Marcus (Eds.), *Psychoanalytic reflections on the Holocaust: Selected essays* (pp. 113–134). New York, NY: Holocaust Awareness Institute, Center for Judaic Studies, University of Denver (Colorado) and Ktav Publishing House.

LaSala, M. C. (2007). Old maps, new territory: Family therapy, theory and gay and lesbian couples. *Journal of GLBT Family Studies, 3*(1), 1–14.

Legters, L. H. (1988). The American genocide. *Policy Studies Journal, 76*(4), 768–777.

McGoldrick, M., & Shibusawa, T. (2012). The family life cycle. In F. Walsh (Ed.), *Normal family processes: Growing diversity and complexity* (pp. 375–398). New York, NY: Guilford Press.

Miller, D. B., & Joe, S. (2008). *Life span: Young adulthood*. Washington, DC and New York, NY: NASW and Oxford University Press.

Mullaly, B. (1997). *Structural social work: Ideology, theory and practice* (2nd ed.). Toronto, ON: Oxford University Press.

Neugarten, B. L. (1996). *The meanings of age: Selected papers of Bernice L. Neugarten*. Chicago, IL: University of Chicago Press.

Niederland, W. G. (1989). Trauma, loss, restoration, and creativity. In D. R. Dietrich & P. C. Shabad (Eds.), *The problem of loss and mourning: Psychoanalytic* perspectives (pp. 61–82). Madison, CT: International Universities Press.

Perlman, H. H. (1965). *Social casework: A problem-solving process*. Chicago, IL: University of Chicago.

Poston, W. C. (1990). The biracial identity development model: A needed addition. *Journal of Counseling & Development, 69*, 152–155.

Rhodes, S. (1977). A developmental approach to the life cycle of the family. *Social Casework, 58*, 301–311.

Robbins, S. P., Chatterjee, P., & Canda, E. R. (2011). *Contemporary human behavior theory: A critical perspective for social work* (3rd ed.). Boston, MA: Pearson.

Rogers, A. T. (2016). *Human behavior in the social environment: Perspectives on development and the life course* (4th ed.). New York, NY: Routledge.

Root, M. P. P. (Ed.). (1996). *The multiracial experience: Racial borders as the new frontier*. Thousand Oaks, CA: Sage.

Said, E. (1993). *Culture and imperialism*. New York, NY: Knopf.

Scherz, F. H. (1970). Theory and practice of family therapy. In R. W. Roberts & R. H. Nee (Eds.), *Theories of social casework* (pp. 219–264). Chicago, IL: University of Chicago Press.

Seabrook, J. A., & Avison, W. R. (2012). Socioeconomic status and cumulative disadvantage processes across the life course: Implications for health outcomes. *Canadian Review of Sociology, 49*(1), 50–68.

Smalley, R. E. (1967). *Theory for social work practice*. New York, NY: Columbia University Press.

Smelser, N. J., & Erikson, E. H. (Eds.) (1980). Themes of adulthood in the Freud-Jung correspondence. In E. H. Erikson & N. J. Smelser (Eds.), *Themes of Work and Love in Adulthood* (pp. 43–74). Cambridge, MA: Harvard University Press.

Sokol, J. (2009). Identity development throughout the lifetime: An examination of Eriksonian theory. *Graduate Journal of Counseling Psychology, 1*(2), Art. 14.

Stannard, D. (1992). *American Holocaust: Columbus and the conquest of the new World*. New York, NY: Oxford University Press.

Stiffarm, L. A., & Lane, P., Jr. (1992). The demography of Native North America: A question of American Indian survival. In M. A. Jaimes (Ed.), *The state of Native America: Genocide, colonization, and resistance* (pp. 23–53). Boston, MA: South End Press.

Stouffer, S. A., Suchman, E. A., DeVinney, L. C., Star, S. A., & Williams, R. M., Jr. (1949). *The American soldier: Vol 1. Adjustment during Army life*. Princeton, NJ: Princeton University Press.

Sue, D. W., & Sue, D. (2003). *Counseling the culturally diverse: Theory and practice* (4th ed.). New York, NY: John Wiley & Sons.

Syed, M., & Mitchell, L. L. (2013). Race, ethnicity, and emerging adulthood: Retrospect and prospects. *Emerging Adulthood, 1*(2), 83–95.

Thomas, W. I., & Znaniecki, F. (1918–1920). *The Polish peasant in Europe and America: Monograph of an immigrant group* (Vol. *1–5*). Boston, MA: Gorham Press.

Thornton, R. (1987). *American Indian holocaust and survival: A population history since 1492*. Norman: University of Oklahoma Press.

Tornstam, L. (1989). Gero-transcendence: A meta-theoretical reformulation of the disengagement theory. *Aging: Clinical and Experimental Research, 1*, 55–63.

Tornstam, L. (2005). *Gerotranscendence: A developmental theory of positive aging*. New York, NY: Springer.

van der Kolk, B. A. (1987). *Psychological trauma.* Washington, DC: American Psychiatric Press.

Vandiver, B. J. (2001). Psychological nigrescence revisited: Introduction and overview. *Journal of Multicultural Counseling and Development, 29*, 165–173.

Walsh, F. (2012). The new normal: Diversity and complexity in 21st century families. In F. Walsh (Ed.), *Normal family processes: Growing diversity and complexity* (pp. 3–27). New York, NY: Guilford Press.

Weaver, H. N., & Brave Heart, M. Y. H. (1999). Examining two facets of American Indian identity: Exposure to other cultures and the influence of historical trauma. *Journal of Human Behavior in the Social Environment, 2*(1–2), 19–33.

Wellman, B., Wong, R. Y.-L., Tindall, D., & Nazer, N. (1997). A decade of network change: Turnover persistence and stability in personal communities. *Social Networks, 19*, 27–50.

Worrell, F. C., Cross, W. E., & Vandiver, B. J. (2001). Nigrescence theory: Current status and challenges for the future. *Journal of Multicultural Counseling and Development, 29*, 201–213.

Yellow Bird, M., & Chenault, V. (1999). The role of social work in advancing the practice of Indigenous education: Obstacles and promises in empowerment-oriented social work practice. In K. C. Swisher & J. Tippeconnic III (Eds.), *Next steps: Research and practice to advance Indian education* (pp. 201–235). Charleston, WV: ERIC.

Zastrow, C. H., & Kirst-Ashman, K. K. (2016). *Understanding human behavior and the social environment* (10th ed.). Boston, MA: Cengage Learning.

9

SYMBOLIC INTERACTIONISM

PHOTO 9.1
Social interaction shapes identity: On the streets of Zagreb, Croatia.

OVERVIEW AND IN-DEPTH EXAMINATION OF GEORGE H. MEAD

CASE EXAMPLE
THE MULTIPLE PERSPECTIVES OF A HOARDING TASK FORCE

As a member of a hoarding multidisciplinary task force in rural Nebraska, a city code inspector was called in to deal with a crisis involving an elder, John, engaged in hoarding behaviors. John had stacks and stacks of newspapers and only a "path" where he could walk back to his kitchen. John cared for several cats, but they had defecated on the paper stacks and on the floor where they could find a place to do so. The inspector also remarked that she felt like she was in a gerbil cage; mice had literally made "nests" in John's home and had shredded many of the papers. The inspector deemed John's home as a fire hazard and unsafe to live in; her responsibility as a member of the task force was to remove massive amounts of flammable items. When the inspector approached John to discuss the clean-up of his home, he became very upset and threatened to commit suicide if anything was removed. John's reactions caught the inspector off guard and so she called the mental health social worker on the task force and said, "I am standing on John's front lawn saying that we have to haul away all these flammable items and John is threatening to kill himself." The inspector noted, "I need to know how to call someone that can help John and these animals, because I can't. This is not what I do."

Hoarding multidisciplinary task forces consist of a variety of professionals, such as code inspectors, social workers from adult protective services and area agencies on aging, mental health professionals (many of whom may be social workers), animal control officers, public health nurses, and police officers. Each professional has a specific role and interpretation of John's hoarding situation. Animal control officers are concerned with the health and well-being of animals, city code inspectors are concerned about physical safety and the violation of housing codes, social workers in adult protective services are concerned about older adults' risk to self-neglect or abuse, and the person engaged in hoarding behaviors may indeed want no interference or help from the task force (Koenig, Chapin, & Spano, 2010; Koenig, Leiste, Spano & Chapin, 2013).

Discussion Questions

The following questions are put forth to help you explore the roles, perspectives, or interpretations of different task force members regarding this hoarding case:

(1) Based on this case example, what was the city code inspector's role?

(2) How does the city code inspector's role impact her interpretation of John's situation?

(3) What actions is she charged with carrying out based on her interpretation of John's situation?

(4) How might the city code inspector's interpretation (or definition) of John's situation differ from that of the mental health professional and the animal control officer?

(5) How might these various definitions lead to different actions for addressing John's situation?

Symbolic interactionists believe that we decide how to act according to how we "define the situation" that we find ourselves in. There can be multiple interpretations of a particular situation, such as John's hoarding behavior, and this is illustrated in the variety of perspectives of multidisciplinary hoarding task force members. Task force members' definitions of John's hoarding behavior also influence their subsequent actions, are shaped by the role they play on the task force, and by their interactions with John. For example, the code officer interprets John's behavior as a fire hazard, however, when John threatens suicide at the thought of losing his hoarding "stuff," the code officer shifts her view of John's situation to a concern for his mental health. She is able to take on John's role, to put herself in John's shoes, and to reach out to the task force for help in working with John.

One of the key founders of symbolic interactionism, George Herbert Mead, (featured as an in-depth theorist within this overview) taught that in human behavior, such as John's hoarding behaviors, there is always an interpretation of what we do and in how we perceive what others do. It is through the mind that individuals tell themselves how others see things and how other people's perspectives operate. As others act, we put ourselves into their perspectives and we begin to understand the meaning their acts have for them. And, by taking the role of the other, we also engage in self-discovery and develop our own perspectives.

Symbolic Interactionism: Social Work Relevance and Historical Roots

Although misunderstood and at times undervalued by social work scholars, we have chosen to include symbolic interactionism because it is a theory with great applicability to social work practice, policy, and research. Social work scholars have used numerous symbolic interactionist concepts (e.g., self, identity, role, stigma, and primary group), but often they do not acknowledge the roots of these concepts. Historically, sociologists who embraced symbolic interactionism once partnered directly with social workers (e.g., in the settlement house movement). The fruits of this partnership have influenced social work practice over time and with all kinds of social systems (e.g., individuals, families, small groups, and communities) (Forte, 2004a, 2004b).

Symbolic interactionism is an interpretivist theoretical approach that can be linked to Max Weber's writings. Weber, as part of the German idealist tradition, suggested that in the human sciences we are concerned with *Verstehen* or understanding (Gerth & Mills, 1970; Weber, 1949) and that an interpretive approach is needed in human and social sciences. This is in contrast to the natural sciences, which are concerned with *Erklären* or logical explanation and causality. According to this tradition, there is a fundamental difference between nature and culture; natural laws are inappropriate to the realm of human affairs characterized by the freedom of the human spirit (See Figure 9.1). Symbolic interactionists basically agree that the human and social sciences require methods of inquiry that are different from the natural sciences (Dilthey, 1976a, 1976b). Interestingly enough, the natural and social worlds have come closer together largely due to the recognition by many thinkers that positivist science's age old claims to certitude and objectivity cannot be sustained and that findings in the natural sciences are themselves social constructions and human interpretations. All forms of scholarly inquiry are interpretations.

FIGURE 9.1 ■ Contrasts Between the Social (Verstehen) and Natural (Erklären) Worlds

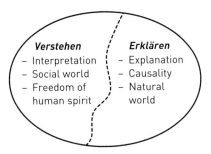

Symbolic interactionism, as an American perspective on life, society, and the world, stems from the thought of George Herbert Mead, a faculty member for many years at the University of Chicago. Mead's teachings are encapsulated in a posthumous work, *Mind, Self and Society* (1934). This book was compiled by grateful students from Mead's papers and lecture notes. One student, Herbert Blumer, is credited, in large measure, for compiling Mead's work. Blumer (1969, p. 2) delineated three basic interactionist assumptions: (1) that human beings act toward things on the basis of the meanings that these things have for them; (2) that the meaning of such things is derived from, and arises out of, the social interaction that one has with one's companions; and (3) that these meanings are handled in and modified through an interpretive process used by the person in dealing with the things she encounters.

Key Concepts in Symbolic Interactionism

In this section, several key concepts in symbolic interactionism are described; these concepts have been chosen for their centrality in understanding symbolic interactionism and for their application to social work practice (Burrell & Morgan, 1979; Charon, 2001; Crotty, 1998; Martindale, 1960). Key concepts that will be discussed include

- social interaction,
- the combined role of thinking and acting,
- definition of the situation,
- everything about humans is a process and is constantly changing,
- the role of the active human being, and
- taking the role of the other (or role-taking).

Social Interaction

Symbolic interactionism views social interaction as central to everything humans do. Instead of only focusing on the individual (e.g., psychodynamic theories) or on society (e.g., critical theories), symbolic interactionism focuses on the nature of social interaction and the dynamic social activities taking place among actors. In focusing on the interaction itself, the symbolic interactionist creates a more active image of humans and rejects the image of the passive, determined organism. People are constantly undergoing change through social interaction, and society arises and changes through this interaction. Interaction means that actors constantly influence one another—they are not simply influenced by others.

Symbolic interactionists view symbols and language as central to social interaction and what it means to be human. Symbols are defined as words, objects, and actions agreed on by people to represent or stand for an idea; they represent something more than what is immediately perceived. For example, a thumbs-up may stand for approval or "going for it" in reaching a goal. The word "woman" stands for one-half of the human race. Words are symbols, but so are many objects that people may make into symbols (e.g., no8do, which is a symbol representing the King of Spain and reflecting a historical period of unity between Muslims, Jews, and Christians in Seville, Spain; see Figure 9.2 of a drawing of No8do with Seville, Spain, depicted in the background).

FIGURE 9.2 ■ Drawing of No8do, With Seville, Spain in background

© N. Corey Koenig

People understand the use of symbols. We do not simply respond to symbols, but we can describe them to ourselves and others, and apply them to thousands of situations where they seem to fit. Symbols are therefore social objects used by the actor for representation and communication. Through symbols, we are able to tell others something about what we think, what we are, and intend and feel, and we are able to communicate to ourselves (to think) about our world. Each person depends on society for symbols (and language), and the complexity of society demands and depends on humans to develop symbolic communication.

The Combined Role of Thinking and Action

Interactionists believe that as humans evolved with language and the ability to reason, they were able to turn back on nature itself, actively directing how natural forces act. Humans are not simply shaped by nature and culture, but they can learn, understand, build, invent, shape, and act upon their environments and even their own heredity. We act based on how we are thinking in a specific time and situation, even though our thinking may be influenced to some extent by our social interaction. Mind is action, and whatever self we develop is a process, not a static entity.

As a seminal writer of symbolic interactionism, Mead viewed human behavior as much more than a response to physical stimuli and thereby distanced himself from strict behaviorists. For Mead, behavior included action that is not directly seen, action that takes place within the actor, and action we might call thinking or minded action (Mead, 1938). In contrast, John B. Watson, as a major proponent of behaviorism, discounted all behavior except that which can be directly observed. Mead believed that without an understanding of mind, symbols, and self, human behavior cannot be understood for what it is. To measure physical behavior without trying to understand *thinking* is to ignore the centrality of what it means to be human. Strict behaviorism ignores our uniqueness as a species and treats humans as identical with all things in nature.

For Mead, both mind and behavior are generated by the ongoing interplay of human communication (1934). As animals, humans interact with each other (or in groups) through both gestures and language. Like other animal species, humans use body language, vocal tone, facial expression, and so on to communicate. But unlike other animals, humans also use sophisticated language that conveys comprehension and meaning. Both lingual and nonlingual communication are relational processes, but the ability to use language permits greater awareness of oneself and the ability to consider the perspectives of others. Language is also essential for thought, and thought gives rise to the mind. Mead's *social* behaviorism thus prioritizes thought, and it also recognizes the influence of social forces in producing thought and the shared meanings it generates.

Definition of the Situation

People don't sense their environment directly, they *define their situation* as action unfolds. We decide how to act according to our definitions of the situation that we find ourselves in. In social behavior, there is always an interpretation to be included in what we do and in how we perceive what others do. Humans use perspectives to understand how people act in situations; we use perspectives to define our world and these are always social, dynamic, and guiding rather than determining (Shibutani, 1955).

Symbolic interactionists believe that there is an objective reality that exists independent of our interpretation or definition, and that as these definitions develop, they do so at least partially in relationship to something real or physical. However, we do not respond to this reality directly; instead, we define the situation as it exists and this is highly influenced by our social life. Humans therefore exist in an objective and social reality and also have the ability to create a reality in interaction with themselves; each person develops her or his own reality. We learn in social interaction about the world, but then we think about it and arrive at our own interpretations of it. How we act depends on how we define our situation right now, our interaction right now and our thinking process right now (Mead, 1932).

Everything About Humans Is a Process and Is Constantly Changing

Darwin influenced Mead in helping him to understand that the universe is dynamic, not static, and that everything about humans is a process rather than stable and fixed. Society is not a static entity out there, influencing us, but a developing process, characterized by ongoing human interaction. Symbolic interactionists support an emergent human view, in contrast to a stable human view (Warriner, 1970). A stable human view takes its lead from natural sciences, drawing on a biological perspective, which views humans as having a permanent nature in which the human is always acting according to earlier influences. The stable human view is physicalist, deterministic, and mechanistic and has dominated science and philosophy. The emergent human view emphasizes immediate situational factors as causes, and examines social and spiritual characteristics of humans, and accepts unpredictability in understanding human action.

Mead's idea of the self is also something that is not static or atomized but is always socially engaged and in process (1934). To understand the process-self, Mead uses the terms "I" and "me." The **"me"** is the socialized self: the more conventional, habitual part of the self that behaves according to internalized roles. The **"I,"** on the other hand, is the response to the "me": this is the conscious, intentional aspect of the self that is free, indeterminate, and creative. The "I" is always in the present moment, able to make choices about future thought and behavior. Mead's process-self is thus conditioned—that is, socially influenced—but not determined. As such, it is always developing in relation to its social context.

The Role of the Active Human Being

In symbolic interactionism, people are active participants in what they do and are at least somewhat free to interact, think, define, and make decisions in the present based on the immediate situation. We are in fact integral to our environment, rather than people who simply respond to the environment. We define our environment in relation to our goals in a particular situation rather than act passively in relationship to the environment. We are able to define our past in terms of the present rather than see the present as caused or determined by the past. Human acts are symbolic in character rather than primarily physical; and social interaction is viewed as the process from which personality and society emerges. The symboling process involves the capacity to see things not as they are but as they have been or might be in the future, and includes humans using sound and language to communicate with others and to create worlds that never existed in physical reality.

Taking the Role of the Other, or Role-Taking

This concept is intimately connected to every other concept and is pivotal in understanding symbolic interactionism. Role-taking is a mind activity and involves imagining the world from the perspective of others and directing one's actions accordingly. We imagine another person's perspective, and we communicate that perspective to our individual self on the basis of what we see and hear the other do. It is through the mind that individuals tell themselves how others see things and how other people's perspectives operate. As others act, we put ourselves into their perspectives and we begin to understand the meaning their acts have for them. And, by taking the role of the other, we learn about our own perspective on all things.

Taking the role of the other is what people do in every social situation. It is how children grow through play when they try to think and act like Mom or Dad, a pilot, teacher, or guitarist. It is what people do when they try to figure out what the other person is thinking on a date or when a politician tries to appeal to those she wants to influence. Table 9.1 depicts developmental stages of the emergence of self as depicted by symbolic interactionism and which is dependent on the role-taking process.

Mead argued that growth and development occur first through role-taking; we come to know other people first, before we come to distinguish and understand ourselves. In this sense, the society shapes the individual (Mead, 1934). The child first imitates the acts of others, and in the early pre-symbolic stage, assumes the action, but not yet the perspective of the other. From simple imitation comes the earliest glimmers of the object we call self. The child directs imitative acts toward self and then with self, develops mind and symbols, followed by the capacity to take on the perspective of others. Understanding not

TABLE 9.1 ■ Stages of the Emergence of the Self as Depicted by Symbolic Interactionism	
Stages	**Description**
Preparatory Stage	Child imitates the acts of significant others, rather than actually understanding their perspectives. When we imitate others' acts toward self, we also begin to be aware of the self as an object.
Play Stage	Child takes the role of significant others and sees, directs, controls, and analyzes self from the perspective of important individuals; yet, no organized perspective of the self has formed.
Game Stage	Child's selfhood matures into an organized whole and is able to generalize attitudes of members of the whole (e.g., in the community) and react to one's self from the standpoint of those generalized attitudes.
Reference Group Stage	An individual's self is not a single whole but is divided between various social worlds. Here, the self we communicate changes depending in part on which group's perspective is being assumed in a given situation. We are able to take the role or perspective of one of several groups depending on the situation.

only the perspective of others, but the whole social milieu, or "game," is what Mead calls the "**generalized other**" (Mead, 1934, p. 154). A fully matured self requires individuals to have this broad perspective, including an understanding of their roles within the group, which permits intentional choice.

Taking the Role of the Other and the Looking Glass Self

Taking the role of the other is important for action we take toward the self in all situations. We direct ourselves and engage in self-control, in part, based on what we think others will think of our acts. Some scholars indicate that we may be most likely to base our actions on the views of significant others, those we look up to, or **reference groups** outside of our particular situation (Charon, 2001; Martindale, 1960). In all communities, the person must assume the perspective of that community toward herself as others act toward her. We will admonish and analyze ourselves as others would, recognize our rights and duties in relation to the community, and direct self according to the community's general perspective. What we think of self, our self-judgment, is in large part a looking glass image, gained through the eyes of others whose roles we take.

George Herbert Cooley (1902) is generally credited with the development of the concept of the **looking glass self**. He posited that the self is inseparable from social life and arises reflectively in terms of the reaction to the opinions of others on the self—namely, the imagination of our appearance to the other person, the imagination of that person's judgment of those appearances, and some self-feeling such as pride or shame. According to Cooley, from early childhood our concepts of self develop from seeing how others respond to us. However, it should be noted that Cooley argued that people actively and autonomously interpret and select whose appraisals will affect them. In the development of self, there is a balance between the autonomous and social dimensions (Franks & Gecas, 1992).

Cooley went beyond the looking glass self to develop a general theory of society and an explanation of **primary groups** characterized by face-to-face interactions, small numbers of people involved, and the relative permanence and intimacy among participants. Examples of primary groups include the family, neighborhood, play group of children, and a group of elders. In such primary groups, there is an intimate fusion of the individual and group that is fundamental in forming participants' ideals (e.g., subordinating individual interests to the group, supplanting egoism and greed, and developing ethical principles such as justice, service, and kindness) (Cooley, 1909).

Erving Goffman and Symbolic Interactionism

Goffman, influenced by the Chicago School of Sociology, expanded on symbolic interactionist themes and developed a dramaturgical approach that analyzed the social order of human interactions, which includes common rituals and routines. He viewed social life as a drama on stage, a kind of religious ceremony filled with everyday rituals (e.g., the common pattern of averting eye contact between strangers who meet on a city sidewalk). For Goffman, the self is something that must be produced anew on each and every occasion of social interaction. Whenever we interact with others, we are not only performers but an audience for their performances as well. Everything from the individual to society to social interaction depends on authentic performances and mutual trust (Goffman, 1959, 1967).

Goffman studied not only the rules that are developed within our social interactions, but he was interested in how we adapt or conform these rules to our purposes. Roles and institutional patterns do not determine or necessarily predict individual behavior; instead, they provide a framework within which the process of social life is acted out. Goffman discussed three concepts that are clearly relevant to social work practice: (1) face, (2) stigma, and (3) total institution.

First, Goffman described how over time we learn to have feelings attached to the selves we present to others and we care about how others see us and about the positive social value we claim through our performances. Goffman called this "face" (1967); for example, we may become attached to the image of a geek that earns us the respect of our peers and we are mobilized in the interaction order that sustains this claim about ourselves. When we fail to fulfill social interactions and do not, for example, have the answers to a teacher's questions, we are embarrassed and flustered over the projected self we have shattered and the face we have lost. Goffman suggests that this emotional attachment to projected selves or faces is most fundamental to the social control that leads us to regulate our own conduct. This concept of "face" is what deters us from misrepresenting ourselves to others because of the danger of being discovered "in the wrong face" and exposed as a dishonest performer. Our emotional attachment to face leads us to avoid situations in which we would be "out of face" and in which others would refuse to recognize and respect the self we present (e.g., a straight "A" student would avoid a difficult teacher, a person who doesn't know eating etiquette would avoid an elegant dinner party).

Second, Goffman (1963) described a social stigma as any aspect of an individual's identity that is discredited, rejected, or devalued in his or her social context. Goffman distinguished between visible stigmas (e.g., physical disability, race, age or gender) and nonvisible stigmas (e.g., sexual orientation, religious affiliation, or mental illness). Individuals who have a nonvisible stigma can choose to "pass" or reveal their stigma in order to manage their identity when interacting with others. Goffman (1963) indicated that those who have a particular social stigma often prefer the company of those who share that stigma instead of engaging in uncomfortable interactions with "normals." Managing a social stigma can be difficult and lead to interpersonal discrimination. Like the socially stigmatized, most of us learn from others' hints, glances, and tactful cues about what our places are and we generally keep them. Social life is typically uncluttered and orderly because the person stays away from places, topics, and times where he is not wanted and where he might be disparaged for going. He cooperates with this social order to save face.

Third, Goffman discussed the concept of the total institution. In his book *Asylum*, Goffman (1961) illustrates how residents' social life in a mental institution can pervert the morality of the interaction order. These residents start with at least a portion of citizen rights or freedoms and end up stripped of almost everything. Cut off from contact with the outside world, they are subject to the authority, indoctrination, and discipline of a small staff who control almost every aspect of their lives. This is the nature of a total institution. Defined by their presence in the hospital as very sick, they do not get support from staff or others in their attempts to project a more viable self. Residents adjust in various ways. They may conform (behave as a "normal" resident) or engage in unauthorized means. Goffman's work focused upon these adjustment processes, revealing what he calls the under-life of the organization or the ways in which the people make out in an attempt to defend themselves and their sense of self against the onslaught of the system. Goffman's study of total institutions sheds light on the subjective experiences of people in these systems. Other examples of total institutions include prisons, mental hospitals, homeless shelters, concentration camps, ships, monasteries, and so on in which people spend whole periods of their lives sleeping, playing, and working within institutional boundaries (DeWard & Moe, 2011).

Summary of Overview

This overview has discussed the potentially wide-ranging relevance of symbolic interactionism for social work practitioners who work with individuals, families, small groups and communities, and within institutional settings. Although this theory has been at times undervalued or misunderstood, social work scholars have drawn upon numerous symbolic interactionist concepts including the looking glass self, stigma, role, and reference groups. Our overview examines major symbolic interactionist themes including social interaction, the combined role of thinking and action, the definition of the situation, everything about humans as a process which is constantly changing, the role of the active human being, and role-taking. Further, we spotlight Charles H. Cooley and Erving Goffman as theorists who have greatly influenced the development of symbolic interactionism.

CRITIQUE OF SYMBOLIC INTERACTIONISM

What Does This Theory Say About Human Behavior?

Symbolic interactionists adhere to ontological assumptions in which individuals create their own interpretations and meanings of reality through dialogue with others and through self-reflection (Burrell & Morgan, 1979). And, from an epistemological standpoint, the knowledge of self, society, and the universe represents human interpretations that are dynamic and constantly evolving. This development of self and meaning-making that occurs through social and intrapersonal (within the person) dialogue is a hallmark of symbolic interactionist thought. Interactionists view the world as having a personal, subjective quality to it and even though they may support an objective reality, this reality is one in which no one "has the corner on the truth." Instead, all humans have are evolving interpretations of that reality. Whose interpretation of reality is most important in social work practice? If the client and social worker have different interpretations of reality and of how growth and change might best occur, whose interpretation counts the most?

The following case example demonstrates the ethical dimensions of social work practice and challenges us to explore the world, experiences, and interpretations of clients' views of their own healing and growth. In keeping with Erving Goffman's concept of stigma and what is "normal," this case encourages us to take pause in judging or stigmatizing a client's behavior and to refrain from acting on our own interpretation of what is "best" for the client.

ETHICS SPOTLIGHT
BURNING SAGE ON THE VA GROUNDS

A Native American client, Iona, is a resident in the homeless program at the Veterans Administration (VA) hospital located in a small town. Iona asks the social worker if she can burn sage and conduct ceremonies on the VA property to aid in her recovery from substance abuse. The social worker speaks with the treatment team about Iona's request, but the team is concerned about how it will "look" to others if they allow these "unusual" indigenous ceremonies to be conducted in full view of other residents and staff. Consequently, they are reluctant to approve Iona's request. Treatment team members, many of whom identify as being Catholic, express their confusion as to the meaning or significance of these ceremonies for Iona. The team social worker, who worked with Iona in the hospital before her transfer to the homeless program, explores with Iona the meaning (and symbolism) of these ceremonies for her recovery and discovers that the burning of sage is viewed by Iona as a cleansing ritual for herself and the surrounding environments. The social worker feels that even though he does not share Iona's spiritual beliefs, he has a responsibility to help advocate for Iona and assist the treatment team in understanding and appreciating the meaning of these ceremonies for Iona and her culture.

In small groups, discuss the following questions:

(1) What is your interpretation or view of Iona's situation?

(2) What are the social worker's ethical responsibilities in working with Iona? Use social work values from the NASW *Code of Ethics* (2017) (e.g., service, social justice, dignity and worth of the person, self-determination, cultural and spiritual competence, importance of human relationships, and integrity) to support your answer.

(3) When the client's meaning and identity are stigmatized or not understood by a social agency and administrators, what might be the role of the social worker?

(4) How do Catholics understand the use of incense? And, how might this compare or contrast with Iona's meaning for burning sage? How might these different spiritual perspectives on the ritual of burning incense lead to different kinds of actions for Iona and the social worker?

How Does This Theory Address Growth and Change?

Symbolic interactionists are concerned with how humans think, learn, solve problems, engage in role-taking, and act upon their social and natural environments. Humans are not simply shaped by nature. Interactionists do not believe that human behavior is determined or caused by past experiences; instead people are largely free, creative, and self-directed. They make choices in specific situations about how to interpret or draw upon their past, as they live and grow in the present and plan for the future. In this way, symbolic interactionism counters psychodynamic theory, which emphasizes the deterministic impact of childhood experiences on adult functioning. Symbolic interactionism also counters behaviorism, which views behavior as determined by observed, physical stimuli.

Interactionists have also been influenced by Darwin in their thinking about the universe as dynamic; everything in nature involves a dynamic process that is constantly changing. This idea of an ever-changing universe was revolutionary for its time period, and interactionists viewed this process as applicable to society. Societies are understood to encompass a process of individuals interacting, cooperating, role-taking, and communicating; the actions that take place among people are an important influence on the direction of individuals and society. For interactionists, truth, our symbols, and our narratives about how we interact with each other are constantly growing and changing.

How Holistic Is This Theory?

As we have noted throughout this text, social work practitioners highly value holistic thinking in which human beings are understood within the context of intimate relationships and larger socio-political, cultural, and natural environments. Because symbolic interactionists dually focus on interaction within an individual (thinking) and interaction with intimate others as well as the larger society and our natural environment (Stedman, 2002), their ideas are immediately understood to be holistic and can be applied in multiple ways and across varied contexts (e.g., the growth and development of an individual's identity and sense of self [as it occurs within the context of social interaction], the birth of a couple's first child, a college classroom, and larger social problems such as poverty, discrimination, and inequality, crime, or access to health care). Symbolic interactionism has wide-ranging applications to individuals, families, small groups, communities, and societies and is consistent with social work's expansive perspective, which includes micro-mezzo-macro and global social work practice.

By its very nature, symbolic interactionism makes connections between personal experience and larger social problems. For example, interactionists have shed light on a broad range of problems in society such as the stigmatization of those with mental health needs as well as the societal conditions that contribute to this and other forms of stigmatization (e.g., based on race, gender, sexual orientation and sexual expression, ability, or religious belief). Symbolic interactionists engage in critique of how societies have defined those who are different (e.g., as illegal aliens, infidels, savages, or enemies). From an interactionist perspective, these definitions of differences among people have provided societal justification for stealing land, segregating people, or refusing to develop social policies and practices that work for equality for all groups. Interactionists have also explored the broad role of education and communication in our society to help explain how individual freedom is possible. Because symbolic interactionists examine the intricate relationships and interactions that occur between individuals and society, this perspective has been viewed as less relevant to understanding the intrapsychic elements of an individual; interactionists would likely view practices of mental health assessment and diagnoses, so prominent in the helping professions, as a form of context stripping. Instead, symbolic interactionists put forth a holistic view of human behavior that supports the idea that individuals' growth and behavior cannot be understood apart from their social context.

How Consistent Is This Theory With Social Work Values and Ethics?

Symbolic interactionism is consistent with several core social work values delineated in our *Code of Ethics* (NASW, 2017) including social justice, self-determination, the dignity and worth of each person, competence, and the importance of human relationships. In particular, Goffman's work on stigmatization and total institutions puts forth a potentially scathing critique of society's treatment of those on the margins and provides social workers with a broad framework for challenging unjust social policies and institutional practices regarding their treatment of disenfranchised persons (e.g., those who are mentally ill, imprisoned, or in foster care group settings). In doing so, social workers uphold their core value of social justice in which they strive to ensure that all members of our society have the same human rights, protections, and social benefits.

Interactionists view humans as free and able to make their own decisions; this idea is consistent with social work values of self-determination and the dignity and worth of each person. Symbolic interactionists believe that individual freedom leads to action and the capacity for self-reflection—a central idea in social work practice. As social workers, we must cultivate self-reflection in order to engage in professional action, to become competent in our practice, and as a means of addressing personal biases and prejudices. These self-reflective skills enable us as social workers to develop increased sensitivity and respect for the dignity and worth of all clients no matter what their individual differences. And, our capacity to regularly examine personal biases for their impact on our practice contributes to our overall trustworthiness and integrity as professionals. Finally, symbolic interactionism, with its emphasis on the centrality of social interaction and the importance of primary groups, which help to form individual's ideals and shape the growth and development of individuals and society, supports the importance of relationships as a core social work value.

What Sources of Knowledge Does This Theory Support?

Symbolic interactionists support knowledge from multiple sources including clients, our professional expertise and growing practice wisdom, and empirically based research studies. Because interactionists take into account both observable and covert or hidden human behaviors, (e.g., how people think or engage in self-reflection), this perspective honors the multiple meanings or many truths that emerge from clients' narratives as they are told and reflected upon in any given moment, and as they change over time. Interactionists also value a professional social worker's knowledge and perspectives, being mindful that this knowledge is always incomplete, evolves over time, and is influenced or shaped by dialogue between you as the social worker, your clients, and others in your social milieu.

Symbolic interactionism is critical of traditional social science's emphases on the use of scientific methods that underscore fixed, or unchanging causal relationships as an effective means for studying human behavior. Interactionists view natural laws as inappropriate for studying human affairs characterized by the freedom of the human spirit. Consequently, they care about finding ways to study humans' constantly evolving social and internal dialogue, interpretations of situations, actions, and plans for the future.

Interactionists value scholarly, empirically based inquiry that examines the in-depth narratives humans share as a means of defining their situations within broader societal contexts. Grounded theory methods, which ensure that theories, ideas, and truths (with a small *t*) emerge from the "ground up," or from the participants who share them (in contrast to the interpretations of experts) are highly respected. Grounded theory is a specific type of research inquiry that seeks to ensure that tentative conclusions, perspectives, and theories inductively emerge from the data (e.g., from the narratives and perspectives of participants who share them, and not from some other source) (Glaser & Strauss, 1967). The nature of grounded theory, or ethnography, is to get inside, or as closely as possible, understand the perspectives of others (Hammersley, 1985).

APPLICATION OF SYMBOLIC INTERACTIONISM THEORY TO SOCIAL WORK PRACTICE

Symbolic interactionism has a pervasive, yet ubiquitous role in the intellectual history of social work. For the most part, human behavior courses cover concepts like reference groups, stigma, role, identity, and self-esteem, without tying them directly to writers in symbolic interactionism whose work focused on understanding how these concepts impact the interactions between people and their environments. The relationship between social workers and sociologists who developed these ideas has been complex and fraught with tensions. The following is a very brief overview of some of the themes that account for the tensions and contributions of the two disciplines of social work and sociology.

Earlier, in Chapter 3, which focused on historical context, we examined the paradigm shift that occurred in the late 1800s and early 1900s. In essence, this was a period of time when the emergence of the social sciences challenged existing theological, and moral, understandings of the human condition. These broad intellectual tensions played out between sociologists and social workers. Between 1874 and 1879, sociologists and social workers created a national conference in which they discussed new conceptions of both social problems and individual behaviors (Bruno, 1948). This early alliance ended due to significant differences between the two groups because most sociologists were invested in developing a trajectory as an academic discipline focusing on a "value free science" perspective. They saw themselves applying statistical analyses as a means to produce new scientific knowledge that created novel understandings of individuals in society. And, this new knowledge was to be based on quantitative methods that placed an emphasis on the value of science. Therefore, they were much more focused on macro-level social phenomena that allowed for collection of observable data that could be subjected to statistical analyses (Munson, 1978). In addition, they located themselves in academic settings emphasizing themselves as individualists, where analysis, not action, was valued. These themes were seen as useful to reinforce their goal to be accepted as a legitimate academic discipline. Finally, Seigfried (1996) argues that sociologists' stance toward women was rooted in the prevailing sexist notions that informed behavior during this period of time.

Social workers in the early 20th century were committed to the application of ideas to human problems and were deeply connected to a strong value base that emphasized creating outcomes based on the amount of "good" that was engendered by their collective action. For these early social workers, their applications of ideas were directly connected to actions involving the translation of their thinking into policy, programs, and direct services for a broad range of marginalized people whose needs included both charity (Charity Organization Societies) and social justice (Settlement House Movement). Unlike the sociologists, social work practice was located in community-based agencies rather than universities; it patterned itself after psychiatry and psychology, where the emphasis was on developing a set of skills that were identifiable as "professional" in nature (Forte, 2004a).

By the late 1800s, a confluence of some sociologists, social workers, and philosophers came together in joint efforts to combine knowledge and action. In particular, the work of symbolic interactionists at the University of Chicago, including George Herbert Mead, Herbert Blumer, and W. I. Thomas, had emerged. Unlike some of the other sociologists, the "Chicago" symbolic interactionists were moving toward a much more applied approach to their discipline. According to Forte (2004a), sociologists including Herbert Blumer, Charles Horton Cooley, W. I. Thomas, Ernest Burgess, Robert Park, and Erving Goffman were examining the application of sociology to the microsystem level. For this group, core concepts of symbolic interactionism included symbols, interaction, attitude, socialization, role-taking, self, generalized other, reference group, role, and definition of the situation (Lauer & Handel, 1983). Forte (2004a) notes that with the inclusion of pragmatism into the mix, through their interactions with philosopher John Dewey and social activist Jane Addams at Hull House in Chicago, these interactionists were provided opportunities for the integration of research, theory, policy analysis, and direct practice. Their differing but complementary perspectives opened up new opportunities for the further development of these ideas and their translation into service to the poor on both micro and macro levels. Finally, social work's focus on practice that was community based, action oriented, collectively focused, and agency based patterned itself after psychiatry and psychology, where the emphasis was on the development of the skills necessary for "professional" practice (Forte, 2004a).

Symbolic Interactionism in the Social Work Literature

What follows is an attempt to identify and describe the emergence of the overlap between sociologists, in the symbolic interactionism movement, and the various social workers, who work cooperatively with symbolic interactionists or borrowed their ideas to develop their own thinking about practice in multiple arenas—individual, group, community, broader social policy, and research. At the individual level, social workers began to look at what symbolic interactionism said about the influences that occurred between individuals and their environments.

Two of the major social work thinkers, Mary Richmond and Jane Addams, acknowledge the importance of utilizing a focus on both person and environment when developing strategies to try to help clients. Richmond (1917) used a more medically based perspective in her attempt to arrive at the "social diagnosis," which included both aspects of individuals while at the same time acknowledging the importance of the physical, social, and cultural environments as factors shaping the workers' understanding of the needs of their clients. Jane Addams, in her individual and group interactions with clients, emphasizes the importance of understanding the cultural and social conditions in which both Hull House and its clients existed. Interestingly enough, both of these social work pioneers recognized the importance of focusing on the interactions between individuals and their environments (P/E) as essential for achieving both individual charity and social action to impact growth and development for their clients (Thompson, Spano, & Koenig, in press).

A second example of the use of symbolic interactionist concepts can be seen in the emergence of the "functional" perspective beginning in the 1920s, spearheaded by the work of Jessie Taft and Virginia Robinson, faculty members at the Pennsylvania School of Social Work. The functional school had several important concepts connected to symbolic interactionist thinking. First, the functional school emphasized the importance of the relationship between the worker and the client as a product of their interactions. Those interactions were a product of the immediate context in which the worker and the client found themselves. More specifically, what happened in a social work relationship was directly connected to the realities of both the client and the worker within the context of an agency that was providing the services. These systems created a context that shaped all of the interactions making up a professional relationship. It also assumed that clients were active participants in their own growth process and that growth for the client was a by-product of the interactions in the professional relationship. All of these elements carry one central theme, namely that professional helping needs to be focused on the interactions among the actors, not isolated on one system or the other. In other words, it is not the nature of the client, the professional, or the larger environment, in and of themselves, that accounts for the process of change. It is the interaction among the systems that creates possibilities for growth and development (Robinson, 1962).

A third example of the impact of symbolic interactionism on social work thinking involves the work of Helen Harris Perlman, who was on the faculty at the University of Chicago. Perlman's body of work is extensive, influential, and very practice focused, including her book, *Relationship: The Heart of Helping People* (1979). This book provides a wide array of topics, including the nature and importance of the helping relationship, the role of self-awareness, the importance of both client and professional perspectives on the relationship, core skills for developing a relationship, modeling relationships in professional helping, and the role of hope in helping. Her understanding of professional relationships rests on fundamental notions inherent in social interaction (symbolic interaction). First, relationship is a process that unfolds over time and is constantly changing. Second, relationship involves the interaction between clients and workers in a process of defining and developing their interactions; it belongs to neither one nor the other. Third, relationship is a central driving force in creating change no matter what the setting or the level of practice (micro or macro). Her work connects to the symbolic interactionist perspective related to the "I," "me," and "generalized other." Its legacy is to acknowledge the importance of these dimensions in the relationship as well as placing that relationship in a larger social context.

Finally, Max Siporin published an article focused on therapeutic process in clinical social work relationships in which he tracks social work's long-standing commitment to understanding the connections between processes, relationships, and the production of outcomes in therapeutic relationships (Siporin, 1983). He uses the following definition of process, which refers to a "flow of change through phases of time—a sequence of progressive movement from a beginning, through the middle, to a definite end" (Siporin, 1982, pp. 178–179). Siporin (1972) also focused his attention on what was called a situational assessment and the usefulness of ideas from symbolic interactionism to provide tools to examine the relationships that exist between individuals and their social contexts. When taken together, Siporin's two articles allow us to both examine the dynamics existing in professional relationships, as well as the evolution of our understandings of the interactions between clients and their environments. These themes can be identified in additional social work writers: Howard Goldstein, Gordon Hamilton, William Gordon, Harriet Bartlett, Carol Germain, Alex Gitterman, Hans Falck, Ruth Middleman, Harry Specht, Ruth Smalley, and others (Siporin, 1983).

Another area of social work practice where symbolic interactionism had very direct influence is in the Settlement House Movement. In the early 20th century, many of the settlement houses were incubators for the translation of the social sciences. Hull House was one of the better-known examples of how social science concepts were moved from the universities into communities. The relationship between John Dewey and Jane Addams represents a long and productive connection between social work and both symbolic interactionism and pragmatism. In the settlement house movement, relationships were defined as dynamic and indispensable aspects for bringing about change. Relationships were built on the idea that people were capable of bringing about changes in their environment by activating their existing capacities and/or developing new capacities out of the context of relationships in which they were respected and treated as equals. From pragmatism, social workers took the importance of both critical reflection and action as essential elements contributing to the dynamic growth of both individuals in environments.

Summary

From symbolic interactionism, some social workers drew upon ideas that rooted observable behavior in the context of person/environments transactions. In addition, these ideas began to explain the active processes that included people's individual capacities to make meaning of their environments rather than simply being passively impacted by their environments. Symbolic interactionism specifically defined environments as including designed physical environments; places, physical buildings, and objects; social environments; individual people, groups, communities, and culture; and abstract environment, including anger, compassion, loyalty, love, and hate (Greene, Saltman, Cohen, & Kropf, 1994). While this perspective predated any thought of systems theory, it in fact not only includes the fundamental ideas of systems theory but further operationalizes the processes that go on between people and their environments. These processes are mutually interactive and have consequences in both directions. Ideas from symbolic interactionism provide practical, applicable, and useful understandings of the nature of the interactions between people and their environments and allow social workers to be focused on the transactions between people in their environments in their practice.

Application of Symbolic Interactionism to Case Examples

This section of the chapter focuses on taking key concepts from symbolic interactionism and applying them to case examples to provide you with opportunities to understand the application of this theory to practice. Table 9.2 is a summary of the assumptions outlined by Greene et al. 1994 that connect symbolic interactionism to social work practice.

TABLE 9.2 ■ Assumptions Undergirding Symbolic Interactionism
1 Human beings are self-conscious, reflective, and have the capacity to think.
2 Personality development is a process of learning to assign meaning to symbols. This learning process is a product of the interactions with real and symbolic others.
3 Individual and group meanings are a product of human interaction.
4 Behavior is symbolic and largely rests on linguistic processes.
5 The self is a social structure developed through social interactions with others and is a product of incorporating the attitudes, perceptions, and actions of others and the internalized meanings we create.
6 Deviance is non-normative behavior based on norms constructed by the larger society.
7 Differences among people are the result of learning different symbolic vocabularies for giving meaning to life experiences.
8 Change results from creating new conceptions of meaning anchored in the present, not in the past.

At the heart of the discussion of this first example is Mead's conception of the "I," "me," and the "generalized other." The "I" is that internal component of human experience that responds to the attitudes expressed by those in our environment. The "me" is the organized response we develop in reacting to our understanding of how others behave toward us. Another way to express this is to say that each of us has a private self that generates internal dialogue only we can hear, creating idiosyncratic self-perceptions, while at the same time our public self consists of our observable interactions with others based on the feedback others have given us about how they see us (Robbins, Chatterjee, & Canda, 2012). The "I" and the "me" interact with each other when we are doing self-reflection. This self-reflection leads to the evolution of new meanings that emerge from the interactions between the "I" and the "me." These two components account for meaning making at the micro level, including interactions with other individuals, family members, and other primary groups. In addition, Mead also defined the "generalized other" as the larger social context that gives meaning to our individual behaviors. Its importance relates to the influence our larger, cultural norms have in shaping behavior.

The following brief interaction illustrates how these interact to create specific meaning in any given situation. Imagine yourself walking down the corridor headed for class.

You encounter a good friend and classmate coming toward you. You both smile at each other and as you approach give each other a hug. You say, "I'm so glad to see you. You really look great today." She responds, "I'm glad to see you too, but I didn't have time to get my outfit together today, and I'm having a really bad hair day." According to Mead's theory, this simple exchange is made up of a complex set of interactions between both actors' respective "I" and "me." In this instance, the greeting offered by the first person represents a combination of how they feel about the other person and what they learned about how they should behave when they meet someone they know and like (Berne, 1961). For the second person, the message may be clearly understood, but the meaning assigned to the interaction reflects her own internal experience of herself (I), which is shared in the observable response (me). For example, if this woman has been given messages that suggest she does not measure up to "acceptable" community norms for female attractiveness, she may not allow herself to take in the compliment, which could account for her answer. In other words, their interaction can be understood as a product of their public and private selves, which focused on micro-level interactions. In addition, both people are acting in a social context that creates Mead's "generalized other," which consists of norms considered to be appropriate in their larger social context. In this instance, if the person offering the greeting is male there are certain norms defining appropriate behaviors related to greeting females. If the greeter is female, there are alternative norms shaping her definitions of acceptable behavior in this situation. Thus, the larger community norms form the "generalized other" that provides the context for this simple social interaction and defines what is acceptable or deviant.

Case Example: Elsie Whitmore and Katie

The following case example involves a student, Katie, placed in a hospital setting, who is interviewing a 70-year-old, African American woman, Elsie Whitmore, whose husband had a serious stroke, leaving him paralyzed on the left side of his body. He has lost his ability to speak, making communication particularly difficult. The student social worker is responsible for developing a discharge plan within the next few days. Mrs. Whitmore is extremely distraught, not only because of her husband's condition, but due to the reality that she is going to have to make a decision that will deeply affect the direction for both their lives. During the interview, Katie is continually confronted with questions related to a central theme that run through Mrs. Whitmore's responses: "What do you think I should do?" And, "You are the expert in these situations, tell me what you think I should do."

In the next supervisory session, Katie shares a number of concerns with the supervisor. First, she expresses great discomfort about Mrs. Whitmore placing her in the position of being an "expert" who should take the lead in making decisions in the situation. Katie's discomfort emanates from having learned that client self-determination is a central value in social work's *Code of Ethics* (2017), and that this value should be respected in working with clients. In addition, she struggles with her own perception of herself as being seen as an "expert" given her neophyte status and her concerns about her current level of competence. How does she reconcile the tension between supporting her client's autonomy and her client's deference toward her worker as the expert? Second, what do you do if clients' experiences diverge from your own life experience?

How do you encourage a client to share important aspects of her internal dialogue that create her unique story in a way that allows you to come to understand the meaning she has assigned to these events and how they have shaped her interactions with others? Finally, what happens to the worker and client's relationship if the worker accepts leadership in making this decision and it does not go well for the client? How will they reconcile their conflicting meanings of the nature of an "expert" as they move forward in the relationship between them?

The use of symbolic interactionism as a framework for understanding and analyzing the situation provides a supervisor with a way of understanding the subtext of these interactions. For example, often students struggle with taking on their new role as a social work professional. In this situation, the student's struggle focuses on the discrepancy between the "I" that is fraught with uncertainty that comes with this transition to a new professional role. This internal dialogue creates challenges because the newly emerging "me," impacted by the client's perception of the student as a professional, creates significant conflict within the student but accurately reflects the different meanings each holds about their interactions in this situation. In other words, if the student's internal dialogue centers on fears related to a lack of competency, then this conflicts with the client's internal dialogue focusing on the need to rely on the student as an expert. The use of symbolic interactionism provides the field instructor with a framework that suggests exploring the student's current beliefs about her or his professional competence as they impact the interactions in the current relationship with Mrs. Whitmore. Developing new meanings surrounding the title "expert" are central to being able to change the interactional pattern, thus allowing the student to respond more effectively to achieve the goals in this specific situation. In addition, the supervisor can explore with the student the broader influences (e.g., the agency context) that contribute norms that bear directly on the meaning of appropriate behavior for professional staff. Finally, as you may have noted, the gender of the social work student has been left ambiguous. Exploration of the broader social norms (generalized other), reflecting different norms applied to men and women in professional positions, may also be at play as students attempt to take on this new professional role.

Case Example: A Week in the Life of a Child Welfare Worker

This final example is offered to demonstrate how symbolic interactionism can be helpful in understanding, organizing, and analyzing complex situations in ways that can be translated into actions by practitioners working at various levels and contexts. What follows is a fairly common but complex situation in which social workers often find themselves.

You are the social worker in a medium-size child welfare agency in which you provide services ranging from doing child abuse investigations; to recruiting, training, and supporting foster families; to forming case management functions for both the foster children and their families while the child is in placement; and finally, working with the biological families after the child is returned home. Your specific function is to assess the needs of the child's biological family, develop appropriate responses to that assessment, and monitor progress being made toward the child's eventual return to their family by meeting regularly with both the foster family and the biological family.

The following excerpts represent events that occur during one week. Each excerpt will be connected to elements of symbolic interactionism, and you will be asked how those concepts could be useful in shaping your practice.

Monday's Situation. You are in an all-staff meeting attended by department directors, administrators, and direct service staff. The executive director hands out an excerpt from the local newspaper that reported that African American children are 3 times more likely to be taken into care than White children. She cautions the staff about problems the agency . . . biased practices. She also asserts that this "problem" reflects the country's broader issues related to racism, but not those of the agency. You have been made aware in your professional education that these problems do in fact exist, and your current caseload reflects this narrative.

DISCUSSION QUESTIONS

Drawing upon ideas from symbolic interactionism, discuss the following questions:

1. Symbolic interactionism suggests that reality is constructed through interactions among people and their environments. How might the assertion that the problems with racism exists in the larger society, but not in the agency impact dialogue among agency staff? How could you enter into conversations with people whose perspectives reflect different interpretations of the meaning of this information?

2. Symbolic interactionism assumes that the individuals in this agency will give different meanings to the information that has been shared and that those meanings can be modified through a process of dialogue. As you sit in this room with your colleagues, how do you prepare yourself to use a reflective process that allows you to understand the meanings others attribute to this situation? How would you construct a dialogue designed to reflect social work's core values? Given the agency likely reflects the values of the larger society, the generalized other, what resources might be identified to address the stresses that exist between individual beliefs and the larger social context as it relates to racism?

Wednesday's Situation. You arrive at 6 p.m. at the Wilsons's home, an African American family with four children. Both Mr. and Mrs. Wilson are present along with their four children:

- Tamika, a 14-year-old who was removed from the home as a result of poor school attendance and fighting on school grounds. She is on a home visit as part of the reentry treatment plan.

- Jamaal, a sixth-grader who appears to be fairly withdrawn and detached in his interactions with both the family and yourself.

- Danielle, a 7-year-old who is academically behind other students in her class according to her teacher, and on two occasions she has gotten into altercations during recesses.

- Franklin, an 18-month-old who suffered with colic during the first six months of his life and has since been diagnosed with a serious heart defect.

In your prior three meetings with this family some basic themes emerged. First, Mr. Wilson has expressed his concern that he and his family were targeted by protective services because they are African American. He continues to assert that his daughter's "problems" with fighting at school were rooted in racist attitudes reflected in the school's culture. He also asserts that Tamika stays at home to help his wife care for Franklin, and that "She's the oldest girl and needs to be at home to help her mother because Franklin is a handful and that's what kids are supposed to do." Second, Mr. Wilson expresses his doubts as to whether or not a young, White, unmarried social worker is going to be able to help him and his family deal with their current circumstances. Finally, Mrs. Wilson expresses her concern that the financial burdens caused by Franklin's illness are becoming more overwhelming and creating increased tensions in the family.

DISCUSSION QUESTIONS

Drawing upon ideas from symbolic interactionism, discuss the following questions:

1. Symbolic interaction assumes that reality is a negotiated process reflecting multiple perspectives of reality. As a worker, how can you engage in a process that encourages this family to share their meanings of the reality they face? How can you integrate the meanings you make of the situation and your agency's reality as it reacts to concerns about the newspaper article on racism with that of the clients' meanings as they play out in your work with this family?

2. How do the symbolic interaction concepts of roles, role-taking, role-making, and socialization play into the family's responses to their current situation?

3. How are the interrelationships between this family and their environments interacting to create both challenges and possibilities for this family in this situation?

Thursday's Situation. You are sitting in the break room at your agency having a cup of coffee with a group of colleagues. One of your colleagues brings up the Monday meeting and the concerns expressed by the executive director regarding the accusation that racial prejudice is involved in the delivery of child welfare services. Wilma, a social worker whose career includes 20 years in the child welfare system, suggests that there are significant barriers for many clients, including both institutional and interpersonal racism that add to already difficult challenges people of color face when they're dealing with the child welfare system. Margaret, a somewhat less experienced but deeply committed social worker, responds to the allegation by acknowledging larger systemic racist policies. However, she asserts that she has not witnessed, nor participated in any interpersonal prejudice that she sees as "unprofessional" behavior. She strongly asserts that it would be unthinkable for her as a social worker to hold, let alone act on racist beliefs. The remainder of the group distribute themselves along a continuum from race is always an important factor in their work, to race is not a factor in their work because they have dealt with their prejudices through education and training.

DISCUSSION QUESTIONS

Drawing upon ideas from symbolic interactionism, discuss the following questions:

1. How can symbolic interactionism concepts including self, role-taking, and socialization be used to understand and impact the discussions between yourself and your professional colleagues?

2. If your colleagues constitute a reference group, a collection of individuals with whom you want to interact, how will you manage the need to negotiate your own perspectives with those whose perspectives differ significantly from your own?

3. How does democratic activism, which is committed to dealing with inefficient practices and to the improvement of social membership for all, provide a means to understand how to create conscious, deliberate, and intelligent collective responses to complex phenomena like racism?

Chapter Summary

In this chapter we addressed aspects of symbolic interactionism as it relates to social work practice. The chapter provided an overview of symbolic interactionism that included key ideas and assertions undergirding this theory. First, human behavior is an interpretation of what we do and how we perceive what others do (p. 258). Second, our minds are vehicles designed to tell us how others see things and how all other people's perspectives operate (p. 262). Third, as others act, we put ourselves into their perspective in order to understand the meaning their acts have for them (i.e., role-taking, p. 262). Fourth, by taking the role of others, we engage in self-discovery and develop our own perspectives (p. 262). Fifth, because symbolic interactionism is an interpretive theory it differs from a natural science approach. It is devoid of claims of objectivity (pp. 257–258). Sixth, among its most important concepts are social interaction (pp. 259–260), the combined role of thinking and acting (p. 260), the definition of the situation (p. 260), everything about humans is a process (p. 261), and taking the role of other, role-taking, are all essential for the development of individuals and the larger society (pp. 262–263). When taken together, these assertions put forward a an intricate understanding of society and individual development as complex interactional processes that fits very well with social work's focus on persons/environments.

We also presented thinking of three prominent symbolic interactionist thinkers, Mead, Cooley, and Goffman. Each of these sociologists added new dimensions to our understandings about human behavior. Mead provides an understanding about how individuals interact with each other based on their perceptions of themselves and also their perceptions of those in their environments. Both Cooley and Goffman focused work on addressing the interactions between individuals and larger social systems, generalized others, to explain both positive and negative impacts of these larger social systems. More specifically, these three wrote about the self, identity, role, stigma, and primary group.

In the critique section, we pointed out that symbolic interactionism is a theory that supports the notion that there is more than one "truth" and it is based on the subjective understandings people develop. This is significantly different from positivistic approaches that tend to see objectivity and the search for one "Truth" as both possible and desirable. For this reason, symbolic interactionism can be especially helpful for social workers working with marginalized people whose "truths" are often subjugated by the larger society, including some agencies in our social welfare system (e.g., prisons, psychiatric facilities, and child welfare agencies).

Symbolic interactionism looks at human behavior as an interactive process that goes on between people and their respective environments. Humans are seen as active participants who shape, as well as are shaped by, their environments. And, growth and development is an active process that can be created in the present—not solely a product of our history.

Symbolic interactionism has wide-ranging applications across all levels (micro to macro) as well as across most aspects of our life tasks and social interactions. It clearly breaks down both the internal processes as well as the more visible interactions among people by connecting thinking, feeling, and acting into the calculus for understanding how we create meanings and how those meanings play out in both our private and public lives.

We have provided numerous examples about how symbolic interactionism can be used to explore, understand, and analyze our work with our clients, their families, and the organizations in which both they and we exist. Symbolic interactionism represents a form of systems theory that has had an impact on social work for over 100 years. Unlike current iterations of systems theory, symbolic interactionism provides the impetus for being able to break down interactional processes in ways that allow social workers to use it with clients. In addition, symbolic interactionism is useful in identifying elements of practice, including defining relationships, helping to provide a rationale for focusing on the present to identify capacities and resources that can be used in the change process, and in supporting active participation of clients in their own growth and development.

Key Terms (in order of appearance)

Symbolic interactionism   259

Interactionists   260

"Me"   261

"I"   261

Generalized other   263

Reference groups   263

Looking glass self   263

Primary groups   263

References

Berne, E. B. (1961). *Transactional analysis in psychotherapy.* Toronto, CA: Ballantine Books.

Blumer, H. (1969). *Symbolic interactionism: Perspective and method.* Englewood Cliffs: Prentice Hall.

Bruno, F. J. (1948). *Trends in social work as reflected in the proceedings of the National Conference of Social Work, 1874–1946.* New York, NY: Columbia University Press.

Burrell, G., & Morgan, G. (1979). *Sociological paradigms and organisational analysis: Elements of the sociology of corporate life.* Burlington, VT: Ashgate Publishing.

Charon, J. M. (2001). *Symbolic interactionism: An introduction, an interpretation, an integration.* Upper Saddle River, NJ: Prentice-Hall.

Cooley, G. H. (1902). *Human nature and the social order.* New York, NY: Charles Scribner's Sons.

Cooley, G. H. (1909). *Social organization: A study of the larger mind.* New York, NY: Charles Scribner's Sons.

Crotty, M. (1998). *The foundations of social research: Meaning and perspective in the research process.* Thousand Oaks, CA: Sage.

DeWard, S. L., & Moe, A. M. (2011). "Like a prison!": Homeless women's narratives of surviving shelter. *Journal of Sociology and Social Welfare, 37,* 115–135.

Dilthey, W. (1976a). The rise of hermeneutics. In P. Connerton (Ed.), *Critical sociology: Selected readings* (pp. 104–116). Harmondsworth, UK: Penguin.

Dilthey, W. (1976b). *Selected writings.* Cambridge, UK: Cambridge University Press.

Forte, J. A. (2004a). Symbolic interactionism and social work: A forgotten legacy, Part 1. *Families in Society, 85,* 391–400.

Forte, J. A. (2004b). Symbolic interactionism and social work: A forgotten legacy, Part 2. *Families in Society, 85,* 521–530.

Franks, D. D., & Gecas, V. (1992). Autonomy and conformity in Cooley's self-theory: The looking-glass self and beyond. *Symbolic Interaction, 15*(1), 49–68.

Gerth, H. H., & Mills, C. W. (Eds.). (1970). *From Max Weber: Essays in sociology.* New York, NY: Oxford University Press.

Glaser, B. G. & Strauss, A. L. (1967). *The discovery of grounded theory: Strategies for qualitative research.* Chicago, IL: Aldine.

Goffman, E. (1959). *The presentation of self in everyday life.* New York, NY: Doubleday.

Goffman, E. (1961). *Asylums.* Garden City, NY: Doubleday.

Goffman, E. (1963). *Stigma.* Englewood Cliffs, NY: Prentice Hall.

Goffman, E. (1967). *Interaction ritual.* New York, NY: Random House.

Greene, R. R., Saltman, J. E., Cohen, H., & Kropf, N. (1994). Symbolic interactionism: Social work assessment, language and meaning. In R. R. Greene (Ed.), *Human behavior theory: A diversity framework* (pp. 59–75). New York, NY: Aldine de Gruyter.

Hammersley, M. (1985). Ethnography: What it is and what it offers. In S. Hegarty & P. Evans (Eds.), *Research and evaluation methods in special education* (pp. 152–163). Philadelphia, PA: Nefar-Nelson.

Koenig, T. L., Chapin, R. & Spano, R. (2010). Using multidisciplinary teams to address ethical dilemmas with older adults who hoard. *Journal of Gerontological Social Work*, *53*, 137–147.

Koenig, T. L., Leiste, M. R., Spano, R. & Chapin, R. K. (2013). Multidisciplinary team perspectives on older adult hoarding and mental illness. *Journal of Elder Abuse & Neglect*, *25*, 1–20.

Lauer, R. H., & Handel, W. H. (1983). *Social psychology: The theory and application of symbolic interaction* (2nd ed.). Englewood Cliffs, NJ: Prentice Hall.

Martindale, D. (1960). *The nature and types of sociological theory*. Cambridge, MA: Riverside Press.

Mead, G. H. (1932). *The philosophy of the present*. (A. E. Murphy, Ed.). Chicago, IL: Open Court Publishing.

Mead, G. H. (1934). *Mind, self and society*. Chicago, IL: University of Chicago Press.

Mead, G. H. (1938). *The philosophy of the act*. (C. Morris, Ed.). Chicago, IL: University of Chicago Press.

Munson, C. E. (1978). Applied sociology and social work: A micro analysis. *California Sociologist*, *1*, 91–102.

National Association of Social Workers (NASW). (2017). *Code of ethics*. Washington, DC: Author.

Perlman, H. H. (1979). *Relationship: The heart of helping people*. Chicago, IL: Chicago University Press.

Richmond, M. E. (1917). *Social diagnosis*. New York, NY: Russell Sage.

Robbins, S. R., Chatterjee, P., & Canda, E. R. (2012). *Contemporary human behavior theory: A critical perspective for social work*. Upper Saddle River, NJ: Pearson.

Robinson, V. P. (1962). *Jessie Taft, therapist and social work education: A professional biography*. Philadelphia: University of Pennsylvania Press.

Seigfried, C. H. (1996). *Reweaving the social fabric: Pragmatism and feminism*. Chicago, IL: University of Chicago Press.

Shibutani, T. (1955). Reference groups as perspectives. *American Journal of Sociology*, *60*, 562–569.

Siporin, M. (1972). Situational assessment and intervention. *Social Casework*, *53*, 91–109.

Siporin, M. (1982). The process of field instruction. In B. W. Sheafor & L. E. Jenkins (Eds.), *Quality field instruction in social work* (pp. 178–179). New York, NY: Longman.

Siporin, M. (1983). The therapeutic process in clinical social work. *Social Work*, *28*, 193–198.

Stedman, R. C. (2002). Toward a social psychology of place: Predicting behavior from place-based cognitions, attitude, and identity, *Environment and Behavior*, *34*, 561–581.

Thompson, J. B., Spano, R., & Koenig, T. L. (in press). Back to Addams and Richmond: Was social work really a divided house in the beginning? *Journal of Sociology and Social Welfare*.

Warriner, C. K. (1970). *The emergence of society*. Homewood, IL: Dorsey Press.

Weber, M. (1949). *The methodology of the social sciences*. Glencoe, IL: Free Press.

10

BEHAVIOR THEORY, THE COGNITIVE TURN, AND THE INFLUENCE OF MINDFULNESS

PHOTO 10.1
Sending wishes to the universe in search of
enlightenment: Gas lanterns, Ston, Croatia

283

CASE EXAMPLE
TORI'S FEAR OF CHURCHES

A woman, Tori, in her early 30s, worked with a social worker to address her aversion to Christianity and to "ever stepping foot inside a church again." Tori had served as a director of Christian education in a conservative Lutheran denomination in the early 1980s and had worked with a pastor whose sexual behavior toward female parishioners was abusive and unethical. She had also been involved in the decision-making process to have this pastor officially defrocked; however, the institutional response was inadequate and the Lutheran district officials were ill-equipped to address such dire, unethical behavior within its leadership. The pastor could no longer work as an independent pastor, but district officials had "allowed" him to be sent off to work as a lay minister in a rural area in the same state where he had committed these sexually abusive offenses.

The entire process of working in the church, confronting the pastor, and engaging with church officials to have the pastor defrocked had taken three years. Tori, who had been a vibrant leader in the congregation, was soured and dismayed at this wholly inadequate, bumbling, sexist, and painful decision-making process. She developed an aversion for the physical sight of churches, felt a sense of suffocation upon entering any church structure, and could not participate in any worship activities for her own spiritual nurturance.

Over the course of exploring Tori's spiritual and religious experiences, the social worker, a conservative Mennonite, developed a strong therapeutic relationship with Tori. Tori expressed her motivation to overcome her fear toward churches so as to find spiritual meaning and support within a religious community again. As the social worker and Tori were separated by over 1,000 miles in distant communities, their work was primarily done by phone and through e-mail.

The social worker worked with Tori to implement homework assignments where she explored ways to expose herself slowly to institutional religion and churches again. She drove by churches and spoke with people about their religious beliefs. However, she was still uncomfortable stepping foot in a church again.

As they continued to discuss Tori's fears, the social worker and Tori developed a plan to meet in Washington, D.C., for a local conference and then, to walk down to and enter into the imposing National Cathedral, with its beautiful stained glass windows and numerous smaller chapels. And, as a way to "practice," Tori went with a friend down to the cathedral the day before she was to officially meet with her social worker; this gave Tori a chance to explore her fears ahead of her designated meeting. Tori and the social worker knew entering this massive church structure would evoke strong feelings of fear for Tori, but they also held out hope that they could talk through these fears while inside the cathedral and beyond as a means of working through the fear. Over time, Tori was able to enter church structures without fear or aversion and, as a testament to her growth, she currently leads a study abroad graduate course to Rome, Italy, where she visits a diverse range of cathedrals, deeply reflects on their significance, and encourages her students to do the same.

Exposure-based strategies, rooted in behaviorism and cognitive-behavioral approaches to practice, are viewed as some of the most effective strategies for combatting fear (Dobson & Dobson, 2009; Farmer & Chapman, 2016; Richard & Lauterbach, 2007). These strategies encourage clients to confront feared thoughts and situations as a way to manage unwanted physiological responses (e.g., increased heart rate, breaking out into a sweat, inability to sleep) and to decrease other fear-based responses (e.g., avoiding churches or crowded places). Because they encourage clients to take risks to face their fears, these strategies require that the social worker and client work out a unique intervention tailored to the client's particular set of fears. Consequently, exposure-based approaches necessitate a strong social worker–client relationship. As noted in Tori's example, the strong relationship developed over time with the social worker, combined with her courage and desire to overcome aversion to church structures is commendable and led to creative, individually tailored strategies that she developed collaboratively with the social worker (e.g., speaking with others about their cherished religious beliefs, walking down to the National Cathedral). These planned strategies assisted Tori in reducing her avoidance of church structures and led to new learning in which she is currently able to intimately explore churches for herself and with students within a different cultural context.

INTRODUCTION AND HISTORY OF BEHAVIORISM

In this chapter, we will examine the history of traditional behavior theory as well as discuss three generations of behavioral therapies that developed out of and are loosely associated with the original behavior theory as described by behaviorists such as Watson, Pavlov, and Skinner. **Behaviorism/behavior theory**, emerged in the late 19th century as a reaction to depth psychology and other traditional forms of psychology that supported ideas that could not be easily operationalized and tested through experimentation (See Chapter 5, on traditional psychodynamic theory, which examines intrapsychic and unconscious elements of human functioning that are less conducive to measurement, for example, defense mechanisms). Behaviorism was a movement in psychology and philosophy first coined by John B. Watson (1913) in his Behaviorist Manifesto. This Manifesto

- rejected introspective methods for examining inward human experiences and mental activity;

- viewed psychology's main goals as understanding, controlling and predicting behavior solely through observation and measurement; and

- saw no notable distinctions between non-human and human behavior.

Watson believed that psychology had failed miserably in attempting to conduct experimental research on the subjective experiences of human beings. Additionally, psychology needed to take as its starting point not subjective experiences such as consciousness, but it should instead start with observable human and animal behavior. Consequently, Watson turned to and relied on the results of replicable lab experiments from animal research conducted by Pavlov, Thorndike, and others as a means of developing his behaviorist ideas (Hauser, 2017).

BEHAVIOR THEORY AND THREE GENERATIONS OF BEHAVIOR THERAPY

What follows is (1) a description of early behavior theory (e.g., Watson, Pavlov, and Skinner), and (2) the development of three generations of behavior therapies, which have challenged the purer form of behavior theory and have attempted to expand on early behaviorism by taking into account cognitive and other processes as they impact emotions and behavior (Hauser, 2017; Moran, 2008; Spiegler & Guevremont, 2010).

Early Behavior Theory

Two key behaviorist subtheories are described here to help portray the development of early behavior theory and its emphasis on eliminating or reducing clients' problematic behaviors. These include respondent or classical conditioning and operant conditioning.

Respondent or Classical Conditioning

Both Watson and Pavlov investigated the stimulus-response (S-R) procedures of **respondent or classical conditioning**. Pavlov studied dogs' salivation reflex by placing food within the view of the dog, which elicited the dog's salivation. This, in turn, established the relationship between the unconditioned stimulus (food) and the unconditioned response (salivation). A second event (e.g., the ringing of a bell) occurred at the same time as the food was presented to the dogs. By doing this over time, the bell or conditioned stimulus was able to bring about the conditioned response of salivation, even without the presence of food. Today, behavior therapies use ideas from respondent conditioning to help people face a variety of anxieties and phobias. For example, social workers may work with soldiers, originally conditioned in combat to respond to loud noises by "running for cover" due to incoming mortar blasts, by helping them develop different, less disruptive, responses to the original stimulus (i.e., loud noises). These combat-era veterans, who may be experiencing symptoms of posttraumatic stress, typically want to function in their communities without unnecessarily responding or overreacting to loud noises that are likely to occur in daily living.

Although behaviorism in its pure form originally rejected the systematic examination and impact of inward human experiences and cognitive activity on human behavior, this stance was not to be upheld for long. Both Edward Tolman (1948) and Clark Hull foreshadowed the expansion of behaviorism to include cognitive elements. Although they both accepted the stimulus-response (S-R) framework of Watson, they were much more willing to explore internal mechanisms including thoughts or other mental activity that might intervene or interact with the stimulus and response (e.g., the cognitive processes that intervene between the soccer player's foot and ball when kicking it to a teammate). Kicking a ball is more than a stimulus-response activity and requires thinking on "one's feet" about the strategies involved for optimally kicking the soccer ball to a teammate who might be likely to move the ball down the field.

Operant Conditioning

Operant conditioning refers to the extent to which human behavior functions within the environment and produces consequences for the person engaged in a particular behavior. Operant conditioning is understood to play the largest role in impacting human behavior and was developed by Skinner (1937) based initially on his study of animal (not human) behavior (e.g., Skinner conducted experiments with rats and discovered that they learn effectively if rewarded frequently, and rats' behaviors could be shaped through the use of rewards).

Operant conditioning, used readily with people who face addictions, addresses the modification of voluntary behavior (i.e., drinking alcohol or using drugs) by altering consequences. The key tools of operant conditioning, reinforcement and punishment, either provide positive consequences (delivered following a response) or negative consequences (withdrawn following a response) for a particular behavior. Consequences that strengthen subsequent behavior are called reinforcers; consequences that weaken behavior are called punishers. When a behavior subsequently weakens, the person may discontinue the behavior and the behavior is viewed as extinguished. Finally, shaping occurs when new patterns are developed by reinforcing desired behaviors and not reinforcing others. Skinner (1957) even viewed highly developed human behavior such as a child's development of speech as the end result of shaping (Chomsky, 1959). Shaping has also been used extensively in the field of education (e.g., in foster care and alternative school settings) (Corbett & Abdullah, 2005; Hauser, 2017; Skinner, 1987). Skinner labeled his approach "radical behaviorism," because even though he understood that inner processes exist within human beings, he viewed these as irrelevant to his central focus on the prediction, control, and experimental analysis of human behavior.

THE COGNITIVE TURN AND THE FIRST GENERATION OF BEHAVIOR THERAPIES

Prior to 1960, learning theories were heavily influenced by key ideas within behavior theory (e.g., classical and operant conditioning) and within psychodynamic theory (e.g., the concept of drives). However, Noam Chomsky published a decisive criticism of B. F. Skinner's book, *Verbal Behavior* in 1959, which precipitated behavior theory's turn toward the impact of cognitive processes on behavior. In this review, Chomsky critiqued existing behavior theories that were focused on purely stimulus-response in that they could not account for the process of language acquisition. In essence, Chomsky argued that how children develop language is much more complicated than simple stimulus and response and that, in effect, children engage in a nuanced set of internal processes (e.g., thinking, reflecting, and learning through direct consequences) in order to develop their language skills.

Chomsky's argument contributed significantly to the so-called cognitive turn or revolution and represented the beginning of three generations of behaviorally rooted therapies and/or models (Hayes, Luoma, Bond, Masuda, & Lillis, 2006). It is in this context that Albert Bandura studied learning processes that occur in social environments (e.g., through observation of behavior and the performance of behavior or modeling) and developed social learning theory (Bandura, 1977b; Bandura & Walters, 1963), which he later relabeled as **social cognitive theory** to reflect his growing interests in how control of behavior shifts from external sources to the individual through such cognitive processes as self-regulation and self-efficacy (Bandura, 1977a; Bandura, 1986). Bandura's ideas about modeling, or learning that occurs by observing behavior, led to the development of therapies that helped people learn different responses to their experiences of fear and anxiety (e.g., in order to conquer a fear of flying, a person may learn new responses by observing others who fly with little fear).

Another key element of Bandura's theory and of other first-generation therapies (e.g., early behavior modification and exposure-based approaches as described in our chapter's opening case example) is that they divert from traditional behavior theory, which views behavior as solely governed by reinforcements and instead emphasizes the mutual influence of the environment on the individual's behavior and cognitive processes, and the impact of individual behavior and cognitive processes (as well as other personal factors) on the environment (Grusec, 1992). For example, gender role development may first occur through a child observing a same-sex parent who serves as a model for how to act based on gender. However, this is only one of many models (e.g., other family members and friends) from which a child may learn about gender roles; children may "bend" those gender roles, defining them in a way that is unique to their experience and personality, thereby influencing and changing how society views gender roles (Lombardo, Meier, & Verloo, 2009; Miller, 2011).

COGNITION AND SECOND-GENERATION BEHAVIORAL THERAPIES

The first generation of behavior therapies drew on core ideas (e.g., classical and operant conditioning), which were developed through experimental research. However, and as we have seen, these early behavioral concepts needed to be expanded upon in order to take into account the role of human cognitive processes on behavior. Researchers and practitioners alike realized this need and developed cognitive behavior approaches such as rational emotive and cognitive therapies, thought-stopping, and stress inoculation as avenues for reducing or eliminating psychological distress such as depression, anxiety, or phobias (see Beck, 1967; Ellis, 1957, 1962; Meichenbaum, 1977). Unfortunately, cognitive behavior approaches were unable to make strong research-based links to cognitive development theories such as Piaget's (1964) ideas about **cognition**, cognitive structures, or schemas, in which a person's mind intellectually develops and adapts to its environment and grows in capacity for abstract thought and reasoning. Piaget's ideas are not easily operationalized and do not directly address how events or experiences shape, regulate, or alter human cognition and behavior (Hayes et al., 2006). In response, cognitive behavior therapists created their own cognitive models that were not tied to cognitive development theories as described by Piaget and others, but instead addressed cognitive processing or thinking difficulties such as overgeneralizations, emotional reasoning, and irrational thinking. For example, the goal for the social worker who uses Albert Ellis's rational emotive behavior therapy (REBT) is to challenge and change (or modify) clients' irrational thinking and beliefs (e.g., "I must get an *A* on every college course" or "I must be in a relationship in order to be worthwhile") in order to help resolve emotional and behavioral problems (Ellis, 1962).

THIRD-GENERATION BEHAVIOR THERAPIES

Third-generation behavior therapies are viewed as controversial in that they veer from the primary goal of first- or second-generation approaches that seek to eliminate or reduce clients' problematic behaviors and psychological distress. In contrast, the "goal in third generation therapies is for clients to actively accept various forms of psychological discomfort or pain . . . as inevitable instead of viewing them as obstacles to achieving their goals" (Spiegler & Guevremont, 2010, p. 384). Third-generation therapies include acceptance and mindfulness-based strategies that encompass an expanded view of psychological health grounded in assumptions that pain, suffering, and discomfort are inevitable and cannot be completely eliminated but instead can be accepted and cognitively defused (i.e., letting go of the idea that one's thoughts accurately encompass all of one's experience, "I am not my thoughts") so as not to interfere with life goals. These third-generation therapies support Buddhist concepts such as clients' self-awareness and moment-to-moment acceptance of "what is," even when painful; these therapies encourage clients to practice mindfulness, intentionally paying attention to what is happening in the moment and without judgment, as a means to live a meaningful life even with pain and suffering. Examples of these therapies include dialectical behavior therapy (DBT) (Linehan, 1993), acceptance and commitment therapy (ACT) (Hayes et al., 2006), and mindfulness-based cognitive therapy (MBCT) (Segal, Williams, & Teasdale, 2001).

Summary of Overview

In this chapter, we have discussed how behaviorism emerged in reaction to the prevailing depth psychology, which underscored the centrality of subjective experiences, unconscious mental processes, and their impacts on human behavior. In contrast, traditional behavior theorists, such as Pavlov and Skinner, were interested in being able to predict and control animal as well as human behavior; their ideas regarding classical and operant conditioning and how behavior is shaped by consequences were used to help clients eliminate or reduce problematic behaviors (e.g., anxieties, phobias, and addictions). However, when Skinner (1957) put forth a stimulus-response view of how humans develop language, Chomsky (1959) responded with a pointed critique indicating that children's language development involves a more complex set of internal processes including thinking, reflecting, and learning through direct consequences.

Chomsky's argument greatly influenced behavior theory's turn toward cognitive processes as central to human behavior and represented the beginning of three generations of behavior therapies. The first generation of therapies stressed the importance of modeling or learning that occurs by observing behavior (Bandura, 1986); the second generation of therapies addressed cognitive processing or thinking difficulties such as overgeneralizations and irrational thinking (Beck, 1967; Ellis, 1962); and the third generation of therapies are viewed as more controversial because they do not seek to eliminate or reduce clients' distress, but instead encourage clients through acceptance and mindfulness-based strategies to acknowledge suffering or psychological discomfort as inevitable, not as obstacles to reaching personal goals (Hayes et al., 2006). What follows is an in-depth discussion of mindfulness from both Eastern and Western perspectives and as illustrated through the writings of Thich Nhat Hanh and Jon Kabat-Zinn.

IN-DEPTH: MINDFULNESS EAST AND WEST

Mindfulness is a concept and a practice with a long history that has deep roots in Buddhist traditions (Greater Good Science Center, 2017). Starting around the 1970s to the 1980s, a number of Western scientists and practitioners in the medical and mental health fields became interested in the idea of mindfulness as a therapeutic tool. In subsequent decades both the research on mindfulness, as well as the incorporation of mindfulness into treatments for everything from breast cancer to posttraumatic stress disorder, has exploded. At present, thousands of research articles and books have been published on the topic (a simple search in Social Work Abstracts & PsychInfo for articles with the word "mindfulness" in the title produced approximately 8,500 results!) (Hickey, 2010). The most cursory review of the research literature will show studies demonstrating the usefulness of mindfulness for boosting the immune system, reducing stress, decreasing depression and anxiety, increasing attention, improving memory and emotional regulation, and many, many more helpful things. One must wonder if mindfulness has become a panacea for the harried, overworked, overstressed, 21st-century lifestyles in the so-called developed world. With so many articles and books written on the topic, and with so many practitioners using mindfulness as a therapeutic tool, it is important to understand exactly what mindfulness is and from where it comes. To accomplish this we will offer a two-part in-depth section, each part representing, arguably, the most prominent and referenced thinker in the field (Maex, 2011). In order to understand mindfulness from a Buddhist perspective, the first section will focus on the ideas of Vietnamese Buddhist monk and teacher/activist Thich Nhat Hanh. The second will introduce Jon Kabat-Zinn, one of the first to take the idea of mindfulness and turn it toward science and mental health/medical practice.

Mindfulness East: Thich Nhat Hanh

Mindfulness is a concept that is deceptively simple, yet subtle in its complexity and depth. Hanh uses many descriptions and stories to illustrate the idea of mindfulness (Hanh, 1975). Essentially, mindfulness is about being alive in the first place—for when we are not mindful we are not essentially alive. Hanh defines mindfulness as "keeping one's consciousness alive to the present moment" (p. 11). As an example, he tells the story of washing the dishes—and there are two ways to wash the dishes. "The first is to wash the dishes in order to have clean dishes and the second is to wash the dishes in order to wash the dishes" (p. 4). The first way is to wash them in a mind*less* fashion, letting the moment escape into a seemingly endless concatenation of thoughts, likely focused on what one hopes to do when *finished* washing the dishes—perhaps having some tea. Well, says Hanh, if you cannot be present and conscious while washing the dishes, chances are that you will not be present and conscious while drinking your tea either. In both cases, the mind will wander ever backward, and then forward, and then backward again—rehearsing events, anxieties, or relationships from the past, then projecting a million potential futures in order to coerce the world into fulfilling one's greatest desires. Meanwhile the dishes—or the tea—and the only moment in which one actually has the capacity to live in—the *present*—passes ever onward, tragically unnoticed.

Hanh offers a very different perspective on the second way to wash the dishes. This way is to wash with full conscious awareness. "The fact that I am standing there and washing these bowls is a wondrous reality. I'm being completely myself, following my breath, conscious of my presence, and conscious of my thoughts and actions" (Hanh, 1975, p. 4). Hanh not only finds awareness of the present moment to be enlivening, but what one "wakes up to" is a beautiful and valuable present existence. The point is to be present in every moment of our existence—with family, with friends, while working, when doing something profound, and, yes, when doing mundane things like washing dishes. "We must be conscious of each breath, each movement, every thought and feeling, everything which has any relation to ourselves" (p. 8). The opposite of this sort of thinking is "machine thinking," like letting an "autopilot" run our lives. Being present is waking up to the miracle of being alive. "All is miracle" (p. 12). Being mindful, whether about the dishes or anything else, is about becoming a Buddha, about finding an enlightened reality open to everyone. "The word "budh" means to wake up, to know, to understand. A person who wakes up and understands is called a Buddha" (Hanh, 2005, p. 23).

Becoming enlightened in this way is more than just a healthy way to pay attention and be more intentional—it is about finding what Buddhist monk and teacher Chogyam Trungpa calls the peace of "shunyata" (emptiness) (Trungpa, 1993). Shunyata is about extinguishing the wily human ego. It contrasts with this human tendency to want, to desire, to crave after things and status and for something else, something more, or something later: to be waiting until we get that just-right job, or finish that next graduate degree, or buy that perfect house in order to find satisfaction (which will never come). The four noble truths of Buddhism state that living a good life is about finding the way out of suffering caused by the "fire" of craving desire—this is done by living mindfully, by acknowledging this aspect of the human condition and embracing the enlightened way (Hanh, 1975; Maex, 2011). This is the path to finding one's true self.

How Should Mindfulness Be Practiced and Cultivated?

"The mind is like a monkey swinging from branch to branch through the forest," says Hanh in describing the tendency of the human mind to wander from topic to topic, emotion to emotion, and desire to desire (1975, p. 41). What can be done to calm the monkey? Practice **meditation**, because each of us needs to realize the "total rest" of mindfulness. By total rest Hanh does not mean just relaxation (though this is included), and he does not mean the tossing and turning of sleep, but the total rest of the mind, simply observing itself. A full discussion of meditation styles and techniques is well beyond the scope of this chapter, but here are three basics: first, meditation can be done by sitting in a lotus or half-lotus position (traditional), but it can also be done walking, lying down, or otherwise. Second, meditation is about "letting go" of everything while focusing on one's breathing. Third, meditating means observing one's thoughts, emotions, and sensations in the present moment. This is the way to find peace.

> If you cannot find peace in these very moments of sitting, then the future itself will only flow by as a river flows by, you will not be able to hold it back, you will be incapable of living the future when it has become the present. Joy and peace are the joy and peace possible in this very hour of sitting. If you cannot find it here, you won't find it anywhere. (Hanh, 1975, p. 36)

Meditation is the practice of cultivating peace and joy by acknowledging the reality of our thoughts and emotions and desires, yet without chasing them all down as the mind jumps from branch to branch. Instead, over time the ability to concentrate will develop, along with new self-awareness, which creates the possibility for intentional choice of thought and behavior in one's relationships, work life, in the community, and so on.

The Bodhisattva Ideal: Mindfulness as a Moral and Spiritual Path

Far from being considered merely a "pill" or technique for personal gain, Buddhist conceptions of mindfulness lead to moral and spiritual development. "When your mind is liberated your heart floods with compassion" (Hanh, 1975, p. 58). Practicing mindfulness leads to a new outlook on life that starts with compassion for oneself, realizing all that one has gone through in this life, all that one has suffered (and/or currently suffers). But this new perspective does not stay immature or self-centered. One also develops great compassion for others, recognizing their suffering and that they have gone through many trials as well. "Now you look at yourself and at others with the eyes of compassion, like a saint who hears the cry of every creature in the universe" (p. 50). This is the Bodhisattva ideal—the enlightened perspective of one who "attends to the cries of the world," "beholding all sentient beings with compassionate eyes" (Hanh, 1975, p. 59). The compassionate individual recognizes the interdependencies of all people (and non-humans!). This is considered a sacred moral and spiritual calling—to offer service to others. As one finds personal liberation, this generates the compassionate call to assist others in the same process of awakening, to help alleviate their suffering, to share and spread the way of peace and joy.

Enlightened living is intended to be done in community. "Meditation is not to get out of society, to escape from society, but to prepare for a reentry into society. We call this 'engaged Buddhism'" (Hanh, 2005). Mindful individuals develop the understanding (rooted in compassion and interdependency) that there is no escape from the world, from other people (most often), and certainly not from oneself! Mindfulness makes it possible/easier to *be* in the world, to engage in one's community, to help make the world a better place. Hanh, for instance, did not retreat to a cave for his life, but he engaged his community, locally and globally. He has traveled the world speaking, offering hope and peace related to a wide variety of topics from the Vietnam War to consumer materialism to environmental degradation. In each instance, he does not go around pointing fingers at putative bad guys (whether criminals, democrats, republicans, corporations, etc.). Instead, he begins with compassion, first recognizing his own culpability in various problems, then "becoming one" with others—even criminal perpetrators—recognizing as well his own potential to do what they have done were he to have been raised in theirs or a similar situation. The call to compassionate engagement can take many forms, depending on the individual, but all will have in common the seeking of a more peaceful, flourishing society and earth.

Mindfulness West: Jon Kabat-Zinn

Jon Kabat-Zinn was perhaps the first, and certainly the most prominent, Westerner to "go East," learn the mindfulness traditions, then return to use mindfulness as medicine (Hickey, 2010). There are now hundreds of hospitals and clinics that utilize his Mindfulness-Based Stress Reduction (MBSR) programs, and thousands of practitioners who apply his ideas to their own medical and mental health–related practices. Many more have simply read his books and developed their own mindfulness meditation practices on their own. Kabat-Zinn has translated ancient wisdom into palatable ideas and techniques for Western culture and medicine.

So what is Kabat-Zinn's understanding of mindfulness? First, he is clear to state that it does not imply that one needs become a Buddhist or a monk, nor does it mean one must engage in some "weird cryptic activity" (Kabat-Zinn, 1994). He continues by summarizing overlapping ideas with Hanh about the nature of the mind: it wanders as it moves from past to future and back again, and as it desires and grasps for that always greener grass on the other side of the fence. Mindfulness "has everything to do with examining who we are, with questioning our view of the world and our place in it, and with cultivating some appreciation for the fullness of each moment we are alive" (p. 3). He seeks a perspective on mindfulness that is not particularly Eastern, which avoids any ideologies or beliefs systems, and is decidedly not mystical. Mindfulness, for Kabat-Zinn, is simply about intentionally maintaining awareness of the present moment. Doing this permits an individual to step out of the robot-like, autopilot mode that we tend to live in, and begin to realize the possibilities for personal growth. It is a way to get "unstuck," to get back in touch with our vitality and to begin to improve our relationships with family, work, and even with ourselves. "I like to think of mindfulness as simply the art of conscious living" (p. 6). In its most simplistic form, mindfulness is just about stopping, about stepping out of the rat race that so commonly describes our lives.

Kabat-Zinn is quick to note that, while simple, mindfulness is often not easy (1994). Cultivating present awareness takes work, and practice over time. It involves a certain amount of dedication and persistence to perform well. For instance, mindfulness requires the discipline of persistence—committing to practice and sticking with a meditation schedule of some sort. It also may be emotionally challenging as one becomes more acutely aware of emotions that may have long been bottled up or otherwise avoided—these tend to rise right to the surface of consciousness during mindfulness practice. Thus, pain may be involved, but it is also a hopeful path to healing.

On the other hand, there is a quizzical and even humorous side to mindfulness since it is, literally, about just sitting there. Stopped. Not doing anything. Taking note of the present. Nothing more. Kabat-Zinn tells the story of an older monk sitting with a younger apprentice. As they meditate in the full lotus position with their shaved heads and saffron robes, the younger one looks up quizzically at the older one, who turns toward him and says "nothing happens next, this is it" (p. 14). The present author has had similar experiences conducting meditation groups in counseling practice. There would often come a point, usually a few weeks into weekly sessions, when people would look at *me* quizzically, wondering if they were doing it (meditation) wrong because they weren't getting anywhere, and all of their problems weren't solved. This is when I would offer some kind of comment like the Buddhist monk (not that I'm any sort of sage), usually with a smile, indicating that "nope, this really is it. There is nothing more to come." During at least one session we all broke out into laughter at the seeming silliness of "just sitting there." It was a great moment, and we all got to experience it because we were all mindfully enjoying it in the present. But there is a common misconception that mindfulness practice should lead to some sort of special experience or revelation. The only thing special, according to Kabat-Zinn, that one should expect, is to actually *be* there (wherever you are).

So what is the point of just sitting there, fully aware of the present moment, if it does not lead to some esoteric, mind-bending experience? Kabat-Zinn's answer, in a nutshell, is that awareness creates choice: increasing our knowledge of how we feel, what (and who!) we think about, how our bodies feel, and so on opens up myriad possibilities for intentional living (1994). For instance, in our various relationships, whether with romantic partners or coworkers, we have a tendency to see them through "dream glasses." These glasses represent our own biases and projections, so that when we interact with other people they prevent us from really knowing them for who they really are. Instead, what we see is what we "dream" of seeing—the other person gets reduced to some aspect of *us*: our expectations, disappointments, biases, stereotypes, needs, desires, and more. In contrast, mindfully relating to others helps us to *stop* our own automatic processes, to become aware of our own expectations, biases, and emotions, and to actually make intentional choices about how we relate to other people.

Meditation is a key discipline for developing the aforementioned relational capacities (Kabat-Zinn, 1994). Meditation, for Kabat-Zinn, can mean many things and involves many positions, including walking, but it must center upon the breathing and generating conscious awareness in the present moment. He describes the mind in meditation like waves on the sea: "you can't stop the waves, but you can learn to surf" (p. 30). This doesn't mean that the mind can never become calm, just that it often is not, and meditation is not about forcing calmness (an oxymoron to be sure). If the mind is wandering, full of emotion, then mindfulness is simply being aware of what the mind is thinking about in its wanderings and paying attention to the emotions that are surfacing—then letting go and "surfing" the waves as they come. "[M]editation is not about feeling a certain way. It's about feeling how you feel" (p. 33). We so often attempt to duck and dodge our feelings—mindfulness is about acknowledging them as they are, but without judgment.

Another key to mindful living (and meditation) for Kabat-Zinn is non-judgment. When sitting in mindfulness meditation, people often expect to quickly experience the full benefits of a calm, controlled, conscious mind. Practice can help in developing these capacities, but there will always be days, moments when the mind simply is not calm, and resists awareness, even for practitioners of many years. The crucial skill, given this reality, is non-judgment. When certain unwanted thoughts arise, perhaps about a current or past relationship problem, or when one becomes aware of experiencing distressing emotions, it is easy to judge thoughts and emotions as negative and unwanted, and to judge the self for having them, for not being "better" at being mindful. The same judgment can occur in the other direction, say when one remembers an accomplishment and the concomitant positive emotions. In this case too, non-judgment means simply taking note of what has "come up" and returning one's attention to breathing. One need not pursue it, letting the mind wander off down memory lane and straight into unawareness. In general, Kabat-Zinn invites people to be patient with themselves as they develop their mindfulness meditation practices and (hopefully) transformed lifestyles. He invites everyone to open themselves to the present moment and to hope for new and creative possibilities in life.

In summary, this in-depth section has examined the mindfulness writings of Thich Nhat Hanh and Jon Kabat-Zinn. As noted in our overview, mindfulness has become a central component of the third generation of behavior therapies such as dialectical behavior therapy (DBT), acceptance and commitment therapy (ACT), and mindfulness-based cognitive therapies. What follows is a social work critique of behavioral theory and its subsequent three generations of behavior therapies.

CRITIQUE OF BEHAVIOR THEORY AND BEHAVIOR THERAPIES

What Does This Theory Say About Human Behavior?

Two Dimensions of Theoretical Assumptions

In this section, we will discuss the two dimensions of theoretical assumptions (see Burrell & Morgan, 2003) as applied to behavior theory and three generations of behavior therapies, as well as the ontological elements of behaviorism. Although social work scholars describe the purpose of behavior theory and therapies as helping to change human behavior, their understanding of behavior change is largely focused on observable indicators of individual behavior and does not typically address community or societally based change (Chavis, 2011; Nagel, 1988). Regarding the two dimensions of theoretical assumptions introduced at the beginning of this book (i.e., the subjective–objective dimension and the stability–radical change dimension), behavior theory and therapies view an individual's behavior as real, measurable, and testable consistent with assumptions about objectivity within the natural sciences. However, although behavior theorists and therapists are pointedly interested in changing, controlling, or predicting individual behavior, this view about "change" does not extend to the larger social world and cannot be equated with radical change as described by Burrell and Morgan or societal change as depicted by critical theories (e.g., Marxism, critical feminist, or queer theories) (see Chapter 4). For our purposes, Table 10.1 has been altered to depict the more narrowly focused assumptions of behavior theory and therapies as applied to individuals.

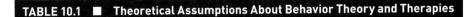

TABLE 10.1 ■ Theoretical Assumptions About Behavior Theory and Therapies

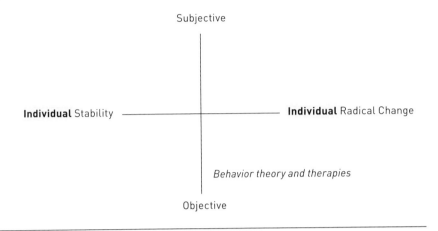

Ontology

Ontology is concerned with the essence of reality; behaviorists, whose historical roots involve observation, prediction, and the control of animal behavior, assume that the lessons learned from animal research can be readily translated to human beings. For behavior theorists (as well as two of the three generations of behavior therapists), human behavior is understood to be tangible, concrete, and observable and, therefore, can (and should) be changed and/or controlled. It is only in the more controversial third generation that behavior therapists begin to take into account and engage in clinical strategies that support acceptance (and not necessarily behavior change and control) of the moment-to-moment reality of clients' experiences of suffering and other difficulties.

How Does This Theory Address Growth and Change?

Behavior theory and all three generations of therapies place a strong emphasis on the expertise of the social work professional in assessing, diagnosing, and treating clients. The notion that the seeds for a person's growth and change can be found within the person would be largely dismissed by behaviorally oriented practitioners in favor of social workers' capacities to contribute to their clients' growth through accurate application of behavioral techniques. This is reflected in the variety of clinical skills and practices (e.g., accurate assessment and development of a treatment plan) that a social worker must develop, for example, in using cognitive behavioral techniques with clients. Behavior approaches are also rooted in the expertise of quantitative findings that further support a "top down" approach (not starting with clients' wisdom, experiences and/or meaning-making narratives) for what works in practice-based settings, in contrast to what might work in clients' natural environments.

Numerous empirically based studies support improvement in client outcomes in areas such as depression, anxiety, marital distress, attention deficit hyperactivity disorder, substance abuse, panic disorders, phobias, and posttraumatic stress disorder (Mitte, 2005; Powers, Vedel, & Emmelkamp, 2008; Thomlison & Thomlison, 2011). These studies do support client growth and change, however, they lack "staying power" and continue to be less effective in follow-up studies when the client is no longer in the protected environment of the social worker's office (Mace & Critchfield, 2010). Our discussion in the holistic section of this critique is relevant here. By emphasizing solely individual change and growth, behavioral approaches do not include strategies for impacting pivotal social or environmental change.

How Holistic Is This Theory?

ETHICS SPOTLIGHT

BEHAVIORAL TREATMENT FOR DAVID'S ANXIETY

David and his wife, Karen, had just sold their house and used the proceeds from the house to buy a trailer home. They were headed for Texas to join a retirement community and had agreed to stop at a hospital in Kansas in order for David to undergo surgery. Their plans were to travel to Texas after the surgery; their trailer home was parked in a long-term lot on the hospital grounds. Yesterday, David had spinal cord injury surgery to correct for the narrowing of his spine (stenosis). Unfortunately, the surgery was unsuccessful and David became paralyzed from "the middle of his chest on down." He is no longer able to walk, has trouble breathing, expresses anxious thoughts and feelings about being very limited in taking care of himself, and is worried about being able to use their trailer home due to its lack of handicapped accessibility. As a social worker trained in third-generation behavioral techniques, you explore strategies with David such as meditation and mindfulness exercises for helping him to accept changes to his body and to assist in coping with his anxiety.

Discuss the following questions:

(1) What do you think are the causes of David's anxiety?

(2) How might a behaviorally oriented approach help David deal with his anxiety? What are the strengths and limitations of this approach in helping David grow and change?

(3) As a social worker who practices from a holistic perspective, taking into account the core social work values of social justice and the importance of human relationships, what other elements of David's situation (e.g., unexpected changes in his health and mobility, his relationship with his wife, and his need for resources to outfit his trailer with handicapped equipment) need to be addressed? And, can these elements be easily addressed with behavior therapy? Why or why not?

The acknowledgment of humans' holistic capacities to be both shaped by *and* to creatively act upon their environments is not a major centerpiece of behavior theory or the three subsequent generations of behavior therapies. In its original conception, behavior theorists focused much more on the deterministic role of the environment in shaping human behavior and did not view humans as having free will or as able to reason, act upon, and creatively change their environments. This original conception is one-sided, views human beings as androids, and lacks a holistic emphasis on the combined and mutual interactions that occur between people and their environments. However, this purer, traditional behavior theory quickly gave way to a cognitive turn (see Bandura's writings), which acknowledges humans' capacities for thinking, reflecting, and engaging in observations of others' behaviors as a way to influence their own behavior. Bandura (1977a, 1977b; 1986) also broadly recognized the impact that humans could have on their environments, thereby asserting a more holistic approach to human behavior. Although the subsequent three generations of behavior therapies loosely developed from behavior theory, these therapies are individually focused and continue to be critiqued for the directive or leading role of the therapist regarding what behaviors should be accepted, targeted, and/or changed (Rogers & Skinner, 1956). Further, behavior therapies place little emphasis on the impact that humans can have on impacting or changing their environments.

How Consistent Is This Theory With Social Work Values and Ethics?

In this section, behavior theory and therapies will be scrutinized for their consistency with three core social work values: professional competence, cultural competence, and client freedom or self-determination. Behaviorally oriented social workers view their use of behaviorist interventions with clients as demonstrating the greatest level of professional competence because of the strong level of outcome studies that support these approaches. Some might even say that if we do not use a behavioral approach in our practice, we are not making use of ample empirical evidence and are not providing our clients with the "best" services (Thyer, 2011). However, although there have been some gains in helping clients maintain behavior changes, follow-up studies continue to show that clients who initially benefit from behavioral approaches are often not able to sustain these gains after treatment has ended and when they return to live and function in their natural, social environments (Mace & Critchfield, 2010). Some authors have also expressed concerns about the lack of applicability of behaviorist approaches to social work practice with diverse client populations based on gender, race, ethnicity, sexual orientation, and sexual expression (Chavis, 2011). Finally, scholars such as Carl Rogers, who famously developed a client-centered psychotherapeutic approach, critiqued behaviorism for its failure to acknowledge human beings' freedom or self-determination in creatively problem-solving and in responding to their own unique needs. In a published dialogue between Carl Rogers and B. F. Skinner, Rogers challenged Skinner's emphasis on the prediction and control of human behavior and stated,

> It is my hope that we have helped to clarify the range of choice which will lie before us and our children in regard to the behavioral sciences. We can choose to use our growing knowledge to enslave people in ways never dreamed of before, depersonalizing them, controlling them by means so carefully-selected that they will perhaps never be aware of their loss of personhood. We can choose to utilize our scientific knowledge to make men [sic] happy, well-behaved, and

productive, as Skinner earlier suggested. . . . Or at the other end of the spectrum of choice we can choose to use the behavioral sciences in ways which will free, not control; which will bring about constructive variability, not conformity; which will develop creativity, not contentment; which will facilitate each person in his self-directed process of becoming; which will aid individuals, groups, and even the concept of science to become self-transcending in freshly adaptive ways of meeting life and its problems. The choice is up to us, and, the human race being what it is, we are likely to stumble about, making at times some nearly disastrous value choices and at other times highly constructive ones. (Rogers & Skinner, 1956, p. 1064)

What Sources of Knowledge Does This Theory Support?

From an epistemological standpoint, behavior theorists ask the question, "How do we know what we know?" Their response is that behaviorism privileges empirically based, quantitative studies that demonstrate the strongest level of outcome research results of any practice-based social work approach or model (Reid, 2004; Thyer, 1991, 2011). Behaviorism represents a positivist perspective on knowledge that places types of knowledge in a kind of hierarchy (see Diagram 10.1).

Behaviorists view quantitative studies as more important than all other forms of inquiry and knowledge, including clients' voice and expertise about their own experiences and behaviors, qualitative studies that explore the meaning of experiences from the point-of-view of the research participants, and social workers' expertise and practice wisdom.

DIAGRAM 10.1 ■ Behaviorism's Hierarchy of Knowledge

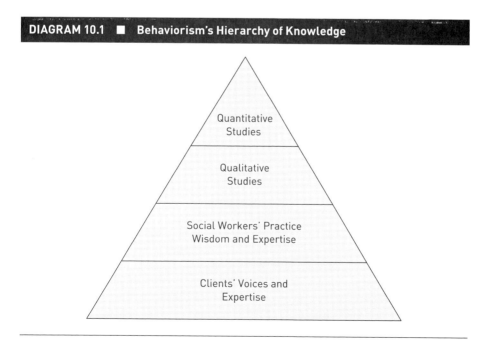

Quantitative Studies

Qualitative Studies

Social Workers' Practice Wisdom and Expertise

Clients' Voices and Expertise

APPLICATION OF BEHAVIORISM TO SOCIAL WORK PRACTICE

Behaviorism in Practice: An Historical Context

Earlier in the chapter, you were provided with an overview of the evolution of behaviorism. We presented the notion that this intellectual history can be divided into three separate generations: (1) First-generation therapies, understandings, and applications emerged in the 1950s and 1960s and included concepts related to stimulus control, reinforcement and punishment, aversion therapy, exposure therapies, and modeling as presented in behaviorism. These approaches emphasize treating clients' directly observable problem behaviors as opposed to changing the external environmental conditions that influence them. The emphasis is on changing the person to conform to the environment with little or no attention to the costs that may be inherent in the existing environments (e.g., social injustice, unfairness, and discrimination). (2) Second-generation approaches, which emerged in the mid-1960s, introduced the place of cognitive thinking as an important component for understanding humans' behaviors. These approaches focused on the interactions of thoughts and beliefs as integral elements for understanding people's behaviors. They moved beyond the stimulus response (S-R) paradigm, which informed the first-generation therapies, to include thinking as a behavior that could be targeted as a part of the change process in both the persons and their environments. (3) By the 1990s, a third generation of behavioral therapies was developed with the primary goal of not only eliminating problem behaviors but also reducing them with a clear understanding that some forms of psychological discomfort and pain may need to be actively accepted by clients. What connects these three generations is the ongoing commitment to understanding human behavior in context with what we now call behaviorism to inform our understanding of the interactions between people and their environments.

Probably more than most other practice theories/models, behavioral approaches to social work practice have engendered powerful responses, both embracing and rejecting this approach to practice. Social work's ambivalence toward behavioral-based models is a complex mix of critiques based on ideological differences, conflicting appraisals about how behavioral approaches tend to focus on persons as targets for change, while ignoring the environment as needing change, and its adherents' claims of empirical superiority over other approaches. As we will see in the next section, these strong reactions are connected to broader historical themes that were impacting and continue to impact social work.

Behavioral Social Work in the 1950s and 1960s

During the first historical period, behaviorists' stronghold was in psychology and until the 1950s and 1960s it had a relatively small footprint in the intellectual traditions of social work. However, by the 1960s, social work was embroiled in its ongoing search for legitimacy based on efforts to codify various models that would give social work legitimacy in its efforts to seek "expert" status among the professions. This led to a mix of both new models and refinements of older models that could be used to bring about change. Among the many were *The Problem-Solving Model* (Helen Harris Perlman), the *Psychosocial Approach to the Practice of Casework* (Florence Hollis), the *Functional Approach to Casework Practice* (Ruth E. Smalley), *Behavior Modification and Casework* (Edwin J. Thomas), *Crisis Intervention as a Mode of Brief Treatment* (Lydia Rappaport), and *Theory and Practice of Family Therapy* (Francis H. Scherz). What each of these authors shared was their intent to emphasize the use of specific models that reflected the application of a set of skills that could be mastered through educational programs providing their acolytes with specific knowledge, values, and skills that were unavailable to those without these credentials. They were professional "experts," not just well-meaning community members.

Behavioral Social Work in the 1970s to 2000

During the second historical period, behavioral social work writers frequently made very broad assertions that often resulted in strong responses to their colleagues. For example, Bruce Thyer begins a chapter on social learning theory and social work with the following sentence: "The purpose of the practice of social work is to change behavior" (Thyer, 2011, p. 437). Thyer and Hudson (1987) then go on to define behavioral social work as

the informed use by professional social workers of assessments and interventions based on empirically derived theories. These theories include, but are not limited to, respondent learning, operant learning, and observational learning. Behavioral social workers may or may not subscribe to the philosophy of science known as behaviorism. (p. 1)

KEY ETHICAL QUESTIONS RELATED TO BEHAVIORISM

Thyer's (2011) first sentence, which defines the purpose of social work as being to change behavior, begs certain key questions with ethical implications that must be addressed by social workers if they are going to translate this assertion into social work practice. These questions include:

(1) Whose behavior needs to be changed?

(2) Why does the behavior need to be changed?

(3) Who decides what the new behavior should be?

(4) What are the responsibilities that flow from the reality that a professional relationship inherently has a power imbalance favoring professionals?

(5) And, in whose interest is it to change behavior?

The following practice example is offered to help illustrate the importance of these key questions. Please use the above questions, along with your understanding of behaviorism as it applies to the following case situation.

THE CASE OF MATTIE AND HER FAMILY

Mattie is a 13-year-old child who was brought into foster care placement approximately six months ago. Her records indicate that both her mother and father have had a history of being physically abusive, however, her treatment plan states that the reunification of this child with her family is the final goal for this intervention. She has made a good adjustment to the foster family and up until now has been willing to work toward improving her grades at school as well as getting her angry outbursts under control in the foster home. Her teacher, Ms. Sorenson, acknowledged that she was making significant progress at school even though she still remains about one grade level behind her peers.

Approximately one month ago, during a supervised visitation she was told by her parents that her father has Stage IV lung cancer. They told her that the doctors are not positive about his prognosis but they believe he has less than a year to live. Since this information has emerged, Mattie's behaviors have reverted to levels present at the time of her initial placement. Her teacher says that she is falling behind in all areas of her schoolwork, and when she tried to speak with Mattie about what she needs to do, Mattie gets either explosive with her anger or overwhelmed with her sadness, and sits silently weeping, unable to respond with any words. Ms. Sorenson believes that if Mattie can't get quickly refocused she may not successfully complete the school year.

Her foster parents are also concerned about Mattie's deteriorating behavior in their family. She has had several outbursts where she has exhibited verbally, and on one occasion, extremely physically aggressive behavior toward her 11-year-old foster sister. They too see her behavior reverting to levels she exhibited when she was first placed in their home.

Practice-Based Questions

Having explored key ethical questions above, now answer the following practice-based questions related to the case example:

(1) How does behaviorism help you move from focusing on Mattie's individual development of these learned behaviors toward examining the interactions among all of the actors in this illustration in order to help them cope with this difficult situation?

(2) Should the social worker, the foster parents, and the teacher focus their attention on Mattie?

(3) Should they be looking at their own behaviors as a means to improve the situation, and if so, what is it they can do to help her learn new behaviors to cope with the situation? And, what would be "desirable outcomes" toward which they should be directing their work with Mattie and her family?

In order to apply behaviorism to social work practice, fundamental ethical questions must be asked about how behaviorism should be used, when or under what circumstances it should be used, and who should have a say in what behaviors are changed. Unfortunately, Thyer's (2011) assertion that social work's purpose is to change behavior provides little guidance to connect our actions to the application of behavior theory to practice.

Another historical theme impacting social work was the emergence of the concept of "accountability" in the social services. By the 1970s, under the leadership of Richard Nixon, social services of all kinds were subject to public scrutiny related to the costs of both clinical programs and social policy outcomes. Accountability was translated into the production of measurable results that demonstrated not only the effectiveness but also the efficiency of those services to the public. These larger trends created an increased focus on the production of measurable outcomes for the services and policies being provided to clients. Behavioral practice helped focus practitioners and planners on the production of data that emphasized the efficiency of the services they delivered. Second-generation behaviorists emphasized the collection of information to provide evidence to support the use of specific techniques to demonstrate client progress toward specified goals. These second-generation efforts reflect the influences of cognitive theories including those of Aaron Beck (1967), Albert Ellis (1962), and Donald Meichenbaum (1977). Their work produced the cognitive approaches of rational emotive therapy and cognitive therapy, as well as problem solving, thought stopping, and stress inoculation (Tomlinson & Tomlinson, 2011).

These approaches, along with the inclusion of some first generation S-R approaches, made significant inroads into health, mental health, residential treatment for children and adolescents, and prisons. For example, from the 1970s until the present, most residential facilities, group homes, and foster families who treat children with the diagnosis of SED (severe emotional disturbance) are required to have some form of behavioral management system in place in order to be licensed by their respective states. Most school systems use behaviorally-based approaches to work with children who have developmental, emotional, or behavioral disorders. Most correctional facilities, whether juvenile or adult, have very clear and specific regimens to shape client behaviors as a central feature to their efforts to change client behaviors. And finally, even those social workers who are in private practice are beginning to experience the influence of insurance companies that dictate which models for treatment should be used with certain diagnoses (e.g., the use of cognitive behavioral therapy as a means to treat depression). Failure to use this approach can lead to nonpayment for their services.

Current Applications for Behavioral Social Work

Current behavioral social work draws upon the third generation of behaviorism, combined with frameworks emphasizing mindfulness as drawn from Eastern traditions and the use of a dialectical approach that highlights the tensions between change and acceptance. Together, (1) behaviorism, (2) mindfulness, and (3) dialectical approaches represent the three quite disparate streams of ideas shaping behavioral social work in the 21st century. We will examine each of the three elements and then examine how they interact in case illustrations.

Social Work Behaviorism. Current behavioral social work uses the second-generation behavior therapy assumptions, which include cognitive as well as behavioral dimensions resting on assertions identified by Thyer (2011). The following four are particularly relevant to our current discussion: (1) Human behavior consists of both observable behavior and unobservable behavior including overt acts, covert speech, thoughts and cognitions, feelings, and dreams; (2) Human behavior is learned throughout the lifespan based on the incorporation of both ideas and experience; (3) The processes involved in developing human beings' behavior transcends cultures; and (4) There are three major empirically supported learning processes that constitute behavior theory and earlier behavior therapy, (a) *respondent learning*, a Pavlovian response, where a neutral stimulus, the sound of a bell, is paired with an unconditioned stimulus, a dog salivating due to hunger, the sound of the bell eventually will cause the dog to salivate even when no food is present; (b) *Operant learning*, a form of learning in which behaviors are strengthened or weakened by altering the consequences that follow those behaviors; and (c) *observational learning*, which involves individuals acquiring behaviors by observing other people, which they then translate into social roles and behaviors.

Social Work Behaviorism and Mindfulness. A second source of thinking that has had an impact on social work behaviorism comes from the emergence of a group of social work writers, many of whom are rooted in the inclusion of spirituality into their social work perspectives. Canda and Warren (2013, p. 2) defined mindfulness as "a mode of awareness in which a person pays purposeful and kind attention to oneself in the present moment and situation with nonjudgmental acceptance and without clinging to the flow of thoughts, feelings, and habitual reactions." Another prominent writer, Baer (2010) describes mindfulness as a complex process that includes "paying attention to present moment experiences, labeling them with words, acting with awareness, avoiding automatic pilot, and bringing an attitude of openness, acceptance and willingness, allowing non-judging, kindness, friendliness, and curiosity to all observed experiences" (p. 28). What both of these authors share in common is a sense of the importance of living in the present moment and reducing the judgments we experience both internally and as it relates to our environment. These skills are essential for both clients and professionals in order for them to develop an awareness of the importance of remaining in the present rather than drifting back into the past or perseverating about the yet to be determined future. In essence, we neither can undo the past nor can we control events in the future. The only place that change can occur is in the present moment by consciously making decisions to change or accept the situations in which we find ourselves.

Social Work Behaviorism in Dialectics. The third major source of ideas impacting current use of social work behaviorism relates to the concept of dialectics. Koons (2008) defines **dialectics** as a Western philosophy that postulates that the truth, in any situation, lies between the opposing tensions experienced in that situation. Therefore, the helping situation creates dynamic tensions that shift and change over the course of the work. And, as the tensions change, so do the definitions of what the truth is in any given situation. For example, if clients have a very clear picture of themselves as having no worth, then this represents their truth. If the social worker takes a stance that emphasizes the client's inherent dignity, irrespective of past behaviors by others (i.e., sexual abuse, rape, verbal abuse, and physical abuse) or her or his own behaviors (drug abuse, physical abuse, disrespectfulness toward others, and self-harming behaviors), this may trigger tension for the client who must now resolve her or his conflicting perceptions. According to dialectics, growth occurs as a worker provides an external positive perspective, supported by evidence that challenges clients' internal perspectives that are driven by an inability to see themselves as worthwhile human beings. It is the tension between these two "truths" that eventually leads to growth and development.

Practice Models Incorporating Behaviorism, Mindfulness, and Dialectics

There are four major models that are linked to more current understandings of behaviorism. The reality is that they bear little resemblance to the early work of behaviorists in the first generation. Rather than focusing solely on stimulus and response, they incorporate the cognitive aspects of behaviorism that are central in the transition to the second and third generation of behaviorists including Beck (cognitive behavioral therapy, CBT), Ellis (rational emotive therapy, RET), Linehan (dialectical behavior therapy, DBT), and Hayes (acceptance and commitment therapy, ACT). For the purposes of illustration, we will be focusing on two of these models: CBT and DBT. CBT is a therapeutic model in which negative or unhelpful thinking is challenged as a means of changing emotions and behavior patterns. DBT can be defined as a therapeutic model that examines problematic, learned behaviors and helps the client replace these behaviors with more adaptive behaviors. It includes both an examination and focus on private thoughts as well as the more observable behaviors that occur in the public sphere. The following example describes a situation in which some of the basic techniques from these two models will be applied. This example represents a composite illustration consisting of some of the common themes emerging when working with individuals who had sexual abuse as a part of their history.

CASE EXAMPLE
ELLEN'S PATH TO RECOVERY

Ellen is a 32-year-old woman who was seen over a period of 18 months. In the beginning she was struggling with persistent panic attacks, making her unable to perform daily tasks related to being a wife, mother, and a student trying to finish her undergraduate degree. In addition, she was struggling with flashbacks, self-doubt, obesity, concerns related to sexuality, and depression. She had been married for 14 years and had two sons, ages 13 and 11, and a daughter, age 9. Her relationship with her husband was quite volatile and often included both verbal and, on some occasions, physical altercations between them. Her oldest son was beginning to refuse to help her around the house and was expressing more and more overt anger both toward her and his siblings. His anger often led to physical altercations between the two boys as well as verbal aggression toward her daughter. There was one instance of a physical altercation between the oldest son and his father.

She came in voluntarily to seek assistance with managing her current complex family situation but also expressed concerns about being insecure because of her own "awful" upbringing. She often referred to herself as "damaged goods." What precipitated her coming in at this particular time was that she and her sister had spoken to each other two weeks prior to the appointment. Her sister was undergoing treatment for drug abuse and a recent suicide attempt. Her sister told her about being sexually abused by their father. Until then, neither sister knew that they were having a shared experience.

Her family of origin consisted of her two parents and her sister, who was three years younger than the client. Her mother was in the home taking care of domestic chores as well as tending to a small garden from which she earned some money by canning vegetables for her neighbors. Her father worked on their small farm and also was employed

(Continued)

(Continued)

in various businesses in a larger community about 15 miles away. Her struggles began at the age of 6 when her father approached her to engage in overt sexual contact including masturbation and oral sex. These advances became a consistent pattern for the next four years. As she got older, she began to resist her father's efforts. The result was twofold: first he put her in a root cellar and threw snakes into the root cellar to terrorize her so that she would be compliant to his wishes; the second thing he did was to tell her that he would leave her sister alone if she would acquiesce to his advances. This pattern persisted until she married and left home at the age of 17.

This concludes the overview of the case situation. What follows are a series of individual vignettes from weekly sessions that demonstrate the use of behavioral, mindfulness, and dialectical elements drawn from dialectical behavior therapy (DBT) and cognitive behavioral therapy (CBT) that were used at various points in the helping process.

During the first three months of their work together, Ellen and her social worker, Leo, focused much of their attention on handling the panic attacks, which were interfering with Ellen's capacity to attend class. She reported that she had no idea what triggered these panic attacks, but they made it impossible for her to remain in the classroom. Leo's assessment of the situation indicated that Ellen could not provide reliable information about the sequence of events that led to her panic attacks. He decided to use a DBT technique, "chain analysis," as a way to develop her understanding (Linehan, 2015). This involved an examination of what might be creating her current vulnerability to panic attacks. Step one, she was asked to describe the internal and external aspects she experienced that led to the panic attack. Step two, she was asked to describe the prompting events that led to the panic attacks, which included being in a large group of relatively unfamiliar people, a sense of feeling trapped because she was embarrassed to leave class, and a head full of internal dialogue going on about her fear she would fail the course. Step three, she was asked to identify the factors happening before the event that made her feel vulnerable. In this instance, she repeated the elements she identified in step two, but there appeared to be no clear pattern that initiated her awareness that a panic attack was imminent. However, with additional questioning Leo learned she was placed on anxiety medication approximately a month before the panic attacks began increasing in frequency. And, she had gained approximately 40 pounds in the past four months, which she connected to her sister sharing with her that she too had been sexually abused by their father. This led to a sense of utter despair as she realized that her submitting to her father's demands for sexual contact had been unsuccessful in protecting her sister. Step four, she was able to describe in great detail both her feelings and body sensations as well as identify her thoughts as her anxiety intensified. However, she was unable to identify any single factor in the environment that triggered this process. Step five, she was able to describe the internal feelings related to her body (excruciating headache, stomach upset, cramping in her legs, and her jaw aching from clinching it). The following description includes both behaviorism, as applied to the panic attacks, and mindfulness as a replacement strategy for the panic attacks themselves.

With this information, she and Leo began developing specific strategies that could be applied when she began to experience this process leading to a panic attack. Through discussions with Ellen, Leo learned that Ellen had a "safe place" she went to when she was overwhelmed by her experiences in her family. This place was next to a small stream surrounded by large boulders, through which a creek gently flowed down toward a small lake on their property. With this information, Leo began a process of teaching her how she could take her mind back to that place in order to calm herself. Once she learned that skill, they added a series of breathing meditations in which she learned to concentrate on the sense of her breathing by focusing on the feeling of the air going in and out of her nostrils. By using this meditational technique, along with careful review of the material provided in steps one through five, she was able to recognize when the attacks were likely to come and was able to engage in her breathing meditation as a way to reduce both the intensity of the panic attacks and their frequency. Within four to six weeks, she was able to remain in classes for the rest of that semester. And, she did finish her degree the following year.

The next instance occurred toward the end of the first year. Ellen had separated from her husband and was living, with her three children, in an apartment. The separation occurred after her husband got into a physical altercation with her oldest son and the police were called. The court issued a restraining order, resulting in reduced contact during the last two months. Ellen had a conversation with her attorney and indicated she intended to return to her husband with her three children. The attorney called the child welfare worker and both adamantly felt that this decision could endanger both Ellen and the children. Ellen insisted that she felt she could care for her children and that she needed to give it "one more try." Both her attorney and the child welfare worker called Leo knowing that he had a good working relationship with Ellen and that she trusted him. They both argued that Leo should try to convince her that this was a dangerous decision for both herself and her children that should not be allowed to occur.

Ellen found out about the phone calls made to Leo and showed up in his office with no appointment. She stood defiantly in front of him, daring him to talk her out of her decision. Leo responded by saying he had no intention of trying to talk her into or out of anything. She agreed to sit down and talk for about 30 minutes. During their time together Leo had come to believe that she did have the capacity to make good judgments in relation to her life and that if she felt she needed to return to her husband then there must be important reasons for her to do so. He simply asked her to ensure that she make a reasonable safety plan for herself and her children given that there was the potential for some harm to occur if she implemented her plan. By the end of the discussion, her tone had changed from angry defiance to curiosity about why he chose to trust her when everyone else was telling her this was a bad idea. This allowed him to point to numerous examples of both her effort and progress toward changing her situation. She and her children returned to the husband's residence and within three days they left, never to return again.

In this example, we see the power of dialectics as a tool to assist individuals whose lives have been deeply affected by trauma. Ellen's life history was cluttered with an endless series of traumatic events related to physical and sexual abuse. She was manipulated by nearly all the adults in her life and came to believe that she had no capacity to make judgments. Her core beliefs included the notion that she was "damaged goods" and lacked the capacity to make good judgments about her life and those of her children. Leo's firm affirmation that while he didn't fully understand her decision and did have concerns, he was completely convinced that there was something important that Ellen needed to accomplish in order for her to take charge of and move forward in her life. In that moment her own "truth," that she was in some way broken, was pitted against Leo's "truth" that she had the capacity make decisions in her best interest. This exchange proved to be pivotal in the remainder of her work with Leo. Time and again Ellen's belief, her thesis, that she was damaged, was met by Leo's antithesis, that she had capabilities, potential, and capacities that could be used to help her change her life.

CHAPTER SUMMARY

Social work behaviorism, in its broadest sense, is used by a significant number of social workers in a broad array of programs. Whether or not social workers identify themselves as social work behaviorists, these ideas have had a profound impact on many of our agencies' programs and the professionals who work in those programs. It would be difficult to find schools, child welfare agencies, mental health centers, and correctional programs that do not integrate important aspects of behaviorism.

Social work behaviorism has a history that reflects emphasis on outcomes that are observable and/or measurable. This makes the models that flow from this theory particularly attractive to funders and agency leaders who are constantly under pressure to demonstrate measurable outcomes to the larger community. It also emphasizes the importance of demonstrating that what we do is useful in bringing about change. However, the theory itself does not answer many of the central questions that social work professionals need to address in their work with their clients. The case of Mattie earlier in the chapter provides a series of questions that may be helpful for those who have an uneasiness with a literal translation of this theory into practice. Social work values need to play a central role in deciding when it's appropriate to use the technologies that behaviorism provides.

We have noted the evolution of behaviorism from its early stimulus-response beginnings to the inclusion of both observable and non-observable behaviors as a part of its theoretical base. The role cognition plays in shaping both behaviors and feelings in the human experience have strengthened our capacity to utilize this approach. Its current iterations, including CBT, DBT, and ACT, expand our focus in ways that redefine behavioral work to include the perception that not all of our experiences, for example, psychological pain, are problems to be overcome but rather conditions, part of the human experience, and that suffering is a part of our existence.

Key Terms (in order of appearance)

Behaviorism/behavior theory 285	Operant conditioning 287	Meditation 291
Respondent or classical conditioning 286	Social cognitive theory 288	Dialectics 304
	Cognition 288	
	Mindfulness 290	

References

Baer, R. A. (Ed.). (2010). *Assessing mindfulness and acceptance processes in clients: Illuminating the theory and practice of change*. Oakland, CA: New Harbinger.

Bandura, A. (1977a). Self-efficacy: Toward a unifying theory of behavioral change. *Psychological Review, 84*, 191–215.

Bandura, A. (1977b). *Social learning theory*. Oxford, England: Prentice-Hall.

Bandura, A. (1986). *Social foundations of thought and action: A social cognitive theory*. Englewood Cliffs, NJ: Prentice-Hall.

Bandura, A., & Walters, R. (1963). *Social learning and personality development*. New York, NY: Holt, Rinehart & Winston.

Beck, A. T. (1967). *Depression: Causes and treatment*. Philadelphia: University of Pennsylvania Press.

Burrell, G., & Morgan, G. (2003). *Sociological paradigms and organizational analysis*. Burlington, VT: Ashgate Publishing.

Canda, E. R., & Warren, S. (2013). Mindfulness-based therapy. In *Encyclopedia of Social Work*. Washington, DC & New York, NY: National Association of Social Workers & Oxford University Press. doi:10.1093/acrefore/9780199975839.013.988

Chavis, A. M. (2011). Social learning theory and behavioral therapy: Considering human behaviors within the social and cultural context of individuals and families. *Social Work in Public Health, 26*, 471–481.

Chomsky, N. (1959). A Review of B. F. Skinner's Verbal Behavior. *Language, 35*(1), 26–58.

Corbett, B. A., & Abdullah, M. (2005). Video modeling: Why does it work for children with autism? *Journal of Early Intensive Behavior Intervention, 2*, 2–8.

Dobson, D., & Dobson, K. S. (2009). *Evidence-based practice of cognitive-behavioral therapy*. New York, NY: Guilford Press.

Ellis, A. (1957). Rational psychotherapy and individual psychology. *Journal of Individual Psychology, 13*, 38–44.

Ellis, A. (1962). *Reason and emotion in psychotherapy*. New York, NY: Stuart.

Farmer, R. F., & Chapman, A. L. (2016). *Behavioral interventions in cognitive behavior therapy: Practice guidance for putting theory into action*. Washington, DC: American Psychological Association.

Greater Good Science Center (GGSC). (2017). *Mindfulness*. GGSC: University of California, Berkeley. Retrieved from http://greatergood.berkeley.edu/topic/mindfulness/definition#what_is

Grusec, J. E. (1992). Social learning theory and developmental psychology: The legacies of Robert Sears and Albert Bandura. *Developmental Psychology, 28*, 776–786.

Hanh, T. (1975). *The miracle of mindfulness: An introduction to the practice of meditation*. Boston, MA: Beacon Press.

Hanh, T. (2005). *Being peace*. Berkeley, CA: Parallax Press.

Hayes, S. C., Luoma, J. B., Bond, F. W., Masuda, A., & Lillis, J. (2006). Acceptance and commitment therapy: Model, processes and outcomes. *Behavior Research and Therapy, 44*, 1–25.

Hauser, L. (2017). Behaviorism. *The Internet Encyclopedia of Philosophy*, ISSN 2161-0002. Retrieved February 11, 2017, from http://www.iep.utm.edu/

Hickey, W. (2010). Meditation as medicine: A critique. *Crosscurrents, 60*(2), 168–184.

Kabat-Zinn, J. (1994). *Wherever you, go there you are: Mindfulness meditation in everyday life*. New York, NY: Hyperion Publishing.

Koons, C. R. (2008). Dialectical behavior therapy. *Social Work in Mental Health, 6*(1–2), 109–132.

Linehan, M. M. (1993). *Cognitive-behavior treatment of borderline personality disorder*. New York, NY: Guilford Press.

Linehan, M. M. (2015). *DBT® skills training: Handouts and worksheets* (2nd ed.). New York, NY: Guilford Press.

Lombardo, E., Meier, P., & Verloo, M. (2009). *The discursive politics of gender equality: Stretching, bending and policymaking*. London and New York, NY: Routledge.

Mace, F. C., & Critchfield, T. S. (2010). Translational research in behavior analysis: Historical traditions and imperative for the future. *Journal of the Experimental Analysis of Behavior, 93*, 293–312.

Maex, E. (2011). The Buddhist roots of mindfulness training: A practitioner's view. *Contemporary Buddhism, 12*(1), 165–175.

Meichenbaum, D. H. (1977). *Cognitive behavior modification: An integrative approach*. New York, NY: Plenum.

Miller, P. H. (2011). *Theories of developmental psychology*. New York, NY: Worth Publishers.

Mitte, K. (2005). Meta-analysis of cognitive behavioral treatments for generalized anxiety disorder. A comparison with pharmacotherapy. *Psychological Bulletin, 13*(5), 785–795.

Moran, D. J. (2008). The three waves of behavior therapy: Course corrections or navigation errors? *The Behavior Therapist, Special Issue*, Winter, 147–157.

Nagel, J. J. (1988). Can there be a unified theory for social work practice? *Social Work, 3*, 369–370.

Piaget, J. (1964). Development and learning. In R. E. Ripple & V. N. Rockcastle (Eds.), *Piaget rediscovered* (pp. 7–19). Ithaca, NY: Cornell University Press.

Powers, M. B., Vedel, E., & Emmelkamp, P. M. (2008). Behavioral couples therapy (BCT) for alcohol and drug use disorders: A meta-analysis. *Clinical Psychology Review, 28*, 279–288.

Reid, W. J. (2004). Contribution of operant theory to social work practice and research. In H. Briggs & T. Rzepnicki (Eds.), *Using evidence in social work practice: A behavioural approach* (pp. 36–53). Chicago, IL: Lyceum.

Richard, D. C. S., & Lauterbach, D. L. (2007). *Handbook of exposure therapies*. Boston, MA: Academic Press.

Rogers, C. R., & Skinner, B. F. (1956). Some issues concerning the control of human behavior: A symposium, *Science, 124*, 1057–1066.

Segal, Z. V., Williams, J. M. G., & Teasdale, J. T. (2001). *Mindfulness-based cognitive therapy for depression: A new approach to preventing relapse*. New York, NY: Guilford Press.

Skinner, B. F. (1937). Two types of conditioned reflex: A reply to Kornorski and Miller. *Journal of General Psychology, 16*, 272–279.

Skinner, B. F. (1957). *Verbal behavior*. New York, NY: Appleton-Century-Crofts.

Skinner, B. F. (1987). Skinner on behaviourism. *Oxford Companion to the Mind*. New York, NY: Oxford University Press.

Spiegler, M. D., & Guevremont, D. C. (2010). Third-generation behavior therapies: Acceptance and mindfulness-based interventions. In M. D. Spiegler (Ed.), *Contemporary Behavior Therapy* (pp. 383–416). Boston, MA: Cengage Learning.

Thomlison, R. J., & Thomlison, B. (2011). Cognitive behavior theory and social work treatment. In F. J. Turner (Ed.), *Social work treatment: Interlocking theoretical approaches* (pp. 77–102). New York, NY: Oxford University Press.

Tolman, E. C. (1948). Cognitive maps in rats and men. *Psychological Review, 55*, 189–208.

Thyer, B. A. (1991). Behavioral social work: It is not what you think, *Arete, 16*(2), 1.

Thyer, B. A. (2011). Social learning theory and social work treatment. In F. J. Turner (Ed.), *Social work treatment: Interlocking theoretical approaches* (pp. 437–446). New York, NY: Oxford University Press.

Thyer, B. A., & Hudson, W. W. (1987). Progress in behavioral social work: An introduction. *Journal of Social Service Research, 10*(2/3/4), 1–6.

Trungpa, C. (1993). *Glimpses of Shunyata*. Nova Scotia, Canada: Vajradhatu Publications.

Watson, J. B. (1913). Psychology as the behaviorist views it. *Psychological Review, 20*, 158–177.

THEORIES OF CULTURE AND WHITE PRIVILEGE

PHOTO 11.1
A gathering place for homeless people from many different countries: Casa della Caritá mural, homeless shelter in Milan, Italy

©Terry Koenig

CASE EXAMPLE
WHITE AND UNAWARE

I am a White female of German and French descent. Although I grew up in an urban area in the South, where I was exposed to racial and ethnic diversity through forced bussing of African American kids to my mostly White and Jewish junior high, I was largely unaware of the narrow understandings I had of race and ethnicity, let alone other intersectionalities related to religious beliefs, sexual orientation or expression, gender, and (dis)ability and their impact on people's views, opinions, and decisions. It was not until I began working as a new social worker in an outpatient rehabilitation unit that my understanding of race and ethnicity began to shift and change. I distinctly remember being called by an exasperated, White physical therapist, Doug, because his client, an African American man with an above-the-knee amputation, was now refusing to do his weight lifting and other strength exercises in order to prepare for his new prosthetic limb. Doug had pleaded with his client, Ray, to no avail, and he was now reaching out to me as the new social worker to see if I could "talk some sense" into Ray.

When I met with Ray, he was not talkative, and together we struggled to discuss recent changes in his motivation for working hard in physical therapy. Without success in physical therapy, Ray would most likely be turned down to receive a prosthetic limb; this concerned me. What spilled out over the course of about three sessions with Ray was that he thought God was somehow punishing him for a prior infidelity in his marriage and that he "deserved" to lose his leg and not be able to walk. Ray's views of God were even more distressing to me; I was uncomfortable with the prominent and, in my view, negative role of religion in Ray's life. Growing up White and loosely Protestant, religion had not played a significant role in my views or decision-making. I was ill-prepared to assess the impact of Ray's religious beliefs on his motivation to work hard in physical therapy. It was only through careful listening to Ray (and in working through my own distress in clinical supervision) that I began to explore the importance of Ray's religious beliefs and the strong relationship he had with his pastor and members of his Black church. I encouraged Ray to reach out to his pastor to talk through his beliefs about being punished for infidelity; Ray, in turn, was able to experience forgiveness and to regain motivation for his physical therapy.

Discussion Questions

(1) How would you describe the social worker's self-awareness in relationship to this case?

(2) What role do you think race plays in this case?

(3) How did (or might) the social worker's White privilege (unearned benefits or advantages) affect her work with Ray?

(4) Discuss the social worker's influence or power in her professional relationship with Ray.

(5) If Ray had not experienced forgiveness by his pastor and church, how might this have impacted the White social worker's (and Ray's) views of the Black church?

Newer writings on cultural competence encourage social workers to develop their own critical consciousness (see Chapter 4, "Critical Theories," for an in-depth examination of critical consciousness) in which they become increasingly aware of how social and political structures affect their personal ideas, insights, and emotional reactions within their practice (Fook & Gardner, 2007; Mattsson, 2014). The purpose of this chapter is for us to

(1) examine the development of our own critical consciousness (e.g., self-awareness, White privilege, and White identity development) as social workers;

(2) explore through the use of the dual perspective how people from diverse backgrounds or intersections (e.g., race/ethnicity, gender, age, sexual orientation and gender expression, (dis)ability, religion or spirituality) function within a majority or sustaining system that may share different values than their nurturing system (e.g., family and friends); and

(3) examine how as social workers we might work with our clients, who represent a myriad of diverse characteristics and experiences (e.g., intersectionality), and who have often faced oppression and discrimination.

CRITICAL CONSCIOUSNESS FOR OURSELVES AND OUR CLIENTS

Scholars have begun to suggest that in order for social workers to fully engage in a process of cultural competence, they must examine their own place in society as diverse human beings as well as examine the experiences, identities, and larger social contexts of their diverse clients (Lee & Greene, 2004; Mattsson, 2014; Samuels & Ross-Sheriff, 2008). By doing so, social workers engage in cultural humility, which involves making an ongoing commitment to critical self-reflection. What is implied here is that in order for us to move from a *naïve consciousness,* in which we are unaware of the conditions we and our clients live in (e.g., unearned race privileges due to being White, our social policies' and agencies' invisibly, or consciously engaging in oppression of diverse clients) to *critical consciousness,* in which we and our clients become self-aware and aware of oppressive social structures, we must first turn this process of critical consciousness on ourselves. We represent professionals with power and control to influence social policy, our agencies, and our practices with clients. This power is based on our role, but for the majority of social workers who are White (Fook & Gardner, 2007), this power is also based on our whiteness.

For the purposes of this chapter, we will define key terms based on the current social work literature and professional social work standards:

Culture can be defined as "the totality of ways being passed on from generation to generation. . . . Culture includes, but is not limited to, history, traditions, values, family systems, and artistic expressions of client groups served in the different cultures related to race and ethnicity, immigration and refugee status, tribal status, religion and spirituality, sexual orientation, gender identity and expression, social class, and abilities" (National Association of Social Workers [NASW], 2015 p. 12).

Diversity, "more than race and ethnicity, includes the sociocultural experiences of people inclusive of, but not limited to national origin, color, social class, religious and spiritual beliefs, immigration status, sexual orientation, gender identity or expression, age, marital status and physical or mental disabilities" (NASW, 2015, p. 9).

Cultural competence "refers to the process by which individuals and systems respond respectfully and effectively to people of all cultures, languages, classes, races, ethnic backgrounds, religions, spiritual traditions, immigration status, and other diversity factors in a manner that recognizes, affirms, and values the worth of individuals, families, and communities and protects and preserves the dignity of each" (NASW, 2015, p. 13).

Cultural humility, necessary for developing cultural competence, involves the social workers' "lifelong commitment to self-evaluation and self-critique, to redressing the power imbalances in . . . [professional/client relationships and in] developing advocacy partnerships with communities on behalf of" the clients social workers serve (Tervalon & Murray-Garcia, 1998, p. 117).

Intersectionality, highlighted in the in-depth theorist (i.e., Kimberlé Crenshaw) section of this chapter, can be viewed as an approach to social work practice "which examines forms of oppression, discrimination and domination as they manifest themselves through diversity components. These diversity components include multiple identities such as race and ethnicity, immigration, refugee and tribal status, religion and spirituality, sexual orientation, gender identity and expression, social class, and mental or physical disabilities" (NASW, 2015, pp. 16–17). Social workers using an intersectionality approach integrate "various diversity components and identities . . . [and practice] from a holistic point of view" (p. 17).

WHITE PRIVILEGE AND WHITE IDENTITY DEVELOPMENT

White social workers' attention to their whiteness and its privileges is a critical element in their development as culturally competent practitioners. **White privilege** can be defined as unearned and invisible social privileges due to one's White skin color. Some authors refer to White privilege as a kind of invisible knapsack (McIntosh, 1989); whiteness is all around us, yet hard to see (Lipsitz, 2006). The reality is that most White individuals cannot identify how they experience being White, nor do they identify belonging to any ethnic or racial group. These blinders (or naïve consciousness) contribute to their inability to understand how whiteness occupies a dominant position in societal structures and in their own lives. Hence, White individuals may continue to view society as a meritocracy where no matter what our identities, our background, and experiences, if we work hard, we will obtain the "good life."

Some scholars (Hardiman, 1982, 1994; Helms, 1990, 1994; Sue, Rasheed, & Rasheed, 2016) have described models of **White identity development** that depict the White person's journey from being naïve or unaware of their whiteness and privilege to an increasing cultural awareness of their dominance, coupled with action to address social injustices experienced by diverse and often marginalized groups of people.

HELMS'S WHITE IDENTITY DEVELOPMENT MODEL

Helms (1990, 1995) understood that members of any racial group go through a racial identity development process that must be viewed in the context of power imbalances that exist among racial groups in American society. Helms created an influential and widely used White racial identity development model in which she described the general developmental issue for Whites as the abandonment of entitlement (in contrast to developmental issues for people of color, which involve overcoming internalized racism). Helms described two phases involved in developing a healthy White American identity: (1) a progressive abandonment of racism, and (2) the development of a nonracist White identity. Six ego statuses, distributed equally between the two phases, are described: contact, disintegration, reintegration, pseudoindependence, immersion/emersion, and autonomy. These ego statuses are not linear stages; they are fluid, and individuals may exhibit different statuses at the same time. A person is considered to have developed a mature identity if they are able to call on these statuses to assist in coping with racial material. Each status will be described, along with strategies used for coping within a particular status.

Phase One: Progressive Abandonment of Racism

(1) Contact status. At this stage, people are oblivious to or in denial about racism, have minimal experiences with persons of color, and believe everyone has an equal chance of success (meritocracy). White people in this stage avoid perceiving themselves as having power due to their dominant group membership and may not view themselves as having biases or prejudices. In this stage, a person may declare being "color blind," viewing race and culture as unimportant. They may remark, "I don't notice a person's race at all," or "You don't act Black."

(2) Disintegration status. Obliviousness may eventually break down and a healthy resolution might be to confront the myth of meritocracy. This is a process and can involve ambivalence, lead to avoiding contact with persons of color, or the person may seek reassurance from others that Whites are not to blame for racism.

(3) Reintegration status. The person regresses or swings back to idealized beliefs in White superiority, denigrates and demonstrates intolerance for minority groups, and retreats into a dominant ideology as a way to resolve dissonance created from the previous stage. In this status, a person may say, "My ancestors owned slaves, but I have never owned slaves. Discrimination against Blacks no longer exists. Instead, I experience reverse discrimination as a guard in the prison because most of my fellow guards are Black and I am White. They do not treat me well and are physically and verbally abusive to me."

Phase Two: Development of a Nonracist Identity

(4) Pseudoindependence status. People are likely to be propelled out of the reintegration status and into this phase because of a painful or insightful encounter in which they become aware of the unfairness of treatment of racial minorities. This may lead them to identify with the plight of persons of color, to make conscious decisions to interact with minority group members and attempt to understand racial, cultural, sexual orientation, and other forms of diversity. The well-intentioned White person may unknowingly perpetuate racism by helping minorities "adjust" to the larger, dominant society instead of challenge prevailing White standards. In this status, the person is likely to understand diversity at an intellectual, not experiential or emotional level. This point about conflict between helping others "adjust versus changing institutional structures," is often ignored in the agencies that employ us. Yet, this is a central theme for most social workers in their practice. How to combine reflection and action in these circumstances is fraught with ethical dilemmas. These dilemmas represent fundamental tensions that overwhelm many practitioners as they seek to help their clients and themselves to work toward social justice.

(5) Immersion/emersion status. This status is marked by a shift in trying to change people from diverse backgrounds, but instead to engage in self-growth and change, to confront personal biases, and incorporate emotional and experiential understandings of racism and oppression. Helms believed that this status required an emotional catharsis, a kind of rebirth or release of emotions that had been denied or distorted. These affective experiences are necessary for developing a nonracist White identity and for taking action to redress injustices.

(6) Autonomy status. As people become increasingly aware of their whiteness and accept their role in perpetuating racism as well as exhibit determination to abandon White entitlement, they enter the autonomy status. They become increasingly knowledgeable about and value diversity, are no longer uncomfortable with the realities of race, and exhibit behaviors (e.g., seeking to create and live in integrated communities including in their work and personal living spaces) and integrate practices that reflect active efforts to include marginalized perspectives.

PRAXIS AS ACTION-AWARENESS-REFLECTION-DIALOGUE

Social workers can strengthen their critical consciousness through **praxis**, defined as a process of action-awareness-reflection-dialogue (Diagram 11.1), which, includes a commitment to human well-being and when applied consistently to their social work practice can function as a means of more effectively working with diverse clientele (Davis, 2012; Freire, 1970). Praxis can be illustrated in the following case example.

DIAGRAM 11.1 ■ Praxis as Action-Awareness-Reflection-Dialogue

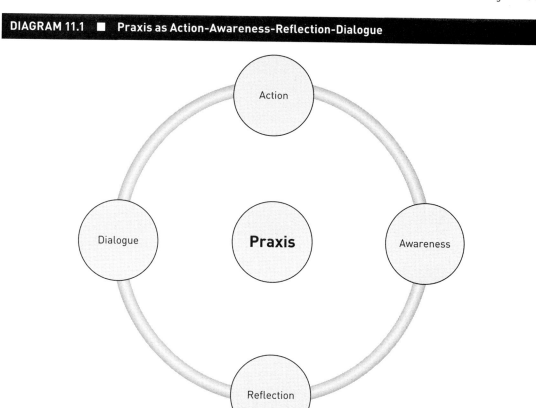

CASE EXAMPLE
PRAXIS FOR A WHITE SCHOOL SOCIAL WORKER

A new, White social worker assigned to work in a predominantly African American, inner-city high school makes a conscious decision to take *action* and reach out to African American students to establish relationships with them. She talks informally with students both before and after class, on breaks, and in brief presentations and discussions she facilitates in the classroom. She also conducts visits to students' homes. As she engages in these actions, the social worker becomes increasingly *aware* of the strengths, issues, and problems faced by her students and their families. Along with developing greater awareness, the social worker also chooses to engage in a process of self-*reflection* to examine what strategies

(Continued)

work well in establishing relationships with her students and their families, how her whiteness may affect her interactions with them, and which interactions appear to be difficult or awkward. She further explores these difficulties and successes in *dialogue* with fellow social workers and teachers in the school district, but she also engages in dialogue with her students and their families to obtain their feedback about her interactions and attempts at establishing beginning relationships with them.

Discussion Questions

(1)   How did this social worker take action to develop relationships with clients? What else could she do?

(2)   As a White social worker, imagine what might be awkward or difficult in your interactions with the African American students and families? How might teachers or other colleagues respond to your efforts?

(3)   What would be hard about reaching out to the African American students and families to get their feedback on your interactions with them?

(4)   As you continue to engage in dialogue with these students and their families, how might this change your social work practice with them?

White social workers who commit themselves to becoming aware of their White identity development and engage in self-consciousness raising about unearned, often invisible benefits of being White and their experiences with social injustice have an opportunity to use their privileged positions to act to address discrimination and oppression at individual, community, and larger societal levels (Bricker-Jenkins & Joseph, 2008; Davis & Gentlewarrior, 2015).

The Dual Perspective

American society has experienced increasing diversity due to growth in existing marginalized populations and increased numbers of people from new racial and ethnic groups, and it reflects other forms of diversity or intersections (e.g., based on gender, age, sexual orientation and gender expression, (dis)ability, religion, or spirituality). Social workers serve many of these diverse groups and consequently need to understand how they function within a broader American societal context. As social work educators, Norton (1978, 1993) and others (Chestang, 1972) put forth the **dual perspective** as a conceptual framework that enables us to look at the interactions between diverse groups and their nurturing systems (e.g., family and immediate community) and larger American society, which represents the dominant or sustaining system that may share different values, customs, and beliefs from a minority person's nurturing system (see Diagram 11.2). Although critiqued in the profession of social work for its emphasis on differences between people (instead of common human needs that unify all people), the dual perspective provides social workers with a way to conceptualize how family and immediate community environments of many marginalized groups may not match those of the larger society on all dimensions (e.g., values and religious beliefs).

DIAGRAM 11.2 ■ The Dual Perspective

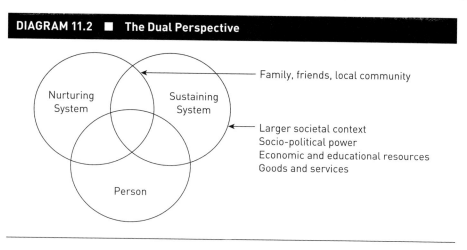

Using concepts from systems theories, the dual perspective indicates that all people are embedded in at least two interacting social systems: (1) their immediate cultural or racial environment, represented by family and their immediate community who are most involved in shaping a person's identity (the nurturing system); and (2) the economic, educational, and political systems of the wider society (the sustaining system) in which people obtain resources such as employment and housing. The dual perspective is influenced by Erikson's (1963) notion that children are first socialized by significant others and their immediate family and community

and by a central concept in symbolic interactionism, the generalized other, in which how one views oneself is shaped by one's relationship to the larger society (Mead, 1934). What Chestang (1972) and Norton (1978) add to our understanding of the generalized other is that those who represent diverse, marginalized groups develop a second more immediate generalized other rooted in the love and care of their families and local community environments, which largely shapes their identity, and can help to buffer and even restore their identity or sense of self when faced with negative attitudes or destructive views coming from the dominant, societal generalized other as described by Mead. To successfully function in both the sustaining and nurturing systems, those from marginalized groups must develop adaptive coping skills and engage in a process of bicultural socialization. This bicultural or dual socialization occurs for those in marginalized groups when they integrate positive qualities of their nurturing system with the dominant, sustaining system.

Norton (1978) describes a tripartite process of growing "conscious" awareness and knowledge (i.e., professional self-awareness; and awareness of the client's nurturing and sustaining systems) that is necessary for social workers if they are to use the dual perspective in their practice. She states,

> The dual perspective is the conscious and systematic process of perceiving, understanding, and comparing simultaneously the values, attitudes, and behavior of the larger societal system with those of the client's immediate

family and community system. It is the conscious awareness on the cognitive and attitudinal levels of the similarities and differences in the two systems. It requires substantive knowledge and empathic appreciation of both the majority societal system and the minority client system, as well as a conscious awareness of the social worker's own attitudes and values. Thus the dual perspective allows one to experience each system from the point of view of the other. (Norton, p. 3)

The dual perspective provides the social worker with a practice-based framework for

(1)   assessing the client's family and community systems without judgment;

(2)   comparing and contrasting these systems with behaviors and beliefs that are viewed as acceptable in the larger, dominant society which may, in turn, erect institutional and other barriers that further oppress diverse clients; and

(3)   examining areas of difference or conflict that might impact the client's particular circumstances.

Using the dual perspective allows the social worker to begin where the client is, to heighten awareness of her own values and biases in working with clients, and to deepen her empathy and understanding as to the total life situation (e.g., social interactions and behaviors) of the client.

Finally, the dual perspective helps social workers from a dominant, privileged position to discover and more closely examine structural barriers and injustices within the wider, sustaining system that may impact on the diverse group's opportunities as well as experiences with oppression. And, social workers who are themselves members of diverse groups or reflect a range of intersectionalities will want to use the dual perspective as a framework that helps them to pay close attention to their own values and beliefs as they interact with the client's nurturing and sustaining systems.

Summary of Overview

In this overview, we have examined social work's expanded view of culture as encompassing many different forms of diversity including, but not limited to, race and ethnicity, sexual orientation, gender and gender expression, age, (dis)ability, and class. We note that as social workers, we need to develop our own critical consciousness through praxis, a process of action, self-awareness, self-reflection, and dialogue with others. Personal and professional self-awareness and self-reflection are paramount in order for us to engage in a lifelong journey toward cultural competence. Because the majority of social work professionals are White and concomitantly few social work educational programs have thoughtfully examined White privilege and White identity development, these perspectives feature prominently in this chapter. We end our overview by discussing the dual perspective as a practice framework that was developed by social work scholars and supports key elements of social work practice such as "starting where the client is," deepening our holistic understanding of a client system's total life situation, and closely assessing the structural barriers within the wider sustaining system that may impact on clients' opportunities and experiences with oppression.

IN-DEPTH THEORIST: KIMBERLÉ CRENSHAW AND INTERSECTIONALITY

Intersectionality has multiple theorists who have proposed a number of ideas over time about just what it means, who it addresses, and what it should be used for. The primary theorist in this area for several decades is Kimberlé Crenshaw, and we will primarily highlight her work. It is worth noting at the outset that intersectionality, while "theoretical," is more of a concept, or analytical tool, than a broad theory that attempts to offer an explanation of human development or identity formation. In other words, as Crenshaw states, intersectionality does not offer a "totalizing theory of identity" (2013), instead it addresses an often ignored element in overlapping identities or intersections that compound experiences of discrimination (e.g., race and gender).

Crenshaw, who received her undergraduate degree at Cornell University and graduated from Harvard Law School, is a Distinguished Professor of Law and teaches courses on civil rights, critical race studies, and constitutional law at both UCLA and Columbia University; she is considered a leader in the critical race theory movement (Crenshaw, Gotanda, Peller, & Thomas, 1996). Crenshaw's conceptual development of intersectionality is born from her thoughtful analyses of the shortcomings of the law in its capacity to address the compounding effects of gender and race discrimination. For example, she experienced this first-hand as she served on the legal team for Anita Hill, who accused the then–Supreme Court nominee Clarence Thomas of sexual harassment. Thomas's case reflected the ongoing tensions between race and gender in which feminists were opposed to his nomination, but the Black community wanted to see him elected as only the second African American to serve on the Supreme Court. For an up-close look of Crenshaw's views on intersectionality specifically related to race and gender, see her TED Talk at https://www.ted.com/talks/kimberle_crenshaw_the_urgency_of_intersectionality#t-179435.

The idea of intersectionality originates with Crenshaw's critique of feminist and anti-racist stances, which recognize and analyze people's experiences and privileges in society along sociopolitical axes in isolation from one another (Crenshaw, 1989). These single-axis analyses, argues Crenshaw, are inadequate to address the complexities of Black women (among others), who are "multiply burdened" by being both Black and female. As such, the very structure used to identify and analyze subordination must be changed; this gives rise to the concept of intersectionality. Failure to reconstruct this underlying analytic device enacts the theoretical erasure of the realities of Black women's lives, as the assumption of mutually exclusive categories ignores their disadvantages vis-à-vis more privileged groups, the point being that their intersectional disadvantages are greater than the disadvantages raised by the mere concatenation of individual categories.

So what is intersectionality? Simply put, intersectionality is a framework providing a constellation of intersecting sociopolitical categories for the analysis of power dynamics in human relationships, institutions, and communities that lead to oppression and discrimination (Cho, Crenshaw, & McCall, 2013). "Intersectional" denotes the idea that a single category such as race alone is not sufficient to enlighten the nature of subordination and exclusion experienced by individuals and groups in society. Instead, we must consider the multiple categories an individual belongs to in order to recognize the nature of their experience. For instance, Black women belong to at least the categories of "Black" (race) and "female" (gender), each of which carries meanings in societal structures and relationships that lead to disadvantage, discrimination, and often violence. The combination of being Black and female is significantly more disadvantageous and dangerous than being either Black and male, or female and White. There are overlapping experiences between White women and Black women, and between Black women and Black men. As Crenshaw notes,

> Yet often they [Black women] experience double-discrimination—the combined effects of practices which discriminate on the basis of race, and on the basis of sex [gender]. And sometimes, they experience discrimination as Black women—not the sum of race and sex discrimination, but as Black women. (1989, p. 149)

Moreover, the societal privileges (and associated safety and well-being) of an individual who is not only Black and female, but perhaps also lesbian and (dis)abled, are radically diminished the more intersecting "burdens" she carries. Each category she belongs to intersects with the others to put her in a position with regard to societal privileges that is extremely disadvantaged compared to others who do not have the same number of factors burdening them.

Crenshaw's critique originated in the legal field as it pertains to laws and policies that offer consideration of only single factors such as race or gender, but not both; Crenshaw offers social critique as her concept addresses the feminist community (and others) who also only consider single factors, one at a time, as burdens to individuals in society (1989). Crenshaw raises questions about who is legitimately considered to be a woman. And what defines womanhood? Her answer is that even the feminists (then, and many still now) define "woman" along White, middle-class norms, which exclude the identity and experiences of *Black* women. For instance, White, middle-class women have not had the same historical burden in the labor force as Black women, who for generations have either been forced or otherwise required to work outside the home in order to make ends meet and whose families were ravaged by slavery. So when White feminists advocate for equality with regard to work, they ignore the perspectives of Black women, who cannot be seen or heard because they do not fit White feminists' assumptions about womanhood. White feminists, in other words, have ignored the multiple privileges they have compared to women who are Black, lesbian, poor, disabled, and so on.

Intersectionality illuminates multiple forms of subordination and disadvantage experienced by Black women, which extends beyond the critique of White feminists and economics to focus on violence—racialized police violence in particular.

> The resurgent racial justice movement in the United States has developed a clear frame to understand the police killings of Black men and boys, theorizing the ways in which they are systematically criminalized and feared across disparate

class backgrounds and irrespective of circumstance. Yet Black women who are profiled, beaten, sexually assaulted, and killed by law enforcement officials are conspicuously absent from this frame even when their experiences are identical. (Crenshaw & Ritchie, 2015, Chapter 1, para. 5)

Black women face violence on many different fronts and in many different ways (Crenshaw, 2016). Recent events include the church shooting in Charleston, Virginia, where six of the nine people killed were Black women. But the violence endured by Black women occurs primarily in their everyday lives and rarely makes news headlines. This includes instances of being shot during routine traffic stops, and raped, brutalized, and dehumanized by police. To make things worse, Black women are also surveilled, arrested, and incarcerated at much higher rates than Whites and Latinas (Crenshaw, 2013). Of course, violence represents only one dimension of disadvantage and subordination that Black women face, which raises broader issues surrounding privileges and advantages in society, who has them and who does not.

It is often assumed that a nation state (or other society) presents its citizens with an **equal playing field** such that each person in the society has equal rights and an equal opportunity to take advantage of the societal benefits such as opportunities for education, employment, safe living conditions, health care, recreational opportunities, social status and respect, and so on. Intersectionality highlights differences in peoples' ability to participate in society according to their relative social status. We know the increasing differences in life outcomes with regard to global wealth and income distribution (among other things) are such that the combined wealth of the richest 85 people is equal to the poorest half of the world's population (approximately 3.5 billion) (Oxfam, 2014).

Using intersectionality as an analytical tool can foster a better understanding of growing global inequality. First, economic inequality does not fall equally on everyone. Rather than seeing people as a homogeneous, undifferentiated mass, intersectionality provides a framework for explaining how social divisions of race, gender, age, and citizenship status, among others, positions people differently in the world, especially in relation to global social inequality. (Collins & Bilge, 2016, Chapter 1, para. 28)

So we see that along multiple dimensions that inequality persists, and intersectionality offers an analytical tool for describing and explaining how and why. In order to elucidate intersectionality further, six core ideas can serve as guideposts (Collins & Bilge, 2016). Each of the six ideas is not always present in a given analysis, and all six may not present themselves at the same time. But each serves as thematic of intersectionality. The six include social inequality, power, relationality, social context, complexity, and social justice—we'll consider each of these in turn.

First, intersectionality is concerned with various forms of social inequality (Collins & Bilge, 2016). Wealth and income, as just mentioned, form one clear domain in which great inequality exists between the rich and poor. Additional social inequalities exist with regard to peoples' ability to access transportation, child care, health care, education, employment, and so on. Intersectionality encourages understanding social inequality from multiple dimensions, not just race or class, but the interactions of multiple categories including, but not limited to, ability, gender, age, race, ethnicity, and sexual orientation.

The second dimension follows from the first: social inequality raises questions about who has power and how that power is used in social, political, economic, and other arenas (Collins & Bilge, 2016). Power analyses are concerned with macro-level structures associated with nation states and sociopolitical ideologies, but also consider dynamics on an individual or group level. Power is associated with being a member of various groups, such as being a citizen of a particular nation state. People who are United States citizens, for example, enjoy benefits that are not necessarily available to residents who are not citizens. Globally speaking, U.S. citizens—along with many from similar developed nations—enjoy rights and benefits that residents of other countries do not have. U.S. citizens tend to consume luxury goods that are often produced by people in other countries who do not have the power (in this case, the financial ability) to purchase the very goods they have just produced (shoes would be one example). On an individual level, power dynamics play out in many ways, from the scourge of sexual harassment to the privileges some enjoy when interviewing for a job.

Third, the idea of relationality rejects binary thinking such as the prioritization of theory over practice, male over female or White over Black. "The focus of relationality shifts from analyzing what distinguishes entities, for example, the differences between race and gender, to examining their interconnections" (Collins & Bilge, 2016, Chapter 2, para. 10). Interconnections, as Crenshaw (above) emphasizes in her work, characterize intersectionality. Instead of looking at single dimensions such as social class, in order to gain perspective on the power dynamics involved in a given situation, intersectionality involves seeking to develop deeper understanding through analyzing the interactions or transactions in relationships, whether individual or large scale.

Fourth, intersectionality requires one to analyze the social and historical context of any relevant relationship or situation (Collins & Bilge, 2016). Far from idle or endless wandering in abstraction, intersectionality starts with concrete situations such as the experience of poverty due to an individual's inability to find work. It considers the race, class, gender, and more of the individual in the specific micro and macro sociopolitical world she finds herself in, which is shaped by real relationships with their concomitant power dynamics and a community shaped by laws and policies and cultural norms, all of which comprise context for understanding. Context provides grounding for intersectional analysis.

Fifth, the preceding four aspects of intersectionality offer complexity for understanding the dimensions of marginalization, exploitation, and abuse (Collins & Bilge, 2016). Intersectional analysis is not easy as it involves multiple factors and a lot of information for processing. That said, there is no way around this, especially as one takes intersectional analysis and applies it toward social work practice of various sorts.

Finally, the sixth theme of intersectionality is social justice. Social justice involves attention to equality and fairness (Collins & Bilge, 2016). For instance, in the United States, everyone has the right to vote, but not everyone has equal access to voting. This returns us quickly to the idea of an equal playing field. Intersectional analysis attends to this field in multiple dimensions, highlighting the unfairness and unequal starting points of the "players" in their global or local socioeconomic and political contexts.

CRITIQUE OF THEORIES OF CULTURE, WHITE PRIVILEGE, DIVERSITY, AND INTERSECTIONALITY

What Does This Theory Say About Human Behavior?

In this section, we will discuss the two dimensions of the assumptions behind theory: the stability–radical change and objective–subjective dimensions (see Chapter 2). Our chapter on White privilege, White identity development, and intersectionality supports what can be viewed as radical change over maintaining the status quo or stability within our larger society. These theories and/or concepts (i.e., intersectionality) indicate that individuals from dominant groups in our society must engage in a process of ongoing, critical self-awareness and reflection in order to grow and change within themselves and in addressing unjust societal structures that harm marginalized groups. In its current form, the dual perspective continues to emphasize minority persons' adaptation and integration within the larger, dominant society in contrast to examining dominant societal members' responsibilities in advocating for and acting to change the larger society to be more responsive to those with minority group status.

All of our theories and/or concepts support self-awareness and self-reflection as pivotal to our professional development as social workers who are on a lifelong journey toward cultural competence. Further, writers who discuss the need for the social worker to cultivate ongoing critical self-reflective skills indicate that this is required even for those social workers from diverse backgrounds who must also hone their critical self-reflective skills. As Sakamoto (2007) remarks, we cannot assume a "race to innocence" in that those social workers from diverse or minority backgrounds are not exempt from becoming oppressive to other clients; they may not be any more prepared than those in the dominant group to address their clients' multiple forms of diversities or intersectionalities and the accompanying discrimination and oppression at both personal and systemic levels.

White privilege, White identity development, and intersectionality support subjectivity or reality based on the meanings we create in a process of ongoing dialogue with our clients. Knowledge is developed through our personal experiences, and yet, this is never the only kind of knowledge we draw upon. We can easily compare our subjective experiences with larger, objective societal data. For example, we can help an African American man, recently released from prison, who comes to see us in our clinical practice to address not only his "adjustment" to the larger, more dominant society, but also by acknowledging the "school-to-prison" pipeline that contributes to disproportionate numbers of African American men being incarcerated within our prison system. This aggregate data about incarceration rates of African American men are important to examine in light of our clients' individual experiences as it is these connections between subjective and objective experiences that help clients and ourselves to move from naïve consciousness to critical consciousness; personal experiences of oppression are then connected to larger unjust societal structures. In contrast, although the dual perspective acknowledges sociopolitical and economic power within the dominant, sustaining societal system, proponents of this theory emphasize the minority person's capacities to adapt to the sustaining system in order to function successfully in our larger society.

How Does This Theory Address Growth and Change?

All of our theories and/or concepts support growth and change at some levels (e.g., for professional social workers, clients, and/or the larger community and society). However, the focus of growth and change for the social worker (through a process of critical self-reflection) is markedly different between the dual perspective and our other theories or concepts (i.e., White privilege, White identity development, and intersectionality). In the dual perspective, the social worker must develop critical self-reflection for the purpose of nonjudgmentally assessing the values, behaviors, and beliefs of the client's nurturing system and as an avenue for comparing and contrasting this system with what is viewed as acceptable in the larger, more dominant society (sustaining system). Although there is an acknowledgment that the client may face institutional barriers in the sustaining system, the goal of such professional self-awareness and reflection is to assist the client in successfully adapting or integrating into the wider society. In the dual perspective, there is virtually no discussion about how professional social workers and clients might act to change dominant systems to be more amenable to the needs of clients who represent marginalized groups.

In contrast, proponents of White privilege, White identity development, and inter-sectionality support development of critical self-reflection for those in dominant as well as minority positions as a means of creating personal, interpersonal, and agency-based change. In particular, White social workers, as members of the dominant group, have choices about what they can do with their privilege. As put forth by Davis and Gentlewarrior (2015), they can (1) cultivate self-reflection in order to develop a more nuanced understanding of their position in a particular context thereby fostering their empathy for those who experience oppression; (2) develop relationships, dialogue with, and listen to the experiences of people from diverse backgrounds as well as challenge prejudicial comments of those in dominant positions; and (3) advocate within our agencies for hiring, promoting, and supporting people from minority groups as well as nurture White people in their growth and commitment to these agency-based practices who can, in turn, spend their privilege to challenge unjust structures and systems (Fook, 2012).

How Holistic Is This Theory?

In order for us to take the journey from a naïve consciousness, in which we are asleep and unaware of the oppression of others in less powerful positions, to a critical consciousness, we must think holistically. (Take note of the holistic symbolism in the painting on the outside of a Buddhist temple near the South/North Korean border). White privilege, White identity development, and intersectionality emphasize the development of a critical consciousness that is only possible when we holistically make connections between our personal and structural spaces in society and the spaces that others in minority positions struggle to claim or cannot inhabit. If we represent the dominant position as White social workers, there are no immediate benefits that come to us in choosing to examine the positions of others who represent marginalized groups. However, as professional social workers bound by a shared set of values, which involve serving those on the margins and respecting their dignity and worth, we are required to engage in an ongoing process of waking up to the invisible, unmarked, and unearned personal and structural privileges that White people experience and to then compare and contrast these experiences with those of persons representing marginalized groups. This holistic process of making connections can assist us in taking actions to change or improve our larger social structures into being more just and sensitive to the needs of others from diverse groups.

Although the dual perspective does support the social worker's development of a critical consciousness, its purpose is in large measure not to change the wider, dominant society. Instead, this perspective supports our capacity to think holistically about our clients' nurturing systems and how the values and beliefs of their families and immediate community might create conflict for diverse clients as they attempt to function successfully in the larger society. By its very nature, intersectionality encourages us to take a holistic approach to social work practice that involves examining various forms of oppression as they manifest themselves through diverse, multiple identities such as refugee and tribal status, religious belief, age, gender, sexual orientation, class, race, and/or ethnicity. In addition to these multiple identities, we might ask ourselves what other characteristics might be important to consider such as height, weight, marital status, and history of sexual or physical abuse.

PHOTO 11.2
Holistic symbol adorning South Korean Buddhist temple

How Consistent Is This Theory With Social Work Values and Ethics?

In this section, White privilege, White identity development, intersectionality, and the dual perspective will be examined for their congruence with four key social work values: integrity, social justice, client freedom or self-determination, and the dignity and worth of each person. Social workers who practice with integrity monitor their own practice so that it remains consistent with the profession's mission and values. All of our theories and/or concepts speak to the importance of social workers' development of critical thinking and self-reflection, which leads not only to an awareness of one's position in society (e.g., as a member of a dominant or marginalized group) but also to critical reflection on unjust social structures that harm those in less powerful or marginalized positions. Through the cultivation of this critical consciousness, which occurs in dialogue with colleagues and clients, social workers are able to actively strengthen their professional integrity by examining their personal biases and prejudices and correcting for mistakes as they commit to ongoing personal and professional growth. Although the dual perspective falls short in directly supporting professional integrity, which contributes to the social workers' actions in combatting unjust societal structures, White privilege, White identity development, and intersectionality challenge social workers to act for the purpose of supporting client growth and in making changes to our larger social systems, which often contribute to hidden, unjust practices.

Early writings on the dual perspective emphasized minority groups' adaptation and integration into the wider society, thereby contributing to views that those in marginalized positions have inherent deficits in being able to engage in healthy adaptation. Although this pathology-based view has been amended in more current literature and social work scholars acknowledge that members of marginalized groups can engage in healthy integration into the larger society, one question remains: Do we want people who represent marginalized groups to "fit" into, adapt, and integrate into the larger, dominant society as suggested by the dual perspective? By taking this position are we indeed denying self-determination to those who represent diverse groups? Although the dual perspective represents a kind of systems or person-in-environment approach, it places minimal emphasis on the dominant group's role in being sensitive to and respecting the dignity and worth of those in marginalized positions. In contrast, intersectionality asks us to be aware of the complex identities of human beings so as to limit stereotyping of any group of people in favor of treating each person with dignity and respect. In other words, professionals need to guard against overgeneralizations (e.g., not all police officers are racist; not all African American women give the same meaning to their experiences with race and gender discrimination).

What Sources of Knowledge Does This Theory Support?

All of these theories and/or concepts support multiple types of knowledge. In particular, White privilege, White identity development, and intersectionality demand that as social workers we do our own self-reflective work first in order to understand our place in society as members of a dominant group that has benefited from unearned privileges. As we develop our own critical consciousness, knowing that privilege is by accident of birth and that those in marginalized positions are harmed by larger unjust social structures that limit their opportunities, this personal knowledge can then be drawn upon or used in our work with clients. These theories and/or concepts also support knowledge that is developed relationally and in dialogue with others. As social workers, there is no way to "know" for certain if the work we are doing with clients respects and takes into account their unique circumstances, identities, and diversities. We have to ask and engage in ongoing dialogue with our clients as to their assessment of our capacities to engage meaningfully with them. Consequently, both the client's voice and the social worker's voice (developed through an ongoing process of critical self-reflection) are pivotal elements of knowledge. What some researchers have shown us is that the knowledge obtained in the social work classroom does not easily translate into the agency-based settings in which we practice. This kind of knowledge gleaned from research studies helps us to holistically integrate what we are doing in social work education with the realities of a resource-starved practice environment in which few opportunities are sustained with professionals over the long haul to help them continuously develop, correct for, and sharpen their critical awareness of oppression.

APPLICATION AND DEVELOPMENT OF DIVERSITY IN SOCIAL WORK PRACTICE

Introduction

In this section of the chapter, we will be using the definitions that you learned in the preceding sections including diversity, cultural competence, White privilege, and

White identity development as they relate to their translation into practice. In addition, we will introduce the concept of **White fragility** defined as a "state in which even a minimum amount of racial stress becomes intolerable, triggering a range of defensive moves . . . such as anger, fear, guilt, and behaviors such as argumentation, silence, and leaving the stress-inducing situation" (DiAngelo, 2011, p. 54). We will begin with a set of six assumptions about what diversity means and how diversity connects to social work education and social work practice. We will specifically address the roles played by "White fragility" and "White privilege" as they relate to the development of critical thinking skills, which we define as a process that can be used to assist you to integrate your personal and professional development. Finally, we will provide case examples and exercises that can help you begin using critical thinking processes on a regular basis to increase both your awareness and skill levels into your practice with a clear understanding that this is a lifelong process, not something that you are going to master solely during your social work education.

Assumptions About the Integration of Diversity Into Social Work Practice

- Changing practice behaviors, as well as adding new practice behaviors (thinking, awareness, and reflection are included here as behavior) are essential to ethical practice.

- Inclusion or omission of diversity perspectives respectively supports or reduces discrimination experienced by our clients in our professional relationships. Here, in the realm of diversity, the feminist adage "the personal is political" frames the importance of diversity in social work practice.

- Our growth as professionals is directly related to our progress in dealing with our own personal worldviews, which are shaped by the "isms" embedded in our own personal narratives. Therefore, our personal growth directly interacts with our professional growth.

- Social constructionism asserts that knowledge is developed within particular social contexts related to diversity. That knowledge base is rooted in the NASW Code of Ethics (2017) which impacts our skills as professionals.

- The integration of culture and diversity into a framework for social work practice is not just mastery of content. In order to achieve more positive outcomes, we must understand, develop, and translate into action critical thinking skills including awareness, reflection, and action.

- The material in this section focuses on practice at all levels (micro, mezzo, and macro). The translation of diversity into practice is a lifelong process. It is not simply mastery of content. The outcome is to develop a more sophisticated level of understanding that includes continual movement toward more effective strategies to include diversity in our practice.

The preceding assumptions about the integration of diversity into social work practice represent a complex set of tasks and processes long identified and described in social work literature (Council on Social Work Education, 2015; Lee & Greene, 2004; Leigh, 1998; Lum, 2003; NASW, 2015; Rothman, 2008; Sue & McGoldrick, 2005). Not only is the subject matter on diversity complex, but it is particularly vexing because it takes place within a national dialogue that has failed to address fundamental issues of oppression related to race, ethnicity, gender, age, social class, and (dis)ability. These "isms" are at the heart of challenges related to social structures as well as interpersonal dynamics. In addition, social work education and practice mirror many of the same larger prejudices that create tensions between the needs of individuals to receive services and efforts to create social change to increase the level of social justice afforded for the majority of our clients.

As you experience your classrooms and practicum, you will notice that there is often significant variance regarding the levels of attention provided to diversity content and often little discussion of what is necessary to do in order to deal with our own narratives as they enter into our practice as social workers. In one study focused on social work graduates, researchers found that 76% of the respondents indicated that diversity was a focus in their master's-level education. Yet, 22% of the respondents indicated that they did nothing when facing differences in their interactions with fellow student colleagues and only 13.5 percent of those even discussed those differences with fellow students. In this particular study, 46% of the practitioners indicated they were uncomfortable talking about cultural and racial issues with student group members (Rittner, Nakanishi, Nackerud, & Hammons, 1999; Vodde, 2000). In another study examining social work education, Pinderhughes (1989) noted that even when content on diversity and oppression is provided, "practitioners must be willing and able to reflexively evaluate their experiences with power, status differences in participation in oppressive strategies as well as their own privilege" in order for this to be relevant in practice (p. 20).

Our own experience of teaching social work includes similar experiences to those reported in the literature. It is often uncomfortable for students and faculty to honestly discuss the kinds of issues that are necessary for the inclusion of diversity in practice. One applicable concept put forward by Robin DiAngelo (2011) identifies "White fragility," which refers to the discomfort Whites have with frank discussions about race given that they live in environments where they are isolated from the discomfort created by acknowledging racial tensions in our society. Davis and Gentlewarrior (2015) examine the role of White privilege in clinical social work practice and Vodde (2000) urges the examination of White privilege in social work education.

In social work education there are often two strategies that contribute to the problems created by White fragility. For example, it is not uncommon for schools of social work to depend on the recruitment of faculty and practitioners of color to teach diversity classes. As we have noted, these courses, when they move beyond simply focusing on content, toward requiring direct engagement of both the teachers' and the students' personal narratives as a part of the dialogue, create significant levels of discomfort that gets reflected in course evaluations. Second, another commonly used strategy is to "infuse" material on diversity in all courses. Unfortunately, we have not always provided the necessary preparation for teachers to deliver this material beyond recitation of content. Because of its potential to create discomfort, there is unevenness in its presence in courses across the curriculum, including practicum, and those teachers who teach "diversity classes" run the risk of the potential for "ghettoization" of diversity content.

ETHICS SPOTLIGHT

TATTOOS AND TRANSFORMATION IN SOCIAL WORK EDUCATION

The following case example provides a look at how challenging diversity issues may be in social work education.

My own consciousness was raised as I watched my White son wrestle with the discrimination that his wife, who is from another country, experienced (and he did not) while on the job market as an architect. I also have beautiful, mixed-race grandchildren. These personal experiences informed my professional interests in developing international educational programming as a way to expose social work students to broader worldviews and led me to change my human behavior courses to include readings and discussions of critical theories and how one "wakes up" to oppression. I had always felt comfortable working with doctoral students to observe my teaching, and in my opening class session on critical theories I had invited a White male doctoral student, Gavin, to observe my class as a part of completing his requirements for another course.

In our introduction to critical theories, I directly asked my students: "Can you describe an experience of waking up to your participation in oppression?" Sean, a White male student, jumped at the opportunity to discuss his waking up to oppression and what he now understood as uncalled-for violence through his membership in a gang. An articulate young man from the East Coast, sleeved with tattoos on both arms from wrists to shoulders, he described his participation in a gang in which they had committed violent acts against those from other racial groups. One night, his gang got into an armed street fight with an African American gang and they exchanged racial slurs, including his use of the "N" word; Sean's gang nearly killed a man. As he recounted this violent scenario, Sean reflected on how ashamed he was of his former racist views and actions and that this scenario is what had led to his awakening or transformation and his desire to now study social work.

After our class session, I discussed Sean's story with my outside observer, Gavin, who reported being deeply offended that Sean had used the "N" word and that by allowing this to occur, as a professor, I was complicit in participating in racism. When I asked Gavin to tell me how he had understood Sean's story, I was surprised to learn that he had stopped listening after Sean had used the "N" word because it was so offensive to him; Gavin had no idea that Sean's story was a confession and renouncement of his former racist views. Sean had not used racist slurs toward others in the classroom; he instead had openly discussed his racism—something I had hoped that as a class (in which we had developed ground rules for open and respectful communication) we would be able to do. From my viewpoint, Sean's disclosure was in part a reflection and product of my own awakening and growth.

After my brief discussion with Gavin and on the following day, I received a call from one of our department's White administrators, Elizabeth, stating that word had "gotten out" about what had happened in my class and that I was being accused of being complicit to racism in the classroom. I agreed to meet with Gavin and Elizabeth in the hopes that we would be able to process and develop an understanding of Sean's story of racism within the context of our class discussion on critical theory. What ensued was frankly unbelievable to me. Gavin came into our meeting 30 minutes late, inebriated, and red in the face. When asked to directly express his concerns to me as the instructor, he was unable to do so, but he eventually admitted that he had not heard the rest of Sean's story nor was he aware of its broader context. However, the White administrator felt sorry for Gavin and concerned as to what she viewed as the "devastating, emotional impact" of our discussion on Gavin. Shortly after our meeting ended, and in ongoing dialogue with

(Continued)

(Continued)

Elizabeth about the difference between classroom discussions about racism and the directing of racist slurs toward others, Elizabeth asked me to meet with Gavin to help him understand these differences. Unfortunately, Gavin refused to meet with me and was not required to process his classroom observation as part of his course requirements.

Discussion Questions

(1) Was what Sean said morally wrong? Was it racist? Why or why not? (Ground your answer in an understanding of differences between classroom discussions of racism and racist slurs.)

(2) How does White privilege operate in this case example?

(3) Using Helms's model of White identity development, how might you characterize Sean's, Gavin's, Elizabeth's and the professor's White identity development? What status best defines them? Be sure to give a reason for your answer.

(4) As you examine the process of praxis (i.e., action-awareness-reflection-dialogue), what elements of praxis are missing or incomplete in this case example?

(5) What do the organizational responses in this case reflect about White fragility and the institution's readiness to engage in the development of critical consciousness for its students as well as for faculty and staff?

(6) What needs to happen in order for growth (e.g., professional competence and integrity) to occur among all the actors in this case?

Finally, when we examine the assumptions that underlie the inclusion of diversity in social work practice, we find long-standing tension between the process aspects of developing diversity and the outcome statements reflected in referring to culturally competent practice. In reality, there are a series of processes and skills necessary to develop, prior to achieving increased levels of competence in relationship to our practice. Unfortunately, what often happens is that cultural competence is defined as the absorption of content related to various populations who experience oppression. For example, in the NASW *Code of Ethics*, we find a listing of specific groups of people for whom we should be advocating for in order to achieve a more socially just world (NASW, 2017). There is an assumption that if we master content related to diversity, this will somehow prepare us to translate that content into action. As noted above, that is not likely to happen. As we stated earlier in this chapter, the process needed to integrate diversity into our practice consists of the capacity to think critically. What this means is that the process includes the following steps: (1) The development of awareness and understanding, about how our own identity has been developed prior to examining the roles that identity plays in others' lives; (2) the capacity to reflect on how our current understandings of ourselves as cultural beings interacts with those individuals whose identities are different from our own; and (3) a willingness to take action that translates our current levels of awareness and understanding of ourselves and others while paying careful attention to examine the consequences of these interactions. In essence, the means by which we include diversity in social work practice creates the capacity to start with the process of critical thinking that leads to new understandings flowing from an emerging critical consciousness about ourselves, which impacts our work with clients. What this approach requires is the acknowledgment that we must start with our own personal narratives and only after getting "our own house in order" can we begin to make any progress toward understanding how to include diversity in our practice.

Table 11.1 is designed to illustrate the translation of Freire's (1970) ideas into a series of processes that represent one way for social workers to move from naïve consciousness to critical consciousness. The intent is to suggest that this is not a linear process but rather a fluid interaction among the following components: experience, awareness, reflection, dialogue, and action. The absence of any one of these five components will hinder our ability to continue to grow and develop our understandings of the role of diversity in social work practice. As we said in an earlier chapter on critical theory, this is central not only to incorporating diversity into our practice but to all areas of professional learning.

TABLE 11.1 ■ Diversity Competency Process

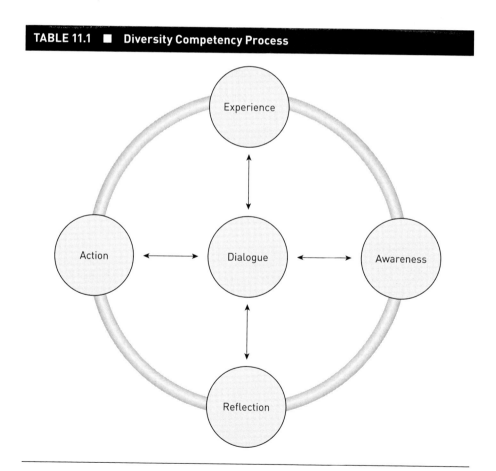

CASE EXAMPLE
STUDY ABROAD AS CONSCIOUSNESS RAISING

What follows provides an opportunity to translate what these processes look like as they play out in our lives. An American social work faculty person took responsibility for a study abroad program in Costa Rica. The instructor and students were engaged in a wide range of activities that including lectures, visiting social agencies, interacting with Costa Rican students and faculty, and some contact with clients. One of the major challenges was that the faculty member had a very limited command of Spanish. One afternoon, the instructor and three students stopped at a local grocery market to make some purchases. When the instructor attempted to pay the cashier for the items, he was unable to communicate effectively with the cashier relating to the purchase. His attempts to explain his needs were unsuccessful, and the cashier became more and more frustrated because others were waiting to pay for their purchases. She repeated her demands more loudly and displayed her frustration with the instructor. After a few minutes the instructor was able to determine how much was owed and completed the purchase (experience).

Upon returning to the hotel, the instructor excused himself from the students and went to his room to begin to examine the experience. At one level his own awareness of his discomfort with his own language skills surfaced based on this encounter. In some ways it tapped into his own fear that he might run into a situation that involved students needing help and his own language skills would not allow him to be of assistance in his role as a group leader. At another level, he was embarrassed about the fact that he was becoming an impediment to the other people in the store and felt powerless to be able to "fix" the situation (awareness). With this awareness, he began to reflect on strategies that would need to be put in place to avoid this kind of situation in the future. In addition, his reactions triggered recollection of similar circumstances he had seen in the United States. There have been occasions he had witnessed when a Spanish-speaking person was struggling to make purchases in American grocery stores or department stores, and English-speaking store clerks behaved in a similar fashion. What his own experience reflected was parallel to the American experience, the vulnerability that comes with limited language skills in relation to the dominant group (reflection). The instructor promised himself that he would not stand by idly and watch this scenario unfold in his own country. The instructor met with the students during the course evaluation that included a discussion about this incident to engage students' exploration of vulnerability they experienced on the trip in their new role as "outsider" and their own sense of vulnerability (dialogue). The outcome was that he had regular opportunities in grocery stores and other venues to step in to assist Spanish-speaking individuals when they faced the overwhelming sense of vulnerability based on their struggles to master the dominant group's language (action).

White Privilege

At the beginning of the chapter we introduced the concepts of White privilege and White identity development. In this section we will look at how the process of White identity development interacts with social work practice. First, it is important to understand that race is only one aspect of diversity. The concept of intersectionality, as discussed in the preceding section, is central to the development of a more nuanced understanding that constitutes diversity in social work practice. Therefore, layering in multiple aspects of the human condition is central to practice because individuals have both shared and unique experiences as it relates to their definition of themselves. It is essential to recognize there are both intragroup differences, as well as differences among groups who are dissimilar from each other. Race, gender, sexual orientation, culture, religion, and ability levels are all important aspects of diversity that shape who we are as individuals.

The following exercise builds on the material related to White identity development, providing an illustration of an individual's reflections on oppression from the dominant, White male, heterosexual position. It reflects a particular point in an ongoing process rather than an end product.

Stages in the Change Process: Reflections on Intra- and Interpersonal Oppression From a Dominant Position

As we noted in this chapter there are two significant domains related to oppression. The first domain, micro, has to do with our own internal beliefs that shape our interactions with others, focused on interpersonal biases. Moving from naïve consciousness to critical consciousness involves an ongoing process of challenging our understanding of the world and the role oppression plays in our interactions with others. For example, if we are attending the gathering of people largely drawn from the dominant culture and we hear a racist or sexist joke, we are forced to decide how to respond. If we remain silent, that has consequences, or if we challenge the inappropriateness of the statements, that too has consequences for our interpersonal relationships. The second domain, macro, focuses on the institutional arrangements that embody and translate oppression. For example, the distribution of opportunities provided by the economic, political, and social welfare systems create inherently unequal access in our society. The choice to fund schools through property tax illustrates the inherent inequality to access quality education.

The following is an example focusing on the first domain related to oppression (micro) embedded in the process of the emergence of White identity in relationship to moving from naïve consciousness toward critical consciousness. It illustrates how we can engage in an active process that allows us to utilize critical thinking skills to alter our own narrative, and thereby our interactions with others to reduce the oppression in our interactions with others.

1. The process begins with both *ignorance* and a level of *certainty*: I am an Italian American, White, Catholic, male, and heterosexual. These lenses provide minimal exposure for me to create awareness of my privilege and its impact on others. Therefore, I did not feel the need to reflect on how my actions were affecting others or contributed to their oppression. My White privilege allows me to remain comfortable, and I am certain that I am not a part of

the problem. The issues are externalized and foreign to me. However, there are some feelings of uneasiness beginning to seep into my consciousness as I watch events unfold in the larger society and interact with new African American friends in graduate school, as well as a new wife and two children, a son and a daughter.

2. *Personal sensitization* of daily events: I begin to see daily interactions that reflect some of the broader social concerns being raised by women, people of color, and gays and lesbians, resulting from their experience of oppression. My conscious mind allows me to interpret the interactions as products of racist institutional systems. However, when our joint bank statement is issued in my name only, or when we buy a car and the salesperson looks at me quizzically when I insist that it should be titled in both my wife's and my name, I begin to connect some of the dots. Or, I also make connections when we are called to the school because my second-grade daughter is hanging upside down on the monkey bars while wearing tights and a dress only to be lectured by the teacher about her "unladylike" behavior. The effects of these experiences include uneasiness and concern that I'm not doing it the "right" way. I find myself distancing from others for fear I will somehow offend them. And, intermittent waves of guilt emerge as I begin to see the unintended, but very real consequences of my behaviors on people in my own immediate family as well as my circle of friends.

3. The personal sense of *ownership* of oppression begins to emerge in my own life: The realization that in my daily interactions I have failed to see how I have exercised privilege in ways that have disadvantaged others. This realization creates waves of shame, sadness about current blocks in relationships, a sense of lost opportunities, and a longing to go back and redo. This is followed by an increasing sense of fear that something needs to be done and I don't have the answers. White fragility sets in and becomes a constant. Yet even with these strong feelings I am unable to fully acknowledge the consequences of my belief that I live in a society based on meritocracy. This is followed by an increasing sense of fear that something needs to be done and I don't know what to do or how to be with others.

4. A powerful process of struggling to *redefine* my role in the world: In the beginning, early attempts are all focused on trying to figure out what these changes should be, but later I come to understand this is a joint interactive process that requires direct engagement with the "others" that understand what needs to happen. This realization heightens the fear of being attacked, the target of anger, sense of separation from others, and a deep sense of isolation and incompleteness. Guilt gives way to fear with the realization that I have to act.

5. *Confusion* coming from a lack of role models: I experienced an urgent need to move toward closure by discovery of "magic" models that will return

the level of certainty to my interactions with others. The first step involves trying to have the people I have offended provide the answers, but it is not their work, it is mine that needs to be the focus. When this fails there is an increasing level of desperation and need to fix it now! In addition to confusion, I experience a sense of being overwhelmed by the tasks and some anger. "What you want from me?" is a central theme (White fragility).

6. Attempting to *reach out to others*: There is an emerging need to connect with both those who have experienced oppression and those who benefit from the oppression. The first instinct is that connecting with those who have experienced oppression should be the first step. This proved to be the "easy" way out. It represented a safer approach than reaching out to my fellow oppressors, who were neither interested in, nor open to, any discussion. And, in some ways this created the most personal risk since my life was embedded in these oppressive systems. My fellow members of the dominant group had the power to push back and they did so. Suddenly I found myself with no comfortable ground—not the oppressors or the oppressed.

This process continues from its onset, five decades ago to the present moment incorporating higher levels of understanding in a broader array of areas in which emerging critical consciousness can be applied in my social work practice.

White Privilege: An Institutional Exploration

Figure 11.1 was adapted from Miller and Garran (2008) as a way to map the interaction of systems that support racism. Our intent is to take this basic framework and broaden it to be used beyond racism to multiple issues of oppression and intersectionality. Our intent allows for the inclusion of the impacts of higher-level systems that exist far beyond the point of our face-to-face interactions with a given client.

This figure can be used as part of an assessment tool in working with clients in order to determine which institutional arrangements are operating to create barriers to their growth and development. However, the purpose here is to ask you to begin to look at your own life space as it relates to the elements in Figure 11.1 in order to make connections between your own narrative and the arrangement of the institutional systems that shape your opportunities and barriers. For example, if you are a White male or female student how do those characteristics impact your access to housing and neighborhoods? How does it connect to upward mobility? Your educational opportunities? And your access to jobs? How does your gender interact with race (intersectionality) to impact the range of opportunities available to you? How does your belief in a meritocracy impact your understanding of these institutional interactions?

FIGURE 11.1 ■ Mapping Systems That Impact Oppression

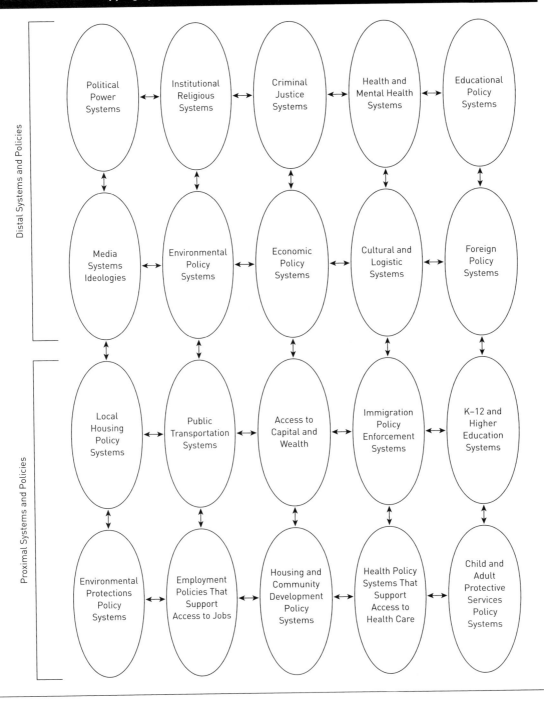

Exercises

As a homework assignment, examine Figure 11.1 and answer the above questions for yourself. Then, get together in small groups in the classroom and share your observations of what you learned and how you experience doing the exercise. If you have some levels of discomfort, or questions about what privilege means in your life, you are on the right track. This assignment is designed to increase your awareness, your ability to reflect on this awareness, and most importantly to begin to take action in the form of honest discussions about what this might mean for you both personally and professionally.

CHAPTER SUMMARY

In this chapter we have provided a range of theoretical ideas and exercises that are designed to help you come to grips with some of the most important and difficult challenges we all face in our roles as social workers. We make the case for understanding concepts like culture, cultural competence, White privilege, intersectionality, and White fragility, among others, as crucial for guiding a process by which we can begin to understand how our own challenges impact our work with clients. These ideas are designed to help us move toward greater awareness and understanding of how our own experiences shape our worldview, which drives our interactions with clients. The intent is to use these ideas in ways that allow us to develop our own critical consciousness as a tool to view our own experience in the light of the larger social economic and political systems that disenfranchise large segments of the population from experiencing a measure of social justice, dignity, and respect.

We emphasize the importance of focusing on the reality that social workers are predominantly White, and therefore, the above concepts are aimed at that reality and our need to help support examining how to move ourselves through a process that raises our own awareness and develops a more holistic approach to understanding clients' life spaces while taking into account the structural barriers in the larger social systems that impact opportunities and oppression.

The middle part of the chapter puts forth an examination of Crenshaw's critique of our current social use of a single axis analysis to understand oppression. She argues that simply focusing on one aspect, like race, fails to capture the level of complexity of individuals' experiences. She puts forward the notion of intersectionality or the layering in of multiple aspects of who most people are as a way to understand how the oppression is more than the sum of its individual parts. For example, a woman may have to deal with multiple levels of oppression if she is also African American and lesbian. The use of intersectionality provides a much more nuanced examination of the person's experience and how the various elements interact to create multiple barriers that impede growth and development.

The final section of the chapter provides a series of exercises that you may find helpful as you begin your own process of creating new levels of awareness that you can translate into actions that can help you improve your practice. The intent is to help you start with your own work in order to have access to alternatives that will improve your work with clients. We are proposing what can be a very uncomfortable examination of your own fears about powerful issues like racism, sexism, and homophobia. Unfortunately, there is no easy path and what we have laid out requires painful honesty with ourselves about who we are and how our perceptions contribute to either sustaining or hopefully changing our interactions with others.

Key Terms (in order of appearance)

Culture   313
Diversity   313
Cultural competence   314
Cultural humility   314

Intersectionality   314
White privilege   314
White identity
    development   314

Praxis   316
Dual perspective   318
Equal playing field   323
White fragility   329

References

Bricker-Jenkins, M., & Joseph, B. (2008). Progressive social work. In T. Mizrahi & L. Davis (Eds.), *Encyclopedia of social work* (pp. 434–443). Washington, DC: NASW Press.

Chestang, L. W. (1972). *Character development in a hostile environment*. Chicago, IL: University of Chicago, School of Social Service Administration.

Cho, S., Crenshaw, K. W., & McCall, L. (2013). Toward a field of intersectionality studies: Theory, applications, and praxis. *Signs: Journal of Women in Culture and Society, 38*(4), 785–810.

Collins, P. H., & Bilge, S. (2016). *Intersectionality.* Cambridge, UK: Polity Press.

Council on Social Work Education (CSWE). (2015). *Educational policy and accreditation standards.* Washington, DC: Author.

Crenshaw, K. (1989). Demarginalizing the intersection of race and sex: A Black feminist critique of antidiscrimination doctrine, feminist theory and antiracist politics. *University of Chicago Legal Forum, 1*(8), 139–167.

Crenshaw, K. (2013). From private violence to mass incarceration: Thinking intersectionally about women, race and social control. *Journal of Scholarly Perspectives, 9*(1), 21–50.

Crenshaw, K. (2016). *TED talk: The urgency of intersectionality.* Available at https://www.ted.com/talks/kimberle_crenshaw_the_urgency_of_intersectionality#t-179435

Crenshaw, K., Gotanda, N., Peller, G., & Thomas, K. (Eds.). (1996). *Critical race theory: The key writings that formed the movement.* New York, NY: New Press.

Crenshaw, K., & Ritchie, A. (2015). *Say her name: Resisting police brutality against Black women.* New York, NY: Center for Intersectionality and Social Policy Studies.

Davis, A. (2012). *Process, power, and possibilities: Exploration of experienced white social workers' cultural competence in clinical practice.* Dissertation, ProQuest LLC, UMI #3496020.

Davis, A., & Gentlewarrior, S. (2015). White privilege and clinical social work practice: Reflections and recommendations. *Journal of Progressive Human Services*, *26*(3), 191–208.

DiAngelo, R. (2011). White fragility. *International Journal of Critical Pedagogy*, *3*(3), 54–70.

Erikson, E. H. (1963). *Childhood and society*. New York, NY: W. W. Norton & Co.

Fook, J. (2012). *Social work: Critical theory and practice*. London, UK: Sage.

Fook, J., & Gardner, F. (2007). *Practicing critical self-reflection: A resource handbook*. Maidenhead, UK: Open University Press.

Freire, P. (1970). *The pedagogy of the oppressed*. New York, NY: Continuum International Publishing Group.

Hardiman, R. (1982). White identity development: A process oriented model for describing the racial consciousness of White Americans. *Dissertation Abstracts International*, *43*, 104A. (University Microfilms No. 82-10330). Amherst, MA; University of Massachusetts.

Hardiman, R. (1994). *White racial identity development in the United States*. Washington, DC: National Multicultural Institute.

Helms, J. E. (1990). *Black and White racial identity: Theory, research and practice*. Westport, CT: Greenwood.

Helms, J. E. (1994). The conceptualization of racial identity and other racial constructs. In E. J. Trickett, R. J. Watts, & D. Birman (Eds.), *Human diversity: Perspectives on people in context* (pp. 285–311). San Francisco, CA: Jossey-Bass.

Helms, J. E. (1995). An update of Helms's White and People of Color racial identity models. In Ponterotto, J. G., Casas, J. M., Suzuki, L. A., & Alexander, C. M. (Eds.) *Handbook of multicultural counseling* (pp. 181–198). Thousand Oaks, CA: Sage.

Lee, M., & Greene, G. (2004). A teaching framework for transformative multicultural social work education. *Journal of Ethnic and Cultural Diversity in Social Work*, *12*(3), 1–28.

Leigh, J. W. (1998). *Communicating for cultural competence*. Boston, MA: Allyn & Bacon.

Lipsitz G. (2006). *Possessive investment in whiteness: How white people profit from identity politics*. Philadelphia, PA: Temple University Press.

Lum, D. (2003). *Culturally competent practice: A framework for understanding diverse groups and justice issues* (3rd ed.). Pacific Grove, CA: Brooks/Cole-Thomson Learning.

Mattsson, T. (2014). Intersectionality as a useful tool: Anti-oppressive social work and critical reflection. *Affilia*, *29*(1), 8–17.

McIntosh, P. (1989). White privilege: Unpacking the invisible backpack. *Peace and Freedom, July/August*, 10–12.

Mead, G. H. (1934). *Mind, self and society*. Chicago, IL: University of Chicago Press.

Miller, J., & Garran, A. M. (2008). *Racism in the United States: Implications for social work practice* (1st ed.). New York, NY: Wadsworth.

National Association of Social Workers (NASW). (2015). *Standards and indicators for cultural competence in social work practice*. Washington, DC: Author.

National Association of Social Workers (NASW). (2017). *Code of ethics*. Washington, DC: Author.

Norton, D. G. (1978). *The dual perspective: Inclusion of ethnic minority content in the social work curriculum*. New York, NY: Council on Social Work Education.

Norton, D. G. (1993). Diversity, early socialization, and temporal development: The dual perspective revisited. *Social Work*, *38*(1), 82–90.

Oxfam. (2014). *Inequality and Extreme Poverty* (fact sheet). Oxfamamerica.org.

Pinderhughes, E. (1989). *Understanding race, ethnicity and power: The key to efficacy in clinical practice*. New York, NY: Free Press.

Rittner, B., Nakanishi, M., Nackerud, L., & Hammons, K. (1999). How MSW graduates apply what they learned about diversity to their work with small groups. *Journal of Social Work Education*, *35*(3), 421–431.

Rothman, J. C. (2008). *Cultural competence in process and practice: Building bridges*. Boston, MA: Pearson.

Sakamoto, I. (2007). A critical examination of immigrant acculturation: Toward an anti-oppressive social work model with immigrant adults in a pluralistic society. *British Journal of Social Work*, *37*, 515–535.

Samuels, G. M., & Ross-Sheriff, F. (2008). Identity, oppression, and power: Feminisms and inter-sectionality theory. *Affilia, 23*, 5–9.

Sue, D. W., & McGoldrick, M. (2005). *Multicultural social work practice*. Hoboken, NJ: John Wiley & Sons.

Sue, D. W., Rasheed, M. N., & Rasheed, J. M. (2016). *Multicultural social work practice: A competen-cy-based approach to diversity and social justice*. Hoboken, NJ: John Wiley & Sons.

Tervalon, M., & Murray-Garcia, J. (1998). Cultural humility versus cultural competence: A critical distinction in defining physician training out-comes in multicultural education. *Journal of Health Care for the Poor and Underserved, 9*(2), 117–125.

Vodde, R. (2000). De-centering privilege in social work education: Whose job is it anyway? *Race, Gender & Class, 7*(4), 139–159.

EMPOWERMENT THEORY AND THE STRENGTHS PERSPECTIVE

PHOTO 12.1
Good and magical Korean dragon wielding power and vitality: Naksan Buddhist Temple, South Korea

CASE EXAMPLE
EMPOWERMENT FOR JESSIE AND HER ADULT CHILDREN

Jessie is a 75-year-old woman who provides care for her husband, John, who served in combat in Vietnam as an aerial photographer and participated in highly classified and dangerous missions. In one incident, John's plane crashed into a banana field, severely injuring John, the pilot, and others. Although John has moderate cognitive impairments and is not able to easily engage in conversations with medical staff or with Jessie, he is physically able to walk and his behavior is erratic, with poor judgment and decision-making skills. In the early days after Vietnam, John had been diagnosed with organic brain syndrome, a catch-all diagnosis used by veterans' hospitals and reflecting uncertainty as to the reason and nature of John's medical condition.

As a social worker, you get to know Jessie in the geriatric clinic, as she brings John in frequently for outpatient appointments. Over time, Jessie becomes much more open with you. She shares that their two sons will no longer visit them. When you inquire about why this might be, Jessie tells you that John has been violent from the early days of their marriage and since returning home from combat. John frequently punched holes in their walls and was verbally threatening and physically violent to both Jessie and their young sons. Early in their marriage, Jessie sought help from medical professionals who told her that her duty was to care for John and to "put up with his violent behavior" because he was a combat veteran. Jessie now realizes that this professional advice was harmful and contributed to her choice to tolerate John's violent behavior in the middle of trying to care for two young sons. She now views this decision as a huge mistake; she confides in you that she has "had enough" and is considering placing John in a nursing home so that she can develop meaningful relationships with her adult sons and with her now-growing number of grandchildren.

Discussion Questions

(1) From your viewpoint, what does it mean for Jessie to become empowered?

(2) Consider the individual, historical, political, and systemic elements of Jessie's story. In other words, how has Jessie experienced oppression as a woman and as a wife? How does Jessie's historical and sociopolitical context affect her experiences and decisions (e.g., discuss medical staff views of John's behavior and Jessie's responsibilities)? And, how has Jessie's self-esteem and confidence likely been affected by her life experiences?

(3) How has Jessie's conflict with her adult children contributed to her awareness of or "waking up" to John's abusive behavior?

(4) What actions should Jessie take? And which actions best reflect empowerment for Jessie and/or for her adult children? For example, consider the following questions: (a) Should Jessie place John in a nursing home or not? (b) Should Jessie confide to her adult children that the medical staff "laid a load of guilt on her"? (c) The medical staff offered no supportive or in-home medical services and insisted that Jessie take care of John by herself. What empowering actions could a VA social worker advocate for or help Jessie pursue? (d) Should Jessie tell her adult children to forgive her and reconsider visiting with her and John? Why or why not?

HISTORICAL CONTEXT FOR EMPOWERMENT THEORY

Since the inception of social work as a profession in the 1890s, a determined group of social work practitioners and scholars have viewed clients, such as Jessie in the case example above, as having multiple capacities, possibilities and strengths, no matter how disadvantaged or marginalized they might be in American society (Simon, 1994; Solomon, 1976). Over the entirety of social work's growth as a profession, these empowerment-oriented social workers have faced tensions and disagreements with their more dominant counterparts who operated out of a paternalistic, professional-as-expert stance toward clients who needed their help, viewing them as victims, as sick and having pathologies and deficits, or their environments as needing liberation. These social workers who reflected a paternalistic or savior mentality supported programs and policies that unintentionally or purposefully limited clients' and communities' power and freedom to make their own choices (Gutierrez, 1990; Hegar & Hunzeker, 1988).

Although the definition of empowerment within social work has changed over time and has multiple meanings—for example, as a feeling of increased personal power (Pinderhughes, 1983; Sherman & Wenocur, 1983), as the development of skills to fulfill valued social roles (Solomon, 1976), or as increasing critical consciousness, which leads to personal and collective political power (Freire, 1970; Gutierrez, 1990)—for our purposes, **empowerment** is broadly defined as "a process of increasing personal, interpersonal, or political power so that individuals can take action to improve their life situations" (Gutierrez, 1990, p. 149). This process occurs when people are able to engage in dialogue with others to develop a critical consciousness or awareness of how personal experiences and problems are connected to larger unjust societal and political structures. (See Chapter 4, "Critical Theories," for a detailed discussion of critical consciousness.) This critical consciousness then contributes to a reduction in self-blame and sparks people's freedom to participate in and take action to change their life situations (Gutierrez, 1990; Simon, 1994).

What follows is a discussion of key themes in empowerment theory as articulated by social work scholars over the past 130 years. Although the idea of an "empowerment approach" in social work practice was not coined until Solomon's (1976) groundbreaking book, *Black Empowerment: Social Work in Oppressed Communities*, these key themes have been present in the profession of social work from its very beginning (Hardina, Middleton, Montana, & Simpson, 2007; Simon, 1994).

KEY THEMES IN EMPOWERMENT THEORY

Key themes in an empowerment theoretical approach to social work practice are presented below with a detailed description of each theme. These themes include the following:

(1) Social work practice as fundamentally hopeful; social workers believe that individuals and environments have a myriad of strengths, capacities, and resources and can be transformed;

(2)   A dual working focus on individuals and their social, political, and physical environments;

(3)   Collaborative partnerships with clients, client groups, and constituents;

(4)   The operating assumption that clients are active subjects and claimants; and

(5)   The focus of social work's professional energies toward historically disempowered groups and individuals.

First, social workers who practice from an empowerment theoretical perspective are fundamentally hopeful; only social workers who believe deeply that people can change, and that agencies, communities, and other environments can be transformed have been able to work from an empowerment perspective in a sustained fashion (Gutierrez, Parsons, & Cox, 1998; Koenig & Spano, 2007). Empowerment-oriented social workers support clients' capacities, growth, and change and attempt to avoid two polarities: (1) a fatalistic tendency that views the world as powered by economic and political forces beyond our individual control; or (2) a pollyannaish view that humans through hard work and ambition can accomplish anything, thereby ignoring the potency of historical forces, societal structures, and contexts (Freire, 1970).

Second, social workers understand individual, human experiences and their linkages with the larger social and political context. Individual growth and social change are interdependent, mutually reinforce one another, and are each insufficient without the other (Freire, 1990; Gutierrez, 1990; J. A. B. Lee, 2001). This holistic perspective acknowledges that social work practice includes a working focus on individuals and their social, political, and physical environments (Parsons & East, 2013). Social workers who practice within the empowerment tradition work within a myriad of settings, such as voluntary social work agencies, outpatient and inpatient medical and mental health clinics, sectarian and secular agencies, social movement offices, public welfare agencies, private practice settings, and within employee assistance agencies and unions. And, these empowerment-oriented social workers also believe that social investigation, in which information on social problems and needs is thoroughly documented, is what will help bring about greater justice and equity for marginalized populations (Chambers, 1963; Leiby, 1978; Lubove, 1975).

Third, social work's empowerment tradition has supported jointly developed partnerships between clients and workers anchored in clients' own experiences and hopes (Reynolds, 1934; Rose, 1990; Simon, 1990). The purpose of these partnerships has been to foster clients' own strengths in searching for and consolidating their self-esteem, health, and community and social power (Weick, 1994). Obstacles to collaboration are many in the agency-based contexts in which social workers practice. Because social workers function as intermediaries between the "haves" (the enfranchised) and the "have nots" (the disenfranchised), some scholars have doubted whether equality could even exist between clients and workers (Reynolds, 1934). In their attempts to gain social and professional status, many social workers have also viewed striving for client–worker equality as "giving up" professional power which can, in turn, lead them to maintain a kind of separateness from their clients or downplay clients' own wisdom and healing capacities (Koenig & Spano, 1998; Weick, 1982). Simon and others view this power dynamic as unavoidable, but that social workers and clients alike can view themselves as equal in dignity and worth and as fellow travelers who each bring specialized knowledge and skills to bear on the clients' desired goals (Hasenfeld, 1987). Empowerment-oriented practitioners have viewed group work—where clients can interact with similar others as a way to raise their consciousness about their oppressors' views of them—as deficient, dependent, or lacking in internal wisdom and strength (Gutierrez, 1990). In turn, social workers have self-reflective work that they must do to challenge their own superiority or to explode dualistic characteristics that separate the "helpee" from the helper or the inferior from the superior (Freire, 1990).

Fourth, clients are active subjects and claimants who yearn for freedom, justice, and fulfilment. From an empowerment approach, clients have a legitimate claim on resources as a member of the community (Falck, 1988). One of our responsibilities as social workers is as "educators for democracy," helping clients as citizens to understand and exercise their civil, social, and legal rights; freedoms and responsibilities; and to assert their claims for resources, power, and relationships (e.g., the rights to an accessible educational system that prepares all citizens for critical thinking and full participation in society; rights to affordable housing) (Addams, 1910; Harrington, 1962; Marshall, 1950, 1977; Richmond, 1922). Clients as subjects need material goods and services. They are citizens who exercise rights and responsibilities that are stipulated by specific social and legal policies, and claimants who make demands on society that reflect their emergent or full comprehension of both needs and rights (Chambers, 1963; Simkhovitch, 1938; Simon, 1994).

Fifth, the focus of empowerment-oriented social workers is on historically disempowered and stigmatized groups and individuals (Goffman, 1963; Solomon, 1976). Some would say that if we are not serving those who are marginalized or have experienced oppression, are we really doing social work? Social workers have had to make painful choices about whom to serve. Empowerment social work has had two missions: addressing the needs of the most desperate among us and who live at the edges or margins of our society, and building a more just and humane social world.

POSITIVE PSYCHOLOGY

Social work, as a professional practice and academic discipline, has generated its own theories and perspectives such as empowerment theory and the strengths perspective (see next section). These theories are closely related to similar theories generated in other disciplines such as psychology. It is worth noting first that the strengths perspective and empowerment theory, while closely related, are not identical (as this chapter should make clear). Similarly, positive psychology and its subfields are not identical to either the strengths perspective or empowerment theory. That said, they may be considered like cousins—they are in the same family of ideas. In contrast to the strengths perspective and empowerment theory, positive psychology tends to focus less on sociopolitical issues (e.g., systemic racism; economic marginalization) related to human behavior and problem solving and is more positivistic in its research platform. It also tends to be more concerned with existential issues as they pertain to human health and happiness. Positive psychology is similar to strengths/empowerment with its shift away from pathology/disease, toward an emphasis on prevention and overall well-being.

Emerging in the mid to late 1990s, positive psychology was generated in response to many years of development in research and professional practice that focused primarily on pathology and problems (Compton, 2005). Following World War II, psychologists (and other helping professionals) invested resources in a benevolent attempt to define war-related psychological maladies (such as "shell shock," later re-conceptualized as posttraumatic stress disorder) and discover effective treatments for them (Seligman & Csikszentmihalyi, 2000). In addition, psychotherapists of all sorts, including social workers, were able to find work as counselors treating not just World War II veterans but many other people suffering from various mental illnesses that were being similarly investigated and addressed. **Positive psychology**, in contrast to this traditional, medical model approach, made a sharp turn away from a focus on disease processes and treatments toward considering positive aspects of human life and relationships. Instead of thinking about what is wrong with people, positive psychologists think about what is *right* with people. Positive psychologists are interested in the "good life" and the personal attributes and social conditions that make it possible. "Psychology should be able to help document what kinds of families result in children who flourish, what work settings support the greatest satisfaction among workers, what policies result in the strongest civic engagement, and how people's lives can be most worth living" (Seligman & Csikszentmihalyi, 2000, p. 5).

Positive psychology has been defined as "the study of the conditions and processes that contribute to the flourishing or optimal functioning of people, groups, and institutions" (Gable & Haidt, 2005, p. 103). There are several key areas within the field of positive psychology. At the more subjective level, researchers are exploring people's experiences of well-being, contentment, hope, and satisfaction in life (Seligman & Csikszentmihalyi, 2000). Related personal traits are also being studied, such as interpersonal skills, perseverance, courage, spirituality, wisdom, and forgiveness. Positive psychology also addresses groups and communities, researching civic virtues, diversity, responsibility, and civility. In one sense, positive psychology is the study of human happiness and what makes humans happy. But it is also much more than that. It does not concern itself with just hedonism or short-term pleasures, but it is more interested in longer-term gratifications—those things that seem to always involve investment and work—which provide meaning and richness in life that are related to spiritual development (e.g., participating in something "larger" than oneself and one's own needs, family relationships, intellectual and physical development, and civic duties) (Seligman, Parks, & Steen, 2004).

APPLIED POSITIVE PSYCHOLOGY

Positive psychology has been applied in many different subfields, from early child development to psychotherapy. Much of the groundwork for the application of positive psychology has been developed already with traditional methods that focus on pathology. These include the ideas around operational definitions, research methods, and interventions (Seligman, 2003). Martin Seligman, one of the founders of positive psychology, offers three "pillars" of the field related to application. The first is *assessment*. Questionnaires have been developed (among other tools) to assess the psychological health of individuals, communities, or even entire nations. The hope is for the reach of positive psychology to influence even economic systems as they affect the well-being of individuals and groups within their bounds. The next application is *intervention*. Intervention is the process of building upon the strengths and virtues of individuals, groups, and communities once these have been determined via assessment. A final application concerns the *development* of well-being over the lifespan of the relevant individual or group. This involves considering conditions that enable or disable the strengths and virtues that foster healthy communities and well-being over time.

Seligman (2003) also identifies four primary aims of applied positive psychology. The first is to ameliorate and improve individual and/or social disorder by fostering prevention strategies. The second is to help professional practitioners become more oriented toward health and well-being (as opposed to problems and pathology) by training them to systematically build upon existing strengths. Third, he hopes to decrease the "promiscuous victimology" that has emerged in the social sciences (and related helping professions) as a result of the ideologies of passivity and pathology evident in disease and problem-focused models. Finally, the fourth aim of positive psychology is to move beyond the "egocentric" to the "philanthropic." What Seligman has in mind here is a move from people merely seeking pleasurable/enjoyable activities for themselves (i.e., their perceived self-centered ego needs) as a way of life, or as a therapy or means of coping, toward seeking self-transcendent activities that are other-focused, which consider the needs of others and take action to address them. There is a considerable body of research showing the benefits of helping others. For instance, Jonathan Haidt (2000) conducted a study showing elevated positive emotional responses and inclinations toward positive actions in response to hearing about or witnessing benevolent deeds, such as stopping one's car in the middle of a snowstorm to help an elderly woman shovel her driveway.

CONCERNS ABOUT POSITIVE PSYCHOLOGY

Positive psychology raises a few concerns and misunderstandings that warrant attention. First, it has been suggested that if there is now a *positive* psychology, does this mean that all other psychology is somehow *negative*? Proponents of positive psychology answer with a definitive "no" (Seligman & Pawelski, 2003; Gable & Haidt, 2005). Psychology in its various subdisciplines, before and continuous with the positive psychology movement, has been successful and beneficial, which led to and supports positive psychology. Positive psychologists don't take an either/or view between themselves and the rest of psychology, they just have their own emphasis. Not to mention that taking a "negative" view of non-positive psychology would seem rather inconsistent with the main tenets of positive psychology in the first place! A second concern is that positive psychology is just pollyannaism or positive thinking warmed over. Gable and Haidt (2005) reply that there are big differences between mere positive thinking and positive psychology. Positive thinking is merely an "armchair" activity that attempts to see the world through rose-colored glasses regardless of the difficulties and challenges of the "real" world. Positive psychology, on the other hand, will have none of that. Instead, it is tied to a rigorous program of empirical research and professional practice. Further, positive psychology, as with the strengths perspective, acknowledges and incorporates realistic appraisals about problems that impact people's everyday lives.

A third and final concern for our purposes asks whether positive psychology should take a back seat to research and practice that focuses more on alleviating human suffering. Seligman and Pawelski (2003) state that positive psychology is actually one of the best ways to help alleviate suffering. "Persons who are impoverished, depressed, or suicidal care about far more than merely the relief of their suffering. These persons care—sometimes desperately—about strength and virtue, about authenticity, about meaning, and about integrity" (p. 162). For many, the alleviation of suffering depends on building up strengths to develop happiness and a life worth living. This highlights the reorientation central to positive psychology—the change from just thinking about alleviating symptoms (certainly not a bad thing in itself), whether in individuals, families, or other groups, to imagining new futures based on existing assets and strengths. In fact, there is a subfield of positive psychology called prospective psychology, which makes a break with retrospective ideas such as those of Freud or behaviorism, both of which attempt to explain human behavior (or disorders, or well-being) primarily in terms of causal antecedents. **Prospective psychology**, in contrast, suggests that humans, as conscious animals possessing free will, actually thrive in conditions where they can exercise their capacities to creatively imagine new futures (Seligman, Railton, Baumeister, & Sripada, 2013). In fact, Seligman states that one of the aspects that makes humans human is the ability to synthesize existing emotion, experience, and information to project possible future actions, interactions, and states of affairs.

In general, positive psychology offers an interesting and useful approach to thinking about human happiness and well-being that re-centers research and professional attention to subjects such as positive emotions, healthy relationships, imagination, resiliency, character strengths, optimism, and virtue as they pertain to living a good life that has value and meaning. Positive psychology overlaps with similar ideas within empowerment theory, the strengths perspective, and the strengths model (which will be discussed in our upcoming in-depth section in this chapter).

Summary of Overview

In this overview, we have closely examined the roots of empowerment theory in the profession of social work dating back to the 1890s. Five themes of empowerment theory were discussed, including that social work practice (1) is fundamentally hopeful and that individuals and environments have a myriad of strengths, capacities, and resources and can be transformed; (2) maintains a dual working focus on individuals and their environments; (3) involves collaborative partnerships with clients and constituents; (4) views clients as active subjects and claimants, and (5) focuses on historically disempowered groups and individuals. This overview concludes by examining one stream of thought, positive psychology, which runs in tandem with empowerment theory and contributes to our understanding of individual, family, community, and societal well-being and health.

IN-DEPTH THEORISTS
FOR THE STRENGTHS PERSPECTIVE

This section of the chapter looks at the evolution of the strengths perspective through the eyes of some of its major contributors and its very close connection to empowerment theory in relation to social work practice. More specifically, we will focus on a cadre of academics and practitioners who, over the last three decades, have worked very closely together to develop the conceptual framework for a strengths-based approach to social work practice. In addition, we will look at the development and application of the strengths-based model for case management in numerous fields of practice including mental health, child welfare, health, and aging. The following case example provides a somewhat typical set of circumstances in which both the strengths perspective and its application to practice emerged.

CASE EXAMPLE
WILLIE'S REFERRAL

One of the authors directed a group home for children, ages 8 to 18, who had the diagnosis of SED (i.e., severely emotionally disturbed). In addition to the categorization of these children based on pathology, our state delineated six levels of treatment, from family foster care as the "least restrictive" to residential institutional care, the "most restrictive level of care." This also paralleled the least expensive to most expensive levels of care. As the state became less willing to pay for its child welfare institutions, it developed a strategy of simply moving children by changing their diagnosis to allow them to be placed at a lower level of care. This meant that children who had been receiving services on a 24-hour, seven-day-a-week schedule, with a full array of psychiatric services including medication, now became the purview of community-based group homes whose per diem was less than one-fourth the amount of the residential facilities. These situations were typical in the 1980s when states looked to close psychiatric facilities for adults as well as children. And, some states moved toward the privatization of these services as a way to reduce their financial obligations to these vulnerable groups. In essence, the environmental changes occurring in the political systems, driven by neo-liberal influences, were having a direct impact on both adults and children who needed mental health services. Therefore, as social workers we needed to re-examine both what we were doing and how we were doing it given these changes.

Our agency received a referral on a 13-year-old African American male who had been in seven different placements prior to coming to our group home. In each instance, his behavior was initially disruptive and led to his running away from his placements in both foster families and other group homes. Like many of our clients, Willie could be combative, express anger, and verbalize disdain for any staff members or residents in the facilities in which he had been placed. His case file contained nearly 210 pages of documentation focused on all his personal faults, foibles, and flaws. At our initial staffing to review his application, the staff was nearly

(Continued)

(Continued)

unanimous in its belief that Willie could not make it in our "open" group home because there was no way to stop his running nor could the staff see any way to manage his difficult behaviors. I asked the staff to read his case file one more time and to come back with at least one example of a capability, capacity, coping strategy, or creativity demonstrated by this child.

Of the six staff who participated in the evaluation, only one found a glimmer of hope embedded in this sea of pathology called the case file. Gretchen, one of our staff who had met Willie, listened to him talk about his interest in drawing and music. In one of the prior group homes he had kept a notebook of his "secret" sketches for which he had been admonished. What ensued was a conversation among the staff about how we might reach out to Willie to encourage him in music and art. We had access to university students who were looking for opportunities to engage young people in projects. This led to us setting up a series of opportunities that were presented to Willie in a meeting that led to his decision to "give it a try." In addition, we talked at length about ways each of us could turn his propensity for running into an acknowledgment of his need to control what he expected to be rejection by staff and the other children. We invited one of our current residents to "host" his visit. That individual was attending the same school with Willie and agreed to be his "lunch buddy." Finally, I met with Willie and openly discussed his propensity for running. I assured him that he was in complete control of whether or not he stayed with us by literally showing him how the front door opened and closed and how to use the locking mechanism. I also told him that if he felt the need to test our commitment to him staying that he should do so. But, I asked that he take my card with him because I would come and get him at any time. He did run one time and was back within one half hour; he never ran again.

This simple, everyday example of what goes on in the child welfare system is the reality that many of us face who are trying to shift from pathology-based approaches to a strengths-based perspective for social work practice. The use of a strengths-based approach in this situation required that we acknowledge the larger systemic problems that we faced and that were having a direct impact on our ability to serve children (e.g., a detailed, child welfare case file emphasizing long-standing problems and pathologies and a child welfare system pressuring us to admit children that stretched the limits of our group home resources). These systemic factors only added to the problems our clients were experiencing. There was no way for us to immediately impact the larger social forces, but we used our understanding of those forces to shape our responses in this individual context. For example, we acknowledged that we were getting different kinds of kids because of the fiscal restraints being placed on our child welfare institutions. This was both a source of stress and also creative thinking about how we acknowledge the environmental impacts and work to stretch the limits of our abilities to continue to provide quality services by identifying and using existing community capacities (e.g., art students).

Once the staff was able to reframe some of Willie's behaviors, like running, we could then develop reasonable responses that could be reshaped in ways to help him reach his potential. Also, by searching out one or two examples of what might be his potential, we were able to make changes in how we attempted to meet this young man's needs. Some have asserted that this is "simply good social work"; rather, we would argue it is good social work but not simple. It requires the acknowledgment of the level of intrusion that the medical model, with all its pathological baggage, has made on the agencies in which we work and clients whom we are committed to serve.

Embedded in the above example are some of the following principles of strengths-based work. First, we must take into account the transactions in the person/environment (P/E) matrix in order to maximize their potential for a positive fit. Second, as the staff of a group home we needed to recognize how quickly we can buy into the medical model (pathology-based) as represented in most client files and stop to critically analyze how to read those files in order to find possibilities, potentials, and capacities in the people and their environments. Third, as we shall see, strengths-based practice is a product of shifting the focus of professionals from individually oriented assessment, treatment planning, and evaluation toward group efforts developed with the idea that having multiple inputs from others improves our services, shifting our attention to improving health, and introducing hope and belief in clients' abilities to grow and develop.

Early Writers Contributing to the Development of the Strengths Perspective

The strengths perspective has a parallel intellectual history to the Functional School in social work. Like the Functional School, which was primarily based at the Pennsylvania School of Social Work, the strengths perspective has evolved in the context of the University of Kansas (KU) School of Social Welfare. Both these innovations challenged the existing models by attempting to shift from pathology-based practice to the notion of human growth and development as a normal condition for human beings. Both perspectives have been the subject of intense debate within the profession.

The early conceptual underpinnings and philosophical moorings for the strengths perspective were provided by Ann Weick and Dennis Saleebey, both of whom were members of the faculty in the KU School of Social Welfare and later became partners for the remainder of their personal lives. While each of them came with their own unique views of social work, their writings create two differing, but complementary, perspectives that continue to influence the evolution of the strengths perspective. It must be noted that their work was embedded in the larger matrix of social workers who made, and continue to make, seminal contributions toward thinking about strengths-based work. The following is a list of both academic and community-based practitioners who play important roles in shaping and translating Weick and Saleebey's theoretical and conceptual work into practice. Among those most prominent in the early work included Charles Rapp, Rick Goscha, Ronna Chamberlain, Pat Sullivan, Wally Kisthardt, Ed Canda, and Jim Taylor. In the following discussion, we will focus more narrowly on the early writings of Ann Weick and Dennis Saleebey, examining both their individual contributions as well as identifying places where their perspectives explicitly overlap.

Ann Weick

Ann Weick was born in 1941 and raised on the West Coast. She graduated from the University of Oregon in 1963 and entered the Peace Corps, working as a social worker in Konya, Turkey, in an orphanage. In 1965, she entered the University of California–Berkeley MSW program and received her degree in 1967. For the next five years she worked in various federal government programs that were a part of the War on Poverty.

In 1972, she entered Brandeis University, receiving her doctorate in social work in 1976 and began her career at the University of Kansas that same year. In 1987, she became the dean of the KU School of Social Welfare and remained in that position until her retirement nearly two decades later (Lieberman, 2015).

During the decade of the 1980s, Weick maintained a significant role as a scholar whose writing laid the groundwork for the emergence of the strengths perspective. First, her focus had its roots in feminist thinking, which emphasized analyses of the use of power to oppress women. Second, she wrote extensively on the shortcomings of a medical model for social work practice based on Western conceptions of science as sources for both knowledge and values. Third, she spoke directly to the environmental constraints under which most social programs labored as it related to their social control functions. Fourth, she also put forward alternative conceptions for a new model for social work practice (Weick, 1982, 1983a, 1983b, 1987; 1994). Finally, her grounding in feminism required the critique of larger social systems as essential to understanding the challenges of the individuals embedded in those systems, especially those from marginalized groups in society, which emphasized the centrality of the person/environment focus for practice.

Each of the themes identified above are woven into the development of the strengths perspective and its application in the strengths-based model for social work practice. For example, her early work looked at issues related to the power dynamics in social work practice. She critiqued the traditional medical model from the standpoint that professional power is used to shape and constrain women who seek social services. She asserted that expert power through the use of knowledge and language is closely associated with influence that social workers exercise over less powerful clients. In essence, social agencies representing dominant social values and theories developed in the dominant society (i.e., sexism) are used to coerce female clients to behave in "acceptable" ways as they express their social roles, which "results in women being treated in stereotyped, growth-limiting ways" (Weick, 1983a, p. 177).

In her 1983 article, Weick focused on a reconceptualization of our understanding of human behavior as cyclical rather than the understandings provided by linear age stage models. In that article, she questioned the consequences and usefulness of sequential growth theory as it relates to the development of social roles. She argued for a focus on life events as a process that takes place in a larger social context rather than a lockstep linear understanding of human growth and development. She viewed this process of growth and development as a series of adaptations to maintain a balance, adapting to new sets of circumstances as they arise irrespective of our age or stage of development. The underlying assumption of her cyclical model is that there is a concurrent need for both stability and adaptability throughout our lives. In her view, "true adaptation, whether psychological or physiological, requires us to build and maintain a central core of meaning or stability but at the same time to be prepared to make at least marginal shifts in that core" (Weick, 1983a, p. 133). What Weick's cyclical model does is to acknowledge that human growth and development is always a product of the interactions between people and their environments without prescribing the specific expectations for achieving an acceptable balance between personal growth and social roles. In some instances, environmentally prescribed social roles (e.g., women socialized to defer to men) may enhance or create barriers to individual growth and development; therefore, practitioners need to explore both the opportunities and barriers that are put forward in social interactions and roles, especially as they relate to larger issues that confront many marginalized groups with whom we work.

A second assumption of Weick's model identifies specific tasks of adulthood including the following themes: "the capacity for intimacy, the capacity to nurture, engagement in productive activity, establishment of balance between dependence and independence and the capacity to transcend personal concerns" (1983a, p. 134). She acknowledges that these fundamental tasks are active throughout all periods of our lives, which unlocks them from a sequential framework. Weick suggests that the central themes will require new adaptations based on all these tasks that play out in various stages of our lives. Hence, identity development is not simply isolated in adolescence; each of us face changes requiring that our identity be examined as circumstances change throughout our lives. For example, if two people are in a relationship and they decide to become parents, they must incorporate new understandings of themselves and their interactions to adapt to these new roles. Weick also points out the importance of issues related to gender, and we would add all forms of diversity, as key factors in shaping the process and its outcomes. We will come back to this later in the chapter as we explore newer writing on how this contributes to the strengths perspective.

Weick applies these ideas to practice by identifying two different ways in which social workers support the growth process. She notes that the provision of tangible resources is one central function of social work. These services are absolutely essential in making it possible for people to engage more freely in their own growth and development as well as in impacting their environments. In addition, social workers provide assistance for people in the growth process as they move through problems that may be caused by such factors as their personal history, personality styles, and belief systems as well as by a wide range of physical and social factors in the person's environment. Her perception of the dynamics of change challenges social workers to create options and supports for clients' struggles that may counter prevailing perceptions and expectations. She also urges social workers to support the dignity and authenticity of clients' struggles to demonstrate an affinity with social work's belief in people's inherent strengths and about their capacity to determine the direction in their own lives (Weick, 1983b).

In conclusion, this brief synopsis of some of the central principles within Weick's writing articulates basic pillars of the strengths perspective. Her insistence on understanding how power plays out in a social work relationship, her articulation of what is now called anti-oppressive practice, her advocacy for the inclusion of a social constructive stance toward knowledge and values, and her steadfast efforts to understand change as a product of social interaction made central contributions to the development of the strengths perspective.

Dennis Saleebey

Dennis Saleebey was born in 1936 in San Diego, California. His father died when he was very young, and he was adopted by his stepfather, Ted Saleebey, with whom he shared a loving and lasting relationship. Dennis graduated with his Bachelor of Arts degree from the University of California–Santa Barbara (1958). He received his MSW from the University of California–Los Angeles (UCLA) in 1960. He received a PhD from the University of California–Berkeley in 1972. He was known by his colleagues for his self-effacing humor, his voracious appetite for reading and thinking, and his generosity with both his talents and his ideas. Dennis died in 2014, approximately six weeks after the death of his wife, Ann Weick.

Dennis's substantial contribution to the social work literature began in the early 1970s. His contributions focused on providing foundational critiques of social work's problems and potentials. For example, in an article published in 1972, he and Mary "Ski" Hunter, who also taught human behavior, looked at the context of clinical social work relationships. They asserted that (1) face-to-face situations have powerful control over individuals' thoughts and actions and constrict freedom of action and decision, (2) individuals can be made aware of the elements of control over them, and (3) individuals can be taught to neutralize or subvert the elements of power in a given context. They went on to prescribe strategies to subvert these inequalities. Some of the strategies included the provision of information to clients, treating clients to think independently, demystifying authority (including in the helping relationship), and stress inoculation (e.g., skills and techniques to create awareness of cues indicating presence of stress and how to manage it). Clearly, these were a significant departure from the kinds of foci suggested by the more individually based models for clinical work (Hunter & Saleebey, 1983).

During the next decade, he continued to look at practice with a wary eye. His concerns about the proper balance between social control and social reform led him to articulate cautions related to social work practice. First, therapy is limited, but necessary. He recognized that people were in pain, suffered, and needed help. He said, "They cannot wait for the revolution" (Saleebey, 1987, p. 19). Second, he cautioned that therapy is not, and never will be, political action, but radical approaches to therapy may be a precondition for creating individual and collective action.

Another example of his practice focus is the use of insight as social critique in clinical practice. He, like many other social work writers, was concerned about the profession's drift into a much narrower view of clinical practice that stripped the importance of context, which raised questions about whether social work would remain relevant to its original person-and-environment focus (Saleebey, 1987). He turned the concept of insight away from its more traditional psychological roots toward insight about institutions, organizations, and cultural norms that oppressed social work clients. He substituted critical consciousness, critical reflection, and praxis as a focus for bringing about both individual and social change (1987). His early connections between the writings of Paulo Freire and social work practice represent a much more radical view of the profession's purpose than most mainstream writers. Additionally, he admonished the profession to avoid "context stripping," which was becoming more prevalent in practice with the rise of neoliberalism in a larger professional and social political context.

During the early 1990s, Dennis had completed the first edition of *The Strengths Perspective* textbook that would subsequently have five iterations. In addition, he continued to write in numerous professional journals about the philosophy of social work and how these debates were impacting the profession's movement toward integrating its knowledge and values with its mission, especially as they related to the achievement of social justice (Saleebey, 1987, 1990, 1993). Some of the themes in his writing took on weighty issues, such as the fundamental nature of human inquiry. In essence, he was first concerned about the impacts of social work's utilization of a positivist approach as foundational for making decisions in social work practice. This positivist approach contends that all knowledge assumes an objective reality based on the perceptions of the senses, which can be systematically gathered and accumulated, and its validity put to the test by standard method and instrumentation. Second, Saleebey put forward social constructivism as an approach more consistent with social work's purposes; social constructionism understands knowledge as a product of social interactions among human beings who arrive at their own individual understanding of the world. Where positivists assert there is one "Truth," social constructivists assert that there are many "truths," each having its own validity. Finally, he raised concerns related to the utilization of theory in social work practice. He critiqued the use of normative theory, which "explains relationships in a systematic way, between discrete groups of uniformities that, without theory, would seem to stand in no relationship to each other (Saleebey, 1993, p. 8). His critique focused on the reality that most normative theory is drawn from beliefs lodged in the dominant groups in society and has the consequence of disadvantaging marginalized groups of people. He argued that social work needed to utilize generative theory. For Saleebey, generative theory focuses on interactions between people and their environments, emphasizing the role of dialogue among people as the primary means to generate meaning in any given situation, and is subject to an evolutionary constructive process that better accounts for metaphysical aspects of human interaction (1993).

CASE EXAMPLE
COMPETING CREATION STORIES

Why is this rather heady debate of importance to a practitioner? The following example may be helpful. Imagine you are meeting with a 20-year-old Native American woman, Carole, who has been struggling with issues related to her place in the world. She is attending a university geography class in which her professor insists that Native people originated in Central Asia and migrated from Central Asia to the Americas. As part of class discussion, Carole chose to share one of her creation stories, from her own tradition, which asserts her people were born deep in Mother Earth and brought to the surface to populate their land. The professor insists that the article she provided to the students proves that Native peoples' DNA can be traced from Central Asia, and science disproves the creation "myth" that exists in Carole's tribe. Carole is very distraught and uncertain about whether she should continue her education if it requires that she abandon her core beliefs; her parents warned her to be wary of Whites who would try to convince her not to be "Indian." Presume you are seeing her in your role as a social worker at the university's health center. Here are some questions that relate to the tensions between positivist and social constructivist "theories" outlined above:

1. What is your internal reaction to the dilemma? Are you drawn toward one understanding of the creation story?

2. If Carole asked you to share your reaction, how would you respond?

3. As a social worker, how does respect for human dignity, self-determination, social justice, and honesty shape your response?

4. What are the tensions, if any, that you experience between your professional and personal belief systems (e.g., your views of science and religion)?

This example steps into large questions about the nature of knowledge, how knowledge and values interact, and how you choose to interpret or give meaning to your experience and those of clients. And, what are the consequences for clients when our voices are more powerful? All of these questions shape our practice behaviors as we work with clients.

Summary of Weick and Saleebey's Early Contributions

These two scholars began their journeys in somewhat different places. Ann's approach emerged from her interest and experience as a woman with strong feminist beliefs and significant concerns about the impact of science and social work's alliance with a medical model. Dennis took a more philosophical stance rooted in epistemological and ontological questions related to social work's emphasis on being a profession. However, Weick and Saleebey share some common themes. First, they were both interested in fundamental questions about the nature of social work and the consequences of how knowledge, values, sanction, and purpose shaped the profession's challenges and potential. They both focused on how these elements of social work interacted to either support the mission of social work, through the realization of its core values, or how our current perceptions of the fundamental elements of social work worked against the interests of our clients. Both raised questions that led them down paths—toward finding new ways to realize the attainment of core social work values in our mission statement, to examine how current practice either liberated or oppressed our clients, to explore how we could move toward new language and understandings that would change our behaviors in ways that would support work toward social justice, and to support mutuality and respect based on the relationship developed between social workers and our clients' systems (Weick & Saleebey, 1995, 1998). These questions became foundational to the translation of answers into perspectives that could be used in practice by social workers at all levels of practice and with a broad range of clients.

CRITIQUE OF EMPOWERMENT THEORY AND THE STRENGTHS PERSPECTIVE

This critique is focused on empowerment theory and the strengths perspective.

What Does This Theory Say About Human Behavior?

Empowerment theory and the strengths perspective offer a realistic, yet optimistic view of human behavior, focused on people's capacities to change. They offer a thoughtful balance of ideas that can help individuals and groups discover their individual and community strengths, and with an understanding of how those individuals and groups fit within a larger sociopolitical environment. Both empowerment theory and the strengths perspective view human behavior as related to (if not caused by) unjust sociopolitical and institutional structures such as economic stratification, gender inequality, homophobia, and racial segregation.

With regard to the question of objectivity and subjectivity, these theories tend to offer something of value in either direction. The strengths perspective, with its empirical research base (Rapp & Goscha, 2012, 2014), offers objective evidence that social work practice focusing on people's strengths, whether individual or social, is effective. The ideas inherent to this perspective also offer a subjective dimension as practitioners assist each client or group. For example, a worker may know from research that helping people find resources in their community tends to be an effective practice. The worker can then invite the client to discover particular resources that may be helpful to that particular client, given the client's particular goals and context.

With regard to stability and radical change, both the strengths perspective and empowerment theory fall into the radical change category. The roots of both are "critical" in nature, meaning they derive from ideas that practically denote radical change itself, such as Marxian thought, feminisms, and social constructionism. Whether doing individual or community-level practice, both are always concerned with sociopolitical context. Race, class, gender, age, ability, ethnicity, and so on are always at the forefront of these ideas, along with hope for change that makes for a more just, equal, and free society. Unlike behaviorism, for instance, which focuses on reinforcement and punishment as causal factors for human behavior, strengths/empowerment approaches focus on sociopolitical factors. Given behaviorism's very objective focus for the cause of human behavior, its treatments reflect the same as proponents utilize reinforcement (though not much punishment) as a therapeutic tool. Strengths/empowerment "treatments" also reflect their assumptions/ideas about human behavior by bringing the sociopolitical dimension to bear as a therapeutic or change-oriented tool. They are more balanced between the objective–subjective dimensions not because they (at least the strengths perspective) have no empirical research base, but because their entire orientation is more directed toward enabling the individual to join with the worker in co-creating the intervention or "therapy" itself, in light of multiple sociopolitical causal factors.

Empowerment/strengths approaches offer more than just the idea that individuals can adapt to unjust sociopolitical structures by, say, discovering/developing a personal ability, or doing mindfulness exercises. By explaining human behavior in terms of sociopolitical structures, they aim to assist people by helping them to understand their sociopolitical context, as well as how to adapt to it and change it. Consider a client who is anxious and depressed, for instance. These theories would suggest that people experience anxiety and depression because they are part of an oppressed, exploited, or marginalized group. Perhaps they are anxious because they do not have adequate child care, sufficient income to pay the bills, and a reliable car (economic oppression). They may be depressed because they do not see a path forward that offers anything better. There is an overlap here with an aspect of positive psychology—one of its subfields is called "projective psychology" and states that people are happiest and healthiest when they are able to creatively imagine desirable possible futures for themselves and their families (Seligman et al., 2013). When people are unable to do this, they tend to become depressed and immobilized. Our particular client may have also been denied employment (or full employment, or employment that pays a living wage with adequate benefits) because she or he belongs to a minority racial/ethnic group. The combination of economic oppression, racial oppression, and perhaps gender oppression (among others) could be quite disabling—not to mention the possible stigma associated with being diagnosed with mental illness. Even if the depression and anxiety are not clearly caused by one or more forms of oppression, oppression, marginalization, and exploitation are always relevant. For instance, say this client is depressed and anxious due to biological reasons alone. Having a mental illness is a stigmatized, marginalized position, and the individual still exists in a sociopolitical context that could be the focus of the social work intervention. Of course, the radical change hoped for must be generated *with* the client, not just *for* the client, so whatever intervention or change process takes place it will necessarily involve the client's values, goals, and the life they hope for and imagine for themselves.

How Does This Theory Address Growth and Change?

Empowerment and strengths-based theorists and practitioners understand that individual and collective empowerment occur in tandem with each other and contribute to change at personal, community, organizational, and even societal levels. For example, empowerment-oriented clinical practices for women who have experienced poverty, trauma, and face mental health concerns support group dialogue and consciousness raising among women to help them grow, change, and take action to address oppressive, sexist, societal structures within their personal lives and in their communities. These practices are in contrast to blaming these women for their "personal problems" or privileging "assessment and diagnoses" from professionals-as-experts (East & Roll, 2015; Kabeer, 2012). Individual growth and change does not occur in isolation and typically involves dialogue with similar others, which, in turn, contributes to the development of a critical consciousness or awareness of oppression and subsequent opportunities to take action and garner resources to reach personal and collective goals (Simon, 1994). What follows is a case example that encourages us to take an empowerment oriented perspective in linking individual pregnancies to larger school policies about sex education.

ETHICS SPOTLIGHT
COMPREHENSIVE SEX EDUCATION IN A MIDWESTERN HIGH SCHOOL

You are a social worker in a small Midwestern high school and have noticed the increase in adolescent pregnancies in your community. You meet with school administrators and teachers to try to convince the school to offer comprehensive sex education as a means of empowering students with education about their bodies and intimate relationships and based on its positive impact in reducing adolescent pregnancies. The school agrees, in turn, to provide this comprehensive sex education for its students, but it faces immediate resistance from parents who view sex education as a private matter and do not want the school to provide this comprehensive education.

(1) What do you think you should do in this case situation? (Base your response on values in the NASW *Code of Ethics*. For example, how might the values of dignity and worth of each person, self-determination, and service be applied to this case example?)

(2) In this case, what does empowering students and their families look like?

We know that individual adolescents who are exposed to comprehensive sex education that addresses much more than reproduction—for example, the use of contraceptives and other forms of birth control, sexualization (the use of sexuality to influence a person's behaviors or attitudes), intimacy (emotional openness and closeness with another person), and sensuality (psychological and physical enjoyment of one's body) (Koenig & Spano, 2003)—contributes to a lower risk of pregnancy, human immunodeficiency virus (HIV), and sexually transmitted infections (STIs) in contrast to those engaged in "abstinence only" education (Chin et al., 2012). We can see how an empowerment oriented approach through social work advocacy for comprehensive sex education can impact and change not just individual students but a school, and even an entire community.

How Holistic Is This Theory?

Empowerment theory and the strengths perspective reflect in great measure a holistic approach to social work practice in that they are concerned about a dual focus on people and their environments, and they acknowledge people's strengths and resiliencies even in the face of hardships and vulnerabilities. Unfortunately, some authors assume that the use of an empowerment approach or the strengths perspective in social work practice implies that practitioners never address clients' problems, needs, and difficulties nor assist them in addressing or resolving those problems (Bransford, 2011). This kind of dichotomous or black-and-white thinking reflects an incomplete and inaccurate view of empowerment-oriented or strengths-based work as an integrative approach (Koenig & Spano, 1998). Empowerment and strengths-based approaches are specifically designed to work with people who are often on the margins and have experienced interpersonal and societal oppression and discrimination. The very nature of social work then requires that we acknowledge our clients' difficulties or problems and simultaneously press on with them to meet these challenges, paying close attention to what resources, capabilities, and strengths they might bring to bear on obstacles in their environments.

Finally, some authors also wrongheadedly separate individual or personal empowerment from collective or societal empowerment (Lee, 2001; Lee, Weaver, & Hrostowski, 2011). Empowerment-based approaches and the strengths perspective acknowledge that empowerment is not likely to be achieved alone. Instead, it is through our dialogue with and support from others that we begin to understand our personal experiences as linked to larger, often unjust societal structures and behaviors. We wake up to our experiences of oppression through our interactions with others like us. Individual and collective empowerment are unescapably linked together.

How Consistent Is This Theory With Social Work Values and Ethics?

Empowerment theory and the strengths perspective are very consistent with social work values in that they attempt to take seriously the voice and expertise of clients and communities who are on the margins of our society. In doing so, social workers respect the dignity and worth of every person and know that in order to practice with integrity and honesty, they must engage in a self-reflective process that pays attention to areas for their ongoing professional growth and development as they continue to learn from and serve diverse clients. This requires social workers to maintain an attitude of openness and humility in their work.

In some instances, empowerment theory or at least the word *empowerment* has been "turned on its head" and insidiously used by government officials and policy makers to insist that their new policies and programs can help ensure that low-income and other marginalized groups are "empowered" so that they no longer need support from the welfare state. In this way, these programs and policies reflect a lack of governmental will and support for social justice in that they have been designed to shrink or eliminate resources and services for some of the most vulnerable among us (e.g., single women and children). For example, TANF's (Temporary Assistance for Needy Families) impact on low-income families involves giving parents governmental resources for a limited period of time, but then not supporting their educational efforts to increase their wages or forcing them to "go to work" in dead-end jobs and without financial support for child care and for services to support families with children who have complex health needs (Butler, 2013).

What Sources of Knowledge Does This Theory Support?

The discussion above can be extended here into the epistemological realm with similar conclusions. Empowerment theory and the strengths perspective support many different ways of knowing and include all of the above, from client's voice to experimental research (Barry et al., 2003; Goscha, 2009; Radohl, 2013; Rapp, 1995; Rapp & Goscha, 2012, 2014; Stanard, 1999). Any form of research that enhances our ability to strengthen and empower individuals, groups, and communities can be valid from these perspectives. That said, these perspectives, because they have been derived historically and conceptually from critical theories, feminisms, social justice philosophies, and so on, tend to lean toward more qualitative forms of research, especially those involving client voices and the perspectives of vulnerable and marginalized populations. Many researchers of this sort find the research itself to be empowering as it generates knowledge from sources traditionally underrepresented in quantitative literatures. Moreover, drawing from the aforementioned theoretical roots, strengths and empowerment-based approaches also value "research" beyond what is typically validated in the social sciences, such as scholarly work in history, philosophy, visual and literary arts, and so on. Overall, many forms and ways of knowing can inform professionals whose aims align with empowerment theory and the strengths perspective.

APPLICATION OF THE STRENGTHS PERSPECTIVE

This section of the chapter is devoted to connecting empowerment theory to the development and implementation of strengths-based work. We will try to clarify elements of the strengths perspective that represent a paradigm shift from more pathology-based perspectives, which have dominated practice over the last 70 years. In addition, we will examine how the strengths perspective has been translated into what Charles Rapp and his cadre of colleagues identify as a strengths-based model that they have applied to their recovery-oriented work in mental health services. Finally, we will identify some newer writings that we believe may add depth to our understanding and implementation of the strengths perspective.

Assumptions Underpinning the Strengths Perspective

Earlier in our overview of the chapter, we identified five key empowerment themes that directly connect to our conception of social work practice. In their chapter on strengths and empowerment, Miley, O'Melia, and DuBois (2017) examine Saleebey's (2006) writing to develop a set of assumptions based on the strengths perspective and that undergird practice. We have developed Table 12.1 to help you see the connections and compatibility between empowerment theory and the strengths perspective.

TABLE 12.1 ■ Comparisons Between Empowerment Theory and the Strengths Perspective	
Themes in Empowerment Theory	**Assumptions of the Strengths Perspective**
Social work practice is fundamentally hopeful; social workers believe that individuals and environments have a myriad of strengths, capacities, and resources and can be transformed.	Clients have existing reservoirs of resources and competencies to draw upon; each client has a distinct capacity for growth and change.
There is a dual working focus on individuals and their social, political, and physical environments.	Individual and societal problems occur within transactions between systems rather than residing in deficient system functioning.
Collaborative partnerships with clients, client groups, and constituents are the vehicle for service delivery.	Collaboration augments existing strengths to build new resources for clients.
The operating assumption is that clients are active subjects and claimants.	Clients know their situations, and given options, can define the best solutions for their challenges.
The focus of social work's professional energies is put toward historically disempowered groups and individuals.	The strengths perspective maintains the attitude that positive change builds on a vision of future possibilities.

Elements of the Strengths Perspective

In 1996, Saleebey put forward what he saw as the elements of the **strengths perspective**. These key elements demand different ways of understanding clients and our work with them:

- Clients must be seen in the light of their capacities, talents, competencies, possibilities, visions, values, and hopes no matter how difficult their current situation.

- The strengths approach requires acknowledging what people know and what they can do however difficult that may seem.

- It requires accurate accounting of resources that exist within and around our client systems.

- We must "suspend our disbelief in clients." This often requires suspending judgments about the meaning we assign to people's behavior, which are often drawn from normative theories that can disadvantage clients.

- It requires that we carefully examine our agency bureaucratic structures and organizational dynamics, which may be diametrically opposed to the strengths perspective.

- It requires that we examine our own professional language and the metaphorical devices that we use to understand helping processes. Often our models are drawn from narrowly focused, individualized approaches, which tend to be context stripping, are deficit-based, and exclude ideas of resilience, possibility, and transformation.

CASE EXAMPLE
EMMA AND THOMAS'S FIRST SESSION

The following case example provides a comparison between how using pathology-based models in working with clients can be differentiated from the strengths perspective based on the worker translating the above outlined assumptions about the nature of the work.

A social worker in a mental health clinic meets with a 30-year-old woman named Emma. She was referred to the clinic for assistance with depression that interferes with her ability to care for her daughter, a 6-year-old first grader who has demonstrated some behavioral concerns in her classroom. Emma appears to be overwhelmed by her current circumstances, including holding a responsible position in a local social service agency, living with her mother, with whom she has a troubled relationship, her fear that she may lose her daughter if "people" find out she is somehow a "bad" mother, and finally, in her words, I have been "diagnosed as a borderline personality disorder." Her social worker, Thomas, listens carefully to her description of the situation and her fears about what the consequences might be for their professional relationship. He returns to the themes outlined above and begins exploring each of the areas she has chosen to share with him. He asks her to talk about her work at the local agency, and he learns that she has been employed for over a decade in the agency and that she has been able to develop solid professional relationships that have allowed her to be promoted to the supervisory level in the agency. She is making an adequate living for herself and her daughter but at this point they are living with her mother, who is a source of great concern to her because of her mother's interactions with Emma's daughter. When asked if she had thought about how she would want that situation to change, she was very clear in stating that she thought it was best for her and her daughter to have their own place to live. Thomas acknowledged and supported the notion that it is often stressful for parents to find their own way when their own parents intercede in ways that contradict and confuse their grandchildren.

At the end of the session, Thomas returned to Emma's statement about her fear of being labeled as having a "borderline personality disorder." He asked what "people" had used that particular language in relationship to her. She said with a great deal of emotion that she had participated in numerous staff meetings in her agency and there were several occasions when consultants used that label in disparaging ways toward clients whose behaviors often mirrored some of her own. In addition, she interpreted the conversations of her colleagues and consultants, not only to be disparaging, but also that they communicated some level of cynicism and lack of hope with regard to these people making any progress. At the end of the first session, Thomas asked Emma if she would come and sit next to him in order to be able to look at, and talk through, what their options might be to deal with the fact that his agency requires diagnoses for clients to be able to access resources. Thomas took the lead in identifying three different diagnostic options that would help her access resources yet minimize the negative

impact these labels might have related to her self-perception. In addition, Thomas talked with her directly about the importance and power of language and its role as potentially disempowering people in professional relationships. Finally, they agreed that once every three months they would revisit this issue to see if there were changes required.

Discussion Questions

The above example is a summary of the first meeting between Thomas and Emma. Now, ask yourself, how did Thomas's work explore potential resources and capacities in Emma's environment? How did he affirm her capacity to grow and develop? In what ways did Thomas affirm interactions between Emma and her social context with a focus on potential capacities and resources? How did he affirm her knowledge of her situation and explore avenues that might provide the best solutions? In what ways did Thomas communicate a positive attitude as Emma articulated her solutions? Finally, how did his tone suggest he focused on mastery and competence rather than deficits?

Implications for Translating These Elements Into Practice

There are several key consequential changes flowing from an examination of both the assumptions and elements undergirding the strengths perspective's translation into practice. First, to implement the strengths perspective, we must take into account the reality that our professional world generally stands in direct conflict with the principles articulated in the strengths perspective. The language we use is deeply rooted in the medical model's focus on deficits that exist in individuals, not on the interactions between individuals and their environments. Weick asserts that the only way to escape the conceptual and language problems is to "overturn the medical model" (Weick, 1983b). For Weick, both the language and its conceptual limitations establish the potential for oppression as a central dynamic in the helping relationship. Saleebey critiques professional language and concepts focused on the development of a replacement document for the DSM-IV, now the DSM-V, which solely focuses our attention on pathology. He proposed the creation of a "diagnostic strengths manual" that requires a new lexicon of categories focused on capabilities, capacities, possibilities, and potential (Saleebey, 2001). This would create wholly different information which radically shifts our efforts directed toward change from remedial actions to reduce deficits toward emphasizing the development and access of capacities focused on helping client systems achieve their potential (Saleebey, 2001). These changes may appear to be straight forward and easily achieved. However, you will see innumerable instances in both classroom and field experiences where the vast majority of our efforts focus on understanding and remediating "problems and deficits" that riddle both individuals and their environments.

CASE EXAMPLE
IT'S ALL IN THE NAME

The following case example illustrates how this pervasive and nearly invisible atmosphere pervades our thinking as professionals. One of the authors was asked to provide training for staff at an agency that identifies itself as providing services for the community, for individuals, and for families where the presenting problem is familial sexual abuse. Staff members asked this consultant specifically because they identified themselves as having a strengths-based approach to providing services in this area, and they knew that this was the consultant's own perspective. The consultant began the workshop by asking them to describe how they experienced their work with clients and what challenges they believed were important for them to face. They began immediately talking about how they had good success in recruiting and retaining clients to attend their "victim" groups but they found it particularly difficult to get individuals to attend their "perpetrator" groups. What ensued was a three-hour conversation about what was underneath the language being used, and how those perceptions were playing out in their relationships with clients. There was a great deal of heated debate about the need to acknowledge that children are victimized when familial sexual abuse occurs, and that adults need to be held accountable by acknowledging their misuse of power in their relationships. All of their arguments reflected ubiquitous beliefs about the meaning they assigned to the people they served, with little or no understanding of the consequences for identifying people as "victims" as well as "perps." Nor could they recognize their

own challenges related to identifying "victims" and "perps" as having capabilities, capacities, potential, and competencies, given their perceptions of these people. While changing our language, in this instance, from victim to survivor, from perps, to mothers and fathers, is not the end product, it represents the beginning stage for helping workers develop the critical self-reflection needed for making significant changes in perceptions that, in turn, allow for changes in their behaviors.

Second, we need to examine the institutions in which we are working to determine how their structures and functions support or deter attempts to utilize the strengths perspective. At one point in that initial meeting, part of the discussion focused on the shared concerns of staff and administrators who were fearful that their community would see them as "soft on crime." If you believe the public interprets your actions as failing to protect children who are victims, and refusing to punish parents as perpetrators, then it may be difficult to operationalize the strengths perspective, because organizations need community support and resources. The agency's need for resources often constrains its willingness to challenge community beliefs because they fear being viewed as somehow responsible for any reoccurrence of abuse.

Third, part of the discussion that linked language with meaning unearthed workers' ongoing struggle with the fundamental sense that given the adults' harmful behavior, they could not be trusted. This made it especially difficult for workers to address their own instincts to somehow manage the relationship, by utilizing their power, thus making authority a central driving force in the relationship rather than trust and empathy. In the end, this stance hindered their ability to "suspend their disbelief in clients," which affected their own hopefulness, as well as that of clients, that somehow this would be a safe and fertile relationship that would support growth and development.

Finally, the group, family, and individual sessions deeply focused on the problems and pitfalls being experienced by these families. Workers were often overwhelmed by the intensity and chaos that often accompanies these situations. Therefore, social workers' attention focused on "harm reduction," which left little time to develop an inventory of resources, capabilities, and capacities that might exist in their environments. The consequence was that both families and individuals tended to perpetuate their isolation from their environments rather than identifying and reaching out to potential resources that could support their attempts to grow and develop.

The Strengths Model

As we mentioned earlier in the chapter, the Strengths Model for practice grew simultaneously with its conceptual underpinnings of the strengths perspective. This is somewhat unique given that most conceptual frameworks develop prior to any significant progress in their translation and implementation into practice. In contrast, the strengths perspective was conceived and developed in a culture that contained both theoreticians and practitioners. This rather unique arrangement allowed both practitioners and academics to provide ongoing and consistent feedback that identified both progress and challenges emerging from their attempts to translate the ideas and actions in the field of recovery oriented mental health services (Rapp & Goscha, 2012, Saleebey, 1992; Sullivan & Rapp, 1992).

The Strengths Model grew out of early work, in 1982, to build on case management efforts to translate this approach into services for people with chronic psychiatric disabilities. The University of Kansas, School of Social Welfare, received a small contract from the state to develop a pilot case management program that collaborated with local mental health centers (Rapp & Goscha, 2014). Ronna Chamberlain, who at that point was a doctoral student, and Charles Rapp, a faculty member in the School, quickly observed that the mental health systems were designed to provide services using a brokerage model. The existing mental health systems focused on having very low expectations that concentrated on remediating perceived deficits and separated people from their communities while blaming them for not doing better in the existing systems (Rapp & Goscha, 2014). They saw a need for a fundamentally different approach that required developing a new set of principles based on the strengths perspective. Six fundamental principles of the **Strengths Model** (Rapp & Goscha, 2014, p. 42) were articulated:

- People with psychiatric disabilities can learn, grow, and change.
- The focus is on individual strengths rather than deficits.
- The community is viewed as an oasis of resources.
- The client is a director of the helping process.

- The worker/client relationship is primary and essential.

- The primary setting of our work is in the community.

These ideas presented a radically different approach from existing practice strategies in the field of mental health. However, they aligned quite closely with the principles of a strengths perspective including the following:

- Every individual, group, family, and community has strengths.

- Trauma and abuse, illness, and struggle may be injurious but they may also be sources of challenge and opportunity.

- Assume that you do not know the upper limits of the capacity to grow and change and take individual, group, and community aspirations seriously.

- We best serve clients by collaborating with them.

- Every environment is full of resources.

- Caring and caretaking provide an essential context for human well-being.

While there are variations in the wording between the principles in the Strengths Model and strengths perspective, there are certain basic themes that transcend both. First, empowerment content for both the community and individuals is the natural and appropriate outcome of creating positive interactions supporting the idea that people should have an active role in making choices about their current situation and their own vision for their future. Second, **resilience** rests on the notion that both individuals and communities have a reservoir of resources that can be brought to bear in any situation, and they exist, not only within the individual, but also in the environments. Third, **membership** emphasizes the notion that there is interdependence between individuals and community, and that those connections must be acknowledged and nurtured in order for both to be healthy. Fourth, health and wellness of individuals and communities are a mutual product of interactions designed to reduce tensions among the systems rather than assigning pathology to one or the other. Finally, both the strengths perspective and the Strengths Model are built on the notion of social constructionism that requires the definition of the current situation, what needs to be done, and the eventual goals as emerging from a co-constructed process involving all of the relevant systems starting with professionals and clients.

Personal Attributes Necessary for Strengths-Based Practice

Rapp and Goscha (2014, p. 47) provide an excellent statement defining their view of the Strengths Model:

Strengths-based practice is not about helping people feel good about themselves while living in substandard conditions or remaining in entrapping environments. Strengths-based practice is about helping people realize they have the power to affect their own lives and exert some control in carving out their future. This does not mean that people will not have challenges, struggles, or face difficult barriers in achieving the life they want. This is part of the human condition we all face. The identification and use of strengths is helping people change narratives about themselves and their world so they can navigate the difficulties of life like everyone else.

In order to operationalize this perspective, an emphasis is placed on the learning of skills that goes beyond what is often the focus of many professional programs. In other words, to move beyond what is often called the "core dimensions of helping," to include the skills identified in our earlier chapter on diversity, we must address the following elements.

First, we need to develop a level of self-awareness that allows us to understand how social contexts and narratives shape our encounters with clients, and how our own belief systems interact with our professional roles in ways that either promote or reduce issues related to oppression, social justice, freedom, and respect among other values. Second, we will want to commit ourselves to exploring the consequences of what we are doing and its impact or lack of impact on client systems based on the application of critical thinking skills. This requires the examination of elements in the environments as well as the persons with whom we work with an eye toward understanding the impact of our actions. Third, self-reflection is necessary in order to focus on the connection between our own beliefs about what "should" be, and how those beliefs shape our work, with specific attention related to social justice, autonomy, service, respect for human dignity, and diversity. Fourth, we need courage to analyze our own actions, within the systems that employ us, when those systems negatively affect our clients' lives. Then, we recognize that our translations of strengths-based practice are likely to stand in clear opposition to the best interests of the systems that employ us. In other words, we often speak with our client systems about the courage it takes for them to create change in their lives. We must be willing to show that same kind of courage in facing the resistance we will likely encounter if we challenge agency and community systems on behalf of our clients.

Classroom Exercise

This exercise focuses on identifying and understanding the translation of the principles of both the strengths perspective and Strengths Model for practice. The first task is to choose a current or former practice situation in which you participated in as a worker, or use one of the case examples in the book and put yourself in the place of the worker. Once you have identified the basic elements of the situation, you should describe what actually happened for both the worker and the client systems. Then, take the principles of the strengths perspective and Strengths Model identified in the chapter and attempt to apply them to this situation. You should focus on the fundamental elements of empowerment in your case example and discuss how you did or did not apply them, and how consistent your work is with strengths-based principles. The focus should be on *your* perspectives and *your* reflection on your interactions. For example, did you choose to read existing assessments prior to meeting with the client system? If so, how did that decision shape your perspective and was it useful in your efforts to empower the individual, group, or community with whom the work occurred? How did the agency system within which you were working support and/or hinder the work? Identify at least two or three changes that would be necessary for you to address in order to increase the likelihood of positive outcomes for clients by using the principles in this chapter. What would be the immediate steps you would take to effect those changes? Identify the impact of your own internal perceptions on your actions as you attempted to "help" in this context.

The second step is to use your analysis of the case that you chose above and share that analysis in the classroom. Bring your analysis of what happened to class and share your reflections with the other members of the class by forming groups of three or four people. Each person shares their analysis and reflections, and the group is responsible to help the presenter to expand options based on their own understandings of the principles in the chapter.

CHAPTER SUMMARY

The following is a summary of four major segments in this chapter. We started with an examination of empowerment theory and its long-standing connections to social work. Empowerment theory addresses key themes related to (1) a fundamental belief that individuals and environments have capacities and strengths that can be transformative, (2) a dual focus that includes *both* persons and their environments, (3) relationships between professionals and client systems that need to be collaborative, (4) clients as active participants and claimants of resources, and (5) social workers' energies focused on marginalized populations of people at the individual, group, and community levels.

We then examined positive psychology as a potential source of ideas that are congruent with both empowerment and the strengths perspective. More specifically, positive psychology aims (1) to ameliorate and improve social disorder by fostering prevention strategies, (2) to help move professionals away from a pathology focus toward health and well-being, (3) to decrease the use of ideologies that engender passivity and pathology among marginalized populations, and (4) to help move people beyond an egocentric (individual) focus toward seeking, considering, and addressing the needs of others.

We examined the work of Ann Weick and Dennis Saleebey as the progenitors for the development of the strengths perspective in social work. We tracked their scholarly paths from their early stages, with Weick's emphasis on critical theory (feminism) and Saleebey's concerns focused on epistemological and ontological questions that were shaping social work's direction. Their work overlapped when assessing questions about the role played by values, knowledge, mission, sanction, and skills as they interacted in practice. They both agreed that "overturning the existing medical model" needed to be achieved. They critiqued its attentions to pathologies, problems, and deficits rather than on potential, possibilities, and capacities. Both found agreement about the role of social constructionism as a linchpin for developing a knowledge base for transformational social work. They both agreed that the utilization of empowerment and critical theories required social work to focus on both person and environment as central to supporting human growth and development and social justice.

We examined the underpinnings of the strengths perspective and its application in the Strengths Model as it relates to empowerment theory and social work's tensions between social control and social change. We provided a beginning translation of the strengths perspective and Strengths Model by using examples of how powerful and difficult it can be for professionals to shift from the existing medical model to a strengths-based paradigm. We provided examples of the power of language (e.g., victim) in influencing our perceptions and behaviors in practice. These changes provide new meanings that reflect knowledge and value formulations that then impact our actions and expectations as practitioners.

Finally, we identified essential skills required to operationalize strengths-based work. These skills include self-awareness, commitment to monitoring outcomes of our work, self-reflection, and courage to analyze and act in ways that hold our agencies accountable in our work on behalf of clients. These skills move beyond the "core dimensions" of helping and are essential for us to engage in if our goal is to operationalize meaningful human growth and the realization of social justice in our social work mission.

Key Terms (in order of appearance)

Empowerment   345

Positive psychology   348

Prospective psychology   350

Strengths perspective   363

Strengths model   367

Resilience   368

Membership   368

References

Addams, J. (1910). *Twenty years at Hull-House*. New York, NY: Macmillan.

Barry, K. L., Zeber, J. E., et al. (2003). Effect of strengths model versus assertive community treatment model on participant outcomes and utilization: Two-year follow-up. *Psychiatric Rehabilitation Journal, 26*(3), 268–277.

Bransford, C. L. (2011). Reconciling paternalism and empowerment in clinical practice: An intersubjective perspective. *Social Work, 56*, 33–41.

Butler, S. (2013). *TANF time limits and Maine families: Consequences of withdrawing the safety net*. Maine Equal Justice Partners. Retrieved January 14,

2018, from https://www.mejp.org/sites/default/files/TANF-Study-SButler-Feb2013.pdf

Chambers, C. A. (1963). *Seedtime of reform: American social service and social action, 1918–1933*. Minneapolis: University of Minnesota Press.

Chin, H. B., Sipe, T. A., Elder, R., Mercer, S. L., Chattopadhyay, S. K., Verughese, J., Wethington, H. R. et al. (2012). The effectiveness of group-based comprehensive risk-reduction and abstinence education interventions to prevent or reduce the risk of adolescent pregnancy, human immunodeficiency virus, and sexually transmitted infections: Two systematic reviews for the guide to community preventive services. *American Journal of Preventive Medicine*, *42*, 272–294.

Compton, W. (2005). *An introduction to positive psychology*. Belmont, CA: Wadsworth.

East, J. F., & Roll, S. J. (2015). Women, poverty, and trauma: An empowerment practice approach. *Social Work*, *60*, 279–286.

Falck, M. (1988). *Social work: The membership perspective*. New York, NY: Springer.

Freire, P. (1970). *Pedagogy of the oppressed*. New York, NY: Continuum.

Freire, P. (1990). A critical understanding of social work. *Journal of Progressive Human Services*, *1*, 3–9.

Gable, S., & Haidt, J. (2005). What (and why) is positive psychology? *Review of General Psychology*, *9*(2), 103–110.

Goffman, E. (1963). *Stigma: Notes on the management of spoiled identity*. Englewood Cliffs, NJ: Prentice-Hall.

Goscha, R. J. (2009). *Finding common ground: Exploring the experiences of client involvement in medication decisions using a shared decision making model*. Doctoral dissertation, University of Kansas, Lawrence, KS.

Gutierrez, L. M. (1990). Working with women of color: An empowerment perspective. *Social Work*, *35*(2), 149–153.

Gutierrez, L. M., Parsons, R. J., & Cox, E. O. (1998). *Empowerment in social work practice: A sourcebook*. Pacifica Grove, CA: Brooks/Cole.

Haidt, J. (2000). The positive emotion of elevation. *Prevention and Treatment*, *3*, http://journals.apa.org/prevention/volume3/pre0030003c.html

Hardina, D., Middleton, J., Montana, S., & Simpson, R. (2007). *An empowerment approach to managing social services organizations*. New York, NY: Springer.

Harrington, M. (1962). *The other America*. New York, NY: Macmillan Publishing.

Hasenfeld, Y. (1987). Power in social work practice. *Social Service Review*, *61*, 469–483.

Hegar, R. L., & Hunzeker, J. M. (1988). Moving toward empowerment-based practice in public child welfare. *Social Work*, *33*, 499–502.

Hunter, M., & Saleebey, D. (1983). Subversion of inequitable situations: Approaches for the powerless and oppressed. *Journal of Social Welfare*, *9*(1), 17–24.

Kabeer, N. (2012). Empowerment, citizenship and gender justice: A contribution to locally grounded theories of change in women's lives. *Ethics and Social Welfare*, *6*(3), 216–232.

Koenig, T. L., & Spano, R. (1998). Taoism and the strengths perspective. *Social Thought*, *18*, 47–65.

Koenig, T. L., & Spano, R. (2003). Sex, supervision, and boundary violations: Pressing challenges and possible solutions. *The Clinical Supervisor*, *22*, 3–9.

Koenig, T., & Spano, R. (2007). The cultivation of social workers' hope in personal life and professional practice. *Journal of Religion and Spirituality in Social Work*, *26*, 45–61.

Lee, J. A. B. (2001). *The empowerment approach to social work practice: Building the beloved community* (2nd ed.). New York, NY: Columbia University Press.

Lee, J., Weaver, C., & Hrostowski, S. (2011). Psychological empowerment and child welfare worker outcomes: A path analysis. *Child Youth Care Forum*, *40*, 479–497.

Leiby, J. (1978). *A history of social welfare and social work in the United States*. New York, NY: Columbia University Press.

Lieberman, A. (2015). Ann T. Weick. *Encyclopedia of social work*. Washington, DC: National Association of Social Workers and Oxford University Press.

Lubove, R. (1975). *The professional altruist: The emergence of social work as a career, 1880–1930*. New York, NY: Atheneum.

Marshall, T. H. (1950). *Citizenship and social class and other essays*. Cambridge, UK: Cambridge University Press.

Marshall, T. H. (1977). *Class, citizenship and social development*. Chicago, IL: University of Chicago Press.

Miley, K. K., O'Melia, M. W., & DuBois, B. L. (2017). *Generalist social work practice: An empowering approach* (8th ed.). Boston, MA: Pearson.

Parsons, R. J., & East, J. (2013). Empowerment practice. *Encyclopedia of Social Work*. Washington, DC: NASW & Oxford University Press.

Pinderhughes, E. (1983). Empowerment for our clients and for ourselves. *Social Casework, 64*, 331–338.

Radohl, T. B. (2013). *The role of personal medicine in shared decision making and mental health recovery*. Doctoral dissertation, University of Kansas, Lawrence, KS.

Rapp, C. A. (1995). The active ingredients of effective case management: A research synthesis. In L. Giesler (Ed.), *Case management for behavioral managed care* (pp. 5–45). Washington, DC: Center for Mental Health Services.

Rapp, C. A., & Goscha, R. J. (2012). *The strengths model: A recovery-oriented approach to mental health services* (3rd ed.). Oxford & New York: Oxford University Press.

Rapp, C. A., & Goscha, R. J. (2014). Three decades of strengths: Reflections of the past and challenges of the future. In A. P. Francis, V. Pulla, M. Clark, E. S. Mariscal, & I. Ponnuswami (Eds.). *Advancing social work in mental health through strengths-based practice* (pp. 39–53). Brisbane, Australia: Primrose Hall Publishing Group.

Reynolds, B. C. (1934). Between client and community. *Smith College Studies in Social Work, 5*, 5–128. (Reprinted, 1982). Silver Spring, MD: National Association of Social Workers.

Richmond, M. (1922). *What is social casework?* New York, NY: Russell Sage.

Rose, S. (1990). Advocacy/empowerment: An approach to clinical practice for social work. *Journal of Sociology and Social Welfare, 17*(2), 41–51.

Saleebey, D. (1987). Insight as social critique: Prospects for a radical perspective in clinical practice. *California Sociologist, 10*, 11–26.

Saleebey, D. (1990). Philosophical disputes in social work: Social justice denied. *Journal of Sociology and Social Welfare, 17*, 29–40.

Saleebey, D. (1992). *The strengths perspective*. Boston, MA: Allyn and Bacon.

Saleebey, D. (1993). Theory and the generation and subversion of knowledge. *Journal of Sociology & Social Welfare, 20*, 5–25.

Saleebey, D. (2001). Commentary: The diagnostic strengths model, *Social Work, 46*, 183–187.

Saleebey, D. (2006). *The strengths perspective* (6th ed.). Boston, MA: Allyn & Bacon.

Seligman, M. (2003). Forward: The past and future of positive psychology. In C. L. M. Keyes & J. Haidt, *Flourishing: Positive psychology and the life well-lived* (pp. xi–xx). Washington, DC: American Psychological Association.

Seligman, M., & Csikszentmihalyi, M. (2000). Positive psychology: An Introduction. *American Psychologist, 55*(1), 5–14.

Seligman, M., Parks, A., & Steen, T. (2004). A balanced psychology and a full life. *Philosophical Transactions: Biological Sciences, 359*, 1379–1381.

Seligman, M., & Pawelski, J. (2003). Positive psychology: FAQs. *Psychological Inquiry, 14* (2), 159–163.

Seligman, M., Railton, P., Baumeister, R., & Sripada, C. (2013). Navigating into the future or driven by the past. *Perspectives on Psychological Science, 8*(2), 119–141.

Sherman, W., & Wenocur, S. (1983). Empowering public welfare workers through mutual support. *Social Work, 28*, 375–379.

Simkhovitch, M. (1938). *Neighborhood: My story of Greenwich house*. New York, NY: Norton.

Simon, B. L. (1990). Rethinking empowerment. *Journal of Progressive Human Services, 1*, 27–39.

Simon, B. L. (1994). *The empowerment tradition in American social work: A history*. New York, NY: Columbia University Press.

Solomon, B. B. (1976). *Black empowerment: Social work in oppressed communities*. New York, NY: Columbia University Press.

Stanard, R. P. (1999). The effect of training in a strengths model of case management on outcomes in a community mental health center. *Mental Health Journal, 35*(2), 169–179.

Sullivan, W. P., & Rapp, C. A. (1992). Reconsidering the environment as a helping resource. In D. Saleebey (Ed.), *The strengths perspective in social work* (pp. 148–157). New York, NY: Longman.

Weick, A. (1982). Issues of power in social work practice. In A. Weick and S. T. Vandiver (Eds.). *Women, power and change* (pp. 173–185). Washington, DC: National Association of Social Workers.

Weick, A. (1983a). The growth-task model of human development. *Social Casework, 64*, 131–137.

Weick, A. (1983b). Issues in overturning a medical model of social work practice, *Social Work, 28*, 467–471.

Weick, A. (1987). Reconceptualizing the philosophical perspective of social work. *Social Service Review, 61*, 218–230.

Weick, A. (1994). Overturning oppression: An analysis of emancipatory change. In L. V. Davis (Ed.), *Building on Women's strengths: A social work agenda for the 21st Century* (pp. 211–227). New York, NY: Haworth Press.

Weick, A., & Saleebey, D. (1995). Supporting family strengths: Orienting policy and practice toward the 21st century. *Families in Society, 76*(3), 141–149.

Weick, A., & Saleebey, D. (1998). Postmodern perspectives for social work. In R. G. Meinert, J. T. Pardeck, & J. W. Murphy (Eds.), *Postmodernism, religion and the future of social work*. Binghampton, NY: Haworth.

13

COGNITIVE AND MORAL DEVELOPMENT THEORIES

PHOTO 13.1
Buddha statue representing perfect knowledge that leads to enlightenment: Seoraksan National Park, South Korea

CASE EXAMPLE
BUYING FRIENDSHIP

Alex was referred to me by the occupational therapist in our rehabilitation center. The occupational therapist was somewhat reluctant to refer Alex because of his diminished judgment and problem-solving skills, but she wanted to honor his wishes to live independently. Alex had suffered a traumatic brain injury after falling off of the back of an armored personnel carrier while serving in Desert Storm. He was paralyzed from the waist down, used crutches for short distances, and had an electric wheelchair that he could propel faster than I could walk. He was determined to buy his first home, and he was asking me as his outpatient rehabilitation social worker to help make this happen. We developed a plan together that involved cleaning up his credit and finding a real estate agent who would take him, wheelchair and all, to visit properties for sale. Alex bought his first house and we obtained remodeling financial support to widen doorways and hallways to make his home wheelchair accessible. We agreed to meet every two weeks to discuss his transition to independent living and to problem-solve regarding any issues he faced as a new home owner. Soon our visits became less frequent and it appeared that Alex had successfully made this transition. However, a few months later, he came into the outpatient clinic stating that he had been "kicked out" of his own home. He had invited a family to live with him, had helped to buy them a van, and they had mercilessly barred him from returning to his own residence. As I talked with Alex, he told me that he really wanted the family to live with him; he wanted friendships and relationships, and if by offering his home he could obtain these relationships, Alex was willing to do this.

Discussion Questions

(1) If you were to do an assessment of Alex's bio-psycho-social-spiritual functioning, what are key elements that you would want to explore? And, why?

(2) How do you think Alex's brain injury impacts his cognitive functioning (e.g., thinking, judgment, and decision-making)?

(3) What is the relationship between Alex's cognitive impairments and his moral development (e.g., Can Alex thoughtfully decide what is in his best interest?)?

(4) Knowing now the negative consequences of Alex's decision to live independently, do you think the social worker did the "wrong thing" by helping him to find a home? Please explain your answer.

Alex's situation reflects complex interactions among his cognitive (or biological) functioning (e.g., due to his brain injury), psychological and social functioning (e.g., his desire to have friends and to be liked), and spiritual or moral functioning (e.g., willing to sacrifice himself, to even "pay" for friendship, as a way to meet his needs). In particular, Alex's behaviors and desires to make his home available to a family so as to have relationships places him squarely in what our featured in-depth theorist, Carol Gilligan (1982), would say is an ethic of care. Alex desires to be responsible to and in what he hopes will be caring relationships; and he has made an ethical choice to let this family live with him in spite of potential negative consequences for himself. As a social worker, one of the most challenging elements of Alex's case is engaging in an ongoing assessment of whether or not he is cognitively able to "think through" his decision and act in his own best interests.

In this overview, we will discuss **cognitive development**, understood as the emergence and maturation of thought processes such as reasoning, language, problem solving, and memory (Hussey, 2016); we will also closely examine Jean Piaget's theory of cognitive development (1936). Second, we will make links, as Piaget and other scholars (e.g., Kohlberg) do, between cognitive and moral development; and we will discuss Lawrence Kohlberg's pivotal moral development theory that flows from and extends Piaget's ideas. Finally, we will point to current trends that call for the expansion of moral concerns beyond justice and care; the possibility of a moral core in infancy; the persistence of virtue and character in moral development; and the shift to studying culturally diverse groups for their strengths and unique contributions to moral development.

PIAGET AND COGNITIVE DEVELOPMENT

Jean Piaget's **cognitive development theory** (1936) delineates four stages that we all move through as we interact with our environments to develop our intelligence and knowledge. Piaget was one of the first theorists to view children as more than just little adults. Children think differently than adults do about the world, make observations, and conduct experiments to deepen their own learning processes. As they experience the world, the new information children obtain is used to modify and add to their existing understandings or "schemas." Piaget identified the following four stages:

In the first stage, the sensorimotor stage (birth to 2 years), infants know the world through their sensations and actions (e.g., grasping, sucking, looking, and listening). They learn that objects continue to exist even if not observed (i.e., object permanence), develop an awareness as separate and distinct from others, and that their actions can cause things to happen.

In the second stage, the preoperational stage (ages 2 to 7 years), children begin to think symbolically using language and pictures to represent objects. They do struggle to see things from another person's perspective, are viewed as egocentric, and think in very concrete terms (e.g., have difficulty with the concept of constancy and will view two equal lumps of clay differently; if one is flattened and the other is smashed into a ball, the child will view the flattened clay as larger).

In the third stage, concrete operational stage (ages 7 to 11), children's thinking becomes more logical and organized. They can use inductive logic—reasoning from a specific example to a general principle, but still struggle with abstract thinking. Their earlier egocentrism begins to disappear as they are able to see a situation from another person's point of view. At this stage, children also begin to understand the concept of conservation (e.g., two glasses of water are actually of equal amounts even though one container may be taller and therefore *look* larger).

In the fourth stage, formal operational stage (ages 12 and up), adolescents and young adults are able to think about social, political, moral, and philosophical issues that require abstract thinking and they are able to begin to reason from a general principle to a specific example (to use deductive reasoning). Youth and adults at this stage are able to see a number of solutions to a specific problem, can plan for the future, and reason about hypothetical situations.

In summary, it is important to note that Piaget viewed children's intellectual growth as becoming qualitatively different over time (Inhelder & Piaget, 1958; Piaget, 1936). As children grow, they do not just stack new knowledge and ideas on top of their existing knowledge. Instead, fundamental changes occur for children, not just in how much more information they have at age 2 versus age 9. Children grow in their capacities to think differently, to use reason, and to engage in abstract thinking for problem solving, future planning, and other efforts.

FROM COGNITIVE TO MORAL DEVELOPMENT THEORY

Piaget and other scholars (Rest, 1979) make links between cognitive development, which includes logical reasoning, and moral development. **Moral development** can refer to the emergence, change, and understanding of how human beings develop morality over the course of their lives. For Piaget, moral development involved a three-step process of moving from an external locus of control to an internal locus of control for assessing "right from wrong" (Piaget, 1932/1955). This progression defined Piaget's **moral development theory** and also reflected growth in reasoning—from concrete to more abstract forms of reasoning. In effect, growth in cognitive development is linked to and necessary for moral development to occur. Kohlberg (1969, 1971) draws upon these ideas to develop his moral development theory.

THE EMERGENCE OF KOHLBERG'S MORAL DEVELOPMENT THEORY

Both Piaget and Kohlberg were influential in shaping scholarship about moral judgment and moral development. Up until their writings, subjective moral values were assessed based on observable behavior and rarely were these values (e.g., social justice or loyalty) studied in their own right. Both tried to understand morality from participants' own viewpoints and based on their pressing concerns and perceived possibilities for action. Piaget (1932/1955) introduced a method for studying children's moral judgment by presenting a story to evoke discussion and explanation of their views, and he noted age-related differences in the types of responses to these stories, with older children better able than younger children to integrate experiences into their logic and moral thinking.

Kohlberg's dissertation work (1958) began a second phase in moral development research in which he argued that morality cannot be assessed without knowing a person's intentions and viewpoints, and he maintained that behavior has an underlying structure and occurs within a context in which humans learn, play, and act. Kohlberg was regularly called on to counter behaviorism (see Chapter 10, on cognitive behavioral theory), which focused only on observable responses to stimuli. Kohlberg built on Piaget's work, but he chose to present older male participants (ages 10–16) with complex, hypothetical moral dilemmas and interviewed them about what they thought should be done and why. Kohlberg found that Piaget's understanding of moral development did not adequately describe his participants' reasoning and moral judgment. Instead, Kohlberg identified numerous features of participants' responses that represented a progression in their development (1973) and seemed to cluster into six stages (See Table 13.1). These stages, which represent Kohlberg's **moral development theory**, are grouped into three levels: the pre-conventional level, the conventional level, and the post-conventional or principles level (Colby, Kohlberg, Gibbs, & Lieberman, 1983; Kohlberg, 1976, 1981, 1984).

TABLE 13.1 ■ Kohlberg's Stages of Moral Development		
Stage Description	**Examples of Moral Reasoning: Why He *Should* Steal the Drug**	**Examples of Moral Reasoning: Why He *Should Not* Steal the Drug**
Preconventional Stage One: Avoid punishment Stage Two: Seek rewards **Conventional** Stage Three: Gain approval/avoid disapproval Stage Four: Conformity to rules **Post-conventional** Stage Five: Social contract Stage Six: Individual principled conscience	If he lets his wife die, he'll get in trouble. If he gets caught, he could give the drug back and he wouldn't get a long jail sentence. He should show his wife how much he loves her. It would be his responsibility if she dies; he can pay the druggist later. Because he vowed to take care of his wife, he is justified in taking it, even though stealing is wrong. His wife's life is more important than the druggist's profits.	He might get caught and sent to jail. The druggist needs to make money. If his wife dies, he can't be blamed. It's the druggist's fault for being selfish. It's always wrong to steal; he'll always feel guilty. Extreme circumstances don't justify stealing. He'll lose respect for himself. He should think about the long-term consequences. Other people may also need the drug. He should consider the lives of everyone involved—not just his wife's.

Source: Adapted from *Life-Span Development* by John W. Santrock, Copyright ©1989. Used with permission of The McGraw-Hill Companies.

In Table 13.1, the first column refers to these stages. The second and third columns refer to participants' responses to Kohlberg's ethical dilemma involving Heinz who must make the decision about whether or not to steal a life-saving drug for his wife (who will die without the drug) (Kohlberg, 1981). Heinz does not have the money to buy this drug and the druggist, who discovered the drug, is charging ten times what the drug cost him to make. Heinz is desperate, cannot get all the money together from his friends. and so steals the drug. Should Heinz have stolen the drug for his wife? Why or why not? The second column provides reasons why Heinz should steal the drug. The third column provides reasons why Heinz should not steal the drug.

Kohlberg described justice as the central, universal principle in the development of these stages of moral judgment. He defined justice as the "primary regard for the value and equality of all human beings and for reciprocity in human relations" (Kohlberg & Hersh, 1977, p. 56); Kohlberg viewed the most just solution as one that incorporates an expanded capacity for empathy, taking into account others' perspectives and rights.

Kohlberg's stages are grouped into three levels and are defined as follows. In the preconventional level, children interpret cultural rules and definitions of good and bad or right and wrong in terms of the consequences of their actions (e.g., for punishment or rewards by those who have more power and make the rules). This level is divided into two stages:

Stage One: The punishment-and-obedience orientation. At this stage, children are interested in avoiding punishment and will engage in unquestioned deference to power and authority.

Stage Two: The instrumental-relativist orientation. Children will take actions based on satisfying their own needs and may trade needs (e.g., "You scratch my back and I will scratch yours.") Their actions are not done out of loyalty or gratitude to others.

In the conventional level, the person is focused on maintaining social order and conforming to the expectations of one's family, group, or country regardless of consequences. There are two stages at this level:

Stage Three: The interpersonal concordance or "good boy–nice girl" orientation. Good behavior is based on the approval of others, and one earns approval by conforming to what the majority views as pleasing and nice.

Stage Four: The "law and order" orientation. At this stage, the person views right behavior as doing one's duty, showing respect for authority, and maintaining the social order for its own sake.

In the post-conventional, autonomous, or principles level, a person views moral values and principles as having validity apart from the authority of the group or society that one identifies with. This level also has two stages:

Stage Five: The social-contract, legalistic orientation typically with utilitarian overtones. At this stage, right behavior involves upholding individual rights agreed upon by one's society with an awareness of the relativism of personal values. People at this stage support democratic rules for reaching consensus and for changing laws.

Stage Six: The universal-ethical-principle orientation. People define right in this stage based on their conscience and abstract ethical principles that appeal to universality and consistency (e.g., equality of human rights, respect for the dignity and worth of human beings, and using the categorical imperative in which you "act only according to that maxim [or moral rule] whereby you can, at the same time, will that it should become a universal law" (Kant, 1785/1993, p. 30).

Kohlberg (1976) described his moral development theory as representing stages in which individuals would first consider their own self-interests (Stages One and Two), then, see themselves as group members who share expectations (Stages Three and Four), and finally, would make moral commitments and hold to standards of a good or just society (Stages Five and Six). Kohlberg also maintained several assumptions about moral development. First, he believed that moral reasoning develops over time through a series of stages that are structured, organized systems of thought. Second, people are consistent in their level of moral judgment and the stages form an invariant sequence in which movement is always forward never backward (unless under extreme trauma) (Higgins, 1995). Third, Kohlberg's stages are universal and cut across all cultures. Kohlberg (1969) was ahead of his time in studying other cultures. However, he believed that some of the cultures he studied (e.g., a Malaysian aboriginal group on Formosa and African American children in the inner city) moved through these stages of moral development more slowly because they were "culturally deprived." Over the years, Kohlberg revised his stages, changed the basis for claiming that higher stages are more conceptually adequate than lower stages, altered his thinking to more adequately explain how moral reasoning is what most strongly influences moral behavior (Arnold, 2000), and changed his methods for assessing participants' responses to his hypothetical ethical dilemmas.

PUBLIC EDUCATION AS THE JUST COMMUNITY

In addition, Kohlberg has been a leading advocate for public education as a place for nurturing students' moral development (Power, Higgins, & Kohlberg, 1989). Because Kohlberg believed that children have the capacity to grow in their moral reasoning and to use more adequate and complex reasoning in solving moral problems, he developed moral education curriculum for public schools, which he described as "just communities." Kohlberg drew upon John Dewey's ideas to support his views about education. Dewey stated that "the aim of education is growth and development, both intellectual and moral. Ethical and psychological principles can aid the school in the greatest of all constructions—the building of a free and powerful character" (1895/1964, p. 207).

From Kohlberg's perspective, teachers can provide opportunities for students to consider genuine moral conflicts faced by the school community. Teachers can stimulate students' moral development by helping them think through problems that need to be solved within the school community. Kohlberg critiqued current public school systems, which seemed more interested in telling students what to think and instead he proposed the creation of a **just community** that involved helping students discover *how* they arrive at solutions to moral problems. From Kohlberg's perspective, schools need to provide an atmosphere in which problems are settled based on principles, not based on power or conventional right answers.

EXTENSIONS FROM PIAGET AND KOHLBERG

In this section, two key areas that represent extensions of Piaget and Kohlberg are discussed. First, the work done by Rest and others provided a standardized method for assessing moral judgment (See the Defining Issues Test [DIT] as described by Rest, 1979, 1986.) Numerous studies using the DIT, conducted within various regions of the United States, provided ample support for the developmental or progressive nature of moral judgment (e.g., as related to age and years of education). Studies using the DIT broke new ground in examining diverse elements of moral judgment (e.g., there is no support for the notion that moral judgment is more related to personality than to cognitive development, and some educational interventions seem capable of facilitating slow growth in moral development). These findings also critiqued Kohlberg's emphasis on distinct stages of moral development noting that these progressive stages are not likely to be mutually exclusive, but instead they overlap and mix in complicated ways; any links between moral judgment as delineated by distinct, step-by-step stages and moral behavior continue to be contested by scholars (Rest, 1986; Rest, Narvaez, Bebeau, & Thoma, 1999).

Second, Carol Gilligan established the **moral orientations theory** as applied specifically to girls' and women's experiences (see Gilligan, 1982). Gilligan's work challenged Kohlberg's sole reliance on a justice orientation in moral development; instead her research asserted the importance of a care orientation and a responsiveness to relationships that guided moral judgments for girls and women (Gilligan & Antonucci, 1988). Gilligan's model, which will be discussed in detail in our in-depth section, includes three broad perspectives: (1) self-survival, (2) caring for others (feminine goodness), and (3) interdependence of self and others (balancing care of self with care of others).

In part, Gilligan's model provided a critique of Kohlberg's only-male study samples for developing his moral development theory. Women (and also people from diverse racial and ethnic groups) were measured against this male "standard" of moral development and were not treated as subjects with their own voices and perspectives (Brown, Tappan, & Gilligan, 1995; Snarey, 1995). Gilligan's research also relied on the narratives that her study participants shared with her about real-world, ethical dilemmas such as whether or not to have an abortion in the first trimester of pregnancy (Gilligan, 1982). Gilligan's study methods were in direct contrast to Kohlberg's use of hypothetical dilemmas, and her work not only challenged a sole justice orientation to moral decision-making but also led the way for scholars to examine a range of moral concerns that are discussed in our upcoming section on current trends (Gilligan, 1977; Gilligan & Belenky, 1980; Snarey, 1995).

CURRENT TRENDS IN MORAL DEVELOPMENT

Several major trends will be discussed in this section: (1) emotion, intuition, and the expanding of moral concerns; (2) the moral self in infancy; (3) the persistence of virtue and character in moral development; and (4) the role of culture and context.

Emotion, Intuition, and the Expanding of Moral Concerns

Scholars have expanded on traditional moral domains of justice and care (Piaget, Kohlberg, and Gilligan) to take into account the role of intuition and emotion (e.g., empathy and guilt) in moral decision-making (Lapsley & Carlo, 2014). This work has attempted to integrate emotions within the context of a person's genetic makeup, temperament, and socialization by parents, peers, and society (Carlo & Randall, 2001). Others have described moral judgments as intuitive and automatic. Moral reasoning often occurs *after* people make an intuitive moral decision (Haidt & Kesebir, 2010). A major purpose of these developments has been to expand the full range of moral concerns to include those found in religious practices and among political conservatives (e.g., purity and loyalty to the group; see moral foundations theory). **Moral foundations theory** (MFT) incorporates the following five sets of what Graham et al. (2011) refer to as universal "moral intuitions," including harm/care, fairness/reciprocity, ingroup/loyalty, authority/respect, and purity/sanctity.

The proponents of MFT describe themselves as reacting to the dominance of Kohlberg's (and Gilligan's) views of moral growth and development as occurring when people move beyond the authority of the group or society in which they identify with in order to determine, through the use of abstract principles, right or moral behavior. They describe these traditional scholars as having enshrined political liberal ideals; their measures of an individuals' moral development identifies political conservatives as often unable to attain the highest levels of moral development (i.e., Kohlberg's post-conventional level—Stages Five and Six). At Kohlberg's post-conventional level, people become fully aware of the relativism of personal values and draw on abstract ethical principles to attain the good or just society.

Moral Self in Infancy

Although not readily acknowledged in its beginnings, research on the development of a moral core in infancy is now gaining traction (Emde, Biringen, Clyman, & Opperheim, 1991). This research draws on holistic views of interactions between the infant's biological tendencies (e.g., for exploration and mastery) and early socialization that occurs, for example, with sensitive and responsive parents (Warneken & Tomasello, 2007). By the second year of life, the interactions among the young child's biological, emotional, and social systems contribute to morally significant knowledge about empathy, sharing, and rule violations, and some scholars point to the existence of a natural propensity for altruism (Brownell, 2013; Hamlin, 2013; Warneken & Tomasello, 2007). Even with this increased focus on genetics in early infant development, authors continue to acknowledge the role of complex contextual factors such as parenting relationships (Kochanska, 2002) on moral development.

Persistence of Virtue and Character

Theorists have always understood that our schools could influence a child's moral development. However, they did not particularly value an educational focus on helping children develop a "bag of virtues" or character traits and indicated that these were very subjective (e.g., what appeared to be honesty, could also be viewed as insensitivity to others) (Kohlberg & Mayer, 1972). In more recent years, there has been a renewed interest in character and virtues, but in the context of efforts to examine moral identity and those who exemplify a moral life (Hardy & Carlo, 2005). Scholars have begun to identify patterns of character traits or virtues that reflect individuals who exhibit strong and committed moral actions, thereby linking moral reasoning with moral behaviors (Laible, Eye, & Carlo, 2008; Matsuba & Walker, 2004).

Culture and Context

As discussed earlier, scholars such as Kohlberg have viewed moral growth and development as universal—therefore, cutting across all cultures. Unfortunately, these same researchers viewed those from low-income or aboriginal communities as "culturally deprived" and slower to develop morally. This universality was not without its critics who noted that evidence for moral stages was gleaned predominantly from White, male, middle- and upper-class subjects (Haan, Aerts, & Cooper, 1985; Snarey, 1995). More current research efforts study the unique characteristics and strengths of specific cultures, examining them not in comparison with White communities but as their own subject and in their own right (e.g., examining specific cultural beliefs, customs, and practices that define a cultural groups' unique way of addressing moral growth and development) (Knight & Carlo, 2012).

Summary of Overview

In this overview, we have discussed cognitive and moral development featuring both Piaget and Kohlberg. We have paid special attention to the growth in cognitive reasoning and the concomitant progression of moral development. We have also examined two extensions of this seminal work in Rest's development of a standardized method for assessing moral judgment and Gilligan's moral orientations theory as applied specifically to girls' and women's moral development. Gilligan's work challenged Kohlberg's sole reliance on a justice orientation in moral development, asserted the importance of a care orientation, and foreshadowed the systematic exploration of a range of moral concerns. Finally, our overview concludes by examining current trends in moral development (e.g., the examination of a moral core in infancy, the persistence of virtue and character in moral development, and the exploration of culturally diverse groups for their unique contributions to moral development).

IN-DEPTH: CAROL GILLIGAN AND WOMEN'S MORAL DEVELOPMENT

Carol Gilligan, who obtained her doctoral degree in psychology in the late 1960s and was the mother of three young sons, recalled in a foreword to her book, *Joining the Resistance* (2013), how she met Lawrence Kohlberg, a well-known psychologist through a friend at a party. She stated that Kohlberg's

> theory of moral development captured the passion for justice that had inspired me along with many members of my generation to take action on behalf of civil rights and to protest what we saw as an unjust war. When he offered me a job as a research assistant, I accepted and thus became involved in the lively discussions provoked by his claim, following Socrates, that virtue is one and its name is justice. Moral development follows a single path, leading beyond self-interest and societal conventions to a principled understanding of justice as fairness. (p. 1)

Gilligan further described how both Erik Erikson and Lawrence Kohlberg had become

> fathers to me in the sense of showing me a way into psychology that engaged my interests, and by their example encouraged me to pursue my own questions. I did not anticipate that by following in their footsteps (as they had followed Freud and Piaget), I would find myself in forbidden territory. It was one thing to bridge men's lives into history and generalize from men's experience. To do so with women broke a silence. (p. 2)

It is Gilligan's scholarship on women's voices and their real-world moral situations that challenged Kohlberg's exclusive reliance on White male study participants in the development of his moral development theory, which viewed justice as the orienting principle of moral growth and maturity (Kohlberg, 1958, 1969). Gilligan asserted that men and women are different, at least when it comes to moral development and concomitant identity formation. Her central concern, dating back to the 1970s, has been to listen to and express women's voices in an attempt to center women's moral development on its own terms and not in contrast to exclusively male voices. It should be noted that it was not until the 1970s that the dominance of all-male samples in research studies was beginning to be remedied with samples that included diverse study participants (e.g., based on gender, race/ethnicity and class) (Giammarco, 2016).

As stated previously, Gilligan began her career as a graduate student of Lawrence Kohlberg, whose six-stage model of moral development was revolutionary in its use of longitudinal research methods that assessed moral development with study participants over a 30-year period. From the very beginning and throughout his career, Kohlberg's work faced critical debate from his colleagues and was viewed as controversial for many reasons (e.g., Kohlberg relied on abstract principles such as justice that he thought reflected the highest stages of moral development; he engaged in discussions [not quantifiable questionnaires] with study participants about how they would work through an ethical dilemma; and he viewed his theory as universal and applicable to all groups of people, including women and people of color).

One of the primary criticisms of his work came from Gilligan, who argued that since he and his research participants were all male, they could not accurately represent a female perspective on moral development. In sum, she stated that Kohlberg's perspective is a male perspective, which is by nature *individualistic*, based on *reasoning*, and is *justice-focused*. In contrast, a female perspective is concerned instead with caring and responsiveness to others, or a *care* ethic. In addition, women's identities are concerned with forming intimate relationships and in developing interdependence—a balance between caring for self and caring for others. Gilligan initially developed a three-stage moral development theory for females, but like other stage-based theorists who initially understood their stages to be in a linear sequence (including Kohlberg), her stages were re-conceptualized as perspectives with overlapping concepts or themes. The first perspective centers on finding one's own happiness and avoiding harm to self. The second centers on caring for other people. The third is to attempt a balance of interconnectedness between oneself and other people (see Table 13.2).

TABLE 13.2 ■ Gilligan's Stages of Moral Development

Stage Description	Basis of Moral Reasoning
Stage 1: Self survival *Transition from selfishness to responsibility for others*	Morality is based on what is best for oneself and the pragmatics of survival.
Stage 2: Caring for others (feminine goodness) *Transition from feminine goodness to truth*	Morality is based on meeting other people's needs and caring for the dependent and unequal.
Stage 3: Interdependence of self and others	Morality is based on caring for self and others; it involves an ethic of care based on nonviolence.

Source: Adapted from Gilligan, C. (1993). *In a different voice: Psychological theory and women's development* (2nd ed.). Cambridge, MA: Harvard University Press.

By centering women as the authors of their own moral life, Gilligan's moral development theory provides an important perspective in the field of moral psychology. Her work paved the way for current trends that expand on a range of moral concerns (e.g., centering diverse cultural and ethnic groups and examining other key orientations such as virtue or purity). In this section we'll explore her ideas in more depth using her example of a woman, whom we will call Isabelle, facing the decision of whether or not to have an abortion. So what, based on Gilligan's view, is different about women's, or the female *voice* when it comes to moral judgment and decision-making? Gilligan uses interviews with women who faced an abortion decision in order to support her ideas—we'll summarize one of those stories here and reference it for our discussion as well (Gilligan, 2012).

According to Gilligan, a man would appeal to abstract principles such as those rooted in Catholic theology, which clearly state that abortion is wrong. Males, says Gilligan, often seek absolutes—objective, universal, and timeless moral truths that can then be applied to real-world situations. These may come from theology (or various religious perspectives), but there are many secular moral/ethical theories as well. Females, on the other hand, are practical—they consider the network of relationships and people who will be affected by the decisions they make. This is the ethic of care. It's like a trampoline, explains Gilligan—what each person does affects everyone else. So when it comes to this woman in the scenario deciding whether to have an abortion or not, she should not simply appeal to male-generated theologies, principles, or moral rules—in fact, to do so would be inauthentic for her as a woman; Gilligan argues that the female voice has been subdued to the point that it often cannot express a truly female perspective in a male-dominated society. Instead, female moral decision-making—about abortion in this case—will have to do with weighing the impact of her decision on herself (something often ignored), her 1-year-old child, husband, as well as extended family, friends, the church, and others. It does not mean she *should* have an abortion—since there is no absolute, abstract "rightness" or "wrongness" about abortion—nor does it mean she should *not* have an abortion. Gilligan's idea is that Isabelle must wrestle with her decision, thinking about those in her relational "care" network. In this sense she expresses her authentic, female moral voice.

CASE EXAMPLE
SHOULD ISABELLE HAVE AN ABORTION?

Isabelle is married to a man who works as a roofer and is presently unemployed. She works full-time as a nurse in order to support her husband and 1-year-old child. She is also Catholic, has a spinal disorder, and has just become pregnant with her second child. At her first prenatal appointment, her doctor tells Isabelle that if she continues with the pregnancy it will result in her spinal disorder becoming significantly worse, potentially to the point that she will not be able to work or care for her children.

Discussion Questions

(1) What should Isabelle do?

(2) On what basis should Isabelle make her moral decision? In other words:

   a. Should Isabelle place her own health needs first? Why or why not?

   b. If she makes the decision to keep her baby, how might this affect relationships with her husband and 1-year-old child?

(3) How might you apply Gilligan's theory to this case? What perspective do you think best applies to Isabelle's situation (e.g., avoiding harm to self, caring for others, or finding a balance between self-care and care for others)?

What has taken place historically for women, according to Gilligan, is that their voices have not been expressed and therefore not heard (Gilligan, 1982). Our male-dominated society has prevented women's perspectives from being developed and included in public and private discourse. When it comes to moral judgments and maturity, women's perspectives have been devalued as inferior or even deviant because they are not the same as men's perspectives (e.g., by Freud, Kohlberg, and other prominent theorists). Women have been told that they must be selfless, their only function in society and the family being to do what they are told and consider only the needs of other people. In the abortion example just discussed, a woman who has no sense of her own voice will simply comply with what men have pre-decided for her—the female voice having become co-opted by men, speaking as if through a male ventriloquist. Next, we will explore in more detail the nature of Gilligan's moral development theory as delineated in three perspectives.

THE FIRST PERSPECTIVE

Gilligan's central theme is that women's moral development and decision-making is different from men's, and that it should be valued, validated, and inserted into both public and private discourse.

When one begins with the study of women and derives developmental constructs from their lives, the outline of a moral conception different from that described by Freud, Piaget, or Kohlberg begins to emerge and informs a different description of development. In this conception, the moral problem arises from conflicting responsibilities rather than from competing rights and requires for its resolution a mode of thinking that is contextual and narrative rather than formal and abstract. (Gilligan, 1982, p. 19)

By "contextual" and "narrative" Gilligan means that women's moral decision-making is firmly grounded in their social context: family, friends, and community—a network of relationships. And, in one of her pivotal studies, Gilligan's (1982) research methods involve asking women to describe real-world moral dilemmas regarding their pregnancy (instead of asking them to respond to hypothetical dilemmas). Gilligan is primarily concerned with the details of real-life stories.

In Gilligan's research, women's moral judgment and decision-making, particularly in considering abortion, tends to focus on the words *selfishness* and *responsibility*. "The inflicting of hurt is considered selfish and immoral in its reflection of unconcern, while the expression of care is seen as the fulfillment of moral responsibility" (Gilligan, 1982, p. 73). Gilligan calls this dichotomy of selfishness and responsibility a false one that traps women as they feel a constant pressure to selflessly take care of others, while also avoiding harm to others at any cost. What falls through the cracks is their own voice and identity. Gilligan's project is to transcend this form of thinking, and she finds that in her research with women facing the abortion decision that she has discovered a female perspective does just that. In short, it is a move, or a developmental path, from the selfishness/responsibility (false) dichotomy, to a more adequate, or sophisticated understanding of human relationships as *interdependent*. The focus in either case is between the self and the other (or others) in relationship, and the development is from a place of oppression, or being trapped, to transcendence or liberation. But before we get to the liberated state, the third stage or perspective of Gilligan's female moral reasoning, let's discuss this first perspective more fully.

The initial perspective women have when considering an abortion, or any moral question, is with caring for the self (Gilligan, 1982). "The concern is pragmatic and the issue is survival. The woman focuses on taking care of herself because she feels that she is all alone" (p. 75). In this first perspective, women will consider primarily their own desires, wants, and needs. So when it comes to abortion, women may express their lack of desire to become a mother and all of the responsibilities that come with that role. They may be young and hope to finish school, start college, explore life, relationships, perhaps travel—in any case, they do not want to be saddled with the overwhelming duties of motherhood. Moreover, having a baby in socially and economically undesirable circumstances can pose problems for women. For instance, young women (and their children) may become socially isolated and economically trapped if they have a baby as a teenager and the father is not willing or able to be supportive. On the other hand, some women find that the idea of having a baby could reduce their sense of isolation, loneliness, and meaninglessness. The child could provide connection and offer purpose in life. The dichotomies of selfishness/responsibility and self/other should be apparent here: the woman is concerned for her own well-being but faces responsibility to others in her network of relationships and perhaps to her unborn child, depending on her views of pregnancy. This is obviously an enormous adult moral decision-making process. And in the first perspective one may conclude that abortion is the best way to care for oneself, to start over and open up new possibilities, freed from all the burdens of motherhood.

THE SECOND PERSPECTIVE

The transition from first to second perspectives is marked by a judgment of the first perspective as being overly selfish as it focuses primarily (perhaps solely) on caring for oneself (Gilligan, 1982). "The criticism signals a new understanding of the connection between self and others which is articulated by the concept of responsibility" (p. 74). The second perspective is characterized by a turn toward being concerned primarily (though not always) with the child, who is dependent upon the mother for survival. This is a move from self-focus to a more conventional female voice—the voice of responsibility to care for others. In this second perspective, women are embracing the societal values of the male-dominated culture. As such, there is an increased concern about being accepted by others. Acceptance requires conformity, so the moral deliberation refocuses on what one has been told to do, and the identity one has been given as a female.

Gilligan's point is not just to note differences between men and women but to recognize that men's perspectives have typically been normalized. This means that the male perspective has been considered the one, real, and correct perspective—simply "the way it is." And when men have the power in society, any and all other perspectives become suppressed and rejected. This is how women's voices fail to be heard; how their perspectives fail to "exist." When women, who are more concerned with relationships than rules, and who mature not to some notion of individualistic autonomy but to a sense of social connection, attempt to participate in moral dialogue, or even make decisions about their own lives, their perspectives have been rejected, marginalized, and labeled deficient. So when women, in the second perspective, take on their given female role, it is to deny the self, to accept the male moral standards of reasoning, as well as the conclusions based on that reasoning. These state that a woman's value is not her own but only in her ability to do for others. One caveat related to this second perspective is that Gilligan (2012) remarks that men may also make moral judgments based on a care orientation; however, due to societal constraints about gender roles, it can be difficult for men to acknowledge that their moral judgments are also deeply impacted by their responsiveness in relationships.

In the abortion dilemma, the second perspective will often result in decisions not to have an abortion, out of a sense of responsibility to others and a denial of the needs of the self. That said, the complex relationships that surround the abortion dilemma may also lead a woman in the second perspective to have an abortion—possibly one that she does not want. Gilligan (1982) discusses a situation where a woman who is having sex with a man who is married and has children becomes pregnant and wants to keep the baby. The woman, considering the needs of others, felt a responsibility to her lover (who wanted the abortion), as well as to his wife and children—their lives potentially becoming disrupted by the birth of her child. Her choice, in this case, was to go along with what her lover wanted and to set circumstances such that the relationship with him would continue as it had for some time. However, making the decision to have an abortion out of pleasing others led to resentment, which undermined the very relationship she hoped to preserve.

THE THIRD PERSPECTIVE

The transition from the second to the third perspective is marked by a move from being good (or being perceived as good) to finding truth (Gilligan, 1982). The *truth* in this perspective has to do with the woman's inner judgment—with finding her own voice. There is tension between the needs of the self and the needs of the other (or others) in her moral deliberation, her process. The third perspective involves a re-emergence of the concept of selfishness—the question of her own needs resurfaces, but with a new, more developed orientation. Not merely an either/or, the self/other tension begins to transcend the dichotomy that previously had her thinking only of the needs of herself, or only the needs of others. How can she be responsible to and for herself while at the same time expressing her genuine concern for those she cares for? Answering this question, she will not be so concerned with how she is judged by others but by the real (or *true*) intentions she has and the consequences her choices will have for both herself and for others. In the abortion case example, Isabelle will now consider her own needs, perhaps to avoid becoming severely disabled and unable to care for her first child. She will also consider, in her truth seeking and consequence-finding, to consider giving birth to her second child in spite of her own health risks. But what impact would having that child have on her first child, her husband, and herself, especially if she can no longer care for any of them because she is permanently and severely disabled? Would it be right to "sacrifice" three people's well-being for her own moral belief (as a Catholic) that abortion is wrong? This third perspective highlights not only these elements but also the woman's conscious, intentional, and honest participation in *her own* decision-making process. She is no longer merely a puppet of male-dominated perspectives, going along with what others would have her do, failing to take responsibility for herself, her family, and her choices. And she expresses an authentic feminine moral discernment by considering not just abstract principles but the real-world consequences of her actions on the actual people in her particular family and social context. Moreover, in doing so she is not merely performing a cost/benefit calculus; she is expressing her care and concern for others— her moral compass—in a practical and mature way.

ADOLESCENT GIRLS AND AUTHENTICITY

As Gilligan and colleagues (Brown & Gilligan, 1992, 1993; Brown et al., 1995) continued to develop their ideas about women and moral development, they studied girls on the edge of adolescence through adulthood and discovered progressive development in their strengths and resilience (e.g., growing independence from external authority, and a broadening of their own viewpoints, taking into account diverse ideas and feelings). They also noted a loss of voice as these same study participants entered adolescence. Gilligan continued to use her narrative methods, considered by some scholars as less than rigorous, but reflecting Gilligan's intentions of encouraging her study participants to "take the lead" in identifying real-life moral situations that they faced in their struggle to find an authentic voice and to be taken seriously. Finally, Gilligan and colleagues examined pivotal relationships between girls and women that help girls navigate adolescence, resist attempts by society and self to bury their voices, author their own stories, and thereby strengthen their own authority and sense of responsibility in taking action to address their moral concerns (Gilligan, 2013; Taylor, Gilligan, & Sullivan, 1997).

CRITIQUE OF COGNITIVE AND MORAL DEVELOPMENT THEORIES

What Do These Theories Say About Human Behavior?

In order to closely examine what cognitive and moral development theories say to us about human behavior, we will want to return to our two key dimensions of theory: the subjective–objective dimension; and the stability–radical change dimension. Piaget conducted detailed observations of his own and other children, and Kohlberg conducted numerous studies that supported the notion of a tangible, structured, and objective quality to cognitive and moral development (e.g., Piaget described schemas as growing understandings and modifications children make over time in their cognitive development; Kohlberg referred to an invariant sequence of moral development that all children move through as they grow into adulthood). Each scholar identified stages in their corresponding theories that reflected progressive development linked to a child's age, intelligence, and educational level and their interactions with the larger environment. Both struck a kind of balance between stability and radical change in that as children develop both cognitively and morally, they are understood to integrate and further differentiate concepts within earlier stages of development, and they continue to move forward in their cognitive and moral growth (Kohlberg, 1969; Piaget, 1960).

It is Gilligan whose theory appears to embrace greater subjectivity. For example, Gilligan broke new ground in moral development research by actually asking study participants to share their real-world stories of difficult ethical decisions. Gilligan was also reluctant to refer to "distinct stages" in her moral development theory and instead described three different moral perspectives that women (and men) may exhibit in an ethic of care. Further, as Gilligan continued to develop her scholarly ideas, she studied the silencing of authentic voices of adolescent girls that occurs within American society and she examined how these girls navigate and grow even within this troubling context (Brown & Gilligan, 1992, 1993; Gilligan, 1991; Brown et al., 1995).

How Do These Theories Address Growth and Change?

The theories that Piaget, Kohlberg, and Gilligan put forth describe individual cognitive and moral growth that occurs for children as they move into adulthood. Kohlberg examined how children move from one stage to the next (with some transitions and overlaps between stages) and found that when they are challenged by others to consider concepts that are similar, but yet different enough from their current stage of development (e.g., from Stage Three to Four) children are able to increase their moral thinking and judgment to one level higher (Kohlberg, 1969; Rest, 1968; Rest et al., 1979). Further, Power, Higgins, and Kohlberg (1989) discussed their creation of "just communities" in schools. They discovered that upward stage change was possible and lasting when students and teachers alike engaged in moral dilemmas that challenged them. By exposing students to multiple viewpoints and different stages of reasoning, teachers and overall school communities provided fertile ground for growth in individual moral reasoning and in social cooperation.

Gilligan, less wedded to a sequence of growth representing distinct stages, discussed "perspectives" that women (and men) develop as they learn to balance care of self with care for others. She and her colleagues also studied girls on the edge of adolescence through adulthood and discovered that girls face a crisis in adolescence regarding connections with others and in which they have to struggle with excluding themselves or being excluded by others (i.e., by being a good woman versus being selfish). Their research points to a loss of voice that girls experience as they enter adolescence and that the relationships between girls and women is particularly pivotal in helping them navigate and grow during this critical juncture (Brown & Gilligan, 1992, 1993; Gilligan, 1991). At the same time that adolescent girls describe a loss of voice, a struggle to face conflict, and need to be taken seriously, adolescent girls also demonstrate developmental progression in that they become less dependent on external authorities, less locked into their own viewpoint and more aware of differences between societal and cultural groups, and more differentiated from others in their thoughts and feelings (see Belenky, Clinch, Goldberger, & Tarule, 1986/1997). Finally, Brown, Tappan, and Gilligan (1995) discuss an educational intervention in which adolescent girls are given opportunities to share their own stories about real-life moral experiences. Through the use of a narrative approach (e.g., journaling, the development of skits and video), these students can author their own stories, thereby strengthening their own authority, self-reflective skills, and responsibility in taking action to address their moral concerns.

How Holistic Are These Theories?

Holistic thinking is a hallmark of cognitive and moral development theories, and there are several potential dichotomies that have been averted in the conceptual thinking represented by these theorists (e.g., person and environment, emotion and cognition, and care of self and care of others). Although our key theorists discuss *individual* cognitive and moral growth and development, all acknowledge the important role that our social *environments* (e.g., the impact of family, peer, and school relationships) play in shaping this development. In particular, Gilligan's narrative approach to moral development serves as a means for participants to author and engage in social interactions with others in the larger environment regarding their personal stories of facing moral situations. Gilligan also discusses the importance of schools in providing adolescent girls opportunities for interacting with female teachers and other female leaders in developing their authentic self, which includes balancing care of oneself with care for others.

Kohlberg's justice communities also support individual moral development within the context of school communities. Individual development occurs through ongoing discussions with teachers and peers that challenge and encourage student growth in moral reasoning. These theories and their practices are consistent with social work's person-in-environment approach to practice. Even among theorists who reflect newer or persistent trends in moral development that emphasize neuroscience and genetic influences (e.g., an infant moral core and early capacities for empathy), scholars are aware and acknowledge the importance of parents/caregivers in nurturing the moral development of a young child.

Although Kohlberg (and Piaget) are criticized and, at times, misunderstood for their primary emphasis on cognition and moral reasoning in their theories, they do acknowledge the role emotions play in moral development (Kohlberg, 1969). Kohlberg viewed cognitive reasoning as in the driver's seat of moral development; he did not ignore emotions but thought that feelings were known and expressed through thoughts. For Kohlberg, cognition and affect are just different perspectives on the same mental events. It should be noted that Kohlberg, unlike other moral theorists (Rest, 1979), did not try to find out whether children were sensitive enough to see a moral problem, nor did he assess study participants' empathy related to moral situations. A few overarching criticisms of our moral development theorists are worth describing in this section of our critique. First, our moral development theorists admit that there are long-standing difficulties within the field in describing or assessing the relationship between moral judgment and action (Arnold, 2000). Kohlberg does attempt to bridge judgment and action through his just communities, in which students and teachers alike are supported to act on their moral judgments and decisions within the context of a school community. Gilligan viewed that the nurturing of adolescent girls' relationships with women could help girls to engage in public resistance to negative gender stereotypes that idealize women or encourage inauthentic relationships. Second, both Kohlberg and Gilligan focus on a particular type of moral concern—respectively, justice or care—and other theorists have been quick to point out the limitations of only addressing these two types of moral concerns (Graham et al., 2011). In fact, there are other moral concerns such as purity, loyalty, exemplary moral character, virtue, and a moral core in infancy that need to be addressed in order to develop a more holistic picture of moral growth and development.

How Consistent Are These Theories With Social Work Values and Ethics?

In this section, we will examine our theories for their attention to five core social work values (i.e., service, social justice, dignity and worth of each person, the importance of relationships, and competence). *First*, Kohlberg and Gilligan are not only researchers, but they created real-world opportunities for children and adolescents to sharpen their moral reasoning skills. For example, Kohlberg and colleagues demonstrated a commitment to teacher training and curriculum development in their efforts to create just communities within school settings (Higgins, 1995). Gilligan developed a narrative approach for helping adolescent girls create skits or plays that are performed for the public and that enact their real-world moral dilemmas and decisions (Brown et al., 1995). These efforts reflect a value of serving their communities by providing services and/or interventions within schools and other community-based contexts to support ongoing moral growth.

Second, Kohlberg maintained that social justice, which he defined as doing no harm and treating people with fairness, is the central universal and organizing principle of his moral development theory. However, Kohlberg's theory is based exclusively on studies with White middle- and upper-class, male participants and consequently, scholars have engaged in substantial critique of the limits of his moral development theory as applied to other diverse groups (e.g., indigenous people; African American children in urban, low-income neighborhoods; and women) (Gilligan, 1982; Kohlberg, 1969; Snarey, 1995). Kohlberg believed that these diverse groups do progress through his theoretical stages to develop moral reasoning, but often at a slower rate. By centering White, male, and middle- to upper-class youth in the development of his theory, his theory views people from racial, ethnic, class, or gender diversity as often morally deprived. Kohlberg's theory privileges White male perspectives and in doing so runs counter to our *third* featured social work value of the dignity and worth of *all people.*

Fourth, Piaget, Kohlberg, and Gilligan do acknowledge the importance of family, peer, and other social relationships in influencing moral growth and development. However, it is Gilligan who places an ethic of care and our responsiveness to others in relationships as her central theoretical principle, which guides moral growth and development. In her theory, social workers will need to become competent, our *fifth* value, in self-reflective, relationship building, and group work skills so as to assist youth and adults in balancing their care of self with caring for others. It is in this final section that we spotlight a case that features the moral tensions between care of self and care of others.

ETHICS SPOTLIGHT
HIGHER EDUCATION AND YULI'S FAMILY

Every semester and especially in my graduate social work classroom, women (and men) describe struggles in caring for their families and caring for themselves by pursuing their goals to obtain a higher education degree. Last year, one of my students was a first-generation Latina college student, Yuli, who was married and had two young children. In the process of discussing the intersection of gender and race related to ethical decision-making, Yuli described how her husband, Marcelo, also Latino, was "only willing to *let me* go to college if I continued to care for our two small children and home in the same way that I had done before starting college." Yuli was willing to acquiesce to Marcelo's demands that she not shirk her family-based responsibilities. However, many of the women in my class expressed shock and dismay at Marcelo's demanding and chauvinistic behavior. Yuli also remarked that her husband was not willing to support her by helping more around the house and with the care of children. Yuli further confided that she was worried about their relationship because Marcelo seemed unwilling to adjust to or support her strong commitment and drive to reach her dream of obtaining a graduate social work degree.

(1) Describe in everyday language what you think is going on in this situation.

(2) How does Yuli define caring for herself?

(3) From Yuli's viewpoint, how does her self-care conflict with her family obligations (care of others)?

(4) How does her husband, Marcelo, see their situation? How do many women in the class view Yuli's situation?

(5) As you reflect on this case example, consider all possible outcomes. What do you think is likely to occur in this situation, and why? Base your answer in Gilligan's ideas about the tensions between care of self and care for others.

What Sources of Knowledge Do These Theories Support?

In this section, we will engage in an in-depth exploration of the empirical evidence that guides or supports the moral development theories of Piaget, Kohlberg, and Gilligan. We will also address the importance these theories place on the expertise of clients and their lived experiences and on your expertise as a social worker.

Piaget examined a child's mind on its own terms and in doing so had a major role in transforming the study of cognitive and moral development. He moved beyond, for example, counting the number of right answers that children obtain on an intelligence test (see Piaget, 1928) and was instead able to identify maturational differences in children's cognitive development that were impacted by their interactions with the environment (Kohlberg, 1969). Piaget also introduced methods for studying moral judgment by presenting and discussing stories with children as his research subjects. These children helped Piaget understand their unique viewpoints. And, although Piaget's research methods lacked systematic rigor (e.g., he studied his own and other children), Piaget pointed researchers to a key empirical test of cognitive development theory—namely, to look at age-related changes that mark a child's growth and development. His research was novel in that he attempted to explore cognitive and moral growth and development from young research participants' perspectives and attempted to honor their lived experiences. This was a dramatically different approach from the behaviorists of Piaget's time, who focused only on the researchers' skills in observing behavior that occurred within the social environment (Rest, 1979).

Kohlberg began by replicating Piaget's work, but he used a new research method for assessing moral judgment that involved presenting boys (ages 10–16) with hypothetical moral dilemmas and interviewing them about what they thought should be done and why. Kohlberg used a longitudinal approach and followed his study participants for 30 years—beginning with his 1958 dissertation study and ending in 1987 with the publication of his methods for assessing moral judgment as developed across the lifespan (Higgins, 1995). Kohlberg's findings provided the foundation for his moral development theory, had a profound effect on the field, and although there are new trends in moral development theory, his ideas continue to have influence today. As might be expected, Kohlberg's ideas stimulated much critical debate. Here are some key points from the critics.

First, Kohlberg's research methods were novel in that they involved discussing hypothetical moral dilemmas with study participants and taking into account their perspectives and beliefs; however, this made it hard to develop a standardized way to measure his theory of moral judgment. It was also difficult to use his methods in discussing moral reasoning with young children, and some criticized him for not using real-world dilemmas in the development of his six-stage theory (Giammarco, 2016; Gilligan & Belenky, 1980; Rest, 1979).

Second, when Kohlberg initially proposed his theory, he thought his highest levels of moral development (Stages Five and Six) would be most typically reached in late adolescence or early adulthood. Scholars have found that it is rare for participants to display five- or six-stage reasoning—even among those with advanced moral or theological training (Giammarco, 2016). And, it is likely that there is a much more gradual progression in moral reasoning, with stops and starts in growth, rather than linear and discrete stages.

Third, Kohlberg's (1958) study used only White male participants, thereby limiting the generalizability of his theory to women and to other diverse populations. Gilligan (1982), as one of Kohlberg's greatest critics, argued that Kohlberg's theory was entirely centered on an individualistic, detached, justice-focused approach to moral reasoning that contrasted with women's care orientation in taking into account their relationships with others as they make moral judgments. Scholars continue to debate whether or not Kohlberg's stages are universal and applicable to all forms of human diversity; Gilligan's critique of Kohlberg remains valid in that his theory does not represent the full range of moral concerns (e.g., the role of caring and empathy, or virtuous character) (Arnold, 2000). Kohlberg responded to these criticisms by later describing his assessment as a limited measure of justice reasoning rather than reflecting an overarching theory of moral maturity (Kohlberg, 1984).

In summary, both Piaget and Kohlberg valued the expertise and perspectives of their research participants; and as noted in the overview, Kohlberg also pursued the development of moral education in public schools believing that students could strengthen their moral reasoning and judgment. In this way, he drew upon the expertise of teachers and others as guides for students in challenging them to think critically for themselves. Gilligan's work is perhaps the most sensitive to the experiences, responsibilities in relationships, and narratives that her research subjects shared about how they make moral judgments when faced with difficult decisions. By eliciting participants' real-world stories to develop her "ethic of care" orientation to moral development, Gilligan took on the role of a practitioner–scholar and she followed her study participants' lead in understanding their moral judgments and in developing her theory.

APPLICATION OF COGNITIVE AND MORAL DEVELOPMENT THEORIES TO SOCIAL WORK PRACTICE

This chapter, like many of the preceding chapters, starts with a brief examination of social work's intellectual history with its deep roots in both theology and social science traditions. These two disparate traditions or paradigms continue to have relevance not only as a part of our history but also in current practice. Each paradigm provides an array of explanations for the human condition, and both have continued to compete for social workers' attention. The emergence of the social sciences occurred in the late 1800s, challenging the primacy of theological traditions and at the same time that social work positioned itself to move into the 20th century as one of the emerging professions. The focus began shifting from the imposition of religious values as a leading force in working with various marginalized people in society toward the implementation of "scientific principles" that would allow for a more comprehensive view based not on morality but professional expertise as the rationale for practice. For example, in the mid-1800s, workers in the Association for Improving the Conditions of the Poor (AICP) described their helping relationships as "moral character development," a less than veiled understanding of their intention to make the poor behave in ways more acceptable to wealthier elements in society, which included the AICP's "friendly visitors." Both the processes and the outcomes were established by the friendly visitors prior to even meeting with their clients. Success meant that the poor would be "better off" if they behaved more like the visitors—most of whom were upper-middle-class women.

With the assent of the social sciences as a rival explanation for human behavior, social work shifted its attention and included this new knowledge as the basis for its expanded and more complex understanding of human beings within their environments. This also opened the door for social work to join with other groups from emerging professions, including business, law, dentistry, bureaucracy, medicine, political leadership and civil service. Social work's expanded emphasis focused on concepts of rationality, objectivity, and skills rather than moral reeducation as a means to create change.

Tensions created by these two paradigms remain with us today. On a daily basis, social workers are faced with decisions where tensions emerge between the application of scientific principles or theologically derived concepts in their work with clients. Each paradigm provides potentially useful information. For example, science provides useful alternatives to examine what *can* work in the situation but cannot answer our questions related to *should* we do something. Theology, on the other hand, articulates how individuals *should* live in the world, but it may be less useful in identifying complex environmental issues that create both opportunities and barriers to people behaving the way they "should."

Cognitive and moral developmental theories provide a range of perspectives for helping us to understand the complex interactions between individuals and their environments. At the beginning of the chapter we saw how Alex and his social worker were doing an intricate dance trying to determine what he could do (his desire to live independently) with the worker's concern for his safety and dignity as he attempted to achieve this goal. Cognitive testing may help determine some aspects of Alex's capacity for thinking and decision-making, which would interact with the worker's stance about his moral right to exercise self-determination. Another example of this intricate dance between cognitive and moral capacities involves a social worker who is working with an 11-year-old female who has been referred because she is in her 10th week of pregnancy. At this point in time she has not told her parents or anyone else about her condition and is adamant that no one be told. In this instance, the worker would need to make an assessment of the 11-year-old girl's cognitive capacity for understanding the nature of her pregnancy and the consequences that would come depending upon the choices she pursues. It is also incumbent upon the worker to determine how to apply ethical principles with regard to her autonomy and privacy as they engage in the work. In addition, the worker must manage the impact of the girl's cognitive development (her understanding of what it means to be 11 years old and pregnant) as well as examining what ethical principles of privacy and self-determination mean in this context. In our daily practice, we are often faced with challenges that require us to understand cognitive functioning as it relates to moral development given that the people we work with (e.g., clients, colleagues, administrators, and community members) bring their own thinking and values into any dialogue in which we engage. Understanding how these processes interact is essential for engaging in effective practice.

Cognitive and moral development frameworks provide tools for helping us understand value-laden situations and arrive at strategies that reflect our own perspectives about what we believe we should do in response to those understandings. They also allow us to listen to how our clients think about their world and the meaning and importance they give to their understandings. In some ways, it is nearly impossible to "start where the client is" without understanding the pivotal roles played by cognitive and moral development theories.

Assumptions Connecting Cognitive and Moral Development to Social Work Practice

The following four assumptions undergird the use of cognitive and moral development theories in practice:

- Cognitive and moral development theories provide ways to incorporate the interactive effects of knowledge and values in practice. They do so by providing a clear understanding of how people think and the meaning they assign to events in their world.

- Understanding cognitive and moral development allows us to employ an interactive approach to track how our personal and professional views interact with those of our client systems (moral dialogue).

- Cognitive and moral development theories are applicable to all levels of practice (micro/macro), all fields of practice (health, mental health, child welfare, schools, and corrections), and shape our professional roles from clinical practice to policy analysis.

- Cognitive and moral growth and development can only be fully understood when placed in the context of individual human diversity (e.g., gender, race, culture, and sexual orientation). The tensions created by the larger social context within which practice occurs contribute to conflicting interests among clients, agencies, workers, and professional organizations. The combination of individual experiences of marginalization and larger societal barriers like institutionalized racism, sexism, homophobia, and xenophobia often interact, creating chasms between workers and their client systems regarding both their understanding and meaning of their respective experiences.

The remainder of the chapter will involve translating Kohlberg's and Gilligan's perspectives on moral development for use in social work practice. Specifically, we will apply the concepts of cognitive and moral development to the understanding of what we call "moral dialogue."

Application of Kohlberg's and Gilligan's Cognitive and Moral Development Theories

Table 13.3 represents a syntheses of the narrative discussions provided earlier in the chapter on Kohlberg's and Gilligan's theories. This table focuses on the role of gender in cognitive and moral development. Table 13.3 identifies five dimensions of Gilligan's and Kohlberg's perspectives related to gender and includes their assumptions, their focus, their characteristics, and problems as they relate to their application in practice.

TABLE 13.3 ■ Gender Differences: Gilligan and Kohlberg	
Responsibilities/Caring (female)	**Rights/Justice (male)**
Assumptions	**Assumptions**
1. Awareness of psychological and social intervention of human behavior 2. Individual focus 3. All decisions are based on "relationship" (closeness)	1. Highest stage of ethical decision-making is application of broad moral principles 2. Broader social rules 3. Based on an "objective" assessment and application of rules (distance)
Focus	**Focus**
Caring, responsibility, nurturance aimed at meeting people's needs	Reasoning based on moral principles emphasizing justice, equality, individual rights
Characteristics	**Characteristics**
1. Moral reasoning based on a web of complex relationships (contextual) 2. Focus on compassion 3. Actual consequences 4. Needs 5. Mercy	1. Individual rights and use of rules and principles 2. Focus is on reasoning 3. Abstract principles 4. Fairness 5. Justice
Problems	**Problems**
1. Doing for others may limit individual autonomy 2. Case by case decisions may lead to unfairness	1. Individual freedoms may cause problems for others 2. Short-term harm to individuals to create long-term goals

First, in our discussion we are focusing on only one aspect of diversity in relationship to cognitive and moral development, namely gender. Remember that there are numerous other essential elements that impact cognitive and moral development including race, culture, sexual orientation, and age to name just a few. Each of these lenses are legitimate perspectives for examining the usefulness of any theory addressing cognitive and moral development. Choosing gender related to Kohlberg's and Gilligan's theories is simply a vehicle to illustrate how any of the above-listed elements could be used in your practice.

Second, the use of any schematic, like Table 13.3, requires placing ideas in categories, for example, male/female, which creates a binary view suggesting they are mutually exclusive. In fact, both Gilligan and Kohlberg acknowledged the reality that not all men, nor all women think within the male/female perspectives. For most people, it is more useful to think of the influence of gender as existing on a continuum to avoid inaccurately presuming that gender is the sole determinant of cognitive and moral development.

Third, our work nearly always involves fundamental value conflicts related to the application of our obligations to clients. For example, whether to protect a person's privacy or limit individual freedom is a common ethical dilemma that requires the application of cognitive and moral theory to analyze the situation. If we apply Kohlberg's characteristics emphasizing individual rights, the use of rules and principles focused on reasoning, and using fairness as a way to achieve social justice, we will develop a plan that maximizes social justice. If we apply Gilligan's understanding of moral development, we would emphasize the influence of relationships in the person's social context, focus on compassion, emphasizing mercy and attempting to meet people's needs (caring rather than social justice). Each approach is justifiable; however, each approach leads to very different consequences for our work with clients and must be measured within the context of our professional Code of Ethics (National Association of Social Workers [NASW], 2017). What these tools provide is not a resolution to the issues that you face as a practitioner, but instead ways to examine the process that you apply as you think through these difficult situations. The following case example is an opportunity to use these tools and examine their limitations.

This case example is provided to illustrate the application of some of the more abstract and complex theoretical ideas (e.g., justice and caring orientations as described by Kohlberg and Gilligan) presented in this chapter. This case situation involves the work being done by a social worker in an afterschool program in a large Midwestern city.

CASE EXAMPLE
RUDY'S MUSIC LESSONS

Bob Harkness is working in an afterschool program for "at risk kids" in a middle school populated by low-income families whose children have both academic and social challenges in their classrooms. Bob has been working with Tatyana Gomez, a young mother of three children, the eldest of whom is 12-year-old Rodolfo (Rudy). Rudy's younger sisters are in primary school but not in the same building with their brother. Rudy came to Bob's attention because he had gotten into some altercations with classmates, both in class and in the halls of the school. Rudy is a quiet, sensitive boy who is being picked on by some of his classmates who called him "gay." Rudy retaliated on several occasions. Bob found Rudy to be intelligent, reflective, and articulate. He was able to talk about both his relationships to classmates and his own internal dialogue. He reluctantly shared that he was deeply interested in music, which opened him up to name-calling by his peers.

Bob met with Rudy's mom on a regular basis to map strategies to try to help Rudy find alternative ways to navigate this intense situation. They spent nearly a month and a half attempting to find both public and private resources that might be used to support Rudy's interest in music. The situation was especially difficult given that the family was on Temporary Assistance for Needy Families (TANF), which provided only very basic resources for this family. One afternoon, Tatyana came bounding into Bob's office with a broad smile, announcing that she had some really good news. She had been approached by a woman who needed a person to do her laundry and this additional income would allow her to pay for Rudy's music lessons. They completed the applications, and Tatyana left Bob's office to tell Rudy about this great opportunity. After she left, Bob's colleague, Angela, who had helped him search for resources dropped in unexpectedly. Since she had assisted him and knew the family's situation he shared the good news about Rudy's music lessons. As Bob talked with his colleague, he began to experience some uneasiness about what had just happened in his interactions with Tatyana.

The following questions began to emerge. First, now that he knew that Tatyana had additional income, what should he do with that information? If he kept this private and it later emerged that Tatyana was now over the TANF limit in terms of the money she was earning, could she be charged with fraud and receive financial penalties that would hurt the whole family? Second, if he shared the information with his supervisor, she might require that he report this to the agency administering her TANF benefits, in which case, they would lower her payments to offset the

new income and Rudy and his family would be harmed. In addition, he was concerned about the damage this might create to the positive working relationship he had with the family. Finally, if he kept the information private, might he lose his job?

A second group of questions need to be addressed. First, how does Bob's own definition of these issues inform his actions about the best way to proceed in this situation? For example, if he believes that it is not fair that Tatyana receives so little help that she can hardly feed and clothe her family let alone enhance their lives, how should Bob proceed (Kohlberg's justice orientation)? Second, he also believes that he has worked very hard to develop a caring relationship with this family. Should that be protected at all costs (Gilligan's caring orientation)?

Now, imagine yourself as Bob's supervisor. He comes to you, shares all of the above information, and asks you how he should answer the preceding questions related to this case example. How would your position as a supervisor in the agency impact how you frame the moral questions and define both the appropriate processes and outcomes? Use ideas from both Kohlberg's and Gilligan's moral development theories to inform your responses to these questions.

Summary of Cognitive and Moral Development Theories

Piaget argued that cognitive development means more than simply adding new knowledge on top of existing knowledge. He viewed children, ages 7 to 11, as moving from experiential learning relying on the use of inductive logical reasoning (i.e., moving from a specific example to a more general principle) to more abstract reasoning. Adolescents and adults develop the capacity to think about social, political, moral, and philosophical issues that require abstract thinking and can use deductive reasoning (e.g., moving from general to specific levels).

The work of Piaget and Kohlberg demonstrates how cognitive growth, reflected in the development of abstract reasoning, is linked to moral development. The fundamental point is that both cognitive and moral development reflect internalized ways of thinking that give meaning to concepts like mother, son, doctor, social worker, and a thousand other labels we use on a daily basis. Our meanings are shaped by the larger social context in which we live, and social norms (values) inform us about how we should or should not behave in relation to others in our environment.

Moral Dialogue

The last section of this chapter introduces the concept of moral dialogue as a way to operationalize elements of cognitive (Piaget) and moral (Kohlberg and Gilligan) theories in relationship to ethical decision-making in social work practice. Moral dialogue shares some common characteristics with cognitive and moral development including the following:

- All three view growth and development built on the notion that processes emerge over time in predictable and measurable stages.

- All three view development as a product of interactional processes between people and their environments.

- All three acknowledge the importance of how we think and the role of values in developing our understanding of events.

Moral dialogue is a concept that first appeared in the social work literature in 2003 based on the work of Spano and Koenig. Its focus was specifically on developing a bridge between broad value statements in the NASW Code of Ethics and the concrete application of the Code to specific interactions among clients and their environments. They defined moral dialogue as "including the ongoing interactions about what should or should not be done among workers and other relevant actors in the ethical decision-making process" (Spano & Koenig, 2003, p. 98). They conceived each practice context as having four interacting and often conflicting and competing systems: clients, workers, agencies, and the profession. These potentially incompatible worldviews frequently left workers with little guidance about how to traverse conflicts presented in nearly all practice situations. Finally, they emphasized that the relationship between the client and worker needed to be seen as a **fiduciary relationship**, requiring professionals to act in the best interest of their clients. They used five fundamental aspects essential to social work practice: awareness, reflection, willingness to engage in dialogue, investment in relationships with clients and others in their environments, and adequate cognitive and verbal skills.

Table 13.4 titled, "Tracking the Ethical Decision-Making Process," provides a tool social workers can use to ask clients questions that solicit their perspectives on dilemmas. This tool also includes self-reflective questions that workers can ask themselves as a means for guiding awareness, self-reflection, and critical thinking as they play out in the client/worker relationship. In essence, this tool or set of questions tracks the thinking, at both the conceptual and moral levels in a given situation, from a transactional standpoint simultaneously looking at both clients' perspectives and workers' perspectives.

TABLE 13.4 ■ Tracking the Ethical Decision-Making Process	
Client Perspective	**Worker Perspective**
1. What are you struggling with?	1. As I listen to what the client is struggling with, what am I reacting to and why?
I am frustrated because they want to send my son to a nursing home, and I can care for him better in my home.	She has her own health challenges, and I wonder if she can realistically care for her son.

Client Perspective	Worker Perspective
2. What hard choices are you facing?	**2. What are the similarities and differences between the way I see the hard choices and the way the client sees them?**
My Catholic faith says I have a duty to care for my children. I know them and they know and trust me. He will be less scared if he knows he is with me.	I believe relationships are important. The woman defines herself as the best caregiver for her son. My concern is that she will place his needs first and her health will decline.
3. Does anyone else need to be involved in the decision-making process? Who? How? When?	**3. Do I think anyone needs to be involved in the decision-making process? Who? How? When?**
I have a group of women from my church who will help prepare some meals for us. My neighbor said he would watch him while I go to church.	Having some aid for meal preparation could be helpful, but how reliable are these women given their ages (77–89)? Can the neighbor actually care, on a regular basis, for her son given his current needs? How can she keep up her church activities, (e.g., attend mass, altar society, and meal preparation for funerals)? Finally, how can she attend to her own medical needs?
	How is my perspective different than the client's perspective? If there are multiple perspectives, am I drawn to a particular person's perspective? Why?
	I have serious concerns about her ability to care for him on a permanent basis. Her walking is impaired by her arthritis and bad shoulders, and her physical conditions don't allow her to lift him or protect herself if he gets agitated.
4. Given the choice, what decision best fits for you?	**4. As you hear the client say what is best for him or her, does it reflect values and beliefs different or similar to your own?**
I am determined to take my son home with me because I am his mother and taking care of my children is who I am.	Her definition of what is best concerns me because she may be placing her own life at risk, but I can see how this perspective fits with her definition of herself as a caregiver and therefore is congruent with her role as a woman.
	Do I feel the need to challenge or support the client's direction based on my beliefs?
	I feel it is important to question the mother about balancing her needs with those of her son. Exploring what possible resources exist in her environment could help her and ease my conscience about whether this will harm her.
5. Given the choices, what course of action best meets your needs?	**5. Does the client's definition of the appropriate balance between her or his needs and those of other fit with or challenge my own beliefs about balancing my needs with those of people closest to me?**

(Continued)

TABLE 13.4 ■ (Continued)

Client Perspective	Worker Perspective
I think my needs can best be met by caring for my son at home.	The mother's way of balancing her needs and those of her son challenges my perspective on caring for myself. I believe that many women care for others because they are expected to do so. However, some women want companionship and so this is why they provide caregiving. What I do know is that the outcomes are unpredictable either way, so I must protect their right to choose either way.
6. Based on what you believe is right and wrong, how does this course of action fit for you?	**6. Do my beliefs about right and wrong differ from the client's beliefs of right and wrong? Do I feel a need to challenge the beliefs expressed by the client and/or the course of action the client is taking?**
Caring for my son is what I should do as a mother and a Catholic woman. My church says I should care for those less fortunate, especially in my family.	In some ways, I believe that caregiving is often unequally assigned to women, who are socialized to surrender their own needs to tend to the needs of others. I am unclear how "free" most women feel to do caregiving even when they know their own needs are being sacrificed.
7. What are the consequences of your decision?	**7. Now that the decision is made, what do I think about the outcomes as reported by the client? Do I agree with the client's report about outcomes? How will these differences or similarities affect our future work together?**
People were right about how hard it would be for me to take care of my son. Some of the people in my life got mad because I could not do things that I had been doing for them. I have been with my son for his medical appointments and feel more comfortable about how to take care of him. I have also met some really nice folks at the Alzheimer's support group and that helps.	His mother had some struggles in the beginning before we connected her to community resources, but she seems to be relieved and, for the most part, at peace with her decision. I remain conflicted about the social norms that expect women to do caregiving just because they are women, but I am able to see that this is a process and respecting women's rights to choose confers dignity and respect to them.

Source: Spano, R., & Koenig, T. L. (2003). Moral dialogue: A worker-client interactional model. *Social Thought, 22,* 91–104.

The following case example is used to illustrate application of moral dialogue in direct practice. Lillian is a 96-year-old White woman who is currently living in her own home, drives her own vehicle, but struggles with a number of physical ailments that make her daily activities more difficult. She is currently receiving visiting nursing services to deal with her arthritis and ligament damage in one shoulder and both knees. She has limited financial resources but does in fact own her two-bedroom home. Therefore, her resources are such that she exceeds the limits for any outside financial help. She has a 75-year-old widowed son, with no children, and who has been diagnosed with dementia. Doctors have determined that he needs nursing home care. He may be eligible for a Medicaid bed in a local nursing home, however, his mother insists on taking him home with her because she does not want him to be dependent on the "state." The staff is unanimous in their view that she should not take him home given her own health challenges. The staff social worker, Wilma, assigned to this situation is an experienced professional who brings a feminist perspective to her practice.

As we said earlier in our book, social work practice requires that as workers we are aware of and monitor the impact of our professional status and power on our work with clients. This is accomplished by reflecting on the interactions between ourselves and our clients. It is also essential to apply critical thinking skills in order to identify broader, structural barriers impacting our clients as well as shaping our own views of the situation.

If you read the left side of Table 13.4 from top to bottom, you will see a series of questions designed to help Lillian define what she is struggling with, and how she views what we call "hard choices." We often talk about "starting where the client is," and moral dialogue provides an opportunity for us to begin by hearing the client's definition and understanding of her challenges. Questions 1 and 2 focus on listening to Lillian's understanding of her situation and Wilma monitoring her own reactions to what is being said by Lillian to ensure that she is not imposing her views on her as the client. All too often professionals lose track of what clients are saying because they are preparing the next question based on their concerns about what the client had just shared. In this instance, Wilma's strong feminist belief that society takes advantage of women in relationship to caregiving could easily be imposed upon Lillian and unfairly impact her decision-making. The third question focuses on assessing the interactions between Lillian and her environments in order to determine both capacities and barriers to her goal. Her understanding of the resources and her willingness to engage resources are central to the success or failure of her plan to care for her son. The worker's responsibility is to join in the assessment process to clarify what could be potential barriers or gaps in Lillian's thinking, understanding that there are likely to be tensions between professionals and clients about the meaning given to their actions. In this instance, Wilma has some concerns about the long-term impacts this decision will have on Lillian's health. She will need to guard against allowing her own concerns to undercut Lillian's right to make her own decisions. Her challenge is to help Lillian plan and take as many contingencies into account as possible.

As a client articulates a plan that fits for her, questions 4 and 5, fundamental value conflicts about what should and should not be done, are likely to be laid on the table. Ideally, the worker helps the client think through the underlying values and beliefs driving her decision-making, and the worker's responsibility is to separate her own values and beliefs from those of the client. However, if there is a danger to Lillian or her son as a result of her definition of the situation, Wilma has a responsibility to balance Lillian's freedoms with the worker's responsibility for protection of human life. Question 6 asks the client to determine if the plan fits with what she believes to be the "right" thing to do and how authentically it reflects her understanding of the situation. Again, the worker's task is to reflect on her own beliefs and how they might intrude inappropriately in the client's plan especially if they challenge what she believes to be the right course of action. Question 7 shifts to evaluation of the interactions. Given that this entire framework is based on a process designed to clarify the impact of cognitive capacity and moral development, it is essential to track that process from beginning to end. We know that it is difficult, if not impossible, to predict human behavior; therefore, it becomes important to return to an evaluative process focused on what actually happened, how it fit with our understanding of what was done, and if our actions achieved the client's goals and what we hoped indeed would happen (consequential analysis).

CHAPTER SUMMARY

This chapter has explored cognitive and moral development theories as articulated by Piaget, Kohlberg, Rest, and Gilligan. In addition, we put forward a moral dialogue framework as a means for translating moral theory into social work practice.

The first section of the chapter examines Piaget's three-step process that moves the locus of control from the individual to the interactions between individuals and their social environments. His contribution was to create a model that tracked cognitive development from birth through adulthood. Kohlberg's contribution to moral development was to put forward the belief that we could not assess moral development without understanding the person's intentions and viewpoints. His research involved providing hypothetical questions for participants, all White males, who were asked how they would act in a hypothetical situation. What emerged was an underlying six-stage model of moral reasoning. The links between cognitive and moral reasoning were further developed by the work of James Rest, who expanded on Kohlberg's moral developmental theory.

Kohlberg's seminal work was harshly criticized by his peers who argued that his qualitative approach to theory development was inadequate because it did not allow for the rigorous quantification of participants' responses and, therefore, it could not be easily replicated. Another substantive challenge came from Carol Gilligan, who focused on the fact that participants were all White males and Kohlberg's ethical dilemmas were hypothetical rather than real events emerging from the participants' own lives. Her research demonstrated that women have a different understanding of moral structure, which she called perspectives that focus on "caring" rather than Kohlberg's principle of social justice. There continue to be questions about roles played by culture, race, and religion as they impact cognitive and moral development.

Finally, we examined the concept of moral dialogue developed by Spano and Koenig (2003), which attempts to connect cognitive and moral development to a framework of questions that guide a process whereby social workers can focus on cognitive and moral aspects of practice situations in order to manage their interactions with clients in ways that translate into our profession's Code of Ethics and as it relates to specific practice situations.

Key Terms (in order of appearance)

Cognitive development 377	Moral development 378	Moral development theory
Cognitive development theory	Moral development theory	(Kohlberg) 379
(Piaget) 377	(Piaget) 378	Just community 381

References

Arnold, M. L. (2000). Stage, sequence, and sequels: Changing conceptions of morality, Post-Kohlberg. *Educational Psychology Review, 12*(4), 365–383.

Belenky, M. F., Clincy, B. M., Goldberger, N. R., & Tarule, J. M. (1986/1997). *Women's ways of knowing: The development of self, voice and mind.* New York, NY: Basic Books.

Brown, L. M., & Gilligan, C. (1992). *Meeting at the crossroads: Women's psychology and girls' development.* Cambridge, MA: Harvard University Press.

Brown, L. M., & Gilligan, C. (1993). Meeting at the crossroads: Women's psychology and girls' development. *Feminism and Psychology, 3,* 11–35.

Brown, L. M., Tappan, M. B., & Gilligan, C. (1995). Listening to different voices. In W. M. Kurtines and J. L. Gewirtz, J. L. (Eds.), *Moral development: An introduction* (pp. 311–335). Boston, MA: Allyn & Bacon.

Brownell, C. (2013). Early development of prosocial behavior: Current perspectives. *Infancy, 18,* 1–9.

Carlo, G., & Randall, B. A. (2001). Are all prosocial behaviors equal? A socioecological developmental conception of prosocial behavior. In F. Columbus (Ed.), *Advances in Psychology Research, 2,* 151–176.

Colby, A., Kohlberg, L., Gibbs, J., & Lieberman, M. (1983). *A longitudinal study of moral judgment.* Chicago, IL: The University of Chicago Press.

Dewey, J. (1895/1964). What psychology can do for the teacher. In R. D. Archambault (Ed.), *John Dewey on Education: Selected Writings* (pp. 207–209). New York, NY: The Modern Library, Random House.

Emde, R. N., Biringen, Z., Clyman, R. B., Oppenheim, D. (1991). The moral self of infancy: Affective core and procedural knowledge. *Developmental Review, 11,* 251–270.

Giammarco, E. A. (2016). The measurement of individual differences in morality. *Personality and Individual Differences, 88,* 26–34.

Gilligan, C. (1977). In a different voice: Women's conceptions of self and morality. *Harvard Educational Review, 47,* 481–517.

Gilligan, C. (1982). *In a different voice: Psychological theory and women's development.* Cambridge, MA: Harvard University Press.

Gilligan, C. (1991). Joining the resistance: Psychology, politics, girls, and women. *Michigan Quarterly Review, 29,* 501–536.

Gilligan, C. (2013). *Joining the resistance.* Malden, MA: Polity Press.

Gilligan, C. (2012, April 23). *Carol Gilligan on women and moral development.* Big Think. YouTube video.

Gilligan, C., & Antonucci, J. (1988). Two moral orientations: Gender differences and similarities. *Merrill-Palmer Quarterly, 34,* 223–237.

Gilligan, C., & Belenky, M. (1980). A naturalistic study of abortion decisions. In R. Selman & R. Yando (Eds.), *New directions for child development, Clinical-developmental Psychology,* Vol. 7, San Francisco, CA: Jossey-Bass.

Graham, J., Nosek, B. A., Haidt, J., Iyer, R., Koleva, S., & Ditto, P. H. (2011). Mapping the moral domain. *Personality and Social Psychology, 2,* 366–385.

Haan, N., Aerts, E., & Cooper, B. (1985). *On moral grounds.* New York: New York University Press.

Haidt, J., & Kesebir, S. (2010). Morality. In S. T. Fiske, D. Gilbert, & G. Lindzey (Eds.), *Handbook of social psychology* (5th ed.; pp. 797–832). Hoboken, NJ: Wiley.

Hamlin, J. K. (2013). Moral judgments in preverbal infants and toddlers: Evidence for an innate moral core. *Current Directions in Psychological Science, 22,* 186–193.

Hardy, S., & Carlo, G. (2005). Moral identity: What is it, how does it develop, and is it linked to moral action? *Child Development Perspectives, 5,* 212–218.

Higgins, A. (1995). Educating for justice and community: Lawrence Kohlberg's vision of moral education. In W. M. Kurtines and J. L. Gewirtz, (Eds.), *Moral development: An introduction* (pp. 49–81). Boston, MA: Allyn & Bacon.

Hussey, D. L. (2016). Adolescents: Practice interventions. In *Encyclopedia of Social Work.* New York, NY: National Association of Social Workers and Oxford University Press.

Inhelder, B., & Piaget, J. (1958). *The growth of logical thinking.* New York: Basic Books.

Kant, I. (1785/1993). *Grounding for the metaphysics of morals* (3rd ed.). Translated by J. W. Ellington. Indianapolis, IN: Hackett.

Knight, G. P., & Carlo, G. (2012). Prosocial development among Mexican American youth. *Child Development Perspectives, 6,* 258–263.

Kochanska, G. (2002). Mutually responsive orientation between mothers and young children: A context for early development of conscience. *Current Directions in Psychological Science, 11,* 191–195.

Kohlberg, L. (1958). *The development of modes of moral thinking and choice in the years 10 to 16.* Unpublished doctoral dissertation. Chicago, IL: University of Chicago.

Kohlberg, L. (1969). Stage and sequence: The cognitive-developmental approach to socialization. In D. A. Goslin (Ed.), *Handbook of socialization theory and research* (pp. 347–480). Chicago, IL: Rand McNally and Company.

Kohlberg, L. (1971). From is to ought. In T. Mischel (Ed.), *Cognitive development and epistemology.* New York, NY: Academic Press.

Kohlberg, L. (1973). The claim to moral adequacy of a highest stage of moral development. *Journal of Philosophy, 70,* 630–646.

Kohlberg, L. (1976). Moral stages and moralization: The cognitive developmental approach. In T. Lickona (Ed.), *Moral development and behavior: Theory, research and social issues* (pp. 31–53). New York, NY: Holt, Rinehart & Winston.

Kohlberg, L. (1981). *Essays on moral development: Vol. I. The philosophy of moral development: Moral stages and the idea of justice.* San Francisco, CA: Harper & Row.

Kohlberg, L. (1984). *Essays on moral development: Vol. II. The psychology of moral development: The nature and validity of moral stages.* San Francisco, CA: Harper & Row.

Kohlberg, L., & Hersh, R. H. (1977). Moral development: A review of the theory. *Theory into Practice, 16*(2), 53–59.

Kohlberg, L., & Mayer, R. (1972). Development as the aim of education. *Harvard Educational Review, 42,* 449–496.

Laible, D., Eye, J., & Carlo, G. (2008). Dimensions of conscience in mid-adolescence: Links with social behavior, parenting and temperament. *Journal of Youth and Adolescence, 37,* 875–887.

Lapsley, D., & Carlo, G. (2014). Moral development at the crossroads: New trends and possible futures. *Developmental Psychology, 59*(1), 1–7.

Matsuba, M. K., & Walker, L. J. (2004). Extraordinary moral commitment: Young adults involved in social organization. *Journal of Personality, 72,* 413–436.

National Association of Social Workers (NASW). (2018). *The code of ethics.* Washington, DC: Author.

Piaget, J. (1928). *The child's conception of the world.* London, England: Routledge & Kegan Paul.

Piaget, J. (1932/1955). *The moral judgment of the child.* New York: Free Press.

Piaget, J. (1936). *Origins of intelligence in the child.* London, England: Routledge & Kegan Paul.

Piaget, J. (1960). Cognitive development in children. In R. Ripple & V. Rockcastle (Eds.), *Piaget rediscovered: A report on cognitive studies in curriculum development.* Ithaca, NY: Cornell University School of Education.

Power, P. C., Higgins, A., & Kohlberg, L. (1989). *Lawrence Kohlberg's approach to moral education: A study of three democractic high schools.* New York, NY: Columbia University Press.

Rest, J. R. (1968). *Developmental hierarchy in preference and comprehension of moral judgment.* Unpublished doctoral dissertation. Chicago, IL: University of Chicago.

Rest, J. R. (1979). *Development in judging moral issues.* Minneapolis: University of Minnesota Press.

Rest, J. R. (1986). *Moral development: Advances in research and theory.* New York, NY: Praeger Press.

Rest, J., Narvaez, D., Bebeau, M., & Thoma, S. (1999). A Neo-Kohlbergian approach: The DIT and schema theory. *Educational Psychology Review, 2*(4), 291–324.

Rest, J., Turiel, E., Kohlberg, L. (1979). Relations between level of moral judgment and preference and comprehension of the moral judgment of others. *Journal of Personality, 37,* 224–252.

Santrock, J. W. (1989). *Life-span development.* New York, NY: McGraw-Hill.

Snarey, J. (1995). In a communitarian voice: The sociological expansion of Kohlbergian theory, research and practice. In W. M. Kurtines and J. L. Gewirtz, (Eds.), *Moral development: An introduction* (pp. 109–133). Boston, MA: Allyn & Bacon.

Spano, R., & Koenig, T. L. (2003). Moral dialogue: A worker-client interactional model. *Social Thought, 22,* 91–104.

Taylor, J. M., Gilligan, C., & Sullivan, A. M. (1997). *Between voice and silence: Women, girls, race and relationship.* Boston, MA: Harvard University Press.

Warneken, F., & Tomasello, M. (2007). Helping and cooperation at 14 months of age. *Infancy, 11,* 271–294.

GLOSSARY

American Holocaust refers to the genocide committed by American Europeans against First Nations people. Scholars estimate that two-thirds to nearly 99% of all indigenous people in North America were destroyed between 1500 and 1900. (Chapter 8, p. 223)

Anthropocentric understands human beings as the most significant entity of the universe and that interpretations about the world should all be understood through the lens of human beings' values and experiences. (Chapter 7, p. 168)

Assistentialism involves the use of well-meaning professionals as instruments of control to keep people in their respective socioeconomic positions. (Chapter 4, p. 84)

Attachment theory examines the caregiver's emotional availability and response to the child's needs as a way of providing a "safe haven" for the child. (Chapter 5, p. 109)

Banking model of education involves the teacher filling the students with prefabricated information (e.g., facts, dates, and names), all devoid of any meaning it might have to a particular group. Education thus becomes an act of depositing in which the students are the depositories and the teacher is the depositor. (Chapter 4, p. 86)

Behaviorism/behavior theory are used as interchangeable concepts for the purposes of this chapter. This theory's early development began in the late 19th century with Watson, Pavlov, and Skinner; and then took a cognitive turn representing the beginning of three distinct generations of behavior therapies and/or models. Early behavior theory emphasized eliminating or reducing clients' problematic behaviors through respondent or classical conditioning. The first generation of behavior therapies still drew on core ideas of the original theory (e.g., classical and operant conditioning) but diverted from traditional behavior theory by emphasizing the mutual influence of the environment on an individual's behavior and cognitive processes. The second generation of researchers addressed cognitive processing and thinking difficulties such as overgeneralization and

irrational thinking as factors in the change process. Third-generation theorists are viewed as more controversial because they do not seek to eliminate or reduce clients' distress, but instead they encourage clients through acceptance and mindfulness-based strategies to acknowledge suffering or psychological discomfort as inevitable, not as obstacles to reaching personal goals. (Chapter 10, p. 285)

Birth trauma is the literal or metaphorical significance of the separation of self from the mother at birth. (Chapter 5, p. 114)

Cognition, as understood by Piaget, focuses on the structure or schema in which a person's mind intellectually develops and adapts to its environment and grows in its capacity for abstract thought and reasoning. Later additions developed by Albert Ellis, including rational emotive behavior therapy, addressed cognitive processing or thinking difficulties such as overgeneralizations, emotional reasoning, and irrational thinking. (Chapter 10, p. 288)

Cognitive development refers to the emergence, development, and maturation of thought processes such as reasoning, language, problem solving, and memory. Cognitive development is understood to occur optimally within the context of a nurturing socioemotional environment. (Chapter 13, p. 377)

Cognitive development theory (Piaget) delineated four stages that we all move through as we interact with our environments to develop our intelligence and knowledge. These four stages include (1) the sensory motor stage (birth to 2 years), in which infants know the world through their sensations and actions; the preoperational stage (ages 2 through 7 years), in which they begin to think symbolically using language and pictures to represent objects. They can be viewed as egocentric and think in very concrete terms; (3) the concrete operational stage (ages 7 through 11), children's thinking becomes more logical and organized and they use deductive reasoning;

and (4) the formal operational stage, where individuals are able to think about social, political, moral, and philosophical issues that require abstract thinking, such as reasoning from general principles to a specific example. (Chapter 13, p. 377)

Colonialism is defined as a "sustained series of events enacted by an invading power [viewed as superior] on another culture [viewed as inferior or different], which facilitates and perpetuates the development of a worldview" (Chenault, 2011, p. 20) or ideology that supports oppression and unjust social structures. (Chapter 8, p. 224)

Colonization is the ongoing process and maintenance of oppressing a group, culture, or nation and involves multiple layers of domination and exploitation to make sure that oppressive conditions (e.g., violence, abuse, dehumanization) stay in place. (Chapter 8, p. 224)

Countertransference is the same phenomenon as transference except that it refers to the professional attributing character traits and feelings of significant others to the client. Countertransference is a very common phenomenon, and Freud believed that this contributed to "blind spots" in the practitioner's own work with clients. He suggested that practitioners participate in their own analysis to enhance self-reflective capacities and address those "blind spots." (Chapter 5, p. 104)

Critical consciousness is a politically active form of critical thinking that avoids such pitfalls as group think, hasty generalizations, and irrational fanaticism. People can engage in a process to move from naïve consciousness to critical consciousness. (Chapter 4, p. 80)

Critical theories have their roots in Karl Marx, who viewed getting and keeping economic power as the motive behind all social and political activity (e.g., education, religion, and government). In the narrow sense, critical theory refers to several generations of German philosophers and theorists whose roots are in the Western European Marxist tradition and who developed theoretical strategies for critiquing Western culture. In their broad meaning, critical theorists encourage us to analyze power, but within an expansive range of relationships and across multiple dimensions of the domination of humans in modern society (e.g., race, feminist, queer, and post-colonial). (Chapter 4, p. 72)

Cultural competence "refers to the process by which individuals and systems respond respectfully and effectively to people of all cultures, languages, classes, races, ethnic backgrounds, religions, spiritual traditions, immigration status, and other diversity factors in a manner that recognizes, affirms, and values the worth of individuals, families, and communities and protects and preserves the dignity of each" (NASW, 2015, p. 13). (Chapter 11, p. 314)

Cultural humility, necessary for developing cultural competence, involves the social workers' "lifelong commitment to self-evaluation and self-critique, to redressing the power imbalances in . . . [professional/client relationships and in] developing advocacy partnerships with communities on behalf of" the clients that social workers serve (Tervalon & Murray-Garcia, 1998, p. 117). (Chapter 11, p. 314)

Culture can be defined as "the totality of ways being passed on from generation to generation. . . . Culture includes, but is not limited to, history, traditions, values, family systems, and artistic expressions of client groups served in the different cultures related to race and ethnicity, immigration and refugee status, tribal status, religion and spirituality, sexual orientation, gender identity and expression, social class, and abilities" (NASW, 2015, p. 12). (Chapter 11, p. 313)

Culture of silence develops because individuals are blamed for their lot in life with no recognition that they have little valid opportunity to act differently. They remain silent because they have internalized the mythologies of the oppressors. (Chapter 4, p. 82)

Deep ecology, developed by Norwegian philosopher Arne Naess, is a perspective that supports the flourishing of both human and nonhuman life. For Naess, this requires deep questioning in the public sphere (e.g., in bar rooms, classrooms, and around family tables) about our relationship to the natural world. Naess also encourages hard questions about what actions can be taken to effect change. Social workers who espouse a deep ecological perspective understand non-human life, in all its richness and diversity, as independent and intrinsically valuable beyond its usefulness for humans. (Chapter 7, p. 173)

Deep green ethics are ecocentric and holistic in their consideration of entire ecosystems (e.g., the complex interrelationships between species, geography, and climate). They are inclusive because they do not ignore the sentience, self-determination, or suffering of *individuals* within species, but consider the needs of the individual in light of the health of the entire species in its particular habitat. Deep green thinking also means that there is at least the potential for humans to "lose" when conflicts arise between human needs (and wants) and the needs of other species or ecosystem health. Deep green ethics are non-anthropocentric and transcend mid-green perspectives by ascribing intrinsic value to entire species, habitats (including non-biological elements), and ecosystems themselves, from micro to macro (including the idea that the entire earth is itself an ecosystem). (Chapter 7, p. 172)

Diagnostic school is a school of thought in social work practice that emphasized the expertise of the social work professional in assessing, diagnosing, and treating clients. The diagnostic school has been prominent in social work's history and still impacts the profession today (e.g., psychodynamic theory). (Chapter 2, p. 30)

Diagnostic theory of case work is the application of Freudian and/or medical ideas to case work that include diagnosis and treatment of disease. (Chapter 5, p. 105)

Dialectics is a Western philosophy that postulates that the truth, in any situation, lies between the opposing tensions experienced in that situation. (Chapter 10, p. 304)

Diversity is more than race and ethnicity; it includes the sociocultural experiences of people inclusive of, but not limited to, national origin, color, social class, religious and spiritual beliefs, immigration status, sexual orientation, gender identity or expression, age, marital status, and physical or mental disabilities. (Chapter 11, p. 313)

Dual perspective is a conceptual framework that enables us to look at the interactions between diverse groups and their nurturing systems, and larger American society, which represents the dominant or sustaining system that may share different values, customs, and beliefs from a minority person's nurturing system. (Chapter 11, p. 318)

Ecofeminist approach challenges the status quo of patriarchal or masculinist thinking, which can lead to domination and exploitation of not just women and other human populations, but also the natural environment. Ecofeminist analyses include the concerns of individuals to the sociopolitical institutions and structures that lead to thought and action that propagates continued oppressions of various groups of people, non-human animals/species, and the land. (Chapter 8, p. 173)

Ecological social work is defined as a social work's interest in ecology (the study of macro biophysical and social systems, their relationships, and interdependencies) in contrast to "person-in-environment thinking that only includes human individuals and groups in their respective sociopolitical environments." The term ecology involves a concern with an entire biotic community which includes humans, but also non-human species as well as habitats, geophysical systems and their interrelationships with their biological inhabitants. (Chapter 7, p. 168)

Eco-maps are practice strategies or tools, developed as part of the Life Model, that offer a graphic representation of all the elements of a case system (e.g., individual, family, group, community, social network, or organization). They also document the relationships among all the interacting elements of the case system and point to the variety of ways that a client system can deal with stressors that require growth and change. (Chapter 6, p. 156)

Ecosystems theory represents social work's translation of systems' abstract concepts from GST and ecological theory for use in social work practice. This theory examines the transactional space between individuals and their environments. (Chapter 6, p. 141)

Ego, whose functions include the use of judgment, frustration tolerance, problem solving, and relationship skills, erects protective defenses against anxiety and mediates the demands of the id and the superego. (Chapter 5, p. 103)

Ego defense mechanisms, which operate unconsciously as a means of protecting the ego from intolerable anxiety, can be either maladaptive or adaptive and serve as healthy coping mechanisms. (Chapter 5, p. 103)

Ego psychology is a major stream of psychodynamic theory that emphasizes human potential, strengths, and resilience. This practice model was taken up by social workers in the 1940s and centers on the ego as a mediating hub for a system of functional, protective, coping mechanisms. Ego psychology uses practice interventions designed to enhance motivation, problem-solving skills, and self-esteem and works in tandem with the strengths perspective. (Chapter 5, p. 106)

Elizabethan poor laws represent a 250-year compilation of rules, regulations, and laws that came in response to larger social changes impacting society. They also represent our beliefs about human behavior, codified in administrative rulings to deal with social changes that impacted English society. (Chapter 3, p. 55)

Empowerment is "a process of increasing personal, interpersonal, or political power so that individuals can take action to improve their life situations" (Gutierrez, 1990, p. 149). This process occurs when people are able to engage in dialogue with others to develop a critical consciousness or awareness of how personal experiences and problems are connected to larger unjust societal and political structures. (Chapter 12, p. 345)

Environmental ethics, developed over the past century, is a history of thinking that began with a purely anthropocentric ethic, then to one that transcends concern just for ourselves (humans) to include non-human animals (zoocentrism), all life forms (biocentrism), and eventually entire ecosystems (ecocentrism). One convenient way to think about this development is to consider it in three rough stages as a movement from "light green" or "shallow" environmentalism, to a "mid-green" ethic, and finally to a "deep green" ecological ethic. (Chapter 7, p. 170)

Environmental social work is rooted in a systems perspective, which views nature as its own system. This was a monumental step forward in that it insisted that the profession include the natural world in its understanding of social work practice. However, this approach represents a "shallow ecology" (light green ethics) in that it is "concerned with ecological problems because of their impact on human beings" (Besthorn, 2012, p. 250); the environment is still viewed as an object, with endless resources that humans can act upon and use. (Chapter 7, p. 196)

Epistemology is concerned with how we know what we know and involves distinguishing justified belief from mere opinion. (Chapter 1, p. 15)

Equal playing field is the assumption that each person in society has equal rights and an equal opportunity to take advantage of societal benefits such as opportunities for education, employment, safe living conditions, health care, recreational opportunities, social status, respect, and so on. Intersectionality highlights differences in peoples' ability to participate in society according to their relative social status. (Chapter 11, p. 323)

Evidence-guided practice (EGP) is an approach in which social work interventions are suggested, not prescribed by research. EGP acknowledges the especially broad nature of the social work profession and the multiple types of knowledge and skills that social workers need in working with clients and communities (e.g., critical thinking, legislative advocacy skills, and respecting and drawing upon clients' expertise about their life experiences). (Chapter 2, p. 36)

Fallibilism, a key term in the philosophy of pragmatism, means that ideas are not considered finished or perfect as they stand but are always in process and able to be revised and improved. (Chapter 1, p. 20)

Family life course perspective developed from life course theorists who began to question important assumptions upon which the earlier conceptions of family development had been based. For example, they challenged what was assumed to be "normal" family development, the impact of divorce on family development, the role diversity plays in families, how sexual orientation impacts family life, the role of spirituality in family development, and the role that poverty plays in family functioning. These current scholars put forth a much more complex understanding of the context in which families exist and how varied social changes impact family development. (Chapter 8, p. 241)

Family life cycle is a framework, rooted in psychodynamic theory, that describes common themes and tasks that need to be addressed in order for a family to successfully negotiate the various stages through which it must move to meet its needs as well as the needs of its individual members. Writers who developed this early framework based their inquiry on what they referred to as "normal" or "traditional" families that included two parents who are White, heterosexual, with only the father working outside the home. (Chapter 8, p. 236)

Fiduciary relationship refers to the relationship between professional social workers and their clients that requires professionals to act in the best interests of their clients. Therefore, social workers are urged to use five fundamental practice skills, including awareness, reflection, willingness to engage in dialogue, investment in relationships with clients and others in their environments, and adequate cognitive and verbal skills, to track the value dimensions of their practice as they unfold in their day-to-day work irrespective of their level of practice or field of practice. (Chapter 13, p. 402)

Functional school is a school of thought in social work practice that has provided a meaningful historical alternative to the diagnostic school. This school is rooted in the belief that everyone, no matter how difficult their life circumstances, has a place within them that propels them toward growth and change. (See our in-depth section on Otto Rank in Chapter 5, on psychodynamic theory.) This view of growth and development has been supported by empowerment theory and the strengths perspective. (Chapter 2, p. 30)

Functional theory of case work centers on Robinson and Taft's ideas on the psychology of growth, emphasizing creativity and the sociocultural influences on human development (contrast with the diagnostic theory of case work). (Chapter 5, p. 105)

General systems theory (GST) puts forth the idea that all living and nonliving matter can be regarded as systems that are holistic and whose elements interact with each other; GST views behavior as a consequence of the total situation in which a person (e.g., biological, psychological, social, and spiritual systems), group, or other social system (e.g., community) finds itself. (Chapter 6, p. 142)

Generalized other is a product of a process whereby a child imitates the acts of others, and in the early pre-symbolic stage, assumes the action, but not yet the perspective of the other. From simple imitation come the earliest glimmers of the object we call *self*. The child directs imitative acts toward self and then, with self, develops mind and symbols, followed by a capacity to take on the perspective of others. The capacity to understand not only the perspective of others but also the whole social milieu is called the "generalized other." (Chapter 9, p. 263)

Genograms are practice strategies or tools, developed as part of the Life Model, that help the client identify generations within a family, major family events, intergenerational communications, family aspirations, alignments, and role assignments as part of the assessment process. Their purpose is to provide both the worker and the client with a graphic representation of the potential resources and barriers that can be brought to bear in a current situation. In addition to producing information,

the diagram can be used to develop mutuality in the relationship between the worker and the client and as a tool to track changes as the work unfolds. (Chapter 6, p. 158)

Gilligan's moral orientations theory was established by Gilligan and applied specifically to girls' and women's experiences. Her research asserted the importance of a care orientation and a responsiveness to relationship that guided moral judgment for girls and women. Her stage model included (1) self-survival, (2) caring for others (feminine goodness), and (3) interdependence of self and others (balancing care of self with care of others). Her research and subsequent development of the moral orientation theory challenged Kohlberg's reliance on only male subjects for his research, and his use of theoretical questions rather than those actually rooted in the subjects' experiences. (Chapter 13, p. 382)

Guilt problem is the conflict of the will arising from competing desires to conform either to the self (authenticity) or to external social groups (e.g., parents). (Chapter 5, p. 114)

Historical context connects the events occurring in the larger society with their impact on human behavior in the social environment. It is the "dirt" in which the ideas about human behavior in the social environment are grown. It consists of understanding how economic, religious, political, and social welfare systems interact and how these interactions shape our understanding and application of that material to human behavior. (Chapter 3, p. 48)

Historical trauma, first developed by Maria Yellow Horse Brave Heart, refers to indigenous and other people's experiences of oppression and suffering, which led to collective and compounding emotional and psychic wounding—both over the life span and across generations. (Chapter 8, p. 223)

"I" is the internal component of human experience that responds to the attitudes expressed by those in our environment. Components of this element of the person are often held privately. (Chapter 9, p. 261)

Id, or unconscious, houses key drives (e.g., sex and aggression) that seek gratification. (Chapter 5, p. 103)

Imperialism refers to practices, attitudes, and perspectives supporting the rights or sense of entitlement of one culture (e.g., European Americans) to dominate or rule over another culture (e.g., First Nations people). Imperialism serves as a foundation for colonialism. (Chapter 8, p. 224)

Indigenous decolonization describes the conscious actions and planned strategies that indigenous people engage in (e.g., teaching language skills to revitalize a tribal language) to reconnect with and reclaim their knowledge, philosophies, and practices. (Chapter 8, p. 225)

Interactionists are adherents of symbolic interactionism and believe that as humans evolve with language and the ability to reason, they are able to turn back on nature itself, actively directing how natural forces act. Humans are not simply shaped by nature and culture, but they can learn, understand, build, invent, shape, and act upon their environments and even their own heredity. (Chapter 9, p. 260)

Intersectionality is an approach to social work practice "which examines forms of oppression, discrimination and domination as they manifest themselves through diversity components. These diversity components include multiple identities such as race and ethnicity, immigration, refugee and tribal status, religion and spirituality, sexual orientation, gender identity and expression, social class, and mental or physical disabilities" (NASW, 2015, pp. 16–17). (Chapter 11, p. 314)

Jacksonian era is the period between the 1830s and 1850s during which significant social change began occurring that affected peoples' understanding about new social problems that challenged the very foundations of American society. The pattern of responses centered on the use of institutional structures to control and correct marginalized groups' behaviors particularly around mental health, corrections, and children's welfare. (Chapter 3, p. 59)

Just community represented Kohlberg's attempt to establish curriculums in the public school system based on his belief that children have the capacity to grow in their own moral reasoning and to use more adequate and complex reasoning in solving problems. From Kohlberg's perspective, teachers could provide opportunities for students to consider genuine moral conflicts faced in the school community. The emphasis was on students' learning processes in going through and arriving at a course of action rather than providing students answers to the dilemmas they faced. (Chapter 13, p. 381)

Liberatory model of education, which is in contrast to a banking model, involves the leveling of the relationships between teachers and students in which they work collaboratively to engage in creative thinking directed toward mutual humanization. (Chapter 4, p. 87)

Life course perspectives, distinct from life span theory, emphasize human development as understood within a broader historical, social, and cultural context. They address four elements that cut across the full span of a person's life (i.e., historical and geographical location, social embeddedness, agency and personal control, and timing). (Chapter 8, p. 218)

Life Model of social work practice represents social work's translation of systems theories for use in social work practice. This model integrates social work's dual purpose of social change and individualized treatment with the ecological perspective as a predominant conceptual framework for social work practice. (Chapter 6, p. 149)

Life span theories, which originated with the work of Erik Erikson, emphasize the role of the ego in shaping human development. Erikson was also one of the first scholars to put forth the idea of eight physical and psychological developmental stages (in which the ego assists the individual in attaining a balance between two opposing basic personality traits) as occurring throughout adulthood and in adaptation to the larger social environment. (Chapter 8, p. 214)

Light green ethics limits direct value only to human beings. Non-human animals, and all other biological species, habitats, and ecosystems, have value only as they pertain to the use and service of humans. This is called *instrumental value*: anything non-human has value only as it is instrumental for our use. (Chapter 7, p. 170)

Looking glass self is inseparable from social life and arises reflectively in terms of the reaction to the opinions of others on the self; namely the imagination of our appearance to the other person, the imagination of that person's judgment of those appearances, and some self-feeling such as pride or shame. This concept of self is a balance between autonomous and social dimensions of our experience. (Chapter 9, p. 263)

Massification defines people as "objects" who are unable to take responsibility for their own liberation. In contrast, as "subjects" people can participate in democratic dialogue seeking to jointly take risks to develop their own consciousness and well-being. (Chapter 4, p. 85)

"Me" is the organized response we develop in reacting to our understanding of how others behave toward us. (Chapter 9, p. 261)

Meditation represents a range of practices that involve both physical and psychological activities designed to determine what is happening in an individual's mind at any given moment in time. Its focus is on the current state of one's mind by paying attention to the thoughts and emotions that are present without judgment. (Chapter 10, p. 291)

Membership emphasizes the belief that there is an interdependence between individuals and community, and that those connections must be acknowledged and nurtured in order for both to be healthy. (Chapter 12, p. 368)

Meta-theory is a theory concerned with the investigation, analysis, or description of theory itself. (Chapter 1, p. 4)

Mid-green ethics extends value to include non-human animals, with special attention to individuals as opposed to entire species. Biocentric views basically extend the concern for human rights and welfare to non-human animals, however, there is still no inherent value ascribed to habitats, nonliving things, or ecosystems. (Chapter 7, p. 171)

Mindfulness is a concept with a long history and deep roots in Buddhist traditions. Mindfulness is a complex set of processes that includes paying attention to the present moment of our experiences, labeling them with words, acting with awareness, avoiding automatic pilot, bringing an openness, acceptance, and willingness, and allowing nonjudgment, kindness, friendliness, and curiosity to all observed experiences. (Chapter 10, p. 290)

Moral development refers to the emergence, change, and understanding of how human beings develop morality over the course of their lives. In the field of moral development, morality guides individuals' beliefs and actions about how to treat one another with respect to justice, social welfare, and people's rights. (Chapter 13, p. 378)

Moral development theory (Kohlberg) consists of a developmental process with six stages and three levels: *preconventional level*, characterized by Stage One, avoiding punishment, and Stage Two, seeking rewards;

conventional level, which includes Stage Three, gain approval/avoid disapproval, and Stage Four, conformity to rules; and *post-conventional level,,* with Stage Five, social contract, and Stage Six, individual principles of conscience. Kohlberg (1976) described his moral development theory as representing these stages in which individuals would first consider their own interests (Stages One and Two), then see themselves as group members who share expectations (Stages Three and Four), and finally, make moral commitments and hold to standards of a good or just society (Stages Five and Six). (Chapter 13, p. 379)

Moral development theory (Piaget) made links between cognitive development, which includes logical reasoning, and moral development. Piaget outlined a three-step process of moral development that moved from an external locus of control to an internal locus of control for assessing "right from wrong." This progression in moral development also reflected growth in reasoning—from concrete to more abstract reasoning. In effect, growth in cognitive development is linked to and necessary for moral development to occur. (Chapter 13, p. 378)

Moral dialogue is the concept that attempts to help track the ongoing interactions of values in the context of the social work relationship. It includes the ongoing interactions about what should or should not be done among social workers and other relevant actors in an ethical decision-making process rooted in the NASW *Code of Ethics*. It focuses professionals' attention on the multiple systems interacting with often largely conflicting value configurations. (Chapter 13, p. 402)

Moral foundations theory asserts that moral reasoning often occurs *after* people make an intuitive moral decision. The major purpose of these developments has been to expand the full range of moral concerns to include those found in religious practices and among political conservatives (e.g., purity and loyalty to the group). Scholars refer to universal "moral intuitions" including harm/care, fairness reciprocity, in group/loyalty, authority respect, and purity/sanctity. (Chapter 13, p. 383)

Naïve consciousness occurs when people are unaware of the conditions in which they live and how those conditions oppress them. (Chapter 4, p. 82)

Nigrescence theory, first developed during the civil rights movement in the United States, refers to a French term for turning or becoming Black and depicts a process of moving from Black self-hatred to an affirmation of a Black identity. (Chapter 8, p. 220)

Ontology is concerned with the very essence of reality. Some assume that reality is external to an individual and consists of concrete, tangible, and objective structures. Others view humans as creating their own meaning or understanding of reality and this is constantly changing. A key idea in ontology is whether or not reality exists outside of our awareness of it. (Chapter 1, p. 15)

Operant conditioning refers to the extent to which human behavior functions within the environment and produces consequences for the person engaged in a particular behavior. Key tools of operant conditioning include reinforcement and punishment—either providing positive consequences (delivered following a response) or negative consequences (withdrawn following a response) for a particular behavior. Consequences that strengthen subsequent behavior are called reinforcers, and consequences that weaken behavior are called punishers. (Chapter 10, p. 287)

Oppression is viewed as "a condition of powerlessness that cuts across every system within a culture" (Chenault, 2011, p. 20) and, in turn, requires holistic, structural responses and practice-based strategies at multiple levels (e.g., individual, family, and community-based change efforts; and social and political action) in order to adequately combat and eradicate. (Chapter 8, p. 224)

Person-in-environment (PIE) perspective involves reciprocity between individuals and environments: individuals can impact various elements of the environment, and the environment can exert conducive or inhibiting influences on the individual. PIE is a crucial and defining principle of social work practice and is associated with the earliest definitions of the scope and purpose of social work. (Chapter 6, p. 141)

Perspective (or epistemological approach) is defined as a worldview or way of perceiving the world (e.g., positivism, social constructionism, and pragmatism). (Chapter 1, p. 4)

Positive psychology is a psychological perspective that focuses on human flourishing and optimal functioning, as opposed to disease and pathology. (Chapter 12, p. 348)

Positivism is a philosophy that believes there is, in large measure, an objective truth that can be discovered through systematic inquiry. This philosophy values quantitative scientific methodologies that can describe and predict outcomes. (Chapter 1, p. 15)

Practice model (e.g., cognitive-behavioral, narrative, and task-centered) describes how social workers can apply and implement theories in their practice. Further, perspectives, theories, and practice models interact with and can inform each other. (Chapter 1, p. 4)

Pragmatism is a philosophy that views humans as biological organisms who interact with their environments, including non-human species, in various interdependent relationships. Humans are constantly evolving, engage in imperfect problem solving using a broad range of ideas, and are on an ethics-based quest for democracy, freedom, and justice for all people. (Chapter 1, p. 18)

Praxis is defined as a process of action-awareness-reflection-dialogue, which social workers can participate in to more effectively work with diverse clientele. (Chapter 11, p. 316)

Primary groups are characterized by face-to-face interactions including family, neighborhood, play groups of children, and groups of elders, among others. In these groups there is an intimate fusion of the individual and group that is essential to forming participants' ideals, including developing ethical principles such as justice, service, and kindness. (Chapter 9, p. 263)

Progressive era included the period from 1895 until the beginning of World War I. It was marked by significant changes in society based on industrialization, urbanization, and immigration. This era's most important contribution was the development of systematic collection of information about the conditions in which the poor lived and marked the beginning of the shift toward the use of social science as a rival explanation to theology for understanding the human condition. (Chapter 3, p. 61)

Prospective psychology is the idea that humans thrive best in conditions where they can exercise their capacities to creatively imagine new futures. (Chapter 12, p. 350)

Psychodynamic theory, based on the work of Sigmund Freud, examines intrapsychic and unconscious processes that contribute to human functioning and includes current developments (e.g., infant research and attachment theory; and influences of social constructionism, feminist and other diversity perspectives). Psychodynamic theory has also been extended to include four core models (i.e., ego psychology, drive theory, object relations, and self-psychology). (Chapter 5, p. 102)

Reason involves the capacity for humans to consciously make sense of their world by establishing and verifying information; changing and adapting beliefs, practices, and institutions based on new and existing information; and by drawing on multiple and integrated sources of knowledge to engage in creative activities and address problems. Reason is closely associated with human activities such as art, science, language, and philosophy and helps us in developing our capacities to make holistic connections and to integrate these multiple sources of knowledge. (Chapter 2, p. 32)

Reference groups are collections of individuals with whom we identify, or look up to, and whose beliefs impact our individual decision-making. They have a powerful impact on what we think of ourselves; our social judgments are, in large part, understood through the eyes of others. (Chapter 9, p. 263)

Resilience rests on the notion that both individuals and communities have a reservoir of resources that can be brought to bear in any situation, and they exist not only within the individual but also in the environment. (Chapter 12, p. 368)

Resistance involves the individual's means of coping with anxiety by refusing to engage in self-reflection or self-analysis that could lead to change and growth. Freud viewed self-reflection as necessary for client growth. A person's resistance to growth can be viewed as normal and reflects how difficult it is for people to make life changes. (Chapter 5, p. 104)

Respondent or classical conditioning was largely developed by Watson, Pavlov, and Skinner. This approach involves establishing a relationship between an unconditioned stimulus (food), Pavlov's dog experiments, with an unconditioned response (salivation). Today, behavioral therapies use ideas from respondent conditioning to help people face a variety of anxieties and phobias. (Chapter 10, p. 286)

Scientific revolution was a movement consisting of individuals from both the natural and social sciences who put forward alternative views for understanding human behavior and environmental conditions that rivaled those held by theologically based paradigms. They redefined human behavior and social conditions as subject to being understood by science and therefore transformed these conditions to problems that could be solved. (Chapter 3, p. 61)

Shared decision-making model (SDM) is a social work practice model used in the mental health field that basically states that there are two "experts" involved in making decisions about the use of psychiatric medications: the psychiatrist *and* the client. SDM, now a few decades in the making, contrasts with conventional psychiatric practice that placed minimal importance on clients' life goals, interests, and values when prescribing medications. Research is currently being conducted to consider empirical questions about SDM, such as whether clients adhere to their medications more when SDM practices are used, or whether clients show more improvements in their symptoms when SDM practices are used instead of the older, "one expert" practice. This SDM model is consistent with social work ethics, such as client self-determination, and may serve to significantly improve the lives of many people suffering with mental illnesses. (Chapter 1, p. 12)

Social cognitive theory, developed by Albert Bandura, studies learning processes that occur in social environments. It reflects the growing interest in how to control behavior and examines shifts from external sources to the individual through such cognitive processes as self-regulation and self-efficacy. (Chapter 10, p. 288)

Social constructionism is a philosophy that acknowledges the importance of subjectivity, multiple ways of knowing, and that knowledge is time and context-bound. Social workers who use this philosophy are more likely to value a different array of therapeutic methods, which are conceptualized and researched to take into account a wide range of situations faced by unique client groups. (Chapter 1, p. 15)

Social Gospel movement involved a group of social reformers driven by theological beliefs that were focused on social salvation. They attempted to bring about reforms related to improving urban housing, calling for shorter working hours and better working conditions for women, and unemployment insurance. (Chapter 3, p. 60)

Stability–radical change dimension examines whether the assumptions of a particular human behavior theory emphasize stability, integration, and the nature of social order and equilibrium; or whether the theory emphasizes conflict, coercion, and change as a way of understanding human affairs. (Chapter 2, p. 25)

Strengths Model is a social work practice model, based on the strengths perspective, which focuses on services for diverse client groups (e.g., people with psychiatric disabilities). (Chapter 12, p. 367)

Strengths perspective is a social work practice perspective that requires that everything you do as a social worker will be predicated, in some way, on helping to unearth and embellish, explore, and exploit client strengths and resources in service of assisting them to achieve their goals, realize their dreams, and shed the irons of their own inhibitions and misgivings and society's domination. It is a versatile practice approach relying heavily on ingenuity, creativity, and the courage and common sense of both clients and their social worker. It is a collaborative process requiring clients and workers to be purposeful, engaged agents and not functionaries. This approach honors the innate wisdom of the human spirit and the inherent capacity for transformation of even the most humble and abused. (Chapter 12, p. 363)

Structural functionalism, a type of systems theory developed by Herbert Spencer, views society as a self-regulating system that can be understood by studying its various elements and their interactions. Spencer applied Darwin's human evolution to the development of societies and believed that all systems strive for unity, stability, and order as a way to survive. (Chapter 6, p. 137)

Subjective–objective dimension examines whether the assumptions of a particular human behavior theory treat the social world just like the natural world as being real and external to the individual (objective) or whether the world ought to be viewed as having a more personal (subjective) quality to it, one in which individuals create their own meanings. (Chapter 2, p. 25)

Superego is a person's conscience or seat of morality. (Chapter 5, p. 103)

Symbolic interactionism is an interpretivist theoretical approach based on Max Weber's writings. George Herbert Mead was the American sociologist who expounded on Weber's writing and popularized symbolic interactionism in the United States. This theory assumes that human beings act toward things on the basis of the meanings that those things have for them, that meaning is derived from and arises out of social interactions, and that meanings are grounded on and develop through the interpretive process based on life experience. (Chapter 9, p. 259)

Theory (e.g., learning theory, feminist, and moral development) is defined as a set of statements aimed at explaining or proving why something happens. (Chapter 1, p. 4)

Transference occurs when clients ascribe or transfer character traits and attitudes of significant others in their past to the social worker. If the social worker does not understand how she or he is perceived by the client, then it is very difficult to be helpful in the therapeutic process. Practitioners using a psychodynamic approach view transference as necessary in order to help clients explore their distorted views of ambivalence, love, or hatred toward others. (Chapter 5, p. 104)

Transtheoretical perspective puts forth an overarching therapeutic approach composed of five common factors that are interdependent and interactive: client, practitioner, the client–practitioner relationship, model/technique, and client feedback. (Chapter 2, p. 38)

Unworthy poor are people who had no physical or mental defects but were without employment, or engaged in stealing, abuse, assault, lying, and cheating. The unworthy poor had no claim on the community for assistance and in fact were to be punished because their maladies were created based on their own choices for which they should take full responsibility. (Chapter 3, p. 54)

White fragility is defined as a "state in which even a minimum amount of racial stress becomes intolerable, triggering a range of defensive moves . . . such as anger, fear, guilt, and behaviors such as argumentation, silence, and leaving the stress-inducing situation" (DiAngelo, 2011, p. 54). (Chapter 11, p. 329)

White identity development model is a framework that depicts White individuals' journey from being naïve or unaware of their whiteness and privilege to an increasing cultural awareness of their dominance coupled with action to address social injustices experienced by diverse and often marginalized groups of people. (Chapter 11, p. 314)

White privilege is unearned and invisible social privileges due to one's White skin color. (Chapter 11, p. 314)

Will psychology is Otto Rank's understanding of the will as the center of the psyche—a volitional, life-giving, transformative force. (Chapter 5, p. 112)

Will therapy is Rank's philosophy of helping that focuses on the relationship between the client and social worker, the content of which centers upon existential themes (e.g., freedom and authenticity) that are particular to each individual client. (Chapter 5, p. 115)

Worthy poor include those individuals who are physically and/or mentally challenged, orphaned, or unable to care for themselves based on circumstances beyond their control. (Chapter 3, p. 54)

INDEX

Note: Page numbers in *italic* refer to figures and tables. Page numbers in **bold** refer to glossary entries.